IMPERIAL AND SOVIET RUSSIA

Imperial and Soviet Russia

Power, Privilege and the Challenge of Modernity

David Christian

St. Martin's Press
New York

IMPERIAL AND SOVIET RUSSIA
Copyright © 1986, 1994, 1997 by David Christian
Figures copyright © Longman Australia Pty Ltd 1994

The book is published by arrangement with Longman Australia Pty Ltd,
Melbourne, Australia, which originally published it under the title *Power
and Privilege.*

St. Martin's Press, Scholarly and Reference Division,
175 Fifth Avenue, New York, N.Y. 10010

First published in the United States of America in 1997

This book is printed on paper suitable for recycling and
made from fully managed and sustained forest sources.

Printed in Hong Kong

ISBN 0–312–17351–2 (cloth)
ISBN 0–312–17352–0 (paper)

Library of Congress Cataloging-in-Publication Data
Christian, David, 1946–
Imperial and Soviet Russia : power, privilege, and the challenge of
modernity / David Christian.
p. cm.
Includes bibliographical references and index.
ISBN 0–312–17351–2 (cloth).   ISBN 0–312–17352–0 (paper)
1. Russia—History—Alexander II, 1855–1881. 2. Russia—History–
–Alexander III, 1881–1894. 3. Russia—History—Nicholas II,
1894–1917. 4. Soviet Union—History. 5. Communism—Soviet Union.
I. Title.
DK220.C48 1997
947.08—dc21   96–50058
                                                            CIP

Contents

List of Tables	vi
List of Figures	vii
Acknowledgements	viii
Introduction	1
1. Medieval and Early Modern times	7
2. The Russian Empire in the Early Nineteenth Century	39
3. The 'Great Reforms' and the Rise of a Revolutionary Movement	71
4. Economic and Social Change Before 1914	100
5. The 1905 Revolution	128
6. The Final Decade of Tsarist Rule and the February Revolution	153
7. 1917	180
8. Civil War and the Origins of a New Social Order	207
9. The New Economic Policy	234
10. Collectivization and Industrialization	265
11. The Stalinist Political Order	293
12. The Great Patriotic War	324
13. Reforming the Stalinist System, 1953 to 1964	351
14. Consolidation, Stagnation and Change, 1964 to 1982	377
15. *Perestroika* and the End of the Soviet Experiment, 1982 to 1991	402
Conclusion: the Failure of the Soviet Experiment	431
Statistical Appendix	435
Annotated Bibliography	438
Chronology	447
Glossary	456
Index	461

List of Tables

1.1	Regional populations of Inner Eurasia 1000AD–2000AD	8
4.1	Index numbers of economic growth, 1861–1913	111
4.2	Rates of industrial growth, 1885–1913	113
5.1	Changes in the structure of the ruling group, 1850–1900	132
6.1	Trotsky on the numbers striking for political reasons, 1903–17	159
9.1	The Soviet economy under the New Economic Policy	236
10.1	Transformation of the Russian class structure	266
10.2	The meaning of collectivization	273
10.3	Index numbers of Soviet economic development, 1928–80	277
10.4	Increases in output between 1928 and 1940	278
10.5	Comparative historical aggregate levels of GNP	279
10.6	Output per unit of labour and capital, 1928–40	282
14.1	The slowdown – Soviet economic growth, 1951–85	390
15.1	Annual rates of growth of the Soviet economy, 1986–91	420
15.2	Growth of Soviet budget deficits	423

List of Figures

1.1	Regional populations of Inner Eurasia	9
1.2	Kievan Rus', eleventh to thirteenth centuries	11
1.3	The expansion of Muscovy from the thirteenth century	22
2.1	Social structure of Russia after the Napoleonic Wars	40
2.2	Urbanization in Russia and the USSR, 1860–1990	43
2.3	Typical layout of a nineteenth-century Russian village	44
2.4	The natural geography of the Russian and Soviet Empires	47
2.5	Distribution of family labour by season and type of work	55
2.6	Distribution of family labour by age and gender	55
2.7	Budget of the Russian government in 1846	59
4.1	Main industrial regions of European Russia before 1917	105
4.2	The trans-Siberian railway and the Far East	108
4.3	Economic growth of the Russian Empire, 1861–1913	112
7.1	Petrograd during the October Revolution	202
8.1	The Civil War, 1918–20	227
9.1	Economic growth during NEP, 1920–6	245
10.1	Social structure of the Soviet Union in 1970	266
10.2	The meaning of collectivization	274
10.3	Soviet economic growth, 1928–40	279
12.1	The changing western boundaries of the Soviet Union, 1917–46	328
12.2	The Great Patriotic War, 1941–45	334
12.3	Evacuation of Soviet industry to the east	335
14.1	Declining growth rates, 1951–85	390

Acknowledgements

Many thanks to Linda Bowman, who read and commented on a first draft of this revised version, to Stephen Wheatcroft, who helped me with information on statistics, and to Graeme Gill, for some useful ideas on Stalinism. Richard Sakwa made some very helpful criticisms of a later draft. I have not accepted all the suggestions that these kind readers made, so they are fully absolved from remaining errors of fact or interpretation. I owe a lot to my students at Macquarie University, whose questions and comments have helped me to clarify my ideas on modern Russian and Soviet history. I also want to thank my colleagues, the late Bill Edmonds, and also George Parsons and Mervyn Hartwig, all of whom taught Russian history with me at various times. But not just them: the community of historians at Macquarie University is my community, and I owe a debt to all of them in different ways, for their friendship and the many ideas I have stolen from them. The most important debt of all is to my family: to Chardi, Joshua and Emily, who made me realise that there is much more to life than Russian history.

The author and publishers would also like to thank Addison-Wesley Longman Australia for permission to reproduce the maps and tables in this book.

Introduction

■ Themes

This book is a history of the Russian and Soviet Empires from the mid-nineteenth century to the end of the Soviet era in 1991. It focuses on the complex and painful transformation of lifeways, politics, economics and ways of thinking that occurred as a traditional agrarian society entered the modern world. In particular, the book tries to explain the peculiar form this transition took in the tsarist and Soviet empires. In Western Europe, the Americas, and many other parts of the world, the transition to modernity occurred within the economic and social structures known in Marxist theory as 'capitalism'. However, in the lands ruled by the tsarist empire, a flourishing but embryonic capitalism was aborted in 1917, and replaced by the economic, social and political structures known as 'communism'. As a result, the people of the Soviet Union entered the modern world along very different pathways from the people of the non-communist world. The Communist government promised to create a society that would be more egalitarian and more humane than capitalism. However, its achievements fell far short of its Utopian ambitions, and in the late 1980s the entire experiment collapsed.

Why did the tsarist lands go down this distinctive path towards modernity? Was this particular trajectory pre-determined by tsarist history, or was it the result of a particular crisis? How different was the Communist path to modernity from that of capitalism? How distinctive was the life-experience of those who lived through the Communist era? Why did the realities of Soviet socialism fall so far short of its ideals? Tackling these questions is important not just in order to understand something about the history of the Russian and Soviet empires. These are also questions about the nature of the strange new world that has emerged in the twentieth century, and about the possibilities and limitations of hopes for human progress.

This book offers some answers to these important questions. Though it tells a story, it is more concerned to make sense of that story than to tell it in encyclopedic detail. Because of the nature of its main themes, it concentrates on the relationship between changing lifeways, ideologies, and political and economic structures. We will explore how people lived, how their lives were transformed by economic change, and how economic change was affected by the ideas and ambitions of governments. Concentrating on these themes means neglecting other aspects of Russian and Soviet history. The book will not offer systematic or detailed coverage

1

of topics such as international relations or religious, cultural and intellectual history, except where these topics help illuminate our central themes. The book also makes little attempt to deal with the distinctive histories of the many lands that made up the tsarist and Soviet empires. It focuses mainly on the Slavic populations of these empires.

The justification for concentrating on these central themes is the author's belief that they are fundamental. Understanding them allows us to understand change in many other areas. Whether this is true or not the reader will have to judge.

■ The Argument

Running through the book is a single, coherent, argument. It is hoped that this argument will help explain the complex links between Communist ideology and the realities of social and economic change in the Russian and Soviet empires. Here, I will offer a bald summary of the key ideas that underlie this argument, in the hope that this will help clarify the more detailed (and nuanced) account of later chapters.

The book's argument highlights certain general features of the transition to modernity. Above all, it focuses on the emergence of new ways of mobilizing resources through commercial exchanges rather than by direct appropriation; and on the impact these changes had on the nature of political and social systems. The two themes are linked. All states depend on the ability to mobilize resources, but the ways in which they mobilize resources vary greatly and so do the political structures best suited to the task of rule. A third theme links these two: that of inequality. Historically, state power has always sustained the privilege of the ruling groups who have controlled, and benefited from their control of state power. What is it that links political power and economic privilege? And why did the Soviet attempt to break that link fail?

In order to function effectively, states have to be able to defend themselves against internal and external challenges. They also have to earn legitimacy by providing religious, economic and military services. And to fulfil these functions, they have to mobilize human and material resources of various kinds. In other words, all states need a machinery of coercion, a machinery of persuasion, and some mechanism for mobilizing resources. Historically, states have also mobilized resources for a fourth, and less obvious, purpose: to sustain the privileges of those who make up the state. If we think of states not as abstractions, but as alliance systems, then the reasons for this become obvious. The power of states depends on the cohesion of those who control them, and that cohesion depends on the existence of shared goals that bind the ruling group together. Most potent of all these ties is privilege: the privilege of shared wealth, status and authority. Privilege binds together the ruling groups who are the foundation of any successful state system. This is why privilege and state power have always been closely linked.

However, the precise nature of the links between privilege and state power have changed profoundly in the modern era. Ultimately, this change reflects a change in the ways in which resources are mobilized. Wealth can be mobilized in many different ways, but for our purposes it will be helpful to distinguish between two main methods: 'direct' and 'indirect' mobilization. 'Direct' mobilization depends on the use of some combination of force and persuasion to make people hand over resources. These surrendered resources may take the form of tributes or taxes or (in the case of military recruitment or slavery) human beings. Direct mobilization was the dominant form of state mobilization throughout most of the pre-industrial era, from the appearance of the first states some 5000 years ago until recent centuries.

It is important to note two central features of direct mobilization. First, direct mobilization depended largely on the coercive or persuasive power of states. This, in turn, required a degree of unity and discipline amongst those who stood to gain most from the process of mobilization. For these reasons, direct mobilization implied the existence of a privileged class. It depended on inequality. Second, for reasons that still puzzle economic theorists, direct mobilization is better at mobilizing existing wealth than at generating new wealth. As Russian serf-owners knew in the nineteenth century, you can force serfs to work, but you cannot force them to work *efficiently*. For this reason, economic growth, when it occurs within a system of direct mobilization, tends to be *extensive* rather than *intensive*. That is to say, it depends on increasing inputs of labour or land or wealth, rather than on increases in productivity. States relying on direct mobilization can use the wealth generated by already-existing methods, and they can expand it by taking in new lands or conquering new populations; but they have rarely been good at introducing new and more productive techniques. This is why economic growth has been so slow and erratic in the pre-industrial world. It depended largely on conquest and population growth, and when population growth slowed or there were no new lands to conquer, it petered out.

'Indirect' mobilization does not depend on the direct use of force or persuasion. Instead, it depends on commercial or market exchanges that generate profits. Through apparently equal exchanges of goods, labour and services, entrepreneurs generate the forms of wealth known in economics as 'profits'. One way of distinguishing the modern from the pre-modern world is to say that the dominant style of mobilization in the modern world is indirect. Certainly, modern states rely on direct mobilization when they tax. However, their power depends less on their powers of direct taxation than on the wealth mobilized indirectly by entrepreneurs using wage labour in a competitive market.

The great strength of indirect mobilization is that when it is practised on a large scale, it seems to encourage not just the *mobilization* of wealth, but also the *creation of new wealth*. It encourages innovations that tend to raise productivity and therefore makes it possible to increase the wealth generated from a particular amount of labour, land or cash. It is this fabulous capacity to generate new wealth that explains many of the distinctive features of the modern world. And this is why it may be appropriate to think of the transition to modernity as a transition from direct to indirect forms of mobilization, from the collection of tributes to the generation of commercial profits.

How do such changes affect the existence of privilege? Is a world of indirect mobilization likely to distribute resources more evenly? Or is it also bound to be a world of inequality? This immensely important question has preoccupied economists since the eighteenth century. Many economists, including Adam Smith, have argued that indirect mobilization, by its very nature, requires more egalitarian social, economic and political relationships than direct mobilization. Its capacity to generate wealth depends on the free economic activity of free individuals. Political equality appears, therefore, as a necessary precondition for economic growth. This argument is central to modern liberalism.

However, socialists have tended to see 'indirect mobilization' in a different light. The freedom of the market is, in their eyes, the freedom to grow rich, and ultimately that freedom must be enjoyed by some people at the expense of others. Socialists have argued, therefore, that market economies are quite as inegalitarian as the pre-modern world. Both direct and indirect mobilization lead to inequality. They have therefore tried to look to a world beyond that of direct or indirect mobilization, a world in which resources will be mobilized in the interests of all members of society.

Socialist thinkers naturally asked: what were the conditions under which it would be possible to build a more egalitarian world? Most modern socialists argued that it would be possible to build such societies by exploiting the fabulous wealth-generating capacity of market societies ('capitalism', in the terminology of Marx), while rejecting its inequalities. It was this idea that was tested in the historical experiment launched by the Bolsheviks in 1917.

What went wrong? One possible answer is that the experiment was tried not in a developed capitalist country with high levels of productivity, but in a country where capitalism was only beginning to make an impact and productivity levels remained low. In the nineteenth century, Russian society, despite its traditional social, economic and political structures, began to feel the economic and the military impact of the emerging 'capitalist' societies of Europe. Commercial activity increased throughout the Empire. At the same time, tsarist governments began to understand the immense political and military power being generated by the capitalist societies of western Europe. (Defeat in the Crimean War provided a painful wake-up call.) Partly through spontaneous change, partly through deliberate government encouragement, the importance of market activity increased, and so did the importance of indirect forms of mobilization. The Russian government stimulated commercial activity by abolishing serfdom, a system dominated by direct mobilization. The abolition of serfdom forced both peasants and nobles to engage increasingly in market activities. The government also supported other entrepreneurial activities such as the building of railways.

By the early twentieth century, the forms of indirect mobilization known as 'capitalism' were beginning to dominate the economic life of much of the Russian Empire. Yet the Empire's social and political structures still belonged to a traditional world of direct mobilization, and levels of productivity lagged behind those of Western Europe. This clash between modern economic methods and traditional social and political structures eroded the power of the traditional tsarist state.

In February 1917, three years into the Great War, the tsarist government collapsed. Eight months later, a socialist government took its place. This attempted to build a society free of the inequalities of capitalism. Yet, if the government was to survive, and provide a decent living for those it ruled, it, too, would have to mobilize resources for defence, administration and welfare. It would have to do this despite the fierce opposition of wealthier capitalist states and of its internal rivals, and despite the low productivity of the Russian economy. The challenge, then, was to find a form of mobilization that was as effective as capitalism in generating new wealth, but did not require the creation of new forms of inequality. Could the Communists find a new 'engine of growth' free of the inequalities of both direct and indirect forms of mobilization?

After experimenting for a time with a mixed economy that depended on both direct and indirect forms of mobilization, the Soviet government abandoned all forms of indirect mobilization in 1929. In effect (though this is not how Soviet leaders saw it), the government of Stalin re-established the primacy of direct over indirect forms of mobilization. Economically, the experiment seemed to succeed. Growth rates were rapid, and the Soviet Union built up a powerful defence establishment. Yet in other ways, the experiment was less successful. Increased reliance on methods of direct mobilization revived the harsh inequalities of the pre-industrial world. The Stalinist labour camps were the most brutal symbol of this reversion to pre-modern methods of rule. Stalinist methods of rule tarnished the early idealism of the communist experiment, though many convinced themselves that they were merely living through a harsh transitional stage. Even more dangerous for Soviet elites was the gradual realization that, despite their initial successes, the Soviet economy, like most economies that depended mainly on direct mobilization, was not good at generating *new* wealth. By the 1960s, most Soviet economists and most western observers understood that Soviet economic growth depended to a dangerous extent on increased inputs rather than on increased efficiency. Economic growth in the Soviet Union was still extensive rather than intensive. And extensive growth, by its very nature, is less sustainable than intensive growth, and more constrained by the availability of existing supplies of raw materials, labour and cash. Eventually, like the tsarist government before it, the Soviet government would find it harder and harder to compete economically and militarily with capitalist societies that enjoyed higher rates of innovation and higher levels of productivity.

In other words, the Stalinist decision to avoid the capitalist path of 'indirect mobilization' entailed a return to traditional methods of 'direct' mobilization. This strategy undermined both the egalitarian aims of communism and its ability to match the economic and military power of its capitalist rivals. While the many inequalities of Soviet society undermined the legitimacy of communist ideology, sluggish growth rates undermined the economic, political and military power of the communist state.

This, in general terms, is the explanation this book will offer for the failure of the Soviet experiment to break the traditional link between power and privilege. The book begins by describing in some detail the society in which the communist experiment of the twentieth century was launched.

■ A Note on Dates and Placenames

Until 1 February 1918, Russia used the Julian calendar, which lagged behind the Gregorian calendar used in western Europe by almost two weeks. This can sometimes create confusion, particularly in dealing with 1917. According to the Gregorian calendar, the October Revolution took place in November 1917, and some sources use this dating. In this book, all dates are those used by contemporaries. I use the Julian calendar (the Old Style, or OS) up to 1 February 1918, and the Gregorian calendar (the New Style, or NS) after that date. The day after 1 February 1918 was 15 February 1918.

In the Soviet period, and again during *perestroika*, governments freely changed the names of major cities. St Petersburg, founded by Peter I in 1703, became Petrograd in 1914 at the start of the First World War. After Lenin's death in 1924, it became Leningrad. Then, in September 1991 it became St Petersburg once more. I have tried to use the names in use during the period under discussion. So in discussing 1917 I refer to Petrograd, while the chapter on the Second World War uses the name Leningrad.

■ *Chapter 1* ■

Medieval and Early Modern Times

■ The Setting of Russian History

The continent of Eurasia is the largest landmass on earth. It consists of two distinct regions. Around the eastern, southern and western edges of Eurasia there are several coastal sub-continents: China, South-East Asia, India, the Middle East and Europe. These regions I will call 'Outer Eurasia'. At the heart of Eurasia there lies a vast flatland, the largest in the world. This stretches from the Arctic Sea to the arc of mountains which extends from the Balkans, through the Caucasus and Tien Shan ranges, to north-eastern China. I will call this region 'Inner Eurasia'. This was the stage on which the history of Russia and the Soviet Union was enacted.

The differences between Inner and Outer Eurasia have shaped the entire history of Eurasia.[1] Because it lies further south, most of Outer Eurasia enjoys warmer climates than Inner Eurasia. More sunlight means more photosynthesis and more plant growth. Most of Outer Eurasia is also coastal, so it is well-watered. High rainfall and plenty of sunlight make for productive agriculture. These factors help explain why Outer Eurasia has been for several thousand years a region of densely populated agrarian civilizations. Most of the population of Eurasia has always lived in Outer Eurasia. As a result, the coastal civilizations of China, India, the Middle East and the Mediterranean, dominated the history of the entire continent.

Settled agriculture was harder in the cold, dry heartland of Inner Eurasia. For this reason, the societies of Inner Eurasia remained nomadic for longer than in Outer Eurasia. Their populations also remained smaller (Table 1.1). Until the middle of the first millennium of the modern era, most people in Inner Eurasia lived in small societies of nomadic gatherers and hunters or pastoralists, though some also engaged in small-scale farming.

From about 1000 BC, armies of pastoral nomads dominated the steppelands and semi-deserts that stretch across the southern parts of Inner Eurasia. These were nomadic or semi-nomadic peoples, whose wealth consisted mainly of large herds of livestock. Scythians, Hsiung-

Table 1.1   *Regional populations of Inner Eurasia 1000AD–2000AD (millions)*

Date	West of Urals	Caucasus	Central Asia/ Kazakhstan	Mongolia	Siberia	TOTAL
1000	4.00	0.50	2.50	0.50	0.10	7.60
1100	6.00	0.70	2.60	0.65	0.12	10.07
1200	9.00	1.00	2.80	0.80	0.14	13.74
1300	9.00	1.25	3.00	0.85	0.16	14.26
1400	9.00	1.00	3.20	0.70	0.18	14.08
1500	12.00	1.25	3.50	0.60	0.20	17.55
1600	15.00	1.50	4.00	0.60	0.22	21.32
1700	20.00	1.75	4.50	0.60	0.30	27.15
1800	36.00	2.00	6.00	0.60	1.00	45.60
1900	100.00	7.50	11.00	0.70	6.00	125.20
2000	190.00	32.00	60.00	3.00	40.00	325.00

Source: McEvedy and Jones, *Atlas of World Population History*, pp. 78–82, 158–65.

Nu, Sarmatians, Huns and Turks, all created empires that squeezed tributes from local populations of farmers, traders or other pastoralists. Occasionally, armies of pastoral nomads even invaded parts of Outer Eurasia. Some, such as the Huns, helped destroy the Roman Empire.

While pastoral nomads ruled the steppelands, agriculture spread along the southern rim of the steppe and in the northern forests. Agriculture spread most rapidly in the north and west, in the regions dominated today by European Russia, Belarus and Ukraine. Here the local populations included Finnic-speaking natives and growing numbers of Slavonic-speaking immigrants from the south and west. During the first millennium AD the region to the west of the Urals became the largest consolidated farming area in the whole of Inner Eurasia. This was where the 'neolithic' revolution made its first large-scale conquests in the harsh lands of Inner Eurasia. With the spread of farming, this became the most populous region of Inner Eurasia. Eventually, though with great difficulty, the governments of the region turned their demographic superiority into military and political superiority to create the Russian and Soviet Empires. The spread of agriculture in the forest lands of western Inner Eurasia was, therefore, of great importance for the future history of Eurasia as a whole. Figure 1.1 illustrates the demographic superiority enjoyed by the lands west of the Urals from as early as 1000 AD.

By the ninth century of the modern era, the forest lands west of the Urals were a region of many small chiefdoms. Their people lived in villages and fortified townships or *grady*, so that visiting Scandinavian

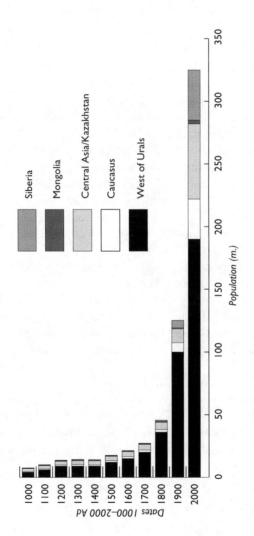

Figure 1.1 *Regional populations of Inner Eurasia*

merchants called the area *Gardariki*, 'the land of forts'. Its people lived off farming, and from fishing, hunting and forest products such as furs and honey. Occasionally, they raided neighbouring tribes for goods or slaves. Many paid tributes to pastoral nomadic peoples to the south and east, such as the Khazars. Much about this region is reminiscent of seventeenth- and eighteenth-century Africa, or seventeenth-century Canada.

■ Kievan Rus'

The first ruling group to combine these small agrarian societies into a larger political system appeared in the ninth century AD. Its influence extended along the river system from the Viking lands of the Baltic to the Byzantine Empire in the eastern Mediterranean, 'from the Varangians to the Greeks' as the medieval chroniclers put it. It also controlled the northern reaches of another major trading system, along the river Volga (see Figure 1.2). After c. 900, when its capital became Kiev, this group survived for almost four hundred years. Its first rulers were probably Viking warriors and merchants keen to exploit the region's abundant human and material riches. However, the ruling groups they led included native chiefs, and many of their followers came from the Slavic, Finnic and Turkic populations of the vast region they controlled.

The first rulers of Rus' mobilised resources crudely and violently. They lived partly off tributes collected from the various peoples they ruled or conquered. Such payments were little more than protection money. As a Soviet historian has written, they were 'a payment for peace and security, a way of avoiding the threat of plunder and devastation by their enemies'.[2] The *Russian Primary Chronicle*, the basic documentary source on early Kievan history, shows vividly the brutal methods the earliest princes of Rus' used to collect tributes from conquered tribes. The following document is from the reign of Prince Igor (913–45), the first ruler of Kievan Rus' for whose existence there is solid historical documentation.

☐ *Document 1.1: Prince Igor gathering tribute, AD 945*

In this year, Igor's retinue said to him, 'The servants of Sveinald are adorned with weapons and fine raiment, but we are naked. Go forth with us, oh Prince, after tribute, that both you and we may profit thereby.' Igor heeded their words, and he attacked Dereva in search of tribute. He sought to increase the previous tribute and collected it by violence from the people with the assistance of his followers. After thus gathering the tribute, he returned to his city. On his homeward way, he said to his followers, after some reflection, 'Go forward with the tribute. I shall

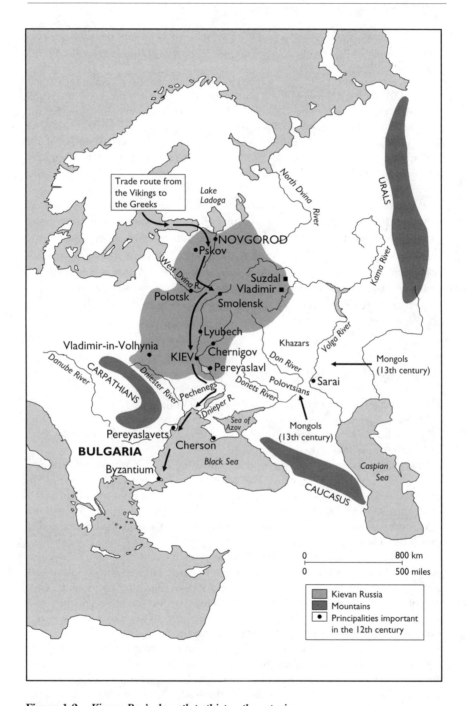

Figure 1.2   *Kievan Rus', eleventh to thirteenth centuries*

turn back, and rejoin you later.' He dismissed his retainers on their journey homeward, but being desirous of still greater booty he returned on his tracks with a few of his followers.

The Derevlians heard that he was again approaching, and consulted with Mal, their prince, saying, 'If a wolf come among the sheep, he will take away the whole flock one by one, unless he be killed. If we do not thus kill him now, he will destroy us all.' They then sent forward to Igor inquiring why he had returned, since he had collected all the tribute. But Igor did not heed them, and the Derevlians came forth from the city of Iskorosten and slew Igor and his company, for the number of the latter was few.[3]

This document shows what the direct mobilisation of resources meant in practice. It shows the role of force in collecting tribute, and the ways in which tribute collecting could provoke resistance. *The Chronicle* goes on to show how Igor's wife, Olga, dealt with this resistance by taking a terrible revenge on those who had killed her husband. This famous story conveys well the role of naked force in the pre-modern world. Document 1.2 describes how Olga tricked a delegation sent to Kiev from Dereva soon after Igor's death.

☐ *Document 1.2: Olga's revenge*

The Derevlians announced that their tribe had sent them to report that they had slain her husband, because he was like a wolf, crafty and ravening, but that their princes, who had thus preserved the land of Dereva, were good, and that Olga should come and marry their Prince Mal ....

Olga made this reply: 'Your proposal is pleasing to me; indeed, my husband cannot rise again from the dead. But I desire to honour you tomorrow in the presence of my people. Return now to your boat, and remain there with an aspect of arrogance. I shall send for you on the morrow, and you shall say: "We will not ride on horses nor go on foot; carry us in our boat." And you shall be carried in your boat.' Thus she dismissed them to their vessel.

Now Olga gave command that a large deep ditch should be dug in the castle within the hall, outside the city. Thus, on the morrow, Olga, as she sat in the hall, sent for the strangers, and her messengers approached them and said: 'Olga summons you to great honor.' But they replied: 'We will not ride on horseback nor in wagons, nor go on foot; carry us in our boat.' The people of Kiev then lamented: 'Slavery is our lot. Our prince is killed, and our princess intends to marry their prince.' So they carried the Derevlians in their boat. The latter sat on the cross-benches in great robes, puffed up with pride. They thus were borne into the court before Olga, and when the men had brought the Derevlians in, they dropped them into the trench along with the boat. Olga bent over and inquired whether they found the honor to their taste. They answered that it was worse than the death of Igor. She then commanded that they should be buried alive, and they were thus buried.[4]

The Chronicle account tells how Olga burnt to death the members of a second delegation, then massacred a third group of Derevlians, before besieging and sacking their capital, Iskorosten. The monks who wrote *The Chronicle* account came from the 'Caves Monastery' in Kiev, which survives to the present day. They admired Olga, partly because she was the first ruler of Rus' to become a Christian. The church made her a saint.

The rulers of Kievan Rus' also used indirect methods of mobilizing resources, for they traded with some of the goods they received as tribute. A famous account of this trade exists, written by the Byzantine emperor Constantine Porphyrogenitus in the mid-tenth century. This describes how, in winter, the princes of Rus' went off on their 'rounds', touring the villages and townships of nearby tribes. From these, they collected furs, honey, wax and sometimes slaves. In April, when the ice melted, they returned to the capital, Kiev. In May, they fitted out a fleet of large canoes, which they loaded with the booty they had collected in the winter. Then, heavily armed against marauding nomadic tribes, they began the dangerous trip down the river Dnieper with its many rapids. On arrival in Constantinople, they exchanged the produce they had collected for the luxury goods of the Mediterranean world.[5] In the early years of Kievan Rus', this trade was probably the main source of income for the princely elite and their retainers.

In the eleventh century, when the Kievan princes began to engage in husbandry and agriculture as well as trade, they found more sophisticated ways of mobilizing resources. The tributes once levied on conquered tribes became regular taxes imposed on the rural population, or revenues from estates worked by slaves or bonded servants. In about 988, the greatest of the early princes of Kiev, Vladimir I (ruled 980–1015), adopted the Orthodox or Byzantine form of Christianity, and Kievan Rus' became a part of Christian Europe. Christianity legitimized the exaction of taxes, for the Orthodox church taught obedience to the will of Christian princes, and received their protection in turn. Ecclesiastical support enabled the princes of Rus' to base their power on consent as well as on coercion.

Under Yaroslav the Wise (1019–54), Kievan Rus' was a civilized agrarian empire. Kiev itself was as wealthy, its architecture as beautiful, and its rulers as well-connected as any in Europe. At its height, Kievan Rus' had a single ruler, the Grand Prince of Kiev, and a single ruling clan, whose members moved from city to city according to complex rules of succession. Nevertheless, Rus' was never really a single state. It was a federation of small city-states, similar to classical Greece. Each had its own elites who lived in the capital city and collected tribute from surrounding villages. The armed might of the princes consisted of little more than a small band of personal retainers, the *druzhina*. Sometimes local militias would support the *druzhina*, though, as the fate of Prince Igor shows, local militias sometimes opposed the princes who tried to collect tributes from them.

What held the *druzhina* together? Ties of kinship counted for something. However, privilege was the primary bond, for members of the *druzhina* shared the tributes exacted with their help. Grand Prince Vladimir I understood as well as anyone that his own power depended on his ability to enrich his followers.

> On one occasion ... after the guests were drunk, they began to grumble against the prince, complaining that they were mistreated because he allowed them to eat with wooden spoons, instead of silver ones. When Vladimir heard of this complaint, he ordered that silver spoons should be moulded for his retinue to eat with, remarking that with silver and gold he could not secure a retinue, but that with a retinue he was in a position to win these treasures, even as his grandfather and his father had sought riches with their followers.[6]

The world of Kievan Rus' seems remote to us now. However, we can glimpse the life of its rulers through the testament that Grand Prince Vladimir Monomakh (1113–25) left his sons. This shows a life dominated by warfare and by hunting, itself a form of military training. The virtues Vladimir admires are bravery, endurance and physical toughness. His testament also reveals Prince Vladimir's profoundly religious outlook. His God is a powerful and fearsome overlord, who demands of his subjects obedience, worship, a sense of justice and charity towards the poor.

☐ *Document 1.3: From the 'Testament' of Vladimir Monomakh*

I, wretched man that I am ... sitting upon my sledge [that is, 'as I approach death'], have meditated in my heart and praised God, who has guided me, a sinner, even to this day. Let not my sons or anyone else who happens to hear this document laugh at its contents. But rather let any one of my sons who likes it take my words to heart and not be lazy, but work hard.

First, for the sake of God and your own souls, retain the fear of God in your hearts and give alms generously, for such liberality is the root of all good. ... Above all things, do not forget the poor but feed them to the extent of your means. Give alms to the orphan, protect the widow, and do not permit the mighty to destroy anyone. Do not kill the just or the unjust person or permit him to be killed. Do not destroy any soul even if he deserves death. ... Receive with affection the blessings of bishops, priests, and priors, and do not shun them, but rather, according to your means, love and help them, so that you may receive from them their prayers ... [for help] from God. ...

Do not be lazy in your own households, but keep watch over everything. Do not depend upon your steward or your servant lest they who visit you ridicule your house or your table. When you set out to war, do not be lazy, do not depend upon your *voevody* [commanders], do not indulge yourself in drinking, eating, or sleeping. Set the sentries yourselves, and at night go to sleep only after you have posted them on all sides of your troops, and get up early. Do not put down your weapons without a quick glance about you, for a man may thus perish suddenly through his own carelessness. Guard against lying, drunkenness, and lechery, for thus perish soul and body. ...

I now narrate to you, my sons, the fatigue I have endured on journeys and hunts ever since the age of thirteen. ... Among all my campaigns there are 83 long ones, and I do not count the minor adventures. I concluded 19 peace treaties with the Polovtsians [steppe nomads] both while my father was living and since then. ...

I devoted much energy to hunting as long as I reigned in Chernigov ... At Chernigov, I even bound wild horses with my bare hands. ... Two aurochs tossed me and my horse on their horns, a stag once butted me, an elk stamped upon me and another butted me with his horns, a boar once tore my sword from my thigh, a bear on one occasion bit the saddle-cloth beside my knee, and another wild beast jumped on my thigh and knocked over my horse with me. ...

In war and at the hunt, by night and by day, in heat and in cold, I did whatever my servant had to do, and gave myself no rest. ... I looked after things myself and did the same in my own household. At the hunt I posted the hunters, and I looked after the stables, the falcons, and the hawks. I did not allow the mighty to distress the common peasant or the poverty-stricken widow, and I interested myself in the church administration and service.[7]

Christianity united the princes of Kievan Rus'. So did kinship, for most princes claimed descent from Rurik, the legendary first ruler of Novgorod. But these ties were fragile, and there were long periods of warfare between rival princes. In the eleventh and twelfth centuries new difficulties appeared. The trade with Byzantium declined and attacks from nomadic tribes to the south increased. Finally, in the early thirteenth century, Kievan Rus' succumbed to a new and more formidable rival: the Mongols.

Why did the Kievan ruling group lose its grip on the territory it had lived off for so long? All ruling groups in this region faced the same basic problems, posed by geography. First, the territory of Kievan Rus' was difficult to defend, as it lacked natural defensive boundaries. Set in the world's largest lowland plain, Kievan Rus' was not protected by large mountain ranges or seas either from Europe in the west, or from steppe nomads to the south-east. So the whole burden of defence fell on the army. To survive external challenges, the rulers of this region needed an exceptionally large and expensive army.

Second, the land was difficult to farm. North of a line running from Kiev to Riazan (see Figure 2.4), the soils are poor, sandy podzols. In the northern parts of Rus', the short growing season meant that farmers had to complete all agricultural work in four to six months, in contrast to the eight or nine months available in western Europe. The winters were also extremely cold. This forced farmers to keep cattle indoors and feed them for long periods. The combination of poor soils and a short growing season kept grain yields low. This meant that the taxable surplus was meagre.

The difficulties of farming in this region meant that any ruling group was bound to weigh heavily on the population it ruled. This, of course, was likely to provoke resistance from below, which meant that rulers in this region faced serious threats both from abroad and from below. So, ruling this territory required exceptional organization, discipline and unity. Not only would ruling elites have to extract a heavy tribute from the population they ruled, but they would also have to pay a heavy price in discipline themselves. All in all, mobilizing the demographic superiority of the lands west of the Urals would not be easy.

None of these problems was critical while there existed no serious rivals to the princes of Kievan Rus'. While their rivals were as weak as they were, they could survive in spite of their small armies and the constant feuding that deprived them of unity, cohesion and group discipline. Once the Mongols appeared, with their much greater discipline and unity, the weaknesses of the Kievan ruling group proved fatal.

■ Rus' under the Mongols, 1240 to 1480

In 1206 in Mongolia, a *Khuriltai*, or gathering of Mongol tribes, elected as their leader a chieftain called Temuchin. They gave him the title of Genghis Khan ('Universal Ruler'). Genghis Khan had earned his position by the skill he displayed as a military leader during the vicious tribal wars of his youth. As leader of a large confederation of pastoral nomadic tribes, he now directed their energies towards further conquest. By his death in 1227, Genghis Khan had conquered Siberia, central Asia and northern China. In 1223, Mongol armies led by Genghis Khan's general, Subodei, also made a first, brief foray into Kievan Rus'. Here they encountered and defeated an alliance of Rus' and Polovtsians (Kuman) on the river Kalka. As a sign of respect for the rank of the princes they captured in this battle, the Mongols executed them without spilling their blood. According to the *Novgorod Chronicle*, 'The princes were taken by the Tatars and crushed beneath platforms placed over their bodies on the top of which the Tatars celebrated their victory banquet'.[8] The arrival of the Mongols marked a new stage in the struggle for control of Rus'.

In 1237, Genghis Khan's grandson, Batu, renewed the attacks on Rus' in a terrible war of conquest through its northern cities. The failure of local princes to unite made Batu's task that much easier. In 1240 Batu's armies sacked Kiev itself. In 1241 Batu established a capital at Sarai on the River Volga (south of modern Stalingrad/Volgograd). The Mongol Empire broke up within a generation of these conquests. Nevertheless, for more than two centuries, much of Kievan Rus' came under the control of Mongol *khanates* or 'hordes' based on the lower reaches of the river Volga.

As usual in this era, the aim of conquest was to collect tribute. Document 1.4 is an account from a Rus' chronicle of the attacks of 1237 on the town of Riazan', south-east of Moscow.

☐ *Document 1.4: Khan Batu attacks Riazan', 1237*

That same winter the godless Tatars [Mongols], with their tsar Batu, came from the east to the land of Riazan', by forest ... and ... sent their emissaries ... to the Princes of Riazan', asking from them one-tenth of everything: of princes, of people, of horses ... And the princes replied: 'When we are gone, then all will be yours.' ... The princes of Riazan' sent to Prince Iurii of Vladimir, asking him to send help or to come himself; but Prince Iurii did not come himself nor did he heed the entreaty of the princes of Riazan', but rather he wished to defend himself separately. But there was no opposing the wrath of God; He brought bewilderment, and terror, and fear and trepidation upon us, for our sins. Then the foreigners besieged the town of Riazan', on December 16, and surrounded it with a palisade; the prince of Riazan' shut himself up in the town with his people. The Tatars took the town of Riazan' on the twenty-first of the same month, and burned it all, and killed its prince, Iurii, and his princess, and seized the men, women, and children, and monks, nuns, and priests; some they struck down with swords, while others they shot with arrows and flung into the flames; still others they seized and bound ... They delivered many holy churches to the flames, and burned monasteries and villages, and seized property, and then went on to Kolomna.[9]

After the first invasions the Mongols established a more regular system of administration and taxation over the lands they had conquered. Usually, they let local princes act as their agents. To these princes they granted a *iarlyk*, or charter, confirming their authority. During two centuries, more than two hundred princes received the Mongol *iarlyk*. They collected taxes levied by the Mongols and helped suppress any opposition. To help them (and to keep an eye on them), the Mongols stationed their own officials and soldiers in the major cities. In return for helping the Mongols, those princes who received the *iarlyk* enjoyed other privileges. If they needed it, they could also call on military support from Mongol armies. In effect, they became subordinate members of the Mongol ruling group.

In their early years, the Mongol rulers were more powerful than the Kievan princes they replaced. The differences between the two groups reflect one of the basic principles governing the success of a ruling group:

the more united and disciplined a ruling group, the more resources it can mobilise, and the larger the armies it can field. The Mongols were more unified, more disciplined, taxed more heavily than the Kievan princes, and had a larger and stronger army.

The Mongols invaded with a disciplined cavalry army much larger than the traditional Kievan *druzhina*. Batu's invasion army of 1237 had 50 000 Mongols and 150 000 auxiliaries. It relied on ferocious internal discipline. A papal envoy, Plano Carpini, described the army as follows after visiting the Mongol Horde in 1246.

☐ *Document 1.5: Plano Carpini on the Mongol army, 1246*

On the subdivisions of the army I will say the following: Genghis Khan ordered that there should be one man in charge of every ten ... and one in charge of every ten groups of ten ... and one in charge of every ten groups of 100 [and so on] ... At the head of the whole army there were to be two or three generals, but they in turn were subordinate to a single leader. In battle, if one, or two, or three members of a group of ten run away, then all other members of the ten are executed even if they have not run; and if all ten run away, then all the other members of their hundred are executed ... in the same way, if one or two from a group of ten enter into battle bravely, and if one member is captured and his comrades do not free him, then they are all executed.[10]

Members of the Mongol elite obeyed a single, autocratic leader, who expected total obedience from his commanders. During the treacherous tribal wars of his youth, Genghis Khan learnt that ties of kinship could be fragile. So he often preferred to appoint as commanders men of low birth who depended entirely on his favour. In their turn, members of the Mongol ruling elite knew that their wealth and status depended on strong leadership. When offered the imperial throne in 1246, Khan Guyuk asked the Mongol tribal leaders: 'If you want me to reign over you are you ready each one of you to do what I shall command, to come whenever I call, to go wherever I may choose to send you, to put to death whomsoever I shall command you?'.[11] They said they were.

Discipline and autocratic leadership enabled the Mongols to impose a much higher level of taxation than their predecessors. Soon after their first invasion, they demanded a tenth of everything in the lands they conquered – crops, animals and people. (They used the people either as soldiers or as slaves.) The terror the Mongols inflicted during the first invasion encouraged prompt payment of the tributes they demanded. Soon, however, the Mongol rulers regularized the system of tribute. In 1257, with the help of Chinese advisers, officials conducted the first census of Rus', and this became the basis for assessing future taxes.

The imposition of this huge fiscal burden provoked resistance, and resistance provoked reprisals. Here is an account from the *Russian Primary Chronicle* of an uprising in Tver in 1327, ninety years after Batu's invasion.

☐ *Document 1.6: The Tver uprising, 1327*

The people, constantly hurt in their pride by the pagans [Tatars/Mongols], complained many times to the grand prince [of Tver] that he should defend them; but he, although he saw the injuries done to his people, could not defend them and ordered them to be patient; but the people of Tver could not endure this and waited for a suitable moment. And it happened that on the fifteenth day of August, in mid-morning, during the market hours, a certain deacon, Tveritin, surnamed Diudko, was leading a small and very fat mare to drink the water of the Volga; the Tatars saw her and carried her away. The deacon was grieved and began to cry out loudly, saying: 'Oh men of Tver, do not let me down!' And a fight took place between them; the Tatars, relying on their unlimited authority, began to use weapons, and straightway men gathered, and the people arose in tumult, and sounded the bells, and assembled in a *veche* [town meeting]; and the entire city turned [against the Tatars], and the people all gathered right away, and there was agitation among them, and the men of Tver gave a shout and began to kill the Tatars, wherever they found them, until they had killed Shevkal himself [the Tatar representative] and all of them in turn … And after they had heard this, the lawless tsar [Mongol Khan] sent an army in winter into the Russian land, with the *voevoda* [commander-in-chief] Fedorchiuk, and five *temniki* [commanders of units of 10 000 soldiers each]; and they killed many people, and took others captive, and put Tver and all the towns to flame.[12]

The Mongols' weak spot was their lack of an effective machinery of persuasion. In the thirteenth century, the Mongols worshipped many gods and expressed interest in many different religions, including Nestorian Christianity. They had no missionary zeal and made no serious attempt to convert the Christian population of Rus'. As a result, they never persuaded them of the legitimacy of Mongol power. The conversion of the Golden Horde to Islam in the late thirteenth and early fourteenth centuries created a permanent ideological gulf between its rulers and the Christian populations of what had been Kievan Rus'. Tatar power over Rus' rested almost entirely on force. When disunity began to undermine their power, the Golden Horde could count on no support from the population of Rus'.

The Mongols did not absorb all the lands of Kievan Rus'. By the fourteenth century, the western parts, including Kiev itself and the Dnieper basin, had fallen into the hands of the grand princes of Lithuania, whose dynasty merged with that of Poland in 1386. These regions later became the core of modern Ukraine. The contrast between the Mongol and Lithuanian political systems is instructive, for the Lithuanian princes had nothing like the power of the early Mongol Khans. The Lithuanian princes had limited wealth, and a council (*rada*) of leading nobles restricted their power.

Further north, the forests of the taiga restricted the mobility and power of the Mongol cavalry. Here the commercial city-state of Novgorod escaped direct Mongol control, though it also paid tribute. Like Lithuania, its political system was far from autocratic. Leading landed families of *boyars* (nobles), together with the city's merchants, ruled through a *veche*, or town council. This imposed severe limits on the financial and political powers of the princes and expelled those who overstepped these limits.

Eventually, the loose oligarchic structures of Novgorod and Lithuania, like those of Kievan Rus', proved fatally weak. By 1500 both regions had been absorbed by a Muscovite ruling group that had acquired a harsher political culture under the supervision of the Mongols.

Those princes who acted as agents for the Mongols also learned their methods of rule. None learnt them better than the princes of Moscow. Eventually, they would use them to form a new ruling group.

The first mention of Moscow dates from 1147. At that time Moscow was a border fortress belonging to Yurii Dolgorukii, grand prince of the principality of Suzdal. A century later Moscow was already a major principality, and Khan Batu's armies sacked it in 1238. In 1327 its prince, Ivan I (1325–40), became chief agent for the Mongols in the north-east of Rus'. So successfully did Ivan collect taxes for his Mongol overlords and himself, that contemporaries called him Ivan Kalita, or 'Moneybags'. Ivan's success had much to do with the loyalty with which he served his Mongol masters. He spent two years early in his life at the capital of the Golden Horde, where he befriended Khan Uzbeq. In 1327 he led a Tatar army that punished the principality of Tver for rebellion (see Document 1.6). In return, the Mongols appointed Ivan grand prince of all the lands of Rus'.

As agents of the Mongol Empire, the prince and his followers shared some of its privileges. They did not suffer from the raids that devastated less submissive areas of Rus', and Muscovy paid only one-seventh of the normal tribute. By the late fourteenth century, the prince himself and the town of Moscow paid no tribute at all. Under these conditions, Moscow's prestige, power and wealth increased, while that of other principalities declined. This made Moscow an attractive place to settle, and many wealthy families migrated there with their followers and settled down as *boyars* of the prince of Muscovy. These favourable conditions also persuaded the Orthodox Church to make Moscow its metropolitan centre in 1326. In return the Church gave the Prince of Moscow its support and its blessing. In the eyes of most Christians this gave the rulers of Moscow a legitimacy that the rulers of the Golden Horde lacked.

The growing power of Moscow's leaders depended not just on their own skills, but also on changes in the nature of the entire ruling group. Indeed, the building of a powerful government was never just the work of rulers. Throughout Russian history, it depended on the outcome of a tense and difficult collaboration between rulers and other members of the ruling group. Where leaders have no bureaucracies to carry out their will, their power depends entirely on gaining the support of clan leaders. In Muscovy, in the fourteenth and fifteenth centuries, there emerged a close-knit group of leading *boyar* clans, each with their own territories and their own followers. The distinctive feature of the Muscovite *boyar* elite was that its leaders were unusually successful in preventing any public display of disunity or conflict. This enabled them to give their united support to the princes of Moscow. The growing power of Moscow's rulers depended largely on the solidarity of a small number of great *boyar* families, bound to each other and to the royal family through networks of intermarriage. Autocracy was the price that leading families willingly paid to ensure stability in a dangerous world. Carefully arranged marriages between leading families provided the adhesive that held the ruling group together.[13]

As the power of Moscow grew, that of the Tatars declined. As with the Kievan princes before them, their main problem was disunity. From the mid-fourteenth century, the Golden Horde split into rival groups which formed distinct Tatar kingdoms. In 1380, at the battle of Kulikovo, a Muscovite army soundly defeated the army of Khan Mamai of Kazan. Two years later the Tatars retaliated, but they were never as strong again. In 1480 the retreat of a Tatar army before another Muscovite army, led this time by Tsar Ivan III, marked the symbolic end of what Russian historians call the 'Tatar yoke'. In fiscal terms, the change meant that the princes of Moscow ceased to pay tribute. It did not mean that they ceased to collect taxes from those they ruled.

 ## Muscovite Russia: The Sixteenth and Seventeenth Centuries

Patriotic Russian historians have portrayed the end of Tatar domination as a moment of national liberation. Unlike the Tatars, the Muscovite ruling group was ethnically and linguistically similar to most of their subjects. As Christians, they could also appear as defenders of the true faith against the infidels. Moscow, they began to claim, was the third Rome, the capital

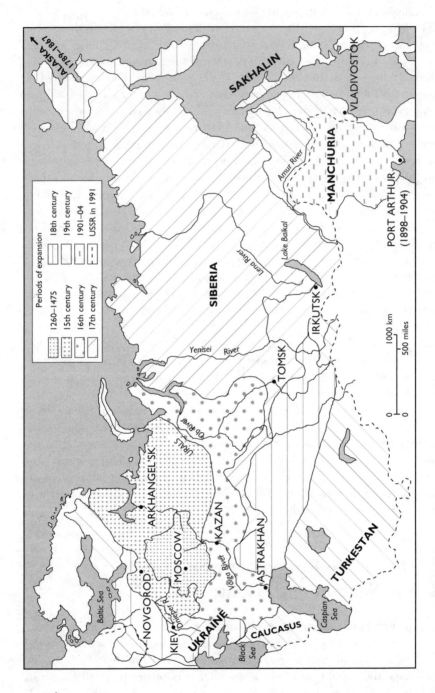

Figure 1.3 *The expansion of Muscovy from the thirteenth century*

of true Christianity. In the eyes of the Christian population, this gave them a legitimacy the Tatars had always lacked.

Nevertheless, they were as much rulers as the Tatars had been. They could be as savage towards their fellow Russians, and they taxed as hard. Liberation had merely substituted a Christian and Russian ruling group for a Tatar and Islamic ruling group. As early as 1389, the will of Prince Dmitrii Donskoi, the victor of Kulikovo, declared that: 'If God should change the Horde [that is, should liberate Russia from the Horde] and my children do not have to give tribute to the Horde, then whatever [tribute] each of my sons collects in his appanage, that shall be his'.[14]

The taxes the Muscovite princes collected even looked like tributes. *Kormlenie*, or 'feeding', was a traditional form of taxation that survived to the sixteenth century. A prince would assign a certain area to one of his nobles. The *kormlenshchik*, or grantee, would then administer this territory, try court cases and collect taxes. In return, he collected whatever he needed to live on from the local population.

☐ *Document 1.7: A* Kormlenie *charter of Ivan III, late fifteenth century*

I, Grand Prince Ivan Vasil'evich of all Russia, have granted to Ivan, son of Andrei Plemiannikov [the villages of] Pushka and Osintsovo as a *kormlenie* with the right to administer justice [*pravda*] [and collect fees for this service] and to collect taxes on the purchase, sale, and branding of horses [*piatno*]. And you, all the people of this *volost'* [district], honor him and obey him, and he will govern you and judge you and will conduct your affairs in every way as they were conducted heretofore.[15]

Such a grant made sense only because everyone understood that the Grand Prince would punish the villages if they did not provide an adequate living for his *kormlenshchik*. In this way, the ruling group as a whole upheld the authority of its individual agents.

The reign of Ivan III (1462–1505) marks the emergence of Muscovy as a powerful and independent state. Muscovy formally rejected the overlordship of the Mongols in 1480. During Ivan's reign Muscovy also absorbed the principalities of Novgorod, Tver and Pskov. The conquest of these weaker states by the autocratic principality of Moscow showed the advantages of strong leadership in a region that lacked natural defensive borders. It also justified Ivan's assumption of the title of Grand Prince of all Russia. Finally, his conquests made available plenty of spare land that Ivan used to support his own nobles in return for service.

Over the next two centuries, the political history of Muscovy consists of attempts to tighten the discipline and unity of the ruling group even further by increasing the power of the Grand Prince of Moscow. The result was the emergence of a peculiarly autocratic political culture in Muscovy. This enabled the ruling group of Muscovite Russia to mobilize the resources needed to defend and enlarge Muscovy's vulnerable borders.

How was Russia's autocratic political culture forged? The process was complex, prolonged and painful, and there was never any certainty that it would succeed. To enhance their authority, rulers had to persuade, cajole and, if possible, compel members of the ruling group to accept that strong leadership was necessary for their own survival. The rulers of Muscovy could not have done this if many members of the group had not understood that this was, indeed, true. Leaders and members of the ruling group co-operated in the building of an autocratic political system.

Because of their strategic position, leaders were in the best position to enhance the unity of the ruling group by increasing their own power. Like Genghis Khan, Muscovy's more able rulers understood that the best way to increase their power was to favour individuals whose position in the ruling group was insecure, against those whose membership rested on birth and kinship. To understand how this process worked, we must distinguish between two sections of Muscovy's ruling elite. At the top of the system was the *boyar* elite. The *boyars* claimed to owe their position to birth, for most were descended from old princely families or their military retinues. They viewed their land as their own property, not as a grant from the prince of Moscow. They also claimed the freedom to transfer their allegiance from one prince to another whenever they wished. So, though the great *boyar* families had laid the foundations for Muscovite autocracy, their obedience was by no means total.

Below the *boyars*, there existed a group of less privileged nobles, who came to be known as 'courtiers', or *dvoriane*. The *dvoriane* were of lower birth than the *boyars*. Most had entered the nobility through service as officers in the army or officials of the state. In return, they received conditional grants of land, or *pomest'ya*, which they kept as long as they served their prince. This meant that they owed their membership in the ruling class and the privileges it brought to the favour of the prince. That favour was conditional. It could be withdrawn as easily as it had been given. This ensured that the *dvoriane* could usually be counted on to obey their ruler without question.

If the *dvoriane* needed a strong ruler to protect their precarious privileges, *boyars* sometimes felt threatened by their ruler's increasing power. So, the best way for rulers to tighten the discipline of the ruling group even further was to favour the *dvoriane* at the expense of the *boyars*. A series of rulers favoured the *dvoriane*, and used the power this gave them to break the independence of the great *boyar* clans.

By the reign of Ivan III this policy was already well established. Ivan III's will differs significantly from those of earlier Kievan and Muscovite princes.

First, it limited the right of *boyars* to leave the service of Ivan's son and heir, Vasilii, and take their land with them. Second, it gave most of the land ruled by Ivan III to Vasilii, the oldest son, instead of dividing it up equally among several sons. These large landholdings, together with the lands conquered from Novgorod and Pskov, gave the rulers of Muscovy the resources needed to buy the loyalty of lesser nobles by granting them *pomest'ya*.

By the reign of Vasilii III (1505–33), the process of disciplining the ruling elite and increasing the authority of the grand prince had already created an unusually autocratic political world. A German traveller, Sigismund von Herberstein, who visited Muscovy in the early sixteenth century, described how its autocratic political culture shaped the world of upper-class men and women.

□ *Document 1.8: Herberstein on the Muscovite nobility under Vasilii III*

In the control which he [Grand Duke Vasilii Ivanovich, the eldest son of Ivan III] exercises over his people, he easily surpasses all the rulers of the entire world ... He obliges all people to do hard service, to such an extent that whomever he orders to be with him in court, or to go to war, or to go on any mission is forced to undertake whatever it may be at his own expense. The younger sons of the *boyars* are excepted, that is, of the nobles of lesser fortune. It is customary to send for them every year, and because they are oppressed by poverty, to support them with a fixed but inadequate salary ... He uses his authority as much in spiritual as lay affairs and freely decrees according to his own will concerning the life and properties of all people.

Of the counsellors whom he had, there is no one of such authority that he would dare to disagree or to resist him in anything. They publicly declare that the will of the Prince is the will of God, and that whatever the Prince does is done by the will of God ...

[While the men in noble families served their tsar, their women lived a life of segregation and isolation, dominated by the demands of family and clan honour.]

Love is lukewarm among most married people, especially among the nobility and the princes because they marry a girl not seen before, and, occupied by services of the prince, they are forced to desert them, contaminating themselves in the meantime with base lust for another.

The condition of women is very miserable, for no woman is thought to be modest unless she lives locked in her home, and unless she is so guarded that she never goes out. They believe, as I have said, a woman is almost totally immodest if she is seen by foreigners or people outdoors. Locked in the house, women spin and sew. Legal and business matters are absolutely never discussed in the home. All household duties are performed by serfs ... But the wives of the poor perform the household tasks and cook.[16]

The main achievement of Ivan IV, 'The Terrible' (1533–84), was to tighten the discipline of the ruling group even further by a violent assault on the *boyar* class. During his own early life he saw the divisive struggles of the great *boyar* clans. Once he became ruler in his own right, Ivan tried to free himself from the power of the major *boyar* families, and increase his own power. He did this in the firm belief that the autocrat should be subject to no one but God, for disobedience and 'internecine strife ... cause kingdoms to crumble'.[17]

Members of the service nobility, such as the writer Ivan Peresvetov, encouraged Ivan's suspicions of the *boyar* class and his preference for warriors from the service nobility.

☐ *Document 1.9: Peresvetov's 'Tale of the Sultan Mohammed', circa 1547*

From earliest times the wise philosophers have disapproved of those men of high rank who find favour with the tsar neither for their services in war nor by virtue of their wisdom. The wise philosophers speak about them thus: 'These are sorcerers and heretics, who take away the tsar's happiness and wisdom, and cast a spell upon the tsar's heart by means of sorcery and heresy, and enfeeble the warriors.' And the *voivode* [ruler] of Moldavia [the fictional mouthpiece for Peresvetov's own views] speaks thus: 'Such as these should be burned by fire or consigned to some other cruel death, so that the evil may not multiply ... for the tsar cannot exist without his warriors ... In his warriors lies the tsar's strength and glory. The tsar should rule his realm by the grace of God and with great wisdom; and he should be generous to his warriors, as a father to his children. In the tsar's generosity towards his warriors lies his wisdom; a generous hand will never be empty and it gathers great glory for itself.'[18]

Though there was some logic to Ivan's treatment of the *boyar* elite, there was also an element of sheer madness. Yet Ivan's madness was itself a symptom of Russia's autocratic culture. The intense pressure on the entire ruling group to display unity and discipline did not suppress all conflict; it just drove conflict underground. In public, the elaborate rituals of autocracy required nobles to display total subservience to their monarch. Privately, there were always hidden conflicts between individuals and families within the nobility. These were fought out in a twilight world of intrigue and plots. In this way, the banning of open conflict, which became a basic rule of Russia's autocratic political culture, made political conflicts all the more vicious. Hidden conflicts created a pervasive atmosphere of paranoia and suspicion that led to outbreaks of savage internal conflict. These aspects of Russia's autocratic political culture help explain the violent conflicts of Ivan's reign, and those of later periods of Russia's history.

Childhood memories of insults and threats from leading *boyars* intensified Ivan's paranoia. During the period of the *oprichnina* (1564–72), he divided the country into two parts. One, the *oprichnina*, he ruled through a group of newly ennobled *dvoriane* and foreign mercenaries. These took oaths of absolute obedience to Tsar Ivan and depended totally on his favour. They even wore a special black uniform, and carried a broom with which they could symbolically sweep away treason. Ivan used the *oprichniki*, as his followers were called, to destroy many *boyar* families. Altogether, 600–700 *boyars* perished together with their families, while many others lost their land. In this gruesome way Ivan proved that the *boyars*, too, depended on his favour. In name, the *boyar* families survived the *oprichnina*, but from then on their dependence on the Tsar was clear. Ivan had almost managed to reduce the *boyars* to the position of *dvoriane*. In doing so, he greatly enhanced his own power as tsar.

However, Ivan IV overdid it. His reign caused such destruction, both internally and through the long series of wars he fought, that it nearly ruined the entire system. In 1598, the death of his son and successor, Fedor I, without an heir, ended the *Rurikid* dynasty that had ruled since the ninth century. Between 1598 and 1613 Muscovy endured the 'Time of Troubles'. This was a confused period of anarchy, foreign intervention and civil war, during which there were several unsuccessful attempts to found new dynasties. As much as one-third of the population of Muscovy may have perished during these terrible years. Polish and Swedish armies invaded the country and, often with the help of leading Muscovite *boyars*, tried to place their own nominees on the Muscovite throne. Finally, in 1613, an assembly of Russian nobles, merchants and officials, the so-called *Zemskii Sobor* or Land Council, elected one of their number, Michael Romanov, as the new tsar. The Romanov dynasty was to survive until 1917.

The experiences of this period were terrible for both ordinary people and nobles. This explains the enthusiasm with which all classes welcomed the new dynasty. There was now a widespread acceptance of the need for internal discipline under an autocratic tsar if there was to be any stability in Muscovy. These attitudes show up in many documents of the period. The following is a message sent to all major towns by leaders of the army that expelled the foreign armies in 1612.

☐ *Document 1.10: Invitation to help elect a new sovereign, 1612*

And you, sirs, should take counsel together with all the people, mindful of God and of our faith, lest we remain without a sovereign in these times of utter ruin, so that by counsel of the entire state we may choose a sovereign by common agreement, whomever God may grant us in his righteous love of mankind, lest the Muscovite state be utterly destroyed by such calamities. You know yourselves, sirs: how can we defend ourselves now, without a sovereign, against our common enemies, the Poles and Lithuanians, and Germans [Swedes], and the Russian rogues who are renewing bloody strife in the state? How can we, without a sovereign, negotiate with neighbouring sovereigns about great matters of the state and of the land? And how can our realm stand firm and unshakeable henceforth?[19]

During the seventeenth century, the new dynasty began rebuilding Muscovy's autocratic political system. An important sign of this was the decline of the *Zemskii Sobor*, a council of nobles and officials which, under other circumstances, might have evolved into a parliament. It had first met in 1550. Thereafter it met periodically for over a century, but it never placed serious limits on royal authority. Indeed, in 1613 it had met specifically to re-establish autocracy. In practice, it became an instrument of royal power, for it provided a way of sounding out opinion and mobilizing support from those lesser members of the ruling class who rarely met the tsar directly.

The revival of autocracy made it easier to mobilize the men, money and equipment needed to supply Muscovy's huge armies. The modernization of Muscovy's army had begun under Ivan IV, who introduced professional units of *streltsy* or musketeers. He also tried to make army service compulsory for all landowners. The size of Ivan's armies and the hardiness of Muscovite soldiers amazed the Englishman, Richard Chancellor, in the 1550s.

☐ *Document 1.11: Chancellor on the Muscovite army, 1550s*

He [Tsar Ivan IV] never goes to the field himself with under two hundred thousand men, yet does he never take to his wars either husbandman or merchant. All his men are horsemen, all archers. Their armour is a coat of mail with a skull on their heads. Some of their coats are covered with velvet or cloth of gold: their desire is to be sumptuous in the field. Partly I have seen it or else I would scarcely have believed it ... They are a kind of people most sparing in diet and most patient in extremity of cold, above all others. For when the ground is covered with snow and is grown terrible and hard with frost, this Russ hangs up his mantle or soldier's coat against that part whence the wind and snow drives and so, making a little fire, lies down with his back towards the weather; his drink is cold water from the river, mingled with oatmeal, and this is all his good cheer, and he thinketh himself well and daintily fed therewith; the hard ground is his feather bed and some block or stone his pillow; and as for his horse, he is, as it were, a chamberfellow with his master, faring both alike. How justly may this barbarous and rude Russ condemn the daintiness and niceness of our Captains who, living in a soil and air much more temperate, yet commonly use furred boots and cloaks?[20]

In the seventeenth century, the use of foreign technology and foreign-trained soldiers and commanders enabled Muscovite armies to challenge the major powers of central Europe, such as Poland and Sweden. Muscovy's military power also underpinned a burst of territorial expansion. By the treaty of Pereiaslavl in 1654, Muscovy absorbed Ukraine, the heartland of Kievan Rus'. Even more spectacular was Muscovite expansion to the east. Ivan IV had conquered the Khanates of Kazan and Astrakhan in 1552 and 1556. These conquests gave Moscow control of the Volga river to the Caspian sea. Cossack troops launched the conquest of Siberia in 1582, and by the end of the seventeenth century Muscovy claimed the whole of this vast new territory. With the conquest of Siberia, Muscovy created a land empire to match the overseas empires of western Europe. It also became the dominant power of Inner Eurasia. The seventeenth century, therefore, marks a crucial turning point in the history of Inner Eurasia. This is when the governments of Muscovy finally turned their demographic superiority over the steppelands into a clear military superiority. This was the most important single achievement of Muscovy's autocratic governments, and it laid the foundations for the military successes of the Russian and Soviet Empires.

The growth of the army demanded huge resources in cash and in men. Of all the methods used by Muscovite governments to mobilize these resources, serfdom was the most important.

In the sixteenth and seventeenth centuries, *dvoriane* were the core of the Muscovite army. Most received temporary land grants to enable them to support themselves and pay for their armour and their mounts. However, land was useless without labour to work it. Peasants settled on the estates of nobles or *boyars* had always paid for their land by supplying produce, or labour or cash. But as the burden of warfare grew during the reign of Ivan IV, so did the burdens of service, and so did the demands nobles made on their peasants. Many peasants responded by fleeing to unoccupied lands or to landlords who demanded less of them. By the end of the reign of Ivan IV whole provinces had been depopulated in this way. This posed severe problems for the government, as *dvoriane* without serfs could not serve the army properly. The government responded with charters banning the movement of peasants except at certain times of the year, such as St George's day, just after the harvest. In 1581, it went further, banning all movement for a year. This limited the traditional freedoms of Russian peasants settled on noble lands, and began the process of transforming them into serfs. The government renewed these bans many times over the next decades, though its efforts had little effect during the Time of Troubles. Then, in 1649, the government declared that the ban on peasant movement was to be permanent.

The law code or *Ulozhenie* of 1649 decreed that peasants were to remain permanently on the lands they occupied in that year. It gave each serf-owning family the right to exploit the labour and produce of the peasants settled on their land, theoretically forever. Article 9 of chapter XI of the *Ulozhenie* declared:

> And whatever peasants and *bobyli* [poor peasants] are listed with any [landowner] in the census books of the previous years of [1646 and 1647], and who subsequent to these census books have fled, or shall henceforth flee, from those men with whom they are listed in the census books: those fugitive peasants and *bobyli*, and their brothers, children, nephews, and grandchildren with their wives and with their children and with all their possessions, and with their harvested and unharvested grain, shall be returned from flight to those men from whom they fled, in accordance with the census books, without time limit; and henceforth under no circumstances should anyone receive peasants who are not his and keep them with him.[21]

To enforce the new laws, the government had to deal with the problem of runaways. In a country as large as Muscovy, it was extremely difficult to stop peasants from fleeing oppressive masters. This was particularly true of the borderlands to the south and south-east, where the Cossacks lived. Here is how the great nineteenth-century historian S. M. Soloviev described the task the government had undertaken.

> The chase after human beings, after working hands, was carried out throughout the Muscovite state on a vast scale. Hunted were city people who ran away from *tiaglo* [tax obligations] wherever they only could, by concealing themselves, bonding themselves [as slaves], enrolling in the ranks of lower grade clerks. Hunted were peasants who, burdened with heavy taxes, roamed individually and in droves migrated beyond 'the Rock' (the Urals). Landlords hunted for their peasants who scattered, sought concealment among other landlords, ran away to the Ukraine, to the Cossacks.[22]

The government also raised resources in other ways. To pay for foreign soldiers and foreign military and industrial technology it had to find cash. But this was not easy in a society in which most people were still self-sufficient. Fortunately for the government, there were some goods that even peasants had to purchase, and Muscovite governments discovered as early as the sixteenth century that they could raise large revenues by controlling the sale and production of these rare commodities. In the seventeenth century, the most important goods of this kind were salt and vodka. Both were vital in daily life. Salt was used to pickle vegetables and meat over the winter, while vodka was a vital ingredient in all social and church ceremonials. Because of their importance, people had to buy vodka and salt even if the government taxed them heavily. By 1700, state controlled taverns or *kabaks* may have generated more than 10 per cent of the government's income. The Muscovite government was already in danger of turning its citizens into alcoholics to pay for its army.[23]

The Church taught the peasantry that it was their religious duty to obey a government established by God. However, as the burden of taxes and serfdom rose, the power of moral and religious exhortations declined. From early in the seventeenth century, peasants began to resist the growing burdens imposed by Muscovy's autocratic state.

Resistance took many forms: flight, the murder of landlords or their bailiffs, and occasionally, large-scale peasant rebellions. After the Bolotnikov uprising of 1606–7, such peasant wars were to become periodic features of Russian political life until the twentieth century. The greatest of these rebellions in the late seventeenth century was led by a Don Cossack leader, Stenka Razin, in 1670–1. Often the moral inspiration for rebellion came from religious dissenters, the so-called 'Old Believers', who had left the official church after the *Raskol*, the religious schism of the mid-seventeenth century. The political inspiration usually came from non-Russian peoples of the borderlands, determined to resist the Muscovite juggernaut.

■ Imperial Russia: The Eighteenth Century

By the late seventeenth century, serfdom and autocracy were the twin pillars of the Russian political and social system. However, it was under Peter I that the Russian ruling group assumed its most united and disciplined form. Peter's reign began with internal squabbles over succession to the throne. Divisions within the government weakened the state and led to military defeats at the hands of the Swedes and Turks.

Peter became sole ruler in 1696, but the huge reforms that characterized his reign did not begin for several years. The trigger for reform was a humiliating defeat at the hands of the Swedes at Narva in 1700. This made Peter face the basic problem of all Russian ruling groups – the task of ruling a poor country with inadequately defended borders.

His reforms clearly show the relationship between these factors and the authoritarian political culture of the Russian ruling group.

Peter began his reforms with the army. In 1698–9 he suppressed a mutiny among the *streltsy* units. He did so with a violence that showed that he would tolerate no indiscipline in his armies. As many as 1200 *streltsy* were executed or tortured to death. Typically, Peter set his nobles an example by personally torturing and executing some of the rebels. After

1700 Peter increased the army's size, tightened its discipline, and hired foreign military experts to train and lead its troops. By 1709 he was able to inflict a serious defeat on the Swedes at the battle of Poltava. His control of the Baltic shoreline was by then so secure that in 1712 he made the port of St Petersburg (which he had founded in 1703) his capital city. It remained the capital until March 1918. By 1721, with the signing of the Treaty of Nystadt, Russia had become the dominant power in northern Europe. Its old rivals, Poland, Sweden and Turkey, entered long periods of decline. In the same year, Peter declared Russia to be an Empire, and assumed for himself the title of 'Emperor'.

Peter's military reforms demanded a huge mobilization of human and material resources, and caused great suffering. The government drafted hundreds of thousands of men to fight in its armies and to carry out immense public works programmes, such as the building of St Petersburg. Thousands died during the building of the new capital because of the appalling conditions under which they had to work. A new system of military recruitment required that every twenty peasant households produce one recruit each year. The recruits served for life, and their families mourned them as if they had died. Money taxes also increased, probably by 200 or 300 per cent during his reign. In 1724, Peter consolidated many new taxes into a single tax on all males, the 'poll tax'. Introduction of the new tax tidied up the system of serfdom, for it tied down even those peasants who had no landlords and had remained outside the net of serfdom. Like the Mongols in the thirteenth century, Peter prepared for the new system of taxation by taking a census of the population.

The population reacted to these burdens with mass flight and many petty acts of desperate violence. There were also larger rebellions in Astrakhan, and in the lands of the Bashkirs south of the Urals. In 1707–8, a Don Cossack *hetman*, Bulavin, led a huge popular rebellion against the government. Like earlier rebel leaders such as Bolotnikov or Stenka Razin, Bulavin promised freedom from serfdom and poverty, and a return to the true faith of the 'Old Believers'. His Utopian promises attracted a motley army of more than 100 000 serfs, slaves, cossacks, steppe nomads, ex-soldiers and religious dissidents. But his army was too indisciplined to challenge Peter's reformed armies. After savage fighting, it was crushed in 1708.

External and internal crises such as those of the early years of Peter's reign demanded exceptional unity and discipline if the system was to survive. Peter showed that he had the ruthlessness and the political skills necessary to forge a more disciplined ruling group and to increase his own power as its leader. Peter made it compulsory for all members of the nobility to serve their whole life long, either in the army or in the government service. In 1721, he introduced a 'Table of Ranks'. This organized the entire ruling elite into a strict hierarchy, as if they were a sort of occupying army. Each noble, in theory, was to start at the bottom and work upwards, and each rank carried its own rights and privileges. Combined with Peter's own policy of favouring ability and service over birth, the Table of Ranks made it much easier for non-nobles to join the ruling group through dedicated service in the army of bureaucracy. This was the opposite of the *boyar* ideal of nobility based on birth. Under the Table of Ranks nobles earned their privileges through service to the tsar.

☐ *Document 1.12: Table of Ranks, January 1722*

The Act decreed:

All state officials, Russian or foreign, who now belong, or have formerly belonged, to the first eight classes, and their legitimate children and descendants in perpetuity, must be considered equal in all dignities and advantages to the best and oldest nobility, even if they are of humble origin … Any military man who is not [himself a hereditary] noble and who attains the rank of a company-grade officer becomes a nobleman; all his children born after the promotion are also nobles.[24]

Peter paid less attention to the persuasive than to the coercive aspects of power. He incorporated the Orthodox Church within the government bureaucracy when, in 1722, he replaced the Patriarch with a civilian official, the Procurator of the Holy Synod. This increased the State's control over the Church, but deprived the church of the prestige it had enjoyed in the past. Peter's own irreligious behaviour, in particular the drunken mock services he held with many of his close followers, also undermined the church's authority. The great church schism of the seventeenth century had further weakened the church's power to support the state. Indeed, most of the so-called 'Old Believers' were convinced that Peter and his government represented the Anti-Christ. The declining prestige of the church made it a less effective instrument of persuasion than it had been in the Muscovite era.

Finally, Peter's policies of westernization exposed members of the Russian ruling elite to the corrosive rationalism of European thought. Peter had forced the nobility to familiarize themselves with the technical knowledge of western Europe and to adopt European styles of dress and manners. Soon, Russian nobles were familiar with the languages of western Europe (particularly French and German), and also with the philosophies and theories of the Enlightenment. Not only did this threaten their traditional faith in autocracy; it also created an ideological gulf between the elite of Russian society and the mass of the population. The cohesive Christian faith of the Muscovite period, which had provided such powerful ideological support for Tsarism, began to disintegrate during the eighteenth century.

Peter's reforms created immense strains and caused much suffering. However, for the ruling group they were a success. The proof of success was the emergence of Russia as the dominant power in eastern Europe.

The long-term results of Peter's reforms were more paradoxical. By tightening the discipline of the ruling class to an extreme degree, Peter's reforms prepared for an eventual reaction against the centre. Most nobles resented the heavy demands Peter's reforms placed on them, particularly for life-long military service. As soon as he died, they began to chip away at the principle of life-long service for the nobility. Peter had unwittingly helped them by encouraging the westernization of upper-class Russian society. Western political theories encouraged Russian nobles to see their own privileges as rights to be defended, even against the autocracy. Eventually, European political ideas provided the basis for a distinctively Russian form of liberalism. The westernization of the Russian ruling group also altered the situation of upper-class women. In Muscovite Russia, women of noble families were kept segregated in the women's quarters of each house (the *terem*). However, from 1718, Peter began to hold social gatherings called 'assemblies'. At these the dress was European and, as in a French salon, women played a major role. From then on, women were much more visible in Russian upper-class society, though their political role remained inferior to that of men.

Building on the achievements of Peter the Great, Russia remained the dominant power in eastern Europe. During the reign of Catherine the Great (1762–96), Russia absorbed much of Poland and conquered the northern shores of the Black Sea. In 1812–15 it was the Russian armies of Alexander I that did most to crush the once invincible armies of Napoleon.

The autocratic traditions of the past also survived. As long as the dangers from both outside and inside were clear to all (as in 1613 or 1700), it was easy to convince members of the Russian ruling class to unite around an autocratic monarch. In the eighteenth century, occasional reminders of these dangers, such as the odd military reversal, or the huge peasant rebellion led by Emelyan Pugachev in 1773–4, helped sustain upper class faith in autocracy. However paradoxical it may seem to those brought up in a liberal democracy, most nobles saw autocratic government as necessary to the preservation of their own privileges. This political outlook is expressed well in a memorandum written in 1799 by a prominent official, Prince Bezborodko.

Document 1.13: Prince Bezborodko on the importance of autocracy in Russia

Russia is an autocratic state. Its size, the variety of its inhabitants and customs, and many other considerations make this the only natural form of government for Russia. All arguments to the contrary are futile, and the least weakening of autocratic power would result in the loss of many provinces, the weakening of the state, and countless misfortunes for the people. An autocratic sovereign, if he possesses the qualities befitting his rank, must feel that he has been given unlimited power not to rule according to his whim, but to respect and implement the laws established by his ancestors and by himself; in short, having spoken his law, he is himself the first to respect and obey it, so that others may not even dare to think of evading or escaping it.[25]

Nevertheless, the successes of the Petrine system reduced the willingness of the ruling group to put up with the ferocious discipline Peter had imposed on them. This relaxation of tension explains why, during the eighteenth century, the Russian ruling group managed to reduce the burden of compulsory service. In practice, it had always been hard to enforce their service obligations. Many nobles simply hid on their rural estates, far from the capital. Besides, during the eighteenth century, conflicts over the succession weakened the monarchy. This was true even of Catherine the Great, for, though she was as able as Peter the Great, she had a weaker claim to the throne. By birth an obscure German princess, she secured the throne through a *coup d'état* against her husband, Peter III. As a result, she had to spend many years consolidating her position by granting favours to her supporters.

Under these pressures, the government freed the nobility from compulsory service by two statutes of 1762 and 1785. From then on the nobility was free to serve or not to serve. Many continued to serve because they needed the salary, while others served out of a sense of moral obligation. But service was no longer a legal obligation. Nobles also received full property rights over their land. They now owned their estates outright, like Muscovite *boyars*, rather then enjoying them in return for service. Meanwhile, the privileges of the upper nobility increased as Catherine extended serfdom to regions previously untouched by it, including Ukraine.

There were slight but significant changes in the political mood of some nobles. Catherine herself helped spread the progressive ideas of Enlightenment philosophers such as Voltaire and Montesquieu. By the end of her reign there existed a minority of dissident nobles committed to ideas such as freedom and democracy, which conflicted with the very foundations of Russian autocracy. One of the first to express these ideas publicly was Alexander Radishchev, whose *Journey from St Petersburg to*

Moscow, published in 1790, attacked both serfdom and autocracy. For the Russian nobility the idea of freedom meant primarily an end to the extreme dependence of nobles on the autocratic monarch. The result of these changes was that the nobility, which Peter had organized like the old *dvoriane,* now began to behave like the old *boyar* class, though the term *dvoriane* was now used for nobles of all kinds.

The growth of the bureaucracy partially counterbalanced the growing independence of some sections of the nobility. Most government officials came from non-noble families. Like sixteenth-century *dvoriane,* therefore, their status depended on loyal service to the crown. As the bureaucracy expanded it took over the governmental functions of the nobles, just as professional soldiers had taken over the military functions of the nobility in the seventeenth century.

The bureaucracy originated from the private officials of medieval princely estates, and the government chancelleries or *prikazy* of the sixteenth century. Catherine the Great expanded its influence greatly in 1775, when she created for the first time a provincial bureaucracy. Civil, judicial, military and police officials now appeared not just in the capitals, but also in the major provincial (*guberniya*) and district (*uezd*) towns of the empire. Here, in the salaried officials of state, the government found a new class as susceptible to discipline as the old *dvoriane*. In the eighteenth and nineteenth centuries the government relied more and more on its officials as the nobility's willingness to serve declined. In the nineteenth century these changes eventually transformed the Russian government into a bureaucratic dictatorship without deep roots in Russian society at large.

■ Summary

This chapter has argued that there is a close link between the difficult ecological and military environment of the lands west of the Urals, and the emergence in this region of an autocratic tradition of government. The harsh climates and poor soils of Rus', the lack of natural defensive borders, and the military threat from steppeland pastoralists, made the task of state building peculiarly difficult. To create a powerful state here, ruling elites had to be exceptionally good at mobilizing the region's scarce resources. To get away with that, they would have to show something of the unity and discipline of an occupying army. This was true on a small scale for the early princes of Kievan Rus', but later rulers faced even greater challenges both from the steppes and from Europe. In periods of apparent success, such as the eleventh and twelfth centuries, when the need for elite self-discipline was less obvious, the unity of elites, and the power of their leaders, could easily be undermined. However, periods of acute external and internal crisis, such as the Mongol invasions, or the various crises of the seventeenth century, encouraged the creation of more disciplined forms of rule in the various lands west of the Urals. It is no accident that it was the most autocratic of these states that eventually established its authority over most of the lands of Kievan Rus'. It did so by building a powerful army supported by the coercive form of direct mobilization known to historians as 'serfdom'.

☐ *Further Reading*

There are many fine histories of Rus', Muscovy, and the many nations later incorporated in the Russian Empire. The best short history in English is still L. Kochan and R. Abrahams, *The Making of Modern Russia*. R. Pipes, *Russia Under the Old Regime*, stresses the importance of Russia's autocratic political traditions. Auty and Obolensky, *An Introduction to Russian History*, and Riasanovsky, *A History of Russia*, are conventional textbooks, with full bibliographies and detailed coverage. Dukes, *A History of Russia*, and Acton, *Russia: The Tsarist and Soviet Legacy*, are more recent. Orest Subtelny's *Ukraine: A History* is the standard modern history of Ukraine. On particular periods or topics, see: Pavel Dolukhanov, *The Early Slavs: Eastern Europe from the Initial Settlement to the Kievan Rus*; Simon Franklin and Jonathan Shepard, *The Emergence of Rus 750–1200*; Janet Martin, *History of Medieval Russia*; R. Crummey, *The Formation of Muscovy 1304–1613*; and J. Cracraft (ed.), *Peter the Great Transforms Russia*.

☐ *Notes*

1. See D. Christian, '"Inner Eurasia" as a Unit of World History', *Journal of World History*, vol. 5, no. 2 (Sep. 1994).
2. I. Ya. Froyanov, *Kievskaya Rus': Ocherki sotsial'no-ekonomicheskoi istorii* (Leningrad, 1974) pp. 113–14.
3. G. Vernadsky *et al.* (eds) *A Source Book for Russian History from Early Times to 1917*, 3 vols (New Haven, Conn.: Yale University Press, 1972) vol. 1, pp. 22–3.
4. S. A. Zenkovsky (ed.) *Medieval Russia's Epics, Chronicles and Tales*, rev edn (New York: Meridian, 1974) pp. 55–6.
5. Vernadsky, *Source Book*, vol. 1, p. 24.
6. S. H. Cross and O. P. Sherbovitz-Wetzor (trans and ed.), *The Russian Primary Chronicle* (Cambridge, Mass.: Medieval Academy of America, 1953) p. 122 (years 994–6).
7. Vernadsky, *Source Book*, vol. 1, pp. 32–3.
8. Zenkovsky, *Medieval Russia's Epics, Chronicles and Tales*, p. 195.
9. Vernadsky, *Source Book*, vol. 1, p. 45.
10. S. S. Dmitriev et al. (eds), *Khrestomatiya po istorii SSSR* (Moscow: gos-oe uchebno-pedagogicheskoe izd-vo min-va prosveshcheniya RSFSR, 1948) vol. 1, p. 49 (trans D. Christian).

11. G. Vernadsky, *A History of Russia* (New Haven, Conn.: Yale University Press, 1953) vol. 3, p. 121.
12. Vernadsky, *Source Book*, vol. 1, p. 53.
13. N. S. Kollmann, *Kinship and Politics: The Making of the Muscovite Political System 1345–1547* (Stanford: Stanford University Press, 1987).
14. Vernadsky, *Source Book*, vol. 1, pp. 57–8.
15. Ibid., p. 120.
16. Ibid., pp. 156–7.
17. Ibid., p. 173, from Ivan's letter to Prince Kurbskii of 1564.
18. Ibid., p. 163.
19. Ibid., pp. 206–7, from Pozharskii's appeal to Sol'vychegodsk.
20. F. Wilson, *Muscovy through Foreign Eyes, 1553–1900* (London: Praeger, 1970) pp. 28–9.
21. Vernadsky, *Source Book*, vol. 1, pp. 225–6.
22. Cited in R. Pipes, *Russia under the Old Regime* (London: Weidenfeld & Nicolson, 1974) p. 108.
23. On the role of vodka in Russian life, see David Christian, '*Living Water': Vodka and Russian Society on the Eve of Emancipation* (Oxford University Press, 1990).
24. Vernadsky, *Source Book*, vol. 2, p. 344.
25. Cited from M. Raeff (ed.), *Plans for Political Reform* (Englewood Cliffs, New Jersey: Prentice-Hall Inc., 1966) p. 70.

■ *Chapter 2* ■

The Russian Empire in the Early Nineteenth Century

■ A Pre-Modern Social Structure

Just after the Napoleonic war, one of Russia's first statisticians, K. I. Arsenev, used the tax censuses of 1812 and 1816 to draw up the following description of Russia's social structure.

☐ *Document 2.1: Arsenev on Russia's population, 1812 to 1816*

All inhabitants of Russia can be divided into two main classes – the productive and the non-productive classes. To the first belong those who either directly or indirectly expand the wealth of the nation, such as agriculturalists, manufacturers, artisans and merchants. To the second class belong all those who live at the expense of the first class: such as the clergy, the nobility, civil and military officials [*chiny*, rank-holders in the *Table of Ranks*], the army and navy, servants, etc.

Here are Arsenev's calculations of the size and main subdivisions of these groups between the censuses of 1812 and 1816.

Non-productive classes	*000s*	*%*
1. Nobility	450	1.1
2. Clergy	430	1.1
3. Military	2000	5.0
4. Officials of various kinds and *Raznochintsy* (people of mixed ranks)	1500	3.7
Total	4380	10.9

Productive classes		
5. Merchants	204	0.5
6. *Meshchane* (town-dwellers)	1490	3.7
7. State peasants	13 100	32.7

8. Landlords' serfs	20 300	50.7
9. 'Free people' (mainly Cossacks)	234	0.6
10. Other categories of peasants	360	0.9
Total	35 688	89.1
Total population	40 068	100.0

Arsenev concluded: 'The non-productive class is to the productive class in the proportion 1:9, so that 9 producers support a single consumer'.[1]

Figure 2.1 uses these figures. However, it changes Arsenev's classification in two main ways. First, it places the merchants with the 'non-productive' classes. Second, it adds a vague but important category of 'borderline' groups. This is to show that the border between the productive and non-productive groups was blurred. For example, most of the 'military' were common soldiers recruited from the peasantry. Many officials, *raznochintsy* and clergy, and even some nobles, also lived in conditions of extreme poverty and squalor.

Arsenev was an intelligent and informed observer. However, some of his classifications are confusing. This is because class was a legal, rather than a socio-economic category in nineteenth-century Russia, as in most pre-modern societies. Like most traditional governments, the Russian government used class labels to fix people's place within a rigid hierarchy of power and privilege. This made sense in a pre-modern

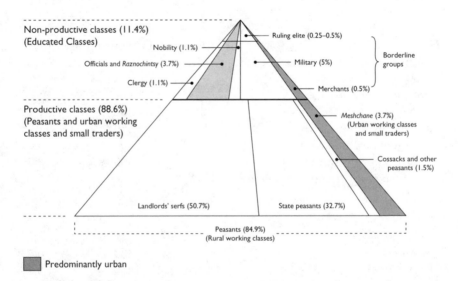

Figure 2.1   *Social structure of Russia after the Napoleonic Wars*

society in which social position depended more on political than on economic forces.

However, particularly in the towns, these traditional labels could not grasp a complex and changing reality. *Raznochintsy*, for example, was a catch-all term for an important but motley group of educated people who were not nobles. They did not hold high rank (*chin*) in the Table of Ranks. So they did not fully belong to the ruling group. Yet they were clearly not peasants or merchants. This made it hard to classify them in law. The term *raznochinets* reflects this vagueness, for it means 'of various ranks'. For the historian, the *raznochintsy* are important as the precursors of the Russian intelligentsia, the group that provided most of the leaders for the Russian revolutionary movement.

Meshchanin was a legal classification that referred to a variety of poorer town-dwellers. It could include labourers and street pedlars as well as artisans, small entrepreneurs and shopkeepers. Yet it did not cover all poorer town-dwellers, for many belonged, in law, to the peasantry. The curious category of 'free people' referred mainly to the Cossacks, the free soldier-peasants of Ukraine, the south-east and western Siberia.

Each person had a precise legal status carrying particular rights and duties. For example, a *meshchanin* could carry on commercial operations only within strictly defined limits. If a business was successful, a *meshchanin* might eventually try to join one of the merchant guilds. This required paying a large entry fee. In return the merchant received new commercial privileges and a new legal status.

The legal barriers between classes limited social mobility. For serfs, bound by law to their master's land, escape was extremely difficult. This is clearest in the rare cases when a serf did succeed in entering another class. Occasionally serf-owners allowed their serfs to undertake small business operations, and sometimes enterprising serfs earned enough to buy their freedom. The following passage shows the complex negotiations this required. It comes from an essay on serfdom written by a liberal-minded official in the 1840s.

Document 2.2: Zablotskii on the difficulties of purchasing freedom from serfdom

The peasant desiring to buy his freedom starts negotiations with his landlord, and these continue for some time and employ various diplomatic niceties. The peasant, for example, finds out when his landlord is short of cash; or the landlord increases his demands just when the peasant is most in need of cash for his business. This leads to many different forms of cunning. The result, usually, is that the peasant buys his freedom, but at a price dependent on the scale of his turnover. No landlord finds it shameful to acquire gratis, in this way, the savings others have accumulated through much blood and sweat and merely as the result of an absurd set of laws. Such are their notions of justice and equity. Indeed, they often boast, when they succeed in tearing huge sums of money from a peasant, just as a horse-dealer boasts when he has sold a horse for a high price.

'I once had a rich peasant,' said Mr M ___, 'who wanted to buy his freedom. We haggled and settled on 16 000 rubles. But the son of a bitch tricked me. It turned out later that he had 200 000 rubles, so I could have asked for up to 150 000! My sister was smarter. She would not let one of her peasants free for less than 30 000 and she was right, as it turned out that his total capital was only 45 000.' Such are the notions of justice held by the landowners! And yet M ___ is no fool, is not lacking in goodness, and is no savage. 'What does it matter to the peasant,' a landlord told us, 'if he pays a third or half of his accumulated capital, when in return he gets his freedom, and in one or two years of good fortune, he can regain his whole fortune?'[2]

Many historians prefer to talk of 'estates' rather than 'classes' when describing pre-modern societies, because of the existence of such barriers to social movement. They use the word 'class' only for modern societies, where social hierarchies are shaped by market forces rather than by legal regulations. The distinction between 'class' and 'estate' is important and useful. However, in a modernizing society such as nineteenth-century Russia, the two overlapped. Indeed Arsenev himself preferred the foreign term *klass* to the traditional Russian term for 'estate'. For this reason, I will use the term 'class' more broadly than most historians. I will use it to include both the legally defined 'estates' of the pre-modern world, and the social and economic groups typical in modern societies.

The social structure that Arsenev described was typical of the agrarian empires of the pre-modern world. Its most important classes were peasants and landed aristocrats. Neither class depended primarily on market forces. Unlike entrepreneurs, nobles had little need to compete on a market. They took most of what they needed to survive from their peasants in the form of feudal dues. As long as their bailiffs squeezed enough from their serfs, most nobles were uninterested in how efficiently their estates operated. Peasants were also protected to some extent from market forces. Many had to earn cash for taxes or special purchases, but they produced most of what they needed from the land made available to them by their landlords. Markets existed, of course. So did entrepreneurs and wage-earners. But as yet these three crucial ingredients of the capitalist 'engine of growth' played only a minor role in Russian society. The 'modern' revolution, which was already transforming the societies and economies of Western Europe, had barely touched the Russia of Pushkin and Gogol. We must now look at this pre-modern world in more detail.

▌The 'Productive' Classes: Agriculture and the Peasantry

How did the 'productive' classes generate the resources that supported Russian society? And how did they live?

Most surplus resources were generated in the countryside, for Russia, like most pre-industrial societies, was overwhelmingly rural. In 1858, 94 per cent of Russians lived in small village communities. Indeed, the best measure of the huge changes that took place over the next hundred years is the relative decline of the rural population and the growth of towns. (See Figure 2.2 and column B of the Statistical Appendix.)

As most Russians still lived in the countryside, we will ignore the urban working classes in this section. (Many were, in any case, temporary migrants from the villages.) We will concentrate instead on the main productive class, the peasantry.

Physically, the village was a group of houses strung along the dirt track that passed for a main road (Figure 2.3). It was usually close to a river. Most villages had fewer than 500 inhabitants. However, they were larger in the steppe lands, where supplies of water were scarce. As a social unit, the village was similar in size to a modern suburban street.

In well-wooded regions peasants built their houses, or *izby*, of wood. In the steppes of Ukraine the scarcity of wood made stone the preferred

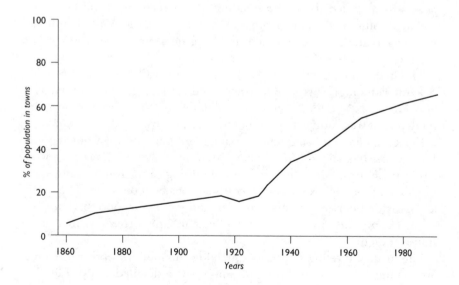

Figure 2.2 *Urbanisation in Russia and the USSR, 1860–1990*
Note. Based on information in the Statistical Appendix

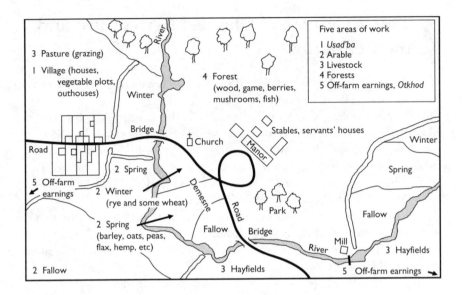

Figure 2.3   *Typical layout of a nineteenth-century Russian village*

material. Elsewhere, stone was a luxury material used for the houses of the nobility or the occasional church. Each house had one or (in richer families) two large living rooms. This was where people slept, ate and spent their leisure time. Dominating the living room was a large brick stove, the *pech'*, which heated the entire building. Other sections of the household included cattle sheds, storage areas for grain, and the *banya*, or bathhouse. In colder regions, these adjoined the living quarters and shared the heat from the *pech'*. Elsewhere, they were separate from the main dwelling.

The land immediately around the house was called the *usad'ba*. Here peasant women grew vegetables and raised cattle, pigs and poultry. They also grew flax and hemp for cloth-making. In southern regions, they tended fruit trees or gardens of melons and gourds.

Villages needed grazing land for cattle and hay-land for winter fodder. Where possible, villagers also made use of local forests. They used wood from the forests for heating, for building and for making farm implements, as well as for village crafts such as boat-building. The forests also provided berries, mushrooms, fish and game, for food; bark for bast shoes (*lapti*); and much more, including the tapers (*luchiny*) that lit the house at night.

Life in such dwellings appears squalid to the modern observer. Here is an account by a modern historian, who made a detailed study of life in a single village in the early nineteenth century. His account avoids the idealization of peasant life common in much writing about rural Russia.

☐ *Document 2.3: A historian's description of the interior of peasant huts
– Petrovskoe village, Tambov province, early nineteenth century*

Inside the huts, the air was fetid from animal and fowl excreta. The walls and ceiling were covered with soot and ash. Smoke, especially in the morning when the stove was lit, filled the top half of the *izba*. In the evening, soot from the *luchinas* stung the eyes. The dirt floor was always damp, and in the spring and autumn it was muddy. It was impossible to keep cockroaches out of the food; they even became a symbol of abundance and material wealth and a sign of good luck. In fact, when moving to a new home, the head of the household would bring a few roaches with him and let them loose. These were the conditions under which all the serfs lived for at least a third of the year.

In contrast, the warm months brought considerable relief from the squalor of the hut, and the psychological effect must have been substantial. Livestock, of course, was moved outside. The stove was heated less often and in summer was used only for cooking. More hours of sunlight reduced the need for *luchinas*. Animal feces were removed from the hut, though with warm weather came the stench of decomposing manure piled in the yard.[3]

The basic unit of village life was the three-generation family or household. On average, the family included five to eight people living under the same roof. The household was much more important than it is in industrial societies today. No institution in modern society (except perhaps the state itself) has the influence the nineteenth-century Russian household had over the life of those within it. The household coped with many tasks that modern society assigns to different institutions. It handled child-rearing, education, food production and money-making, care of the aged, medical treatment, even relaxation. This wide range of functions gave the household an absolute authority over its members that is difficult for us to appreciate. Through its head (usually the father), the household took the most important decision of all in the life of its members, by deciding who married whom and when. The household also decided who stayed at home and who went away for work. The immense authority of the household meant that people saw themselves more as members of a group than as separate individuals.

The need of the household for children meant that childbearing and child-rearing dominated women's lives. Parents needed children for their labour. Besides, everyone knew that large families were usually wealthy, while small families were poor. In part, this was because land was allotted to households in accordance with the number of sons they had. In part, it was because spare labour was a resource that households could use to generate more income. Indeed, labour was the only productive resource peasants controlled, for they had little hope of buying land or borrowing capital. Children were also the only source of security for the old.

For these reasons, the pressure to marry and rear children was overwhelming. In Petrovskoe village in Tambov province, 90 per cent of all women were married by the age of twenty-four in the early nineteenth century.[4] Marriage rates had been high in Russia since at least the sixteenth century. In earlier centuries, the need to settle new lands had encouraged widespread and early marriage, and large families. With the rise of serfdom, landlords encouraged early marriage to increase the numbers of their serfs.[5] As almost half of all children died by the age of five, women had to marry young and keep bearing children as long as possible to make sure some survived to adulthood. So married women spent most of their mature years pregnant and looking after children. In a world without day-care centres or schools, in which few questioned traditional gender roles, the task of child-rearing tied most women permanently to the household.

What sort of life did ordinary men and women expect to live? Most expected to spend most of their life in the village they were born into. However, men in particular travelled extensively outside their village in search of temporary work. People did not expect life to change much during their lifetimes. They lived much as their ancestors had done hundreds of years before them, and expected the future to be much the same.

For most people, life was short. Average life expectancy on the estate of Petrovskoe, in Tambov province, was about twenty-seven years in the first half of the nineteenth century. This compares with over seventy years in, for instance, Australia today. The Russian figure is low because almost 45 per cent of children died before their fifth birthday. On the other hand, those who reached their fifth birthday had a life expectancy of forty years, while those who survived to twenty, could hope to live well into their fifties.[6]

For the peasantry the basic productive resource besides their own labour was the land. The heartland of Kievan Rus' and of Muscovy is a huge plain. For travellers the main variations were in soils, rainfall and vegetation rather than in the shape of the land. These variations created distinct zones running east and west (see Figure 2.4). We can ignore the sparsely populated tundra of the far north and the deserts of the south-east. Apart from these, there were two main inhabited areas – the forested northern zones and the almost treeless steppes of the south, with a transitional area of wooded steppes in between. In the early 1840s the German traveller Baron Haxthausen wrote:

> In the north of Russia the vegetation springs up into a forest; every
> fallow field, every uncultivated spot is covered with wood in a few years
> ... In the Steppes, nature shoots up into grass and flowers; and what a

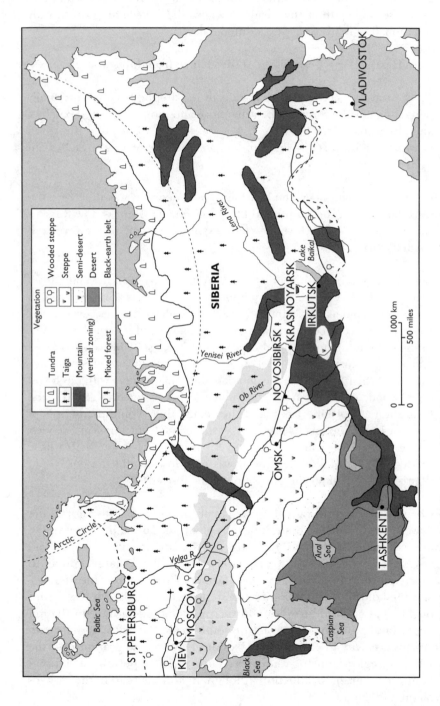

Figure 2.4 *The natural geography of the Russian and Soviet Empires*

luxuriant growth! Plants which with us are at the utmost two feet tall, here rise higher than the head. Nowhere did we see any forest, only occasionally a few bushes and stunted oaks.[7]

Here is Haxthausen's description of the change from forest to steppe:

To the traveller coming from the north the Steppe becomes gradually perceptible by the forests appearing more and more in isolated patches, and the grass plains growing larger in extent. All at once the wood ceases, not a bush is anywhere to be seen, and the Steppe stretches out in its immensity before us.[8]

The forest zone had been the heartland of Muscovy. It was therefore the forests that shaped the traditional life of old Russia. Here is how Russia's greatest historian, V. O. Klyuchevskii, described the role of the forests in Russian history:

Even in the seventeenth century, for a Western European travelling from Smolensk to Moscow, Muscovy appeared an endless forest, in which towns and hamlets were simply larger or smaller clearings. Even today [the late nineteenth century] a broad horizon fringed by a bluish band of forest, is the most familiar landscape of central Russia. The woods offered much to the Russian people, economically, politically and even morally. They built their houses of pine and oak; they heated them with birch and aspen wood, and lit them with birch tapers; they wore boots (*lapti*) made from the bark of lime trees; and they made their domestic utensils of wood or bark. The forests provided a safe refuge from external enemies, taking the place of mountains and fortresses. The state itself, whose predecessor had failed because it was too close to the steppes, could flourish only ... under the protection of the forests.[9]

Changes in soils and rainfall were equally important. In the north, the soils were sandy podzols, but rainfall was plentiful. The steppelands of the south had richer black soils, formed from the composting of steppeland grasses over thousands of years. However, until the late eighteenth century, pastoral nomads prevented farmers from settling the steppes. When they did begin to colonize the steppes, farmers had to cope with droughts that could destroy an entire crop. Poor soils in the north, and droughts and pastoral nomads in the south made agriculture a hard and precarious activity in Russia and Ukraine. However, migration into the black soil regions during the nineteenth century permitted a rapid expansion in grain production, though it also increased the risk of drought and famine.

High latitudes were the other main influence on Russian agriculture. Huge areas in the far north were too cold to farm. Elsewhere, the long winters made farmers concentrate their work into a shorter period than in western Europe. Farmers also had to keep livestock indoors for much longer. These problems still bedevil agriculture in the region today.

The main productive activity of villagers was agriculture, often combined with rural crafts. Agriculture provided the food that sustained most Russians, as well as the surplus products used to pay taxes and feudal dues. Most important of all was the grain (usually rye) that provided most of the food energy in peasant diets. Like peasants in other grain-growing regions of the world, Russian and Ukrainian peasants spent much of their life eating grain. They ate it in bread, in gruel (or *kasha*), in lightly fermented drinks such as *kvas*, or, on festive occasions, in pies or *pirogi*. In the late nineteenth century, potatoes emerged as an important supplement. Vegetables, pickled for winter, provided variety and an essential source of vitamin C. Livestock produce was less important, for large animals were more valuable alive than dead. Meat, meat fat and milk were merely supplements to a largely vegetarian diet. Gathered foods, such as berries, mushrooms, fish and game, occasionally relieved the tedium.

Recent research suggests that Russian peasant diets, though boring, were well balanced nutritionally. Russian peasants probably ate at least as well as their contemporaries in western Europe, and better than many in the Third World today. However, diets were unreliable. Most peasants suffered occasional periods of shortage, and sometimes they endured terrible famines. Poorer families often expected shortages in the spring, as the previous year's stocks began to run out. The following description suggests how families coped with spring shortages. It comes from Smolensk province in the 1870s:

In the autumn, when there is a stock of rye, they eat pure bread, as much as they like, and only a very conscientious peasant eats adulterated bread ... But then the peasants notice that bread is short. They eat less, not three times a day, but twice and then only once. Then they start adding chaff to the pure flour. If there's money left from selling hemp, they use it to buy bread instead of for taxes. If there's no money, they get by. The head of the household finds work, or borrows ... When there's no more bread the children and old folk take their knapsacks and go out 'collecting crusts' [begging] in the neighbourhood.[10]

Agricultural methods were primitive by twentieth-century standards. The main problem was to maintain soil fertility. Without artificial fertilizers, Russian and Ukrainian peasants solved this problem in two main ways. First, cattle and horse manure provided a natural fertilizer. This made livestock a vital element in peasant agriculture. Second, farmers rested their arable land, usually every three years, by leaving it fallow. This meant that a third of arable land was unsown at any time.

The black soil areas of the southern steppes were different. While populations remained small, farmers could cultivate the land more wastefully. They planted crops year in and year out, and simply moved on when output declined. The scattered populations of the northern forests sometimes practised an even more ancient technique, known as slash-and-burn, or swidden agriculture. They burnt down patches of forest, and farmed the ashy soils until they had exhausted their fertility. Then they moved on, returning to the same patch several decades later.

The central regions, which had been the heartland of Muscovy, were more typical. Populations were dense here by the nineteenth century, so there was no room for such wasteful methods. Here, three-field crop rotations were universal. Though farming was never easy in this region, recent research suggests that crop yields were not necessarily lower than in most of western Europe in the same period.[11] However, harvests were less reliable than in western Europe. Every decade, some regions suffered acute famine.

The most distinctive feature of agriculture in this region was the way in which peasants divided the arable land they farmed. Though the land belonged, in law, to landlords or the state, peasants usually controlled how it was farmed. This encouraged the peasants' traditional belief that the land should belong to those who farmed it. Usually, they divided the land into many strips, scattered throughout the village's arable land, and each household received strips from different parts of the arable land. In this way, each household received a fair share of good and bad land.

Methods of farming shaped the lives of peasant families in many ways. The following account, by a modern historian, explains how they shaped the division of labour between men and women in Tambov province.

Document 2.4: Agriculture and the division of labour between men and women

As a consequence of the extremely short growing season – five and a half to six months instead of the eight to nine months in Western Europe – under the three-field system the harvesting of winter and spring cereals and the plowing and sowing of the winter field all came in quick succession within the span of six weeks. From mid-July to the end of August was the harvest season, the *stradnaia pora* as the Russians called it, literally the time of suffering. It was an agonizing period of exertion demanding that numerous tasks be accomplished simultaneously. A work team, or *tiaglo*, of husband and wife together proved the best allocation of labor resources. A single male simply could not complete all the necessary field work if he were to allow the cereals to mature fully yet avoid the danger of an early frost.

There thus emerged in Russia a clear differentiation of field labor by sex. During the harvest season, women used sickles to cut rye, winter wheat, if any, and sometimes oats, while the men reaped the other spring cereals with scythes. Winter crops could not be cut with a scythe because it knocked too many seeds off the stock, but this was not a problem with less ripe spring cereals. The women then tied the grain into sheaves for drying, and the men began plowing the winter field. While they sowed the next year's rye crop, the women started to cart the sheaves from the fields, assisted by their husbands if time permitted. In general, plowing, harrowing, cutting hay, and harvesting with a scythe were men's field work; tending the kitchen garden and hemp field, raking hay, cutting stalks with a sickle, tying them, and transporting them to the threshing floor were women's field work.

A partnership was essential.[12]

The institution that controlled the reallocation of land was the commune. This was an informal meeting of the mainly male heads of households that took basic decisions about the allocation of land and taxes, and the timing of agricultural activities. Dividing the arable land was necessary to make sure each household had enough land to support itself and pay its taxes. All males had to pay the poll tax so, as the number of males changed within a household, the commune could adjust its allocation of strips. Regular re-partition of the land by males, and according to the number of males, meant that men controlled the land. This control underpinned the patriarchal authority of males in the life of the village. The commune also acted to maintain male dominance within the household by supporting the authority of husbands and punishing wives accused of adultery. In the 1880s, a woman named Ferapontova from Russia's northern provinces, made the following complaint to a district constable.

□ *Document 2.5: Defending family values in rural Russia, 1880*

I complained to the township court that my husband beat me, but the court did not resolve the case according to the law; instead, the village elder gathered some people together, came to the home … where I was staying, and amidst a din and shouts they seized me, and ordered my husband to tie my hands with a saddle strap, which is just what he did. Then I was pushed out of the house and, while I was tied up, he thrashed me down the entire street and up to our house, and … he dragged me inside and there, where people had already gathered, threw me on the floor … and, though he didn't beat me further, he mocked me in all kinds of ways, cursing with every possible word. I implore you to carry out an investigation quickly, otherwise I will have to endure still more torture from my husband. Is it possible that they can order people to be tortured and mocked? Save me, for the sake of God, I haven't the strength to bear this torture.[13]

Though to Ferapontova the commune may have symbolized oppression, many Russian intellectuals saw it as the embodiment of working-class equality and democracy. They saw in the survival of the commune a basic difference between Russia and Western Europe, for they believed that the Russian commune had preserved the socialist ideal of collective ownership, which had vanished in Europe. In the 1860s this idea provided the basis for the revolutionary ideology known as Populism (see Chapter 3). Most Russian intellectuals took their ideas on the commune partly from the classic account of the German traveller Haxthausen.

☐ *Document 2.6: Haxthausen on the Russian commune, 1843*

The following information was given to us concerning the division of land in the village communes. The principle is that the whole of the land (tillage, meadows, pasture, woods, streams, and so on) belongs to the population of a village community regarded as a whole, and in using these communal possessions every male inhabitant has a right to an equal share. This share is therefore constantly changing; for the birth of every boy creates a new claim, and the shares of those who die revert to the commune. The woods, pastures, hunting grounds, and fisheries remain undivided and free to all the inhabitants; but the arable land and meadows are divided equally, according to their value, among the males. This equal division is of course very difficult, as the soil differs in quality, and portions of it may be distant or inconveniently situated. The difficulties are great; nevertheless the Russians overcome them easily. There are in each commune skilful land surveyors, who, competently, with insight acquired from the traditional habits of the place, execute the work to the satisfaction of all. The land is first divided, according to its quality, position, or general value, into sections, each possessing on the whole equal advantages. The sections are then divided into as many portions, in long strips, as there are shares required, and these are taken by lot. This is the usual plan, but each region, and frequently each commune, has its local customs ....

The facts here described constitute the basis of the Russian communal system, one of the most remarkable and interesting political institutions in existence, and one that undeniably possesses great advantages for the social condition of the country. The Russian communes evince an organic coherence and compact social strength that can be found nowhere else and yield the incalculable advantage that no proletariat can be formed so long as they exist with their present structure. A man may lose or squander all he possesses, but his children do not inherit his poverty. They still retain their claim upon the land, by a right derived, not from him, but from their birth as members of the commune. On the other hand, it must be admitted that this fundamental basis of the communal system, the equal division of the land, is not favorable to the progress of agriculture, which ... under this system could for a long time remain at a low level.[14]

This extract shows why Russian socialists came to believe that Russia had preserved in the commune a unique basis for socialism. The extract also shows how the commune could hinder technical progress. It was hard to use modern machinery where the land was divided into many small strips. Besides, re-partitions deprived peasants of any incentive to improve land that others might be farming in a few years.

Although primitive, Russian agriculture made efficient use of energy. Modern agriculture has reduced the labour demanded of both people and animals in food production. However, it makes up for this by using energy in other forms. It uses fuel for farm machinery, in transport and distribution and to make fertilizers. Indeed, for each unit of energy put into agriculture, modern agriculture produces less food energy than did traditional peasant agriculture. Judged by its energy cost, it is modern agriculture that is inefficient![15]

In the early nineteenth century, peasants were still largely self-sufficient. They produced much of their own cloth and most of their own clothes. Horses and home-made carts provided transport. Peasants built their own houses, paying others only for special tasks such as the building of the brick stove. Their parents and relations taught the many skills needed in daily life, such as building, carpentry (with an axe), hunting, fishing and baking. For such tasks, schools were not necessary. As for medicine, each family had its own favourite treatments, many of which relied on the healing power of vodka. For more serious treatments, villagers went to the local *znakharka*, or wise woman, who treated the sick, using a combination of herbal lore and charms. The following interview, from the 1890s, gives some insight into the world of a village healer called Marfa.

☐ *Document 2.7: The world of a village healer*

'I remained a widow with six small children, so I had to feed myself somehow.'
'Did you learn to cure from someone?'
'It's from God.'
'Did you begin to cure immediately?'
'How can you do it immediately? No, little by little. It happened that I was treated myself and saw how others cure. So, I watched closely and began to cure myself: I learned from others.'
'Do you treat with herbs?'
'With herbs, with sayings, and I wash with magical water.'

'Would you tell anyone these sayings?'

'Why not? It's not sinful. I get this from God. So, I went among the holy and asked, is it a sin to heal? The old men said, not at all, it's not a sin. You see, I had a dream ... I was in a room and a girl came into the room with a book in one hand and a jug in the other. She looked into the jug and then into the book. Then she says three times, "no, it's not a sin". I asked Father Ambrosia about the dream. He said, "It's alright, it's given from God". The monks, the most holy of them, also said it was alright.'[16]

This extract also hints at the religious world of Russian peasants. Formally, most were Orthodox Christians. In reality, Christianity was less important than the many spirits that lived in the houses, streams and fields of every village. Most peasants believed deeply in the power of magic, of spells and of curses.

Self-sufficiency meant that few goods and services passed through the market, so money was less necessary than in modern industrial societies. Healers, for example, were paid in kind. 'The znakharka took what the family could afford, usually payment in kind – a loaf of bread, five eggs, a length of cotton or wool.'[17] However, there were some items that peasants did have to buy. These they bought in the nearest town, or at a fair or market. They needed vodka for all village and family celebrations, and they bought metal goods such as ploughshares. They also bought salt, the major preservative in a world without refrigerators.

During the nineteenth century, the importance of cash steadily increased. Purchases, money taxes and land shortages forced peasants to seek cash incomes. Wage-earning was possible because the rhythms of agricultural life meant there were slack seasons when peasants had spare time. Agriculture was an erratic activity in comparison with the nine-to-five routine of modern city-dwellers. Work was hard at certain times of the year, such as harvest-time. At other times, particularly during the winter, there was less to do. As a result, Russian peasants (particularly males) were used to periods of intense labour, followed by periods of prolonged idleness or intense festivity. In the early twentieth century, Russian rural sociologists tried to graph these erratic work rhythms (Figures 2.5 and 2.6).

Free labour time and increasing need for money encouraged peasants to find new ways of turning their many skills into cash. The search for cash incomes was the beginning of the profound changes that would eventually turn traditional peasants into modern urban wage-earners.

There were three main ways of earning cash. First, peasants could earn money while remaining in the village. Many earned money by weaving, spinning, carving wooden utensils, making bast shoes from tree bark, or in many other rural trades. Occasionally, whole villages specialized in a trade, such as the making of samovars, the beautiful water heaters used for preparing tea. Some villages even specialized in begging.

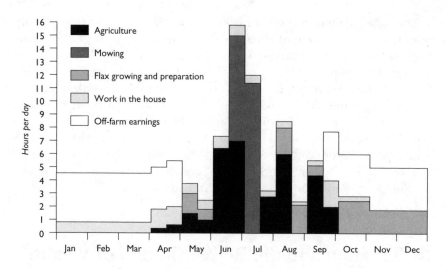

Figure 2.5 *Distribution of family labour by season and type of work*
Source: Adapted from D. Thorner, R. E. F. Smith and B. Kerblay (eds) *A V Chayanov on the Theory of Peasant Economy* (Homewood, Ill.: Richard D Irwin Inc, 1966) p. 151.

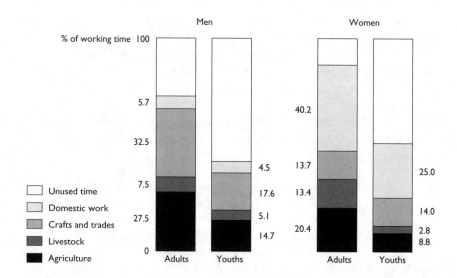

Figure 2.6 *Distribution of family labour by age and gender*
Source: Adapted from D. Thorner, R. E. F. Smith and B. Kerblay (eds) *A V Chayanov on the Theory of Peasant Economy* (Homewood, Ill.: Richard D Irwin Inc, 1966) p. 180.

The second choice was open mainly to the men. This was to seek work outside the village, using the many skills learned in the village. Migratory workers brought in the harvest, carted goods to markets, or hauled barges on the river Volga. In the grain belt of the south, there appeared in the late nineteenth century special markets for the hire of farm labourers.

Third, peasants could go to the towns and find work in building, transport, mining, or in factories. Work in the towns usually required new skills, and often it required a degree of literacy. So urban work was, in this sense, the hardest of the three options. Whatever they did, most migratory workers, even those who worked in the towns, returned to their villages for the spring sowing or for the harvest in late summer.

■ Taxation and the Redistribution of Wealth

The easiest way to understand relations between the productive and non-productive classes of nineteenth-century Russia is to examine the system of taxation. By taxation I mean both the direct and indirect methods used by the ruling group to mobilize resources.

Before 1861, there existed two distinct types of taxation. These were feudal dues and state taxes.

Feudal dues were payments that all serfs had to make to their landlords. Serf-owners could choose to levy them in cash, in kind, or in labour (usually on the landlord's own lands). Serf-owners received these dues by right, just as modern governments receive taxes by right. There were two main groups of serfs – landlords' serfs and state peasants. State peasants belonged to the government. Landlords' serfs belonged to individual members of the nobility, for the right to own serfs was a privilege of the noble estate. From the serf's point of view, the main difference was that the government was more remote, and meddled less in their lives than did individual landlords.

Landlords' serfs had to pay whatever their masters demanded of them. Still, most serf-owners had good reason not to ruin the serfs who were the basis of their own wealth. Where soils were fertile and farming was profitable, many landlords required their serfs to labour on the demesne lands set aside for the landlord's own use. Labour dues of this kind were called *barshchina*. Elsewhere landlords demanded payment in cash, or *obrok*. In practice, landlords could demand any combination of labour and cash dues, as well as payments in kind. Here is a list of the annual payments in kind that serfs paid on an estate in Tambov province in the 1840s, in addition to their normal feudal dues. Each *tiaglo* (an adult male and female couple) paid: 20 metres of linen; two skeins of silken thread;

one skein of ordinary thread; 15 to 25 kilograms of ham; 800 grams of butter; as well as one sheep, one duck, one goose, and one chicken.[18] Serfs on *obrok* suffered less direct interference in their lives than those on *barshchina*. Their landlords often allowed them to work in the towns, and some serfs even became wealthy entrepreneurs.

'Household serfs' had no land and worked for their landlords as maids, butlers, cooks, coach-drivers, or gardeners. They rarely received cash wages but usually received free board and lodging. Of all serfs, household serfs were most vulnerable to the arbitrary power of their owners, and closest in their status to slaves.

State peasants paid feudal dues to state officials, mainly in the form of cash (*obrok*). This usually meant that they suffered less petty tyranny than did landlords' serfs. On the other hand, officials who chose to harass state peasants lacked the landlords' self-interested concern for the well-being of the serfs.

To enforce their fiscal rights, nobles and government exercized a wide range of powers over their serfs. These powers were the basis of Russian serfdom. The law forbade landlords to kill, ruin or injure their serfs, and most landlords had good reason to obey. Otherwise, there were few legal limits on the power of landlords. The only restraints were practical. Landlords could decide how much labour, money and goods to exact from their serfs. They decided how much land to assign to the peasants and how much to set aside for their own use. They could force their serfs to marry. They could dispossess serfs of their land at any time, turning ordinary serfs into household serfs. Serf-owners judged petty offences and could flog their serfs or even exile them to Siberia. They could send male serfs to the army as recruits. They could even sell their serfs, though the law frowned on this practice. Finally, as serfs could not legally own property, unscrupulous landlords extorted large payments from entrepreneurial serfs who made money. In short, the right to tax their serfs gave landlords arbitrary authority over most aspects of a serf's life. Though self-interest forced most landlords to protect their serfs, there were always some who used their powers in brutal and sadistic ways.

Serfdom was not slavery. Most serf communities had considerable freedom to determine how they farmed the land set aside for their own use and how they managed their village affairs. It is also probable that Russian serfs lived better, in a material sense, than many wage-earners in Western Europe. However, serfs had no civil or political rights. In this sense they were similar to American slaves.

Their lack of rights helps explain the Russian peasants' traditional respect for the tsar. They had no legal protection against landlords or government officials. Indeed, Catherine the Great had made it illegal for serfs to complain about their masters. The only source of protection for serfs, therefore, was someone more powerful than the landlords or officials who stood over them. This could only be God – or the tsar. So most peasants retained a touching faith that the tsar would try to help them, if only they could tell him of their real plight. This also explains why most peasant disturbances broke out not because of the intensity of peasant grievances but because, momentarily, peasants came to believe that the tsar would support their protests. The belief that they could get away with protest was usually more important than the intensity of their grievances. They also knew that landlords and officials would try to hide the truth from the tsar and sabotage his efforts at reform. Peasants saw more clearly than many historians that the tsar could be as much the captive as he was the master of Russia's ruling group.

How burdensome were feudal dues? There are no precise calculations. However, we have some indirect evidence. Soviet scholars claimed that the *obrok* payments in four central provinces of Russia amounted to about 20 per cent of average peasant income in the late eighteenth century, and as much as 30 to 40 per cent by the nineteenth century.[19] Where labour dues were the norm, we can estimate the size of the tribute by comparing the number of days worked on the landlords' land with the time peasants spent on the land set aside for their own use.

> If the landlord demands only three days of *barshchina* a week, it is obvious that the peasant cannot work more land for the landlord than he has been given for his own allotment, assuming, of course, that he works as hard as is humanly possible. But peasants often work more land for the landlord than they receive for their own use.[20]

Andrei Zablotskii, the author of this passage, noted cases where the peasants had to work twice as hard for the landlord as for themselves. However, he added that such cases were unusual. These calculations are extremely rough. However, they suggest that feudal dues could account for as much as one-third, and sometimes two-thirds of all the labour and wealth generated by peasant households. This is much more than the 10 per cent tribute levied by the Mongols in the thirteenth century. Such figures show the power of serfdom as a lever for the direct mobilization of resources.

In addition to the feudal dues it levied as a serf-owner, the government also levied direct and indirect taxes on the entire non-noble population. The most direct of all taxes was army recruitment, which was levied not on property but on human beings. Until 1834, those recruited had to serve for twenty-five years. In 1834, the term was reduced to fifteen years. At the end of their term, recruits received their freedom. However, this was small consolation. The high death rate in the army (mainly from disease), meant that few returned to civilian life, and those who did found they no longer had roots there. Recruitment meant severing all ties with one's home village. Indeed the law treated the wives of recruits as widows, and allowed them to remarry. In the 1850s recruitment was the lot of one in twenty-five Russian males.

The nobility and clergy were free from compulsory recruitment and from the payment of direct monetary taxes. The main direct tax, paid by all other classes (except merchants), was the poll tax. Introduced by Peter the Great, it was levied on all males from the 'tax-paying' classes. The other main direct tax was the *obrok*, paid by state peasants. This was the governmental equivalent of the feudal dues received by private landlords. Together, poll taxes and the *obrok* from state peasants accounted for about 25 per cent of ordinary government revenue in the 1846 budget (see Figure 2.7).

The main indirect tax in 1846 was on sales of vodka. This yielded an astonishing 30 per cent of ordinary revenue. To collect the liquor tax, the government used the archaic method of tax farming. In each province, liquor traders bid for the right to become 'tax farmers'. This gave them a monopoly on liquor sales for a period of four years, in return for which

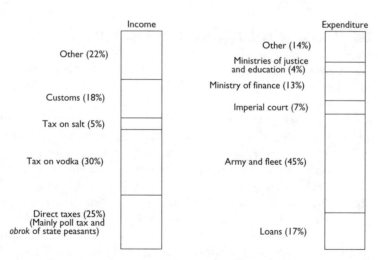

Based on *ordinary* revenue and expenditure (that is, excludes *extraordinary* loans and expenditure)

Figure 2.7 *Budget of the Russian government in 1846*
Source: Based on S. S. Dmitriev *et al.* (eds), *Khrestomatiya po istorii SSSR* (Moscow: gos-oe uchebno-pedagogicheskoe izd-vo min-va prosveshcheniya RSFSR) vol. 2, pp. 607–10.

they paid the government a fixed amount each month. Inevitably, this generated great corruption as the tax farmers looked for ways of raising as much cash as they could within the four years available to them. Like the direct taxes, the vodka tax mainly affected working-class households in the villages and towns.[21] Working-class families also contributed to customs revenues by paying inflated prices for imported goods. Customs revenues accounted for 18 per cent of ordinary revenue in 1846. Altogether, it is likely that peasants and urban workers contributed at least 90 per cent of the government's ordinary revenue.

What did they get in return? Not much. In the same year, 1846, 17 per cent of ordinary expenditure serviced loans, 45 per cent went to the army and fleet, 13 per cent to the ministry of finance, and 7 per cent to the upkeep of the imperial court. Of the remaining 18 per cent, most went to various other ministries. Even the 2 per cent assigned to the ministry of education went to elite schools. The similar amounts assigned to the ministry of justice had no effect on peasants, who came under the jurisdiction of separate manorial or communal courts.[22]

The huge fiscal machinery of the Russian state pumped resources upwards from the peasantry to support Russia's huge armies, and to support the privileged and leisured life-style of Russia's non-productive classes.

■ The Non-Productive Classes

The non-productive classes were a diverse group. The dominant section was the serf-owning nobility, headed by the tsar, the largest of all landowners. I will also examine three other groups within the ruling group, for their importance was to grow steadily as Russia modernized. These were the officials, the intelligentsia and the merchantry. The military never formed a distinct political group, and at the upper levels they merged with the nobility. The clergy, and the Russian Orthodox Church in general, also played a limited role in Russian political life. The church had been firmly subordinated to the government by Peter the Great, and Catherine the Great completed the process by secularizing Church lands. Besides, most parish clergy lived a life little different from that of the peasantry. For these reasons, I will not discuss the military and the clergy separately.

In 1858 there were about one million nobles in the Russian Empire. However, only 610 000 were hereditary nobles, and only 247 000 belonged to the Russian hereditary nobility. (Many of the rest were from the numerous Polish nobility.) Of these, only about 90 000 owned serfs. Even within this smaller group, there were large variations in wealth and privilege. Only about 18 500 serf-owners owned more than a hundred serfs. These were the real nobility. Only they could vote in the provincial assemblies of nobility established under Catherine the Great. Some of the remaining serf-owners were so poor they lived like peasants alongside their own serfs. So it is really these 18 500 (about 0.02 per cent of the total population) who made up the upper crust of Russian society. As this group also dominated the bureaucracy and the army, it is reasonable to describe its members as the 'ruling elite'. Together with their families, they accounted for no more than 0.25–0.5 per cent of the total population.

Even within this elite, there were differences. There was a tiny inner group, close to the royal court. This is the world of Leo Tolstoy, and the Rostov family in *War and Peace*. There was also a larger outer group of rural nobles, often referred to by historians as the 'gentry'. These were the heroes and heroines of Gogol's novel, *Dead Souls*.

What is striking about the upper nobility is not just its fabulous wealth, based on serf labour, but also its Europeanness. Ever since the reign of Peter the Great, the upper nobility had been educated in European traditions. By the nineteenth century, their world was European in clothing, food, education, culture, even language. Many could barely speak the language of their own peasants. Instead, they spoke French or German. They lived on large country estates, or in town houses in Moscow or St Petersburg, or in the spas and resort towns of Western Europe. Their spiritual home was Europe even if their economic home (the source of their wealth) was the Russian countryside.

In the early nineteenth century, the landed nobility still dominated the Russian ruling group. Its upper levels set the tone for the upper classes in manners, dress and attitudes. As serf-owners, they directly ruled half the peasant population. They dominated the upper levels of the bureaucracy and advised the tsar on policy. The autocracy itself was still the representative of noble interests, and tsars saw themselves as leaders of the class of nobles. Tsars also knew that if they neglected the nobility's interests too obviously, disgruntled nobles might simply murder them. This had been the fate of Paul I (1796–1801), the father of Alexander I and Nicholas I who, between them, ruled from 1801 to 1855. The French traveller, de Custine, was thinking of this unspoken threat when he described Russia as an 'autocracy tempered by assassination'.

Under the original Table of Ranks all nobles were also either civil or military officials of the government. After the emancipation of the nobility from compulsory service in 1785, this ceased to be true. From that time, it was possible to distinguish between those nobles who worked as government officials, and those who did not. By the mid-nineteenth century, the number and importance of government officials was growing rapidly. Officials began to form an inner, disciplined core of the ruling group. Whether or not they were of noble rank, most officials were dependent on government salaries for a livelihood. Like the old *dvoriane*, their privileges derived from service. Meanwhile, those nobles who did not serve considered themselves more independent of the government, like the old *boyar* class. During the nineteenth century the gap between the two groups grew wider, as the autocracy relied increasingly on paid officials for the routine execution of government decisions.

At the top of the pyramid the two groups merged. Government ministers and provincial governors usually came from the upper levels of the landed nobility. Below them, serving in the ministries or in the various organs of local government and police, was a larger group of professional bureaucrats. At the lower end of the scale, these exercized purely clerical functions in return for pitifully small salaries. In 1850 there were about 114 000 officials on the government's payroll, but 32 000 were purely clerical. The remaining 86 000 were in the Table of Ranks, but only the upper eight ranks (about 14 000) had noble status.

By the mid-nineteenth century, the Russian government consisted of a disciplined bureaucracy, which gave the tsar advice and carried out the tsar's decisions. There were no elected institutions of any significance. Nor could any group, institution, or individual legally resist the will of the tsar. The main instruments of government were the ministries, which had been founded in 1802. In each province (*guberniya*), the main government official was the governor. The governors represented the tsar, and ruled their provinces as autocratically as the tsar ruled Russia. They, in turn, headed an administration based in the provincial capital, but with branches in the main towns of each district (*uezd*).

About 246 000 merchants belonged to the so-called merchant guilds in 1867. Merchants could not own serfs, nor could they vote in the assemblies of the nobility. Although many were extremely wealthy, they had nothing like the prestige or influence of the bourgeoisie of nineteenth-century France or England. In dress, mental outlook and customs, they, along with the clergy, were the least Europeanized section of the upper classes. Nevertheless, in economic and fiscal matters the government often turned to merchants for advice. As Russia began to modernize later in the century, merchants gained increased influence as industrialists and financiers.

The Russian term 'intelligentsia' has given rise to much dispute among historians. It is simplest to think of the intelligentsia as those members of the upper classes who, though educated, enjoyed neither the material privileges of the nobility nor the political influence of the bureaucracy. It was their half-and-half status, as semi-members of the ruling group, that explains why so many became dissidents.

Members of the intelligentsia were the forerunners of the modern 'white-collar' workers. They were brain workers, living from their education and intellect. This is an extremely large and important group in modern industrialized societies, but it was a small and underprivileged group in most pre-modern societies, including nineteenth-century Russia.

In the mid-nineteenth century, most members of the intelligentsia came from *raznochintsy* groups, such as the children of priests. However, as the century wore on, increasing numbers trained in the universities. By the second half of the century, many worked for the government as statisticians, teachers, doctors, agricultural experts. Others worked as journalists or writers. A minority felt so alienated from the system that they became revolutionaries. Dissident members of the intelligentsia provided most of the leaders of the Russian revolutionary movement, and they made good revolutionary leaders, for they were better educated than their working-class followers, and knew from inside how the system worked.

By comparison with the productive classes, most of these groups enjoyed considerable material, political and psychological privileges. However, their privileges took various forms. Nobles owed their wealth mainly to serf labour. Officials, and most members of the intelligentsia, lived off ungenerous government salaries, though some enjoyed influence as servants of a powerful state. Merchants made their money in business and industry. Within each group there were wide variations in wealth, status and power. At the lower levels, each group merged imperceptibly into the 'productive' classes.

The diverse interests of the various sections of the ruling elite always threatened their solidarity as a group. Even in the eighteenth century, some nobles had resented the immense power of the autocracy and its officials. Merchants resented the exclusive economic privileges of the nobility. Members of the intelligentsia resented the constant petty harassment of a government that respected birth and wealth more than education and expertise. Poor wages, censorship, and bars to promotion were the main grievances of the nineteenth century intelligentsia.

These divisions within the ruling group multiplied during the century. Eventually, they created rifts so wide that the ruling group began to lose the unity and cohesion necessary for its survival.

In the early nineteenth century, these divisions were balanced by powerful unifying pressures. In the first place, all members of the non-productive classes benefited from the massive redistribution of wealth described in the previous sections. They also shared in different ways in the task of government. This was obviously true of the nobility, government officials and the military. But even the intelligentsia, the clergy and the merchantry played important leadership roles in the more specialized areas of culture, religion and the economy. This is the first reason for treating all these groups as members of a single 'ruling group'.

Second, formal institutions bound the group together. The most important were the autocracy and the Table of Ranks. Together, they created structures of leadership, subordination and hierarchy, that incorporated everyone of importance in Russian society. As the literature of the period shows, most upper-class Russians accepted the autocratic political culture that had evolved in Russia since the Middle Ages. They were also intensely conscious of rank. There were even special forms of address for each rank. Members of the first two ranks were addressed as 'Your Supreme Excellency'; those of ranks 3 to 5, as 'Your Excellency'; those of ranks 6 to 8, as 'Your Supreme Honour'; and the rest, as 'Your Honour'.

The third cohesive factor was cultural. In 1850, 90 to 95 per cent of the population was illiterate.[23] In contrast, most members of Arsenev's 'non-productive' classes were literate, and many were well-educated. Their learning was European in content, and taught either by private tutors or in the country's few secondary schools. As a result, the 'non-productive' classes were also the 'educated' classes. They shared a western culture that separated them from the religious, superstitious and pre-literate peasantry. Intellectually, the productive and non-productive classes lived in quite different worlds. In the long-term, the cultural gulf between the upper and lower classes did much to preserve upper-class solidarity against the 'dark masses' they ruled, despite the many potential divisions within the elite.

In the early nineteenth century Russia's educated classes produced a rich literary, philosophical and scientific culture that reflected many of the tensions of a pre-modern society first glimpsing the dangers and opportunities of the 'modern' revolution. Three main issues haunted Russian intellectuals in the early nineteenth century.

1. *The relationship between individuals and the autocracy*
   This issue emerged naturally out of the growing discontent of some educated Russians with autocratic government. Their discontent drew inspiration from the slogans and ideals of the American and French Revolutions, and the tumult of the revolutionary epoch that ended with the defeat of Napoleon in 1815. It was this combination of resistance to extreme forms of autocracy, and attraction to the liberal ideas of revolutionary Europe that laid the foundations of the Russian revolutionary movement.

2. *The relationship of Russia to Europe*
   Ever since the reign of Peter the Great, educated Russians had borrowed extensively from the culture of Europe. Yet ordinary

Russians knew nothing of the culture of Europe. What, then, was Russian culture? What did it mean to be Russian? Did Russia's future lie with Europe or with its own past? This issue merged imperceptibly with a third.

3. *The gulf between the upper and lower classes*
    Did Russia's future lie with the educated elite or with the peasantry? Which group was truest to Russia's essential nature? Or could educated and non-educated Russians combine to produce a distinctive Russian culture in spite of the gulf between them?

These questions fired the revolutionary movement, whose origins lie in this period. Their importance can be seen clearly in the Decembrist revolt of 1825. This was an unsuccessful *coup d'état* led by a small group of young army officers. Most of the Decembrists had participated in the campaigns of 1812–14 against Napoleonic France. On returning to Russia, they were shocked by the contrasts between post-revolutionary Europe and their Russian homeland, with its lack of civil and political freedoms. One of them, A. Bestuzhev, wrote in a letter:

> The war was still on when the soldiers, upon their return home, for the first time disseminated grumbling among the masses. 'We shed blood', they would say, 'and then we are again forced to sweat under feudal obligations. We freed the fatherland from the tyrant and now we ourselves are tyrannised over by the ruling class.'[24]

Another Decembrist, Yakushkin, described his personal experience of the home-coming from France:

> From France we returned to Russia by sea. The first division of the Guard landed at Oranienbaum [a royal palace near St Petersburg] and listened to the Te Deum performed by the Archpriest Derzhavin. During the prayer, the police were mercilessly beating the people who attempted to draw near to the line-up of troops. This made upon us the first unfavourable impression when we returned to our homeland ... Finally the Emperor appeared, accompanied by the Guard, on a fine sorrel horse, with an unsheathed sword, which he was ready to lower before the Empress. We looked with delight at him. But at that very moment, almost under his horse, a peasant crossed the street. The Emperor spurred his horse and rushed with the unsheathed sword toward the running peasant. The police attacked him with their clubs. We did not believe our own eyes and turned away, ashamed for our beloved tsar.[25]

From 1816, groups of young officers formed conspiratorial organizations intending to overthrow autocracy and serfdom. In December 1825, in the confusion that followed the death of Alexander I, they attempted a coup in St Petersburg. However, their mutiny was ill-prepared, and the new Tsar, Nicholas I, crushed it within a few days.

During the oppressive reign of Nicholas I, strict censorship restricted public discussion of issues such as serfdom or autocracy. Censorship expressed one of the basic rules of the autocratic political culture of Russia's ruling group. There must be no public display of division in deeds or words. As in the past, this principle did not suppress conflict. It merely drove it underground. Educated Russians reacted to censorship by debating politics indirectly, through discussions of topics such as Russia's relationship with the West. This issue was debated with particular intensity during the 1840s by small groups of Moscow intellectuals who later became known as the Westernizers and Slavophiles. Broadly speaking, the Westernizers admired the modern world of Western Europe, with its civil and political rights, its rational, scientific and urban culture, and its economic productivity. On the other hand, the Slavophiles admired old Russian culture and saw the West as a corrosive force destroying the communal, rural and religious world of old Russia.

Many of their discussions centred on the role of Peter the Great, for it was during his reign that Russia's elite had first begun to absorb western culture and to separate itself from the mass of the Russian population. For the Westernizers Peter was a hero, the ruler who at last had turned Muscovy towards the higher civilization of Europe. Here is how a Westernizer, the literary critic V. G. Belinsky (1811–48), described Peter's role in Russian history.

☐   *Document 2.8: Russia and the West – a pro-Western view*

Peter the Great was the greatest phenomenon not only in our history, but in the history of all mankind. He was a god who called us back to life, who blew a living soul into the body of ancient Russia, colossal, but sunk in a deadly torpor ...

Everything great, noble, human, and spiritual came up, grew, burst into splendid bloom, and brought forth sumptuous fruit on European soil. The diversity of life, the noble relations between the sexes, the refinement of customs, art, science, the subjugation of the unconscious forces of nature, the victory over matter, the triumph of the spirit, the respect for the human personality, the sacredness of human right – in short, everything that makes one proud of being a man ... all this is the result of the development of European life.[26]

When Slavophiles such as Ivan Kireevskii compared Russia and Europe, they saw something very different.

☐ *Document 2.9: Russia and the West – a Slavophile view*

Theology in the West assumed the character of rational abstractness; in the Orthodox world it retained an inner wholeness of spirit ... In the West, there were universities for scholasticism and law; in ancient Russia – monasteries for prayer ... There, the rational and scholastic study of higher truths; here, the striving toward an active and complete understanding of them ... There a state organization based on violent conquest; here, one based on the natural development of the people's way of life, permeated with the unity of a fundamental belief. There, a hostile division of classes; in ancient Russia, their harmonious association in all their natural variety ... There, a propensity in the law toward the appearance of justice; here, a preference for the essence of justice. There, jurisprudence strives for a logical code; here, instead of formal connections, it seeks the intrinsic bond between legal principles and the principles of faith and custom ... There, improvements were always accomplished by forcible changes; here, by harmonious natural growth ... There, the precariousness of each individual regulating himself; here, the firmness of family and social bonds ... There, the foppery of luxury and the artificiality of life; here, the simplicity of basic needs and the courage of moral fortitude.[27]

■ Towards the Modern World

In retrospect, we can see that in debates such as these, educated Russians were beginning to grapple with the issue of modernity. Europe represented a new world of industry, urbanization and science. Russia represented a traditional world of peasants, religion and autocracy. In discussing the relationship of Europe and Russia, or the Europeanized upper classes to the peasantry, intellectuals were trying to make a choice, for it still seemed there was a choice to be made. Should Russia keep what was best in the traditional world? Or should it welcome the changes that were already transforming Europe? We can see now that the choice was unreal. Sooner or later, willingly or not, Russian society would be transformed. However, debates such as those between the Slavophiles and Westernizers shaped Russia's response to modernity and affected the way in which Russian society entered the modern world. They could not prevent modernization, but they could and did affect its course.

■ Summary

This chapter has described the economic, social and political structures of the Russian empire in the early nineteenth century. Most of those structures were still typical of the pre-modern world. A small ruling group unified by the structures of autocracy, lived off resources mobilized directly from a large, agrarian population through the system of serfdom. Most of the peasant population lived lives little different from those of the Middle Ages. The family, the household and the village were the crucial institutions of rural life. Largely self-sufficient peasants used traditional ways of working the soil, and levels of productivity were little higher than those of the Middle Ages. Serf-owning nobles extracted surplus resources from the peasantry directly. The government also relied largely on direct mobilization through the poll tax and the dues it levied on state serfs.

However, new forces were already beginning to undermine the traditional patterns of Russian politics and the Russian countryside. In some areas, particularly near the larger cities, market forces were beginning to transform village life. Some peasants already earned much of their income through artisan work or wage-work in nearby towns, while the government's revenues came, increasingly, from commercial sources, such as the sale of alcohol. At the upper level of society, the military successes of the Russian government in the previous century, and the increasingly Westernized outlook of Russian elites, undermined the autocratic political culture of Russia's ruling group. The government became aware of how threatening these various changes might be to its own power only in the middle of the nineteenth century.

☐   *Further Reading*

In the last 25 years, there has been a lot of good social history written about nineteenth-century Russia, so it is easier now to understand the life of ordinary Russians. Particularly vivid are the accounts in S. L. Hoch, *Serfdom and Social Control*, C. Worobec, *Peasant Russia*, and D. Ransel, *Village Life in Late Nineteenth-Century Russia*. B. Eklof and S. P. Frank (eds) *The World of the Russian Peasant*, is a fine collection of essays, as is Kingston-Mann and Mixter (eds) *Peasant Economy, Culture, and Politics of European Russia*, while Atkinson, *Women in Russia*, and B. E. Clements *et al.* (eds) *Russia's Women: Accomodation, Resistance, Transformation*, are just two of many good recent studies on the history of women in Russia. On some basic aspects of peasant material life, see R. E. F. Smith and D. Christian, *Bread and Salt*. On serfdom, Blum, *Lord and Peasant*, is old but still very valuable, while Kolchin, *Unfree Labor*, is a remarkable recent comparison of slavery and serfdom in Russia and North America. R. Pipes, *Russia Under the Old Regime*, has some good discussions of class structure. The best general histories of the era are Saunders, *Russia in the Age of Reaction and Reform*, and the more encyclopedic Seton-Watson, *The Russian Empire*, whose focus is mainly political.

☐ *Notes*

1. Adapted from S. S. Dmitriev *et al.* (eds), *Khrestomatiya po istorii SSSR* (Moscow: gos-oe uchebno-pedagogicheskoe izd-vo min-va prosveshcheniya RSFSR, 1948) vol. 2, pp. 402–3 (trans D. Christian). Arsenev's figures are very rough, and I have corrected totals. It is characteristic of the attitudes of the time that government censuses counted only males, as it was males who paid the poll tax. So the above figures have been doubled to estimate the total population.
2. A. P. Zablotskii-Desiatovskii, 'O krepostnom sostoyanii', in *Graf P.D. Kiselev i ego vremya* ... (St Petersburg: Tipografiya M. M. Stasulevicha, 1882) vol. 4, pp. 289–90 (trans D. Christian).
3. From S. L. Hoch, *Serfdom and Social Control in Russia: Petrovskoe, a Village in Tambov* (Chicago: University of Chicago Press, 1986) p. 62.
4. Hoch, *Serfdom and Social Control*, p. 76.
5. P. Gatrell, *The Tsarist Economy 1850–1917* (London: Batsford, 1986) p. 52.
6. Hoch, *Serfdom and Social Control*, p. 68.
7. A. von Haxthausen, *The Russian Empire: Its People, Institutions, & Resources* (London, 1856) vol. 1, p. 344 (reprinted London: F Cass, 1968).
8. Ibid., vol. 2, p. 70.
9. V. O. Klyuchevskii, *Kurs russkoi istorii*, in *Sochineniya* (Moscow: Mysl', 1987–90) vol. 1, p. 83 (trans D. Christian).
10. A. N. Engel'gardt, *Iz Derevni*, 41–3, cited from R. E. F. Smith and David Christian, *Bread and Salt: A Social and Economic History of Food and Drink in Russia* (Cambridge University Press, 1984) p. 337.
11. Hoch, *Serfdom and Social Control*, pp. 30, 56.
12. Ibid., pp. 91–2.
13. Cited in S. P. Frank, 'Popular Justice, Community, and Culture: 1870–1900', in B. Eklof and S. P. Frank (eds), *The World of the Russian Peasant* (Boston: Unwin Hyman, 1990) p. 143.
14. G. Vernadsky *et al.* (eds), *A Source Book for Russian History from Early Times to 1917*, 3 vols. (New Haven, Conn.: Yale University Press, 1972) vol. 2, pp. 554–5.
15. See C. Tudge, *The Famine Business* (Harmondsworth: Penguin, 1979) pp. 11–13.
16. Cited in R. L. Glickman, 'The Peasant Woman as Healer', in B. E. Clements, B. A. Engel, and C. D. Worobec (eds), *Russia's Women: Accommodation, Resistance, Transformation* (Berkeley: University of California Press, 1991) p. 154.
17. Ibid., p. 157.
18. Zablotskii, 'O krepostnom sostoianii', p. 280.
19. P. G. Ryndziunskii, *Utverzhdenie kapitalizma v Rossii* (Moscow: Nauka, 1978) p. 56.
20. Zablotskii, 'O krepostnom sostoianii', p. 277.
21. See D. Christian, '*Living Water': Vodka and Russian Society on the Eve of Emancipation* (Oxford University Press, 1990) chs. 5–7.
22. Dmitriev, *Khrestomatiya*, vol. 2, pp. 607–10 for the 1846 budget.
23. *The Fontana Economic History of Europe* (Glasgow: William Collins, 1973) vol. 2, p. 801.
24. T. Riha (ed.), *Readings in Russian Civilization* (University of Chicago Press, 1964) vol. 2, p. 299.

25. A. Mazour, *The First Russian Revolution: The Decembrist Movement* (Stanford University Press, 1937) p. 55.
26. Vernadsky, *Source Book*, vol. 2, p. 568.
27. Ibid., p. 576.

■ *Chapter 3* ■

The 'Great Reforms' and the Rise of a Revolutionary Movement

In the early nineteenth century the Russian Empire was a major world power. It owed its strength to the formidable armies that had helped defeat Napoleon, and to the autocratic governments that mobilized the resources needed to support these armies. Yet in the 1850s Alexander II launched a 'revolution from above' which transformed Russian society. His government began by abolishing serfdom. Then it introduced reforms in local government, the law, censorship, banking, taxation and the army.

Most historians regard the 'Great Reforms' as a watershed in Russian history. In the view of Soviet historians, they marked the end of almost 1000 years of feudalism. Most Western historians have seen the reforms as a large, if hesitant, step towards modernization. One western historian, Terence Emmons, has described them as 'probably the greatest single piece of state-directed engineering in modern European history before the twentieth century'.[1]

Why did the Russian government introduce such dangerous and far-reaching changes? Were the reforms a first attempt to bring Russia into the modern world? If so, how successful were they?

In discussing these questions, we will bear in mind the striking parallels between the era of the 'Great Reforms', and the era of *perestroika* in the late 1980s. In both periods, a new generation of young, reforming politicians launched sweeping changes from above, after a prolonged era of political oppression and economic stagnation. In one case, the reformed system survive for another 60 years; in the other case, it collapsed.

■ Causes of the Reforms

To explain the 'Great Reforms', we must begin by distinguishing between the real problems of the government (as far as we can assess those problems now), and the government's own assessment of its problems. Soviet historians wrote within a Marxist theory of history that stressed the

71

role of objective historical laws. As a result, they usually emphasized the long-term changes that made reform inevitable. Western historians have mainly stressed the government's subjective assessment of its problems. Both approaches are necessary. No one doubts that the Russian government faced serious long-term problems that would eventually undermine its stability. Yet the timing and nature of reform depended on how particular politicians assessed the nature and urgency of these problems.

In retrospect, we can see that serfdom posed economic, political, military and moral problems, that had to be tackled sooner or later if Russia was to survive as a great power in a modernizing world.

A minority of educated Russians had argued since the eighteenth century that serfdom was an inefficient way of using labour. In 1766 Catherine the Great organized an essay competition on the question: 'Whether it is more beneficial to society for the peasant to own land, or only movable property, and the degree to which his rights should extend over either type of property'. The winner, a Frenchman, put the case for free labour clearly.

☐   *Document 3.1: The advantages of free labour in theory, 1766*

Beyond all doubt, the best way to attract, arouse, and encourage the tillers of the soil is to give them ownership of the land they cultivate. Then each one will toil for himself, for his children, for his descendants; in a word, he will enrich the state while increasing property.

But what limits should be assigned to this property? If he owns only movable goods, this can hardly be called property; it holds no attraction for the peasant; he should be given land. But he must be free; freedom and property rights are united in an indissoluble bond. Two thousand peasants doing forced labor will be of less benefit to the state than one hundred husbandmen who see a sure path open to their own enrichment; for the former labor under duress and always seek ways of avoiding hard work.[2]

In other words, the government should encourage peasants to become petty entrepreneurs. This was a way of saying that the direct mobilization of resources through force was less efficient than indirect mobilization operating through market forces and people's real interests.

In the early nineteenth century, educated Russians read the works of the Scottish economist Adam Smith, who also argued that free wage labour was more productive than forced serf labour. Practical experience confirmed these conclusions. Andrei Zablotskii, a progressive government official, described what he was told by a provincial noble in 1840.

☐ *Document 3.2: The advantages of free labour in practice, 1840s*

There is no doubt that free labour is better. It is wrong to suppose that once our peasants are free they will become even lazier. This is untrue! A free man knows that if he does not work he is not going to be fed for nothing, and as a result, he works hard. Here is my own experience: twenty *versts* from my estate of Zemenki, I have some unsettled land which I have worked using my own peasants, not under *barshchina*, but by hiring them under a free contract. The same peasants who idle about on *barshchina* work extremely hard there and are even willing to work on holidays, as long as no one stops them. And they so value this work that they are reluctant even to annoy the overseer.[3]

The low productivity of serf labour threatened both the state and the nobility. Nobles found it increasingly difficult to extract from their serfs the resources needed to support their Westernized life styles. As a result, they borrowed from the State Loan Bank. By 1859, landlords had mortgaged 60 per cent of their serfs. Serfdom was also failing the Treasury. In the 1840s and 1850s the taxes that rose most rapidly were not the taxes based on serfdom – poll taxes, and the *obrok* from state peasants – but those on vodka. By 1855 the government was 54 million roubles in debt. During the Crimean War, it was the rising revenues from vodka sales that saved it from bankruptcy. It was certainly in no position to pay for the military modernization needed if Russia was to remain a military superpower.

Serfdom also restricted growth indirectly. In regions with good soils, some serf-owners exploited serf labour to produce cheap grain for the market. This was a commercial form of serfdom, similar to the commercial uses of slavery in the southern states of the USA. However, because transportation was so primitive, serf-owners who produced for the market had to sell their grain on local markets where prices were low. To survive, they needed the access to wider markets which an extensive railway network could provide. Yet many believed that railways were incompatible with the survival of serfdom for, while serfdom meant tying peasants to the village, railways encouraged migration.[4] Like Nicholas I's minister of finance, Kankrin, they saw railways as 'a malady of our age'.[5]

To more thoughtful Russians, the conclusion was clear. While serfdom remained, Russian agriculture would stagnate and so would the entire Russian economy. A stagnant economy would limit the revenues of both nobles and government, while a fixed tax base left no resources for military reform. Meanwhile, the economies of Russia's European rivals were growing at unprecedented rates. If nothing was done to stimulate the Russian economy, Russia would fall behind the other great powers in economic and military strength.

There can be no doubt that these arguments were correct. Eventually, forced labour would have to give way to wage labour for, as we have seen, wage labour is one of the defining features of a successful modern society.

Nevertheless, these conclusions were harder to see in mid-nineteenth century Russia. Indeed, even amongst educated Russians, only a minority accepted them, and most of these assumed that Russia would remain an agrarian society even after the abolition of serfdom. Supporting the abolition of serfdom did not necessarily mean supporting industrialization. Most provincial nobles found the arguments of economists irrelevant. Serfdom was simply a way of life. Few provincial nobles had read Adam Smith, and they saw no reason to pay for labour when serf labour was free. Besides, Russia's serf economy still had plenty of room for growth, as Lenin's one-time ally, Peter Struve, argued later in the century.[6] In the early nineteenth century many serfs engaged in wage-work or in rural crafts in order to pay taxes and cash dues. Meanwhile, serf-owners set up enterprises such as distilleries or sugar-beet processing plants on their lands. Serfdom was by no means so rigid that it prevented the emergence of some entrepreneurs and wage-labourers, or an extension of market relations.

In the middle of the century, only a minority of progressive nobles and officials really thought that the advantages of free labour justified overthrowing a system that had worked well since the sixteenth century. Though the problem of economic stagnation would eventually have to be faced, it was not yet so serious that it demanded immediate action.

Contemporaries were more impressed with the social and political dangers of maintaining serfdom. Because it depended on forced labour, serfdom generated a high level of class tension. We have already seen that the first large peasant rebellions in Russian history occurred as serfdom was being created. Between 1773 and 1774, the greatest of these rebellions, led by Emelyan Pugachev, had caused the death of 1500 nobles and threatened to destroy the government of Catherine the Great. Ever since, Russian governments had feared the appearance of a new Pugachev. Yet the low productivity of the Russian economy meant that governments and nobles had to tax their serfs hard, even though they knew this might provoke unrest.

In the early nineteenth century, there were ominous signs that the peasantry might hit back. Between 1835 and 1854, the army suppressed 228 peasant disturbances of various kinds. Between 1836 and 1851, serfs killed 139 nobles or their bailiffs and tried to kill seventy more.[7] The government of Nicholas I took these signs very seriously. In the 1840s, Count Benkendorff, the head of the secret police, reported to Nicholas I that:

The whole mood of the people is concerned with one aim – emancipation ... Serfdom is a powder keg under the state, and is the more dangerous because of the fact that the army itself consists of peasants ... It is better to begin gradually, cautiously, than to wait until the process is started from below by the people themselves.[8]

Benkendorff's nightmare vision, of 100 000 serf-owners holding down 30 million serfs with a serf-based army, troubled the sleep of many nobles and officials. During mobilization for the Crimean War in 1854, peasant disturbances broke out in many parts of the Empire. Many peasants responded to rumours that the tsar could be found wearing a golden cap and sitting on top of a mountain in the Crimea, dispensing freedom to all who came to him. To deal with internal disturbances, the government diverted army units that should have been used against the external enemy. In the late 1850s, the number of disturbances rose. Indeed, the Soviet historian, M. V. Nechkina, claimed that by 1859 the country faced a 'revolutionary situation'. The thought of a new peasant war was particularly terrifying for rural nobles living on remote country estates.

But we must not exaggerate. Most peasant disturbances were small-scale affairs. While they posed real threats to individual nobles and their families, none really threatened the government. The so-called 'potato riots' of the 1840s illustrate the limited scale of these disturbances. The potato riots erupted in response to a government decision of 1840 to force state peasants to grow potatoes. Many peasants believed the potato was a fruit of the devil. Others resented government interference in the way they farmed their land. Police reports show vividly the sort of small-scale but desperate resistance peasants could display when faced with changes in the already precarious conditions of their life. The following description, by a Soviet historian, also shows the pathetic lack of organisation characteristic of most peasant insurrections.

☐ *Document 3.3: Potato riots in Vyatka province, 1842*

In order to put an end to these disorders, the governor of Vyatka province, Mordvinov ... arrived in Bykovskoe village on June 12 [with about 300 soldiers]. Finding a gathering of about 600 unarmed peasants, he tried to calm them with the aid of a priest, but the peasants unanimously declared that potatoes were no good for them, and that they would not disperse. After this, the governor announced that he intended to fire on the crowd, but the peasants shouted unanimously: 'Shoot! We still won't surrender.' Finally, the governor, noticing that the peasants had begun to pull down fencing posts in order to arm themselves, ordered a volley of forty-eight shots. This inspired considerable fear amongst the peasants, and they ceased arming themselves. But they still remained on the spot, and when ordered to disperse once more they declared again that they were willing to die.

Seeing neither resistance nor submission from the peasants, the governor, with his troops, went around the village and, arriving at the plot of land set aside for potatoes, ordered some of the other, more obedient villagers to plough the land and sow potatoes, which they did. However, the other peasants remained as before and, when told that the potatoes had been sown, replied: 'Let them sow. We will just throw them out.' Finally, seeing that nothing he had done yet would solve the problem, he ordered his soldiers to charge the crowd in order to bind them. He ordered his soldiers not to use their bayonets, but to use their rifle butts in case of resistance. This action, which the peasants had not anticipated, was carried out quickly, and with complete success. After an extremely brief conflict all those who had put up resistance were thrown to the ground and, with the help of some other peasants, were bound with their own sashes. All 600 were led to the village of Kurchum, where, after the main instigators had been separated out to face a military court, eight others were whipped, and the rest, after repenting in full, were allowed to return to their homes.[9]

Disturbances in the late 1850s were also small-scale. The most organized were the boycotts of vodka sales that spread to almost half the provinces of Great Russia in 1859. However, these were aimed at the corrupt practices of the 'tax farmers' and the high prices they charged for vodka. They were not attacks on the government or on serfdom and do not prove the existence of a serious 'revolutionary crisis'.[10]

As with the issue of economic productivity, there was a real problem, though some exaggerated its seriousness. Unlike the issue of economic productivity, this problem scared both nobles and government, and therefore encouraged the government to act.

The army was the linchpin of the system. As Alexander II's Minister of War, Dmitrii Miliutin, told him in 1867: 'Thanks to the army, Russia became a first class European power [and] only by maintaining the army can Russia uphold the position it has acquired'.[11]

The army had many strengths. It was huge, with one million regular soldiers and many units of Cossacks. The bravery and discipline of its common soldiers remained one of its strengths. Officers maintained discipline with ferocious methods. The punishment for disobedience, for instance, was running the gauntlet. The victim had to run several times between two rows of soldiers who beat him with birch branches as he ran past. In 1831, 2600 mutinous military colonists were punished in this way, and 129 died.[12]

The army looked particularly impressive on the parade ground. Paul I (1796–1801), Alexander I (1801–25), Nicholas I (1825–55) and Alexander II (1855–81) were all connoisseurs of good drill. As a result the army performed splendidly on the parade ground, where it could manoeuvre free from enemy harassment.

The army won most of its victories in the early nineteenth century against inferior opponents such as the declining Ottoman Empire. This disguised its weaknesses. The Crimean War exposed these weaknesses by pitting it against two of the most advanced armies in Europe. Though the French and British armies also displayed spectacular incompetence, the Russian army suffered from specific difficulties of its own. Russian army drill still concentrated on the bayonet, and soldiers lacked training in the use of firearms. Most officers were nobles, who despised formal military training. Many found to their cost that panache was no substitute for expertise in modern warfare. The lack of railways meant that, though Russian armies fought on Russian soil, they found it harder to get supplies to the front than the French and English, who supplied their armies by sea.

The army was also costly. Being a standing army, it remained at full strength even in peacetime. As a result, it gobbled up 40 to 50 per cent of government revenue. The Crimean War drove the government to the verge of bankruptcy.

Military officials realised that serfdom made it difficult to reform the army. They knew that to create a more efficient and less costly army, Russia would have to follow the example of its opponents. It would have to form a small peacetime army with a trained reserve that could be called up in time of war. This meant recruiting soldiers for only five or six years, and allowing them to return to civilian life. However, a reform of this kind was unthinkable under serfdom, for traditionally recruits were freed at the end of their term of service. Such a reform would have led to a gradual, yet automatic emancipation of all male serfs. Besides, the idea of giving millions of serfs military training before returning them to their villages was unappealing to nobles afraid of a peasant rebellion. The conclusion was clear: reform of the army required the abolition of serfdom. These arguments were put to Alexander II in 1855, in a memorandum written by Dmitrii Miliutin, a future minister of war.[13]

Serfdom also inhibited railway building, yet as long as serfdom existed, the government was reluctant to support a large-scale programme of railway construction.

These arguments suggested that the abolition of serfdom was necessary if Russia was to remain a major military power. Yet while Russia's armies appeared successful, these arguments lacked force. It took defeat in the Crimea to persuade the government that the survival of serfdom was undermining the army as well as the economy of the Russian Empire.

Serfdom also raised difficult moral problems. It arose in a world of direct mobilization, where forced labour seemed normal and legitimate.

Though forced labour had declined in Western Europe, it had expanded in Eastern Europe since the late middle ages. In the seventeenth century, few doubted that serfdom, like slavery, was a natural relationship, sanctioned by God. During the eighteenth century, Western European attitudes to slavery began to undermine this confidence. Catherine the Great, who was herself of German origin, had written in her diary that it was 'contrary to the Christian religion and to justice to make slaves of men (who are all free by birth)'.[14] Later, a series of liberal-minded writers put the moral case against serfdom. These included Nicholas Novikov (1744–1818) and Alexander Radishchev (1749–1802), as well as the Decembrists, and both Westernizers and Slavophiles.

By 1850 educated members of the nobility accepted that serfdom was morally indefensible. Unlike American slave-owners, Russian serf-owners made no serious attempt to defend serfdom on moral grounds. When serfdom came under attack, its defenders could fall back only on pragmatic arguments for inaction.

By the early nineteenth century Russian governments understood that eventually serfdom would have to go. While it survived, it would hinder reform of the economy and the army, and Russia would remain a moral pariah to progressively minded Russians and Europeans.

Yet the government hesitated to act. After all, the system seemed to work; and abolition would be risky. 'Why change that political system that made [Russia] a first-class power in the world?' asked a Russian. 'To undermine its foundations, everything that constitutes its strength and essence, is ill-advised and dangerous.'[15] Even Count Benkendorff's metaphor cut two ways: It was dangerous sitting on top of a powder keg; but it might be even more dangerous to shift the keg. So, throughout his reign (1825–55) Nicholas I dithered. He discussed reform endlessly and set up numerous secret committees on the subject. In the end, though, he chose inaction, arguing: 'There is no doubt that serfdom, as it exists at present in our land, is an evil, palpable and obvious to all. But to touch it now would be a still more disastrous evil … The Pugachev rebellion proved how far popular rage can go'.[16]

Nicholas's government was equally afraid of the opposition reform might provoke among the nobility. It would inevitably cause them hardship, and Nicholas had no wish to annoy the nobility. The Decembrist revolt, and the murder of his father (Paul I) and grandfather (Peter III) by disgruntled nobles were reminders of how dangerous that could be. Like Brezhnev's government in the 1970s, the government of Nicholas I preferred the abstract dangers of stagnation to the immediate risks of reform.

Meanwhile, for more than fifty years, Russian governments tinkered with the problem as if defusing a bomb. Their experiments were, in part, a way of avoiding decisive action. However, they suggested some important principles, which guided the government when it finally took action in the 1850s.

In 1803, Alexander I issued the so-called 'law of free cultivators'. This created a legal way for nobles voluntarily to free their serfs. However, very few landlords took up the government's offer. The experiment showed that a voluntary emancipation would not work.

In 1804, in Livonia (modern Lithuania), the government tried to regulate serfdom by introducing inventories that fixed the level of feudal dues and the size of peasant landholdings. In principle, this should have changed serfdom into a rental agreement binding on peasants and their owners. However, the reform satisfied neither the peasants, who wanted full freedom, nor the landlords, who feared losing control of their land. In the 1840s, the government tried a similar reform on an even larger scale amongst the state peasantry of the Russian provinces. Once again, the half-heartedness of the reform generated more problems than it had resolved.

In 1816, in Estonia and Courland (modern Estonia and Latvia), the government experimented with a reform that freed the peasants without any land at all. This protected the landlords' property rights. However, it created a large and discontented group of landless workers, who proved unsatisfactory as wage-labourers and caused much rural unrest. This experiment persuaded the government that it would have to free the peasantry with land. Otherwise, it feared, landless peasants would drift to the towns and create the sort of proletarian class that had fuelled revolutionary upheavals in Western Europe in the early nineteenth century. The proletariat had played a particularly important role in the revolutions of 1848. In seeing dispossessed peasants or 'proletarians' as a dangerous revolutionary class, the Russian government was not alone. In the *Communist Manifesto*, which they wrote in response to the 1848 revolutions, Karl Marx and Friedrich Engels argued that the proletariat would become the main revolutionary class of the modern era.

These experiments convinced the government that reform, when it came, had to be compulsory, that it had to give the peasants real property rights, and that it had to give them enough land to support themselves. They also showed that half-hearted measures would achieve nothing. When it finally decided to act, the government would have to act decisively.

■ The Reform Process

Two events explain why the government chose to act in the 1850s. These were defeat in the Crimea, and a change of political leadership. The second factor was critical because Russia's government was autocratic. Unlike a democratic ruler, an autocrat can take basic decisions without waiting for a broad consensus to emerge. This is why authoritarian governments often make sudden sharp changes in policy.

The Crimean War began in 1853 when France and Britain backed Turkey against Russian claims in what is now Moldova. Lacking any obvious target, the Western allies attacked the Russian naval base of Sebastopol in the Crimea. Its fall in 1855 marked the most humiliating defeat for a Russian army in one and a half centuries. For a government whose power depended on its armies, this was a sign that reform could not be postponed – and most people now understood that reform meant tackling the issue of serfdom.

The death of Nicholas I in February 1855 ended thirty years of economic, political and intellectual stagnation. It also allowed the rise to positions of influence of a new generation of officials. Nicholas' son and successor, Alexander II, probably held views similar to those of his father. However, Alexander's friends and advisers came from a small network of liberal-minded nobles and officials whose views had been neglected in the previous reign. Now, this younger generation of politicians (which included Alexander's brother, Constantine) gained real influence.[17] They had all been committed for some time to the abolition of serfdom, and now they carried the tsar with them. In an autocracy, that counted for everything. With the tsar on their side, progressive officials could push through reform despite widespread opposition.

The new reign began in an atmosphere of greater frankness or *glasnost'* in public debate. The government permitted public discussion of many issues that had once been taboo, including serfdom. The most important single act of *glasnost'* in this period was the speech Alexander II made to a meeting of Moscow nobles in 1856. Alexander said: 'the existing system of serf-owning cannot remain unchanged. It is better to begin abolishing serfdom from above than to wait for it to begin to abolish itself from below. I ask you, gentlemen, to think of ways of doing this. Pass on my words to the nobles for consideration'.[18] This was the first time the government had committed itself publicly to the reform of serfdom. The speech also showed that the government saw the threat of a peasant rebellion either as the strongest motive for reform, or as the best way of persuading the nobility to co-operate.

Now the government had to decide what to do and how. Like Gorbachev's government in the 1980s, Alexander's government had to figure out how to rebuild society without bringing the entire edifice down. Alexander had started an extremely delicate and complex piece of social engineering.

As Alexander's 1856 speech showed, the government's first impulse was to work as closely as possible with the nobility. However, the nobility remained silent, hoping, like Soviet officials in the mid 1980s, that the issue of reform would go away. The government set up a new committee to consider reform but, as one member put it: 'In general the composition of the committee was extremely unfortunate, and thus it was not surprising that for the first half year it only gazed at the beast that was shown it and walked around it, not knowing from which side to approach it'.[19] Finally, in November 1857, in response to a tentative enquiry from the nobility of Lithuania, the government issued the so-called Nazimov rescript. This committed the government to reform, and laid down certain general principles. The reform must grant landlords legal title to all the land they held. However, peasants must receive their houses and the surrounding *usad'ba*. Further, a portion of the landlords' land must be made available for the peasants' use. Finally, peasants were to be placed under the jurisdiction of the peasant commune, though landlords were to keep police powers.

In 1858, provincial assemblies of nobles met to prepare proposals for reform. Broadly speaking, conservative nobles tried to limit the impact of the reform by keeping the nobility's economic and judicial powers over their peasants. Liberal nobles argued for a reform which would grant the peasants genuine liberty as well as full property rights in the land. However, even some liberals argued that peasants must not get too much land. Otherwise, they feared, peasants would have no need to seek wage-labour on the estates of their former masters, and nobles would be deprived of cheap labour.[20] The fears of the nobility were real, and widely held.

☐ *Document 3.4: Gentry fears about emancipation*

A significant majority of estate owners either did not sympathize at all with the enterprise that had begun or at least objected to giving the serfs land along with their freedom. The provincial opposition movement fed the Petersburg movement, which in turn supported the provincial movement. In Petersburg drawing rooms, at court functions, at parades and inspections of the troops, behind the walls of the State Council and the Senate, and in the offices of the ministers and members of the State Council were heard more or less energetic protests against the intentions of the government. These protests expressed in vigorous terms more or less the same idea – that the emancipation of the serfs was premature; the result of the change, said the numerous enemies of the proposed reform, would be that the estate owners would remain without working hands, the peasants because of their natural indolence would not work even for themselves, the productivity of the state would decrease, causing general inflation, famine, disease, and nationwide misery. At the same time would come insubordination on the part of the peasants, local disorders followed by widespread rioting – in a word, they predicted another Pugachev rebellion with all its horrors and with the addition of a 'deeply plotted' democratic revolution.[21]

Like Gorbachev in the late 1980s, Alexander found that the momentum of reform would carry him further and faster than he had originally intended. Two events forced the government's hand: renewed peasant disturbances in the Baltic provinces; and a financial crisis that threatened the government with bankruptcy.

During 1858, new peasant disturbances broke out in Estonia. These persuaded Alexander that he had to offer peasants more than most nobles were willing to concede. The government had to free peasants entirely from the authority of their former masters, and it had to give them substantial amounts of land. By the autumn, General Rostovtsev, the official in charge of the reform process, began to argue that: 'If we deprive the peasants of the land we will set Russia alight'.[22] However, if the government was to be more generous to the peasantry than most nobles wished, it could not expect gentry co-operation. So, from late in 1858, the government took the reins firmly into its own hands. Early in 1859 it closed the gentry committees and set up its own Editing Commission to supervise the final preparation of the reform. The Editing Commission, headed by the liberal official, Nicholas Miliutin, used the material provided by the gentry committees, but it was the government that took the crucial decisions.

Meanwhile, a financial crisis made it impossible for the government to protect either peasants or landlords from the real costs of reform.[23] After the Crimean War, the government knew it had to encourage railway building. Yet the archaic state of government finances attracted investment funds into unproductive and archaic areas such as the infamous liquor tax farms, or the government's own credit institutions, of which the most important were the State Loan Bank, set up in 1786, and the State Commercial Bank, set up in 1817. In 1857, to divert private funds into more productive areas such as railway-building, and to reduce its own interest payments, the government lowered the interest rates it paid on deposits in government banks. Unfortunately, this manoeuvre proved too successful. Investors withdrew money from government credit institutions and by 1859 the government was close to bankruptcy. In that year, on the recommendation of a committee dominated by young officials such as Nicholas Miliutin and two future ministers of finance, M. Kh. Reutern and N. Bunge, the government issued the first long-term government loans. This created a modern national debt for the first time in Russia. In 1860, the government established a new State Bank to manage the national debt. By making the new government bonds extremely attractive, the government avoided bankruptcy, just. But the crisis left it without enough money to help finance the redemption operation. It could not offer former serf-owners the loans they needed to reorganise their estates, or help ease the burden of redemption for peasants. The redemption operation would have to pay for itself. This burdened both peasants and landlords for many decades. Its financial difficulties had forced the government to throw both peasants and landlords on to the market without the safety nets that might have softened their fall.

These pressures moulded the final details of the emancipation act and explain some of its contradictions. Peasant disturbances had forced the government to offer the peasantry more land than it had once intended. But financial pressures had forced it to offer less cash.

■ The Reforms

The emancipation decrees were published on 19 February 1861. Their first article declared: 'The serfdom of peasants settled on estate owners' landed properties, and of household serfs, is abolished forever'. This appeared to mark a decisive break with the past. The reality was more complicated.

What did the 1861 Act do? It is a complex document, composed of twenty-two separate enactments. These changed the legal and economic relationship between serfs, nobles and government. They did so in three stages. (Later acts dealt with the state peasants and other, smaller groups. Household serfs were freed without land and formed a small group of landless wage-workers.)

Stage one was to last two years, from 1861 to 1863. The twenty-three million landlords' serfs were declared legally free. This meant they could own land; they could marry without outside interference; and they could sue and be sued in the courts. However, their economic situation remained much as before for the first two years. The act declared that all the land on landlords' estates belonged to the nobility. This meant that the peasants would have to buy the land they had used in the past. The only exception was the land on which their houses stood, and the *usad'ba* surrounding it (see Figure 2.3). This land immediately became the property of the peasants. Temporarily, peasants had to keep paying all the feudal dues they had paid before the reform. However, the landlord could no longer change their nature or extent. In return, the peasants were to continue farming the land they had used before. Meanwhile peasants and landlords were to draw up inventories of the land used by peasants and the feudal dues they paid. The inventories would then become legally binding agreements.

Stage two was to start in 1863. During this phase, the ex-serfs remained in a state of 'temporary obligation'. Legally, all ties with their former landlords were severed. The landlord could no longer punish serfs for minor offences or failure to pay taxes. These judicial functions were taken over by a communal court. This was to be run by the ex-serfs but supervised by government officials and by a new official, the peace arbitrator, elected from the nobility. However, peasants were to continue paying the old feudal dues to their ex-landlords, on the basis of the inventories drawn up in stage one.

During stage two, the government required landlords and peasants to negotiate the terms on which the peasants would buy land from their ex-landlords. The statutes placed severe limits on these negotiations. The landlords had to sell, and the peasants had to buy. The government specified different maximum and minimum amounts for different regions. It also specified limits within which the price could be negotiated. At first, the government allowed an indefinite period for these complex negotiations on the sale of land, but in the 1870s and 1880s it began hurrying the process of redemption along.

Stage three began once these negotiations had been completed. The government paid the landlords most of the purchase price of the peasants' land. The peasants were then to pay off their mortgages over a period of forty-nine years in the form of 'redemption payments'. These became, in effect, a new form of direct taxation. The government tried to make them roughly equivalent to the old feudal dues. In effect, this meant that peasants now paid the government what they had once paid to their landlords. These arrangements for the purchase of land should have made peasants full owners of their land forty-nine years after they began paying for it. But even then, it was the commune as a whole that would collectively own the land and allot each household a share.

Once stage three began, even the economic ties with the old landowners were severed. Only then could it be said that serfdom had really ended. At this stage, the legal situation of the 23 million ex-serfs became similar to that of the 25 million state peasants. Their legal and economic ties were now with the peasant commune and the government, not with a private landlord. However, though legally free, they remained, in effect, tied to the land. They were tied now, not by the legal bonds of serfdom, but by the obligation to purchase land. The emancipation statute made it almost impossible for peasants to sell their share of allotment land to others. There were several difficulties to be overcome, but the greatest was the obligation (according to article 173 of the statute) to pay half of the total value of the peasant's allotment land, and to find guarantees for the remaining payments, before leaving the commune.[24]

Serfdom was so central to Russian social, political, legal and military structures, that its abolition made further reforms necessary in all these areas. The government also undertook reform as a concession to the growing liberalism of sections of the Russian nobility. As a result, many of the reforms appeared to retreat from the autocratic principle that had governed Russian political life for so long. That is also how many liberally-minded contemporaries saw them. In reality, the government conceded less than liberals had hoped. Indeed, the overall effect of the reforms was to increase, rather than to reduce, the power of the government.

The arbitrary way in which the government handled the 1861 reform persuaded many nobles that they had to find new ways of influencing the government. In the late 1850s, A. A. Golovachev, a liberal noble from the relatively liberal nobility of Tver province wrote:

> If we do not propose measures for the reform of our bureaucratic system, if we leave it with the same rights and responsibilities, what will happen ...? Will not [the peasants] escape the control of one person, whose own interests forced him to consider their welfare, only to fall under the control of another, indifferent to that. If the character of our bureaucracy remains the same as before, then it is clear that this change will not abolish serfdom, but only transfer it and widen its limits, transforming not only the free classes, but even the gentry into serfs [of the bureaucracy].[25]

By 1860, the fear of losing all influence over government decision-making had encouraged many liberal-minded nobles to support a broad but cautious programme of liberal reforms first put forward by nobles from Tver province. This programme asked for full emancipation of the peasantry, the creation of elected local government assemblies, an independent judiciary with the power to prosecute government officials, and freedom of the press. These proposals set the agenda for the reforms the government introduced in the wake of the emancipation act.

The most important of these reforms were the judicial reform of 1864, and the *zemstvo* reform of the same year, which created elected local government bodies.

The 1861 Act deprived nobles of their traditional authority in local government. To restore the balance, a number of liberal nobles proposed the creation of elected local government assemblies representing all classes. Some nobles, such as the nobility of Tver province, even proposed the creation of a central elected assembly to advise the tsar. The government rejected this proposal outright. However, it accepted the idea of elected local government assemblies. These proposals were the origin of the *zemstva*, which the government created in 1864.

At first sight, the *zemstva* looked like genuinely democratic institutions. They were separate from the bureaucracy, and represented all classes. Yet they never fulfilled the hopes Russian liberals placed on them, for the Russian government was too jealous of its own powers to permit them an independent role. It granted the *zemstva* modest powers over local education, health, agriculture, roads and many other aspects of local government. However, their budgets were small, and they had to raise revenue from local taxes. Provincial governors had the power to reverse all *zemstvo* decisions that they found to be 'contrary to the laws and to the general welfare'. *Zemstva* also appeared only in the thirty-four Russian provinces. Finally, elections were indirect, and landowners were over-represented. As a result, in 1874, nobles held some 74 per cent of all positions on provincial *zemstva*. As a step towards more liberal government structures, we must judge the *zemstva* a failure. Nevertheless, their mere existence was an important symbol of the more liberal governmental structures that might have appeared in the 1860s.

The judicial reform suffered a similar fate. It created open courts, jury trials and an independent judiciary. However, the government limited the authority of the new courts. They could try government officials only under special rules and with the government's permission. Certain types of cases had to go to military courts. Besides, the majority of the population, including most ex-serfs, remained under the jurisdiction of special courts. The government also managed to exercise considerable pressure over the formally independent judges. Finally, during the terrorist crisis of the late 1870s, the government introduced martial law to many provinces, thus suspending the activities of the new courts in these regions. Still, despite their limitations, the reformed courts remained a potent symbol of what might have been. For Russia's growing minority of liberals, they were also a symbol of what could still be.

The other reforms of the 1860s suffered from similar ambiguities. Most appeared liberal and progressive when first introduced. Yet in practice most preserved and some enhanced the power of the central government. The government introduced for the first time a public budget of government finances in 1862. In 1863, it granted Russia's universities greater autonomy. In the same year, it abolished the corrupt practice of farming out the collection of its most important indirect tax, on liquor. It was this system that had generated most of the peasant protests in 1859. In place of the tax farms, the government established an excise on liquor distilling, which it collected through its own officials. In 1865, the government issued a new, and more liberal, censorship law. In 1870, it created elective municipal government institutions to match the rural *zemstva*. Finally, in 1874, Dmitrii Miliutin introduced the military reform he had first proposed almost twenty years before. The reform extended military recruitment to all classes. It shortened the period of active service to six years, with a further period in the army reserve. It also introduced elementary education for all recruits, which made the army for a few years one of the most potent educational institutions in the Russian Empire.[26]

■ Assessing the 'Great Reforms'

How successful were the 'Great Reforms'? The government had undertaken a radical overhaul of the social, economic, political and military structure of the Russian Empire. This was a complex, and potentially dangerous task. So the best measure of the government's success is the fact that it survived the reforms unscathed, unlike the reforming government of Mikhail Gorbachev 130 years later. However, the reforms left serious problems for future governments. In trying to balance the interests of nobles and peasants, while retaining its own powers intact, it alienated both the major classes of traditional Russian society. For Russian society as a whole, the reforms mark an important, though painful, step towards modernity.

The nobility lost the basic privileges of serf-ownership. They lost the right to compulsory labour and feudal dues, and they lost their traditional judicial and police powers over the peasantry. In effect, the reforms cut them out of government. The declining influence of the nobility was part of a larger process. Ever since they had emancipated themselves from compulsory service in 1785, nobles had become less necessary to the autocracy. By the middle of the nineteenth century, the government depended more on its bureaucracy than on the traditional nobility. Clear proof of this change in the Russian ruling group had come in 1858, when Alexander II had excluded the nobility from the preparation of reforms that would change their entire status. After this, many nobles began to see the bureaucracy as a symbol of governmental insensitivity to the needs of the noble class.

In the short run, nobles gained from the payments they received in return for the land the government forced them to sell. In the long run, this meant little. By 1871, 248 million roubles of the 543 million paid for nobles' land had gone to repay old debts.[27] The reforms also created serious problems for the nobility. Serf-owners no longer enjoyed a guaranteed income. To survive without free labour, nobles would have to learn businesslike habits of mind. Yet most nobles despised mercantile habits of mind, and few had the training or the inclination to run their estates like businesses. Many failed to adapt. Like Stepan Oblonsky in *Anna Karenina*, or Madame Ranevskaya in Chekhov's play, *The Cherry*

Orchard, they found it easier to sell their land than to economise. In 1862 nobles owned 87 million *dessyatiny* of land (1 *dessyatina* = 1.09 hectares). By 1882, they owned only 71 million *dessyatiny*, and by 1911, only 43 million. The 'Great Reforms' had cast the Russian nobility unprepared into a world where entrepreneurial skills counted for more than birth or rank.

The attempt to reintegrate the nobility into the political system through the *zemstvo* reform failed because it was so half-hearted. Most nobles found that the reforms had reduced both their economic and their political influence, and many lost their faith in a government that seemed to have ignored their interests. The reforms had created a rift between government and nobility which widened, by 1905, into revolution.

Peasants showed what they thought of the reforms in a new wave of disturbances. According to the police, in 1861 there were disturbances on 1176 estates, and troops had to quell disorders on 337.[28] The prospect of paying for land they had always believed to be theirs by right, appalled most peasants.

Serfs also lost the protection of their former masters, and that could mean a lot. The English traveller Mackenzie Wallace described what serfs lost as a result of the reforms.

☐ *Document 3.5: Mackenzie Wallace on the price of emancipation*

If the serfs had a great many ill-defined obligations to fulfill [under serfdom] – such as the carting of the master's grain to market ... they had, on the other hand, a good many ill-defined privileges. They grazed their cattle during a part of the year on the manor land; they received firewood and occasionally logs for repairing their huts; sometimes the proprietor lent them or gave them a cow or a horse when they had been visited by the cattle plague or the horse stealer; and in times of famine they could look to their master for support. All this has now come to an end. Their burdens and their privileges have been swept away together, and been replaced by clearly defined, unbending, unelastic legal relations. They now have to pay the market price for every stick of firewood which they burn, for every log which they require for repairing their houses, and for every rood of land on which to graze their cattle. Nothing is now to be had gratis. The demand to pay is encountered at every step. If a cow dies or a horse is stolen, the owner can no longer go to the proprietor with the hope of receiving a present, or at least a loan without interest, but must, if he has no ready money, apply to the village usurer, who probably considers twenty or thirty per cent as a by no means exorbitant rate of interest.[29]

Most important of all, the land settlement sold peasants less land than they had used before the reform, and did so at artificially high prices. On average, ex-serfs ended up with about 4 per cent less land than they had used before emancipation. In the western provinces they did better than average because the government discriminated against their Polish landlords. Excluding these regions, the average decline in peasant landholdings was close to 19 per cent. In the fertile black soil lands of the central and southern provinces, the peasants lost nearly 25 per cent. It is hard to place an objective market value on the lands they bought, but the best estimates suggest that ex-serfs paid on average 134 per cent of the free market price. In effect, this meant that the government made ex-serfs pay for their personal freedom as well as for their land. It is hardly surprising that many peasants believed for years that nobles and officials had hidden the true emancipation statute.

Population growth during the next half century compounded the problem of land shortage. Between 1858 and 1897, the population of the Russian Empire rose from about 74 million to 125 million. Average peasant land holdings declined by almost the same ratio. By 1900, land hunger was a national calamity. It was worst in the densely settled belt of agrarian provinces immediately south of Moscow. By 1902, the problem of land shortage had turned the peasantry into a revolutionary force far more dangerous than Nicholas I could ever have imagined. The rebellion that governments so feared in the 1850s finally came half a century later.

Nevertheless, the reform clearly meant a lot to peasants once they had absorbed its real meaning. It gave them freedom. It rid them of the arbitrary interference of landlords. It confirmed the autonomy of the commune. Though we cannot quantify these gains, peasants clearly valued them. We can get some idea of the immediate benefits of reform from the following document. In early 1861, the government sent 167 so-called 'heralds of liberty' to the villages to explain the reform to the serfs. One of these, N. V. Sakharov, reported that the men were mainly interested in the land settlement. However, the women were delighted when they realised that they would no longer have to supply their owners with goods in kind. A woman called Lukeria, whom Sakharov described as 'no longer young and, apparently, a bit saucy', checked that this was really true.

☐ *Document 3.6: Peasant reactions to reform*

'Tell me, does this mean that turning chickens over to the lords is now *shabash* [finished]?'
'Now it's *shabash*.'
'And the eggs are *shabash?*'
'And the eggs, too ... '
'And gathering mushrooms and berries for the lords is *shabash?*'

'Yes, all *shabash*.'
'And when will it be *shabash?*'
'From this very moment, it's all *shabash* ... '
'Does that mean that when summer comes, I don't have to go around getting mushrooms and berries for the squires?'
'You can do it for money or go for yourself, if that is your sweet will.'
'You're not kidding?'
'No, it's the solemn truth. See, it's all written in this law book.'

'Hey, girls, see what's turned up for us!' Lukeria joyfully cried, turning to the women. 'Isn't that nice. All right, Aleksandra Sergeevna, here's for you.' And she unceremoniously gave the finger (a greasy finger) in the direction of the manor house.[30]

The most powerful evidence that the peasants felt they had gained something through the reform is that the peasant disturbances which had continued for so long, like approaching thunder, died away to a distant rumble for forty years after 1862. The government had succeeded in the complex task of abolishing serfdom without provoking an immediate rebellion. That was a considerable achievement.

In the short run, it was the government and its officials who gained most from the reforms. Before 1861 the nobility had ruled almost half of the peasantry. Now the government ruled these same peasants through the commune. It also received the equivalent of the old feudal dues in the new form of redemption payments. The reforms had extended the powers of the government in the countryside. Further, the government had retained the political initiative despite the pressure from liberal nobles to concede parliamentary or semi-parliamentary institutions.

In the long term, however, the government paid a heavy price for the inadequacies of the reforms. While its own powers grew, so did the discontent of the two most important groups in traditional Russian society, the nobility and the peasantry. The government finally paid the price in 1905. The seeds of the 1905 Revolution were sown during the era of reform.

Did the reforms push Russia into the modern world? The government's own intentions were uncertain. It hoped for increases in productivity and greater social stability. Yet it had no wish to create an urban industrialized society with a large proletariat like those of Western Europe. Historians have been equally uncertain in their assessments of the impact of the reforms on the process of modernization.

The model of modernization proposed in the Introduction may help clarify this issue. That model suggests that the important question is: did the reforms encourage the emergence of the sort of social structure that drove the capitalist engine of growth? The answer is that they did; but they did so in indirect ways.

The Emancipation Act removed some of the barriers that protected both landlords and peasants from market forces. Landlords could no longer count on feudal dues, while ex-serfs could no longer hope for the protection of their landlords in a crisis. Both had to learn how to earn their incomes in a market economy, either as entrepreneurs or as wage-earners. In this way, the Emancipation Act accelerated the transformation of landlords and peasants into entrepreneurs and wage-earners by increasing the importance of market forces. In doing so, it encouraged the development of all three main ingredients of the capitalist engine of growth: markets, entrepreneurs and wage-earners.

The government itself did not see reform in this way. It clearly hoped to protect both the traditional nobility and the traditional peasantry, for these had been the basis of its power. Yet unwittingly it had encouraged the transformation of Russia's old class structure. Though they marked a step towards the creation of a modern capitalist society, the reforms also threatened the very classes on which the power of the autocracy was based. During the next half century the government slowly realized what a dangerous gamble this was.

The Emergence of the Revolutionary Movement

Though it took decades for most educated Russians to shed their traditional loyalty to autocracy, a minority was so disillusioned by the reforms that they became revolutionary socialists in the 1880s.

Socialism, like liberalism, was a philosophy of emancipation. Both philosophies emerged from the political and ideological conflicts of the American and French Revolutions. However, while liberals defined freedom and equality mainly in legal and political terms, socialists saw them also as economic issues.

For liberals, freedom meant legal guarantees of individual rights (in particular the right to private property), while equality meant equality before the law. Socialists argued that legal and political equality was not enough. In a society based on private property, civil and political rights alone could not prevent those who owned property from exploiting those who did not. Socialists saw private property from the point of view of the proletarians – the growing number of ex-peasants who owned no land and thereby had to live on wages earned by working for those who did have property. True freedom, the socialists argued, required freedom from economic as well as legal or political oppression. True equality meant equality in economic as well as in civil rights. It meant abolishing the right to private property and replacing it with collective ownership of society's resources.

Many liberal-minded Russians took the path from liberalism to socialism because of their disillusionment with the Emancipation Act. They saw that the legal rights granted to the peasants meant little while the peasants remained in grinding poverty.

The lead came from radical journalists. Nicholas Chernyshevskii (1828–89) was the son of a priest, which made him a *raznochinets*. Alexander Herzen (1812–70) was a member of the nobility. Between 1857 and 1867, Herzen published an illegal revolutionary newspaper, *The Bell*, from exile in London. He had been a Westernizer in the 1840s, but lost his faith in the capitalist West after leaving Russia in 1847. In exile, he took up the Slavophile view of the Russian peasant commune as the basis for an egalitarian society, and used it to construct a distinctively Russian brand of socialism. Herzen saw the commune as the basis for a regenerated Russia, free of exploitation and inequalities in wealth. In the 1860s, these ideas provided the core of the Russian ideology of 'Populism'.

By 1861, Herzen and Chernyshevskii, like many others, had decided that the reforms would leave the peasantry as exploited and as unfree as before. They had deprived peasants of the protection of their landlords without giving them enough land to fend for themselves in a world increasingly dominated by market forces. The radicals argued that revolution was now the only way to achieve a genuine emancipation.

In 1861, peasant uprisings in the countryside and student unrest in the universities created an extremely tense atmosphere. In the summer, several revolutionary manifestos appeared, written by radical students. These illustrate well the main ingredients of revolutionary Populism. They also illustrate the emergence of a style of Russian socialism that rejected the Western path to modernity, as the Slavophiles had in the 1840s.

□ *Document 3.7: A revolutionary manifesto, September 1861*

The sovereign has betrayed the hopes of the people; the freedom he has given them is not real and is not what the people dreamed of and need ...

Are the economic conditions and the land situation in Europe the same as they are here? Does the agricultural commune exist there ... ? Can every peasant and every citizen there own landed property? No, but here he can. We have enough land to last us tens of thousands of years.

We are a backward people and in this lies our salvation. We should thank our good fortune that we have not lived the life of Europe. Her misfortunes and desperate straits are a lesson to us. We do not want her proletariat, her aristocracy, her state principle, or her imperial power ...

We want all citizens of Russia to enjoy equal rights; we do not want privileged classes to exist; we want ability and education, rather than birth, to confer the right to high position; we want appointments to public office to follow the elective principle. We do not want a nobility and titles. We want everyone to be equal in the eyes of the law and equal in [the assessment of] exactions, taxes, and obligations by the state.

We want the land to belong to the nation and not to individuals; we want each commune to have its allotment, without the existence of private landowners; we do not want land to be sold like potatoes and cabbage; we want to give every citizen, whoever he may be, the opportunity of becoming a member of an agricultural commune, i.e. either by joining an existing commune or by forming a new commune with several other citizens. We want to preserve communal possession of the land, with periodic redistribution at long intervals.[31]

In 1862, liberals in Tver province had called for an elected assembly representing the entire people. However, the liberals always stopped short of calling for revolution. Student radicals were less restrained. In 1862 a manifesto entitled *Young Russia* contrasted privileged and unprivileged Russia even more brutally than had earlier revolutionary manifestos.

☐ *Document 3.8: A second revolutionary manifesto,* Young Russia, *1862*

Society is at present divided into two groups, which are hostile to one another because their interests are diametrically opposed ....

The party that is oppressed by all and humiliated by all is the party of the common people. Over it stands a small group of contented and happy men. They are the landowners ... the merchants ... the government officials – in short, all those who possess property, either inherited or acquired. At their head stands the tsar. They cannot exist without him, nor he without them. If either falls the other will be destroyed ... This is the imperial party ....

There is only one way out of this oppressive and terrible situation which is destroying contemporary man, and that is revolution – bloody and merciless revolution – a revolution that must radically change all the foundations of contemporary society without exception and destroy the supporters of the present regime.[32]

In the summer of 1862 there were outbreaks of arson in St Petersburg and several provincial towns, and new outbreaks of student unrest. The Polish insurrection of 1863 divided educated Russian society. It turned many liberals into conservative nationalists, but radicalized others. In 1866, a student, Dmitrii Karakozov, tried to assassinate the tsar. While conservatives and moderates rallied to the autocracy, radical students formed small circles of revolutionaries. Together with the illegal newspapers and manifestos, these circles formed the main elements of the populist revolutionary movement throughout its early history.

Populism also attracted many young women, such as Catherine Breshkovskaya (see document 3.9). Populism appealed to radical women because of its progressive ideas on the emancipation of women in a society where most women were denied education and confined to domestic roles.

In the 1870s the populist movement became a real threat to the government. In 1873 and 1874, more than 2000 students 'went to the people'. They travelled through the countryside and small towns trying, without success, to incite a popular uprising. Occasionally peasants were so suspicious of these educated youths from the nobility and intelligentsia that they turned them over to the local police. Even those populists who found sympathetic listeners discovered that the peasantry were pessimistic about the chances of improving their lot. Catherine Breshkovskaya, the daughter of a noble and later a founder of the Socialist Revolutionary Party, spread propaganda in Ukraine, disguised as a peasant. She left vivid memoirs of the world she found in the town of Smela, a centre of the sugar-beet industry.

□ *Document 3.9: 'going to the People', 1874*

Soon we moved to Smela. This enormous country town, which already contained one sugar refinery and six factories, was spread over a wide area. The house of the landlord, with its garden, park, and lake, surrounded by a sea of trees, seemed to draw away from the noisy, dirty streets, which teemed with factory people. The large market place swarmed with traders. The police and fire stations were at the market place. At the end of the place was a pond, its muddy water surrounded by very steep banks. Earthen huts were dug out of these banks, and the shores of the lake were thus lined with habitations resembling dens for animals. In them the workers who came from other places lived – former *dvorovye* [household serfs], who had no land, who had come from northern [provinces]. They lived in these huts with their large families; here they were born and here they died.

In Smela we soon found a corner to live in. No one in the town occupied a whole house. Small rooms were rented, usually without tables or seats. The father of the owner of our hut, an old fighter for the welfare of this community, offered us his own room, a dark den, and himself moved into the passage, where he slept on planks. This old man helped me a good deal in understanding the life of the factory population. They had been brought to Smela, when serfdom still existed, from one of the central [provinces] to work in the factories, having abandoned their land and their houses. With their liberation as serfs they had got new small patches of land, but only large enough to build their houses on, and were still obliged to work in the factories, receiving a ration of bread as wages. I do not remember further details, but I know that the factory population lived in constant fear of losing their work at the whim of managers and directors. Those with large families had an especially hard time. Our old man was always weak from hunger. His son had his own family to care for; his daughter-in-law was unkind; and the old man, who had been twice flogged and sent to Siberia for defending the common interests, was at the end of his days almost a beggar. An old pink shirt, a jacket, and an old peasant coat were his only clothes. He also had a wooden basin and several wooden spoons, which he kindly put at our disposal ....

At noon we ... sat with the old man around the wooden basin and swallowed our soup with great appetites. I talked a great deal with the old man, questioning him concerning the life of the workers and listening to his tales of the past. It was a cruel story. The peasants, transferred from their homes against their wills and placed by their landlords in a position of hopeless slavery, had 'revolted' several times, demanding that they be sent back, and refusing to work in the factory. They were punished for this. Every fifth or tenth man was flogged. Detachments of soldiers were quartered in the place. Like grasshoppers these soldiers devoured everything, leaving not a crust of bread for the inhabitants. The fate of the serf leaders was most terrible. These were the men who had spoken the loudest and had been the most obstinate in defending the rights of the villagers.

To the request that he help me in my revolutionary propaganda in Smela the old man answered: 'I have no strength left. I have been cruelly punished. One soldier stood on one arm, another on the other, and two on my legs. I was beaten, beaten until the earth was soaked with blood. That is how I was flogged. And that did not happen merely once or twice. I was exiled to Siberia, came back, and began all over again; but I can't do it any more.' ...

[Other peasants] made no protest against my proposal to prepare the soil for a general revolt; but it was evident that the recent punishments [after the 1861–63 uprisings] had made a terrible impression on them. They said as one man: 'If everyone agreed to rise at the same time, if you went around and talked to all the people, then it could be done. We tried several times to rise. We demanded our rights to the land. It was useless. Soldiers were sent down and the people were punished and ruined.'[33]

The failure of the movement 'to the people' hardened the tactics of those who remained committed to revolution. A group called 'Narodnaya Volya' ('The People's Will') argued for a campaign of terror and assassination, led by a party of tightly organized professional revolutionaries. In 1881, twenty years after the emancipation statute, they succeeded in assassinating the 'tsar liberator', Alexander II. Several paid for this success with their lives.

The government reacted to the revolutionary movement with increasingly conservative attitudes and methods of rule. The wave of patriotic feeling generated by the Polish revolt of 1863 had already created support for conservative policies. After the attempt on the life of the tsar in 1866, even Alexander II turned away from reform.

His son, Alexander III (1881–94), was much more conservative, partly because of the influence of his former tutor, Constantine Pobedonostsev

(1827–1907). Alexander III managed to suppress the revolutionary movement for over a decade. He also whittled away at the achievements of the reform era. This made sense, for conservatives were becoming aware of how dangerous reform could be for a traditional monarchy. Alexander III's government reduced the already limited powers of the *zemstva* and the reformed courts, and re-established harsher censorship regulations. In the countryside, he created a new semi-official post, that of land captain, in 1889. Reserved for members of the nobility, it restored some of the nobility's administrative and judicial powers over the peasantry. The government began a policy of systematic discrimination against non-Russian nationalities, in particular Jews. This policy, and the accompanying pogroms, or attacks on Jews, did much to discredit tsarism in the last thirty years of its existence, and helped generate new national movements in Finland, the Baltic, Poland, Ukraine and the Caucasus.

The government and the revolutionary movement had joined battle. Temporarily, at least, the government was victorious. However, it was unclear whether either side could gain enough support from the rest of the population to achieve a decisive victory. Beneath that question there lurked an even deeper question: could Russian society and the economy adapt to the modern world without a revolutionary upheaval of some kind?

Political reform seemed to have failed. However, beneath the surface, and even with the support of Alexander III's government, economic and social change accelerated in the second half of the nineteenth century. The next chapter will consider these changes in more detail.

■ Summary

At the heart of the 'great reforms' was the decision to abolish the system of direct mobilization known as 'serfdom'. In the early nineteenth century, an increasing number of government officials realized that Russia's traditional social and economic structures were beginning to undermine Russia's power. Though they only half-understood the nature of the challenge posed by Western Europe, they realized that serfdom inhibited the growth of the economy, limited the government's tax base, and stifled technological innovation. Most important of all, after defeat in the Crimea, the government of Alexander II realized that technological and economic backwardness were beginning to undermine the army, the foundation of the government's authority. Many individuals within the Westernized ruling group also felt that serfdom was no longer morally tolerable, while others feared that its continuance would lead to revolution.

By breaking the ties of serfdom, the reforms forced both nobles and peasants to rely, increasingly, on market forces. Landlords now had to run their estates as commercial enterprises. Peasants found that they could no longer survive just as farmers. In addition, they would have to earn wages, or sell grain, or sell goods manufactured in their own households. Entry into a market economy was painful for both groups, and it began to sap their traditional loyalty to the autocracy. Yet the same changes also helped push Russian society into the modern world, for they stimulated economic growth by increasing the number of those engaging in commercial activities.

The government had a limited understanding of these changes, and an exaggerated confidence in its ability to control them. Most officials assumed that Russia would remain an agrarian country, that nobles and peasants would remain the most important groups in Russian society, and that autocracy would remain the best way of ruling Russia for the foreseeable future. The half-heartedness of the government's break with the past disillusioned those members of the educated classes who sought a more decisive commitment to modernity. In this way, the reforms stimulated the emergence of a revolutionary movement whose first royal victim was to be the reforming tsar, Alexander II.

☐ *Further Reading*

The best general accounts of this period can be found in Saunders, *Russia in the Age of Reaction and Reform*, and Seton-Watson, *The Russian Empire*. For studies on serfdom and social history, see the readings listed under Chapter 2. On the great reforms, see: the recent collection of essays in Eklof and Bushnell, *The 'Great Reforms'*; W. B. Lincoln, *The 'Great Reforms'*, which is particularly good on the bureaucratic infighting; Emmons, *Emancipation of the Russian Serfs*, a good collection of essays and extracts; and the more detailed study by Field, *The End of Serfdom*. The best Soviet study is Zaionchkovsky, *The Abolition of Serfdom in Russia*. On the economic aftermath of the reforms, see Gatrell, *The Tsarist Economy*, Rogger, *Russia in the Age of Modernisation and Revolution*, and Alexander Gerschenkron's essay, 'Agrarian Policies and Industrialization', as well as his classic study of Russian modernisation: 'Problems and Patterns of Russian Economic Development'. On the revolutionary movement, Venturi, *Roots of Revolution* is still of great value despite its age. See also the useful chapter in Lichtheim, *A Short History of European Socialism*, and A. Walicki, *A History of Russian Thought*.

☐ *Notes*

1. T. Emmons, *The Russian Landed Gentry and the Peasant Emancipation of 1861* (Cambridge University Press, 1967) p. 44.

2. G. Vernadsky *et al.* (eds), *A Source Book for Russian History from Early Times to 1917*, 3 vols (New Haven, Conn.: Yale University Press,1972) vol. 2, p. 462.
3. A. P. Zablotskii-Desiatovskii, 'O krepostnom sostoyanii', in *Graf P D Kiselev i ego vremya* ... (St Petersburg: Tipografiya M. M. Stasulevicha, 1882) vol. 4, p. 327 (trans D. Christian).
4. T. Emmons (ed.), *Emancipation of the Russian Serfs* (Hinsdale, Ill.: Dryden Press, 1970) pp. 38–9.
5. Cited in A. Gerschenkron, 'Agrarian Policies and Industrialization, Russia 1861–1917', in *Cambridge Economic History of Europe*, vol. VI, pt 2 (Cambridge, 1966) p. 710.
6. Struve's argument is summarized in the extracts in Emmons (ed.) *Emancipation of the Russian Serfs*, pp. 34–41.
7. S. S. Dmitriev *et al.* (eds), *Khrestomatiya po istorii SSSR* (Moscow: gos-oe uchebno-pedagogicheskoe izd-vo min-va prosveshcheniya RSFSR, 1948) vol. 2, pp. 646–7.
8. N. M. Druzhinin, *Russkaya derevnya na perelome, 1861–1880 gg* (Moscow: Nauka, 1978) p. 12.
9. S. V. Tokarev, *Krest'yanskie kartofel'nye bunty* (Kirov, USSR: Kirovskoe oblastnoe izd-vo, 1939) pp. 89–90 (trans D. Christian).
10. On the liquor riots, see D. Christian, 'The Black and the Gold Seals: Popular Protests Against the Liquor Trade on the Eve of Emancipation', in E. Kingston-Mann and T. Mixter (eds), *Peasant Economy, Culture, and Politics of European Russia, 1800–1921* (Princeton University Press, 1990) pp. 261–93.
11. Cited in Emmons (ed.), *Emancipation of the Russian Serfs*, p. 77.
12. N. Riasanovsky, *Nicholas I and Official Nationality in Russia* (Berkeley and Los Angeles: University of California Press, 1969) p. 14.
13. See the extracts from A. Rieber, introduction to *The Politics of Autocracy. Letters of Alexander II to Prince A I Bariatinskii 1857–1864*, cited in Emmons (ed.), *Emancipation of the Russian Serfs*, pp. 72–80.
14. J. Blum, *Lord and Peasant in Russia* (New York: Atheneum, 1968) p. 537.
15. W. Bruce Lincoln, *The 'Great Reforms'* (Illinois: DeKalb, 1990) p. 29.
16. Cited from N. V. Riasanovsky, *A History of Russia*, 4th edn (Oxford University Press, 1984) p. 327.
17. An American historian, W. B. Lincoln, has shown the importance of this new generation of officials. See *In the Vanguard of Reform: Russia's Enlightened Bureaucrats, 1825–1856* (Illinois: DeKalb, 1982).
18. Vernadsky, *Source Book*, vol. 3, p. 589.
19. A. I. Levshin, assistant minister of internal affairs, 1856–9, cited from Vernadsky, *Source Book*, vol. 3, p. 589.
20. This argument is described (and criticized) by K. D. Kavelin, *Sobranie sochinenii*, vol. 2 (St Petersburg: Tipografiya M. M. Stasulevicha,1898) p. 46.
21. From the memoirs of Senator Ia. A. Solov'ev, cited in Vernadsky, *Source Book*, vol. 3, pp. 592–3.
22. Druzhinin, *Russkaya derevnya*, pp. 16–18.
23. Stephen Hoch has analysed this crisis in an important article, 'The Banking Crisis, Peasant Reform, and Economic Development in Russia, 1857–1861', *American Historical Review*, June 1991, pp. 795–820.
24. A. Gerschenkron, 'Agrarian Policies and Industrialization', p. 752.
25. Emmons (ed.), *The Russian Landed Gentry*, p. 135.

26. However, compulsory education of recruits was abandoned in the more conservative atmosphere of the 1880s. J. Bushnell, *Mutiny amid Repression: Russian Soldiers in the Revolution of 1905–1906* (Bloomington: Indiana University Press, 1985) p. 9.
27. L. Kochan and R. Abrahams, *The Making of Modern Russia*, 2nd edn (Harmondsworth: Penguin, 1983) p. 189.
28. Dmitriev, *Khrestomatiya*, vol. 3, p. 69.
29. Sir Donald Mackenzie Wallace, *Russia on the Eve of War and Revolution*, (ed.) C. E. Black (New York: Random House, 1961) p. 340.
30. Cited from Daniel Field, '1861: "God Yubileya"', in L. Zakharova, B. Eklof and J. Bushnell (eds), *Velikie reformy v Rossii 1856–1874* (Moscow University Press, 1992) p. 74.
31. Vernadsky, *Source Book*, vol. 3, p. 639.
32. Ibid, p. 640.
33. Cited in T. Riha, *Readings in Russian Civilization*, vol. 2 (University of Chicago Press, 1964) pp. 359–61.

Chapter 4

Economic and Social Change Before 1914

▌ The Challenge of the 'Modern' Revolution in the Russian Empire

To understand the revolutionary upheavals of the early twentieth century, it is vital to understand the social and economic changes that were transforming Russian society. This chapter describes those changes, using the theoretical ideas explained in the Introduction.

The Russian government tried hard to control social and economic change and to limit its political impact. However, like Russian society as a whole, the government found itself drifting in currents it could not master as Russia entered the choppy waters of the 'modern' revolution.

Two distinct but related pressures dragged Russian society into the modern world. First, spontaneous forces were transforming Russia's class structure and its economy. The importance of market forces was increasing. So was the number of those who depended on wage-labour or profits for their incomes. The government did not really understand these processes, though it had unwittingly accelerated them by introducing the 'Great Reforms'. The second type of pressure was military. In the second half of the nineteenth century, imperialist wars extended European control over much of the globe. These showed spectacularly the close link between military power and the 'modern' revolution. The sudden decline of ancient agrarian states such as China showed that it was impossible to remain a great power without radical economic and social changes.

How could traditional governments respond to these twin challenges? At the time, it was hard to see any clear answers. In practice, governments responded by borrowing some aspects of Capitalism while rejecting others. However the models described in the Introduction suggest that, in theory at least, two distinct types of response were possible. First, governments could try deliberately to transform the social and economic structures of the societies they ruled, to create modern capitalist societies and stimulate intensive growth. However, this was a dangerous option for traditional governments, as it meant dismantling the social structures on which they based their power. The second option was to rely on traditional methods of extensive growth. Governments could try to mobilize resources on a large enough scale to compete with the more productive economies of the capitalist world. They could pit direct mobilization against indirect mobilization; extensive against intensive growth. In reality, strategies were never this clear. Governments improvised, reacting most of the time to immediate pressures. Only occasionally did they attempt a more planned response to the challenge of modernity. Nevertheless, it will help in discussing economic change if we think of government policies as tending towards one or the other of these abstract solutions.

 # Before 1850: Government Strategies and Spontaneous Modernization

The challenges faced in the late nineteenth century were not entirely unfamiliar. In less serious forms, Muscovite governments had faced similar challenges since at least the sixteenth century. The more energetic Muscovite governments had responded with a two-pronged strategy. First, they borrowed selectively from their more modern neighbours. They borrowed ideas, techniques and experts, particularly if they had military significance. However, they realized that modern ideas could threaten a traditional society, so they tried to limit the impact of foreign ideas by quarantining foreigners and imposing strict censorship. Second, to pay for foreign techniques and to compensate for lower levels of productivity, Russian governments relied on their superior powers of direct mobilization. So, while western ideas and techniques began to enter Russia from the sixteenth century, the state itself became more powerful and more authoritarian. This combination explains why so many foreigners found Russian society so paradoxical a mixture of modern and archaic elements.

As early as 1550, Ivan the Terrible created the first Russian companies of musketeers, the *streltsy*. Russia's use of imported gunpowder technology helped turn the tide against the pastoral nomads who had dominated Inner Eurasia for over two millennia. The *streltsy* played an important role in the conquest of Kazan, the first step towards Muscovy's conquest of the steppelands and Siberia. Characteristically, the import of foreign technologies coincided with a strengthening of autocracy and an intense hostility to European cultural and religious ideas.

In the 1630s, the government of Tsar Mikhail Romanov imported foreign military units trained in European military techniques. To supply them, the government founded a Russian arms industry based in Tula, south of Moscow, with the help of a Dutch engineer, Vinnius. Tula remains a centre of Russian armaments production today. Once again, modernization of technique coincided with the preservation of traditional social, political and cultural structures. The government used the mobilizational power of autocracy and serfdom to pay for foreign expertise. At the same time, Muscovite governments tried to limit the impact of foreign ideas on Russian society. A good symbol of this was the *nemetskaia sloboda*, or 'foreign quarter'. This was a special suburb of Moscow, founded by Tsar Alexei Mikhailovich in 1652, to which all foreigners were confined.

The first Russian ruler to launch a systematic strategy of military and industrial modernization was Peter the Great. Western technology fascinated Peter, particularly Western military and naval technology. He also understood that Western technology and Western education were necessary if Russia was to survive as a great power. However, he used the great mobilizational power of the Russian state to introduce his reforms. Stalin was to imitate this approach over two centuries later.

In 1697–8, Peter undertook the first major trip abroad by a Russian tsar. On his return he sent a number of young Russian nobles abroad to acquire Western learning, particularly technical and scientific skills. He imported foreign army officers and artisans. He built up the iron industry of the Ural Mountains and the armaments industry of Tula to equip Russian armies with Russian-made weaponry. In Moscow, he established a modern textile industry to clothe Russian armies in Russian-made uniforms. By the end of his reign, the Russian Empire had 200 factories and was the world's major producer of iron.

However, though the ideas and technologies were new, the government's methods of exploiting them were traditional. Peter did little to stimulate independent entrepreneurial activity or free wage-labour. On the contrary, he relied on coercion. He forced unwilling nobles to go abroad to get a Western education. He forced merchants to set up enterprises, and most of the funding for economic growth came not from entrepreneurial profits, but from increases in state taxes. Finally, to provide labour, his government mobilized forced labour on a vast scale for projects such as the building of St Petersburg. Peter even created a special class of industrial serfs and assigned them to factories for life.

Peter's reforms worked because the government was so powerful and had such immense human and material resources at its disposal. And they worked because the technological gap between Russia and Western Europe was not too wide in the eighteenth century. Largely because of Peter's reforms, the Russian Empire became a great military power and remained one throughout the eighteenth century. However, this was not a strategy for continuous innovation. Technologies pioneered in the commercial environments of Western Europe often proved sterile in a traditional world in which entrepreneurs and wage-workers played only a limited role. The iron foundries of the Urals or the weapons factories of Tula survived while the government supported them. But they did not stimulate growth in other sectors of Russian industry, and by 1800 Russian iron technology was falling behind that of Europe. Without a flourishing entrepreneurial economy, ideas alone could not stimulate continuous growth.

In the nineteenth century, the technological and military gap between Europe and more traditional societies such as Russia began to widen. Could older strategies of mobilization work in this changed environment?

As the technology gap widened, spontaneous social changes were already undermining traditional Russian social and economic structures. Changes in the world economy and within Russia encouraged the growth of markets, entrepreneurialism and wage-labour, the three major elements of the capitalist engine of growth, despite the government's efforts to preserve traditional social structures.

Though it is impossible to measure the change with any precision, the increased use of cash suggests that market forces were becoming more important from at least the sixteenth century. The government itself stimulated cash transactions because it needed cash to pay for its growing military expenditures. To raise cash it demanded the payment of direct taxes such as the poll tax in cash rather than kind. It also increased its reliance on indirect taxes. These were taxes on the purchase of goods such as salt and vodka. By the middle of the eighteenth century, indirect taxes already produced more revenue than direct taxes.

To pay cash taxes peasants had to earn cash by seeking wage-work, or selling surplus produce or goods produced in local 'domestic industries'. This was particularly true near the large urban centres of Moscow and St Petersburg. The spread of domestic industries corresponds to the phenomenon known in the economic history of Western Europe as 'Proto-industrialization'. This was an early form of industrial development in which merchants used the labour of peasants working in their own households. Proto-industrialization increased the cash incomes of peasant households, multiplied opportunities for small and medium-sized entrepreneurs, and expanded the range of market forces. It may also have encouraged population growth by increasing opportunities to turn spare labour into cash, thereby allowing couples to marry younger.

Meanwhile, the demand of the Russian ruling group for foreign military and luxury goods also stimulated trade. Though subordinate to the government, and usually at its mercy, merchants and entrepreneurs had always played a significant role in Russian life. The Stroganov family, which had made its money trading in salt and furs, had pioneered the exploration of Siberia in the seventeenth century. Merchants ran many of the new industries established by Peter the Great. By the early nineteenth century there existed enough demand for industrial textiles, and enough wage-labour and entrepreneurial capital to stimulate a small-scale industrial revolution in Moscow. In the 1840s textile entrepreneurs introduced steam engines to most of Moscow's textile works. So rapid was the mechanization of textile production in the 1840s that one Soviet historian even argued that Russia's 'industrial' revolution occurred in that decade.[1]

So, through many different channels, and despite the government's efforts, elements of the capitalist package of wage-labour, capitalist entrepreneurs and the market, were appearing in Russian society even before the abolition of serfdom.

 # 1850 to 1914: Economic Change and Government Policy

In the 1850s, the government and most educated Russians supported economic growth, but resisted industrialization. They did not want to create a large industrial proletariat of the kind that had brought down European governments during the 1848 revolutions. They hoped Russia could remain an agrarian society.

However, after its humiliating defeat in the Crimea in 1856, the government understood the need for further economic and social change. It abolished serfdom in part because it had concluded that wage labour was more productive than forced labour. It also supported economic change in other areas. It supported the creation of new banks, and of new industries such as oil extraction. After its embarrassing difficulties in supplying its armies during the Crimean War, it also encouraged railway building. Immediately after the war the government backed a consortium of Russian and foreign capitalists who planned to build a large network of railways. The government guaranteed 5 per cent interest on all capital invested in the project on the understanding that the government itself would eventually assume control of the railways. These terms proved attractive to potential investors, and Russia's railway network expanded from 2000 kilometres in 1861 to more than 30 000 kilometres in 1891.

As in the United States, the economic impact of railways was profound, for they cut transportation costs over the huge Russian land mass. Reduced transportation costs were particularly important for the grain trade, the largest branch of Russian commerce. In the late nineteenth century exports of grain through the Black Sea port of Odessa increased rapidly. In the middle of the century, less than 2 per cent of the grain harvest was exported. By the early 1880s, more than 6 per cent was being exported, and by the late 1890s about 18 per cent was going abroad.[2] The growth in grain exports explains the increased importance of the Straits of Constantinople for Russian foreign policy.

Railway building encouraged the emergence of a new iron and coal industry in Ukraine. In the 1860s, a Welsh engineer called John Hughes built an ironworks in the Donets Basin to supply iron rails for the government. In 1885, a rail link was built between the coal of the River Donets region and the iron ore of the Krivoy Rog region. This encouraged rapid expansion of iron production in Ukraine. By the 1890s Ukraine had replaced the Urals as Russia's major producer of iron (see Figure 4.1). In a similar way, the Baku–Batum railway, opened in 1883,

Figure 4.1   *Main industrial regions of European Russia before 1917*

linked the oil-producing region of Baku on the Caspian Sea to the ports of the Black Sea. This stimulated a rapid expansion of oil exports. By the 1890s, railway construction used about 60 per cent of all iron and steel produced in Russia.[3]

In the 1890s, the Russian government finally accepted that if Russia was to remain a great power it could not remain a country of peasants and farms trading with industrial powers. It must become an industrial power in its own right. As a result, the government began actively to support industrialization.

The tsarist government now adopted a carefully thought-through strategy of industrial development. Sergei Witte, the minister of finance from 1892 to 1903, symbolized the change in policy. Witte's background was unusual for a tsarist minister, for he was not a noble but had made his career in business and railway administration. It was therefore natural for him to encourage closer contacts between the government and business. He also used the government's immense propaganda resources to stimulate business and enterprise through the press, exhibitions, special training programmes, and generous use of government subsidies.

Witte supported industrial growth because he saw more clearly than others that Russia would fall behind its European rivals if it remained an agricultural power. He believed that if Russia did not catch up industrially it would slip into the position of a colony itself, a fate already facing the Chinese Empire. The following comes from a memorandum he wrote in defence of his policies in 1899.

> *Document 4.1: Sergei Witte's 1899 memorandum on industrial development*

The economic relations of Russia with Western Europe are fully comparable to the relations of colonial countries with their metropolises. The latter consider their colonies as advantageous markets in which they can freely sell the products of their labor and of their industry and from which they can draw with a powerful hand the raw materials necessary for them ... Russia was, and to a considerable extent still is, such a hospitable colony for all industrially developed states, generously providing them with the cheap products of her soil and buying dearly the products of their labor. But there is a radical difference between Russia and a colony: Russia is an independent and strong power. She has the right and the strength not to want to be the eternal handmaiden of states which are more developed economically.[4]

Witte did not rely merely on the state to stimulate industrial growth. He believed firmly in the need to stimulate the activities of independent entrepreneurs as well. The government's role was to give industrial growth a kick-start. Eventually, he hoped it could retreat from direct involvement in economic growth. Private entrepreneurs would then take over. Because of this larger perspective, Witte spent much energy encouraging entrepreneurial activity by funding credit institutions, encouraging trade fairs and protecting Russian entrepreneurs from foreign competition through the introduction of tariffs.

However, his strategy also contained some archaic elements. Kick-starting industrial growth required a large injection of cash, and Witte saw the autocracy as the institution best able to mobilize these resources. So Witte believed firmly in the need to preserve the autocracy, and even wrote a famous book in its defence. He also defended traditional institutions such as the peasant commune, which played a crucial role in the collection of government taxes. Like Peter the Great, Witte hoped to use Russia's traditional political and fiscal structures to pay for economic modernization.

The centrepiece of Witte's strategy was the use of government funds to construct the trans-Siberian railway. He hoped this would stimulate growth by providing rapid and cheap transportation for the first time between the western and eastern edges of the Russian Empire. By now, railway building was a familiar element of tsarist military and economic policy. However, Witte gave it a new significance. Instead of encouraging railway building by private entrepreneurs, the government began to take a direct interest in railway building. By 1914, it owned and ran two-thirds of Russia's railways.[5] Construction of the trans-Siberian railway began in 1891, when Witte was minister of transport. It was completed in 1904. In eleven years, the amount of railway track in Russia nearly doubled, rising from 30 000 to 56 000 kilometres. During its construction, government orders for iron, coal, locomotives and equipment boosted the development of Russian heavy industry and engineering. The railway also reduced transportation costs, thereby stimulating trade throughout the Russian Empire. Finally, through freight charges and passenger fares, the railway earned the government large revenues. (See Figure 4.2.)

Witte's policies were expensive. However his predecessors as ministers of finance had worked hard to raise government revenue and balance the budget. The most significant elements in their policies had been high protective tariffs (that is, duties on imports), the export of grain, the borrowing of foreign capital and heavy taxation. From 1877, Witte's predecessors had steadily raised tariffs from the low level typical of the 1850s and 1860s. In 1891, I. A. Vyshnegradskii introduced the highest tariffs in Russia's commercial history. By the 1890s, tariffs accounted for 33 per cent of the value of all imports, while before 1877 they had accounted for only 12 per cent.[6]

Tariffs were not just a way of raising money. They have also played an important role in industrial development in most countries, by protecting

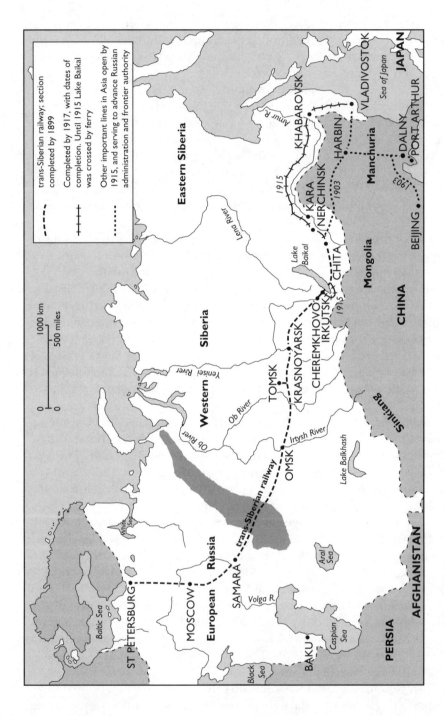

Figure 4.2 *The trans-Siberian railway and the Far East*

infant native industries. One of the first economists to recognise this was the German, Friedrich List (1789–1846), of whom Witte was a great admirer. List argued that high tariffs were the key to American industrial development in the early nineteenth century, for they had protected American industry from the competition of cheaper English imports. German industry had also developed behind the high tariff barriers of the Zollverein customs union established in 1818. Witte argued that tariffs should play the same role in Russia's development.

Witte's predecessors had also advocated the expansion of Russian grain exports. Exports of grain earned the reserves of gold and foreign currency needed to guarantee repayments on foreign loans. Such guarantees were necessary if Russia was to attract foreign loans. Here, too, Witte pursued a traditional policy with a new purpose and new energy. In 1897 he placed the Russian currency on the gold standard. This meant fixing the value of the rouble against other currencies and against gold, so foreign creditors would know the real value of the interest they could earn on Russian loans. As a result of Witte's energetic encouragement of foreign investment, the amount of foreign capital (mainly French and Belgian) in Russian industrial companies rose from 26 per cent in 1890 to 41 per cent by 1915. Foreign shares of Russia's national debt rose from 30 per cent in 1895 to 48 per cent in 1914.[7]

Foreign loans did not come free. Interest payments, like the cost of railway building, had to come from tax revenues. Ultimately, it was peasants and urban workers who paid these costs. As consumers, they paid for the government's economic policy through high tariffs on imported goods, and rising indirect taxes on consumer goods such as vodka. Peasants also paid through the pressure the government applied to make them pay arrears of redemption dues, even when payment became more difficult later in the century.

Witte was well aware that consumers in general and peasants in particular, paid a heavy price for his strategy of development.

☐ *Document 4.2: From Sergei Witte's 1899 memorandum*

Of all charges against the economic policy of Russia, the minister of finance is most keenly aware of the following: that because of the tariff, a Russian pays for many items considerably more than the subjects of other countries; ... that the cost of living also grows for both rich and poor; and that the paying powers of the population are strained to the utmost, so that in many cases consumption is directly curtailed. The minister of finance recognizes that the customs duties fall as a particularly heavy burden upon the impoverished landowners and peasants, particularly in a year of crop failure. These imposts are a heavy sacrifice made by the entire population, and not from surplus but out of current necessities.[8]

The impact of the growing tax burden can be seen most clearly in the methods used to collect direct taxes from the peasantry. Government officials collected taxes in autumn, just after the harvest. This allowed peasants to sell their newly harvested grain to pay their taxes. Of course the autumn was the worst possible time for peasants to sell. Grain was abundant and millions of peasants were selling it, so competition forced prices down and peasants had to sell more. Many sold grain they would eventually need for their own subsistence. By spring, many households had run out of grain and had to return to the market. Now they entered the market as buyers in a seller's market, as increased demand forced prices up. The government and grain merchants gained at both ends of this unpleasant deal. Peasants knew they lost twice, but there was nothing they could do. As they took their rye to market in the autumn, they would say: 'Don't be sorry, Mother Rye, that my path is city-wards. In the spring I will overpay; but I will take thee back!'.[9]

When such methods failed, the government resorted to direct brutality. Members of a commune were collectively responsible for the commune's total payments. In the last resort, the land captains could, and did, inflict mass whippings to force the commune to pay for households that had fallen into arrears.

Though levels of taxation undoubtedly rose in this period, some historians have argued that this did not lead to a decline in average rural living standards. Agricultural output rose fast enough to feed the population most of the time, and opportunities for wage-work meant that many rural families had increasing cash incomes. Nevertheless, there can be little doubt that government policy created genuine hardship for millions of peasants at a time when average landholdings were declining. The difficulties were worst in what Stephen Wheatcroft has described as the 'Central Producer Region', the band of agricultural provinces to the south of Moscow. Heavy taxation was not the only cause of peasant difficulties. Poor harvests were also frequent. However, the government deserved and received much of the blame for the difficulties peasants suffered in these years.

Such methods of paying for modernization forced the government to preserve the more archaic elements of rural life. It had to keep the peasantry tied to the commune, and it had to keep the commune as a device for collecting taxes. Witte's strategy of growth also meant preserving the autocracy, for only an autocratic government could exert this degree of fiscal pressure on the population.

The slump of 1899 increased protests about the results of government economic policy. Famines in the countryside and strikes in the towns finally took their toll. Nicholas II lost his nerve in 1903 and sacked Witte. From then until 1914, the government was too concerned with its own survival to undertake a systematic programme of economic development. Indirectly, though, government policies stimulated further growth through government purchases of military equipment and further expenditure on railways. The dismantling of the commune after 1906 also accelerated economic change in the countryside. Economic growth continued, but it owed less and less to systematic government policies of growth, and more to social and economic changes over which the government had little control.

■ Assessing Economic Growth

How rapid was economic growth between 1850 and 1914? Which sectors of the economy grew fastest? Were Russian productivity levels catching up with those of the capitalist West? The statistics reproduced in the Statistical Appendix and in Table 4.1 suggest some preliminary answers.

Table 4.1 and Figure 4.3 use index numbers to help us compare different rates of growth. Index numbers are ratios. They show how much

Table 4.1   *Index numbers of economic growth, 1861–1913*

	Total ind.	Total agric.	Popn	Urban popn	Volume of grain exports	Railways (length)	Iron	Govt revenue
	A	B	C	D	E**	F	G	H
1861	1.00	1.00	1.00	1.00	1.00	1.00	1.00	1.00
1871	1.49	1.11	1.16	2.12	2.42	6.18	1.33	1.25
1881	2.52	1.12	1.36		3.59	10.50	1.67	1.60
1891	3.99	1.17*	1.62		5.04	13.95	3.33	2.19
1896	5.33	1.96	1.70	4.25	6.47	17.95	5.33	3.36
1901	7.50	1.81	1.83		7.40	25.64	9.67	4.41
1906	8.10	1.89	1.99		7.25	28.91	9.00	5.57
1913	11.65	3.09	2.32	6.96	7.83	31.91	14.00	8.38

Notes:
* A famine year (1890 = 1.49; 1892 = 1.43)
** Figures for 1861–5, 1871–5, 1881–5, 1891–5, 1896–8, 1901–5, 1906–10, 1911–13

Sources: A and B based on R. W. Goldsmith, 'The Economic Growth of Tsarist Russia', in *Economic Development and Cultural Change*, vol. 9 (1960–1), pp. 446–7 (col. 5) and pp. 462–3 (col. 8); C, D, F, G based on Statistical Appendix; E based on G. Pavlovsky, *Agricultural Russia on the Eve of the Revolution* (London, 1930) pp. 113, 267; H based on P. A. Khromov, *Ekonomicheskoe razvitie Rossii v XIX–XX vv* (Moscow, 1951).

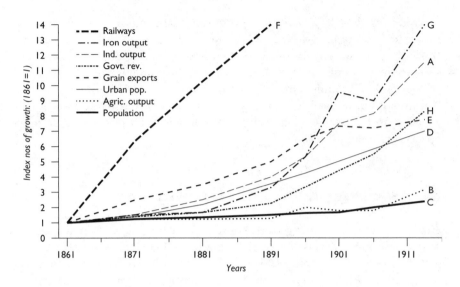

Figure 4.3   *Economic growth of the Russian Empire, 1861–1913*
Note: Based on information in Table 4.1

a given variable has increased since the base year (in this case 1861). I have calculated them by dividing the original figures (most of which come from the Statistical Appendix) by the figure for the base year, 1861.

The population of the Russian Empire (C) more than doubled between 1861 and 1913. However, industrial and agricultural production grew more rapidly. This suggests that output per caput (that is, the amount produced for every individual) was increasing. Clearly, the general level of productivity of the Russian economy increased throughout the period. This shows there was intensive, as well as extensive growth.

All indicators of industrial production show rapid increases. The growth of the urban population (D) shows indirectly the increase in the number of wage-earners and factory workers. However, total industrial production (A) increased even more rapidly than the urban population (D). This suggests that the productivity of the urban work force was increasing more rapidly than its numbers.

Particular sectors of heavy industry, such as iron (G) or the railways (F), grew even more rapidly than total industrial production (A). (Note that the figures in column F look more impressive than they should because growth began from such a low level in 1861.)

When was industrial growth most rapid? Is there any sign of the sudden spurt of growth some historians have detected in the 1890s? Rates of industrial growth in the 1890s (about 8 per cent a year) were indeed remarkable. They have rarely been equalled in the industrial history of

Table 4.2   *Rates of industrial growth, 1885–1913*

Years	Average annual rate of growth of industrial productiion (%)
1885–9	6.10
1890–9	8.03
1900–6	1.43
1907–13	6.25

Source: M. E. Falkus, *The Industrialisation of Russia: 1700–1914* (London: Macmillan, 1972) p. 46.

any country. Nevertheless, the growth rates of the 1890s continued an accelerating trend that had begun even before the 'Great Reforms'. After a decline in growth rates in the first few years of the twentieth century, the acceleration resumed in the years before 1914. The growth of railways followed a slightly different path. Growth was rapid in the 1860s and 1870s, but even in this sector growth was most rapid in the 1890s, during the construction of the trans-Siberian railway.

Accounts of Russian industrial development have often exaggerated the importance of heavy industry and underestimated growth in domestic (*kustar*) and consumer goods industries. This is partly because the government itself focused mainly on heavy industry. Yet domestic industries and consumer goods industries had a far greater impact on the life of most peasants, and probably had a greater impact on the economy as a whole.

'Proto-industrialization', the growth of domestic industries, was as important in Russia's economic history as in that of early modern Europe or many Third World countries today. Available figures suggest that in Russia about 800 000 people worked in domestic industries in 1861, and about 3 million in 1913. These figures are similar to those for the numbers employed in industry and mines (see p. 122). Though *kustar* industries sometimes competed with factories, they could also be part of a larger organization. In Vladimir province in the 1850s, fifty-eight cotton factories had 900 looms and 5800 workers on the premises. They also had another 45 000 looms and 65 000 workers working in peasant homes in nearby villages.[10]

Consumer goods industries, particularly textiles and foodstuffs, also grew at respectable rates throughout the nineteenth century. Populists in the nineteenth century claimed that the self-sufficiency of Russia's peasants severely restricted the demand for consumer goods. As a result, they claimed, Russia could never become a capitalist society. Modern economic historians have often shared this assumption. In reality, even in the early nineteenth century, most peasants had many links with the market, either as wage-earners or as purchasers, and these links multiplied later in the century. Those who earned cash had to spend it. As a result, there was a steady increase in the demand for consumer goods in the towns and in the countryside. Far from stagnating, consumer goods industries flourished throughout the century. In 1913, textiles and foodstuffs made up 50 per cent of total industrial production.[11] Of course, increased expenditure was not necessarily a sign of growing wealth. For many peasant households it was a sign of poverty. They earned and spent more cash because the land could no longer support them.

Until recently, researchers argued that agricultural growth lagged behind population growth in the late nineteenth century, thereby reducing the availability of foodstuffs and depressing average peasant living standards. That in turn was seen as a major cause of the 1905 revolution. Recent research portrays a more dynamic agricultural sector.

Output of grains provides the best single indicator of agricultural output, for grains were the main foodstuff, and accounted for 90 per cent of the sown area even in 1913. Harvests varied wildly from year to year, so it is the longer trends that interest us. In the 1870s and 1880s, grain production per caput may have declined slightly, and between 1889 and 1892 there was a series of four bad harvests, culminating in a major famine. Between 1890 and 1913, per caput grain production rose, even after deducting exports, though there was another brief decline during the crisis of 1905–8.[12] From 1890 to 1913, grain production kept just ahead both of population growth and the growth in grain exports.

Between 1860 and 1914, Russian grain harvests roughly tripled in size. Only about one-quarter of this increase reflects expansion in sown areas. The rest reflects genuine increases in productivity.[13] Much of the gain came from intensive capitalist farming of the newly colonized black earth lands of Ukraine and the south-east. Here, merchants leased land and farmed it commercially. Some gains were realised on the estates of entrepreneurial nobles who produced for the market. Some farmers began to concentrate on commercial crops such as sugar-beet or tobacco. Even peasants improved productivity. Some village communes introduced fertilizers, or drained marshlands, or introduced new crop rotations. Between 1860 and 1910, crop yields on peasant lands may have increased by as much as 50 per cent.[14] Improvements in agricultural productivity were associated with an expansion in the market for agricultural products. During the last two decades before 1914, almost 25 per cent of all grain was placed on the market, either for internal consumption, or for export.[15]

These national figures mask important regional differences. Output in newly colonised regions in Ukraine, the south-east and west Siberia

expanded faster than the average. In contrast, in the belt of agricultural
provinces south of Moscow and along the middle Volga, the 'Central
Producer Region', per caput production fell steadily in the thirty years
before the First World War. This was a region of real agricultural crisis in
the last decades of tsarist rule.[16] It was also the heart of the rural
revolutions of the early twentieth century. The agricultural crisis of the
late nineteenth century was real enough, but it was largely confined to the
Central Producer Region. Livestock was the main resource of peasant
households besides land and their own labour, and it is clear now that the
average numbers of cattle, horses and pigs owned by each household fell
steadily throughout this period.[17] This is a clear sign that peasants were
coming under great economic pressure.

Summing up this complex picture of economic change is not easy. In
an influential essay first published in the 1960s, Alexander Gerschenkron
argued that the economic reforms of Peter the Great set a pattern of state-
led economic growth that would reappear in the late nineteenth century,
and again in the Soviet period, under Stalin.[18] The government
encouraged economic changes, and mobilized the necessary resources. As
the government's aims were military, industrial growth favoured heavy
industry rather than consumer goods industries or agriculture, so it did
little to generate increased consumer goods or to improve living
standards. Instead, living standards declined as taxation increased to fund
growth in the military-industrial sector. This was a style of economic
growth that depended on direct mobilization of resources. The heavy
demands it placed on the population impoverished most people and
generated widespread discontent. Such strategies required governments
able and willing to use force to maintain their power. It was,
Gerschenkron argued, an appropriate strategy for autocratic governments
such as those of the Russian Empire.

Gerschenkron divided the economic history of the late nineteenth and
early twentieth centuries into two main phases. The 'Great Reforms', and
in particular the Emancipation Act, shaped the first phase. During this
phase, he argued, government policies retarded industrial development
by tying peasants to the land. In the late 1880s, the government finally
abandoned its resistance to industrial growth. In the 1890s, the policies of
Witte triggered an unprecedented spurt of rapid industrial growth,
concentrated almost entirely in heavy industry and transportation. Some
economic historians, such as Walt Rostow, argued that the 1890s marked
the point at which the Russian economy 'took off into sustained growth'.
Despite a slump in the early twentieth century, Gerschenkron argued that
growth resumed in the half decade before 1914. By then, he claimed,
Russia was well on the way to successful industrialization. In other words,
Gerschenkron believed that Witte's policies had offered a successful

solution to the dilemma of backwardness. However, the intervention of war and revolution diverted Russian history into new paths.

This has been an influential account of economic growth in Russia before the First World War. However, it now needs serious modification. As even Gerschenkron conceded, the state was not the only significant force for economic growth in the late nineteenth century. We have seen that there was much economic development in areas of the economy of little interest to the government. It now appears that change was less erratic and more continuous than Gerschenkron suggested. Instead of a series of sudden growth spurts, mainly in heavy industry, the economic history of the last century of tsarist rule consisted of a prolonged acceleration in economic output across most sectors of the economy. Finally, Gerschenkron exaggerated Witte's reliance on a traditional mobilizational strategy of growth. In reality, Witte, unlike either Peter the Great or Stalin, was an enthusiastic advocate of capitalism. Though he used traditional mobilizational methods, he saw them as steps towards a capitalist pattern of growth. Gerschenkron's account of the late tsarist period no longer stands, though his analysis of the reforms of Peter the Great and Stalin retains its importance.

Was growth sufficient to allow the Russian Empire to remain a great power? We have seen that there was growth in all sectors of the economy. It was particularly rapid in heavy industry and communications. However, from the government's point of view, the real issue was whether Russia was holding its own as a great power. Was Russia catching up economically with Europe? Did it have the economic foundations necessary for a modern military establishment?

Comparisons are difficult. However, Russia's industrial output per caput (that is, total industrial output divided by population), appears not to have risen any faster than it did among other major industrial powers between 1860 and 1910. On the contrary, Russia fell behind Italy into tenth position.[19] Undoubtedly, Russia's position as an industrial power would have been even worse had it not been for the industrial growth that occurred in this period. However, there was still a long way to go before Russia reached the levels of productivity of capitalist Western Europe. Even in 1913, Russia's economy remained mainly agricultural. Only 18 per cent of the population lived in the towns, and industry still produced only 20 per cent of national income.[20]

These conclusions suggest that the government had at best partial success in stimulating intensive growth. What of the other side of the dilemma? Did it manage to preserve the social foundations for its own power? Here, the success of government strategies is even less certain. The government made strenuous efforts to preserve its own power and to prevent the destruction of the landed nobility and the peasantry. Despite this, Russian society underwent profound changes in this period, changes over which the government had little control.

 ## Economic Growth and Social Change, 1861 to 1914

In its desire to prevent the emergence of a wage-earning urban proletariat, the government of Alexander II had emancipated the serfs in ways that made it difficult for them to leave the land. Though free, most remained tied to allotments controlled by communes. The commune appeared to prevent the emergence of classes of wage-earners and entrepreneurs from amongst the peasantry, by equalizing landholdings between households. This made it difficult for successful households to accumulate land and become small entrepreneurial farmers. Equally, the 1861 Act made it difficult for less successful households to sell their land and become full-time wage-workers.

These aspects of Russian society after 1861 persuaded many contemporaries that Russia had its own, unique, path of development. Populists, in particular, concluded that Russia would never become a 'capitalist' society, but would remain a peasant society. In reality, legislation alone could not prevent social change. After the 1861 act, peasants came under increasing pressure to engage in the market, either as wage-labourers or as petty entrepreneurs or traders. Landlords, too, found they had to enter the market if they were to survive. These processes, in turn, generated new opportunities for other entrepreneurs, and stimulated the growth of the market.

Entrepreneurs increased in numbers and influence during the last century of tsarist rule. The rising entrepreneurial class came from many different groups within traditional Russian society. Three were particularly important: the merchantry, the nobility, and the peasantry.

Officially, the merchant class increased its numbers from about 246 000 to about 600 000 between 1850 and 1900. However, their economic, political and social influence grew even more rapidly as Russia industrialized. Slowly, the traditional merchant class transformed itself into a modern capitalist class of bankers and industrialists. The increase in the number of industrialists can be measured by the increase in medium and large-sized factories. Between 1866 and 1903, the number of factories employing more than sixteen workers increased from 2500 to 9000.[21]

The changing role of the merchantry can be illustrated from the history of the Guchkov family. Fedor Alekseevich Guchkov, an *obrok*-paying serf, founded the family's fortune. In the late eighteenth century, he set up a weaving shop in Moscow, with the permission of his master. Typically, Fedor Alekseevich continued to dress and look like a serf even after he purchased his freedom. His sons began to run the business in the 1820s, and by the 1840s the Guchkovs owned one of the largest woollen factories in Russia. By 1853 his factories employed 1880 workers. His grandsons, Ivan and Efim, were 'modern businessmen who dressed in western clothing, had western educations and had travelled in Europe'. The fourth generation was less actively involved in business, preferring to live off profits from the family concerns. One member, Ivan, took on posts in urban government and state administration. Another, Nikolai, became mayor of Moscow. Alexander Guchkov, the most famous of the Guchkovs, was in turn 'adventurer, public servant, liberal politician of the last years of the Tsarist regime, Octobrist leader in the *Duma*, and minister of war for the Provisional Government'.[22] We will meet this Guchkov again. By 1900 the leading members of the bourgeoisie had clearly 'arrived' in Russian high society. Some, like Sergei Witte, were now playing leading roles within the ruling group.

Not all entrepreneurs were merchants. Some came from the nobility. Not only did many nobles succeed in becoming entrepreneurial farmers; many diversified into industries such as cotton or distilling. Particularly in the black soil provinces of the south, commercial agriculture flourished in the late nineteenth century. Both merchants and nobles engaged in it, hiring labour, using modern agricultural techniques, and producing wheat for the growing export markets of Odessa.

Peasants also became entrepreneurs. On the face of it, the 1861 Act should have ensured that the peasantry remained a homogenous, egalitarian class of self-sufficient small farmers. Land, the basic productive resource, was distributed according to the number of males in a household. This should have ensured a basic equality of wealth, which is why the populists saw in the Russian commune the germs of socialism.

However, the commune was less egalitarian than it seemed. The other major productive resource, labour, was distributed quite unequally as a result of accidents of birth and death. Large families could often generate enough money to buy additional farming equipment, lease additional land or set up small domestic industries. Such peasants became small entrepreneurs. In the villages they were often known as *kulaks*, or 'fists', a term which combined envy and respect. Lenin argued in *The Development of Capitalism in Russia* (1899) that the *kulaks* represented an emerging rural bourgeoisie. Recent research shows that changing fortunes, such as the break-up of large households, could destroy wealthy peasant families as fast as they created them. Few *kulaks* founded long-lived dynasties of entrepreneurs. Despite this, the number of peasant entrepreneurs rose steadily.

So did the number of wage-earners. We have seen that the expansion of wage-labour is a fundamental aspect of modernization. However, as Marx pointed out, from the point of view of those forced to become wage-labourers against their will, the process was extremely painful. This helps explain why so many recently recruited wage-workers were attracted to revolutionary politics. The class of wage-workers expanded in two distinct ways.

First, the number of intellectual wage-workers increased. The late nineteenth century saw the birth of the professions. Lawyers, doctors, teachers, all formed professional associations. The *zemstva* also hired veterinarians, statisticians and agronomists to work with the peasantry. These were known as the 'third element' in the *zemstva* (the first being government officials, the second being elected members). This new class of intellectual wage-workers came mainly from members of the former upper classes. They came from declining noble families or from those borderline classes which had access to education despite their non-noble birth.

Far more important numerically was the rising class of manual wage-workers. These are the groups that Marx called the 'proletariat'. Though many new proletarians came from the towns, most came from the countryside. In a peasant society, creating a class of wage-labourers meant denying peasants access to the land, the primary productive resource in an agrarian society. Creating a class of wage-labourers has always, therefore, required the expropriation of peasants. This was the process that Marx referred to as 'primitive capitalist accumulation'. He meant by this the mechanisms that created the class structure necessary for Capitalism to work. In the Russian Empire, these processes took confusing forms. The 1861 Act, far from creating a large class of landless labourers, forced most peasants to remain on the land. It therefore seemed to prevent the emergence of a proletariat. However, as Lenin pointed out, the 1861 Act merely changed the ways in which the peasantry lost control of the land. Instead of being severed from the land with a single blow, like eighteenth-century English peasants under the so-called 'enclosure' Acts, Russian peasants were squeezed from the land over several decades. As a result, there appeared a vast and growing class of part-time wage-earners, rather than the full-time proletariat that Marx saw in Victorian Britain. These processes had a profound effect on the nature and the grievances of Russian workers.

What pressures forced peasants to earn wages? The most important pressures were rising taxation and land shortage, though rising consumption may also have played a role.

The rising tax burden has already been discussed. Growing land shortage played an even more important role in pushing peasants on to the market as wage-earners and then as consumers. As population grew, the land available per person shrank. Between 1860 and 1900, the average allotment of male peasants had declined by about 46 per cent, from 5.2 to 2.8 hectares. Meanwhile, a growing number of poor peasants did not have the livestock necessary to work and manure their land. By 1900, about 30 per cent of all peasant households did not have a single horse, and 35 per cent had no cows. Such households could no longer survive by farming. Many leased their land to wealthier households and began to live entirely off wages.[23]

These pressures meant that peasants who in the past had supported themselves from their own land now had to enter the market. If they had spare cash, they could lease extra land. If they had surplus grain, they could sell it. Between 1850 and 1914 more and more peasants put grain on the market. In 1850 peasants produced 45 per cent of all marketed grain; by 1914, they produced 75 per cent.[24] However, if they had neither surplus cash nor surplus grain, they had to seek wage-work. This strategy had the greatest effect on village life, for it took peasants away from their families and their villages, sometimes for months or years on end. As noted in Chapter 2, the search for wage-work took three main forms. Each represented one more stage in the severing of ties with the traditional ways of life of rural Russia. Each also represented an increase in the total labour expended.

First, peasants could find work in domestic, *kustar*, industry. There were many types of domestic industry: weaving, spinning, boat-making, or any of the numerous money-making activities that could be carried on in the household or the village. The advantage of domestic industry was that people could stay in the village and continue to farm their allotments. It simply meant making more productive use of the time not used in agriculture. The disadvantage was that domestic industry often involved very hard work indeed, even for the very old and the very young. Workdays of fifteen to sixteen hours were not uncommon in households that spun or wove cloth. The hours became longer when *kustar* industries began to face competition from factories using modern equipment. The agrarian economist, A. V. Chayanov, called this increase in labour time 'self-exploitation'. Here is an account of one such trade by a modern historian.

> In a trade such as the making of wooden spoons, every member of the family had a specific function, well adjusted to his age and capabilities. The youngest children would sort out pieces of wood according to size. Those aged ten to fifteen would shape them roughly. The adult men would give them their final shape with knife and chisel. The women and the old would smooth and polish them; and the daughters of the

family would apply patterns and lacquer. It was this family cooperation which kept costs low and made for prices accessible to the poorest, and also made for great resilience and ability to withstand competition, often also factory competition.[25]

Second, there was rural wage-labour. This usually meant that males of working age left the village for long periods, returning only for the harvest. Meanwhile, the women, the young, and the old took on the burden of farming the family's allotment. However, rural wage-work meant that males who sought work could still make use of the many skills they had learnt growing up in the village, as they tried to find work as farm labourers, ditch diggers, or in building or construction.

To cater for the growing numbers seeking rural wage-work there developed special 'hiring markets' in the commercial grain farming provinces of Ukraine and the south east. Peasants travelled to these in the traditional work-gangs known as *artels*. They travelled by foot or on dangerous home-made rafts known as *duby*. On the day the market began, negotiations would start at a given sign, such as the ringing of a bell. Often, *artel* leaders negotiated with potential employers on behalf of the group as a whole. The following document, from a contemporary source, conveys the relationship between employers and employees in this emerging world of petty Capitalism.

☐ *Document 4.3: A hiring market near Taganrog, early 1860s*

Usually negotiations are conducted with the uncle [the *artel* head]; the others all lay on the ground in very free and easy poses, and only rarely, in chorus, interfere in the conversation, [which is] of extreme interest to them. Their half crude and even insolent treatment of the employer during negotiations represents a strange and funny contrast with their deferential and even servile behavior with regard to that same employer, if, by mutual consent, they become his *batraki* [labourers]. The rude treatment before hire is as if a farewell to freedom, which they sell for four whole months to their employer. The tone of the employer likewise changes somewhat, but in inverse ratio: before hire, he is mainly exhorting, fawning and to the highest degree kind, especially when he contends to the workers, that it is [more] advantageous for them to hire cheaply to him than to another more expensively. After hire he adopts a tone imperious and strict and no longer talks with them amicably, but limits himself to orders.[26]

Finally, there was urban wage-labour. From the peasants' point of view, this option was the most drastic. It was often the resort of the most desperate poor peasants. Factory work not only meant leaving the village for long periods. It also demanded new skills, and devalued the skills of village life. It meant a new living environment, often in unsanitary factory barracks, a different way of using one's labour, and long periods away from one's family and village. Wages were low – a quarter to a third of those in Western Europe. Accident rates were high. Hours of work were long and discipline was harsh. For women workers conditions could be particularly harsh in the towns. Employers often sacked pregnant women. As a result, 'the women workers used to hide (their pregnancy) until their mouths foamed and the child was born at the bench. And after the confinement – back to the bench ... There used to be many women workers who cursed their children'.[27]

There was a steady increase in all three types of wage-work. Between 1860 and 1913 the numbers employed in domestic industry rose from 800 000 to three million (a 275 per cent increase). During the same period, the numbers employed as agricultural wage-labourers rose from 700 000 to 4.5 million (a 543 per cent increase). The numbers in other forms of non-industrial employment (building, transport, domestic service), rose from 1.7 million to 6.9 million (a 314 per cent increase). Meanwhile, the industrial work force – those employed in factories and mines – increased from 860 000 to 3 million (a 275 per cent increase).[28]

These figures show that the total number of wage-earners was far greater than the number of factory workers. Total wage-earners had increased from about 4 021 000 in 1860 to 17 480 000 in 1913 (a 335 per cent increase), and this figure does not include millions more who earned some wages as a supplement to farming.

What is less obvious from these figures is that the various categories of manual wage-work overlapped. Any manual wage-earner might earn money in all these ways during a lifetime. In fact by 1900 most Russian workers were neither peasants nor proletarians, but belonged to a transitional group of peasant-proletarians – 'economic amphibians' as one writer has described them.[29] They spent considerable periods of time earning wages but also maintained an allotment of land in the village. A common pattern was for males to seek work outside the village between the ages of about twenty and forty, and then 'retire' to their villages. As a result, many families were split, with adult males in a town and the rest of the family maintaining the farm. In 1900 only 48 per cent of married wage-earners lived with their families.[30] In these ways, economic change slowly undermined the traditional peasant family. This pattern of making a living remained characteristic until the upheavals of the 1930s introduced a sharper division between rural and urban work.

Not surprisingly, peasant habits persisted in the towns, despite the efforts of factory-owners to re-educate and discipline their work force into modern work habits. It was impossible to stop workers abandoning work and returning to their villages during the harvest. Employers also found their workers' frequent holidays frustrating. In the villages, there were many religious or family festivals during which all work ceased. At first, factory-owners had to accept that they could not expect their workers to do much on those days but drink. However, employers gradually reduced the number of permissible holidays. At a machinery works in Kolomna, the number of work days a year increased from 240 to 260 days in twelve years, an increase of about three weeks in the working year. Still, Russian factory-owners had a long way to go to match the average working year of American workers. At the end of the century this was 283 days, compared with an average of 260 days for Russia.[31]

The following account of the life of an industrial worker shows this odd mix of rural and urban life-styles. It comes from the autobiography of a worker who later became a Bolshevik. The passage also shows how different degrees of urbanization created different groups within the working class.

☐ *Document 4.4: From the autobiography of A. S. Shapovalov*

I was thirteen years old when [in 1884] the railway repair workshop accepted me in its embrace. Although becoming a locksmith coincided with my desires, and although I had not been spoiled by fate and had already graduated from a hard school, still, after one day spent under the authority of the coppersmith, Aleksei Ignatievich Sokolov, I wanted to run away. Instead of giving me a chance to learn a trade, I spent the whole day being sent out to fetch vodka ... Boozeups were organized for any excuse. The birth of a child, a baptism, a funeral, a wedding – all these were marked with boozeups. When a new worker started at the works, he had to buy 'welcoming' drinks for his comrades. When he was discharged, they demanded a 'farewell'. They drank most on the saint's day of the icon which hung in the workshop ...

Only a year later – during which time I had caught severe colds from running in the frost without warm clothing – was I released from the coppersmith Sokolov and transferred to the locksmith workshop.

I heard constantly from the grown-up locksmiths that I should count myself lucky that I was not beaten and was paid thirty kopeks a day on payday, and so I contented myself with the position of a locksmith's apprentice [*slesarnogo uchenika*]. I became coarser, and lowered my standards; I stopped reading books, learnt to smoke, to drink, and to swear with the choicest Russian swear-words ... A work day 'with evenings' (overtime) lasted from seven o'clock in the morning until ten-thirty at night. We also worked on Sundays and all the major holidays, such as Christmas, Easter, and so on. From the constant hard work I became even more coarsened ...

In autumn and winter fist fights used to be arranged. Two opposing teams would line up, 'wall to wall'. When adults joined in, these sometimes became ferocious. At the end of the fights people left with black eyes, broken teeth, bloody faces, broken ribs. Once, after being thrown to the ground, I received such a blow in the spine that I was left unconscious ...

The most backward of the railway workers were the firemen and labourers. They lived in barracks, which were filthy. They were peasants, torn from the plough, who had come to St Petersburg merely to earn a bit and return to their villages. They were extremely hardy and had minimal needs. After working for a bit, and accumulating some money, a fireman would buy a '*troika*' – a suit, polished boots with shining leggings, a crimson blouse, and a harmonica (a 'Talyanka') – and return to his village. In their spare time they wandered the streets in groups and played Russian songs on their 'Talyankas': 'I have been in Petersburg, lots of money have I earned, scarves for the girls I've bought', and so on.

The locksmiths, assistant engine-drivers, and drivers were a sort of aristocracy among the workers … Recognition of their human worth was rare amongst the workers. The master was a 'tsar', a 'god'. Usually, he not only knew what was going on in the factory, but also what was going on in the workers' families. When he walked through the workshop, the workers, before waiting for him to bow, would humbly bow, stutteringly remove their hats and say: 'Good morning, our Lord and Master!' All the foremen and clerks, with rare exceptions, robbed the till mercilessly and took bribes. This inheritance of tsarist slavery also affected the workers. They stole from the workshop everything they could, even the tools of their comrades. 'Don't yawn, and keep a lookout!' became the rule. If someone stole a locksmith's cutter … everyone would laugh when he said, 'Who took my cutter?' To steal, to cheat, to deceive, was thought all to the good. Those who were honest, and correct, who neither lied nor stole, were regarded as fools or eccentrics.[32]

Conclusion: Was There a Viable Strategy of Growth?

Between 1850 and 1914, Russian society saw both the creative and the destructive sides of modernization. Productivity rose in agriculture and even more spectacularly in industry. By 1914, Russia had the heavy industrial basis needed to support a reasonably modern military machine. Yet economic growth had also undermined traditional Russian society. Slowly, sometimes with the support of government policies, sometimes despite them, Russia's social structures were assuming the familiar features of capitalism. As wage-earning increased, as capitalist entrepreneurs acquired more influence, and as market relations extended into every corner of Russian life, the traditional social and economic structures of Russian society lost vitality. Peasants, nobles and government found the sands shifting beneath them. By 1900 many peasants and many nobles had abandoned their traditional way of life. It is no coincidence that in 1905 the tsarist government came close to collapse.

Did this mean that the government had failed to solve the dilemma of modernization? Not necessarily. As we have seen, there was no easy solution to the problems the government faced as Russian society modernized. To survive, it had to preserve the traditional bases of its support. Yet to modernize, it had to allow the emergence of new social and economic forces. Eventually, the government would have to start looking for support amongst these new groups without alienating its traditional supporters. This was a delicate political manoeuvre, and the Meiji dynasty in Japan was one of the few traditional governments to complete it successfully. The crises of the first decade of the twentieth century suggested that the Russian government lacked the insight or the skills needed to imitate the success of the Japanese government. In a sense, the Russo-Japanese war of 1904–5 was a contest between two strategies of modernization. Its outcome was a warning that the Russian government was drifting in very dangerous waters.

■ Summary

In the late nineteenth century, social and economic modernization accelerated. Traditionally, historians have stressed the role played by the Russian government in these changes. They have seen Russian industrialization in the late nineteenth century as an artificial and brutal process, dominated by the state, and harsh in its impact on living standards. Alexander Gerschenkron has stressed the parallels between this period, and the industrialization drives of Peter the Great and Stalin.

There is no doubt that the Russian government began to give active support to industrial growth. By the mid 1890s, under the influence of a commercially-minded Minister of Finance, Sergei Witte, the government had abandoned its traditional hostility to industrialization. It began to support rapid growth in railway-building and heavy industries such as iron, steel and oil. There is also little doubt that the ways it funded economic growth placed a heavy fiscal burden on the Russian population at large. However, recent research has shown that economic growth in this period was more broadly based than was once thought. Much economic growth also took place in sectors of the economy in which the government showed less interest, such as agriculture, peasant industries and consumer goods. By the end of the century, most peasants were deeply involved in the emerging market economy, as entrepreneurs, as sellers of grain or, most commonly of all, as wage-earners. Yet the mechanisms of the Great Reforms forced them still to keep their traditional plots of land. As a result, there emerged a huge class of peasants whose income came as much from wages as from agriculture. There also emerged a dynamic and influential entrepreneurial class recruited from the merchantry, from foreign entrepreneurs, from nobles, and even from peasants. In short, though Russia still lagged behind the economies of Western Europe in levels of industrialization and per caput productivity, by 1900 there had emerged a vigorous young capitalism.

Though economic growth created new opportunities, it was also painful. Peasants found their traditional lifeways undermined by land shortage and rising taxation, and many spent long periods away from the land. In the towns there appeared the beginnings of an urban proletariat. Meanwhile, a nobility forced to rely more on market forces than traditional privileges, found its power, its influence and its privileges declining while the importance of merchants and intellectuals steadily increased. In these ways, economic growth undermined the traditional social structures on which Russia's autocratic government based its power. While ordinary Russians found themselves caught up in the complex changes of modernization, the government still preserved the traditions and methods of a pre-industrial world. The dangers of this mismatch became clear during the revolutionary crisis of 1905.

☐ *Further Reading*

Gerschenkron's essay, 'Problems and Patterns of Russian Economic Development', presents a coherent argument on economic development in the late tsarist period. It makes a good introduction to the issue of modernization, even though many historians no longer accept its general approach. Falkus, *The Industrialisation of Russia*, and Von Laue, *Why Lenin? Why Stalin?*, adopt a similar approach to Gerschenkron. For more recent views, see some of the essays in Kingston-Mann and Mixter (eds), *Peasant Economy, Culture, and Politics of European Russia*, as well as Gatrell, *The Tsarist Economy*. Rogger, *Russia in the Age of Modernisation* is good on both economic and political developments in the late nineteenth century, while Seton-Watson, *The Russian Empire* is more concerned with political and diplomatic history. On the social history, see the works listed under Chapter 2, and the early chapters of Andrle's superb *Social History of Twentieth-Century Russia*. Olga Crisp's essay, 'Labour and Industrialization in Russia', is a pioneering study of changing class structures and lifeways. Thomas Owen, *Russian Corporate Capitalism from Peter the Great to Perestroika*, is the most recent survey of Russian capitalism.

☐ *Notes*

1. V. K. Yatsunsky, 'The Industrial Revolution in Russia', in W. L. Blackwell (ed.), *Russian Economic Development from Peter the Great to Stalin* (New York: New Viewpoints, Franklin Watts Inc, 1974) pp. 111–35.
2. Figures from S. Wheatcroft, 'Crises and the Condition of the Peasantry', in E. Kingston-Mann and T. Mixter (eds), *Peasant Economy, Culture and Politics* (Princeton University Press, 1991) p. 135.

3. P. Gatrell, *The Tsarist Economy 1850–1917* (London: Batsford, 1986) p. 153.
4. T. Riha (ed.), *Readings in Russian Civilization* (University of Chicago Press, 1964) vol. 2, p. 431.
5. M. Falkus, *The Industrialisation of Russia: 1700–1914* (London: Macmillan, 1972) p. 55.
6. Ibid., p. 57.
7. Ibid, pp. 72, 69.
8. T. Riha (ed.), *Readings*, vol. 2, p. 432.
9. J. Mavor, *An Economic History of Russia* (London and Toronto: Dent and Sons, 1925) vol. 2, p. 289.
10. Gatrell, *The Tsarist Economy*, p. 147.
11. Ibid., p. 144.
12. Wheatcroft, 'Crises and the Condition of the Peasantry', p. 133.
13. Gatrell, *The Tsarist Economy*, pp. 100–1.
14. Ibid., p. 122.
15. S. G. Wheatcroft, 'Agriculture', in R. W. Davies (ed.), *From Tsarism to the New Economic Policy: Continuity and Change in the Economy of the USSR* (Ithaca: Cornell University Press, 1990) p. 84.
16. Wheatcroft, 'Crises and the Condition of the Peasantry', pp. 137–42.
17. Ibid., p. 143.
18. Alexander Gerschenkron, 'Problems and Patterns of Russian Economic Development', in M. Cherniavsky (ed.), *The Structure of Russian History* (New York: Random House, 1970) pp. 282–308, and elsewhere.
19. A. Nove, *An Economic History of the USSR*, 3rd edn (Harmondsworth: Penguin, 1992) pp. 4, 7.
20. R. W. Goldsmith, 'The Economic Growth of Tsarist Russia', in *Economic Development and Cultural Change*, vol. 9, 1960–1, p. 442.
21 Lenin, *The Development of Capitalism in Russia* [1st pub. 1899] (Moscow: Progress Publishers, 1956) p. 472.
22. W. L. Blackwell (ed.), *Russian Economic Development from Peter the Great to Stalin*, pp. 154 ff.
23. H. Rogger, *Russia in the Age of Modernisation and Revolution: 1881–1917* (New York: Longman, 1983) pp. 76, 82.
24. Gatrell, *The Tsarist Economy*, p. 139.
25. O. Crisp, 'Labour and Industrialization in Russia', in *Cambridge Economic History of Europe* (Cambridge University Press, 1978) vol. 7, pt 2, p. 337.
26. T. Mixter, 'The Hiring Market as Workers' Turf', in Kingston-Mann and Mixter (eds) *Peasant Economy, Culture and Politics*, p. 301.
27. S. Rowbotham, *Women, Resistance and Revolution* (Harmondsworth: Penguin, 1974) p. 139.
28. Cited in M. McCauley (ed.), *Octobrists to Bolsheviks: Imperial Russia 1905–1917* (London: Edward Arnold, 1984) pp. 137–8.
29. O. Anweiler, *The Soviets, the Russian Workers, Peasants, and Soldiers Councils 1905–1921* (New York: Random House, 1974) p. 21.
30. Crisp, 'Labour and Industrialisation in Russia', p. 368.
31. Ibid., p. 381.
32. S. S. Dmitriev *et al.* (eds), *Khrestomatiya po istorii SSSR* (Moscow: gos-oe uchebno-pedagogicheskoe izd-vo min-va prosveshcheniya RSFSR, 1948) vol. 3, pp. 467–9 (trans D. Christian).

■ *Chapter 5* ■

The 1905 Revolution

The social changes of the late nineteenth century increased the size and the power of classes hostile to autocracy. They also undermined the unity and discipline of the government and its traditional supporters. An increase in resistance from below and a decrease in power above – these were the preconditions for the breakdown of 1905. In 1904–5, military defeat once again exposed the limitations of both government and army. Amidst these growing tensions, it was Nicholas II's refusal to make the necessary concessions that brought the government to the verge of collapse.

■ Working-Class Discontent

The crisis began in 1900, when a sudden economic slump released a wave of working-class discontent that had been building throughout the 1890s.

The industrial boom of the 1890s ended in 1899. Between 1897 and 1901 a run of poor harvests brought famine in their wake. Foreign funds dried up as a result of an international financial crisis triggered by the Boer War in South Africa and the Boxer Rebellion in China. The government reduced its orders for industrial products as tax revenues and foreign investment declined and the Siberian railway neared completion. Annual rates of industrial growth fell from 8 per cent to about 1 per cent. Declining growth brought unemployment and wage cuts, particularly in the metal industries that had grown fastest in the 1890s. The figures on industrial growth rates in Table 4.2 show the effect of the slump.

The slump provoked a wave of strikes among Russia's urban working class. Though still a small proportion of the population, the number of urban workers had increased in the 1890s. So had their industrial might. According to the 1897 census, there were 13.3 million *meshchane* [town-dwellers]. An additional 8.8 million peasants also lived permanently in the towns. These two groups together accounted for 17.6 per cent of the total population. The industrial working class was, of course, smaller. Lenin estimated that in 1897 there were 5.2 million industrial workers and another 700 000 workers in railways and communications. Together, these two groups made up about 4.7 per cent of the total population.[1] The

Statistical Appendix gives the lower (and more widely accepted) figure of 4 million workers, or 3.2 per cent of the population. However, even this figure represents an increase of more than 300 per cent in the size of the urban working class since 1861.

Appalling working conditions gave urban workers plenty of reasons for protest. Even more dangerous for the government was their increased organization. As Marx had argued, the proletariat was a more dangerous revolutionary force than the peasantry, for, though less numerous, they were better able to co-ordinate their actions. The following is from the *Communist Manifesto*.

☐ *Document 5.1: Marx on the power of the proletariat*

With the development of industry, the proletariat not only increases in number; it becomes concentrated in greater masses, its strength grows, and it feels that strength more ... the collisions between individual workmen and individual bourgeois take more and more the character of collisions between two classes. Thereupon the workers begin to form combinations (Trade Unions) ...

Now and then the workers are victorious, but only for a time. The real fruit of their battles lies, not in the immediate result, but in the ever-expanding union of the workers. This union is helped on by the improved means of communication that are created by modern industry and that place the workers in different localities in contact with one another.[2]

The Russian government knew the dangers posed by an urban proletariat. It had tried to limit the growth of such a class in Russia by tying peasants to the land in 1861. It also tried to stifle working-class organisations by making unions and strikes illegal. Despite this, there were illegal unions and strikes throughout the nineteenth century. Many were organized through *zemlyachestva*, associations that helped migrant workers from a particular province or region. The number of strikes grew from twenty to forty a year in the 1870s and 1880s to more than 100 a year in 1895 and more than 200 in 1898. The army, which had been employed earlier in the century to suppress peasant disturbances, now found itself called out to put down strikes. This was usually a more violent business.[3]

Populists had organized the first large strikes in the 1870s, but by the 1890s Marxists were taking over this role. This was a natural development for, while the Populists hoped to build a rural Socialism based on the peasantry, Marx had always insisted that the urban working classes would lead the socialist revolution. Several future leaders of Russian Marxism, including Vladimir Lenin (1870–1924) and Julius Martov (1873–1923), took part in organizing the great textile workers' strikes in St Petersburg in 1896–7.

During the slump, the government did more than the revolutionaries to develop traditions of unionism among Russian urban workers. A Moscow police chief, S. V. Zubatov, suggested that officially sponsored unions might be able to divert working-class discontent into safe channels. His general idea was that, to survive, the autocracy must divide its upper class from its lower-class opponents. In theory Zubatov was certainly correct.

☐   *Document 5.2: S. V. Zubatov on the principle of 'divide and rule'*

The principle of our internal policy must be to balance between the classes, which, at present, hate each other. An autocracy should keep above the classes and apply the principle of 'divide and rule'. Do not leave them time to agree between themselves: that would mean revolution, which we should help along if we were to take one side in this conflict ... We must create a counter-poison or antidote to the bourgeoisie, which is growing arrogant. Accordingly, we must bring the workers over to us, and so kill two birds with one stone: check the upsurge of the bourgeoisie and deprive the revolutionaries of their troops.[4]

Between 1901 and 1903 Zubatov organized several large unions. By 1903 his unions were exploiting the advantage of police sponsorship to organize large-scale strikes, and in June 1903 Zubatov was dismissed. However, his ideas survived. A year later, in St Petersburg, a priest, Father Gapon, organized an officially sponsored union that was to play a major role in the crisis of 1905. Meanwhile Zubatov unions helped organize the large strikes of 1903 in the oilfields of the Caucasus and the industrial regions of Ukraine.

The rising intensity of the strike movement provoked greater violence from the government. The government used troops to suppress strikes nineteen times in 1893, fifty times in 1899, and 522 times in 1902.[5]

Despite rising taxes and shrinking landholdings, there had been no serious peasant disturbances since 1863. However, a string of poor harvests in the late 1890s finally broke the patience of the peasantry. Sporadic attacks on the property of landlords began once more.

☐   *Document 5.3: Peasant unrest, 1898*

In certain provinces, predominantly southern and south-eastern, there has recently emerged a series of peasant disorders in the form of systematic damage to the landowners' fields and meadows, together with the driving away of cattle under the protection of men armed with sticks, staves and pitchforks, and attacks on the landowners' watchmen and guards or considerable illegal timber-cutting in the landowners' woods and brawls with the foresters. When the guards seize the peasants' cattle, the peasants, hoping to free it, often moving by whole villages, carry out armed attacks on the buildings and farm-houses of the landowners and divide up the working and even the living quarters, attacking and wounding servants and guards.[6]

As always, geographical separation and lack of education made it difficult for peasants to co-ordinate their actions. Most revolts were spontaneous, local affairs. At most, the local commune might meet to decide what to attack. However, the barriers to effective rural organization were breaking down. Since the military reforms of 1874, many recruits had learned the rudiments of literacy, and when they returned to the village as reservists they could use their military skills to help organize peasant insurrections. Growing literacy also meant that more peasants could read revolutionary propaganda. Meanwhile, increasing numbers of migratory workers helped spread revolutionary ideas picked up in the towns.

In 1902, there was a wave of peasant revolts in Poltava and Kharkov provinces in Ukraine. During the next three years, disorders spread to other provinces. By 1904 there were rural insurrections throughout the country. In 1905 landlords wrote desperately from Penza province:

> Country houses are being burned and looted; agitators go around in army uniforms; there is no protection; few troops; we urgently beg you to place more army units and cossacks at our disposal; we implore help, otherwise, the province will be utterly devastated.[7]

Workers concentrated mainly on economic goals. Urban workers demanded a shorter working day, higher wages, and improved working conditions. They also had political aims, and expressed them by demanding the right to organize unions and strikes, and to enjoy the civil and political rights needed to defend their economic situation. However, most saw political rights as a means to an end, not an end in themselves.

Peasants wanted more land. They also hoped to reduce the burden of taxes, but this was a secondary demand. Both classes also demanded to be treated with dignity. Demands for more respectful treatment from foremen and bosses were particularly common in industrial disputes.[8] However, in a still hierarchical society, this was so Utopian a demand that it appeared only at moments of extreme crisis.

■ Divisions within the Ruling Group

While working-class pressure mounted, divisions opened within Russia's ruling elites. The social changes of the late nineteenth century had

Table 5.1   *Changes in the structure of the ruling group, 1850–1900*

Class	Size 1850 (000s)	(%)	Size 1900 (000s)	(%)	Increase (%)
Nobility	1000	71	1800	55	+ 80
Officials	114	8	500	15	+ 339
Intelligentsia	50	4	400	12	+ 700
Merchantry/'Bourgeoisie'	246	17	600	18	+ 144
Total	c.1410	100	c.3300	100	+ 134

Source: My estimates based on several different sources including
H. Seton-Watson, *The Russian Empire*, 1801–1917 (Oxford University Press, 1967).

altered the balance of power and influence within the ruling elite. While working-class grievances generated new forms of organization, the grievances of the upper classes widened existing divisions.

Table 5.1 gives rough estimates of the numerical changes within the ruling group between 1850 and 1900. The nobility was the only group whose relative weight within the ruling group had declined. Nobles had also lost the political and economic influence they wielded before 1861. Many were not even landowners, but lived off salaries from the government or institutions such as the universities or the *zemstva*. By 1900 the nobility was no longer a well-defined group with a common culture and common attitudes and problems. Its members could no longer act as the natural leaders of the ruling group.

Document 5.4: P. N. Milyukov on the changing role of the gentry [nobility], 1903

What must be mentioned first is the enormous growth of the politically conscious social elements that make public opinion in Russia. The gentry still play a part among these elements, but are by far not the only social medium of public opinion, as they were before the emancipation of the peasants. Members of the ancient gentry are now found in all branches of public life: in the press, in public instruction, in the liberal professions, not to speak of the state service, and particularly the local self-government. But it would be impossible to say what is now the class opinion of the gentry. The fact is that the gentry are no longer a class; they are too much intermingled with other social elements in every position they occupy, including that of landed proprietors. By this ubiquity the gentry have added to the facilities for the general spread of public opinion; but as a class they influence public opinion in an even smaller measure than in former times.[9]

As the nobility declined, the new upper classes, the merchantry, the intelligentsia and the officials grew in numbers, importance and assertiveness.

The number of officials had multiplied four times since 1861. Officials now enjoyed much of the power once wielded by nobles. With the introduction of martial law to many provinces after 1881, they also took over many functions of the *zemstva* and the courts. By 1900 the bureaucracy and army were the real instruments of the tsar's authority. They remained the most loyal and disciplined sections of the ruling elite until 1917.

The numbers and the influence of the merchantry increased dramatically in the late nineteenth century, which meant that the Russian government could no longer ignore them. The rise of figures such as Witte to positions of great influence and the growing interest of the government in banking, railways and industry marked a significant change in both government attitudes and in the nature and attitudes of the tsarist ruling group. Some entrepreneurs, such as Savva Mamontov or Pavel Tretyakov, became great patrons of the arts. At his estate of Abramtsevo, seventy kilometres from Moscow, Mamontov organized and funded a famous colony of artists, painters and musicians. This included some of the best known names in Russian cultural life, such as the painters, Repin, Serov and Levitan, and the singer, Chaliapin. Tretyakov founded one of Moscow's best known collections of Russian painting. Such people gave the rising capitalist class increased respectability and prestige in upper-class society.

The intelligentsia grew fastest of all. A modernizing economy needed experts of many kinds, and many nobles had been forced to take up intellectual wage-labour of various kinds. Many members of the intelligentsia worked closely with the peasantry and knew their problems. They were also poorly paid, which eroded their sense of loyalty to the system, and encouraged their radicalism. As a result, the intelligentsia provided most leaders of the revolutionary movement and of the left-wing of Russian Liberalism. As Milyukov noted, 'The "men of mixed ranks", the *raznochintsy*, have enormously increased in all vocations; and the democratic spirit brought by them, and fostered by the liberal and radical press, is a distinctive feature of the educated class in present-day Russia'.[10]

Slowly and painfully, what had been a traditional aristocracy dominated by landed nobles was becoming a heterogeneous elite of urban and rural entrepreneurs and intellectual wage-workers. The traditional structures of autocracy had less and less to offer Russia's transformed elites.

The alienation of the educated classes was extremely dangerous, for these were the people who were beginning to dominate the press and the educational institutions of the Russian Empire. The low educational standards of the Orthodox Church and the Church's lack of independence, ensured that it could do little to counterbalance the growing ideological influence of the educated classes. Increasingly, the machinery of persuasion was falling into the hands of opponents of autocracy. Their dissatisfaction with the government was expressed in dissident ideologies and the formation of political parties committed to political reform.

Dissident members of Russia's upper classes took up three distinct ideologies in the early twentieth century – liberalism, socialism and nationalism. After 1900, supporters of each ideology formed illegal political parties. Liberals demanded the granting of basic civil and political rights to everyone. Socialists championed the economic demands of the working classes. Nationalists defended the rights of the many non-Russian inhabitants of the Russian Empire.

In the mid-nineteenth century, Liberalism had been an ideology of disgruntled nobles concerned to reduce the powers of the autocracy and its officials (see Chapter 3, p. 85). Since 1864, the *zemstva* had provided the institutional base for this 'gentry' liberalism. Its chief aim had been to create institutions through which forces outside the bureaucracy could shape government policy. Liberal nobles from the Tver *zemstvo* proposed the creation of a national *zemstvo*, or *Duma*, in 1862, and again in 1895. Though they saw this purely as an advisory body, the government regarded the idea as a threat to autocracy. In 1895, Nicholas II dismissed the idea as no more than a 'senseless dream'. Despite these rebuffs, congresses of *zemstvo* leaders began to meet regularly from 1896 under the leadership of D. N. Shipov (1851–1920). These meetings provided a national forum for a moderate liberalism, whose members were willing to co-operate with an autocratic government.

Radical liberalism emerged later. Its first organizational expression was an illegal paper, *Liberation*, established in 1902 in Germany. The paper's founders were the historian, P. N. Milyukov (1859–1943) and an ex-Marxist, P. B. Struve (1870–1944). In January 1904, at a secret meeting in St Petersburg, supporters formed an illegal political party, the 'Union of Liberation'. Milyukov and Struve led the new party, along with the veteran *zemstvo* leader I. I. Petrunkevich (1844–1928). The 'Union of Liberation' demanded a Legislative National Assembly with real legislative power, elected under 'four-tail' suffrage. By this liberals meant a universal, secret, direct ballot, held in equal electoral constituencies. Their intention was to abolish autocracy, though most favoured a constitutional monarchy of some kind. Like all liberal parties, the 'Union of Liberation' hoped to represent all classes and sections of society. It hoped for the support of Russia's working classes, as well as its national minorities. Despite this, its proposals for the vote did not include women.

□   *Document 5.5: The programme of the Union of Liberation*

The first and main aim of the Union of Liberation is the political liberation of Russia. Considering political liberty in even its most minimal form completely incompatible with the absolute character of the Russian monarchy, the union will seek before all else the abolition of autocracy and the establishment in Russia of a constitutional regime.

In determining the concrete forms in which a constitutional regime can be realized in Russia, the Union of Liberation will make all efforts to have the political problem resolved in the spirit of extensive democracy. Above all, it recognizes as fundamentally essential that the principles of universal, equal, secret, and direct elections be made the basis of the political reform.

Putting the political demands in the forefront, the Union of Liberation recognizes as essential the definition of its attitude in principle to the socio-economic problems created by life itself. In the realm of socio-economic policy, the Union of Liberation will follow the same basic principle of democracy, making the direct goal of its activity the defense of the interests of the laboring masses.

In the sphere of national questions, the union recognizes the right of self-determination of different nationalities entering into the composition of the Russian state.[11]

Despite the efforts of the Union of Liberation, in 1905 there remained two distinct strands within Russian Liberalism. There was a moderate strand, dominated by members of the nobility and organized mainly in the *zemstva*. There was also a more radical strand, dominated by members of the intelligentsia, and organized around the Union of Liberation. Radical liberals were concerned with social as well as political issues, above all with the plight of the peasantry. In November and December of 1904, liberals of both kinds agitated for reform. While a large conference of *zemstvo* liberals met, the Union of Liberation organized revolutionary banquets in imitation of those held during the French Revolution of 1848. At these, speakers attacked the government and demanded basic political and constitutional changes.

On their own, the liberals were unable to shake the government. This drove them closer to more radical groups. By 1905 even moderate liberals saw little alternative to revolution. In July 1905 Petrunkevich said of the liberals: 'Till now ... they had hoped for reform from above, but henceforth their only hope was in the people ... We cannot keep the storm in check, but we must at least try to avert too much turmoil'.[12]

After 1900 two major socialist parties emerged. One adopted the Marxist version of Socialism, which saw the proletariat as the main revolutionary class. The other, the Socialist Revolutionary Party, continued the populist tradition of rural Socialism that had first appeared in the 1860s. I will concentrate mainly on Russian Marxism because of the role it was to play later in Russia's history.

Marxism was a particular type of Socialism. Its founders were two Germans: the philosopher, Karl Marx (1818–83) and his lifelong friend Friedrich Engels (1820–95). They first presented their ideas in systematic form in 1848, in the 'Communist Manifesto'. Marx developed his ideas more thoroughly in the three volumes of *Capital*. The first volume appeared in 1867 and was translated into Russian in 1872. Engels published the second and third volumes after Marx's death. In *Capital*, Marx analysed the nature and evolution of the economy of Great Britain, which he regarded as the most advanced and the most typical of modern capitalist economies.

Marx made an immense contribution to the ideology of socialism (see Chapter 3, pp. 91–2 for a general discussion of socialism). He was impatient with the early socialists who spent much of their time describing what socialist society would be like. Marx saw such writings as 'Utopian' fantasies. He believed it was necessary, first, to show that socialism was possible. Only then was socialism worth fighting for. For this reason, Marx spent most of his life analysing existing societies to see if they contained the materials needed to construct socialism. He argued that during most of human history the socialist ideal of a free and egalitarian society had indeed been Utopian. However, the emergence of 'capitalist' societies made socialism a real possibility for the first time in human history, for capitalism created the building bricks of socialism. For this reason, he claimed that his form of socialism was not Utopian but 'scientific'. In Marx's view, socialism would be founded on the achievements of capitalism.

How did capitalism make socialism possible? Marx argued that capitalism created two necessary preconditions for socialism. The first was material abundance. Marx believed there was no point creating a society based on material equality in an environment of poverty. To try to make everyone equal where there was not enough to go around could only mean making everyone poor, and that was bound to cause new, and vicious, forms of class conflict. Yet this had been the situation in all previous societies. This is why he argued in the *Communist Manifesto* that: 'The history of all hitherto existing society is the history of class struggles'. As early as 1846 Marx wrote: 'this development of productive forces ... is an absolutely necessary practical premise because without it want is merely made general, and with destitution the struggle for necessities and all the old filthy business would necessarily be reproduced'.[13] It followed that socialism could only be built in conditions of high productivity and abundant material wealth. Only then would equality mean an equality of wealth rather than of poverty. Marx saw that modern capitalist society created for the first time in history the high levels of productivity necessary if socialism was to be a realistic vision of the future.

Marx argued that capitalism raised productivity because of the existence of two distinct classes. These were the wage-earners, or proletarians, who did not own productive resources; and the capitalists, who did. In other words, capitalism required inequality. It was therefore incompatible with socialism. This meant that though capitalism created the first precondition for socialism (high productivity), the second precondition for socialism would be the overthrow of capitalism. Marx argued that capitalism also created the conditions for its own demise. As capitalism developed the number of wage-earners would increase. Since wage-earners owned no productive property, they would have no reason to support capitalism. Eventually, the proletariat would be powerful enough to overthrow a system that deprived them of control over productive resources. As Marx wrote in the *Communist Manifesto*, 'What the bourgeoisie ... produces, above all, is its own grave-diggers'.

When Marx was developing his ideas in Europe in the 1840s, his vision of the proletariat as a revolutionary class seemed perfectly reasonable. Indeed, most politicians agreed with him. Many wage-earners were peasants who had recently lost their land, or artisans or small property-owners who had had to sell what they owned. Having owned property, they resented a system that had impoverished and degraded them. During the 1848 revolutions such people were, indeed, a dangerous revolutionary force. However, the belief that proletarians would always oppose capitalism has proved to be wrong. The main reason is that modern capitalism has generated such high levels of productivity that it can redistribute material wealth back to its own wage-earners. This is a central feature of the consumer capitalism of the twentieth century. It creates a class of wage-earners which, far from wishing to overthrow capitalism, sees itself as a beneficiary of capitalism. It was first-generation proletarians who had most reason to strike back at the capitalist system that had ruined them. For second- and third-generation proletarians capitalism seemed normal. Many even saw themselves as better-off than the peasants left behind in the countryside.

Marx's failure to predict the political passivity of second and third-generation proletarians had momentous consequences. It explains the failure of his other prediction: that anti-capitalist revolutions would occur in the most developed capitalist countries. On the contrary, most twentieth-century anti-capitalist revolutions occurred in countries where capitalism was in its infancy, and where most proletarians still had links with the countryside. The result, in Russia as elsewhere, was that socialist governments tried to build socialism without the high levels of productivity characteristic of mature capitalism. They tried to build socialism without the material abundance that Marx himself regarded as the basic precondition for a successful socialist society. Paradoxically, the failures of twentieth-century communism have shown the accuracy of Marx's claim that socialism required a foundation of material abundance.

But this was in the future. For Russia's first Marxists, the general message of Marxism was clear. Capitalism itself would create the preconditions for socialism. It would do so by creating high levels of productivity and by raising the number of wage-earners. The task of revolutionaries was to organize the proletariat for the coming revolution.

However, when they tried to draw up a specific plan of action, Russian Marxists faced some complex problems. In the late nineteenth century the main problem was that most Russian intellectuals did not believe Russia would ever be capitalist. Even those who respected Marx argued that his ideas had little relevance for Russia. For this reason, most populist revolutionaries ignored Marx, at least until the 1880s.

The founders of Russian Marxism were revolutionaries who had become disillusioned with the peasant socialism of populism. In 1883, in exile in Switzerland, they founded a Marxist group called 'Emancipation of Labour', which supported the Marxist idea of a socialist revolution led by the urban proletariat. G. V. Plekhanov (1856–1918) emerged as their leading theorist. For a decade, Plekhanov's group had little influence in Russia, as most Russian socialists continued to believe that Russia would bypass capitalism. However, the industrial upsurge of the 1890s made the Marxist approach seem more relevant to Russia, and the 'Emancipation of Labour' group began to attract disciples among a younger generation of revolutionary intellectuals. Among them were Vladimir Ilyich Ulyanov (who was to adopt the underground name of Lenin) and Julius Martov. They spent much of the 1890s trying to prove that Russia was, indeed, becoming a capitalist nation. It was the young Lenin who clinched this argument with a massive volume called *The Development of Capitalism in Russia*, which he wrote in exile in Siberia between 1896 and 1899.

By 1900, few could doubt that Russia was becoming capitalist. However, its capitalism remained primitive. Neither of Marx's two preconditions for socialist revolution existed. Average levels of productivity were extremely low; and Russia's industrial proletariat was small. Under these conditions, what should a Marxist do? At first sight, it might seem that they should support the development of capitalism, and some early Russian Marxists, including the young Lenin, did just that. Politically, though, this was unattractive. How could a party that supported capitalism hope for the support of the working classes that capitalism exploited? Before 1905, no Russian Marxist had an adequate answer to this question.

Meanwhile, Russia's Marxists concentrated on organizational problems. Everyone expected that eventually a Russian Marxist party would lead a revolution. So it made sense to prepare the organizational structures that would provide leadership when the crisis came. Lenin saw more clearly than most that a working-class party would need the leadership skills of radical intellectuals such as Marx or, indeed, Lenin. Russian Marxists also understood that in tsarism they faced a formidable opponent. To survive, revolutionary parties would need a high level of unity and discipline.

In 1900, Plekhanov, Lenin and Martov founded an illegal newspaper, *Iskra* ('The Spark'), and began smuggling it into Russia. The disciplined network of agents they formed provided the organized nucleus for the Russian Social Democratic Party. This held its founding Congress in 1903. (Technically, this was the Party's second Congress, as a first had met in 1898, only to be dispersed by police.) During the 1903 Congress, the party split into two factions, the 'Mensheviks' and 'Bolsheviks'. The split occurred primarily over the degree of discipline and professionalism required of party members. Lenin led the Bolsheviks (or 'Majoritarians'). He opposed amateurism in revolutionary politics and insisted that the party needed a disciplined core of professionals, most of whom would come from the intelligentsia. This was vital if it was to provide clear theoretical leadership and to survive against tsarist police agents with much experience of fighting and infiltrating such organizations. Lenin's organizational ideal was *Narodnaya Volya*, the populist group that had assassinated Alexander II. However, Lenin rejected *Narodnaya Volya's* populist ideals and their tactics of terror. His opponents, the Mensheviks ('Minoritarians') argued for a greater degree of internal democracy within the Party.

We should not exaggerate the differences between Bolsheviks and Mensheviks in 1903. Many grass-roots revolutionaries ignored the differences, and all Marxists saw the need for a disciplined underground party. On the other hand, even Lenin defended the principle of 'democratic centralism' within the party. This meant that all decisions should be taken democratically by the elected Central Committee of the party, but once taken, such decisions became binding on all party members. The early differences were of degree and emphasis, not of kind.

Personal conflicts overlaid these disputes over party organisation. Plekhanov and Martov sided with the Mensheviks in part because they found Lenin too dictatorial. After 1905, new differences appeared. The most important concerned the strategies appropriate in a country lacking the preconditions for a socialist revolution. By 1912, the split had become permanent. I will discuss these later differences within Russian Marxism in Chapter 7.

In 1900, the Socialist Revolutionary Party was formed. This took up the populist ideal of peasant socialism (see Chapter 3). Its most important thinker and leader was Victor Chernov (1873–1952). The new party imitated the organizational and tactical methods of *Narodnaya Volya*. It formed a terrorist wing, which assassinated many prominent officials, including one of the tsar's uncles, Grand Duke Sergei Aleksandrovich, in February 1905. The SRs, as they were known, also conducted revolutionary agitation among the peasantry. In July 1905, they organized an All-Russian Peasant Union.

Nationalism was as dangerous a force for the government as liberalism or socialism. In 1897, Great Russians made up only 45 per cent of the population of the Russian Empire, yet in the late nineteenth century the Russian government had launched a policy of systematic Russification. As early as 1876, it banned the publication of books or plays in Ukrainian, and the teaching of Ukrainian in elementary schools. It even ordered schools to remove Ukrainian language texts from their libraries.[14] Similar laws were passed in other non-Russian areas of the Empire. Russification was especially brutal in Finland between 1898 and 1905, and it produced a particularly violent nationalist reaction. This culminated in the assassination of the Governor-General of Finland, Bobrikov, in 1904. In Ukraine, the Caucasus, Poland, the Baltic and Finland, the government's policies stimulated demands for greater cultural and political autonomy. Everywhere, nationalist movements emerged first amongst the intelligentsia.

■ Military Disaster: The Russo-Japanese War

As so often in the past, military defeat showed the seriousness of the looming crisis. The Russian government continued to regard itself as a major world power, and was determined not to miss out on the imperialist land-grab of the late nineteenth century. Blocked in the Balkans since the Congress of Berlin in 1878, the logical area for Russian expansion seemed to be in the Far East, in northern China and Korea. Indeed, one of the aims of building the trans-Siberian railway was to ease the task of dominating this region.

After its defeat in the Sino-Japanese war of 1894–5, the Chinese government allowed Russia to build a railway across northern China – that is, Manchuria (see Figure 4.2). In 1898 China granted Russia a twenty-five year lease on the Liaotung Peninsula and the right to build a further railway to Port Arthur. Not content with this, the more ambitious members of the Russian government began to consider expansion into Korea. This group gained the support of the tsar. A project for concessions on the Yalu River (the modern border between China and North Korea) brought the Russians into conflict with the Japanese, who regarded Korea as their sphere of interest. The Russians had little interest in negotiations. They knew their position would improve when the trans-Siberian railway was completed and they could transport more troops. For the same reason, the Japanese wanted a quick decision. So, when negotiations broke down, Japanese troops attacked Port Arthur in February 1904. (See Figure 4.2.)

The war that followed was a series of disasters for the ill-prepared Russian navy and army. The Japanese attack on Port Arthur crippled the Russian Pacific fleet. Attempts to break out in February and August only led to further losses. Finally, Port Arthur surrendered in December 1904. Japanese control of the sea allowed them to bring reinforcements more rapidly than the Russians, who relied on the single track of the trans-Siberian railroad. Russian armies suffered defeats on the Yalu River in April, and twice at Mukden, north of Port Arthur, in August 1904 and in February 1905. The stalemate on land was broken at sea. In October 1904 the Russian Baltic fleet set out to relieve Port Arthur. After circling the world, it arrived three months after Port Arthur had surrendered. In February 1905, the waiting Japanese fleet met the Russian ships in the Tsushima Straits, between Japan and Korea, and within a few hours the entire Russian fleet had been destroyed. Japan's victory was a victory for the Meiji strategy of modernization.

In August 1905, peace negotiations opened in Portsmouth, New Hampshire, with Sergei Witte heading the Russian delegation. Three weeks later, the Russian and Japanese delegations signed a treaty under which Russia withdrew altogether from Manchuria.

For Russia the war had been a disaster, militarily and politically. The minister of internal affairs, V. K. Plehve, said early in 1904 to a critic of the war: 'You are not familiar with Russia's internal situation. We need a little, victorious war to stem the tide of revolution'. Defeat, of course, had the opposite effect. Each Japanese victory encouraged new disturbances. Plehve himself was assassinated in July 1904, not long after the defeat on the Yalu River. Further defeats provoked the series of political banquets organized by the Union of Liberation in November and December. The loss of Port Arthur in December 1904 triggered a new wave of demonstrations.

■ Revolution

An industrial dispute at the Putilov metal works in St Petersburg started the new wave of strikes at the beginning of January 1905. Paradoxically, it was a government-sponsored union, the 'Assembly of Factory Workers', that organized the strikes. This was led by a radical priest, Father G. A. Gapon, who soon found himself at the head of the largest strike in

Russia's history. By 8 January, 111 000 workers were on strike in the capital. The next day, Gapon led a crowd of striking workers towards the tsar's Winter Palace in St Petersburg, carrying a petition to the tsar.

☐ *Document 5.6: The working-class petition of 9 January*

We working men of St Petersburg, our wives and children, and our parents, helpless and aged men and women, have come to you, our ruler, in quest of justice and protection ... We have no strength at all, O Sovereign. Our patience is at an end. We are approaching that terrible moment when death is better than the continuance of intolerable sufferings ...

Our first wish was to discuss our needs with our employers, but this was refused to us: we were told that we have no legal right to discuss our conditions ...

Every worker and peasant is at the mercy of your officials, who accept bribes, rob the Treasury and do not care at all for the people's interests. The bureaucracy of the government has ruined the country, involved it in a shameful war and is leading Russia nearer and nearer to utter ruin. We, the Russian workers and people, have no voice at all in the expenditure of the huge sums collected in taxes from the impoverished population. We do not even know how our money is spent. The people are deprived of any right to discuss taxes and their expenditure. The workers have no right to organize their own labour unions for the defence of their own interests.

Is this, O Sovereign, in accordance with the laws of God, by whose grace you reign? And how can we live under such laws? Break down the wall between yourself and your people ... The people must be represented in the control of their country's affairs. Only the people themselves know their own needs. Do not reject their help, accept it, command forthwith that representatives of all classes, groups, professions and trades shall come together. Let capitalists and workers, bureaucrats and priests, doctors and teachers meet together and choose their representatives. Let all be equal and free. And to this end let the election of members to the Constitutional Assembly take place in conditions of universal, secret and equal suffrage.

This is our chief request; upon it all else depends; this is the only balm for our sore wounds; without it our wounds will never heal, and we shall be borne swiftly on to our death.[15]

The St Petersburg police gave the following account of the events that followed.

☐ *Document 5.7: A police account of Bloody Sunday*

Today, at about 10 a.m., workers began to gather at the Narva Gates, in the Vyborg and Petersburg districts, and also on Vasilievsky Island at the premises of the Assembly of Factory Workers, with the aim, as announced by Father Georgy

Gapon, of marching to Palace Square to present a petition to the Emperor. When a crowd of several thousand had assembled in the Narva district, Father Gapon said prayers and then together with the crowd, which had at its head banners and icons stolen from a Narva chapel as well as portraits of Their Majesties, moved off towards the Narva Gates where they were confronted by troops. Despite pleas by local police officers and cavalry charges, the crowd did not disperse but continued to advance ... Two companies then opened fire, killing ten men and wounding twenty ...

A little later about 4000 workers who had come from the Petersburg and Vyborg districts approached the Trinity Bridge: Father Gapon was also with them. A volley was fired into the crowd, killing five and seriously injuring ten ...

Towards 1 p.m. people began to gather in the Alexander Garden, over-flowing out of the garden itself into the adjoining part of Palace Square. The cavalry made a series of charges to disperse the crowd, but as this had no effect a number of volleys were fired into the crowd. The numbers of dead and wounded from these volleys is not known as the crowd carried off the victims.

The crowd then engulfed Nevsky Prospect and refused to disperse: a number of shots were fired, killing sixteen people, including one woman.[16]

Police estimates of the casualties (130 killed and 450 wounded) are far too low. In reality, many hundreds may have died as a result of police fire and the horrifying sabre charges of the Cossack troops. Along with the victims died the traditional popular belief in the tsar as the people's protector. Father Gapon, although a priest and a believer in autocracy, denounced 'Nicholas Romanov' as a traitor to the people. The United States consul in Odessa reported: 'The present ruler has lost absolutely the affection of the Russian people, and whatever the future may have in store for the dynasty, the present tsar will never again be safe in the midst of his people'.[17]

In January and February peasant revolts broke out in Kursk province. Soon they spread to the Volga region and most of the black earth provinces. On 14 June, mutiny broke out on the battleship Potemkin in the Black Sea. Liberal leaders in the *zemstvo* movement and in various professional organisations put forward constitutional demands. In May an alliance of professional associations, the Union of Unions, was formed in Moscow. It elected Milyukov as its chairman. University students went on strike and made university buildings available for public meetings.

Meanwhile, an important new working-class organization had appeared – the Soviet. The Russian word, 'Soviet', means advice or counsel. It was also applied to meetings, such as the peasant commune. Indeed, it was probably the traditions of the commune that inspired the first Soviet. This was a spontaneous strike committee that emerged in May 1905 in the textile town of Ivanovo, east of Moscow. The committee's members were elected from all workers in the town, just as communes consisted of all heads of households in the villages. Similar institutions soon appeared in other towns. By far the most important met in St Petersburg on 14 October, and rapidly assumed leadership of Soviets throughout the Empire. A young Marxist, Leon Trotsky (1879–1940), became its leader. Trotsky was independent of both Menshevik and Bolshevik factions and one of the revolution's most inspiring public speakers.

In the face of opposition from most sections of Russian society, the government agreed in August to convene an elected, but purely consultative, national assembly. In January this might have worked. By August it was not enough. Printing workers went on strike on 19 September and workers in both capitals soon followed them. On 7 October railway workers went on strike, and within a few days Russia was facing the first general strike in its history. The general strike came under the direction of the St Petersburg Soviet, which acquired more popular support than any of the socialist parties. The strike soon gained the support of most strands of the opposition movement. This rare display of united opposition finally brought the government to its knees.

Of all classes it was the industrial working class that had the most direct impact through the novel weapon of the general strike. In October the strike brought communications of all kinds to a standstill, paralysing the government. On his return from the United States in October, Witte found that even contact with the tsar's palace at Peterhof was possible only by boat.[18]

☐ *Document 5.8: The general strike in Kharkov*

In Kharkov, in the Ukraine, work stopped everywhere: on the railways, in all factories, workshops, in shops of all types, in the University, in all schools, in all administrative offices, even the telegraph offices … the whole population was on the streets, either as sightseers or as demonstrators. From the evening, people began to ransack arms stores and to smash the windows of the large stores and conservative journals. On the 24th, students directed by lawyers, doctors and teachers and helped by workmen and Jews, seized the district neighbouring the University and set up ten barricades made of heavy oak planks, telegraph and telephone poles, electric light standards and large paving stones. The rioters seized the law courts where the archives were and threw them into the streets.

All the police could do was organize a poor demonstration at one rouble a head, with a portrait of the emperor and the national flag. This demonstration failed pitifully before the student's revolvers – they tore the tsar's portrait and the flags to shreds.[19]

Most dangerous of all for the government, even the bureaucracy and army cracked. In the middle of October, the staff of central government institutions, including the Treasury and all the Ministries, went on strike.

Employees of the State Bank even called for a Constituent Assembly. The Russo-Japanese war had drained the army in European Russia of its better trained troops and officers, leaving behind discontented reservists and inexperienced officers to deal with the turmoil in European Russia. Beginning with the mutiny on the battleship *Potemkin* there were ten mutinies in the army and navy in June and July.[20] Nevertheless, discipline held in most units and soldiers continued to suppress demonstrations. The real military problem in October was that there were too few soldiers both to repress disorders and run essential services such as the railways.

Under these conditions, the repressive apparatus was useless. It was impossible to issue orders to troops or to begin transporting troops back from Manchuria. The last time government had broken down like this had been during the Time of Troubles three centuries before.

■ Surviving the Revolution, 1905 to 1906

In October 1905 the government was near to collapse; a year later, it was firmly in control once again. How did it recover its balance?

As early as 1902, the government had begun a large-scale fiscal retreat to relieve the economic pressure on the peasantry. It abolished the collective responsibility of commune members for each other's tax payments; it cancelled all arrears of taxation; and it abolished corporal punishment. Most important of all, a law of November 1905 cancelled remaining redemption payments as of 1 January 1907. These laws dismantled the structures of rural life created in 1861 and granted the peasantry full ownership of the land they had used since then. They reduced the fiscal pressure on the peasantry, but they also weakened the government financially. However, this had little immediate effect on the mood either in the towns or in the countryside.

Witte showed Nicholas how to deal with the immediate political crisis. In the middle of October he persuaded the reluctant tsar to concede the constitutional and political demands of Russian liberalism, which had become by then the demands of most sections of Russian society. On 17 October the tsar issued what is known as the 'October Manifesto'. It granted basic civil liberties. It also promised to create a State *Duma* (or parliament), elected by universal male suffrage and capable of sharing in the law-making process. The Manifesto marked the formal end of autocratic government, as the tsar would now have to share his law-making powers. The government issued the details of the new constitutional system over several months and published them together in the Fundamental Laws of April 1906. The first *Duma* met in May 1906.

The October crisis confirmed what the police chief, Zubatov, had argued some years before: to survive, the autocracy had to divide its opponents. The October Manifesto broke the revolutionary coalition of October 1905. The right-wing of Russian liberalism immediately accepted the Manifesto as a satisfactory end to the revolution. On 4 December moderate liberals formed a new liberal party, the Union of 17 October (or 'Octobrist' Party), and Alexander Guchkov became their leader. Left-wing liberals had already organized the Constitutional Democratic Party (or *Kadets*) at a founding Congress held between 12 and 18 October. The Kadets, led by Milyukov and Petrunkevich, denounced the October Manifesto, as they sought an elected constitutional assembly that would write a new constitution. However, they were willing to end revolutionary activity and accept the new system as a starting point for reform.

Though the October Manifesto ended the upper-class revolution, the working-class revolution gained momentum after October. The Manifesto satisfied few working-class demands, and the St Petersburg Soviet saw little reason to end the General Strike. Peasants interpreted the Manifesto as permission to seize the gentry land they had long believed was theirs by right. So peasant disorders rose to a peak in November and December.[21]

Most dangerous of all for the government, discipline collapsed within the army. Between 15 October and the end of the year, there were at least 211 mutinies, affecting one-third of all military units in European Russia. On the trans-Siberian railroad mutinies of returning troops prevented the return of more disciplined troops from the Far East until 1906. The breakdown of military discipline was a response to the apparent collapse of authority in October. Soldiers mutinied only when they believed that the existing authorities had already collapsed. Like peasants (which is what most of them were), many soldiers interpreted the October Manifesto as permission to ignore authority structures, even within the army.[22]

One of the first, and most violent, of these mutinies occurred in late October at the Kronstadt naval base outside St Petersburg. In the chaos of the mutiny, twenty-six men were killed, and 107 were wounded. Three days later, in the Far East, mutinous troops burned much of the port city of Vladivostok.[23] However, most mutinies were not violent. Instead, troops disobeyed orders and presented their officers with petitions demanding improvements in their conditions. Mutineers usually acted with the unanimity traditional in the peasant commune. Either the entire unit went out or no one went out. Like peasants, too, many mutinous units proclaimed their loyalty to the tsar who they believed had liberated them. In late November garrison mutinies deprived the government of control in ten of the Empire's largest nineteen cities, including Moscow. As November turned into December, the regime's situation was truly desperate: it had lost control over the peasantry, it was losing control over the urban garrisons and therefore over the cities, and the Soviets were operating with near impunity. Mutinous reserves clogged the line through Siberia, many of the Siberian garrisons had mutinied and given revolutionaries the opportunity to seize effective power, and the field army was trapped in Manchuria.[24]

The government's one consolation was that the divisions within the revolutionary coalition were now clear. In October, many employers had supported the general strike and some had even paid their workers half wages. In November, when the same workers struck for the eight-hour day, their employers locked them out. The Kadet leader Milyukov called the November strikes a 'crime against the revolution'.

In December, emboldened by these divisions, the government regained its nerve. Its decisive actions in early December broke the mutinies within the army. On 3 December, the government arrested all 260 members of the St Petersburg Soviet. Between 9 and 20 December, it successfully used troops who only a few days before had been in a state of mutiny to suppress a Bolshevik-led insurrection in Moscow with great bloodshed. Government promises of better conditions may have eased some of the soldiers' grievances, while civilian attacks on soldiers angered them. Similar events occurred in several large cities. News that the old order was back in charge brought mutinous troops to heel.

Liberals made only mild protests at the crushing of working-class strikes and army mutinies. The reappearance of the traditional divisions between Russia's educated elite and its urban and rural working classes now gave the government valuable room for manoeuvre.

Early in 1906, the reimposition of discipline within the army, the return of troops from Manchuria, and the negotiation of a French loan of 2250 million francs by Witte on 3 April, further improved the government's situation. The meeting of the first *Duma*, from 27 April to 8 July, concentrated the minds of Russia's educated elite on constitutional rather than revolutionary activities. With a more secure military and financial position and the qualified support of much of Russia's upper classes, the government could move on to the offensive. However, before it could do that, it had to endure one more serious crisis in the summer of 1906.

The opening ceremonies of the *Duma* in the Winter Palace highlighted the divisions within Russian society, as the minister of finance, Kokovtsov, noted.

☐ *Document 5.9: The opening of the* Duma, *26 April 1906*

St George's Hall, the throne room, presented a queer spectacle at this moment, and I believe its walls had never before witnessed such a scene. The entire right side of the room was filled with uniformed people, members of the State Council and, further on, the tsar's retinue. The left side was crowded with the members of the *Duma*, a small number of whom had appeared in full dress, while the overwhelming majority, occupying the first places near the throne, were dressed as if intentionally in workers' blouses and cotton shirts, and behind them was a crowd of peasants in the most varied costumes, some in national dress, and a multitude of representatives of the clergy. The first place among these representatives of the people was occupied by a man of tall stature, dressed in a worker's blouse and high, oiled boots, who examined the throne and those about it with a derisive and insolent air. It was the famous F. M. Onipko, who later won great renown by his bold statements in the first *Duma* ... While the tsar read his speech addressed to the newly elected members of the *Duma*, I could not take my eyes off Onipko, so much contempt and hate did his insolent face show.[25]

In 1906, there were at least 200 mutinies, affecting more than 20 per cent of army units. Most occurred between April and July, while the *Duma* was in session.[26] Peasant disturbances increased at the same time. Both movements were inspired by the debates over land in the *Duma*, and by what peasants and soldiers took to be the *Duma*'s support for a radical programme of land redistribution. In June, the police reported from Voronezh province that: '[soldiers] are beginning to reason that they are all peasants and shouldn't go against their own, they are talking about the possibility of disobeying orders, about refusing to fire. Moreover, the enlisted men are deeply interested in the debates in the *Duma* and throw themselves upon newspapers that come into their hands, especially newspapers of an extreme tendency'.[27] The following 'instruction' to the peasant Trudovik party expresses well the demands of both peasants and soldiers.

☐ *Document 5.10: Instruction to the Trudovik party from an unidentified regiment of soldiers*

We soldier peasants salute the Trudovick group [in the *Duma*] for its determined action. We will support it in the moment of need if necessary, if it demands all land in communal tenure without redemption, and all liberty. In our view, the land is God's, the land should be free, no one should have the right to buy, sell or mortgage it; the right to buy is fine for the rich, but for the poor it is a very, very bad right ... We soldiers are poor, we have no money to buy land when we return home from service, and every peasant needs land desperately ... The land is God's, the land is no one's, the land is free – and on this, God's free land, should toil God's free workers, not hired laborers for the gentry and *kulaks*. These words pleased us very much, we soldiers even learned them by heart. Deputies, if you will demand this then we, for our part, will lay down our lives to support these demands. Further, we most humbly ask your excellencies, respected deputies, immediately to demand of the authorities that they no longer persecute us for reading newspapers – are we really not men, are we little children that they won't let us know anything ...[28]

While the army remained unreliable, the government had little hope of suppressing peasant revolts, or containing any new waves of insurrection in the towns. Paradoxically, the military organizations of the revolutionary parties did most to restrain mutineers, for they were convinced that the time was not yet right for a general insurrection. The crisis came to a head on 9 July, when the government dissolved the first *Duma*. Two hundred deputies crossed the border to the Finnish town of Vyborg and issued a manifesto calling for passive resistance and a tax strike. This was an extremely dangerous moment for the government, as dangerous as the crises of October and November 1905. As in October 1905, representatives of Russia's educated elite were once again supporting revolutionary activity.

However, there was little response to the Vyborg manifesto. There was a mutiny amongst troops in Kronstadt and Helsinki, and an attempt at a general strike in St Petersburg later in July. However, reluctant and confused leadership ensured that the actions of the government's opponents lacked co-ordination. Most revolutionary parties believed the time was not right for a general uprising, so they restrained their supporters in the towns and in the army. Once the critical moment had passed, soldiers understood there was no alternative but to obey. This transformed them once more into reliable instruments of repression.

The mopping-up of rural insurrections continued throughout the rest of 1906 and into 1907. The government tried oppositionists in courts martial and made free use of the hangman's noose, known as 'Stolypin's necktie' after Nicholas' new prime minister. Between 1905 and 1909, the government executed 2390 people on charges of terrorism, while 2691 died at the hands of terrorists.[29]

The crisis of 1905 showed that the government was extremely vulnerable. It had survived because of the cultural and economic gulf between Russia's educated elites and the mass of rural and urban working people. However, as long as Russia's upper classes remained discontented with the existing political system, there remained the possibility that, in a moment of crisis, they might reluctantly support a working-class insurrection. Meanwhile, the smouldering discontents of urban workers and land-hungry peasants ensured that there was plenty of inflammable material in Russian society. The crisis of 1905–6 showed that if working-class and upper-class dissidents could unify, even temporarily, that might be sufficient to break the discipline of an army consisting mainly of peasants and workers. If the army's discipline broke, the government's situation would be critical.

Yet there is another side to this question. The government's recovery after the crisis of 1905 also suggested remarkable resiliency. The crisis showed that there were many powerful groups, particularly among Russia's educated elites, who were willing and able to back a forward-looking government if it offered them some role in government. Bankers, entrepreneurs, landowners and professionals had little to gain from revolution, and much to gain from political stability. In addition, the economic revival that began from 1907 showed that the rapid economic growth of the late nineteenth century was no fluke. Indeed, the social and economic changes that caused the 1905 revolution were also signs of vigorous modernisation. Though the stresses of modernization would remain acute, there was every reason to think that a competent government would be able to cope with them and preside over a successful transition to some form of mature capitalist society. The question was: could Nicholas provide the skilful leadership Russia needed?

■ Summary

By the early twentieth century, social and economic change had transformed Russia's traditional social structure. This, in turn, undermined the traditional power base of the autocracy. Land hunger generated discontent amongst a half-proletarianized peasantry, while poor working conditions in the towns made Russia's tiny urban proletariat exceptionally militant. While the influence of the government's traditional supporters amongst the nobility declined, that of newer elite groups such as the intelligentsia and merchantry increased. The government's refusal to grant merchants and intellectuals some role in government forced them into opposition, while the loyalty of the nobility was undermined by their declining wealth and influence.

Between 1900 and 1905, an economic slump, endemic conflict in the countryside and the towns, the emergence of illegal opposition movements, and an unsuccessful foreign war, combined to generate a serious crisis. In 1905, the government's inept handling of the crisis forced groups that had little in common with each other into a temporary anti-autocratic alliance. In October 1905, a general strike paralysed the government. On the advice of Sergei Witte, Nicholas II defused the crisis by granting some basic civil and political rights, and agreeing to the creation of an elected legislative assembly, the *Duma*. These concessions split the revolutionary coalition, and by the middle of 1906 the government was once more firmly back in charge. However, as the revolutionary tide ebbed, Nicholas II showed that he was still unwilling to learn the lessons of the crisis he had survived. His attempts to minimize the concessions he had granted, and to preserve what he could of the traditional structures of autocracy, made it more and more difficult to rebuild support for the government in a rapidly changing society.

☐ Further Reading

The standard history of the 1905 revolution is now Ascher, *The Revolution of 1905*. The best study of the army's role is Bushnell, *Mutiny and Repression*. F. S. Zuckerman, *The Tsarist Secret Police in Russian Society, 1880–1917* is a recent study of the police. There are very good sections on the social history of different classes in Andrle, *Social History of Twentieth Century Russia*. R. McNeal (ed.) *Russia in Transition*, contains a useful collection of documents and readings, while M. McCauley, *Octobrists to Bolsheviks*, contains documents. Kochan, *Russia in Revolution*, is a vivid general study of the revolutionary era. There are also general surveys of the period in Rogger, *Russia in the Age of Modernisation*, and Seton-Watson, *The Russian Empire*.

☐ Notes

1. V. I. Lenin, *The Development of Capitalism in Russia* (Moscow: Progress Publishers, 1956; first pub. 1899) p. 506.
2. R. C. Tucker (ed.), *The Marx–Engels Reader* (New York: Norton, 1972) pp. 342–3.
3. J. Bushnell, *Mutiny amid Repression: Russian Soldiers in the Revolution of 1905–1906* (Bloomington: Indiana University Press, 1985) pp. 26–7.
4. Cited in M. Ferro, *Nicholas II The Last of the Tsars* (Harmondsworth: Penguin Books, 1990) p. 78.
5. L. Kochan, *Russia in Revolution 1890–1918* (London: Granada, 1966) p. 47.
6. Ibid., pp. 51–2.
7. D. Floyd, *Russia in Revolt: 1905* (London: Macdonald, 1969) p. 79.
8. V. Andrle, *A Social History of Twentieth Century Russia* (London and New York: Edward Arnold) pp. 103–4, 107.
9. T. Riha (ed.), *Readings in Russian Civilization*, vol. 2 (University of Chicago Press, 1964) p. 425.
10. Ibid., p. 425.
11. G. Vernadsky *et al.* (eds), *A Source Book for Russian History from Early Times to 1917*, 3 vols (New Haven, Conn.: Yale University Press, 1972) vol. 2, p. 425.
12. Kochan, *Russia in Revolution*, p. 99.
13. 'The German Ideology', cited from Robert C. Tucker, *The Marx–Engels Reader* (New York: Norton, 1972) p. 125. The weak phrase 'all the old filthy business', is a prudish translation of Marx's more forthright 'die ganze alte Scheiße'.
14. O. Subtelny, *Ukraine: A History* (University of Toronto Press, 1988) p. 283.
15. Kochan, *Russia in Revolution*, p. 99.
16. M. McCauley, *Octobrists to Bolsheviks: Imperial Russia 1905–1917* (London: Edward Arnold, 1984) pp. 12–13.

17. Kochan, *Russia in Revolution*, p. 92.
18. Ibid., p. 103.
19. Ibid., pp. 103–4.
20. Bushnell, *Mutiny amid Repression*, pp. 55–6, 68.
21. Ibid., p. 75.
22. Ibid., pp. 76–7, 81.
23. Ibid., p. 85.
24. Ibid., p. 109.
25 Cited from Ferro, *Nicholas II*, p. 109.
26. Bushnell, *Mutiny amid Repression*, p. 172.
27. Ibid., p. 176.
28. Ibid., p. 180.
29. Vernadsky, *Source Book*, vol. 3, p. 750.

■ *Chapter 6* ■

The Final Decade of Tsarist Rule and the February Revolution

The survival of the tsarist government was not just a matter of concern for the royal family. In different ways, it would affect everyone in the Russian Empire. In the past, the tsarist autocracy had provided the linchpin for the ruling group that dominated the empire. It had held together the empire's diverse elites, giving them the unity and discipline needed to control the largest land empire on earth. However, by 1900 social and economic changes had so transformed Russian society that the autocracy could no longer perform its traditional role. Its weakness deprived the empire's elites of the unity needed to maintain their power during a period of great instability. Without a government capable of uniting them into a cohesive ruling group, many in the elite believed they faced a period of anarchy and chaos as terrible as the 'Time of Troubles' in the early seventeenth century. They believed with some justice that a breakdown on this scale would threaten all classes of society.

What prospects were there of maintaining stable government despite the tensions of modernization? To survive, a government would have to deal with some of the grievances of a growing working class. It would also have to provide a focus for the diverse and changing interests of an emerging capitalist society. It would have to satisfy the interests and defend the privileges of the rising entrepreneurial and professional classes as well as those of a declining landed aristocracy. Could the tsarist government have done this?

There is every reason to think that it could. The traditional monarchy of Meiji Japan had managed, during a few decades in the late nineteenth century, to transform itself into the government of a rising entrepreneurial class without alienating the remnants of the traditional aristocracy or provoking an explosion of working-class discontent. Though transformed, it had survived. Why should Russia's government not have undergone a similar transformation? The trouble was that these were complex political manoeuvres requiring great political skill and flexibility, and the Russian government lacked both qualities. Its autocratic methods deprived it of the support and advice of many intelligent and perceptive members of the rising intelligentsia and entrepreneurial classes. And Nicholas himself was blind to the problems facing his government. In transforming the basis of its power, the government would have to transform itself, for the main demand of the new elites after 1905 was for greater participation in government. This meant abandoning autocracy in favour of a constitutional monarchy. Yet Nicholas believed his main duty was to preserve the autocratic powers granted to him by God, and pass them on, intact, to his son. He rejected all thought of building coalitions through concessions.

The decade from 1907 to 1917 offered the tsarist government a last chance to avoid revolution.

■ The Stolypin Era: 1906 to 1914

Some of Nicholas' ministers saw the situation more clearly than he did and tried hard to persuade him of the need for reform. Most promising of all was the strategy proposed by P. A. Stolypin, his prime minister from July 1906. Though Stolypin was assassinated in 1911, his policies dominated the era between the 1905 revolution and the outbreak of war in 1914. His strategy had three main elements. He tried to regain the support of Russia's changing elites by taking the *Duma* seriously; he tried to build support amongst peasants through a land reform that would satisfy the more enterprising peasants without alienating the landed nobility; and he repressed any remaining discontent by force. Stolypin's main task was to sell this strategy to both Nicholas and the majority in the *Duma*.

The attempt to construct a workable constitutional system did not get off to a good start. When drawing up the Fundamental Laws early in 1906, Nicholas II did all he could to limit the powers of the *Duma*. The electoral system discriminated in favour of landlords and peasants and against urban workers by setting up separate constituencies (or 'curia') for each class. The new constitution created an upper house, the State Council, many of whose members were to be nominated by the government. Ministers were to remain responsible solely to the emperor. The *Duma* had the power to reject only parts of the state budget. Finally, Nicholas insisted on referring to his own authority as 'autocratic', though he agreed to drop the word 'unlimited' from the traditional formula describing the monarch's power. This now read: 'Supreme autocratic power belongs to the emperor of all Russia' (article 4). The ministerial discussions in April, that preceded this decision, show clearly how little Nicholas understood his situation.

◻ *Document 6.1: Nicholas' views on autocracy and the October Manifesto*

I am filled with doubt. Have I the right, before my ancestors, to alter the limits of the powers they bequeathed to me? This inner conflict still troubles me and I have yet to reach a decision. It would have been easier for me to make up my mind a month ago ... but since then I have received heaps of telegrams, letters and petitions from all parts of Russia and from persons belonging to all classes of society. They express their loyalty to me and, while thanking me for the October Manifesto, ask that I do not limit my powers. They want the Manifesto and preservation of the rights granted to my subjects, but are against any further step being taken which would limit my own powers. They desire that I remain autocrat of All Russia.

I am, believe me, sincere when I tell you that if I were convinced that Russia wanted me to abdicate my autocratic powers, I would do that, for the country's good. But I am not convinced that this is so, and I do not believe that there is need to alter the nature of my supreme power ... It is dangerous to change the way that power is formulated. I know, too, that if no change is made, this may give rise to agitation, to attacks ... But where will these attacks come from? From so-called educated people, from the proletariat, from the Third Estate? Actually, I feel that eighty per cent of the people are with me.[1]

Finally, article 87 tempted the government to rule by decree when the *Duma* was not in session.

◻ *Document 6.2: Article 87 of the 'Fundamental Laws'*

While the *Duma* is not in session, if extraordinary circumstances demand a measure requiring legislative sanction, the Council of Ministers shall submit the matter directly to the emperor. Such a measure, however, may not introduce any changes into the Fundamental State Laws, the establishing acts of the State Council or the State *Duma*, or the laws governing elections to the Council or the *Duma*. Such a measure becomes inoperative if the appropriate minister or chief administrator of a separate department does not introduce in the State *Duma* a legislative bill corresponding to the adopted measure within the first two months of the next *Duma* session, or if it is rejected by the State *Duma* or the State Council.[2]

The first *Duma* met on 27 April. Socialist parties, except for the Mensheviks, boycotted the elections. This ensured a Kadet majority. But even the Kadets were in a radical mood. Their programme, which most *Duma* members supported, demanded changes to the constitution and a radical land reform. The government refused to discuss these demands, though it did consider appointing some Kadet leaders as ministers. When negotiations broke down, the government dissolved the *Duma* on 9 July.

Once it had survived the immediate crisis caused by the dissolution of the *Duma*, the government was firmly back in the saddle. On the day the *Duma* was dissolved, the tsar appointed P. A. Stolypin (1862–1911) as chairman of the Council of Ministers. The second *Duma* met in February 1907. It was even more radical than the first, because the Social Democrats, who had boycotted the first *Duma*, sent delegates to the second. Stolypin dismissed the second *Duma* on 3 June 1907.

On the same day, the government used article 87 to issue a new electoral law, which favoured Russia's traditional classes, the landed nobility and the peasantry. Technically, the government had breached the Fundamental Laws which forbade any tampering with the electoral system without the consent of the *Duma* and the State Council. But there were few protests, and Stolypin's '*coup d'état*' succeeded in its political aims. Under the new law, it took 230 landowners to elect a single deputy; 1000 wealthy business people; 15 000 lower-middle-class electors; 60 000 peasants; and 125 000 urban workers. Here was a clear indication of the government's conservative outlook, even under Stolypin. Though willing to court the emerging business elite, it still found it easiest to work with its traditional supporters, the landed nobility.

The law succeeded in its immediate aim. The third *Duma*, which met in November 1907, was dominated by the moderates in the Octobrist party. For the first time the government found itself dealing with an assembly willing to support some of its legislation. For three or four years it looked as if the *Duma* would hold together a political alliance between the government and the nobles, officials and capitalists who supported the Octobrist Party. However, by 1911, even the Octobrists found the government of Nicholas too reactionary for their tastes. The parliamentary alliance broke down and the Octobrists split into separate factions. In September 1911 Stolypin was assassinated, probably by a police agent. His death deprived the government of its last clear-sighted politician.

From then on the autocracy had as little support amongst Russia's upper classes as it had in 1905. Enthusiastic supporters of autocracy could be found only on the far right of Russian politics, among proto-Fascist, anti-Semitic organisations such as the Black Hundreds, or 'Union of the Russian People', first formed in 1905. By refusing to take the *Duma* seriously, the government had lost the support not merely of the new upper classes of intellectuals and entrepreneurs, but also of its more traditional supporters amongst the landed nobility. It had also deprived itself of their advice and expertise. Now the *Duma* could do little more than parade the divisions within Russia's upper classes.

Peasant insurrections had continued in spite of the abolition of redemption dues from January 1907. Clearly, more had to be done to solve the problem of rural discontent. In 1905 even the Kadets argued for the redistribution of landlords' land to land-hungry peasants. This seemed reasonable enough. As Lenin pointed out, the 30 000 largest landowners in Russia each held enough land to support 330 average peasant households. In 1905 even some big landowners were prepared to accept that the compulsory redistribution of some gentry land was the only way of salvaging something from the wreck. D. F. Trepov, the minister of internal affairs, remarked to Witte: 'I am myself a landowner and shall only be too pleased to give away half of my land for nothing as I feel certain that it is the only way of saving the other half for myself'.[3] However, by 1906 landlords were regaining their confidence in the government and a wholesale redistribution of land seemed an unnecessary sacrifice.

Stolypin adopted an alternative approach to reform that had first been proposed in 1902. Its main attraction was that it did not require the surrender of landlords' land. This meant that it might gain the support of the Octobrist party. Stolypin proposed abandoning the commune and allowing peasants to own their land individually. This would introduce private property into the Russian village.

Though Stolypin's proposal reversed the government's policy on the commune, officials supported it because most had already decided that the commune was economically inefficient and politically dangerous. As one noble put it, the commune had become a 'seed-bed of socialist ideas'.[4]

Stolypin hoped the introduction of private property would create a class of prosperous peasant farmers. These would support the government to protect their own property rights, creating a new and conservative class of small landowners among the traditionally monarchist peasants. The government also hoped the reform would raise agricultural productivity by rewarding more enterprising peasants. As in his approach to constitutional reform, Stolypin showed his conservatism by courting the traditional class, the peasantry, rather than the rising class of wage-earners.

Stolypin introduced the agrarian reform under article 87, in November 1906. The decree made three changes. First, it abolished collective ownership within the family by declaring that land belonged to the head of each household. As most heads of households were male, this gave legal sanction to rural traditions of male control over land. Second, the decree permitted heads of households to demand that their land be separated from the commune's holdings. This turned the land into private, rather than communal, property. Third, the decree allowed the new owner to demand that the various strips of land be consolidated into a single block to form a separate farm or *khutor*. The government also set up special 'land settlement commissions', which helped negotiate and implement the complex rearrangements of landholdings envisaged in the new laws. Though they came into effect in late 1906, Stolypin's decrees acquired full legal force only when passed by the *Duma* in 1910. Joined with these measures were others designed to help migration to Siberia and to raise the productivity of peasant agriculture.

How successful was the reform? It was skilful enough in its intentions to persuade Lenin (who was abroad again after returning briefly in 1905) that it might work. He saw, as did Stolypin, that a class of wealthy and independent peasants might provide powerful support for a strong, conservative government, as it had in France since the French Revolution. However, the process was too slow to save the government. By 1915, about 30 per cent of all peasant households had requested individual ownership of the land, and 22 per cent had received it. Of these, about 60 per cent (or 10 per cent of all households) took the more difficult and costly step of consolidating their land and setting up separate farms. The number of exits declined rapidly after 1910, which suggests that the number would not have increased much even if there had been a generation of peace. Besides, most of these separate farms appeared in the western and southern provinces where individual land-holding was already familiar to the peasants. The reforms had least effect in the overcrowded Central Producer Region, where land shortage and peasant discontent were at their worst. In these areas, the commune provided considerable protection to poorer peasants, and most households clung to it desperately.

The agrarian reform did not create the politically conservative rural society that Stolypin had hoped for, as the renewed peasant insurrections of 1917 proved. Nor had the constitutional reform helped to bridge the gap between the government and Russia's rapidly changing educated elites. As a result, the government remained as isolated as in 1905. Its power rested now on the bureaucracy and the army alone, for the support it could expect from other groups, even from its traditional supporters, was uncertain and hesitant. This was a narrow base for a government about to lead its country into the first great war of modern times.

On the other hand, the government still held some strong cards. Though the army and bureaucracy had cracked under pressure in 1905, both remained powerful and responsive instruments of the royal will. Most important of all, there remained a deep cultural and economic gulf between Russia's educated classes and the bulk of the working population. This made it difficult to organize combined action by all sections of Russia's population. These divisions showed up clearly after the issuing of the October Manifesto and again in the middle of 1906. On both occasions, upper-class revolutionaries tried to restrain working-class insurrections which they feared they could not control.

These deep class divisions offered the government opportunities to survive through a policy of divide and rule. This is why the most dangerous aspect of the government's position was the political naïvety of the tsar. He simply did not see how isolated his government was. He saw no need to balance repression with concessions. In 1909, a French diplomat reported that: 'He [the tsar] is certain that the rural population, the owners of land, the nobility and the army remain loyal to the tsar; the revolutionary elements are composed above all of Jews, students, of landless peasants and of some workers'.[5] Nicholas's assessment deprived him of any incentive to try to consolidate his power basis. It also explained his failure to back perceptive reformers like Stolypin.

■ The Tsarist Government in 1914

On the eve of war, the most ominous sign for the government was the revival of popular discontent between 1912 and 1914. The revival mainly affected the urban population. In his *History of the Russian Revolution*, Leon Trotsky used estimates of the number of strikers, based on police records, as a measure of the political temperature of Russia's workers. These show clearly the change in mood between 1912 and 1914 (see Table 6.1).

Early in 1912, 270 miners died when police and troops suppressed strikes in the Lena goldfields in Siberia. Like the Bloody Sunday massacre of 1905, this provoked sympathy strikes among workers and then among students. Amongst the young workers radicalized by the

Table 6.1   *Trotsky on the numbers striking for political reasons, 1903–17*

Year	No. of strikers (000s)	Year	No. of strikers (000s)
1903*	87	1911	8
1904*	25	1912	550
1905	1843	1913	502
1906	651	1914	1059 (first half of year)
1907	540	1915	156
1908	93	1916	310
1909	8	1917	575 (Jan.–Feb.)
1910	4		

Note:
* Figures for both economic and political strikes

Source: L. Trotsky, *The History of The Russian Revolution* (London: Sphere Books, 1967) vol. 1, p. 49.

crisis was the 18-year-old Nikita Khrushchev, who was working at a mine in the Donbass town of Yuzovka. However, the proletariat was now larger than in 1905, and the strikers were more radical. One sign of their radicalism was the rise in Bolshevik party membership after the post-revolutionary lull, for the Bolsheviks now offered the most radical of all revolutionary programmes. Many new recruits to the party were peasants who had only recently had to sell their land. So it is likely that the revival of working-class discontent reflected in part the anger of these first-generation proletarians. This suggests that the Stolypin reforms, far from solving the problems of discontented peasants, may have driven them to the towns. Here, they posed a greater political threat than in the villages.

In July 1914 a general strike began in the capital. Barricades went up in some working-class districts, and there were violent clashes between workers and police. Militant young workers fresh from the countryside provided energetic leadership and resisted the efforts of socialist parties to call off the strike.

As in 1905, some members of the upper classes supported the strike movement in the hope that it might force the government to take the *Duma* more seriously. A. I. Konovalov, a Moscow capitalist and deputy for the newly formed Progressive or Business Party, even proposed funding the Bolshevik Party to increase pressure on the government. But he was not typical.

This near-revolution collapsed only on the outbreak of war. We cannot know if the crisis could have turned into a full-scale revolution. It showed that many of the discontents of 1905 were still alive. Yet, in contrast to the 1905 crisis, the peasantry remained passive and the army remained loyal. Most important of all, despite the discontents of liberal *Duma* deputies, the class alliance of 1905 between workers and liberal intelligentsia did not reappear.

> No demonstrations, no public meetings, no collective petitions – no expressions of solidarity even barely comparable to those that Bloody Sunday had evoked were now aroused. Thus, in the last analysis, the most important source of the political impotence revealed by the Petersburg strike was precisely the one that made for its 'monstrous' revolutionary explosiveness: the sense of isolation, of psychological distance, that separated the Petersburg workers from educated, privileged society.[6]

Despite everything, traditions of loyalty to Tsarism survived among many sections of the population. These resurfaced immediately after the declaration of war, on 20 July 1914. In the first flush of patriotic enthusiasm, the capital was renamed Petrograd instead of the Germanic 'St Petersburg'. In the *Duma*, criticism of the government ceased. So did the demonstrations and strikes in the capital. Patriotic manifestations took their place. The Octobrist deputy M. V. Rodzianko (1859–1924) described the patriotic demonstrations outside the Winter Palace where, a mere nine years before, the Bloody Sunday massacre had taken place.

☐   *Document 6.3: Rodzianko on the declaration of war*

On the day of the manifesto of war with Germany a great crowd gathered before the Winter Palace. After a prayer for the granting of victory, the tsar spoke a few words, ending with the solemn promise not to end the war while the enemy still occupied one inch of Russian soil. A loud 'hurrah' filled the palace and was taken up by an answering echo from the crowd on the square. After the prayer, the tsar came out on the balcony to his people, the empress behind him. The huge crowd filled the square and the nearby streets, and when the tsar appeared it was as if an electric spark had run through the crowd, and an enormous 'hurrah' filled the air. Flags and placards with the inscription 'Long live Russia and Slavdom' bowed to the ground, and the entire crowd fell to its knees as one man before the tsar. The tsar wanted to say something; he raised his hand; those in front began to sh-sh-sh; but the noise of the crowd, the unceasing 'hurrah', did not allow him to speak. He bowed his head and stood for some time overcome by the solemnity of this moment of the union of the tsar with his people.[7]

The government could also count on the loyalty of its bureaucracy and its army. The Russo-Japanese war was now a distant memory, and reforms had improved the condition of common soldiers, tightened discipline, and raised the level of training and equipment. The Russian army finally abandoned its traditional reliance on the bayonet.

There had also been renewed economic growth in the period after the 1905 Revolution. Growth affected both industry and agriculture. Growth in industrial output in this period may have been as rapid as 6 per cent a year. This is below the remarkable 8 per cent growth rate of the 1890s, but remains impressive. Though the government no longer pursued a systematic policy of industrial growth, government orders for military equipment stimulated growth in heavy industry as the building of the trans-Siberian railroad had under Witte. In agriculture, rising world prices, a string of good harvests, and increased use of artificial fertilizers and agricultural machinery raised productivity during the years of the Stolypin reforms. (See Table 4.1 and the Statistical Appendix.)

Was war likely to weaken or strengthen the government? Immediately, the war rescued the government from a dangerous political crisis. However, it also created new strains. These help explain why the final collapse of tsarism proved so spectacular. At least one tsarist official understood this as early as 1914. He was P. N. Durnovo, who had served in the tsarist police, and also as a government minister and a member of the State Council. Like those other police officials, Benkendorff and Andropov, he knew better than his masters what dangers lurked beneath the surface of Russian society. In 1914, Durnovo submitted to the tsar a memorandum that forecast with astonishing accuracy the crisis the war would generate.

☐ *Document 6.4: Durnovo on the dangers of war*

In the event of defeat [in a war with Germany] ... social revolution in its most extreme form is inevitable ...

It will start with all disasters being attributed to the government. In the legislative institutions a bitter campaign against the government will begin, which will result in revolutionary agitation throughout the country. There will immediately ensue Socialist slogans – which alone are capable of arousing and rallying the masses – first the complete reapportionment of land and then the reapportionment of all valuables and property. The defeated army, having lost its most dependable men during the war, and carried away for the most part by the tide of the general elemental desire of the peasant for land, will prove to be too demoralized to serve as a bulwark of law and order. The legislative institutions and the opposition intelligentsia parties, lacking real authority in the eyes of the people, will be powerless to stem the rising popular tide, which they themselves had aroused, and Russia will be flung into hopeless anarchy, the outcome of which cannot even be foreseen.[8]

■ The Impact of War

Defeats in the Crimea and in Manchuria had cast doubt on the ability of the Russian army to deal with foreign opponents. Mutinies during 1905 had shown that its willingness to suppress internal dissent was not absolute. And there is little sign that ordinary soldiers greeted the outbreak of war with enthusiasm. Nevertheless, in 1914 the Russian army remained an impressive and responsive instrument of the royal will. By March 1917 this was no longer true.

Several factors explain the decline in the army's reliability. The first was the sheer scale of the war. By 1917, 1.7 million soldiers had died. Another 8 million were wounded or incapacitated and 2.5 million were prisoners of war. Irrespective of the human cost of these losses, their military effect was disastrous. In 1914, the army consisted of an elite of professional officers drawn from the ruling class, commanding recruits who underwent three full years of training. By 1917, hastily-trained draftees had swamped the professionals. All too often, young officers drafted from the dissident intelligentsia tried without success to command peasants recently drafted from the countryside and keen to return home. The army was no longer insulated from the grievances or the social divisions of society at large. To some extent this was true of all combatant armies. What made such problems peculiarly dangerous in Russia was the extent of the divisions between Russia's different classes. If discipline cracked, as it had in 1905, the army would cease to be the last defence of the government and become, instead, an instrument of revolution. Conditions at the front also undermined the morale of troops and officers. Most demoralizing of all was the inadequacy of supplies. The supply situation was worst in the earlier stages of the war. In December 1914 only 4.7 million rifles were available for the 6.5 million men mobilized.[9] In July 1915 a Russian general informed the French ambassador, Maurice Paleologue: 'In several infantry regiments which have taken part in the recent battles at least one-third of the men had no rifles. These poor devils had to wait patiently, under a shower of shrapnel, until their comrades fell before their eyes and they could pick up their arms.'[10] There were not enough artillery shells, and clothing was inadequate. In December 1914 General Yanushkevich, the chief of staff, complained that: 'Many men have no boots, and their legs are frostbitten. They have no sheepskin or warm underwear, and are catching colds. The result is that in regiments which have lost their officers, mass surrenders to the enemy have been developing'.[11]

Supplies improved in 1916, but morale did not. In October a government official who visited Riga reported:

> the atmosphere in the army is very tense, and the relations between the common soldiers and the officers are much strained, the result being that several unpleasant incidents leading even to bloodshed have taken place. The behavior of the soldiers, especially in the units located in the rear, is most provocative. They openly accuse military authorities of graft, cowardice, drunkenness and even treason.

Another report claimed that:

> every one who has approached the army cannot but carry away the belief that complete demoralization is in progress. The soldiers began to demand peace a long time ago, but never was this done so openly and with such force as now. The officers not infrequently even refuse to lead their units against the enemy because they are afraid of being killed by their own men.[12]

We should not exaggerate. Similar problems occurred in all European armies during the First World War. In any case, the Russian army did keep fighting even during much of 1917. Discipline held best at the front, where troops faced the enemy directly and understood the dangers of indiscipline. Nevertheless, by February 1917, revolutionary propaganda found an eager audience amongst soldiers at the front and in the rear. The machinery of persuasion was now being turned against the government even in the army. The increase in mass surrenders and desertions was the visible sign of widespread demoralization. This proved most dangerous in units away from the front, particularly in units garrisoning the major towns.

How did the government mobilize the resources needed to fight a modern war? Did it still have its traditional ability to mobilize labour, resources and money on the scale necessary to make up for its relative backwardness?

The 1905 Revolution had undermined the government's fiscal power and its prestige, which made it difficult to mobilize enough manpower and resources for a prolonged war. The government's achievements were astonishing despite these difficulties, but they were not quite enough.

The drafting of men into the army provides a good example. In 1914, the peacetime army consisted of 1.4 million men. Mobilization of reserves immediately added another 4 million, and by the end of the war a further 10 million had been drafted. However, many potential draftees secured exemptions. This was particularly true among the educated and wealthy, but also among skilled industrial workers. As a result, Russia drafted a smaller proportion of its population than the other major combatants: 8.8 per cent, compared with 12.7 per cent in Britain, 19.9 per cent in France, and 20.5 per cent in Germany.[13]

Its efforts to supply the army with ammunition and the industrial towns with food and supplies were also inadequate. In both cases, Russia paid for its relative backwardness. The entry of Turkey into the war on the German side in October 1914 closed the Straits of Constantinople. This was disastrous for Russia, as the straits were the last convenient route for importing western European supplies. Russia was now dependent on its own industry and raw materials. Yet Russian industry could not immediately produce enough weapons, munitions, clothing and boots for the army. By 1916 improved organization of industry, increased industrial output and increased imports had solved many of the supply problems. However, these successes, which prevented a collapse at the front, created additional strains in the rear. These internal strains explain why, when the collapse finally came, it took the form of revolution rather than military defeat.

Supplying the towns was a less immediate priority for the government than supplying the army, but in the long run it turned out to be equally important. Rapid growth in wartime industrial production caused an influx of labour into the towns. Petrograd's population increased from 2.1 to 2.7 million, and Moscow's from 1.6 to 2 million between 1914 and the beginning of 1917.[14] How could this rapidly growing town population be fed? In theory, there should not have been a problem. Wartime harvests were only slightly below the pre-war level. The army's demand for grain was balanced by a decline in civilian demand. Meanwhile, exports of grain had ended. The difficulty was to get the grain from producers to those who needed it.

Part of the problem was that the railway network had been designed to transport grain surpluses north and south, to the ports of the Black Sea or the large cities of the north. Now the government had to move grain to its armies in the west. It had neither the spare railway capacity, nor the organizational capacity to make the switch efficiently. Part of the problem was commercial. Production on the large commercial farms which marketed all their produce declined sharply as their farm labourers were drafted into the army. In the northern and central producer regions, which normally supplied the towns of the north, marketed surpluses declined as the large farms dropped out of the market. Supplies now had to come from peasant farms in the south and the south-east. This meant transporting grain over larger distances than in peacetime. It also pushed up the commercial price of grain, for peasants, unlike commercial farmers, did not have to sell grain. Yet the government offered low prices for grain, and wartime inflation reduced incentives for peasants to sell by raising the real price of industrial goods. Increased production of military equipment reduced production of consumer goods and pushed their price even higher. For most peasants, it made more sense to feed surplus grain to their livestock and pigs. There was little point in selling it at low prices in exchange for over-priced consumer goods from the towns. So trade between town and country began to break down. In 1914, 25 per cent of the grain harvest came on to the market. By 1917 only 15 per cent entered the market.[15] Here was an early example of what the Soviet government was to call a 'procurement crisis' in the 1920s. Not surprisingly, the government gave priority to the army in distributing the available surpluses. As a result, supplies of food to the towns became unreliable late in 1916.

The failures of the mobilization system appear also in the government's search for additional revenue. Customs revenues dropped with the sudden decline in foreign trade (almost half of which had been with Germany). Even more disastrous was Nicholas' high-minded decision, in August 1914, to prohibit the production and sale of alcoholic drinks during the war.[16] It made sense to prohibit alcohol sales during mobilization. The Russo-Japanese war had shown that unless this was done the call-up of reservists would turn into a series of drunken riots. However, it made little sense to prolong the ban during the war, for 30 per cent of the government's revenue came from its monopoly over liquor sales. The ministry of finance clearly hoped to use liquor revenues to pay for war. Indeed, on 26 July, it hastily passed a law raising the excise on liquor through a special session of the *Duma*. However, Nicholas decided in August to make the ban on alcohol sales permanent. He thereby deprived his government of almost one-third of its revenues on the eve of the greatest war Russia had ever fought. In October 1916 the minister of finance, Peter Bark, admitted that it had taken two years for government revenues to recover from the introduction of prohibition.[17] A *Duma* member, A. I. Shingarev, reporting for the *Duma*'s budgetary and financial commission on 18 August 1915, put it like this:

> From time immemorial countries waging war have been in want of funds. Revenue has always been sought either by good or by bad measures, by voluntary contributions, by obligatory levies, or by the open confiscation of private property. But never since the dawn of human history has a single country, in time of war, renounced the principal source of its revenue.[18]

The decision was a characteristic example of Nicholas's political naïvety. Even sadder, prohibition was a failure. For a time there was a real decline in consumption. However, as a contemporary explained, Russian drinkers soon began the search for ways around the new laws.

> At first, instead of vodka, they tried to use various other substances containing alcohol – eau-de-cologne, varnish, or denatured alcohol. But these were hard to get hold of, they were expensive, and they were unpleasant tasting and obviously dangerous to the health of consumers. Then people turned to domestic beers and *braga* [a strong domestic beer], trying to make them as strong as possible, but these couldn't get you drunk enough. Finally ... they learnt how to extract spirits by distilling fermented grains or sugary substances.[19]

Within a few years, distillers of illicit vodka, or *samogon*, had appeared in most villages and towns. Widespread production of poor-quality *samogon* deprived Soviet governments of revenues and left them with a vast, and apparently insoluble, problem of alcoholism, which has lasted to the present day.

Mobilizing cash was as tricky as mobilizing grain or munitions, for the war proved costlier than anyone had imagined. It cost 1655 million roubles in 1914, 8818 in 1915, 14 573 in 1916, and 13 603 for the first eight months of 1917.[20] By 1916, the war alone cost 4.7 times total government expenditure in the last peacetime year, 1913. How could the government pay for so expensive a war? The 1905 Revolution had forced the government to abandon its traditional policy of squeezing the peasantry. Taxing the rich through an income tax seemed reasonable and fair, though it was unlikely to raise much revenue, and might discriminate against wartime manufacturers. In 1916 the government did finally introduce modest income taxes and excess-profits taxes, but these raised little.

The only remedies left were to borrow and to increase the money supply. Both merely postponed the problem. The second method was, in reality, a disguised form of indirect taxation, for it led to rapid inflation. This, in turn, led to a severe decline in real living standards, particularly in the towns. In two and a half years the money supply increased by about 336 per cent and prices rose on average by 398 per cent. Inflation allowed a weak government to increase revenue without appearing to do so.

Increasing demands for revenue generated discontent among those paying it. However, the precise form of discontent reflected the ways in which the government raised its revenues. Rising demand for labour for war production led to rising wages. However, the disguised taxation by inflation raised prices even more rapidly. Combined with the growing difficulties in food supplies, declining real wages created an explosive situation in the major towns by 1916. The Petrograd secret police, who watched the situation closely, reported as follows in October 1916.

☐   *Document 6.5: Living standards in Petrograd, October 1916*

Despite the great increase in wages, the economic condition of the masses is worse than terrible. While the wages of the masses have risen fifty per cent, and only in certain categories 100 to 200 per cent (metal workers, machinists, electricians), the prices on all products have increased 100 to 500 per cent. According to the data collected by the sick benefit fund of the 'Triangle' plant, a day's wages for a worker before the war were [as follows in comparison with current wages] [in roubles]:

[Type of Worker]	[Pre-war Wages]	[Present Wages]
Unskilled	1.00 to 1.25	2.50 to 3.00
Metalworker	2.00 to 2.50	4.00 to 5.00
Electrician	2.00 to 3.00	5.00 to 6.00

At the same time, the cost of consumer goods needed by the worker has changed in the following incredible way [in roubles]:

[Item]	[Pre-war Cost]	[Present Cost]
Rent for a corner		
[of a room]	2.00 to 3.00 monthly	8.00 to 12.00
Dinner (in a tearoom)	0.15 to 0.20	1.00 to 1.20
Tea (in a tearoom)	0.07	0.35
Boots	5.00 to 6.00	20.00 to 30.00
Shirt	0.75 to 0.90	2.50 to 3.00

Even if we estimate the rise in earnings at 100 per cent, the prices of products have risen, on the average, 300 per cent. The impossibility of even buying many food products and necessities, the time wasted standing idle in queues to receive goods, the increasing incidence of disease due to malnutrition and unsanitary living conditions (cold and dampness because of lack of coal and wood), and so forth, have made the workers, as a whole, prepared for the wildest excesses of a 'hunger riot' ...

If in the future grain continues to be hidden, the very fact of its disappearance will be sufficient to provoke in the capitals and in the other most populated centers of the empire the greatest disorders, attended by pogroms and endless street rioting. The mood of anxiety, growing daily more intense, is spreading to ever wider sections of the populace. Never have we observed such nervousness as there is now. Almost every day the newspapers report thousands of facts that reflect the extremely strained nerves of the people in public places, and a still greater number of such facts remains unrecorded. The slightest incident is enough to provoke the biggest brawl. This is especially noticeable in the vicinity of shops, stores, banks, and similar institutions, where 'misunderstandings' occur almost daily.[21]

Whether the government could deal with such discontent when it finally erupted would depend on the loyalty of the troops and particularly on the garrison troops in the rear. However, that was something no one could count on any more.

The government's prospects would also depend on the support it could expect from Russia's upper classes. Yet the divisions between the government and the *Duma*, which had vanished on the outbreak of war, soon re-emerged. There also appeared signs of a growing unity among the disparate elite groups opposed to the autocracy.

The renewed split between the government and its traditional supporters owed much to the obstinacy of Nicholas II. Typical of his attitude is a conversation he had with the British ambassador, George Buchanan, two months before his abdication. Buchanan told the tsar:

'Your Majesty, if I may be permitted to say so, has but one safe course open to you – namely, to break down the barrier that separates you from your people and to regain their confidence.' Drawing himself up and looking hard at me, the Emperor asked: 'Do you mean that I am to regain the confidence of my people, or that they are to regain my confidence?'[22]

The tsar's attitude made it impossible for him to work with the leading politicians of the day, all of whom now saw the need for a proper constitutional government. His refusal to face political realities explains his growing dependence on people who understood the political situation as little as he did. In particular, he relied on his wife, the Empress Alexandra. She, in turn, relied on her spiritual adviser, the dissolute monk Gregory Rasputin, whose influence derived from his ability to control the haemophilia of the heir to the throne, Alexei, through hypnosis. Both Alexandra and Rasputin insisted that the tsar must not concede any of his powers. By 1916, after Nicholas had left for the front, Rasputin in effect chose the various government ministers. While Rasputin exercised such influence, the government was headed by a succession of nonentities whose only qualification for office was that they also refused to see the dangers facing the government. Contemporaries referred contemptuously to their comings and going as 'ministerial leapfrog'.

In July 1914 the upper classes had rallied around the government. The *Duma* met for one day and voted war credits (with moderate socialist leaders abstaining and the Bolsheviks opposing the vote). A provisional committee of *Duma* members was set up under M. V. Rodzianko, the *Duma* president, to organize aid for victims of the war. *Zemstvos* and town councils throughout Russia held conferences to consider how they could support the war effort. By August, an 'All-Russian Union of *Zemstvos* for the Relief of the Sick and Wounded' had been formed. In May 1915 representatives of industry and trade set up another body – the Central War Industries Committee (WIC) – to co-ordinate war production. It included workers' representatives as well as industrialists. In June, the WIC elected Alexander Guchkov, the Octobrist leader, as its chairman. Also in June, *zemstvo* and municipal organizations merged in the All-Russian Union of *Zemstvos* and Cities, or *ZemGor*. In these interlinked organizations, dominated by liberals and industrialists, there emerged the embryo of an alternative government. Despite the lack of government co-operation, these organizations did much to co-ordinate Russia's war effort.

By mid-1915 defeats at the front and bureaucratic muddle in the rear had revived the pre-war demoralisation of Russia's educated elite. When the *Duma* met in August 1915, it was hostile once again. Octobrists, Kadets and some right-wing deputies allied to form the 'Progressive Bloc'. This soon commanded a majority in the *Duma*. The Progressive Bloc fought for the traditional liberal goal of a parliamentary assembly with real authority. Above all, it demanded a 'government of public confidence'. By this, it meant a ministry appointed from the majority group in the *Duma*. In

September 1915, a document began to circulate amongst *Duma* leaders proposing the creation of a new ministry including Guchkov, Milyukov and Alexander Kerensky (1881–1970), the leader of the left-wing Trudovik group in the *Duma*.[23]

There can be little doubt that such a ministry would have been much more competent than the ministries appointed by Nicholas II. It would also have had the support of the *Duma*, of the voluntary organizations such as *ZemGor* and the WIC, and of most educated Russians. It would therefore have been in a better position than the existing government to co-ordinate the war effort. Members of the Progressive Bloc argued that only a government with genuine popular support would be able to lead the country to victory. They were probably right.

Nevertheless, Nicholas rejected their demands. Instead, in late 1915, he dismissed the most liberal of his ministers for opposing his decision to take personal command of the armies at the front. Their replacements were both incompetent and isolated. Leaders of the Progressive Bloc became bitter and pessimistic. Many feared that the tsar's stubbornness was leading Russia to defeat, and perhaps to social revolution. Yet they feared that any attempt to force their demands on the tsar might be equally disastrous. Their mood and the dilemmas facing Russia's upper classes as a whole are expressed vividly in a fable told by a leading liberal, Vasily Maklakov.

☐   *Document 6.6: Maklakov's fable of 'The mad chauffeur', September 1915*

Imagine that you are driving in an automobile on a steep and narrow road. One wrong turn of the steering-wheel and you are irretrievably lost. Your dear ones, your beloved mother, are with you in the car.

Suddenly you realise that your chauffeur is unable to drive ... should you continue in this way, you face inescapable destruction.

Fortunately there are people in the automobile who can drive, and they should take over the wheel as soon as possible. But it is a difficult and dangerous task to change places with the driver while moving. One second without control and the automobile will crash into the abyss.

There is no choice, however, and you make up your mind; but the chauffeur refuses to give way ... he is clinging to the wheel and will not give way to anybody ... Can one force him? This could easily be done in normal times with an ordinary horse-drawn peasant cart at low speed on level ground. Then it could mean salvation. But can this be done on the steep mountain path? ... One error in taking a turn, or an awkward movement of his hand, and the car is lost. You know that, and he knows it as well. And he mocks your anxiety and your helplessness ...

You will not dare touch him ... for even if you might risk your own life, you are travelling with your mother, and you will not dare to endanger your life for fear she too might be killed ... So you will leave the steering-wheel in the hands of the chauffeur. Moreover, you will try not to hinder – you will even help him with advice, warning and assistance. And you will be right, for this is what has to be done.[24]

Fearing a direct attack on the government, leaders of the Progressive Bloc began to attack it indirectly, arguing that, through its incompetence, it was consciously or unconsciously sabotaging the war effort. Their hostility focused on the 'German woman', the German-born Empress Alexandra. In November 1916 Milyukov attacked the government bitterly in the *Duma*.

☐   *Document 6.7: Milyukov accuses the government of treachery*

[The] present government has sunk beneath the level on which it stood during normal times in Russian life ... And now the gulf between us and that government has grown wider and has become impassable. ...

Today we see and are aware that with this government we cannot legislate, any more than we can with this government lead Russia to victory ... We are telling this government, as the declaration of the Bloc stated: We shall fight you; we shall fight with all legitimate means until you go ... When the *Duma* with ever greater persistence insists that the rear must be organized for a successful struggle, while the government persists in claiming that organizing the country means organizing a revolution and deliberately prefers chaos and disorganization, then what is this: stupidity or treason?[25]

Other *Duma* leaders contemplated more direct action. Guchkov began to sound out military leaders such as his old friend, General A. I. Krymov, about a palace *coup* that would remove Nicholas but retain the monarchy. Members of the Union of Zemstvos and Cities (*ZemGor*) discussed similar plans. In December, three members of the inner circle of the ruling elite murdered Rasputin. The murderers were Prince Felix Yusupov, one of the richest Russian landowners, V. M. Purishkevich, a right-wing *Duma* deputy, and Grand Duke Dmitrii Pavlovich, one of the tsar's uncles. This was as near as the ruling class dared come to directly seizing the wheel of government from the 'mad chauffeur'. We can regard the murder of Rasputin as a symbolic attack on the tsar himself.

By this stage, most members of Russia's upper classes had united not in support of, but in opposition to, the government that had traditionally defended their interests. In the *Duma*, *ZemGor* and the War Industries Committee, and through other networks and connections, they already had the ability to form a new government without the tsar. But they dared not take that step alone. The final push came from outside the ruling elite.

■ The February Revolution

The crisis began with demonstrations in the capital. On 22 February, a lockout at the giant Putilov metalworks brought many metal-workers on to the streets. There was nothing unusual about such demonstrations. There had been demonstrations before and during the war. However, this time the demonstrations gained momentum with terrifying speed.

The 23 February (8 March in the Western European calendar) was International Women's Day, a date chosen by the International Conference of Socialist Women in 1910 to commemorate a strike of women textile-workers in New York in 1908. On that day, the Bolsheviks of the Vyborg district called a strike, and large numbers of women textile-workers went on strike. The number of women workers had increased greatly during the war. Many came from the countryside, and many were supporting families alone, as their husbands had left for the front. Once on strike, the women called out the mainly male workers in the metal and munitions factories. A worker from the Nobel works remembered:

> We could hear women's voices in the lane overlooked by the windows of our department: 'Down with high prices!', 'Down with hunger!', 'Bread for the workers!' I and several comrades rushed at once to the windows. … The gates of No. 1 Bol'shaia Sampsonievskaia mill were flung open. Masses of women workers in a militant frame of mind filled the lane. Those who caught sight of us began to wave their arms, shouting: 'Come out!', 'Stop work!' Snowballs flew through the windows. We decided to join the demonstration.[26]

By the 25 February, about 240 000 workers were on strike. Factories stopped work, newspapers did not appear, city transport stopped, banks, shops and restaurants closed. Loose networks of revolutionary socialists from different parties joined together to provide strikers with a degree of organization. Slogans demanding an end to the war and to autocracy now replaced earlier slogans demanding bread and better working conditions.

On 25 February, General Khabalov, the commander of the Petrograd garrison, telegraphed the tsar:

> I report that, as a result of the bread shortage, a strike broke out in many factories on February 23 and 24. On February 24, around 200 000 workers were out on strike and forced others to quit their jobs. Streetcar

service was halted by the workers. In the afternoons of February 23 and 24, some of the workers broke through to the Nevskii [the main street], whence they were dispersed. Violence led to broken windows in several shops and streetcars.[27]

Meanwhile, the tsar ordered the *Duma*, which had convened on 14 February, to close again on 27 February. On 26 February, Rodzianko, the *Duma* president, telegraphed the tsar:

> The situation is serious. The capital is in a state of anarchy. The government is paralyzed; the transportation system has broken down; the supply systems for food and fuel are completely disorganized. General discontent is on the increase. There is disorderly shooting in the streets; some of the troops are firing at each other. It is necessary that some person enjoying the confidence of the country be entrusted immediately with the formation of a new government. There can be no delay. Any procrastination is fatal. I pray God that at this hour the responsibility not fall upon the sovereign.[28]

The tsar commented: 'That fatty Rodzianko has sent me some nonsense, which I shan't even answer'.[29] Instead of making the concessions Rodzianko demanded, he ordered the immediate suppression of the disorders.

General Khabalov already understood how unreliable his troops were. Some regiments drew their recruits from the Petrograd region. Others were billeted with working-class families. Others were wounded evacuees from the front, who had had their fill of military discipline.[30] Cossack regiments had already shown their reluctance to suppress demonstrations. On 25 February, one cossack soldier had even cut down a policeman trying to arrest demonstrators.

Khabalov had hoped to let the momentum of the demonstrations die away without forcing soldiers to choose between obedience and mutiny. Now he reluctantly took the tsar's order as a command to use maximum force. He informed unit commanders that:

> The sovereign has ordered that the disorders be stopped by tomorrow. Therefore the ultimate means must be applied. If the crowd is small, without banners, and not aggressive, then utilize cavalry to disperse it. If the crowd is aggressive and displays banners, then act according to regulations, that is, signal three times and open fire.[31]

The decision to use force was fatal. Reluctant troops now had to choose between mutinying and firing on crowds whose grievances they shared.

On 26 February, troops were ordered to fire on the demonstrators. The next day, one of the garrison units, the Volynskii Regiment, mutinied. The men killed some of their officers, and went over to the demonstrators. Other regiments soon followed their example. Later that day Khabalov cabled the tsar: 'I cannot fulfill the command to re-establish order in the capital. Most of the units, one by one, have betrayed their duty, refusing to fight the rioters'.[32] Within two days, the entire Petrograd garrison of 170 000 troops had mutinied.

The main institutions of government now crumbled. The Council of Ministers ceased to meet. After Nicholas closed the *Duma* on the twenty-seventh, a group of leaders from all parties continued to meet illegally in an effort to control the situation. That evening they decided to try to form a new government 'that corresponds to the wishes of the population and that can enjoy its trust.'[33] The first Provisional Government emerged from this group of *Duma* politicians a week later.

On the evening of 27 February, a group of left-wing socialist intellectuals and worker representatives on the War Industries Committee summoned a meeting of the Petrograd Soviet. This had not met since the government had closed it down in December 1905. Within hours, delegates assembled from the suburbs and factories and from troop units in the capital. Soon the Petrograd Soviet of Workers' and Soldiers' Deputies (to give its full title), was acting as a second alternative government. It met in the same building as the *Duma*, the magnificent Tauride Palace, originally built for the lover of Catherine the Great, Prince Potemkin. On 3 March, V. N. Kokovtsov, a member of the State Council who had just been arrested by the Soviet, described the scene in the palace:

> Even the most vivid imagination could not picture what was taking place within the Tauride Palace. Soldiers, sailors, university students of both sexes, nondescript persons by the score, deputations to see someone, anyone, orators perched upon tables and chairs shrieking unintelligibly, arrested persons like me escorted by guards, ... orderlies and unknown persons transmitting some sorts of orders to someone, a steady hum of voices! It was bedlam. And in the midst of it all wandered members of the *Duma*.[34]

The chaos was not total. On 1 March the Soviet issued Order No. 1. This ordered all troop units to send representatives from the rank and file to its meetings and demanded that troops submit themselves to the authority of the Soviet, 'in all political matters'. By doing this, the Soviet asserted its control over the garrison troops of the capital, thereby bypassing the normal command structure of the army.

Meanwhile, the tsar himself tried to return from army headquarters in Mogilev. However, striking railway workers diverted his train to the ancient city of Pskov. This was the headquarters of General Ruzsky, commander of the northern front. Here the tsar consulted with the army High Command. General Alekseev, the army chief of staff, argued that the army could not suppress the Petrograd insurrection, for any attempt to do so would simply spread disaffection within the army. He advised that the tsar had to resign if the army was to continue fighting at the front.

> The situation apparently does not permit of any alternative solution, and every minute's hesitation only serves to reinforce these demands, which are based on the fact that the army's existence and the work of the railways are actually dependent on the Petrograd Provisional Government. The army in the field must be saved from disintegration.[35]

Most other front commanders supported Alekseev. Indeed, some had already contacted members of the *Duma* about the possibility of removing the tsar. As in October 1905, Nicholas waited until even the army cracked before backing down. One last blow clinched his decision: the news that the old capital, Moscow, had also fallen.[36]

Late on the evening of 2 March, while still in General Ruzsky's train at Pskov, Nicholas II abdicated. His manifesto of abdication transferred power to his brother, the Grand Duke Mikhail Aleksandrovich. The next day, on 3 March, the Grand Duke announced that he would not accept the throne. He transferred power to the provisional committee of the *Duma*, on condition that it transfer sovereignty as soon as possible to an elected constituent assembly. These decisions marked the end of just over three centuries of Romanov rule. The birth of the Romanov dynasty had marked the end of one Time of Troubles; its death marked the beginning of another.

Could the Tsarist Government Have Survived?

By 1914, there were two basic types of political division in Russia. One was the division between Russia's upper classes and the working-class majority. The other division was between the majority of the ruling group and its traditional leader, the tsar. A Russian-American historian, Leopold Haimson, describes the two divisions as follows: 'By July, 1914, along with the polarization between workers and educated, privileged society … a second process of polarization – this one between the vast bulk of privileged society and the tsarist regime – appeared almost equally advanced'.[37]

At times, such as during the October 1905 general strike, divisions within the ruling group appeared even deeper than those between the ruling group and the working classes. In October 1905, the whole of Russian society appeared united in its opposition to the tsar. The collapse of this temporary class alliance after October 1905 revealed the weakness of the revolutionary coalition. The willingness of most educated Russians to support the new constitutional order, despite the government's obvious disdain for constitutional politics, reflected their growing fear that a violent revolution might lead to chaos and anarchy. Unless checked, any abrupt change of government might sweep away the entire structure of privilege on which the position of Russia's educated classes rested.

A clear understanding of the dilemma of Russia's educated elite suggests that the February Revolution could have been avoided. As Maklakov's parable suggests, there remained, even in 1916, a willingness within the upper classes to rally around the tsar, if only he could bring himself to create a genuinely constitutional government. If the tsar had been willing to accept the demands of the Progressive Bloc, this would have greatly narrowed the gulf within the ruling group. The Progressive Bloc, whose members now dominated much of the Russian press, would have swung the media behind the government and behind the war effort. A Progressive Bloc ministry would also have improved the conduct of the war. There was much political and commercial expertise within the *Duma* leadership. Besides, members of the Progressive Bloc already played a crucial role in supplying the armies, through their own business operations and through organizations such as the War Industries Committee. When discontent did break out in the towns, as it almost certainly would have sooner or later, the demonstrators would have faced a united ruling class, unwilling to support a change of government. The history of 1917 would have been very different.

But Nicholas was incapable of seeing this alternative. By February 1917, he had alienated the only groups in the empire who might have been able to rescue him. In doing so, he had prevented the emergence of a stable bourgeois government. His failures as a politician help explain why, when the revolution finally came in 1917, it swept away not only the autocratic government, but the whole traditional ruling group of Russia. Ever since the emergence of Russia's traditional autocratic political system, this had been its weak point. Leaders had great power. But if they did not know how to use their power properly they could threaten the future of the entire ruling group. In the Soviet period, the same rules would apply, but in even more violent circumstances.

■ Summary

After the 1905 revolution the government, led by Petr Stolypin, made some half-hearted attempts to regain the loyalty of educated Russians and peasants. The constitutional experiment gave the educated classes some hope of playing a role in government, while the agrarian reforms were designed to create a conservative class of peasant landholders. However, neither reform succeeded. Nicholas refused to give the Duma any real say in government, while the agrarian reforms could provide no long-term solution to the desperate land shortage of Russia's central regions.

Russia entered the First World War with a traditional autocratic government, unwilling to co-operate with the constitutionally inclined financiers and politicians whose support was vital if Russia was to mobilize successfully for a prolonged war. The government's failure to co-operate with the voluntary organizations that emerged during the war undermined the war effort and alienated groups that desperately wanted to work with the government for victory. Meanwhile, the costs of the war placed huge strains on a society whose economy was still less productive than those of the other major combatants. The urban population felt these strains most acutely. Working conditions declined in the factories, real wages dropped, and the supply system began to break down. When the inevitable crisis occurred in February 1917, the government found that it lacked the support needed to cope with simultaneous strikes and mutinies. Far from supporting the autocracy, the army high command and the *Duma* leadership insisted that Nicholas abdicate. Perhaps the most important single cause of the autocracy's final collapse was Nicholas' failure to understand how deeply Russian society was changing.

☐ *Further Reading*

Hosking, *Russian Constitutional Experiment*, remains the best study of the Constitutional experiment. McNeal (ed.), *Russia in Transition*, gives a good introduction to debates on the hoary old question of whether or not revolution was inevitable, while Haimson, 'The Problem of Social Stability', is one of the key essays in that debate. On economic issues, see Davies (ed.), *From Tsarism to the New Economic Policy*, while Andrle, *A Social History of Twentieth Century Russia,* discusses social issues, including the complex outcomes of the Stolypin reforms. Suny (ed.), *The Russian Revolution*, is a good recent collection of essays mainly on the revolutionary period, while Katkov and Oberlander (eds), *Russia Enters the Twentieth Century*, remains useful and is broader in scope, though it is also much older. Florinsky, *The End of the Russian Empire*, is a fine study of Russia at war by a historian who fought in the Tsarist army. Wildman, *The End of the Russian Imperial*

Army, is the best book on the army, while Stone, *The Eastern Front* is an interesting and provocative study of the Russian military and economic performance during the First World War. Ferro, *Nicholas II*, is a recent biography of the man who reluctantly held the key to Russian history in this period. There are good general surveys of the period in Kochan, *Russia in Revolution*, Fitzpatrick, *The Russian Revolution*, and Rogger, *Russia in the Age of Modernisation*. The most detailed study of the February Revolution is Hasegawa, *The February Revolution*. Mark Steinberg and Vladimir Khrustalëv, *The Fall of the Romanovs,* is a collection of recently released documents. For an introduction to the vast historiography on 1917, see Acton, *Rethinking the Russian Revolution.*

☐ *Notes*

1. M. Ferro, *Nicholas II The Last of the Tsars* (Harmondsworth: Penguin Books, 1990) p. 107.
2. G. Vernadsky *et al.* (eds), *A Source Book for Russian History from Early Times to 1917*, 3 vols (New Haven, Conn.: Yale University Press, 1972) vol. 3, p. 773.
3. G. Katkov *et al.* (eds) *Russia Enters the Twentieth Century* (London: Methuen, 1971) p. 127.
4. S. P. Trapeznikov, *Leninizm i agrarno-krest'yanskii vopros*, 2nd edn, vol. 1 (Moscow: Mysl', 1974) p. 186.
5. D. C. B. Lieven, *Russia and the Origins of the First World War* (London: Macmillan, 1983) p. 55.
6. L. Haimson, 'The Problem of Social Stability in Urban Russia, 1905–1917', cited from M. Cherniavsky (ed.), *The Structure of Russian History* (New York: Random House, 1970) p. 359.
7. Vernadsky, *Source Book*, vol. 3, p. 831.
8. Ibid., p. 797.
9. H. Seton-Watson, *The Russian Empire: 1801–1917* (Oxford University Press, 1967) p. 700.
10. Vernadsky, *Source Book*, vol. 3, p. 835.
11. M. T. Florinsky, *The End of the Russian Empire* (New York: Collier Books, 1961) p. 209.
12. Ibid., pp. 214–15.
13. J. N. Westwood, *Endurance and Endeavour, Russian History 1812–1980*, 2nd edn (Oxford University Press, 1981) p. 186.
14. Seton-Watson, *The Russian Empire*, p. 720.
15. N. Stone, *The Eastern Front: 1914–1917* (London: Hodder & Stoughton, 1976) p. 296.
16. See David Christian, 'Prohibition in Russia: 1914–1925', *Australian Slavonic and East European Studies*, vol. 9, no. 2 (Dec. 1995) pp. 1–30.
17. Even this claim depended on some accounting sleight-of-hand. Bark's report is reprinted in *Krasnyi arkhiv* (1926) vol. 17, no. 4, pp. 51–69.
18. Florinsky, *The End of the Russian Empire*, p. 44.
19. D. N. Voronov, *O samogone* (Moscow–Leningrad: Izdatel'stro Z-oe, 1929) p. 6.
20. Florinsky, *The End of the Russian Empire*, p. 46.
21. Vernadsky, *Source Book*, vol. 3, pp. 867–8.

22. Ibid., p. 876.
23. J. White, *The Russian Revolution 1917–21* (London/New York: Edward Arnold, 1994) pp. 54, 64.
24. G. Katkov, *Russia 1917, The February Revolution* (London: Fontana/Collins, 1969) pp. 249–51.
25. Vernadsky, *Source Book*, vol. 3, p. 870.
26. Cited in S. Smith, 'Petrograd in 1917', in D. H. Kaiser (ed.), *The Workers' Revolution in Russia, 1917 The View from Below* (Cambridge University Press, 1987) p. 61.
27. Vernadsky, *Source Book*, vol. 3, p. 878.
28. Ibid., p. 879.
29. Seton-Watson, *The Russian Empire*, p. 725.
30. A. Wildman, *The End of the Russian Imperial Army* (Princeton University Press, 1980) pp. 157–8.
31. Ibid., p. 136.
32. L. Kochan, *Russia in Revolution, 1890–1918* (London: Granada, 1966) p. 192.
33. From the letter Rodzianko wrote to the Tsar next morning. See M. D. Steinberg and V. M. Khrustalëv, *The Fall of the Romanovs* (New Haven, Conn. and London: Yale University Press, 1995) p. 84.
34. Vernadsky, *Source Book*, vol. 3, p. 883.
35. Katkov, *Russia 1917*, p. 441.
36. T. Hasegawa, *The February Revolution: Petrograd 1917* (University of Washington Press, 1981) p. 490.
37. Haimson, 'The Problem of Social Stability', p. 360.

■ *Chapter 7* ■

1917

In February 1917 the autocracy fell. Yet the traditional ruling group, though weakened and leaderless, survived. It continued to dominate the economy, the army and the new government. In October the ruling group itself lost control of the government. In its place there appeared a new ruling group. This claimed to represent Russia's industrial workers and peasants, though most of its leaders belonged to the radical intelligentsia. They created the first communist government ever formed. In doing so, they set Russian and world history off on new and unmapped paths. Why and how did these momentous changes take place?

■ The Formation of the Provisional Government

By 3 March, two alternative revolutionary governments had appeared. Each had its own supporters within Russian society. Each also controlled the elements of a coercive machinery of power.

On 1 March the provisional committee of the *Duma* formed itself into a Provisional Government. It immediately chose a new Council of Ministers. Under pressure from Milyukov, this excluded Rodzianko, and included some politicians who did not belong to the *Duma*, thereby depriving the new Ministry of the prestige it would have enjoyed as a sub-committee of the Fourth *Duma*.[1] Its chairman was a wealthy landowner, aristocrat and *zemstvo* leader, Prince G. E. L'vov (1861–1925). Milyukov became foreign minister. Guchkov became minister of war. A. I. Konovalov (1875–1948), became minister of trade. Finally, A. F. Kerensky became minister of justice. Landowners, industrialists, intellectuals and members of the radical intelligentsia – this was a representative cross-section of Russia's changing ruling group.

It was to this group that Grand Duke Mikhail Aleksandrovich surrendered supreme power on 3 March, 'until the Constituent Assembly ... shall by its decision on the form of government express the will of the people'. The formal transfer of power gave the Provisional Government legitimacy in the eyes of educated Russians. This secured the loyalty of those who staffed the traditional tsarist machinery of power – army commanders, government officials and police. However, indiscipline in the army and the desertion of many police officials during the February uprising had sapped the power of the old coercive machinery.

Simultaneously, there emerged a second alternative government, the Petrograd Soviet. Most of its leaders came from the moderate socialist parties, the Mensheviks and Socialist Revolutionaries. The Soviet rapidly gained the allegiance of most of the Petrograd working class. On 1 March, it issued its famous Order No. 1. This required that troops obey only those orders which did not conflict with the orders of the Soviet. Soon the Petrograd Soviet secured the allegiance of most of the troops in the capital, and within weeks Soviets sprang up throughout the country. In June, when the first All-Russian Congress of Soviets met in Petrograd, it included representatives from at least 350 local Soviets. Simultaneously, soldiers' committees began to appear at the front. These local institutions gave the Petrograd Soviet the rudiments of a new, and largely working-class, machinery of power reaching across the entire country. In March, this machinery was still ill-organized and unreliable, but it gave the Soviet enough power to impose its will within the capital.

At this stage, the Soviet had more real power than the Provisional Government. Guchkov, the new minister of war, wrote on 9 March: 'The Soviet ... has in its hands the most important elements of real power, such as the army, the railways, the posts and telegraphs. It is possible to say flatly that the Provisional Government exists only as long as it is allowed by the Soviet'.[2] If it had wanted to, the Soviet could have seized power on its own, at least in the capital. Yet the Soviet did not take power. Why not?

Ideological and psychological pressures both encouraged restraint. Most socialist leaders believed that Russia was too backward for a socialist revolution. They remembered that even Marx had warned against trying to build socialism without the necessary preconditions. Capitalism, they believed, still had much work to do before socialism could be built in Russia. Meanwhile, Russia needed the bourgeoisie, who at least had the skills and experience necessary to keep the economy running. The following document comes from the memoirs of a prominent Menshevik and one of the Soviet's early leaders, N. N. Sukhanov.

☐ *Document 7.1: Sukhanov on the Soviet's decision not to take power*

The epoch of worldwide imperialist war could not but culminate in world-wide Socialist revolution ... [But] though our revolution had been consummated by the democratic masses it lacked both the material power and the indispensable prerequisites for an immediate Socialist transformation of Russia. We could only construct a Socialist society against the background of a Socialist Europe and with its help. But as for the consolidation of a bourgeois dictatorship in the present revolution – that was quite out of the question. ...

The Soviet democracy had to entrust the power to the propertied elements, its class enemy, without whose participation it could not now master the technique of administration in the desperate conditions of disintegration, nor deal with the forces of Tsarism and of the bourgeoisie united against it. But the conditions of this transfer of power had to assure the democracy of a complete victory over the class enemy in the near future.

Consequently, the gist of the question was whether propertied Russia would consent to take power in such conditions, and the task consisted of compelling it to embark on this risky experiment as the least of the evils lying before it.[3]

These were the ideological arguments for restraint. However, psychological factors may have been equally important. Most socialist leaders came not from Russia's working classes but from its educated elite. Only seven out of the forty-two members of the Soviet's first Executive Committee were workers. The rest were intellectuals. Despite their radical political beliefs, most socialist leaders shared the culture and outlook of Russia's upper classes and feared that a working-class revolt in backward Russia could lead only to anarchy.

The events of the next few decades showed that these fears had some basis. However, they also raised immediate problems of tactics and strategy. In 1917, the contrast between their radical socialist ideals and their cautious politics put the Socialist Revolutionaries and Mensheviks, who dominated the revived Petrograd Soviet, in an extremely difficult position. Eventually, it lost them the working-class support they enjoyed at the beginning of the year.

In pursuit of a stable bourgeois government, the Soviet had to compromise with the emerging Provisional Government. The delicate negotiations between the Soviet and the Provisional Government took place in the corridors of the Tauride Palace on 1 March, as Kerensky, the only member of both institutions, moved between the two wings of the palace with proposals and counter-proposals.

In return for supporting the Provisional Government, the Soviet made demands of its own. It demanded a general amnesty; the granting of basic civil liberties even to soldiers; the abolition of all legal disabilities based on class, religion and nationality; the right of labour to strike and to organize; and the summoning of a Constituent Assembly. These demands were similar to those of the 'Liberation' Movement of 1905. They were also similar to the programme of the wartime Progressive Bloc in the *Duma*. So the members of the Provisional Government had little difficulty in accepting them. Members of the Soviet made no effort to demand more basic social changes. They did not mention land redistribution, or the nationalization of large industrial enterprises. Indeed, such demands were unrealistic and inappropriate while the leaders of the Soviet hoped to co-operate with a government of the 'bourgeoisie'.

These negotiations laid the basis for what came to be known as 'dual power', *dvoevlastie*. This was an alliance of the Provisional Government and the Petrograd Soviet. Together, they formed an uneasy coalition of institutions and classes, claiming to represent both Russia's traditional elites and its workers and peasants. 'Dual power' recreated the fragile coalition of forces that had nearly brought the tsarist government down in October 1905. In principle, the new government had enough support to create genuinely democratic institutions for the first time in modern Russian history. But was democratic government possible in a country where the gulf between upper classes and working classes was so profound? Would 'dual power' prove any less fragile in 1917 than it had in 1905?

In March each part of the awkward coalition contributed its own supporters and its own machinery of power. Russia's traditional elites mostly supported the Provisional Government. So did the remnants of the tsarist bureaucracy and the high command in the army. The Soviet had the support of urban workers and peasants. It also gained the loyalty of the Soviets which sprang up in the towns and villages and at the front. The factory committees which appeared in large industrial enterprises also supported the Soviet. Both elements in the new coalition benefited from the universal relief at the downfall of the autocracy. The new government could therefore count on a honeymoon period during which it would enjoy the support of most Russians. These were immense political assets. Yet within eight months the power of the Provisional Government/Soviet coalition had shrivelled to nothing. How did this happen?

■ Decline of the Provisional Government

Previous chapters have described the decline of the tsarist political system as the result of two opposite processes. These were: growing disunity within the traditional ruling group, and the increased organization of opposition groups. Similar processes also occurred in 1917, but they were speeded up. To understand the changes that occurred in 1917 we must concentrate on those programmes, events and leaders that did most to organize some social groups and disorganize others.

There were two crucial processes. The first was the decline of the Provisional Government. The second was the rise of an alternative, working-class government led by the Bolshevik Party and based on the Soviets. The two processes were intertwined. However, for the sake of clarity, I will discuss them separately.

The Provisional Government hastened its decline by adopting policies that undermined both its machinery of power and its social support. As the agreement between the Soviet and the Provisional Government showed, it was liberal principles that united the two elements of the 'dual power'. With the end of autocracy, everyone agreed that government by force must give way to government by consent. On 26 April, the new government declared that 'the power of the state should be based not on violence and coercion, but on the consent of free citizens to the power they themselves created'.[4] This meant that the government should rule not through a coercive machinery, but with the consent of the population. But was this possible in a society as divided as wartime Russia and without any traditions of democracy?

The government took its programme seriously. It announced freedom of religion and the press, which deprived it of control over much of the machinery of persuasion. Even riskier was the government's decision to dismantle important components of the traditional machinery of coercion. Within two months it had dismantled two key institutions of tsarist government. It replaced the tsarist system of police with a 'people's militia', and the provincial governors with elected *zemstvos*.

Though admirably democratic, these measures made it difficult for the government to enforce its orders in the provinces. Power slipped from local officials into the hands of the local population.

> The peasant revolution ... destroyed piecemeal the old state apparatus in the countryside – the provincial governors, the district *zemstva*, the *volost'* administration ... the land captains, and the police officials ... It replaced them with a network of ad hoc peasant committees (and later soviets), elected by the communal or village assembly.[5]

By the middle of 1917, the Provisional Government no longer controlled the countryside.

Revolution accelerated the break-up of the army. As in 1905, the collapse of the tsarist government persuaded many soldiers that they need no longer obey their officers. The Soviet's Order No. 1 encouraged this belief. Though aimed at the garrison troops in the capital, it soon applied to rank and file soldiers even at the front. Soldiers began electing soldiers' committees or 'Soviets', which reserved the right to reject officers' orders. Under the agreement between the Soviet and the Provisional Government, the new government also abolished the death penalty at the front. The ending of censorship led to an increase in anti-war propaganda within the army, and rumours of a land redistribution convinced soldiers from rural areas that they had to return home quickly to get their share of land. Under these conditions, it was extremely difficult for officers to maintain discipline. The supply situation also worsened as discipline broke down in the munitions factories of cities such as Petrograd.

These problems would have mattered less if the new government had intended to make peace with Germany. However, most leaders of the new government had agreed to the abdication of the tsar in the hope of improving the army's fighting capacity. Far from ending the war, the Provisional Government intended to fight it more energetically. Amongst Russia's working population this was an extremely unpopular decision. In late April the government learned the extent of popular anti-war feeling when its foreign minister, Milyukov, announced that his government would continue fighting until it could reach a 'just peace'. His declaration provoked massive anti-war demonstrations in the capital. These persuaded Milyukov to resign, together with the minister of war, Guchkov. In June the government tried to rouse patriotic feelings with a huge military offensive on the Galician front. However, this merely showed the extent of anti-war sentiment within the army. Soldiers told General Brusilov, the commander of the offensive: 'What we want is to return home and enjoy freedom and land. Why should we go on being wounded?' Many officers did not know until they attacked whether their men would follow them into battle.[6] Desertions increased rapidly after February. While there had been 195 000 desertions between 1914 and the February Revolution, there were over 365 000 desertions between March and May 1917. Improved discipline reduced desertions in the summer, but in the autumn desertion increased again as discipline collapsed.[7]

By July 1917, the government no longer had a reliable army or a trustworthy machinery of local government. The weakened machinery of power it had inherited in March could no longer maintain the government's authority. To survive, the government would have to depend on popular support.

Yet it alienated its supporters too. The new government hoped to rule with the support of all sections of Russian society. To do so, it would have to offer a programme that satisfied both the upper-class supporters of the Provisional Government and the working-class supporters of the Soviet. In reality, the deep divisions within Russian society made it impossible to construct such a programme. By trying to do so, the government merely alienated both groups. The interests of upper-class and working-class Russians conflicted at so many points that policies that pleased one group inevitably alienated the other. M. T. Florinsky, a Russian historian who fought during the war, writes: 'The conflict between the attitude of the masses and that of the educated classes ... was fundamental, insoluble, fatal ... There was no room for compromise between the two points of view, and the conflict had to be fought out to its bitter end'.[8]

The implications of Florinsky's argument are bleak. It implies that democratic government was impossible in wartime Russia, for it was impossible to rule with the support of both upper and lower classes. All the key political issues of 1917 – war, land, industrial relations and the Constituent Assembly – illustrate the truth of his judgement.

The government lost upper-class support because it failed to protect their property, to maintain order, or to prosecute the war successfully.

In the countryside, the abolition of the tsarist police made it impossible to defend landowners' property from peasant attacks. All too often, the hastily organized 'people's militias' sided with the peasants who supplied most of their recruits. In any case the government's vague pronouncements on the land problem seemed to condone land seizures. These began to spread rapidly in April. In March the police reported peasant disorders in thirty-four districts; in April, in 174; and in July, in 325.[9] Given the momentousness of these events, the massive land expropriations of 1917 were surprisingly orderly.

☐ *Document 7.2: Land seizures in 1917 in Samara province*

The majority of the estates were expropriated just before the start of the autumn or spring sowing. A general gathering of the peasants resolved to place under the control of the commune all or part of the estate property. At a selected time, the peasants assembled their carts in front of the church and moved off towards the manor, armed with guns, pitchforks, axes, and whatever came to hand. The squire and his stewards, if they had not already fled, were arrested and forced to sign a resolution placing the property of the estate under the control of a village committee. The peasants loaded on to their carts the contents of the barns and led away the cattle, excepting the property which had been left for the use of the landowner and his family. Pieces of large agricultural machinery, such as harvesters and winnowing machines, which the peasants could not move or could not use on their small farms, were usually abandoned or destroyed. The Saratov provincial land department left a vivid account of this plundering of the estates in December 1917:

> Yesterday, 26 January, at 12 noon the entire commune of Kolybelka, led by the chairman of the village committee, appeared at my *khutor*. They arrested me and my family, as well as two policemen who happened to be at my house, and left a guard with us with a warning not to go out of the house. They also placed armed guards around my farm and made threats to my labourers. Then they took away all my grain and seed, except forty *pud* of rye, and locked up my barns. I asked them to weigh the grain they had taken, but they refused as they loaded up their fifty-six carts until they were overflowing ... That night some of the peasants returned, broke the lock on the barn and took away my scales and tubs with weights of five *pud* measure.[10]

Traditional power structures also crumbled in the army and in industry. The Soviet's Order No. 1, and the abolition of the death penalty at the front, had reduced the authority of officers. In industry, concessions to labour, such as the eight-hour day and the recognition of factory committees, undermined profitability and labour discipline. In May, the industrialist A. I. Konovalov predicted economic disaster.

☐ *Document 7.3: Konovalov on the economic crisis*

The normal working of industrial enterprises has been seriously interrupted and the energy of the nation must be marshalled to overcome the economic disintegration, to prevent economic ruin overtaking the country, and to adequately defend the country. When we overthrew the old regime we believed absolutely that freedom would bring about a great expansion of the productive forces of the country. Now it is not a question of thinking about developing productive forces, but of making every effort to protect [industry] ... from total ruin. And if the confused minds do not see reason soon, if people do not realise that they are sawing off the branch they are sitting on, if the leaders of the Soviet of Workers' and Soldiers' Deputies do not manage to control the movement and to guide it into the channels of legitimate class struggle, then scores and hundreds of enterprises will close down. We shall experience the complete paralysis of national life and shall embark upon a long period of irreparable economic disaster when millions will be unemployed, without bread, without a home, and when the crisis will affect one branch of the economy after the other, bringing with it everywhere death, devastation, and misery, partly ending credit and producing financial crises and everyone's ruin.[11]

By the summer, landowners, army officers and entrepreneurs began to think that strong government might be preferable to democratic government, particularly in time of war. Many believed the Provisional Government had moved too far to the left. The changing composition of the government reinforced these fears. In April, Milyukov, the leader of the Kadet party, and Guchkov, the leader of the Octobrist party, had both resigned. Intensive negotiations with the Soviet led to the appointment of socialist members of the Soviet to the new cabinet. These included Victor Chernov (the founder of the Socialist Revolutionary Party) and two Mensheviks. Meanwhile, Kerensky, a socialist and a member of the Soviet, became the new minister of war. Despite its socialist majority, the Petrograd Soviet was now playing an active role in a government committed to retaining upper-class support. Early in July, Prince L'vov resigned as premier, and Kerensky took his place.

After the attempted Bolshevik *coup* early in July, the mood of Russia's upper classes underwent a sea-change. Members of upper-class society lost their faith in the Provisional Government and began to dream of a strong, unified government capable of holding the Russian Empire together and preventing anarchy. In early August, the industrialist P. P. Riabushinskii struck a sympathetic nerve at a conference attended by many Kadets, when he said:

> We ought to say ... that the present revolution is a bourgeois revolution, that the bourgeois order which exists at the present time is inevitable, and since it is inevitable, one must draw the completely logical conclusion and insist that those who rule the state think in a bourgeois manner and act in a bourgeois manner.[12]

In September, a Russian journalist, Burtsev, told the American journalist John Reed: 'Mark my words, young man! What Russia needs is a Strong Man. We should get our minds off the Revolution now and concentrate on the Germans'.[13] This more authoritarian mood found a symbolic focus in the personality of General L. G. Kornilov (1870–1918).

Kornilov, a strict military disciplinarian, had persuaded Kerensky to reintroduce the death penalty at the front on 12 July. On 16 July Kerensky made Kornilov commander-in-chief of the army. Kornilov had the support of a newly formed Union of Army and Navy officers. He also received financial backing from a committee of leading financiers, which included Guchkov, and which hoped to overthrow the Soviets. Prominent Kadets such as Milyukov and Rodzianko gave him their moral support.

In August, Kornilov spoke in Moscow of the need to re-establish discipline in the rear as well as at the front. The reception he received in Moscow illustrated the resurgence of right-wing feeling among Russia's upper classes. Here is Trotsky's colourful and ironic account of Kornilov's arrival in Moscow.

Document 7.4: Trotsky on Kornilov's reception in Moscow, August 1917

Kornilov ... was met by innumerable delegates – among them those from the Church Council. The Tekintsi [his bodyguards] leapt from the approaching train in their bright red long coats, with their naked curved swords, and drew up in two files on the platform. Ecstatic ladies sprinkled the hero with flowers as he reviewed this body-guard and the deputations. The Kadet, Rodichev, concluded his speech of greeting with the cry: 'Save Russia, and a grateful people will reward you!' Patriotic sobbings were heard. Morozova, a millionaire merchant's wife, went down on her knees. Officers carried Kornilov out to the people on their shoulders ... From the station Kornilov took his way – in the steps of the czars – to the Ivarsky shrine, where a service was held in the presence of his escort of Mussulmen Tekintsi in their gigantic fur hats ... Kornilov's biography, together with his portrait, was generously scattered from automobiles. The walls were covered with posters summoning the people to the aid of the hero. Like a sovereign, Kornilov received in his private car statesmen, industrialists, financiers. Representatives of the banks made reports to him about the financial condition of the country.[14]

Unfortunately for his admirers, Kornilov proved as incompetent a politician as Nicholas II. One supporter, the former army chief-of-staff Alekseev, said that Kornilov had 'a lion's heart and the brains of a sheep'.[15] When he tried a *coup d'état* at the end of August, he bungled it.

The Provisional Government alienated the left as thoroughly as it alienated the right, though for opposite reasons. The key issues were war, land, industrial relations and the Constituent Assembly.

Continuing to fight the war was dangerous, as most Russian peasants, workers and soldiers had no desire to continue fighting. For peasants (and most soldiers were peasants), the real issue was land. Yet on this issue the government refused to act, even when the Socialist Revolutionary leader, Victor Chernov, became minister of agriculture in May. The government argued that only the Constituent Assembly could undertake so basic a redistribution of Russia's resources. Peasants took the land anyway, knowing the government could no longer stop them. Meanwhile, peasants in the army deserted in increasing numbers to take part in the land repartition which they knew would soon take place.

A Constituent Assembly might have solved some of these problems. Yet the government claimed that wartime conditions made it impossible to hold elections for a Constituent Assembly. Eventually it set up an electoral commission in May, and promised elections for November. However, its hesitation on the issue had planted the suspicion that a 'bourgeois' government was deliberately avoiding elections which would certainly overthrow it.

The government also dithered on the issue of industrial relations and urban living conditions. It had conceded the eight-hour day, the freedom to strike and to organize unions, and the right to form factory committees. Yet as long as it devoted resources to the war the government could do little to improve conditions in the factories, to improve the supply situation, or to raise working-class living standards. Real wages fell more rapidly than ever in 1917, as prices rose. In January 1917 prices were 300 per cent of the 1914 level. By October 1917 they had risen to 755 per cent.[16]

Meanwhile, the supply of food was no better than in March. The American journalist John Reed described the situation in September and October.

☐ *Document 7.5: John Reed on the effects of inflation*

Week by week food became scarcer. The daily allowance of bread fell from a pound and a half to a pound, then three-quarters, half, and a quarter-pound. Towards the end there was a week without any bread at all. Sugar one was entitled to at the rate of two pounds a month – if one could get it at all, which was seldom ... There was milk for about half the babies in the city; most hotels and private houses never saw it for months ...

For milk and bread and sugar and tobacco one had to stand in queue long hours in the chill rain. Coming home from an all-night meeting I have seen the *kvost* [queues] beginning to form before dawn, mostly women, some with babies in their arms.[17]

In its efforts to supply the army, the government also angered workers by trying to reimpose discipline in the factories. In August, industrial workers were treated to the depressing spectacle of a Menshevik minister of labour, M. I. Skobelev (1885–1939), reaffirming the right of management to dismiss workers, and forbidding factory committees to meet during working hours. Skobelev announced that: 'the task of every worker before the country and the revolution is to devote all his strength to intensive labour and not lose a minute of working time'.[18]

Workers saw attempts to reimpose factory discipline as a form of class conflict. Some factory committees tried to increase their control of factories in the belief that they could run them more efficiently than their owners. Failing that, they tried to keep factories running when their owners began to talk of closures. 'It is very likely,' warned one speaker in August, 'that we stand before a general strike of capitalists and industrialists. We have to be prepared to take the enterprises into our hands to render harmless the hunger that the bourgeoisie so heavily counts upon as a counter-revolutionary force.'[19] By backing employers in such conflicts, the Provisional Government alienated its working-class supporters as effectively as its more radical measures had alienated the upper classes.

Finally, for workers and peasants, the Provisional Government lacked legitimacy. The Soviet was 'their' government. As early as April, workers at the Puzyrev and Ekval' factories declared:

The government cannot and does not want to represent the wishes of the whole toiling people, and so we demand its immediate abolition and the arrest of its members, in order to neutralize their assault on liberty. We recognize that power must belong only to the people itself, i.e. to the Soviet of Workers' and Soldiers' Deputies as the sole institutions of authority enjoying the confidence of the people.[20]

By September the Provisional Government no longer had the active support of any large section of society. Nor did it have the coercive machinery needed to impose its will by force. Delivering the death blow proved all too easy.

■ Political Alternatives in 1917

The Provisional Government failed because its attempts to please all classes pleased no one. But what alternative was there? The alternative was a government ruling with the support of either Russia's educated classes or its working classes. Such a government would have to be willing to use force against its opponents. It would have to be relatively authoritarian. But would it be an authoritarian government of the right (like the former tsarist government) or of the left?

At the time, the first possibility must have appeared the most likely, for Russia's upper classes were used to government. An authoritarian government of the right would have meant a dictatorship (probably dominated by the military or a member of the royal family), capable of protecting property, maintaining the powers of the army, and suppressing working class discontent. In essence, this was the programme of Kornilov and his supporters. As Kornilov himself put it:

> It is time to hang the German agents and spies with Lenin at their head, to disperse the Soviet of Workers' and Soldiers' Deputies and scatter them far and wide … I have no personal ambition, I only wish to save Russia, and will gladly submit to a strong Provisional Government purified of all undesirable elements.[21]

Kornilov failed, but his mistakes, unlike those of the Provisional Government, were tactical rather than strategic, for his aims were realistic enough. Russia had a long tradition of right-wing authoritarian government, and during the Civil War several new governments of this kind were to emerge.

The second alternative was an authoritarian government of the left. Such a government would represent the interests of Russia's working-class population – peasants, workers and soldiers. It would therefore represent the interests of most of the population of the Russian Empire. In this sense, it would be far more democratic than the traditional political systems of Russia and Europe. Yet at the time this possibility must have appeared unlikely. There was no precedent for such a government anywhere in the world. There had never existed a socialist government, and few seriously believed a working-class government would have the competence to rule. Why was it this most unlikely outcome that triumphed in October 1917?

■ The Rise of a Left-wing Alternative

In March 1917 the idea that the Bolsheviks would be ruling the country a year later appeared far-fetched. At that time, they were the smallest of the major socialist parties. They had about 25 000 members, and only forty representatives among the 1500 or so members of the Petrograd Soviet. None of their front-line leaders were in the capital. Lenin was in exile in Switzerland. J. V. Stalin (1879–1953) and L. B. Kamenev (1883–1936) were in Siberian exile. G. Y. Zinoviev (1883–1936) and N. I. Bukharin (1888–1938) were also abroad. In February, even Lenin had said in a speech in Switzerland, that revolutionaries of his generation would not live to see the revolution.

How, within eight months, did the Bolsheviks gather enough power to overthrow the Provisional Government? The decline in the power of the Provisional Government provides part of the answer. The gulf that existed between working-class and upper-class Russians is also part of the answer. But the critical element was the leadership of Lenin. Lenin created the Bolshevik party in 1903. He held it together during the years of exile. He gave it a political programme that gained working-class support. Finally, in 1917, he provided decisive leadership at critical moments. We will look first at the Bolshevik Party and its Leninist ideology. Then we will discuss the Party's conduct in 1917.

In the Soviet Union, Stalin transformed Lenin's ideas into rigid dogmas. To understand Leninism, we must shake off the dogmatic approach that sees his ideas as either right or wrong. Instead, we will approach Lenin as one of many Marxists who tried to apply Marx's ideas to a country in which capitalism barely existed. (On socialism and Marxism, see Chapters 3 and 5.) What distinguished Lenin's ideas from those of other Russian Marxists, and gave them such prestige even outside the Soviet Union, is that they worked. They led to the creation of a revolutionary government of the working classes. Whether they succeeded in creating a genuinely socialist society is another matter, and one we will explore later.

At the time of the Bolshevik/Menshevik split in 1903, two features distinguished Lenin's thinking. First, he had an exceptional commitment to party discipline. Second, he believed that intellectuals would provide most of the leaders in a revolutionary working-class party. The 1905 revolution widened the split amongst Russian Marxists, for it posed complex problems of both tactics and strategy. It showed that even if one precondition for socialism was absent in Russia (a high level of productivity), the other (a revolutionary proletariat) was present. What should Marxists do in such a situation? Should they support the further development of capitalism? Or should they use the revolutionary energies of the proletariat to attempt an anti-capitalist revolution?

Marx himself offered few clear guidelines, for in most of his writings he had assumed that the two preconditions would arise together as capitalism evolved. He argued that capitalist societies had appeared through 'bourgeois' revolutions that had swept away the remnants of feudal society and laid the basis for a flourishing capitalism. Such revolutions had occurred in England in the seventeenth century, in France in the eighteenth century, and in much of Europe in 1848. Presumably, 1905 was Russia's 'bourgeois' revolution.

Most Russian Marxists saw a clear distinction between the bourgeois and socialist revolutions. They believed that the bourgeoisie would rule for a long time in the interval between the two revolutions. During this interval, capitalism would flourish and build up both the material and social preconditions for a socialist revolution. However Lenin and Trotsky arrived, by parallel routes, at the belief that in Russia the two revolutions would run into each other. Lenin argued in 1905 that the Russian bourgeoisie was too conservative to push for a radical bourgeois revolution. Russian entrepreneurs would prefer a strong, autocratic government that could encourage economic growth, to a weaker, though more democratic government.

> The big bourgeoisie, the landlords, the factory owners, the 'society' which follows the 'Liberation' lead, ... do not even want a decisive victory. We know that owing to their class position they are incapable of waging a decisive struggle against Tsarism; they are too heavily fettered by private property, by capital and land to enter into a decisive struggle. They stand in too great need of Tsarism, with its bureaucracy, police, and military forces for use against the proletariat and the peasantry, to want it to be destroyed.[22]

Therefore, he argued, it fell to the working classes of Russia to radicalize the revolution. They would have to push the bourgeoisie into making radical political demands that would speed up the development of capitalism in Russia.

In 1905, the revolutionary energy of peasants and workers so impressed Lenin that he began to envisage the creation of a working-class government even during the bourgeois revolution. His slogan in 1905 was: 'A Revolutionary Democratic Dictatorship of the Proletariat and Peasantry'. This would not be a socialist government, but it would be one in which Russia's working classes played a dominant role.

> While recognising the incontestably bourgeois nature of a revolution incapable of directly overstepping the bounds of a mere democratic revolution our slogan advances this particular revolution and strives to give it forms most advantageous to the proletariat; consequently, it strives to make the utmost of the democratic revolution, in order to attain the greatest success in the proletariat's further struggle for Socialism.[23]

Yet how could a working-class government rule in a capitalist society? For a Marxist this was a serious riddle. Most Russian Marxists resolved it by dismissing the prospect of a working-class government in a country as underdeveloped as Russia. This is why, in March 1917, they supported the formation of a bourgeois government.

Trotsky and Lenin came up with a very different solution. They argued that a working-class government might emerge even in backward Russia. However, it could survive only if its creation triggered revolutions in the more developed capitalist countries of Europe. As early as 1905, Lenin wrote: 'a revolutionary-democratic dictatorship of the proletariat and the peasantry ... will enable us to rouse Europe; after throwing off the yoke of the bourgeoisie, the socialist proletariat of Europe will in its turn help us to accomplish the socialist revolution'.[24] The conclusion was clear. The duty of a Marxist party was not to support the bourgeoisie. It was to overthrow the bourgeoisie, even in backward Russia. Revolutions would take place, not in distinct stages, but as part of a continuous process, linking local bourgeois revolutions with a world-wide socialist revolution. To describe this process, Trotsky picked up on a phrase Marx had used as early as 1850: 'Permanent Revolution'.[25]

This line of argument led to a conclusion utterly different from that reached by the moderate socialists. The Mensheviks argued that capitalism barely existed in Russia. Therefore Russia was not ready for a socialist revolution. Therefore Russia's working classes would have to live under a bourgeois government for a long period. Lenin agreed that capitalism barely existed in Russia. But he argued that the rest of Europe was highly developed and ready for a socialist revolution. Therefore it was the duty of Russia's working classes to overthrow their own bourgeoisie and detonate a European revolution. These different conclusions threatened to put Bolsheviks and Mensheviks (and other moderate socialists) on opposite sides of the barricades.

These strategic differences implied different tactics and different programmes. For the moderate socialists, proletarian revolution was a distant dream. For the Bolsheviks it was an immediate reality. They therefore took it seriously, and prepared for it carefully. In the Bolshevik Party, they already had a revolutionary headquarters with the traditional military commitment to discipline, unity and secrecy.

Lenin's insistence on the imminence of a proletarian revolution in Russia also implied a distinctive party programme. The moderate socialists, believing that capitalism would exist for some time, had to devise programmes compatible with capitalism. It made no sense to undermine the rights of bourgeois landlords or bourgeois factory owners if they wanted capitalism to flourish. So they could not promise the peasantry land. Nor could they promise workers' control over the factories. However the Bolsheviks saw no need to compromise with a bourgeoisie they intended to overthrow. They could therefore support workers' control in industry, or peasant control of the land. For Russia's peasants and workers, such a programme had much greater appeal.

The decision of the German Social Democratic Party to support the German government in 1914 confirmed Lenin's fear that, when the chips were down, moderate socialist parties would support the bourgeoisie. From this time, Lenin saw the moderate socialists as enemies, fighting for, rather than against the bourgeoisie. The scale of the war also confirmed Lenin's radicalism, for it persuaded him that the final crisis of capitalism had arrived. In a work published in 1916, Lenin argued that the war arose from the growing conflicts between capitalists over colonial profits. As capitalism came to dominate world markets, the opportunities for easy profits would vanish. Less developed societies would find it harder to develop capitalism on their own territory. For them, the only escape from colonial exploitation would be through an anti-capitalist revolution. Meanwhile, imperialist capitalist powers would have to fight each other for colonies and profits. The war marked the death agony of capitalism. A country like Russia, part-capitalist, part-colony, was where he expected world Capitalism to crack.

By 1917, Lenin believed firmly that a period of world-wide socialist revolutions was imminent. He also believed that a Russian revolution would play a key role in the world-wide socialist revolution. However, he understood that the Russian revolution would not be a socialist revolution. It would be impossible to build Socialism in Russia until the triumph of revolution in the developed capitalist countries of Europe. At best, a proletarian state might survive as an embattled fortress until revolution triumphed elsewhere. In 1916, he wrote, in an eerie anticipation of Cold War rivalries:

The development of Capitalism increases to the highest degree inequalities among various nations ... From this fact an unchallengeable conclusion emerges; Socialism cannot triumph simultaneously in all countries. It will triumph first of all in one or several countries, while the remainder, for some time, will remain bourgeois or pre-bourgeois in character. This will create not only conflict, but direct attempts on the part of the bourgeoisie of other countries to destroy the victorious proletarian socialist state. In these circumstances, war will be necessary and just from our perspective. This will be a war for Socialism, for the liberation of other peoples from bourgeois hegemony.[26]

What sort of society would the revolution create? It would not yet be a classless society. Russia was too backward to do more than lay the foundations for socialism. However, the new society would be more democratic than any that had existed so far, as it would represent for the first time in history the interests of most Russians, rather than those of a privileged minority. Lenin hoped to create a government based on the social support of most Russians. Specifically, he believed the new government would represent an alliance (or *smychka*) of peasants and proletarians. (Peasants used the word *smychka* to describe the yoking together of oxen to pull a plough.) Though democratic, such a government would still need a coercive apparatus, for it would face both internal and external enemies. To fight them, a socialist government would have to use whatever coercive methods it could devise. So even this government would need to build and maintain a coercive machinery of power, and use it against its enemies.

To describe the type of government he expected to create, Lenin borrowed from Marx the provocative label, 'The Dictatorship of the Proletariat'. He used this phrase to describe a government representing the majority of the population (unlike all previous governments), but prepared to use force to control the minority that still opposed it.

When the tsar abdicated, Lenin had been in exile almost continuously since 1900, apart from a brief return in 1905. After the fall of the autocracy, he negotiated frantically to return through enemy country. Eventually the Germans, having decided that Lenin's return could only harm the Russian war effort, gave him safe passage to neutral Sweden. From there, he entered Russia and arrived at Petrograd's Finland station on 3 April.

To his disgust, he discovered that even the Bolsheviks in Petrograd had decided to support the 'bourgeois' Provisional Government. The decision to do so was taken by Stalin and Kamenev after they returned from Siberian exile in mid-March and assumed control of Party affairs. On his arrival, Lenin issued what came to be known as the 'April Theses'. This is an immensely important document, for it contains an outline of the strategy which, within seven months, was to bring the Bolsheviks to power. In the April Theses, Lenin advocated the overthrow of the Provisional Government by the Soviets. To achieve this, he offered a programme designed to gain the support of workers, peasants and soldiers. His programme promised to end the war, to expropriate landowners and capitalists, and to establish a working-class government.

☐ *Document 7.6: Lenin's April Theses*

1. In our attitude towards the war, which under the new government ... unquestionably remains on Russia's part a predatory imperialist war owing to the capitalist nature of that government, not the slightest concession to 'revolutionary defencism' is permissible.

    The class-conscious proletariat can give its consent to a revolutionary war, which would really justify revolutionary defencism, only on condition: (a) that the power pass to the proletariat and the poorest sections of the peasants aligned with the proletariat; (b) that all annexations [that is all plans of the belligerent powers to annex the territory of opponents] be renounced in deed and not in word; (c) that a complete break be effected in actual fact with all capitalist interests ...

    The most widespread campaign for this view must be organised in the army at the front ...

2. The specific feature of the present situation in Russia is that the country is passing from the first stage of the revolution – which, owing to the insufficient class-consciousness and organisation of the proletariat, placed power in the hands of the bourgeoisie – to its second stage, which must place power in the hands of the proletariat and the poorest sections of the peasants ...

3. No support for the Provisional Government; the utter falsity of all its promises should be made clear, particularly of those relating to the renunciation of annexations ...

4. Recognition of the fact that in most of the Soviets of Workers' Deputies our Party is in a minority, so far a small minority ...

    As long as we are in the minority we carry on the work of criticising and exposing errors and at the same time we preach the necessity of transferring the entire state power to the Soviets of Workers' Deputies, so that the people may overcome their mistakes by experience.

5. Not a parliamentary republic – to return to a parliamentary republic from the Soviets of Workers' Deputies would be a retrograde step – but a Republic of Soviets of Workers', Agricultural Labourers' and Peasants' Deputies throughout the country ...

    Abolition of the police, the army and the bureaucracy. (The standing army to be replaced by the arming of the whole people.)

6. ... Confiscation of all landed estates.

    Nationalisation of all lands in the country, the lands to be disposed of by the local Soviets of Agricultural Labourers' and Peasants' Deputies. The organisation of separate Soviets of Deputies of Poor Peasants ...

8. It is not our immediate task to 'introduce' Socialism, but only to bring Socialism and the distribution of products at once under the control of the Soviets of Workers' Deputies.[27]

Despite his prestige, Lenin had to fight hard to get the Bolshevik leaders to accept this radical programme. An ex-Bolshevik, Bogdanov, said of the speech in which Lenin announced the new programme: 'This is the raving of a madman! It's indecent to applaud this claptrap!'.[28] However, many rank-and-file workers and Party members shared Lenin's outlook, and his ferocious argumentation in Party committees, combined with rank-and-file pressure, persuaded a Party conference early in May to adopt the April Theses as official Party policy. This decision distinguished the Bolsheviks from all the other socialist parties.

The decision to overthrow the Provisional Government meant that the Bolsheviks had no need to court Russia's upper classes. Freed from the need to compromise, the Bolsheviks could promise land for the peasants, an end to the war, and improved supplies in the towns. These promises made for a simple, but attractive programme: Soviet power, plus bread, land and peace. Whether they could satisfy these demands was another matter.

Lenin's programme gave the Bolsheviks a huge advantage in the search for working-class support. They picked up support in the factories and from the peasant-soldiers who made up the bulk of army units in the towns and at the front. As the old coercive machinery collapsed these ordinary soldiers came to hold the balance of power in the towns. In 1917, Lenin built his political strategy on this alliance of proletarians, peasants and soldiers. The Party's commitment to revolution also meant that its members could concentrate on the task of seizing power. This project gave the Party an *élan* and a sense of purpose that the moderate socialists lacked.

In the chaotic conditions of 1917 most statistics are guesswork, but it is clear that Bolshevik membership began to rise. The best guess is that in February the Bolsheviks had about 25 000 members, far fewer than either the Mensheviks or the Socialist Revolutionaries. By May, they had the support of most factory committees in the capital. In the same month, soldiers at the Kronstadt naval base, just outside Petrograd, announced that they no longer recognized the Provisional Government, and placed themselves at the disposal of the Soviet. Bolshevik support also increased in the army. By June, the rise in Bolshevik strength was clear to everyone. The first All-Russian Congress of Soviets met in that month. The Bolsheviks had 105 delegates; the Mensheviks, 248; and the Socialist Revolutionaries, 285. Most delegates to the first Congress of Soviets still refused to take seriously Lenin's claim that the Bolsheviks were willing to seize power. When he said the Bolsheviks were willing to take power, most delegates laughed. However, in the same month, demonstrations called by the Petrograd Soviet showed that the Bolsheviks were now a serious political force in the capital. The Menshevik Sukhanov described the (to him) gloomy sight as follows.

☐ *Document 7.7: Sukhanov on the June demonstrations*

But what was the political character of the demonstration?

'Bolsheviks again,' I remarked, looking at the slogans, 'and there behind them is another Bolshevik column ...

Apparently the next one too,' I went on calculating, watching the banners advancing towards me and the endless rows going away towards Michael Castle a long way down the Sadovoy.

'All power to the Soviets!' 'Down with the Ten Capitalist Ministers!' 'Peace for the hovels, war for the palaces!' In this sturdy and weighty way worker-peasant Petersburg, the vanguard of the Russian and the world revolution, expressed its will. The situation was absolutely unambiguous. Here and there the chain of Bolshevik flags and columns was interrupted by specifically SR [Socialist Revolutionary] and official Soviet slogans. But they were submerged in the mass; they seemed to be exceptions, intentionally confirming the rule. Again and again, like the unchanging summons of the very depths of the revolutionary capital, like fate itself, like the fatal Birnam wood – there advanced towards us: 'All power to the Soviets!' 'Down with the Ten Capitalist Ministers!'[29]

In July, Trotsky and his small group of followers joined the Bolshevik Party. This brought together the two revolutionary leaders most committed to an immediate overthrow of capitalism. They were the most determined, and perhaps the most brilliant, of all Russian socialists. Together they were a formidable team.

So powerful was the groundswell of support that it carried the Bolsheviks further than they wished. Lenin understood the danger of trying to seize power prematurely. Such a move might provoke a right-wing reaction strong enough to crush the Bolsheviks permanently. Yet on 3 July, pro-Bolshevik army units in the capital forced the party, against its better judgement, to support an attempted *coup*. The Provisional Government still had the backing of loyal troops, and after two days of rioting pro-government troops suppressed the revolt. The government arrested several Bolshevik leaders, but Lenin and Zinoviev escaped across the Finnish border, a few kilometres from the capital. Kerensky, the new prime minister, published documents claiming that the Bolsheviks were receiving money from the German enemy, and support for the party plummeted.

At the time the 'July Days' looked like a disaster for the Bolsheviks. In reality the damage was limited. A large core of supporters did not waver, and in mid-July the party even held a secret Party Congress in Petrograd. The Bolsheviks also learned a lot about how not to organize an uprising. Besides, Russian society was as polarized as ever. Early in August, when supporters of Kornilov gathered in Moscow, cab-drivers refused to drive them from the station to the Bolshoi Theatre, and restaurant workers refused to serve them.[30]

Ironically, it was Kornilov who saved the Bolsheviks from obscurity. In July, Kerensky appointed him commander-in-chief of the Russian armed forces. Late in August, Kornilov ordered several cavalry units to march on Petrograd, apparently with the aim of crushing the Petrograd Soviet and forming a military dictatorship. However, his move was as ill-prepared as the Bolshevik insurrection of July. In panic, Kerensky called on the Soviet to help defeat Kornilov, and released Bolshevik leaders from prison to help organize resistance. Railway workers diverted or delayed the trains carrying Kornilov's troops. As they waited on railway platforms, Kornilov's soldiers listened to the speeches of agitators sent by the Petrograd Soviet. These explained that Kornilov was using the soldiers to crush the revolution. Many soldiers agreed not to move further; Petrograd was saved; and Kornilov was arrested. It now appeared that the main danger to the Provisional Government came from the right, and Bolshevik support soared again.

Meanwhile, the Bolsheviks were free to organize openly again, except for Lenin, whom the government still planned to arrest. Early in September members of the Petrograd Soviet supported a Bolshevik resolution demanding the transfer of power to the Soviets. As a result, the Bolsheviks secured a majority on the Soviet executive committee and could now claim to represent the majority opinion in the Petrograd Soviet. A few days later, the Bolsheviks secured a majority in the Moscow Soviet.

■ The October Insurrection

Lenin, still in hiding, decided that this was the wave to ride. Signs of growing discontent in the armies of other combatant countries convinced him that the wave of revolution was Europe-wide. Capitalism was close to breakdown, so that a *coup* in Petrograd might trigger a world-wide revolution even if it failed in Russia. The issue was urgent. He wrote to the central committee of the party that the time was now ripe for a direct transfer of power.

☐ *Document 7.8: Lenin on the need to prepare for insurrection*

Without losing a single moment, [we must] organise a headquarters of the insurgent detachments, distribute our forces, move the reliable regiments to the most important points, surround the Alexandrinsky Theatre, occupy the Peter and Paul Fortress, arrest the General Staff and the government, and move against the officer cadets and the Savage Division – those detachments which would rather die than allow the enemy to approach the strategic points of the city. We must mobilise the armed workers and call them to fight the last desperate fight, occupy the telegraph and the telephone exchange at once, move our insurrection headquarters to the central telephone exchange and connect it by telephone with all the factories, all the regiments, all the points of armed fighting, etc.

Of course, this is all by way of example, only to illustrate the fact that at the present moment it is impossible to remain loyal to Marxism, to remain loyal to the revolution unless insurrection is treated as an art.[31]

As always, Lenin saw clearly that power was the issue. Success meant controlling the communications network and getting the support of the Petrograd garrison. With their support, the party would have real political muscle in the capital.

However, the party's central committee in Petrograd was more cautious. Far from accepting Lenin's advice, they decided to ignore his letters. They had had their fingers burnt in July, and had no desire to make the same mistake twice. Kamenev and Zinoviev argued for the formation of a broad coalition of socialist parties, while Trotsky argued that the Bolsheviks should work for a seizure of power by the imminent Congress of Soviets. In frustration Lenin returned secretly to the capital. On 10 October, at a secret meeting of the Central Committee, he bullied most of the committee into supporting a *coup*. However, their decision was still half-hearted. Two members, Kamenev and Zinoviev, voted against the decision and publicized the fact in the press. The rest, except for Trotsky, dragged their heels.

Preparations for the *coup* were rudimentary. The Bolshevik Party was more disciplined than its opposition. However, as the behaviour of Kamenev and Zinoviev showed, Lenin's authority was by no means absolute. Nor did the party have a coercive machinery of its own, except for the Red Guards, a part-time militia formed mainly from younger factory workers. This meant that success depended less on careful military planning, than on working-class support, particularly amongst the garrison troops. With that support they might succeed; without it they would certainly fail. Social support was the key to power. The crucial activity was, therefore, oratorical rather than military, as Bolshevik leaders hurried from factory to factory and barracks to barracks whipping up support for the Soviet.

By the middle of October everyone knew that a *coup* was in the air. Yet no one, not even the Bolsheviks, knew when or how the crisis would break. Kerensky's nerve broke first. On 23 October, he ordered a unit of soldiers to close down the Bolshevik military newspaper. Immediately, the Soviet called upon Red Guards and troops loyal to the Soviet to resist this

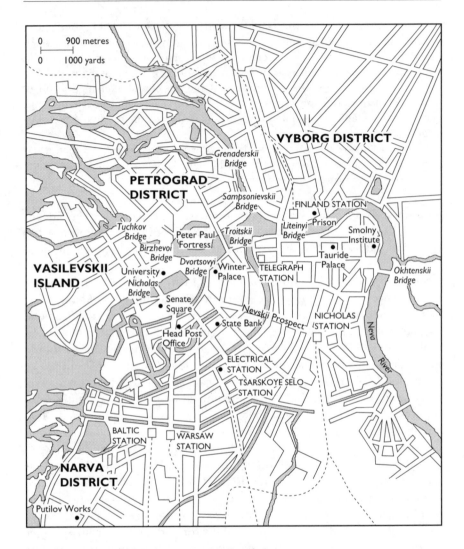

Figure 7.1   *Petrograd during the October Revolution*

attack on its authority and reopen the presses. John Reed described the frantic and chaotic atmosphere in the Soviet headquarters at Smolny (formerly an elite girls school) at this critical moment.

☐   *Document 7.9: John Reed on Smolny during October*

The massive facade of Smolny blazed with lights as we drove up, and from every street converged upon it streams of hurrying shapes dim in the gloom.

Automobiles and motor-cycles came and went; an enormous elephant-coloured armoured automobile, with two red flags flying from the turret, lumbered out with a screaming siren. It was cold, and at the outer gate the Red Guards had built themselves a bonfire. At the inner gate, too, there was a blaze, by the light of which sentries slowly spelled out our passes and looked us up and down. The canvas covers had been taken off the four rapid-fire guns on each side of the doorway, and the ammunition-belts hung snake-like from their breeches. A dun herd of armoured cars stood under the trees in the courtyard, engines going. The long, bare, dimly illuminated halls roared with the thunder of feet, calling, shouting ... There was an atmosphere of recklessness. A crowd came pouring down the staircase, workers in black blouses and round black fur hats, many of them with guns slung over their shoulders, soldiers in rough dirt-coloured coats and grey fur *shapki* pinched flat, a leader or so – Lunacharsky, Kameniev – hurrying along in the centre of a group all talking at once, with harassed anxious faces, and bulging portfolios under their arms.[32]

The activities of the pro-Bolshevik troops were directed not by the Bolshevik Party itself, but by the Military-Revolutionary Committee of the Soviet. The Soviet had created this body on 16 October, nominally to defend Petrograd against counter-revolution. It was led by Trotsky and dominated by Bolsheviks, as the Mensheviks and Socialist Revolutionaries refused to join. On 23 October, in response to Kerensky's attempt to close the Bolshevik press, the Military-Revolutionary Committee appointed commissars, or representatives, to all troop units in the capital. These persuaded most units to obey them rather than the Provisional Government. On the evening of the twenty-fourth, under pressure from Lenin (who was still in hiding), the Military-Revolutionary Committee directed Red Guards and loyal units of soldiers to seize the key points in the city: the bridges, the railway stations, the central post office and the central telephone exchange. There was hardly any resistance as they took over the capital. That night, Lenin himself travelled by tram to Smolny and took charge of the insurrection.

The final task was to seize the Winter Palace, where Kerensky and the ministers of the Provisional Government were meeting. The palace was threatened by artillery from the Peter and Paul Fortress across the River Neva and the guns of the battleship Aurora. Eventually, pro-Bolshevik units stormed it during the evening of 26 October. They arrested all the members of the Provisional Government except Kerensky, who had escaped in a car belonging to the United States embassy. That evening Lenin confessed to Trotsky his astonishment at what had happened. 'You know, from persecution and a life underground, to come so suddenly into power ... *es schwindelt* [it makes you giddy]!'[33]

The October uprising marked the final collapse of the traditional Russian ruling group. The Bolshevik-led Soviet seized power despite its weakness, because the existing government was even weaker. John Reed wrote:

> Wednesday, 7 November [25 October, Old Style], I rose very late. The noon cannon boomed from Peter-Paul [the fortress opposite the Winter Palace] as I went down the Nevsky. It was a raw, chill day. In front of the State Bank some soldiers with fixed bayonets were standing at the closed gates.
>   'What side do you belong to?' I asked. 'The Government?'
>   'No more Government,' one answered with a grin. 'Slava Bogu! Glory to God!' That was all I could get out of him.[34]

■ Summary

Because the crisis of February 1917 had been ignited from below, the *Duma* leaders who dominated the Provisional Government never enjoyed the political initiative. Far from being able to rule decisively in a time of national crisis, they had to compromise with the demands of the Petrograd Soviet, which had acquired great influence as the symbolic representative of Russia's working classes. Given the profound divisions within Russian society on issues such as the war, the Constituent Assembly, land redistribution and power relations within the factories, a government forced to compromise could please no one. Gradually, the dual system of government formed in March lost the support both of Russia's educated elites and of its soldiers, workers and peasants.

Oddly, most socialist parties refused to exploit the government's weakness, for they believed firmly that Russia was not yet ready for socialism. In the meantime, they hoped to forge a government representing all social classes. Only the Bolsheviks argued for an anti-bourgeois government. And even within the Bolshevik Party, there were many who wavered on this issue. Lenin argued that, though Russia remained too backward to build a viable socialist society on its own, it would be able to do so after a wider world revolution which would create a socialist Europe. The duty of Russia's socialists, therefore, was to trigger a world-revolution by overthrowing Russia's own bourgeoisie. Committed to the creation of a working-class government, the Bolsheviks could offer a clear and unambiguous programme of peace, land, Soviet power and workers' control. Lenin's firm leadership on this issue enabled the Bolsheviks to pick up more and more support amongst soldiers and workers disillusioned with the policies of the Provisional Government. In September, Lenin decided that the party had enough power to attempt a *coup*. In October, the support of garrison troops in the major towns was the key to Bolshevik victory. After the successful coup in Petrograd, the Bolsheviks formed a new, working-class government. However, even the most confident of the Bolshevik leaders had little idea how they would survive the national and international conflicts that the October Revolution was bound to ignite.

☐ *Further Reading*

There is a huge literature on 1917, which is surveyed in Acton, *Rethinking the Russian Revolution*. The best recent study in English is White, *The Russian Revolution*, but there are good general introductions in Fitzpatrick, *The Russian Revolution*, and Service, *The Russian Revolution*. There are good collections of essays on the social history of the revolution in Kaiser (ed.), *The Workers' Revolution in Russia*; Service (ed.), *Society and Politics in the Russian Revolution*; and Frankel (ed.), *Revolution in Russia*. A classic study, still vivid and readable, is Chamberlin, *The Russian Revolution*. Carr's multi-volume *History of Soviet Russia* is encyclopedic, but dated in some respects. Trotsky's *History of the Russian Revolution* is well-written and vivid, though it is, of course, the view of a participant. Another vivid partisan account is John Reed, *Ten Days that Shook the World*. On Marxism, see Tucker (ed.), *Marx–Engels Reader*. Two recent biographies of Lenin are Robert Service, *Lenin: a Life*, and D. Volkogonov, *Lenin, A new Biography*. On Lenin's ideas, see Harding, *Lenin's Political Thought*, though Lichtheim, *A Short History of European Socialism*, and Bottomore (ed.), *A Dictionary of Marxist Thought*, are also useful. The best study of the October uprising is probably Rabinowitch, *The Bolsheviks come to Power*, which stresses the extent to which Lenin responded to grass-roots radicalism in the cities. There are several good collections of documents, including, McCauley (ed.), *The Russian Revolution and the Soviet State*.

☐ *Notes*

1. J. D. White, *The Russian Revolution 1917–21* (London/New York: Edward Arnold, 1994) pp. 76–7.
2. L. Kochan, *Russia in Revolution, 1890–1918* (London: Granada, 1966) p. 208.
3. N. N. Sukhanov, *The Russian Revolution: 1917. A Personal Record* (ed. and trans) J. Carmichael (Oxford University Press, 1955) pp. 104–5.
4. From a declaration of 26 April. See L. Schapiro, 'The Political Thought of the First Provisional Government', in R. Pipes (ed.), *Revolutionary Russia* (Cambridge, Mass.: Doubleday & Co, 1967) p. 123.
5. O. Figes, *Peasant Russia, Civil War: The Volga Countryside in Revolution 1917–1921* (Oxford University Press, 1989) p. 31.
6. Kochan, *Russia in Revolution*, p. 245.
7. White, *The Russian Revolution*, p. 130.
8. M. T. Florinsky, *The End of the Russian Empire* (New York: Collier Books, 1961) pp. 228–9.

9. Kochan, *Russia in Revolution*, p. 238.
10. Figes, *Peasant Russia, Civil War*, pp. 52–3. The quotation comes from an account 'written in January 1918 by a small landowner in Samara district about the expropriation of his farmstead (*khutor*)'.
11. 18 May 1917, from M. McCauley (ed.), *The Russian Revolution and the Soviet State: 1917–1921* (London: Macmillan, 1975) p. 67.
12. W. G. Rosenberg, *Liberals in the Russian Revolution: The Constitutional Democratic Party, 1917–1921* (Princeton University Press, 1974) cited from R. Suny and A. Adams (eds), *The Russian Revolution and Bolshevik Victory*, 3rd edn (Lexington, Mass.: Heath & Co, 1990) p. 298.
13. John Reed, *Ten Days that Shook the World* (Harmondsworth: Penguin, 1966) p. 50.
14. L. Trotsky, *The History of the Russian Revolution* (London: Sphere Books, 1967) vol. 2, p. 152.
15. Ibid., p. 147.
16. McCauley (ed.), *Russian Revolution*, p. 72.
17. Reed, *Ten Days*, pp. 37–8.
18. Kochan, *Russia in Revolution*, p. 253.
19. From D. Mandel, *The Petrograd Workers and the Soviet Seizure of Power: From the July Days 1917 to July 1918* (London: Macmillan, 1984) cited from Suny and Adams (eds), *Russian Revolution*, p. 349.
20. S. Smith, 'Petrograd in 1917', from D. Kaiser (ed.), *The Workers' Revolution in Russia 1917* (Cambridge University Press, 1987) p. 66.
21. R. Daniels, *Red October* (New York: Scribner's, 1967) p. 46.
22. V. I. Lenin, *Selected Works* (Moscow: Progress Publishers, 1971) p. 81.
23. Ibid., p. 107.
24. Ibid., p. 103.
25. Marx's address to the 'Communist League' in 1850 concluded that 'Permanent Revolution' should be the 'battle cry' of the proletariat.
26. Cited in R. C. Nation, *Black Earth, Red Star: A History of Soviet Security Policy, 1917–1991* (Ithaca: Cornell University Press, 1992) p. 6, from 'The Military Program of the Proletarian Revolution'.
27. B. Dmytryshyn, *USSR: A Concise History*, 2nd edn (New York: Scribner's, 1971) pp. 368–70.
28. T. Cliff, *Lenin* (London: Pluto Press, 1976) vol. 2, p. 121.
29. Sukhanov, *The Russian Revolution*, pp. 416–17.
30. Diane Koenker, 'Moscow in 1917', in D. Kaiser (ed.), *The Workers' Revolution in Russia 1917*, p. 85.
31. Lenin, *Selected Works*, p. 361.
32. Reed, *Ten Days*, p. 96.
33. Trotsky, *My Life* (Harmondsworth: Penguin, 1975) p. 351.
34. Reed, *Ten Days*, p. 88.

■ *Chapter 8* ■

Civil War and the Origins of a New Social Order

Chapters 1 to 7 traced the emergence and then the decline and fall of the traditional Russian ruling group. In October 1917 a new government claimed power. Most of its leaders came from the radical intelligentsia, yet they claimed to represent the peasants and workers of the Russian Empire. The new ruling elite promised to build an entirely new type of government that would serve the interests not of a privileged minority, but of the working-class majority of society.

The Bolsheviks believed that a mature socialist society, enjoying the support of most of society, would not need to use systematic coercion. The state would simply 'wither away' in Friedrich Engels's famous phrase. However, the Bolsheviks also understood that in the immediate future they would face dangerous enemies. To deal with them, they would need a coercive machinery of some kind. Russia's backwardness and poverty would also make it difficult to build a truly democratic and egalitarian society.

How long would these problems delay the creation of a genuine Socialism? How long would the transition period last? And what type of society would emerge during the transition to true Socialism?

The remaining chapters of this book will describe the outcome of the Bolshevik experiment. They will argue that before the Bolsheviks could build Socialism, they had to face two other hurdles: political survival and economic backwardness. Sadly, the solutions they found to these problems led them far from their original goals, forcing them to build a society whose political culture was depressingly similar to that of tsarist Russia.

How and why were they led so far from their long-term goals? What did they achieve? Were their failures inevitable? Were their socialist ideals unrealistic?

■ The New Soviet Government: The First Six Months

Formally, it was not the Bolsheviks who led the October Revolution, but the Military-Revolutionary Committee of the Petrograd Soviet. In this sense, the October Revolution represented the belated assumption of power by the Soviet and those it represented. The meeting of the Second All-Russian Congress of Soviets on the evening of 25 October confirmed this impression. The Second Congress met in Smolny, the headquarters of the Petrograd Soviet, and the headquarters for the uprising. Of 670 delegates, 300 were Bolsheviks. Another 193 left-wing Socialist Revolutionaries allied with the Bolsheviks in support of the uprising. Altogether, more than 500 delegates supported the creation of a socialist government. However, many of these opposed the violent methods used to assume power.[1]

The congress elected a new executive committee dominated by Bolsheviks and left-wing Socialist Revolutionaries. This replaced the old executive committee elected in June, which had been dominated by moderate socialists. During the night of 25–26 October, as pro-Soviet soldiers stormed the Winter Palace, Menshevik and right-wing Socialist Revolutionary delegates to the congress walked out in protest at the use of armed force. This left the Bolshevik–Left Socialist Revolutionary coalition in charge of a diminished congress. For the moderate socialists, the walkout proved a fatal mistake. As they left the room, Trotsky shouted contemptuously: 'Go where you belong, to the rubbish bin of history!'

Early in the morning of the twenty-sixth, the Bolshevik Kamenev announced to the congress that the Winter Palace had fallen. Its fall meant the end of the Provisional Government. All ministers had been arrested except Kerensky, who had escaped. The Second Congress of Soviets now assumed power in the name of Soviets throughout the former Russian Empire. The announcement came in a decree drafted by Lenin.

> *Document 8.1: The assumption of power by the Congress of Soviets, 26 October 1917 [Old Style]*

To All Workers, Soldiers, and Peasants:

The Second All-Russian Congress of Soviets of Workers' and Soldiers' Deputies has opened. It represents the great majority of the soviets, including a number of deputies of peasant soviets....

Supported by an overwhelming majority of the workers, soldiers, and peasants, and basing itself on the victorious insurrection of the workers and the garrison of Petrograd, the congress hereby resolves to take governmental power into its own hands.

The Provisional Government is deposed and most of its members are under arrest.

The Soviet authority will at once propose a democratic peace to all nations and an immediate armistice on all fronts. It will safeguard the transfer without compensation of all land – landlord, imperial, and monastery to the peasant committees; it will defend the soldiers' rights, introducing a complete democratization of the army; it will establish workers' control over industry; it will insure the convocation of the Constituent Assembly on the date set; it will supply the cities with bread and the villages with articles of first necessity; and it will secure to all nationalities inhabiting Russia the right of self-determination.

The Congress resolves that all local authority shall be transferred to the soviets of workers', soldiers', and peasants' deputies, which are charged with the task of enforcing revolutionary order ...

Soldiers, Workers, Employees! The fate of the revolution and democratic peace is in your hands!

Long live the Revolution!

The All-Russian Congress of Soviets of Workers' and Soldiers' Deputies and Delegates from the Peasants' Soviets.[2]

The congress immediately passed two more decrees drafted by Lenin. These dealt with the issues of peace and land. The first proposed immediate negotiations to end the war 'without annexation and without indemnities'. The second abolished private ownership in the land and allowed local peasant Soviets to take control of all private lands. In effect the decree on land sanctioned the slow takeover of the land that had already begun throughout the empire. Finally, the congress appointed a new government, the Soviet of People's Commissars, or *Sovnarkom*. Lenin became its chairman, and Trotsky its commissar (minister) for foreign affairs. Thus, it was as the dominant party of a government of Soviets that the Bolsheviks first assumed power. As a result, the October Revolution gained the support not just of Bolsheviks, but also of many others who saw it as a victory for the Soviets and for Russia's workers and peasants.

The government did not have a traditional machinery of power. There were no bureaucrats, soldiers or police whose obedience it could take for granted. When the new commissars entered the tsarist ministries, most officials refused to obey them. Clerks emptied ink-wells; bank-tellers refused to cash cheques; guards hid the keys to offices and safes. They had good reason, for the new commissars had no experience of government, and no formal right to issue orders. There was indiscipline even within the Bolshevik Party. Not only did Kamenev and Zinoviev publicly oppose the October insurrection, but Lenin himself disobeyed a Central Committee order to remain in hiding until the insurrection had succeeded. Instead, risking arrest or assassination, he travelled by tram to Smolny on the evening of 25 October. If such indiscipline was possible at the very top of the party, the discipline of distant provincial committees and Soviets was even less certain.

The government's lack of a reliable coercive machinery persuaded many that it could not last more than a few days or weeks. Sukhanov argued that five hundred disciplined troops loyal to the Provisional Government could easily have dispersed the government in the weeks after October. Even Lenin and Trotsky knew that their government might go down as another heroic failure. They half expected it to suffer the fate of the Paris Commune of 1871, whose working-class government had lasted only three months. Both believed that the international revolution would decide the fate of the Russian revolution. In a speech to the Second Congress of Soviets, Trotsky put it bluntly: 'If the rising of the peoples of Europe does not crush imperialism, we will be crushed ... that is unquestionable'.[3]

However, the government had several sources of strength which helped it to survive the crucial six months of its infancy.

In spite of its weakness, the new government wielded considerable coercive power in the weeks after the October uprising. This coercive power rested not on the discipline of a traditional army and bureaucracy, nor on popular support alone, but on the support of groups of armed men. Most important of all were the garrison soldiers in the capital and the major towns. Less important were the armed workers organized in units of Red Guards. As long as it had the active support of these two groups, the government could wield considerable force in the towns. In the weeks after the Petrograd uprising it made free use of that force to spread the revolution throughout Russia. Between October and December, town after town fell to Soviets dominated by local Bolsheviks and supported by local troop garrisons. Where the support of the troops was uncertain, as in Moscow, there were violent and bloody clashes. Elsewhere, the transfer of power in the towns was surprisingly smooth.

Bolshevik influence in the countryside was insignificant. Very few Bolsheviks came from rural areas and most village Soviets preferred the Socialist Revolutionaries to the mainly urban Bolsheviks. In the anarchic conditions of late 1917, however, it was the towns and the railways that held the keys to power, and by early 1918 the Bolsheviks controlled both. The countryside remained a world apart, invaded but never conquered by the armies that marched across it during the Civil War.

In the early months after October, the Bolsheviks, like the Provisional Government before them, took seriously the aim of ruling through popular support rather than through a machinery of power. They certainly used force – in the October uprising itself and, as early as 27 October, to close down anti-Bolshevik newspapers. In December, they created a new secret police institution, the *Cheka*, or All-Russian Commission for Suppression of Counter-Revolution, Sabotage and Speculation. However, the Bolsheviks did not yet start systematically building a new machinery of power. During their first six months in power, they relied on the considerable support that the new government of Soviets enjoyed in the towns and among the rank and file of the army.

During his months in hiding before October, Lenin had written the classic *State and Revolution*. In this almost anarchistic essay, he argued that a socialist government would not be a special organization, separate from and above the people. On the contrary, it would require the direct or supervisory participation of most members of the working-class population. In this sense, it would be the people. In the same way, its army would be the people in arms.

After October, the government acted on these assumptions, partly out of conviction, but partly because it had no other source of power. The land decree turned the administration of the land over to village Soviets. On 14 November the government granted to committees of workers control of the running of factories and enterprises. The first Red Armies were militias. Their recruits were volunteers, their officers were elected by soldiers councils, and they dispensed entirely with the hierarchy of ranks, and the harsh discipline of traditional armies. The Bolsheviks hoped that Bolshevik armies, like those of revolutionary France, would make up in revolutionary *élan* for what they lacked in discipline and training. Working-class democracy would triumph over ruling-class discipline.

The government also continued the process (well advanced by October) of dismantling the old machinery of coercion. They abolished the old legal system, and replaced it with a system of elected 'people's courts'. In early November, they abolished the old class system, along with Peter the Great's Table of Ranks. The old police and bureaucracy disintegrated without any help. In November, the Bolsheviks declared an armistice at the front. This led to the final collapse of the army, as peasant-soldiers deserted *en masse* and the government began active demobilization. Finally, the decrees on land and on workers' control of industry abolished the private property in productive resources (above all, in land and capital), that had been the economic foundation of the old ruling group. These decrees destroyed the power of the main ruling classes of tsarist Russia: the landed nobility and the moneyed bourgeoisie.

The Bolsheviks also began to carry out the long-established socialist commitment to the emancipation of women. The Provisional Government had already granted women the vote. The Soviet government abolished all forms of legal discrimination based on sex, and its Marriage Code of 1918 gave married women complete legal equality with their partners. It also made divorce easier. In 1920 the government legalized abortion. By the standards of the time, this was remarkably advanced legislation.

Within the Bolshevik Party a special Women's Department (*Zhenotdel*) was set up in 1919 under the direction of the most active Bolshevik feminist, Alexandra Kollontai (1872–1952). Lenin and Trotsky wanted to mobilize women in support of the new government. They also shared the traditional socialist belief that the building of Socialism would emancipate women as women, not just as proletarians. Socialist society would allow women to enter the paid work force on equal terms with men. To do this, socialist governments would have to provide extensive social services to free women from domestic labour. However, Kollontai went much further than most Bolshevik leaders in her commitment to sexual liberation and the abolition of the traditional family.

In early 1918 the flimsy fabric of Soviet power rested almost entirely on the popular support of key sectors of the population. The decrees on land and peace earned the sympathy of most peasants and soldiers, and the decrees on factory control consolidated urban working-class support. Most important of all was the support of those with guns: soldiers and Red Guards.

But working-class support was not as total or as enthusiastic as the party might have wished. The peasants' first loyalty remained to the Socialist Revolutionaries. This was shown clearly when elections were held for the Constituent Assembly in November. The Bolsheviks received only 9.8 million out of 41.7 million votes (24 per cent), and 168 out of 703 deputies (24 per cent). The Socialist Revolutionaries had 17.1 million votes (41 per cent) and 380 deputies (55 per cent). The left Socialist Revolutionaries (now allied with the Bolsheviks) had only thirty-nine delegates. The new government also faced the hostility of those working-class organizations, such as the railway unions, which had opposed a violent overthrow of the Provisional Government. By early 1918, many urban workers were already disillusioned at the new government's failure to halt the economic collapse that began in 1917.

In the early months of its existence the new government benefited from the weakness and disorganization of its opponents. The collapse of the old machinery of power left the old ruling classes politically naked. They had neither the organization with which to replace the old coercive machinery, nor the popular support necessary to undermine Bolshevik power. Sukhanov's five hundred disciplined and loyal troops (see p. 209–10) simply did not exist. Few soldiers felt strongly enough to oppose a government that promised them so much, as Kerensky found late in October when he tried to rally Cossack units to retake Petrograd. Further, the conviction that the Bolsheviks could not last long induced a lethargy in their opponents that prevented them from organizing effective resistance.

■ The Drift Towards Civil War

While the new government faced a disorganized enemy, it could survive on a wave of urban working-class enthusiasm. But as working-class enthusiasm waned and its enemies began to organize in earnest, the rules changed. The Bolsheviks now discovered how desperately weak they were. To stay in power, they would now have to impose their will on friends as well as foes. They would have to build a new coercive machinery.

The Bolsheviks' most dangerous enemy in the early months was the German army. Late in November the Bolsheviks announced an armistice, and early in December peace negotiations began at Brest-Litovsk. However, the Germans demanded so high a price for peace that many Bolsheviks found their terms unacceptable. Early in February the Bolshevik delegation, led by Trotsky, marched out of the negotiations, announcing grandly that it would accept 'neither peace nor war'. The German armies exploited this foolish gesture to the full by advancing, unopposed, into Russian territory. The realists in the government, headed by Lenin, rapidly agreed to even harsher peace terms. On 3 March they signed the Treaty of Brest-Litovsk, which surrendered most of the territory conquered by Russia since the seventeenth century, including the Baltic and Polish provinces, Georgia, Finland, and much of Ukraine. Along with 60 million people, the treaty surrendered 2 million square kilometres of land, which had provided almost a third of the Russian Empire's agricultural produce.

This was a heavy price to pay. Still, many Bolsheviks believed that a German revolution would soon render the treaty void. In any case, the treaty bought the Bolsheviks a crucial breathing space. They used it to prepare for the encounter with domestic opponents who, though weaker than the Germans, fought for higher stakes. In March the Bolsheviks moved their capital from Petrograd to Moscow. Here it was less vulnerable to attacks from the west.

Meanwhile, their enemies began to organize. At the end of 1917 several army commanders, including Kornilov, Alekseev and Denikin, had fled to the south of Russia. Here they began to form an anti-Bolshevik Volunteer Army in the lands of the Don Cossacks. They formed an uneasy alliance with the cossacks and through them began to purchase arms and munitions from their former enemies, the Germans.

The Bolshevik declaration of the right of all subject peoples of the Russian Empire to secede encouraged the emergence of separatist movements in Finland, the Baltic and the Caucasus. On 18 December (31 December according to the European calendar) Finland became an independent state. In Ukraine an elected *rada* or parliament negotiated a separate treaty with Germany and set up an independent government that was soon fighting pro-Bolshevik forces.

Left-wing opponents of the Bolsheviks initially put their faith in the Constituent Assembly. This met in Petrograd on 6 January and elected the Socialist Revolutionary Chernov as its president. However, their hopes of forming a new, elected government of the left were soon crushed. After one session, the Bolsheviks used loyal troops to disperse the Assembly. After this, even socialists took up arms against the Bolshevik government. In March, the left Socialist Revolutionaries split with the Bolsheviks over the Brest-Litovsk Treaty and over the Bolsheviks' hostility towards the wealthier peasantry. In July 1918 they led a series of urban uprisings against the Bolsheviks. In June Chernov formed a Socialist Revolutionary government in Samara on the Volga. He soon allied with a conservative government that had been set up in Omsk, in western Siberia. In Arkhangel'sk, in the north, a Socialist Revolutionary government was established in August. Though its leader was a veteran populist, Chaikovsky, it rested on the power of British troops.

On 17 July 1918, local Bolsheviks in Ekaterinburg in the Urals murdered the tsar and his family, fearing that advancing anti-Bolshevik troops might release them. Bolshevik leaders had almost certainly given them permission to do so in the event of a crisis and on hearing of the execution, the leadership gave its formal approval. However there is no proof that Bolshevik leaders issued specific orders for the execution.[4] On 30 August, a left Socialist Revolutionary, Dora Kaplan, shot and wounded Lenin. The Cheka took a terrible revenge, shooting thousands held in Bolshevik-controlled prisons. Feliks Dzerzhinskii (1877–1926), the head of the Cheka, wrote to his wife from Moscow: 'Here there is a dance of life and death, a moment of truly bloody battle'.[5]

In the first half of 1918, foreign powers began to intervene in Russia's increasingly confused affairs. They did so partly to protect foreign interests, and partly to help overthrow a government that had unceremoniously repudiated tsarist foreign debts and tsarist military commitments and nationalized foreign-owned enterprises. British troops landed at Murmansk in the far north in March. British and Japanese troops landed at Vladivostok in the far east in April. In the second half of 1918, Italian, French and American troops also landed in the far east, while British and French troops entered the Caucasus and the Black Sea region. Meanwhile, German armies occupied much of the west of the country and most of Ukraine. All in all, over 250 000 foreign troops from more than fourteen different states took part in the war.[6]

The first direct blow came from an unexpected source. During the war, a Czechoslovak Army of Liberation had been formed in Russia from Czech residents and prisoners of war. By 1918, this numbered 45 000 soldiers. In early 1918 it was the only disciplined army unit left on Bolshevik-controlled territory. In March the Bolsheviks granted permission for it to travel eastward through Siberia so they could travel by sea to join the fighting in France. The Czechs set off on the trans-Siberian railway in a convoy of sixty trains, strung out along hundreds of kilometres. However, in May Bolshevik officials at Chelyabinsk station in the Urals tried to arrest Czech soldiers involved in a fight with Hungarian troops. During the skirmish that followed, the Czechs seized control of Chelyabinsk station, and then of stations from Penza to Irkutsk. With the trans-Siberian railway in their hands, they controlled much of western Siberia and parts of eastern European Russia. After abandoning hope of reaching the far east, Czech soldiers allied with anti-Bolshevik forces, and began to advance westwards from the Urals towards Moscow.

■ War Communism

The Bolsheviks reacted to the crisis of mid-1918 with energy and decisiveness. In doing so, they laid the foundations of a new social order very different from the idealized socialist society they had envisaged before coming to power. Faced with the threat of all-out civil war they began to construct a new coercive machinery. They built an army, a new police system, a disciplined ruling group, and the fiscal machinery necessary to support these structures.

The evolution of the Red Army shows clearly how this transformation occurred. The renewed German attacks in February forced the government to abandon the idea of a 'People's Army'. While some party members persisted with the ideal of a socialist militia, others argued for the adoption of more traditional methods of discipline, training and mobilization. Lenin and Trotsky both supported the more pragmatic approach. So did the 'military specialists', professional soldiers prepared to serve the Communist government. On 8 April Trotsky became commissar for war. In the same month, plans were drawn up to attach Party commissars to each army, to ensure the loyalty of the mainly non-Bolshevik 'military specialists', and the 'revolutionary discipline' of the troops. The role of the military commissars was to prove crucial in maintaining discipline in the Red Armies. Indirectly, the anti-Bolshevik armies recognized this by executing captured commissars.

The crisis of May 1918, provoked by the Czech advance, strengthened the hand of military traditionalists within the party. Though there were bitter clashes within the Party, the traditionalists won the day. At the end of May, the government introduced compulsory military service for the working classes and began to mobilize new Red Armies. Here was one of the many points at which the new government crossed the divide between power based on 'social support' and the establishment of a 'machinery of power'. In mid-March, the various Red Armies probably included only 100 000 to 200 000 men. By August, the Bolsheviks had mobilized 500 000 more. By January 1920 the Red Army was five million strong.[7] Meanwhile, the Communists had also recruited over 48 000 former tsarist officers.[8] Along with compulsory recruitment went other changes. Soldiers' committees disappeared. Ranks and harsh military discipline reappeared, including the reintroduction of the death penalty for desertion.

In August 1918, with the fall of Kazan on the Volga, the situation was so critical that Trotsky personally took charge of the Red troops who faced the advancing Czechs and Whites at Sviyazhsk. This was a crucial period. Trotsky ordered that if any unit retreated without orders its commissar and commander would immediately be shot. When a new regiment of soldiers deserted, seizing a steamer to flee down the river, Trotsky sent one of his own lieutenants, Markin, to stop them. Here is Trotsky's account of what followed.

☐ *Document 8.2: Trotsky at Sviyazhsk, August 1918*

Boarding an improvised gunboat with a score of tested men, he [Markin] sailed up to the steamer held by the deserters, and at the point of a gun demanded their surrender. Everything depended on that one moment; a single rifle-shot would have been enough to bring on a catastrophe. But the deserters surrendered without resisting. The steamer docked alongside the pier, the deserters disembarked. I appointed a field-tribunal which passed death sentences on the commander, the commissary, and several privates – to a gangrenous wound a red-hot iron was applied.[9]

Trotsky's savagery paid off. The Red units held Sviyazhsk and soon launched a counter-offensive. A series of episodes like this shaped a rabble of soldiers and armed workers into a disciplined regular army. Trotsky wrote: 'In the autumn [of 1918] the great revolution really occurred. Of the pallid weakness that the spring months had shown there was no longer a trace. Something had taken its place, it had grown stronger'.[10]

The Bolsheviks had always understood the importance of propaganda. Indeed, the party had largely organized itself around the editorial board and distribution networks of its underground newspapers. After October, the Bolsheviks took immediate steps to seize control of the machinery of persuasion so as to mobilize support. They banned all 'counter-revolutionary' newspapers as early as 28 October 1917 and seized control of all forms of public communication. During the Civil War the Communist government created one of the most sophisticated propaganda machines of the early twentieth century. It established a wide range of government-controlled newspapers. Amongst the most important were the army newspapers, whose correspondents included the writer,

Isaac Babel. The government pioneered the use of posters and encouraged experimentation with new media such as film. It also gained the support of radical artists and of poets such as Mayakovsky (1893–1930). Education itself became an instrument of persuasion, as literacy brigades combined education and propaganda. Propaganda trains and riverboats brought newspapers, books, films and teachers to remote villages and to army units. In 1919 the government nationalized theatres and cinemas. These were the first steps towards the creation of the all-embracing machinery of persuasion of the Stalin era.

The change from spontaneity to discipline affected not just the armies. It affected all areas of life during the Civil War, and in both the Red and White camps. Both sides began to make free use of secret police to arrest suspected traitors, and to arrest and frequently murder the families of opponents or traitors. Rigid press censorship and ubiquitous secret police suppressed internal opposition. In June the Bolshevik government expelled all Socialist Revolutionaries and Mensheviks from the Soviets. (Other non-Bolshevik parties further to the right had already met the same fate.) From now on the government included only members of the Communist Party, the name assumed by the Bolsheviks in March 1918.

In July 1918, the government issued the first Soviet constitution. This described the new governmental structure. On the face of it, the new structure was extremely democratic. Elected Soviets at all levels became the main organs of government. Each elected delegates to the next level of Soviets – district, provincial and republican. Supreme power was held by the All-Russian Congress of Soviets. This elected a central executive committee to take decisions between meetings. The executive committee in turn appointed a cabinet, *Sovnarkom* (*Soviet narodnykh kommissarov*). In reality, the new government was less democratic than it appeared. The banning of all non-communist parties left the Bolsheviks/Communists as the only organized group within the political structure. This was already a one-party state.

The Party also changed during the Civil War. In the early months after the revolution, the rough and ready democracy of the revolutionary underground survived. Election was common in Party appointments. Debate and controversy were endless. Contacts between the centre and local Party cells were sporadic. Local Party officials frequently rejected, criticized, or ignored orders from the centre. At the centre itself, the crucial decisions – over Brest-Litovsk, or the reintroduction of military discipline – provoked bitter controversy and debate.

By the end of the Civil War, the atmosphere of party life was permanently transformed. Numbers had expanded rapidly as workers and soldiers joined the party. Early in 1917, the Party had only about 25 000 members. By 1918 it had almost 400 000 members, and by March 1921 it had almost 750 000. The vast majority of Party members had joined during the Civil War. Inevitably, the Party itself was militarized. During the Civil War, most new Party members were not intellectuals or factory workers but soldiers or bureaucrats. The hierarchical structures of the army and bureaucracy shaped the atmosphere of the Party profoundly. By 1921, Party officials had survived two or three years of bureaucratic and military campaigns, and the unending crises had hardened them to the brutalities of civil war. Party members expected to give and to receive orders, and they expected harsh punishment for indiscipline. To debate or reject the decisions of the centre was now unthinkable. The Civil War buried the democratic traditions of the revolutionary underground for ever, creating instead a new ruling group, organized and disciplined through the Communist Party. By 1921 it displayed the discipline and unity that had characterized Russia's traditional ruling elites. As so often in Russia's past, members of the new ruling group began to see themselves as the desperate defenders of a besieged fortress. Most willingly accepted the discipline their situation demanded.

Characteristic of the changing mood of the Party is the following decision of the Eighth Party Congress, held in March 1919.

> *Document 8.3: On the organization question, eighth Party Congress, March 1919*

#7 Centralism and discipline

The Party finds itself in a situation in which the strictest centralism and most severe discipline are an absolute necessity. All decisions of a higher body are absolutely obligatory for lower ones. Every decree must first be implemented, and appeal to the corresponding party organ is admissible only after this has been done. In this sense outright military discipline is needed in the Party in the present epoch. All party enterprises which are suitable for centralization (publishing, propaganda, etc.), must be centralized for the good of the cause.

All conflicts are decided by the corresponding higher party body.[11]

The demand for strict discipline came as much from below as from above. Local party organizations often wrote to Moscow asking for the appointment of central government officials to help cope with local crises. All sections of the party needed, demanded and accepted a discipline that was increasingly military in its strictness and ruthlessness.

As the party became disciplined, it also became corrupt. Many joined it because the party had become the only avenue to influence and power. Where most goods were rationed, Party members were in a position to make sure they were first in line. Warm leather jackets soon became a symbol of party membership. By 1919 the Party leaders were already discussing the need to remove those who had joined the Party for the wrong reasons, and who were now disgracing it with their corrupt, brutal and drunken behaviour. 'The word commissar has become a curse', said a delegate to the Eighth Party Congress. 'The man in the leather jacket … has become hateful among the people.'[12] The congress decided to renew all Party membership cards in mid-1919 in order to weed out the corrupt. Unfortunately this, the first Party purge, provided as many opportunities for the settling of old scores within the party, as for the removal of corrupt members. It set a dangerous precedent.

The economic structures that emerged during the Civil War were the outcome of two distinct pressures: the need to fight a civil war, and the Party's notions of how to build a socialist society. Where the two pressures conflicted, the needs of defence prevailed. Where the two coincided they created the illusion of a rapid transition to socialism. For a time, the illusion convinced many members of the party that they were building communism itself in the midst of war. It is this uneasy combination of Utopian and practical elements that characterized the economic structures known as 'war communism'.

As with the army, the early economic decisions of the new government were more concerned to destroy old structures than to create new ones. The Bolsheviks expropriated landowners, industrialists and foreign capitalists. The peasants took charge of the land and workers took charge of the factories through the factory committees. As a way of destroying the old ruling elite these measures were extremely successful. Ideologically they seemed progressive, and their implementation fulfilled the promises contained in the Bolshevik Party programme.

However, as methods of organizing a war economy, they were disastrous. Trotsky wrote:

> The spring and summer of 1918 were unusually hard. All the aftermath of the war was then just beginning to make itself felt. At times it seemed as if everything was slipping and crumbling, as if there was nothing to hold to, nothing to lean upon. One wondered if a country so despairing, so economically exhausted, so devastated, had enough sap left in it to support a new regime and preserve its independence. There was no food. There was no army. The railways were completely disorganized. The machinery of state was just beginning to take shape. Conspiracies were being hatched everywhere.[13]

Who would control society's resources after the overthrow of the capitalists and landlords? Socialists agreed in principle that all members of society should have some share in the control of society's resources. But how was this shared control to be exercised? By locally elected Soviets or factory committees? By trade unions? Or by a central government claiming to represent the working class as a whole? Would market forces survive during the transition period or not? Ideology provided no clear-cut answers. Neither Marx nor Lenin offered a blueprint. After October it seems that Lenin was ready for a long transition period in which markets would remain important in the country's economic life. Indeed, he talked much in this period of the transitional era of 'state capitalism'.[14]

In practice, the pressures of Civil War forced the government to assert control from the centre. This meant a return to the direct mobilization of resources. The towns and the countryside posed two distinct problems. Control of the towns gave the Bolsheviks control of the factories, their labour force, and the goods they produced. Far harder was the task of controlling the countryside, and the labour and produce of the peasantry, for as yet the Bolsheviks had little power outside the towns.

In December the government established the Supreme Council of the National Economy, or *Vesenkha*. Its task was to control and plan the economic life of the whole country. Ironically, the new planning agency was modelled on the 'Economic Council' which the Provisional Government had created in July to organize a wartime planned economy like those of Britain and Germany. However, *Vesenkha* lacked the skills, the resources and the power necessary to manage the economy. Nevertheless, the government tried to assert control from the centre. Nationalization of industrial enterprises began slowly and chaotically. The government nationalized railways and the mercantile fleet in the spring of 1918. Local Soviets often decided to 'nationalize' individual enterprises. Then in June, the government decided to nationalize all factories. By September 1919 *Vesenkha* claimed to control 3300 enterprises employing 1.3 million workers.[15] How real this control was is impossible to say. What is clear in retrospect is that these were the first steps towards the vast command economy that was to emerge in the 1930s.

As the government tightened its grip on industrial enterprises, managerial control replaced the factory committees of 1917. As the economic role of the government expanded, that of the market contracted. The breakdown of exchange between town and country, inflation, nationalization of banks, the need to take military rather than commercial decisions, and ideological assumptions about the building of socialism combined to limit the role of money. There emerged a system of semi-controlled barter. Increasingly, goods were produced and allocated by government order, and workers were paid with rationed goods. Eventually, the government tried to abolish private trade, altogether.

Many ideologically minded communists saw in these changes the birthpangs of socialism. In retrospect, though, even most communists came to admit that they were merely the consequences of a deep social came to admit that they were merely the consequences of a deep social and military crisis. Some came to suspect that they had indeed witnessed a birth, but that the terrible agonies of the Civil War had deformed the new-born child.

The government had little control over the countryside, where most of the country's resources lay. The desperate and brutal techniques it used in the rural areas gave it just enough resources to continue fighting the war, but the price the rural population paid was high. The methods of direct mobilization that the government used in the countryside meant that tax-collecting began to take on once more the aspect of medieval tribute collection.

The government tried hard to put down roots in the countryside. It created a new local government institution, the *Volispolkom* (VIK), the executive committee of the *volost'*, or district Soviet. These were elected councils handling the affairs of several villages. During the Civil War, increasing numbers of young peasants who had served in the army and joined the Communist Party entered the executive committees of the new *volost'* Soviets. They became, in this way, the first peasant-controlled organs of Communist Party power in the countryside. However, as they turned into instruments of central power, they lost local support.

In practice, the Communists had to use more direct methods to control the countryside. A first priority was to supply bread to the towns and factories. Here was where their main support lay and here were produced the munitions needed to fight the Civil War. They had no magical solution to the supply problems that had brought down the tsarist government the previous February and had plagued the Provisional Government throughout its short life. On the contrary, land seizures, encouraged by the decree on land, made it even harder to persuade peasants to sell grain for scarce and over-priced factory produce. Like its predecessors, the new government tried to control grain prices. This forced it to deal harshly with grain speculators and hoarders. Eventually, it tried to control the grain trade directly. Here, too, its methods were not new, for tsarist army officers had sometimes procured goods for their regiments by force, and so, occasionally, did the Provisional Government.[16] The Brest-Litovsk treaty, loss of the major grain source of the Ukraine, and the drift into civil war, made the food supply situation critical.

To bypass private traders and grain speculators, detachments of workers and soldiers from the larger towns began visiting villages to buy grain and to confiscate the surpluses of the richer peasants, the so-called *kulaks*. The Cheka began to seize stocks held by hoarders. In June the government tried to split the peasantry. It set up committees of poor peasants, who were encouraged to help seize the grain hoarded by their richer neighbours. For the most part, the peasantry did not divide along class lines. Whatever divisions existed within most villages, they were insignificant in comparison with the far greater division between the village and the outside world. Besides, the land repartitions of 1917 had reduced the differences in wealth within most villages.

The government soon regularized the system of food detachments. Like the *druzhina* of a medieval prince, armed workers or army units began to extract resources from the villages. Soon, grain requisitioning units began to take other goods as well – horses, carts, firewood. They paid if they could, and if they felt well disposed towards the peasants. Otherwise, they took what they needed. Lenin admitted after the Civil War:

> The essence of War Communism was that we actually took from the peasant all of his surpluses and sometimes not only the surpluses but part of the grain the peasant needed for food. We took this in order to meet the requirements of the army and to sustain the workers.[17]

The government labelled this system of forced requisitioning of produce *prodrazverstka*. The fancy label masked a modern form of tribute, for *prodrazverstka* relied on the direct and overt use of force. Often, grain requisitioning detachments received a share of what they collected as a reward. This was an economics that the soldiers of Genghis Khan would have understood perfectly. What justified this primitive system was the absence of any alternative, for existing supply systems had collapsed. In late 1918, the commissar for food supplies, Tsyurupa noted:

> There is complete economic dislocation in the localities. There is no political authority whatsoever; postal and telegraph communications have been disrupted; the technical infrastructure for the collection of grain has been destroyed; there is insufficient administrative personnel; the military authorities interfere in the procurement of grain; the peasants have been intimidated and say they are afraid to transport their grain.[18]

□ *Document 8.4: grain requisitioning detachments*

(a) Harvesting and grain requisition detachments, 4 August 1918

1.   All *guberniya* and *uezd* [provincial and district] Soviets of Workers' and Peasants' Deputies, all committees of the poor, all trade union organisations of workers, together with the local organs of the People's Commissariats of Food and Agriculture are to form immediately harvesting and grain requisition detachments. Detachments of workers and peasants from starving [provinces], sent to requisition grain, are to help in bringing in the new harvest. Form immediately new detachments from among the local peasants and workers to carry out these tasks ...

3. All grain collected by harvesting and grain requisition detachments, is to be distributed on the following basis: firstly, of course, the necessary amount of grain to satisfy the need for food of the poorest strata of the local population is to be distributed. This part of the grain collected is not to be removed but to remain at the local level. All other grain is to be immediately and unconditionally delivered to grain collection centres. The distribution of this grain is to be carried out by the [provincial] food committees on the instructions of the People's Commissariat of Food.

4. Members of harvesting and food requisition detachments, if they are not being rewarded according to previously published decrees ... are to be rewarded, firstly, by an allowance in natura [in kind]; secondly, by payment in cash according to local conditions and; thirdly, by special bonuses for successful and rapid fulfilment of harvesting work and the transfer of grain to storage centres. The extent of rewards and bonuses are to be determined by [provincial] food committees on the basis of instructions from the Commissariat of Food.

Chairman of the Council of People's Commissars
V. ULYANOV (LENIN)

People's Commissar of Food
A. TSYURUPA

(b) Instructions for requisitioning grain, 20 August 1918

1. Every food requisition detachment is to consist of not less than seventy-five men and two or three machine guns.

2. A commander is to head each detachment. He is to be appointed by the chief commissar responsible for the organisation of food armies and a political commissar appointed by the Commissariat of Food. The commander is to control purely military and economic activities. The political commissar's duties are (a) to organize local committees of the rural poor and (b) to ensure that the detachment carries out its duties and is full of revolutionary enthusiasm and discipline.

3. [Province and district] military commanders are to be in charge of all food requisition detachments operating in a given [province or district].

4. Plans for grain requisition in a [district] are to be drawn up by the head of the requisition department appointed by the [provincial] food committee.

5. Food requisition detachments are to be subject only to the orders of their commanders ...

7. The food requisition detachments shall be deployed in such a manner as to allow two or three detachments to link up quickly. Continuous cavalry communication shall be maintained between the various food requisition detachments.

People's Commissar of Food
A. TSYURUPA[19]

Though archaic, *prodrazverstka* seemed to work. Despite its crudeness and brutality, it supplied the towns and armies with just enough food and supplies to keep producing war material and to keep fighting.

For the peasantry, the experience was a harsh disillusionment. This was especially true of the richer peasants, or *kulaks*, whom the Communists treated as class enemies. Peasants began to think they had been granted land only to have its produce seized by force. Often, they reacted with violence. As the Civil War dragged on, more and more bands of peasants took up arms. The largest, such as that of the anarchist leader Nestor Makhno, formed regular armies that took on both Red and White Armies, levied their own taxes, and organized miniature governments. (See Document 8.5.) The peasants also reacted by sowing less. Why produce surplus grain only to have it confiscated? In Ukraine, formerly the bread basket of the Russian Empire, the sown area declined by up to 80 per cent.[20] Peasants reacted to government attempts to control trade by circumventing them. Black markets emerged, trading privately despite government bans. Even Lenin admitted that at least half of the trade between towns and countryside was illegal in 1919.[21]

Most of all, however, the peasants reacted to the Civil War by trying to avoid it. A recent study of peasants in the Volga region concludes that:

> The primary concern of the vast majority of the peasantry was not to get itself involved in the Civil War any more than it had to. The peasants were willing to fight against the landowners in their own localities: they formed their own peasant brigades; and they were even ready to fight for the Red Army as long as it was seen to be defending the revolution in their own locality. But the peasants came to see the Civil War increasingly as an alien political struggle between the socialist parties. Their attitude towards this struggle was one of indifference, as a recruiting officer of the People's Army in Simbirsk province pointed out: 'the mood of the peasants is indifferent, they just want to be left to themselves. The Bolsheviks were here – that's good, they say; the Bolsheviks went away – that's no shame, they say. As long as there is bread then let's pray to God, and who needs the Guards? – let them fight it out by themselves, we will stand aside. It is well known that playing it by ear is the best side to be on'.[22]

■ Military Victory

By late 1918, there were already several anti-communist governments, each with its own armies. Denikin was organizing the volunteer army in the south. Victor Chernov, the leader of the SRs, had formed a Socialist Revolutionary government in Samara on the Volga. Anti-Communist governments had also appeared in Omsk in western Siberia, and in Arkhangel'sk in the far north. As we have seen, in August Trotsky had checked the first anti-Communist offensive at Sviyazhsk, near Kazan.

In November 1918, a new right-wing government in western Siberia, headed by Admiral V. Kolchak, overthrew the 'Directory', which had briefly united the various anti-Communist groups. By early 1919, all anti-Communist forces acknowledged Kolchak as their overall commander. However, even this did not provide the anti-Communist forces with the unity necessary for success. In March 1919 Kolchak launched a new offensive from western Siberia, with Czech support. Soon after, Denikin attacked from the south, and General Yudenich attacked Petrograd from nearby Estonia. This triple offensive was the critical moment of the Civil War. The failure of the Whites to co-ordinate their attacks allowed Communist forces to deal with them one by one.

By June 1919 the Communists had checked Kolchak's forces and begun to turn them back. A Communist counter-offensive led by a young party worker, Mikhail Frunze (1885–1925), soon recaptured the Urals. By November Frunze controlled much of western Siberia, and Kolchak's government collapsed as partisan war erupted throughout Siberia. In November Kolchak fled east along the trans-Siberian railway. In Irkutsk the socialist leaders of an anti-Kolchak revolt tried and executed the Supreme Commander of the White forces in February 1920.

Denikin's advance was at first more successful. By October 1919 his forces had captured Orel, a mere 400 kilometres south of Moscow. In the same month General Yudenich reached Gatchina on the outskirts of Petrograd. From here, Yudenich's men could see the spires of Petrograd's Peter and Paul fortress. This was the high tide for the Whites. Trotsky successfully led the defence of Petrograd, and within a month Red forces had driven Yudenich's army back to Estonia. By 20 October Denikin's armies were also in retreat. In their rear, the peasant anarchist army of Nestor Makhno had risen, threatening their communications with the Black Sea ports. By January 1920, Communist armies had recaptured Ukraine, and in April Denikin resigned his command. The Arkhangel'sk government collapsed early in 1920.

In 1920 the tide briefly turned once more. Polish armies occupied western Ukraine in April and May. Simultaneously, General Wrangel, one of Denikin's lieutenants, led a new offensive northwards from the Crimea. However, in May General Tukhachevsky led the Red Army's counter-attack against the Poles. By July the Poles had retreated to Warsaw. Lenin hoped these advances would spread the revolution westwards into the European heartland of world capitalism. Red Armies now turned on

Wrangel and forced his army to evacuate the Crimea. But Lenin's hopes of a Polish revolution came to nothing. A Polish counter-offensive drove the Russians out of Poland, and in October an armistice brought the Russo-Polish war to an end.

The armistice with Poland ended the Civil War. In eastern Siberia local Cossack armies, supported by the Japanese, survived until February 1922. But in European Russia, the Civil War was over by the end of 1920. The Communists now controlled most of the old Russian Empire except for Poland, Finland and the Baltic States, which had become independent nations.

Something of the confusion and savagery of the fighting during the Civil War is conveyed in the following account. It describes a clash between the forces of Denikin and those of the Ukrainian anarchist, Nestor Makhno, whose armies fought both Whites and Reds. The battle described here was fought on 26 December 1919, in the Ukrainian village of Peregonovka. The author was an anarchist and follower of Makhno, Peter Arshinov.

☐ *Document 8.5: a Civil War battle, September 1919*

The fighting started between 3 and 4 a.m. ... in a hurricane of machine-gun fire on both sides. Makhno himself, with his cavalry escort, had disappeared at nightfall, seeking to turn the enemy's flank. During the whole battle that ensued there was no further news of him. By 9 in the morning the outnumbered and exhausted Makhnovists began to lose ground. They were already fighting on the outskirts of the village. From all sides enemy reinforcements brought new bursts of fire to bear on the Makhnovists. The staff of the insurrectionary army as well as everyone in the village who could handle a rifle, armed themselves and joined in the fighting. This was the critical moment, when it seemed that the battle and with it the whole cause of the insurgents was lost. The order was given for everyone, even the women, to be ready to fire on the enemy in the village streets. All prepared for the supreme hour of the battle and of their lives. But suddenly the machine-gun fire of the enemy and their frantic cheers began to grow weaker, and then to recede into the distance. The defenders of the village realized that the enemy was retreating, and that the battle was now taking place some distance away. It was Makhno who, appearing unexpectedly, at the very moment when his troops were driven back and were preparing to fight in the streets of Peregonovka, had decided the fate of the battle. Covered with dust and fatigued from his exertions, he reached the enemy flank through a deep ravine. Without a cry, but with a burning resolve fixed on his features, he threw himself on the Denikinists at full gallop, followed by his escort, and broke into their ranks .... A hand-to-hand combat of incredible ferocity, a 'hacking' as the Makhnovists called it, followed. However brave the First Officers' Regiment of Simferopol' [the Denikin unit] may have been, they were thrown into retreat, at first slowly and in an orderly manner,

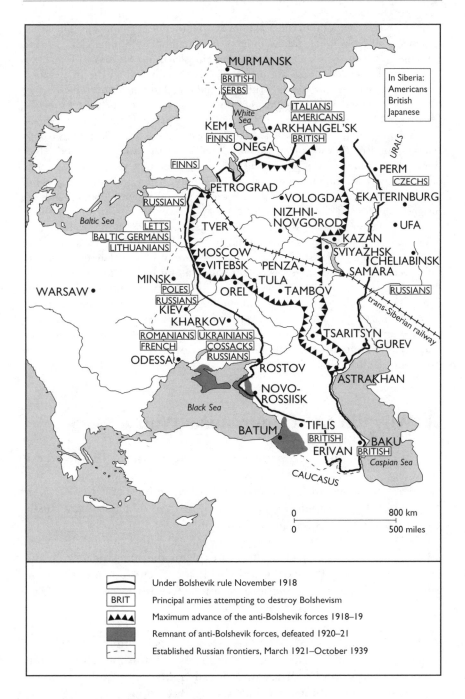

Figure 8.1 *The Civil War, 1918–20*

trying to halt the impetus of the Makhnovists, but then they simply ran. The other regiments, seized by panic, followed them, and finally all of Denikin's troops were routed, and tried to save themselves by swimming across the Sinyukha River.

Makhno hastened to take advantage of this situation, which he understood perfectly. He sent his cavalry and artillery at full speed in pursuit of the retreating enemy, and himself went at the head of the best mounted regiment by a shortcut which would enable him to catch the fugitives from behind. The pursuit continued for eight to twelve miles. At the critical moment when Denikin's troops reached the river, they were overtaken by the Makhnovist cavalry, and hundreds of them perished in the river. Most of them, however, had time to cross to the other bank, but there Makhno himself was waiting for them. The Denikinist staff and the reserve regiment which was with it were surprised and taken prisoners. Only an insignificant part of these troops, who had raged for months in the stubborn pursuit of Makhno, managed to save themselves. The First Simferopol' Regiment of officers and several others were entirely cut down by the insurgents' sabres. The route of their retreat was strewn with corpses for over two miles. However horrible this spectacle was to some, it was only the natural outcome of the duel between Denikin's army and the Makhnovists. During the entire pursuit, the Denikinists had had no thought except to exterminate the insurgents. The slightest error on Makhno's part would inevitably have led to the same fate for the revolutionary insurrectionary army. Even the women who supported the Makhnovist army or fought alongside the men would not have been spared. The Makhnovists were experienced enough to know this.[23]

■ Why did the Communists Win?

In comparison with their opponents, the Communists had three crucial advantages during the Civil War. The social basis of their power was broader; they acted with greater unity and discipline; and finally, their control of the geographical and industrial heartland of European Russia gave them a superior strategic position.

The key areas of Communist support were, of course, among the urban working classes. Working-class support explains the superior morale and discipline of those Red Army units with a high proportion of urban workers. Working-class pride also counted. As Trotsky told a workers' meeting in 1918:

> Although we are still weak, the course of events has raised us up to an immense height. The Russian working class is at this moment the only working class in the entire world which does not suffer political oppression. Yes, things are bad for us right now, but the Russian working class has been the first to draw itself up to its full height and say: 'This is where I begin to learn how to steer the ship of state'.[24]

A small section of the intelligentsia also served the Communists. As the war progressed, so too did many army officers, such as General A. A. Brusilov, who had led the successful offensive of 1915. Some served because the Communists held their relatives hostage. Others, though uninterested in ideology, saw the Communists as national leaders, determined to throw out foreign invaders and re-establish strong government.

The Communists had little support among the peasantry. However, the White Armies failed to exploit this weakness, for most were determined to restore the land to the gentry. As a result, the Reds found it easier to recruit peasants than the Whites. 'It is symbolic that at the critical stages of their campaigns the armies of Kolchak and Denikin were crippled by peasant uprisings behind the White lines. The Red Army also suffered from peasant uprisings, but at the critical moments the rural areas behind the Red lines remained solid. The peasants' dislike of the Communists, it would seem, was not as powerful, and certainly not as ingrained, as their hatred and fear of the old political order.'[25] The Communists were also more successful than the Whites in incorporating younger peasants into the new power structures that emerged during the Civil War. They did this mainly through the army. In the 1920s, ex-servicemen accounted for the vast majority of rural Communist Party members.[26]

Abroad, war-weariness and working-class sympathy for the Communist cause gave the Communists other allies. Domestic opposition to intervention, particularly in England and France, ensured that foreign aid to the Whites was uncertain and small-scale.

As the elections to the Constituent Assembly had shown, the Communists were not as representative of the population as they claimed to be. The Whites, however, were even less representative. They found support mainly among members of the former ruling classes. Even the socialists who joined the Whites after the closing of the Constituent Assembly had to compromise with former landlords, industrialists and army officers.

The policies of the various anti-communist governments also reflected the deep gulf between the old ruling elite and the majority of Russian society. The conservatism of the White governments on issues such as industrial relations and land earned them the active hostility of urban workers. They also failed to pick up the peasant support the Communists were losing. After 1918, the Socialist Revolutionaries, the traditional party of the peasantry, played only a secondary role in formulating the policies of White governments.

Unlike the Whites, the Communists were united. Leading the Red Armies was a single-party government, united under Lenin's leadership. Lenin dominated the government through *Sovnarkom*. His government was guided by a coherent political and social programme worked out over many years. Yet it never followed ideology slavishly. On the contrary, the Communists showed exceptional ability to improvise. The party also displayed a remarkable capacity to close ranks in a crisis. As party members supervised the work of military commanders and government officials at all levels, they instilled their own discipline and energy into the army and bureaucracy. Finally, the government mobilized support by creating a powerful, sophisticated and original propaganda machine.

The White governments never succeeded in creating a unified political programme, or even a unified government. Old divisions within the traditional ruling group could not be smoothed over in a matter of months. Indeed, it was impossible to produce a political programme that could unite ex-radicals, such as the liberal leader Milyukov or the Socialist Revolutionary Chernov, with aristocratic landlords, successful industrialists and conservative army officers. Within the anti-communist governments feuding continued between different factions. Each had its own ideas about how to fight the war and about the sort of society they would build once they had defeated the Communists.

An astute and charismatic leader on the right might have imposed some unity on this motley group, but such a leader did not appear, and the murder of the royal family deprived the anti-Bolshevik forces of the one remaining unifying focus. The Whites paid a high price for their lack of unity and discipline.

Geography exaggerated the disunity of the Whites. By mid-1919 there were White Armies in Arkhangel'sk, in Baltic Estonia, in the Caucasus and in western Siberia, but there was no land connection between the four areas. It proved impossible to co-ordinate the political and even the military plans of such a widely scattered coalition.

While it weakened the Whites, geography favoured the Reds. The Communists never lost control of the heartland of European Russia, dominated by the two capitals – Petrograd and Moscow. Control of the centre meant control of Russia's industrial heartland – Moscow itself, and the armaments factories of Tula and Petrograd. The Reds also held the hub of the railway network, whose various lines converged on Moscow. This eased the task of moving troops from front to front.

■ Direct Mobilization and the Communist Experiment

The advantages of the Reds – strong and united leadership, control of the industrial heartland, and working-class support – meant that they were better able than their opponents to mobilize human and material resources for war. More than anything else, the Communist victory reflected the successful mobilization of resources by a determined and highly militarized ruling group. However, success in the Civil War set a fateful precedent for it meant a return to traditional strategies of direct mobilization, and the autocratic political culture that had sustained them. Eventually, the Communist Party would fall back on these traditions to solve the even greater problems they faced once the Civil War ended. In this way, the Civil War marked a return to the past rather than a leap into the future. The Civil War retreat from indirect to direct forms of mobilization provides a short, sharp epitome of the entire Soviet experiment.

■ Summary

The Bolshevik government survived its first few months because of the support of urban Soviets and garrison troops in the towns, and the disorganization and inertia of its opponents. Under Lenin's leadership, the government made it clear that it would be utterly ruthless where necessary in defence of the revolution; but for a time it also expected to survive on a world-wide wave of working-class enthusiasm. The threat of renewed German advances in the west, and the emergence of organized anti-Bolshevik armies in the south and east disabused the Bolsheviks of this hope. In the middle of 1918, the Communist government began to create a traditional army, based on traditional disciplinary methods, and sustained by the direct mobilization of recruits, grain and war materials. This system of mobilization came to be known as 'War Communism'. Though Communist idealists saw such methods as a hopeful sign of the breakdown of capitalism, they were, in reality, a sign of economic collapse. A combination of ruthless, disciplined government, primitive methods of direct mobilization, and the weakness and war-weariness of their opponents allowed the Communists to win the Civil War. However, the war also left an indelible mark on the party. The party emerged militarized, brutalized, and aware that direct methods of mobilization might be a workable alternative to the methods of capitalism. This legacy was to form an important ingredient of the Stalinist revolution from above of the 1930s.

□ *Further Reading*

The account of the civil war in the second volume of Chamberlin, *The Russian Revolution*, is still worth reading. Two good recent histories are Mawdsley, *The*

Russian Civil War, and Lincoln, *Red Victory*. On the important subject of the role of the peasantry, see the recent study by Figes, *Peasant Russia*. On the role of the Communist government, there is a fine study by T. H. Rigby, *Lenin's Government*. Service, *The Bolshevik Party in Revolution*, surveys the role of the party. R. C. Nation, *Black Earth, Red Star*, provides a brief introduction to international relations during the Civil War. The best introduction to the economics of 'War Communism' is still to be found in Nove, *An Economic History*. There are briefer accounts of the Civil War in Fitzpatrick, *The Russian Revolution*, and White, *The Russian Revolution*, and see also the collection of essays edited by Diane Koenker, *Party, State and Society in the Russian Civil War*.

☐ *Notes*

1. A. Rabinowitch, *The Bolsheviks Come to Power: The Revolution of 1917 in Petrograd* (New York: Norton, 1978) pp. 291–2.
2. Ibid., pp. 303–4.
3. Cited from R. C. Nation, *Black Earth, Red Star: A History of Soviet Security Policy, 1917–1991* (Ithaca: Cornell University Press, 1992) p. 2.
4. M. D. Steinberg and V. M. Khrustalëv, *The Fall of the Romahovs* (New Haven, Conn. and London: Yale University Press, 1995), pp. 293–4, 339.
5. George Leggett, *The Cheka: Lenin's Political Police* (Oxford, 1981) p. 105, cited from W. B. Lincoln, *Red Victory: A History of the Russian Civil War* (London: Sphere Books, 1989) p. 146.
6. Nation, *Black Earth, Red Star*, p. 32
7. J. Erickson, 'The Origins of the Red Army', in R. Pipes (ed.), *Revolutionary Russia* (Cambridge, Mass.: Doubleday & Co, 1976) pp. 307, 317. During the First World War, the Russian army had been 9 million strong.
8. Nation, *Black Earth, Red Star*, p. 18.
9. L. Trotsky, *My Life* (Harmondsworth: Penguin, 1971) p. 418.
10. Cited in Lincoln, *Red Victory*, p. 161.
11. M. Matthews, *Soviet Government: A Selection of Official Documents on Internal Policies* (London: Cape, 1974) p. 134.
12. Cited in Lincoln, *Red Victory*, p. 479.
13. Trotsky, *My Life*, p. 411.
14. M. Lewin, *Political Undercurrents in Soviet Economic Debates* (London: Pluto Press, 1975) p. 76.
15. A. Nove, *An Economic History of the USSR*, 3rd edn (Harmondsworth: Penguin, 1992) p. 62.
16. V. Andrle, *A Social History of Twentieth-Century Russia* (London/New York: Edward Amoded, 1994) p. 78.
17. P. Avrich, *Kronstadt 1921* (Princeton University Press, 1970) p. 9.
18. O. Figes, *Peasant Russia, Civil War: The Volga Countryside in Revolution (1917–1921)* (Oxford University Press, 1989) p. 184.
19. M. McCauley (ed.), *The Russian Revolution and the Soviet State: 1917–1921* (London: Macmillan, 1975) pp. 249–51.
20. B. Dmytryshyn, *USSR: A Concise History*, 2nd edn (New York: Scribner's, 1971) p. 110.

21. Figes, *Peasant Russia, Civil War*, p. 260.
22. Ibid., p. 175.
23. P. Arshinov, *History of the Makhnovist Movement: 1918–1921* (Detroit/Chicago: Black & Red, 1974) pp. 142–5.
24. Cited in Lincoln, *Red Victory*, p. 200.
25. Figes, *Peasant Russia, Civil War*, pp. 4–5.
26. Ibid., p. 225.

■ *Chapter 9* ■

The New Economic Policy

■ Defeat in Victory

The military emergency of the Civil War ended when Wrangel's armies evacuated the Crimea in November 1920, a month after the armistice with Poland. But before the Communist Party could begin to think about the long-term problem of building a socialist society, it had to face the disastrous economic and political aftermath of seven years of war and revolution.

First the Communists had to accept that the world revolution they had hoped for in October 1917 had not occurred. There had been promising flickers of revolution and three great empires had fallen. The German Kaiser had been overthrown in November 1918. In the spring of 1919, Soviet Republics appeared in Bavaria and Hungary. There was even a communist uprising in Berlin in January 1919. In 1920, during the Polish War, the Red Army had tried to export revolution on the point of its bayonets. In March 1921, a further attempt at a communist uprising in Berlin failed. However, by the middle of 1921 all sparks of revolution had been doused. This meant that instead of surviving weeks or months of international isolation, the new government might remain besieged by world capitalism for years or even decades.

The situation inside Russia was equally bleak. H. G. Wells visited the country in 1920 and wrote this description.

☐ *Document 9.1: H. G. Wells on Russia in 1920*

Our dominant impression of things Russian is an impression of a vast irreparable breakdown. The great monarchy which was here in 1914, the administrative, social, financial and commercial systems connected with it have, under the strains of six years of incessant war, fallen down and been smashed utterly. Never in all history has there been so great a debacle before. The fact of the revolution is to our minds altogether dwarfed by the fact of this downfall ... The Russian part of the old civilized world that existed before 1914 fell and is now gone ... Amid this vast disorganization an emergency government supported by a disciplined party of perhaps 150 000 adherents – the Communist Party – has taken control. It has – at the price of much shooting – suppressed brigandage, established a sort of order and security in the exhausted towns and set up a crude rationing system.[1]

The literature on the period – Boris Pasternak's *Dr Zhivago*, Isaac Babel's *Red Cavalry*, Mikhail Sholokhov's *And Quiet Flows the Don* – conveys the same impression of breakdown. The proletariat, the basis of Bolshevik support, had shrunk. The number of workers employed in enterprises with more than sixteen employees fell from 3.5 million to about 1.5 million early in 1921.[2] Many former proletarians were now in the army. Others had left the poorly supplied towns for the villages, to claim a share in the redistributed land. There, at least, they could grow their own food. The population of Petrograd had fallen from 2.5 million in 1917 to 600 000 in 1920.[3] Yet the villages had also suffered, particularly where fighting and requisitioning had been most ferocious. The harvest of 1920 was only 54 per cent of the 1909–13 average. The 1921 harvest was even smaller. Famine affected many areas, and with famine came typhus. In some areas there was cannibalism. Perhaps 6 million people died in what soon turned into one of the worst famines of the twentieth century.[4]

Production had fallen in all sectors of the economy. Even in 1914 Russia was backward by comparison with Western Europe. By 1921, it was even more backward, and the building of socialism seemed more remote than ever. Statistics on economic output tell the sad story (see Table 9.1). By 1921 the Communists had defeated the old ruling group. However, the methods they used had placed an appalling burden on workers and peasants. In the spring of 1921, these accumulated discontents exploded. The continuation of *prodrazverstka* threatened famine in the villages because requisition detachments often took even the grain needed for food, fodder and seed. With the threat of a White victory gone, peasants were no longer willing to tolerate such a system. In February 1921 the Cheka reported 118 separate peasant uprisings in various parts of the country.[5] In Tambov province and parts of Ukraine, peasant armies ruled large areas of the countryside, torturing, mutilating and executing Communist officials or members of food detachments wherever they found them.

The same grievances overflowed into the towns. Russian workers still had close contacts with the countryside. Indeed, these ties had intensified during the years of war and civil war as peasants sought work in the towns and workers sought land in the villages. Besides, by preventing private trade in foodstuffs, Bolshevik policy threatened famine in the towns. Both townspeople and peasants suffered from the activities of the so-called 'cordon' or 'blockade' detachments. These were special army units set up in 1918 to prevent illegal trade by 'sackmen', or peasants with sacks of goods. An English eyewitness recorded this account of their activities at a Petrograd station.

Table 9.1   *The Soviet economy under the New Economic Policy*

Absolute figures	Index numbers (1913 = 100)						
1913	1920	1921	1922	1923	1924	1925	1926
Industrial production 10 251 m. (1926) roubles	14	20	26	39	45	75	*108*
Coal 29 m. tonnes	30	31	33	47	56	62	95
Electricity 1945 m. kilowatt hours	–	27	40	59	80	*150*	*180*
Pig iron 4 216 000 tonnes	–	3	4	7	18	36	58
Steel 4 231 000 tonnes	–	4	9	17	27	50	74
Rail freight carried 132 m. tonnes	–	30	30	44	51	63	–
Cotton fabrics 2582 m. metres	–	4	14	27	37	65	89
Sown area 105 m. hectares	–	86	74	87	93	99	*105*
Grain harvest 80.1 m. tonnes	58	47	63	71	64	91	96

Notes: –figures not available; figures in italics = over 100 per cent of 1913 figure; the 1913 grain harvest was unusually high, so the figures in the final row exaggerate the decline in agricultural production in the early 1920s

Source: A. Nove, *An Economic History of the USSR*, 3rd edn (Harmondsworth: Penguin, 1992) p. 89.

☐   *Document 9.2: The activities of the 'Cordon Detachments'*

At nine [the train] reached the straggling buildings of the Okhta Station [in Petrograd] ... and there I saw a most extraordinary spectacle – the attempted prevention of sackmen from entering the city.

As we stood pushing in the corridor waiting for the crowd in front of us to get out, I heard Uncle Egor [a peasant] and his daughter conversing rapidly in low tones.

'I'll make a dash for it,' whispered his daughter.

'Good,' he replied in the same tone. 'We'll meet at Nadya's.'

The moment we stepped on to the platform Uncle Egor's daughter vanished under the railroad coach and that was the last I ever saw of her. At each end of the platform stood a string of armed guards, waiting for the onslaught of passengers, who flew in all directions as they surged from the train. How shall I describe the scene of unutterable pandemonium that ensued! The soldiers dashed at the fleeing crowds, brutally seized single individuals, generally women, who were least able to defend themselves, and tore the sacks off their backs and out of their arms. Shrill cries, shrieks, and howls rent the air. Between the coaches and on the outskirts of the station you could see lucky ones who had escaped, gesticulating frantically to unlucky ones who were still dodging guards. 'This way! This way!' they yelled wildly, 'Sophia! Marusia! Akulina! Varvara! Quick! Haste!'

In futile efforts to subdue the mob the soldiers discharged their rifles into the air, only increasing the panic and intensifying the tumult. Curses and execration were hurled at them by the seething mass of fugitives. One woman I saw, frothing at the mouth, with blood streaming down her cheek, her frenzied eyes protruding from the sockets, clutching ferociously with her nails at the face of a huge sailor who held her pinned down on the platform, while his comrades detached her sack.

How I got out of the fray I do not know, but I found myself carried along with the running stream of sackmen over the Okhta Bridge and toward the Suvorov Prospect. Only here, a mile from the station, did they settle into a hurried walk, gradually dispersing down side streets to dispose of their precious goods to eager clients.

Completely bewildered, I limped along, my frost-bitten feet giving me considerable pain. I wondered in my mind if people at home had any idea at what cost the population of Petrograd secured the first necessities of life in the teeth of the 'communist' rulers.[6]

In the towns there were other complaints too. Food was scarce (as it had been in 1917). Working hours were long. Wages (now mostly paid in kind) were low. Finally, factory discipline was harsher than ever as the Communists introduced military rule in the factories. There was growing resentment at the new elite of party officials who got a disproportionate share of rationed goods and behaved increasingly like bosses. Many people hoped for a return to the more democratic working-class politics of late 1917 – to freely elected Soviets and factory committees. These were potent symbols of what had proved a brief era of genuine working-class democracy.

In February 1921 there was a rash of factory meetings in Moscow and then Petrograd, protesting against the harsher aspects of War Communism. In March, the naval garrison of the fortress island of Kronstadt mutinied. Kronstadt had been one of the most loyal Bolshevik bases in 1917, and its sailors had fought hard and loyally during the Civil War. This made their mutiny all the more shocking for the Communists. The mutineers demanded a democratic working-class government representing all working-class parties.

Document 9.3: demands of the Kronstadt insurgents, 28 February 1921

1. In view of the fact that the present soviets do not represent the will of the workers and peasants, to re-elect the soviets immediately by secret voting, with free canvassing among all workers and peasants before the elections.
2. Freedom of speech and press for workers, peasants, Anarchists and Left Socialist Parties [that is, not for members of the former ruling group].
3. Freedom of meetings, trade unions and peasant associations.
4. To convene, not later than 1 March 1921, a non-party conference of workers, soldiers and sailors of Petrograd City, Kronstadt and Petrograd Province.
5. To liberate all political prisoners of Socialist Parties, and also all workers, peasants, soldiers and sailors who have been imprisoned in connection with working class and peasant movements [that is, but not upper-class prisoners].
6. To elect a commission to review the cases of those who are imprisoned in jails and concentration camps.
7. To abolish all Political [propaganda] Departments, because no single party may enjoy privileges in the propagation of its ideas and receive funds from the state for this purpose. Instead of these Departments, locally elected cultural-educational commissions must be established and supported by the state.
8. All 'cordon detachments' are to be abolished immediately.
9. To equalize rations for all workers, harmful sectors [that is, types of work] being excepted.
10. To abolish all Communist fighting detachments in all military units, and also the various Communist guards at factories. If such detachments and guards are needed they may be chosen from the companies in military units and in the factories according to the judgement of the workers.
11. To grant the peasant full right to do as he sees fit with his land and also to possess cattle, which he must maintain and manage with his own strength, but without employing hired labour.
12. To ask all military units and also our comrades, the military cadets, to associate themselves with our resolutions.
13. We demand that all resolutions be widely published in the press.
14. To appoint a travelling bureau for control [that is, supervising and checking up on the work of officials].
15. To permit free artisan production with individual labour [that is, hiring labour was to remain illegal]. The resolutions were adopted by the meeting unanimously, with two abstentions.

President of the Meeting
PETRICHENKO

Secretary
PEREPELKIN[7]

The Kronstadt mutiny began on 28 February 1921, a week before the Tenth Congress of the Communist Party met in Moscow on 8 March. On

11 March, more than 300 members of the Congress took the train to Petrograd, where they helped Trotsky and Tukhachevskii prepare the assault on Kronstadt. The issuing of Lenin's decree abolishing grain requisitioning, on 15 March, immediately improved the morale of the Communist troops waiting on the chilly shores of the Baltic. On 17 March Red units, fortified with vodka and dressed in white camouflage, attacked across ice that was breaking up under constant shelling. They suppressed the mutiny only after desperate and bloody fighting in which at least 15 000 defenders died.

The bloody fighting in Kronstadt showed the seriousness of the crisis. Though they had expelled the White Armies, the Communists could no longer contain the discontent their wartime rule had provoked among their working-class supporters. The crisis of the spring of 1921 challenged the ideals of the Communist Party as well as its power. A government claiming to represent the working class now found itself on the verge of being overthrown by that same working class. The crisis had undermined the loyalty of the villages, the towns and, finally, sections of the army. It was fully as serious as the crises faced by the tsarist government in 1905 and in February 1917. Could the Communist government react more successfully than its predecessors? What sacrifices would it have to make to survive?

 # The Introduction of the New Economic Policy

There were two options: advance or retreat. The government could persist with war communism or it could back down.

As early as February 1920, Trotsky had argued for a retreat to indirect methods of mobilization. On his travels around the country as war commissar, he saw clearly the extent of the economic collapse. He saw that, as in 1917, the crucial problem was that of grain supplies – of trade between town and country. Direct control of 25 million peasant farms was as yet quite beyond the government's means. So was the direct control of the grain trade that the government tried to achieve during the Civil War. The alternative, Trotsky argued, was to give the peasants an incentive to produce and sell surplus grain. Instead of requisitioning grain at arbitrary prices, the government should tax peasants in kind, taking a fixed percentage of the grain they produced. It should then let them sell the rest of their produce at free market prices.

The idea was simple. Yet its implications were profound, for it affected the activities of the 84 per cent of people still on the land.[8] Because it satisfied popular demands, it promised to end popular discontent and restore grain supplies to the towns. However, the change would require compromises that many in the Party would find painful. It would mean ending *prodrazverstka,* the foundation of War Communism. The government would have to abandon the attempt to control the rural sector directly. That, in turn, would mean a partial return to a free market in grain, driven by the profits earned by peasant producers and traders. In other words, it meant a partial return to Capitalism.

Trotsky argued for these changes in February 1920, but Lenin would not consider them. Like many others in the party, Lenin resisted the idea of reintroducing capitalism to the countryside after fighting a terrible civil war to overthrow it. Logically, Trotsky then began to argue for an intensified strategy of direct mobilization. If the government refused to abandon war communism, it would have to extend it. The solutions that had worked during the military crisis of 1918 should now be applied to the economic crisis of 1921. Such methods had already produced results on the railways. So Trotsky now proposed militarizing the entire labour force.

By early 1921, Lenin was the realist. During the Kronstadt revolt, he finally saw the force of Trotsky's original idea. To the tenth Party Congress he proposed replacing *prodrazverstka* with a tax in kind. Further, he proposed setting the new tax lower than the existing delivery quotas for 1920–1. He suggested lowering the grain quota by 43 per cent, the quota on potatoes by 45 per cent, and the quota on meat by 74 per cent.[9]

Lenin's proposal marked the end of war communism and the beginning of what the party began to call the New Economic Policy (NEP). It meant a partial return to indirect methods of mobilization, and to the 'state capitalism' that Lenin had talked of in the eight months after the October revolution. As in the past, when faced with widespread rural insurrection, a Russian government had beaten a fiscal retreat. The retreat showed that, though the government now controlled the towns, it did not yet control the countryside.

Other concessions had to follow if the reform was to work. The government abolished the cordon detachments and allowed peasants and small traders to buy and sell produce. It denationalized small non-agricultural enterprises, and leased them, often to their former owners. Small businesses could now employ up to twenty workers and produce goods for a profit.

The sackmen, whose activities it had repressed only months before, now flourished, and a whole class of small traders and entrepreneurs appeared. Following more cautiously in their tracks came larger traders. These two groups came to be known as 'NEP men'. They mediated between town and country, taking on economic tasks that the cumbersome planning system could not handle. The New Economic Policy depended on the success of the NEP men and the wealthy peasants who produced the grain surpluses. Yet it was inevitable that the Communist government would treat their activities with suspicion. NEP men profits were taxed at 50 per cent, their licences had to be renewed frequently, and they could be punished for what the authorities defined as 'speculation'.[10] No wonder they concentrated mainly on quick profits and made few long-term investments.

The government retained control in the urban sectors of the economy. It held what Lenin dubbed, in a crisp military metaphor, the 'commanding heights' of the economy. These included large industrial enterprises, banking, foreign trade, the railways, and large industrial projects such as Lenin's plan for the electrification of Russia. It also held the most important of all economic levers – the state itself. However, it had surrendered the vast agricultural sector and the retail trade based on it to the capitalist instincts of the peasantry and the NEP men. The Party gambled that as long as it held the commanding heights, the capitalist lowlands would remain under its indirect control.

This mixture of party control of the 'commanding heights' and small-scale capitalism in the rural areas and retail trade was the essence of the New Economic Policy. These measures provided a short-term solution to the political crisis of 1921. With the abolition of *prodrazverstka*, popular opposition evaporated. The peasants now had what they had wanted for centuries: ownership of the land and a government too weak to impose heavy taxes.

The economic impact was less immediate. The grain harvest of 1921 was catastrophic, yielding only 37.6 million tonnes, or 43 per cent of the average for 1909–13. In the worst affected areas famine and disease may have killed millions. Eventually the government had to accept famine relief from capitalist America. However, after 1922 the recovery was rapid, particularly in agriculture. It was slower in industry, where restoration of productive capacity was more difficult and more costly.

▮ NEP and Modernization: The Great Debate

Though it solved some short-term problems, the New Economic Policy offered few solutions to the long-term problems facing the government.

The Communist government's long-term aim, and the reason for its existence, was to build socialism. Party members often used the words 'socialism' and 'communism' as synonyms, though in strict usage socialism meant the transitional stage after the overthrow of capitalism, while communism meant the ultimate goal of an egalitarian and classless society. The immediate problem for the government was to build socialism. What did this mean in practical terms?

During the Civil War, the task had seemed simple enough. Many party members believed that socialism would emerge naturally with the overthrow of capitalism. To many, war communism, with its attempt at central planning, its moneyless economy, and its rough egalitarianism, looked like socialism. The collapse of war communism showed that building socialism would not be that easy. Party leaders had to think the problem through more thoroughly.

Marx had insisted that socialism required material abundance. He had also argued that capitalism would generate such abundance by stimulating intensive growth. Yet the Bolsheviks had seized power in backward Russia before capitalism had done its work, in the hope that their uprising would detonate a world-wide revolution. A friendly socialist Europe could then help backward Russia to build socialism. By 1921 it was clear the world-wide anti-capitalist revolution would not occur. This changed the problem entirely. It meant that the Communists now faced the nightmare that moderate socialists had warned against in 1917. They found themselves trying to build socialism in a backward country. Even Marx had said this was impossible. Indeed, he had warned that if they tried to do so, they could only create new forms of class struggle.

What should the Bolsheviks do? The logical answer was to give up. How could they ignore Marx's clear warnings?

In reality, the issue was less clear-cut. For those who had spent their lives fighting capitalism, first in the underground and then during the Civil War, giving up was unthinkable. No one in the party seriously proposed abandoning the socialist project. Besides Marx himself had sometimes been more optimistic about the chances of building socialism under conditions of backwardness. So, the party had to press ahead and find some way of building socialism despite Russia's backwardness. How? This was territory Marx had not charted. One thing was clear. Any path to socialism required overcoming Russia's backwardness quickly. There were three reasons for this. First, the party had to build up Russia's productive resources to provide the economic abundance Marx saw as the basis for socialism. Second, socialist Russia was isolated and vulnerable in a capitalist world. To defend itself, it would need a modern armaments industry and a modern army. Third, modernization was necessary to expand the proletariat, the only class from which the Communists expected solid support.

The problem, then, was how to modernize. During the mid-1920s there took place a wide-ranging debate over strategies of socialist modernization in a backward country. The discussions were profound, committed and original. They took place in newspapers and books, within the party, the planning agencies and the economic ministries. These rich debates pioneered the subject often described in the West as 'development economics', for this was the first time that anyone had discussed the problems of planned industrialization with such urgency, thoroughness and expertise.

Marx's analysis suggested that capitalism itself offered the best strategy for rapid modernization. However, the party's own ideology ruled out a purely capitalist solution. So the Communist government began to look for a non-capitalist engine of growth. The problem, then, was this: was there a socialist engine of growth? If there was, could it match the capitalist engine of growth, which had demonstrated its power so spectacularly during the nineteenth and early twentieth centuries? The fate of the Soviet experiment would turn on the answers the Soviet government found to these questions.

We can simplify the discussion by concentrating on the problem of mobilization. Growth of any kind requires the mobilization of labour, raw materials and cash. We have seen it is possible to mobilize resources through the direct use of power, or indirectly, through the operation of market forces.

The industrialization strategy of Peter the Great had relied on the direct mobilization of resources by the state. The strategy of Sergei Witte had relied on a mixture of direct and indirect mobilization. He had used the state to mobilize cash and grain through taxation and had used these resources for a programme of railway building and industrial development. Simultaneously, he had encouraged the indirect mobilization of resources through the commercial activities of Russian and foreign capitalists.

What mechanisms could a socialist government use to mobilize resources? Could it use market forces? Or would it have to rely mainly on the power of the state? The difficulty was that the Soviet government had fewer options than the government of Sergei Witte, thirty years before. It was also in more of a hurry.

Opportunities for indirect mobilization of resources were limited. There were several reasons for this. The first was ideological. In principle, the Soviet government opposed the use of market forces, for most Marxists saw them as the very essence of capitalism. This is why the government reintroduced markets so reluctantly in 1921. However, Lenin had shown many times that Bolshevik ideology could be flexible when necessary. If they could use market forces to further Socialism, then why not?

The second difficulty was that the Bolsheviks had destroyed the Russian bourgeoisie. Most large entrepreneurs were dead or in exile. What remained was a large class of petty entrepreneurs, consisting of peasants and small retailers, both legal and illegal. Could the government work with such entrepreneurs? If so, what would it gain? Would not a revival of the market lead to a dangerous resurgence of petty capitalism, and eventually of large-scale capitalism?

Third, the chances of working with foreign capitalists were also limited. Witte had mobilized much of the cash needed for developing heavy industry through foreign loans. Yet foreign capitalists were unwilling to lend to the Soviet government. They knew that it was committed to their eventual overthrow. Even more important, the Soviet government had repudiated the massive foreign debts accumulated by the tsarist government. It was a bad debtor.

All in all, a strategy of indirect mobilization through market forces would not be easy for a government committed to building socialism, and even if it worked, it could do so only by encouraging a partial revival of capitalism. The only alternative was the direct mobilization of resources for industrial development.

Here, too, there were serious difficulties. To mobilize enough resources for rapid industrialization the government would have to be immensely powerful. Yet the crisis of 1921 had shown that the Soviet government was very weak, particularly in rural areas. In any case, were the resources there to be mobilized? The revolution had left Russian agriculture even more backward than before the First World War. The large farms that had pioneered modern farming methods and produced the bulk of the grain surplus before the war had vanished. The number of small peasant farms, using primitive methods and producing largely for their own subsistence, had increased from 15 million to 25 million. As a result, the total amount of grain put on the market – the most important measure of rural surpluses – had declined. Even in 1927 only 630 million poods (1 pood = 16.3 kilograms) of grain were marketed. This was only 48 per cent of the 1913 figure of 1300 million poods.[11]

In general terms, then, the problem was this: building socialism required industrialization. Industrialization required mobilizing resources. Yet there seemed to be no way of mobilizing enough resources in a poor country while simultaneously building socialism.

During the debates of the 1920s, two main strategies emerged. Both depended on a mixture of indirect mobilization through market forces and direct mobilization through the use of state power. However, the first leaned more towards market forces, while the second relied more on the mobilizational power of the Soviet state.

The first strategy is associated with the name of Nikolai Bukharin (1888–1938).[12] However, before 1927 it was the official policy of the entire Party leadership, including Stalin. In 1921 most party members saw the

New Economic Policy as a temporary retreat that they hoped to reverse as soon as they could. However, after its introduction, growth was so rapid in industry and agriculture that many began to think that NEP itself might offer a solution to the problem of industrialization. This was the starting point for the 'Bukharinite' strategy of socialist industrialization. The argument went like this.

The success of NEP in its early years (see Figure 9.1) had shown that there were good prospects for mobilizing resources through market forces. The government should encourage the peasantry to prosper and flourish. It should set taxes at a modest level, and allow peasants to sell their surpluses on the free market. It should also promise peasants a stable future. Such policies would earn the support of the peasantry, and encourage them to raise productivity. This would encourage intensive growth in the countryside where most of the country's wealth remained. Increased grain production would feed the growing town population and provide exports to pay for imported modern machinery. A prosperous peasantry would use the income generated by grain sales to buy industrial goods produced by the state-controlled industrial sector. The greater the income of the peasantry, the more they could buy, and the greater the revenues earned by government-run agencies trading in grain and producing consumer goods such as textiles, vodka or agricultural equipment. The government could invest the profits of government

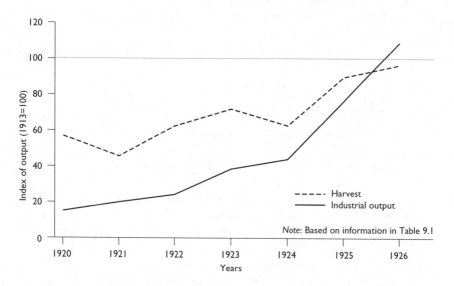

Figure 9.1 *Economic Growth during NEP, 1920–6*
Note: **Based on information in Table 9.1**

enterprises in further industrial growth. In short, trade between government-controlled industries and a flourishing rural sector operating under free market conditions would provide the resources for rapid industrialization.

Though the state would continue to play an active role, indirect mobilization of resources through market forces played the central role in Bukharin's strategy, as it had in Witte's. This strategy had several attractive features. As it depended on the continuation of NEP, it required no social upheavals in the next few years. As Bukharin said, there must be 'no third revolution'.[13] Because Bukharin's strategy required some compromise with capitalism, it would make it easier to deal with foreign capitalist powers. It would therefore allow a lengthy period of co-existence with capitalism, during which it might even be possible to extract foreign loans and borrow foreign technology and expertise.

Ideologically, Bukharin's strategy was attractive for it promised to maintain the *smychka*, the alliance of peasants and proletarians that was the cornerstone of Lenin's strategy in 1917. Lenin's own vague pronouncements on economic policy during the last two years of his life also appeared to support the continuation of NEP for a long time.[14]

To summarize, Bukharin's strategy depended on:

1. maintaining the New Economic Policy for a long time, with private enterprise in the rural sector and retail trade, and socialist control of the urban and industrial sectors;
2. low taxation of the peasantry, and minimal pressure on living standards;
3. slow growth, based on growing exchange between the urban and rural sectors, and led by agriculture and consumer goods industries; and
4. a foreign policy based on peaceful co-existence with capitalism.

However, Bukharin's strategy had some serious weaknesses. Opponents such as Trotsky and Preobrazhensky pointed these out in the debates of the mid-1920s.

First, Bukharin's strategy was slow. Bukharin admitted this when he talked, picturesquely, of 'riding to Socialism on a peasant nag'. His strategy depended on the pace of development of the most backward sector of the Soviet economy – peasant agriculture. It also depended on the ability of Soviet industry to produce consumer goods cheaply. It offered little hope of a rapid build-up of heavy industries such as iron, steel and oil, or of armaments industries. It therefore did little to end the Soviet Union's military weakness. Opponents argued that under Bukharin's strategy, socialist Russia would remain at the mercy of the advanced capitalist nations for decades.

Second, Bukharin's strategy favoured the peasantry, in particular the semi-capitalist *kulaks*. Most party members considered this both dangerous and improper for a proletarian party. The peasantry had been a revolutionary force when they were short of land and sought the overthrow of the landlords. This had been the basis for the Bolsheviks' alliance with the peasantry in 1917. However, after 1917 most peasants were firmly committed to private property in the land. They were, in short, small capitalists. Yet they made up almost 85 per cent of the population. The more they flourished, the more capitalism would flourish with them. From the *kulaks* and the NEP men there would emerge a vast and dangerous class of small capitalists. Their growing economic power would soon enable them to undermine the government's control of the economy and of Soviet society. For a proletarian party keen to abolish private property in productive resources, the resurrection of peasant capitalism was very threatening.

Finally, the economist Eugene Preobrazhensky, a former ally of Bukharin, argued that Bukharin's strategy could not work. The rapid increase in output since 1921 was all very impressive, but it was also misleading. It simply reflected the post-war recovery. Peasants put old fields back into cultivation. Workers and managers repaired factories and locomotives, and drained mines. All this cost very little. However, once recovery was complete, further progress would require the building of new factories, new railways, and the introduction of advanced farming methods. This would demand massive investment funds. Where would they come from? Bukharin's strategy allowed investment funds to rise only 'at the pace of a peasant's nag'. Preobrazhensky argued that the crisis would come in 1926 or 1927, when recovery was complete. At that point, he predicted, rates of growth would fall off rapidly unless the government found new sources of investment funds.

If the left-wing criticisms were accurate, what was the alternative? Bukharin's critics argued that the government had to force the pace at home and abroad. It had to find more resources to fuel industrial growth – and quickly. But where could it find them? Foreign capital could hardly be expected to help much, and there were no longer any large native capitalists. Nor did the Soviet Union have colonies to exploit. (This was not true, of course, as any Ukrainian or Kazakh could have told Preobrazhensky, the economist who made this claim.) This meant that, whether the Party liked it or not, it would have to exact 'tributes' from the peasantry through what Preobrazhensky called 'primitive socialist accumulation'. There was no alternative. The government would have to tax peasants as hard as possible. The left-wing proposed increasing agricultural productivity not with the methods of capitalism, but with the methods of socialism. They argued that it was vital to replace private peasant farming with large collective farms using modern agricultural methods. A more productive rural sector could then provide resources for investment in industrial development. The government should use these resources not for the production of consumer goods, but for heavy industry, electricity, mining, iron and steel, and, of course, armaments. A growing defensive capability would enable the government to adopt a more aggressive foreign policy. Instead of appeasing capitalist powers, it could foment revolution abroad in the hope of provoking socialist revolutions. Socialist revolutions abroad would ease the problems of the Russian government by ending its isolation. Alternatively, the government could attract foreign investment from a position of strength rather than weakness.

To summarize, the Trotsky/Preobrazhensky strategy depended on:

1. the abandonment of the New Economic Policy and a rapid extension of socialism in the countryside;
2. high taxation of the peasantry, and pressure on living standards, particularly in the rural areas;
3. rapid industrial growth led by the heavy goods and armaments industries and supported by collectivized agriculture; and
4. an aggressive foreign policy aimed at ending Russia's isolation through the rapid spread of Socialism.

The left-wing strategy also suffered from serious problems. In particular, it threatened to provoke retaliation from two directions – from Russia's peasantry and from abroad. The right-wing argued that the government was too weak to face either challenge.

Two peasant responses were possible, either of which could bring the government down. First, peasants could simply withdraw from the market. They could stop selling and producing surplus grain. Exports would dry up and the towns would starve. Instead of selling grain, the peasants would eat better themselves or feed surpluses to their livestock, as they had during the First World War. For the government the result would be bread shortages, unrest in the towns, and rapid economic decline – the script of February 1917.

Something like this had already happened during NEP, in the so-called 'scissors' crisis of 1923. Since 1921, agriculture had recovered more rapidly than industry, so industrial production could not satisfy growing peasant demand. As a result, industrial prices rose, while agricultural prices declined. On a graph, the two lines crossed, forming the blades of the 'scissors' from which the crisis took its name. Instead of selling surplus grain in return for overpriced and scarce industrial goods, the peasants stopped marketing grain. Trade between town and country began to break down, which threatened the very foundations of the New Economic Policy. The government moved to force industrial prices down to satisfy the peasantry, and just weathered the storm. Still, the threat remained.

Faced with a government that refused to back down, the peasantry had a second weapon: revolt. This was the script of 1861, 1905 and 1921. The 1921 crisis appeared to show that the Soviet government was too weak to deal with a widespread peasant revolt. But during NEP the Communist Party's influence in the countryside continued to decline. The recruitment of young peasants into the army and the party during the Civil War, and intensive literacy campaigns, had maintained some party influence in the villages. During NEP, demobilization and the ending of literacy programmes, sharply reduced the party's influence in the villages. The countryside became foreign territory, beyond the reach of most party institutions, and beyond the control of its economic planners.

In short, the right argued that the government was too weak and the proletariat too small to risk breaking the *smychka* with the peasantry. The right also argued that the government was too weak to risk a foreign policy that might provoke intervention from imperialist enemies abroad. Stalin, who still supported Bukharin's approach, argued that Russia could go it alone in any case and build 'Socialism in one country'. Stalin opposed this slogan to Trotsky's slogan of 'permanent revolution'.

I have described a complex debate in over-simple terms. In reality, though debate forced opponents apart, the left and right shared much common ground. Above all, they agreed that massive use of force could not solve the problem of modernization. According to Bukharin, Lenin had told him in a private conversation before his death that there must be 'no coercion against the peasantry in building Socialism'.[15] Second, they agreed on the need to maintain a balance between the various sectors of the economy during the period of growth. They realized that unbalanced growth could only cause colossal wastage. Third, both sides agreed on the need to maintain elements of the market within the socialist economy. Stalin eventually found a solution to the difficulties of the 1920s by breaking all three of these rules.

■ The End of NEP

The debate over industrialization was inconclusive. However, the problems facing the government worsened in the late 1920s, and the need to find a solution became more pressing. Several events brought the issue to a crisis by exposing the inadequacies of both strategies of socialist industrialization.

In the mid-1920s, the Bukharinite strategy looked promising. Economic growth was rapid, and the strategy had the support of the main party leaders. A year or two later things looked very different. A decline in the growth rate of heavy industry in 1926 and 1927 suggested that Preobrazhensky had been right: the New Economic Policy could not generate enough funds to sustain industrial growth once post-war recovery was complete. Meanwhile, the international position of the Soviet Union worsened. In May 1927, the British government broke off diplomatic relations with the Soviet Union, creating a serious, if temporary war scare. This reminded everyone forcibly of the Soviet Union's military weakness. The slowdown in industrial growth and the prospect of war persuaded the government to increase investment funds rapidly, particularly for heavy industry and armaments. So it compromised slightly with the left by increasing fiscal pressure on the private sector, on both NEP men and *kulaks*. It increased taxes on private trade and lowered the price the government paid for purchases of grain surpluses – the so-called grain 'procurements'. Even Bukharin accepted that the pace of industrial growth had to increase, and that this meant extracting more resources from the peasantry. The question was how?

Bukharin had warned that lowering procurement prices could make the problem worse. Late in 1927 it became clear that, faced with lower grain prices, and a growing shortage of industrial goods, peasants were marketing less of their recently harvested grain. By January 1928, peasants had placed only 300 million poods of grain on the market, in comparison with 428 million poods in January 1927.[16] The 'procurements' crisis of December 1927 was an ominous sign for the government. It seemed to show that if the government squeezed the peasantry too hard, it would destroy trade between town and country, and the economy would collapse. Yet if it did not squeeze the peasantry, it would not have the resources needed to build up heavy industry. The Soviet Union would remain defenceless against military threats from abroad, and the building of a powerful, secure, socialist society would remain a Utopian dream.

Once again, the government could either advance or retreat. It could resort to more direct forms of mobilization or it could persist with the indirect forms of mobilization it had used since 1921. It could take grain by force, risking peasant hostility and starvation in the countryside. Or it could back down, offering higher prices for grain in order to attract peasants back to the market.

When the procurements crisis first struck, late in 1927, Bukharin argued for retreat. The government should pay the peasants more for grain procurements. However, Stalin argued for advance. Prices should remain as they were. Using a law of 1926 that banned all 'evil-intentioned increases in prices of commodities through purchase, hoarding, or non-placing on the market', Stalin urged party officials to seize hoarded grain.[17] He made it clear that he was not fussy about the methods they used as long as they got results. He even talked, loosely, of collecting 'tribute'. For local Party officials, many of whom had vivid memories of the harsh methods used during the Civil War, the message was clear. The methods of War Communism were back in favour.

In January 1928, Stalin travelled to the Urals and western Siberia to urge Party officials to secure hoarded grain. His 'solution' to the procurements crisis therefore became known as the 'Urals–Siberian' method. At each stop, he lectured local Party bosses.

☐   *Document 9.4: Stalin and the 'Urals–Siberian' method*

You're working badly! You're idle and you indulge the *kulaks*. Take care that there aren't some *kulak* agents among you. We won't tolerate this sort of outrage for long.

Take a look at the *kulak* farms, you'll see their granaries and barns are full of grain, they have to cover the grain with awnings because there's no more room for it inside. The *kulak* farms have got something like a thousand tons of surplus grain per farm.

I propose that:

(a) you demand that the *kulaks* hand over their surpluses at once at state prices;

(b) if they refuse to submit to the law, you should charge them under Article 107 of the RSFSR Criminal Code and confiscate their grain for the state, twenty-five per cent of it to be redistributed among the poor and less well-off middle peasants.

You must steadfastly unify the least productive individual peasant holdings into collective farms.[18]

For peasants, too, the government's actions wakened memories of war communism. Violent conflicts broke out between peasants and Party officials. By mid-1928, there were reports of 150 peasant revolts.[19] This raised worrying questions about the reliability of an army that recruited primarily from the villages.

In the short run the 'Urals–Siberian' method was a success. By the spring of 1928, grain procurements were satisfactory. By the summer, however, it was clear (as Bukharin had warned) that squeezing the peasants would lead them to cut down the amounts they sowed. This ensured that the situation would be even worse later in the year. After the 1928 harvest, there was a renewed procurements crisis. Once again, Stalin insisted on resorting to the forcible methods that had worked a year before.

By now, the split between Stalin and Bukharin was open. Bukharin was appalled at the resort to coercion. In a private letter he referred to Stalin as a new Genghis Khan, bent on extracting tribute from the peasantry by 'military-feudal exploitation'.[20]

The 'Urals–Siberian' method broke the *smychka*. It broke the peasantry's trust in the government, and the trading relationship between town and country that had been the heart of the NEP. Whether Stalin realized where all this was leading is unknown. But the die were cast. The party found itself in the grip of a momentum that was both terrifying and exhilarating, particularly for those on the Party's left-wing.

In 1932, when it was clear where such policies led, a bleak joke did the rounds in official circles:

> *Question*: What does it mean when there is food in the town but no food in the country?
> *Answer*: A Left, Trotskyite deviation.
> *Question*: What does it mean when there is food in the country but no food in the town?
> *Answer*: A Right, Bukharinite deviation.
> *Question*: What does it mean when there is no food in the country and no food in the town?
> *Answer*: The correct application of the general line.
> *Question*: And what does it mean when there is food both in the country and in the town?
> *Answer*: The horrors of Capitalism.[21]

The crisis of 1927 and 1928 affected more than grain supplies. It affected all spheres of Soviet life. The breakdown of food supplies threatened the towns with shortages. By early 1928, many foodstuffs were scarce and queues were lengthening. Some town authorities introduced rationing, and there were food riots in several towns, including Moscow.[22] Work discipline began to break down in response to shortages, poor housing, and attacks by the government on bourgeois managers. Combined with the war scare of May 1927, these problems increased tensions within the leadership. To deal with opposition both within the Party and in the villages, the government increased the powers of the secret police, or GPU, to supervise all areas of Soviet life.

In the middle of 1928, the government tried, for the first time, to blame the country's difficulties on sabotage. It staged the first of the great show trials, the so-called 'Shakhty' case. The prosecution accused fifty-three engineers and managers from the mines of the Donets Basin (or 'Donbass') region, of 'wrecking' and sabotage. Three of the accused were German advisers. This ensured that the foreign press would cover the trial with horrified fascination. In the Soviet Union, the trial encouraged disgruntled workers to blame their troubles on class enemies. The court finally sentenced five of the accused to death and they were executed within weeks.

■ NEP and the Changing Political Structure

Political developments eventually offered the government an escape from the terrible dilemmas of the late 1920s. To understand how, we must retrace the history of the new ruling group under the New Economic Policy.

While the government retreated on fiscal and economic issues in 1921, politically it held firm. Lenin talked of the need for heightened discipline during a retreat. Yet the Kronstadt mutineers, and even sections of the party, had called for a relaxation of party control, believing that socialism was inseparable from increased democracy. Many believed that autocratic methods were permissible only in an extreme crisis such as the Civil War. With the war over many party members expected the restoration of democracy, at least for the working classes. They hoped to reduce the powers of the centre, and to allow more freedom to debate policy at the grass-roots level of politics. The Workers' Opposition, the most influential group of this kind within the party, was led by Alexandra Kollontai and Alexander Shlyapnikov. It demanded greater power for trade unions and other working-class organisations.

Frightened by the implications of the Kronstadt revolt, the party majority opposed such liberalism. Concessions to the peasantry were sacrifice enough. There was no need to weaken the government as well. During the Civil War, the party had banned the activities of other parties, though Mensheviks and Left SRs had continued to work within Soviets. Early in 1921, even this limited tolerance of non-communist parties ended. The party imprisoned or expelled all the leading figures in non-communist parties. This left the Communist Party with a monopoly on political power and undisputed control over the levers of power. At the same time, the party maintained the monopoly over the press and other means of communications that it had established during the Civil War. In 1922, it created *GlavLit* (the Main Directorate of Literature), whose task was to supervise the censorship of all forms of literature. Though censorship was relaxed in the 1920s, the government now had the machinery with which, eventually, it would prevent the public expression of any views that diverged from its own.

The leadership also increased discipline within the party. The tenth Party Congress denounced the views of the Workers' Opposition and passed a resolution on 'party unity'. This was a classic expression of the need for discipline and unity within a beleaguered ruling group, and of the complementary need to break the organizational potential of rival groups.

Document 9.5: Resolution of the tenth Party Congress on party unity, March 1921

1. The Congress directs the attention of all members of the Party to the fact that the unity and solidarity of its ranks, guaranteeing complete confidence between members of the Party and work that is really enthusiastic, work that genuinely embodies the unified will of the vanguard of the proletariat, is especially necessary at the present moment, when a number of circumstances increase the waverings among the petty-bourgeois population of the country [the Party's jargon for the peasantry and NEP men].

2. ... All class-conscious workers must clearly recognise the harm and impermissibility of any kind of factionalism, which inevitably leads in fact to a weakening of amicable work and a strengthening of the repeated attempts of enemies who have crept into the governing Party to deepen any differences and to exploit it for counter-revolutionary purposes. The ability of the enemies of the proletariat to exploit any departures from a strictly maintained Communist line was most clearly revealed at the time of the Kronstadt mutiny, when the bourgeois counter-revolution and the White Guards in all countries of the world showed their readiness even to accept the slogans of the Soviet regime in order to overthrow the dictatorship of the proletariat in Russia ...

6. ... The Congress gives instructions that all groups which have been organized on the basis of any platform whatever should be immediately dissolved and commissions all organisations to watch out very closely so that no factional demonstrations may be permitted. Nonfulfilment of this decision of the Congress must incur unconditional and immediate expulsion from the Party.

7. In order to bring about strict discipline in the Party and in all Soviet work, and to achieve the greatest possible unity by removing all factionalism, the Congress empowers the CC [Central Committee] to apply, in the case (or cases) of violation of party discipline or reappearance of, or connivance at, factionalism, all measures of Party punishment right up to expulsion.[23]

The decrees passed at the tenth Party Congress showed that the Party intended to maintain the high levels of discipline and unity established during the Civil War. This enhanced the power of party leaders over the rank and file. Party members understood the dangers of such autocratic methods, but many also saw the need for them. 'In voting for this resolution,' said Karl Radek (1885–1939), 'I feel that it can well be turned against us, and nevertheless I support it ... Let the Central Committee in a moment of danger take the severest measures against the best Party comrades, if it finds this necessary .... Let the Central Committee even be mistaken! That is less dangerous than the wavering which is now observable.'[24] Radek himself was to become a victim of the 1921 law. The party expelled him in 1927, and he died in prison in 1939.

There was a less obvious consequence of these changes that was to prove immensely important. The banning of open political conflict between or even within political parties did not mean the banning of conflict. Vicious conflicts continued, but they took place out of the public gaze. We have seen already that this was a characteristic feature of Russia's autocratic political culture. By demanding total unity, the party did not end internal conflict. It ensured a public façade of unity, but drove conflicts underground, where they encouraged plotting and paranoia. This mood of furtive conflict explains the extreme suspiciousness of the party in the 1930s and the savagery with which the leadership lashed out at suspected opponents.

However, the very fact that open political struggle was now impossible weakened dissidents and enhanced the power of leaders. How did the party leaders exercise their authority? While the party was small, undisciplined and weak, Lenin dominated it through his skill in argumentation within elected party bodies such as the annual congresses or their various standing committees. He was a skilful backstairs politician, always willing to manoeuvre and apply pressure on delegates if necessary. However he had no means of guaranteeing loyalty, apart from his own personal prestige. As a result, debates at congresses remained energetic and serious while Lenin was active. Something of the ideal of 'democratic centralism' survived, at least at the upper levels of party life.

At lower levels, the party had changed greatly. Party numbers grew rapidly during the Civil War. This posed new organizational problems and generated new forms of power within the party. Before his death in March 1919, Y. M. Sverdlov (1885–1919) had handled most of the party's organizational tasks. After his death, the eighth Party Congress set up three new subcommittees of the Central Committee to handle day-to-day governmental tasks. These were the Politburo (Political Bureau), which took the major policy decisions; and two housekeeping committees, the Orgburo (Organisation Bureau) and the Secretariat. These two bodies kept records on the rapidly growing party membership, and assigned party workers to particular party tasks.

The role of the Secretariat turned out to be peculiarly important, for its powers of appointment gave it great influence over the careers of professional party workers at all levels. It rapidly acquired extensive patronage over the nationwide network of party secretaries, who were the backbone of party life. Party secretaries in turn acquired immense power over rank-and-file members. At the provincial level they soon exercised something of the arbitrary authority of the tsarist provincial governors.

Indeed, it is helpful to think of two distinct layers of government. The central government took general policy decisions. However, at the provincial level regional party secretaries were the real bosses, controlling and sometimes stifling the implementation of central government orders.

In the early 1920s, both central and provincial party officials began drawing up lists of key positions in all areas of government. They also drew up parallel lists of officials suitable for appointment to these positions. These lists, the *nomenklatura*, remained the best guide to the dominant figures in the Soviet ruling group throughout Soviet history. Like the Petrine Table of Ranks, they listed those positions and individuals that members of the ruling group regarded as important. Through these mechanisms, the Secretariat gained control of the *apparat* (the party machine) of professional party workers. Meanwhile, the party *apparat*, with the Secretariat at its head, and regional party secretaries as its key link in the provinces, emerged as the backbone of the Soviet political system.

These mechanisms gave the centre great power over the rank and file of the party. They also reduced the level of democracy within the party and the government, while enhancing the influence of particular central and regional party bosses. Trotsky, who had supported central authority during the Civil War, began to criticize these developments as early as October 1923, when he could already sense the ground shifting under his own feet.

> Document 9.6: Trotsky on the bureaucratization of the party, October 1923

Even during the harshest days of War Communism, the system of appointments within the Party was not practiced on one-tenth the scale it is now. The practice of appointing secretaries of province committees is now the rule. This creates for the secretaries a position that is essentially independent of the local organizations. In the event that opposition, criticism, or protests occur, the secretary, with the help of the center, can simply have the opponent transferred ... The secretary, appointed by the center and thereby virtually independent of the local organizations, is in turn a source of subsequent appointments and dismissals within the province itself. Organized from the top down, the secretarial apparatus has, in an increasingly autonomous fashion, been gathering 'all the strings into its own hands'. The participation of the Party ranks in the actual shaping of the Party organization is becoming more and more illusory ...

The bureaucratization of the Party apparatus has reached unheard-of proportions through the application of the methods of secretarial selection. Even in the cruelest hours of the Civil War, we argued in the Party organizations, and in the press as well, over such issues as the recruitment of specialists, partisan forces versus a regular army, discipline, etc.; while now there is not a trace of such an open exchange of opinions on questions that are really troubling the party. There has been created a very broad layer of Party workers, belonging to the apparatus of the state or the Party, who have totally renounced the idea of holding their own political opinions or at least of openly expressing such opinions, as if they believe that the secretarial hierarchy is the proper apparatus for forming Party opinions and making Party decisions. Beneath this layer that refrains from having its own opinions lies the broad layer of Party masses before whom every decision stands in the form of a summons or command.[25]

In the early 1920s open conflict was already being driven underground. Meanwhile, the Secretariat, through its control of the *nomenklatura*, was beginning to function as a disciplined inner elite of the party. In many ways, its role was similar to that of the bureaucracy in the tsarist ruling group in the late nineteenth century. However, it took some time for party members to appreciate the extent of the power this gave to the Secretariat, and to those who dominated it.

These changes in the structure of the party gained importance with the removal of Lenin. He had a stroke in May 1922, from which he never fully recovered, and he died in January 1924. During his illness the various party bosses began jockeying for position.

Each of the major party leaders – Trotsky, Zinoviev, Kamenev, Bukharin, Stalin – had their own particular sources of power, their own 'fiefdoms' as they were known informally. Grigorii Zinoviev (1883–1936) headed the prestigious Party Organisation of Petrograd (renamed Leningrad after Lenin's death in 1924). Lev Kamenev (1883–1936) headed the influential Moscow Party Organisation. Both had supported Lenin since 1903, and Zinoviev had been a member of the party's central committee since 1912. Lev Trotsky (1879–1940) remained commissar for war. He enjoyed immense national and international prestige as the leader of the October insurrection and organizer of victory in the Civil War. However, he had joined the Bolsheviks only in 1917. Nikolai Bukharin (1888–1938) was the youngest of the party leaders. He edited *Pravda*, the party newspaper, and had considerable influence as a theorist.

Joseph Stalin (born in Djugashvili, 1879–1953), like Zinoviev and Kamenev, was a long-time party member. He had supported Lenin ever since 1903, and joined the party central committee in 1913. From 1917, he was commissar for nationalities, and therefore responsible for the creation of the USSR in 1924. He played a leading role in the military campaigns of the Civil War, which brought him into conflict with Trotsky. From 1919, he belonged to the Politburo and the Orgburo. In May 1922 he became the general secretary of the Communist Party. This placed him at the head of the Secretariat. Party comrades referred to him condescendingly as 'Comrade Card-Index'.[26]

Though Stalin dominated the *apparat*, this did not guarantee that he would emerge as Lenin's successor. Equally important, Stalin had the political skills necessary to maximize the power the Secretariat gave him without ever overplaying his hand. Like all great politicians, Stalin knew precisely how much power he had at any moment, and where his power ended. Where he had enough power, he acted decisively. Where he did not, he manoeuvred discreetly; so his public defeats were very rare. His successes were visible; his failures were not. Though it may sound paradoxical, it was Stalin's political restraint that eventually built up an impression of limitless power. The fact that the immense leverage available to the Secretariat was not widely recognized in the early 1920s – on the contrary many regarded both Stalin and his official position as dull and insignificant – gave him a further advantage. His rivals failed to take Stalin seriously until it was too late. In his account of 1917, which appeared in 1922, the Menshevik Sukhanov, wrote: 'Stalin … during his modest activity in the executive committee [of the Petrograd Soviet] produced – and not only on me – the impression of a grey blur, looming up now and then dimly and not leaving any trace. There is really nothing more to be said about him'.[27]

The struggle for leadership was played out by a succession of changing political alliances between the party bosses. While Lenin was dying, Trotsky appeared the obvious successor. This made him vulnerable. As early as 1923, Zinoviev, Kamenev and Stalin – the Bolshevik old guard – formed a 'triumvirate' of allies against the newcomer Trotsky. Though popular within the army and within many sections of the party, Trotsky never had the numbers within the party apparatus. His defeat in 1925 was marked by his removal as commissar of war. This began a long odyssey whose next stage led him to exile in Alma-Ata in Soviet Central Asia in 1928. In 1929 the government expelled him from the Soviet Union, dumping him unceremoniously in Turkey. After periods of exile in Turkey and Norway, he died in Mexico in 1940 at the hands of a Stalinist assassin.

Zinoviev and Kamenev fell out with Stalin in 1925. In 1926, they tried to ally with Trotsky and the so-called 'left opposition' against Stalin and Bukharin. In November 1927, the Party expelled them along with Trotsky. The fifteenth Party Congress, which met in December, confirmed the expulsions. The third phase of the leadership struggle began during the procurements crisis of 1927, when Stalin and Bukharin fell out. Stalin turned on his rival in 1928, and in the middle of 1929 Bukharin lost his place on the Politburo.

Party leaders fought out their rivalries within the party and in articles and books of polemics on party policy. However, it was votes at the congresses that decided the outcome of the struggles. On the face of it, this was proof of considerable intra-party democracy. These procedures also allowed the victorious alliances to claim that they represented the will of the entire party, and to brand their opponents as minority factions whose actions breached the 1921 anti-faction ruling.

The reality was more complex. Delegates to the congresses were of course elected by their local party organizations. However, the Civil War habit of electing those the centre wanted elected had taken firm hold, particularly in the provinces, and it was Stalin, through the Secretariat, who benefited from this tradition. Increasingly, opposition leaders claimed that the votes that defeated them reflected not the free decisions of independent-minded party delegates, but the disciplined behaviour of a unified party machine directed by the general secretary.

There was certainly some truth to this. The Secretariat's power of appointment and transfer gave the machine wide disciplinary powers over party members. In 1925, a delegate claimed that many voted against their own convictions for: 'not everyone will hold up his hand in opposition in order to be sent, as a result, to Murmansk or Turkestan'.[28]

Other changes enhanced the patronage available to the party machine. The existence of a one-party state gave the Communist party control over all positions of influence within the Soviet Union. The Party controlled careers in the military, industry, education, the arts and sciences. From now on, anyone with any ambition had to reckon with the party, and people found that if they were not party members their careers would falter. The party and the party machine had become the key to success in any sphere of Soviet life.

The nature of the party also changed during the 1920s in ways that enhanced central control. First, it expanded in size. At the end of 1917, there were about 250 000 members. By 1921, there were over 700 000. By 1930 there were almost 1.7 million. These figures underestimate the numbers who joined, for many left again during periodic purges. By the late 1920s, those who had joined the party before 1917 represented no more than one per cent of the membership. Most party members had joined during the Civil War or the 1920s. This cohort of party members was very different from the pre-1917 cohort. They had not joined an underground revolutionary party, but the most powerful political institution in Russia. They were joining the institution most likely to provide them with a life of power and privilege. It is a fair assumption that many joined not out of idealism, but in the hope of making a good career. This made them peculiarly susceptible to the patronage wielded by the Secretariat.

Second, the composition of the party had changed. The old Bolsheviks came largely from the intelligentsia. They were committed revolutionary intellectuals who expected to be able to debate the policies of the government they had helped create. Those who joined in the Civil War and the 1920s came from Russia's working classes. They were mostly young. They had only limited education, and recruitment during the Civil War accustomed them to obedience rather than to debate.

These changes transformed the new ruling group of Soviet Russia. The relation between general secretary and provincial party secretaries recreated something like the alliance between autocrat and lesser nobility that had been the basis for the power of both Ivan IV and Peter I. This mixture of backgrounds allowed party leaders to play newer members against their rivals just as Ivan IV had used the *oprichniki* against the *boyars* (see Chapter 1).

Lenin had always understood the need for a disciplined leadership. However, to his credit, he also glimpsed some of the dangers this posed. As early as the end of 1922, he wrote from his sickbed: 'Comrade Stalin, having become Secretary [General], has unlimited authority concentrated in his hands, and I am not sure whether he will always be capable of using that authority with enough caution'.[29] A month later, Lenin demanded that the party remove Stalin from his post as general secretary. Away from the centre of power Lenin began to see the basic paradox of autocratic government: the more powerful the leaders the greater the group's chances of survival, but the smaller its capacity to protect itself against the caprice of its own leader.

Fortunately for Stalin, his rivals took no action against him. Then, in March 1923, Lenin suffered a further stroke that finally put him out of action. Having survived this crisis, Stalin could consolidate and build on the power he held as general secretary.

However, patronage was by no means the only source of his power. Policies counted, too. By 1928, Stalin was becoming identified with a forceful economic strategy that had great appeal to many party members. He offered a clear way out of the dilemmas of the 1920s. He claimed that Soviet Russia could build socialism without foreign help and without relying on market forces. It simply had to return to the forceful methods that had worked so well during the Civil War. This approach appealed greatly to *praktiki* within the party. His resistance to demands for greater democracy within the party earned him the support of the crucial provincial party secretaries, for it shielded them from excessive scrutiny. His approach to the peasantry increased the influence of the secret police and earned him valuable support within the police apparatus. He also managed better than any of his rivals to present himself to the Soviet public as the legitimate heir of Lenin. His lecture series 'Lessons of Leninism' did much to create the notion of Leninism as a distinct body of ideas. In short, despite the great influence he wielded through the Secretariat, Stalin, like any other politician, had to negotiate, compromise and coax potential supporters to get the congress or central committee votes that built up his power and buried his rivals.

The Crisis of Modernization: From Indirect to Direct Mobilization

Stalin's rise to power transformed the situation of the Soviet ruling group. It gave it once more the unity, strength and sense of purpose it had shown during the Civil War. This, in turn, offered a way out of the economic crisis. Both strategies of growth available in the 1920s assumed that the party was too weak to take on the peasantry directly.

By the late 1920s changes in the political situation of the party offered it a third strategy – to tackle the peasantry head on and take what was necessary by force as it had during the period of war communism. Strategies of direct mobilization appeared once more on the party's agenda, with Stalin as their main sponsor. The precondition for such strategies was a strengthened ruling group and a powerful and ruthless leadership. By 1929 the *nomenklatura*, organized through the Secretariat at both the national and the provincial levels of government, provided the spine of such a system. The emergence of Stalin as undisputed leader gave the system a unity and decisiveness it had lacked during the power struggle. Meanwhile the other key organs of coercive power – the army and the police in particular – had had a decade of relative stability in which to consolidate, grow and develop their own traditions. The party was larger than in 1921. Its rank-and-file members were also more committed to a system that offered them a degree of wealth, status and power unthinkable under any other system. Not only was the government more unified and disciplined than in 1921, it was also far more disciplined than the tsarist elite had been for well over a century before its demise. The new system had one further advantage. The old ruling group had hesitated to encourage economic modernization, because modernization threatened the position of its most influential members, above all, the landed nobility. The Soviet elite came overwhelmingly from the working classes and the intelligentsia. Both groups were products of economic modernization. Their numbers and influence were likely to grow as Russia modernized, and their commitment to the system would grow with each success, instead of being eroded by the very process of modernization.

As leader of such a group, Stalin was in a position to pursue the twin goals of industrial growth and military power more ruthlessly than any Russian ruler since Peter the Great. During the 1930s he showed that he had the will, the strength and the ability to do so.

■ Summary

When they seized power, the Bolsheviks hoped that a world-wide revolution, and the creation of socialist governments in the economically advanced societies of Europe would ease the task of building socialism in backward Russia. By 1921, it was clear that the revolution had succeeded only in the economically backward lands of a contracted Russian Empire, which were now devastated by seven years of war, civil war, and famine. This was an appalling environment in which to try to build Socialism. In 1921, the Communists faced the even more immediate challenges of economic breakdown and widespread hostility. Alienated by the brutalities of the Civil War, peasants, urban workers, and even many soldiers, demanded the creation of a more democratic working-class government. Politically, the Communist leaders made no compromise. They maintained a one-party state, and demanded total discipline and unity within the Communist Party. Economically, however, they abandoned the direct mobilizational methods of 'war communism', and allowed a revival of petty trade. These changes laid the foundations for the era of the 'New Economic Policy'.

The decision to allow private trade allowed a revival of agricultural and then industrial production. Indeed, growth was so rapid that some party members began to think that it might be possible to build at least the foundations of socialism within the structures created under the NEP. In this way, communism could perhaps survive, even in backward Russia, until the next wave of international revolution broke the power of international capitalism. Such optimism began to wane in the late 1920s. Critics of NEP argued that flourishing markets in agrarian produce benefited not the urban proletariat, but a revived class of rural entrepreneurs. They insisted that the government had to find resources quickly to invest in industrial growth, so as to lay the foundations for a future socialist society and to build a powerful defence base. Yet the government found it extremely hard to secure the necessary resources. By the late 1920s, relations between the Communist government, and the peasantry, who still made up over 80 per cent of the population, were breaking down. The government tried to buy rural produce at low prices in order not to cut into investment funds. Peasants responded by cutting back production.

The party itself was divided by a vicious power struggle after the death of Lenin in 1924. Though it was not obvious at the time, it turned out that Stalin was in the best position to succeed Lenin. As General Secretary, he exerted enormous patronage over the new recruits who were beginning to dominate the party's middle and lower levels. This influence allowed Stalin to dominate the party congresses which selected party leaders and took fundamental policy decisions. Stalin also committed himself publicly to the optimistic notion, popular amongst many new party members, that socialism *could* be built in the Soviet Union, even without a world revolution. By 1929, Stalin had defeated his rivals. United under his forceful leadership, the party could now deal more decisively with the crisis caused by the gradual breakdown of the NEP. In 1928 and 1929 Stalin began to experiment once more with the direct, coercive, mobilization of resources from the countryside. These experiments prepared the way for the 'revolution from above' and the creation of the Stalinist system.

☐ *Further Reading*

There are general surveys of the 1920s in Hosking, *The First Socialist Society*, Fitzpatrick, *The Russian Revolution*, and Ward, *Stalin's Russia*. The economic aspects of NEP are dealt with very well in Nove, *An Economic History of the USSR*, though there is a more detailed account in Erlich, *The Soviet Industrialization Debate*. The political and social aspects are dealt with in Siegelbaum's fine study, *Soviet State and Society between Revolutions*. Andrle, *A Social History of Twentieth Century Russia* is also good on social change. See also the collection of essays edited by Sheila Fitzpatrick, *Russia in the era of NEP*. On the breakdown of NEP, Reiman, *The Birth of Stalinism* has been very important, while Cohen's biography of Bukharin, *Bukharin and the Bolshevik Revolution* was very influential when it first came out. Lewin's study of *Lenin's Last Struggle* is far more important than its title suggests. On the countryside during NEP, see the important study by the Soviet historian, Danilov, *Rural Russia under the New Regime*. The standard history of the party is Schapiro, *The Communist Party of the Soviet Union*.

☐ *Notes*

1. H. G. Wells, 'Russia in the Shadows' (London, 1921) quoted in A. Nove, *An Economic History of the USSR*, 3rd edn (Harmondsworth: Penguin, 1992) p. 61.
2. L. Siegelbaum, *Soviet State and Society between Revolutions, 1918–1929* (Cambridge University Press, 1992) p. 27.
3. J. N. Westwood, *Endurance and Endeavour: Russian History 1812–1980*, 2nd edn (Oxford University Press, 1981) p. 277.
4. R. W. Davies, M. Harrison and S. G. Wheatcroft, *The Economic Transformation of the Soviet Union 1913–1945* (Cambridge University Press, 1994) p. 64.
5. P. Avrich, *Kronstadt 1921* (Princeton University Press, 1970) p. 8.
6. L. Lih, *Bread and Authority in Russia, 1914–1921* (University of California Press, 1990) pp. 193–4, citing Paul Dukes, *Red Dusk and the Morrow: Adventures and Investigations in Red Russia* (New York, 1922) pp. 196–8.
7. M. Matthews, *Soviet Government: A Selection of Official Documents on Internal Policies* (London: Cape, 1974) p. 148.

8. V. P. Danilov, *Rural Russia under the New Regime*, trans O. Figes (London: Hutchinson, 1988) p. 47.
9. Nove, *An Economic History of the USSR*, p. 79.
10. V. Andrle, *A Social History of Twentieth-Century* Russia (London/New York: Edward Arnold 1994) p. 133.
11. M. Lewin, 'The Immediate Background to Soviet Collectivisation', in *The Making of the Soviet System* (London: Methuen, 1985) p. 93.
12. On Bukharin, see the superb biography by Stephen Cohen, *Bukharin and the Bolshevik Revolution* (Oxford University Press, 1980).
13. M. Lewin, *Political Undercurrents in Soviet Economic Debates* (London: Pluto Press, 1975) p. 42.
14. On these, see M. Lewin, *Lenin's Last Struggle* (London: Pluto Press, 1975).
15. Lewin, *Political Undercurrents*, p. 18.
16. Nove, *An Economic History of the USSR*, p. 149.
17. Ibid., p. 150.
18. Cited in D. Volkogonov, *Stalin: Triumph and Tragedy*, trans H. Shukman (Rocklin, Calif.: Prima Publishing, 1992) pp. 164–5.
19. M. Reiman, *The Birth of Stalinism* (Bloomington: Indiana University Press, 1987) p. 53.
20. Cohen, *Bukharin and the Bolshevik Revolution*, pp. 306–7.
21. A. Koestler, *The Invisible Writing* (London: Hutchinson, 1969) p. 72.
22. Reiman, *The Birth of Stalinism*, p. 70.
23. Matthews, *Soviet Government*, pp. 149–51.
24. Cited in L. Schapiro, *The Communist Party of the Soviet Union*, 2nd edn (London: Methuen, 1970) pp. 215–16.
25. L. Trotsky, *The Challenge of the Left Opposition (1923–25)* (New York: Pathfinder Press, 1979) pp. 55–6, from Trotsky's letter to the Central Committee of 8 October 1923.
26. C. Ward, *Stalin's Russia* (London: Edward Arnold, 1993) p. 35.
27. N. N. Sukhanov, *The Russian Revolution: 1917. A Personal Record*, (ed. and trans.) J. Carmichael (Oxford University Press, 1955) p. 230.
28. E. H. Carr, *Socialism in One Country* (Harmondsworth: Penguin, 1970) vol. 2, p. 231.
29. V. I. Lenin, *Selected Works* (Moscow: Progress Publishers, 1971) p. 682.

■ *Chapter 10* ■

Collectivization and Industrialization

■ A Social Revolution

The October Revolution had launched a basic transformation of Russian society. By 1921, revolution and civil war had removed the upper classes of tsarist society. Most of the landed nobility, the bourgeoisie and the clergy had vanished, through emigration, expropriation or death. Yet there remained a large class of small property-owners, NEP men and, above all, peasants.

In 1929 the Soviet government launched a final assault on the remnants of capitalism. It banned the activities of NEP men, expropriated *kulaks*, and forced the rest of the peasantry into collective farms. 'Collectivization' and 'dekulakization' were the beginnings of a 'revolution from above', which within a few years completed the work of the 'revolution from below' begun in 1917. After the revolution from above, there were no longer any classes living off the ownership of property. All members of Soviet society lived from wage-labour. (Collective farmers were a partial exception. For many years they received payment not in wages but in shares from the farm's surplus after procurements.) The distinction Arsenev made in the early nineteenth century between 'productive' and 'non-productive' classes lost its force in the Soviet Union after 1930.

After the proclamation of the Stalin Constitution in 1936, the Soviet government recognized the existence of only two classes. These were the proletariat (the urban working classes) and the peasantry (the rural working classes). It also recognized the existence of a 'stratum' recruited from both working classes: the Soviet 'intelligentsia'. This was a larger group than its tsarist counterpart, for it included all white-collar workers, from scientists and artists to clerks and typists. Table 10.1 summarizes the social results of these changes. Figure 10.1 illustrates them graphically.

The revolution from above also created the basic institutions of Soviet society. These were: collective and state farms; a command economy geared for rapid industrial growth; and a centralized political system headed by the general secretary of the Communist Party, controlling a rigidly censored communications system, and supported by secret police

Table 10.1   *Transformation of the Russian class structure*

Class (including members of families)	1913 (%)	1939 (%)	1970 (%)
1 Nobility, clergy, merchants, professionals, senior civil servants	4.9	–	–
2 Peasants:			
Individual	78.1	2.6	–
Collective	–	47.2	20.0
3 Urban workers	14.7	32.5	55.0
4 Intelligentsia (office workers, specialists)	2.3	17.7	25.0
Total	100.0	100.0	100.0

Source: B. Kerblay, *Modern Soviet Society* (London: Methuen, 1983) p. 212.

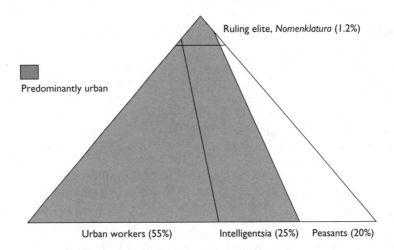

Figure 10.1   *Social structure of the Soviet Union in 1970*
Source: Based on B. Kerblay, *Modern Soviet Society* (London: Methuen, 1983) p. 212.

with an extensive network of informers. Despite the peculiarities of the Soviet system, it inherited many of the methods and attitudes of Russia's traditional political culture. The Stalinist government, like that of Peter the Great, had built a huge and powerful fiscal system, and a coercive machinery strong enough to contain the vast social pressures it generated. In doing so, it shaped a more disciplined ruling group and built a defence establishment that re-established the country as a great power.

In the last resort, the difficulties facing the Soviet government in the late 1920s all turned on the fiscal problem. Somehow the government had to mobilize the resources needed to pay for the modernization of the economy and the army. As the peasantry still made up almost 85 per cent of the population, and much of the country's wealth remained locked up in the countryside, the main task was to extract more labour and resources from the peasantry.

By 1928 neither of the major strategies considered in the 1920s seemed adequate. Stalin's achievement was to find a third strategy. This contained elements of both the right- and left-wing strategies, but applied them with a brutality that would have appalled most participants in the debates of the 1920s. We do not know when Stalin began to conceive of such an approach. However, it was probably the success of the 'Urals–Siberian method' early in 1928, along with memories of the Civil War, that persuaded him of the potential of a more direct approach to mobilization. Michael Reiman, a Czech historian of this era, has written:

> From [Stalin's] point of view, achieving the maximum version of the plan was merely a question of mobilizing material and financial resources. Since Stalin had accumulated extensive experience during 1928, when he intervened forcibly in economic and social life, he lost all respect for the mysteries of the economic process. He openly expressed his contempt for the 'fetishism of doctors' robes and hidebound textbooks.' In his thinking, Stalin put one factor first, one he understood and was familiar with: the 'will of the party'. What could be done economically was decided in a totally new way (although the War Communism of the first years after the revolution served as a model) – through total mobilization of the machinery of administration and repression.[1]

The procurements crisis of 1927–8 had threatened the economic logic of NEP, which depended on continuing trade between town and country. As a result of poor harvests, low official prices for grain, and severe shortages of industrial goods, peasants marketed less grain than the previous year. How could the party solve the problem of procurements, the key to the larger issue of socialist industrialization?

In theory, every party member knew the answer. Indeed, Lenin had described it in one of his last articles, 'On Co-operation'. It was to collectivize agriculture. Slowly, and gently, the government would persuade peasants to give up small-scale private agriculture and join together in collective farms. The government would subsidize collective farms, provide them with modern equipment, and offer credits and technical support. Benefiting from economies of scale and better technique, the collective farms would generate the surpluses the state needed to industrialize. As they flourished, more and more poor peasants would see the advantages of joining them. Meanwhile, richer peasants would find it harder to compete with collective farms. Private agriculture would wither and die.

This optimistic scenario promised to solve both the economic and the political problems the party faced in rural areas. Stalin put it like this in December 1927:

> The way out is to turn the small and scattered peasant farms into large united farms based on cultivation of the land in common, to go over to collective cultivation of the land on the basis of a new higher technique. The way out is to unite the small and dwarf peasant farms gradually but surely, not by pressure but by example and persuasion, into large farms based on common, cooperative, collective cultivation of the land ... There is no other way out.[2]

Unfortunately for the government, peasants saw things differently, and few joined collective farms. As late as 1928, individual peasant households still farmed 97 per cent of the area under crops. Yet the procurements crisis demanded a solution, for it affected all aspects of Soviet society. What was to be done?

From early in 1928, Stalin had experimented with the use of direct force as a solution to the rural crisis. In some areas local officials had used various forms of pressure to increase the numbers of collective farms. Elsewhere, they bore down heavily on *kulaks* and NEP men. In a brutal way, force appeared to work. It helped the government to extract more cash and more grain from the countryside.

Stalin took the critical decisions late in 1929. On 7 November 1929, after the harvest was in, he published a famous article called 'The Great Turn'. This announced an all-out drive to collectivize agriculture, expropriate the richer peasants (*kulaks*), and abolish the private sector in the countryside. Party officials and government agents who for two years had visited the villages to deal with the procurements crisis now appeared once more. But this time their job was to achieve total collectivization before the spring sowing. With them went a special levy of some 27 000 industrial workers, many with military experience, known as the '25 000ers'. At village meetings, party officials encouraged the heads of less wealthy peasant households to join collective farms. They then encouraged them to take over the land and livestock of richer households as the basis for the new collective farms. Often this meant depriving richer neighbours of their homes in the middle of a Russian winter. Many who suffered were not *kulaks* but merely the victims of village quarrels. Many were 'former people', former landlords, priests, White army soldiers or merchants; while others were just outsiders, such as teachers or vets.[3] The policy of systematically eliminating the richer peasants was known as 'dekulakization'. As in 1918, the government tried to divide the peasantry the better to rule them. To add insult to injury, government officials, led by the official 'Militant League of the Godless', attacked traditional religion, deported priests as *kulaks*, and often confiscated church bells.

The government succeeded in imposing its will partly because of the strategic weaknesses of all peasantries – their illiteracy, their geographical dispersion, and their inability to co-ordinate resistance. In the 1920s, Russia's 124 million peasants were scattered over 614 000 rural settlements, whose average size was 200 people, or thirty to forty households.[4] Besides, in 1926 over half of all peasants were under twenty years of age.[5] Most had been born after the 1905 revolution. These factors help explain not only the weakness of the peasantry, but the speed with which many adapted to their new conditions of life after collectivization.

The formal results of the collectivization campaign were spectacular. By February 1930 the government claimed that 50 per cent of peasants had joined collective farms. However, many collective farms existed only on paper and the process of collectivization was disorderly and chaotic. Such was the uncertainty in the spring of 1930 that officials began to fear for the spring sowing. It may have been this that induced Stalin to slow the pace. In a famous article published on 2 March 1930, Stalin claimed many local party officials had become 'dizzy with success' and committed serious excesses. 'Collective farms,' he wrote, 'must not be established by force. That would be foolish and reactionary. The collective farm movement must rest on the active support of the main mass of the Party'.[6] Party officials reacted quickly by easing pressure on the peasants. By July collective farms included only 24 per cent of peasant households and commanded 34 per cent of the sown area. However, the party had not abandoned the goal of total collectivization and the retreat in 1930 proved temporary. Renewed pressure raised the figure to 53 per cent of peasant households (and 68 per cent of the sown area) in July 1931, and 90 per cent (and more than 94 per cent of the sown area) in July 1936.[7] By 1936, the government had completed collectivization. Rural capitalism was dead in the Soviet Union.

Collectivization replaced the 25 million small peasant farms of the 1920s with three new institutions. These were: collective farms (*kolkhozy*); state farms (*sovkhozy*); and machine tractor stations (MTS). By the middle of the 1930s, there were about 250 000 *kolkhozy*, covering most of the country's farm land. Most included whole villages. Members of the *kolkhozy* collectively leased from the state the land their families had farmed for generations. They received a share of the farm's produce after it had supplied its procurement quotas to the government and the machine tractor stations. The *sovkhozy* were state enterprises, and their members were state employees, receiving wages. Most *sovkhozy* were created from former gentry estates. The machine tractor stations hired out tractors, machinery and skilled operators to the *kolkhozy*, most of which lacked modern equipment and skills. The MTS grew from a mere eight in 1928 to 7069 by 1940.[8]

What really happened in the villages? The government claimed that collectivization had the support of most poor and middle peasants. In reality, most peasants resisted collectivization, not just the minority of *kulaks*. Their resistance, which often took violent forms, turned mass collectivization into a virtual civil war. This pitted the new Soviet ruling group, dominated by the 1.5 million-strong Communist Party, against the country's 120 million peasants, from Ukraine, to Kazakhstan, to Siberia. As collectivization began, Bukharin said to Kamenev, 'He [Stalin] will have to drown the risings in blood'.[9] He was not far from the truth. Resistance took many forms. Often women led the assault, as officials were usually reluctant to use violence against them. The following account comes from a Ukrainian village.

A crowd of women stormed the *kolkhoz* [collective farm] stables and barns. They cried, screamed, wailed, demanding their cows and seed back. The men stood a way off, in clusters, sullenly silent. Some of the lads had pitchforks, stakes, axes tucked in their sashes. The terrified granary man ran away; the women tore off the bolts and together with the men began dragging out the bags of seed.[10]

There were many direct attacks on party officials. In response, officials sought the protection of secret police officials or army units, and collectivization began to look like a military operation. Faced with armed officials determined to impose their will, many peasants tried to hide their grain in the ground. Others slaughtered their cows, pigs, poultry and even horses rather than turn them over to a collective farm. Many did so because excessive procurements left them with no fodder. Others did so to reduce their stocks and avoid being labelled as *kulaks*.

The party defined all who opposed collectivization as enemies of the Soviet regime. It even coined a special category of 'sub-kulaks'. This included those who, though not *kulaks*, displayed *kulak* attitudes by opposing collectivization. In this way, dekulakization subjected many poor and middle peasants to the fate of the *kulaks*: expropriation, exile, exclusion from collective farms, imprisonment and often death.

For most peasants and most consumers collectivization was a disaster. Total grain production declined and did not return to the 1928 level until the late 1930s. The setting-up of collective farms, many now headed by Party officials from the towns with little agricultural experience, disrupted traditional agricultural routines. Meanwhile peasants had slaughtered almost half their livestock. As livestock accounted for about half of the total value of agricultural means of production, this meant the loss of about one-quarter of agricultural capital.[11] This was a catastrophe for an agricultural country and condemned a whole generation of Russians to a meatless diet.

The human costs were even more horrifying. Collectivization affected all peasants in some way or another. Material standards of living fell sharply in the towns, and even more rapidly in the countryside. The economic historian, Alec Nove, has written of this period: '1933 was the culmination of the most precipitous peacetime decline in living standards known in recorded history'.[12] While grain harvests fell, state procurements rose. In Ukraine, the northern Caucasus, the Volga provinces, and parts of Central Asia, the imposition of excessive procurements quotas created a terrible famine in the winter of 1932–3. Recent estimates suggest that 4–6 million may have died in these man-made famines.[13]

Meanwhile, dekulakization deprived about one million peasant households or about 5–6 million individuals of their land and houses. Of these, several hundred thousand had died within two years, some of destitution, others in the rapidly growing labour camps (see Chapter 11).[14] Conditions in the camps were such that large numbers died of hunger or overwork or from brutal camp discipline. The memoirs of the writer, Arthur Koestler, who visited the Ukraine during 1932 and 1933, hint at the reality of life in the Soviet countryside in this period.

☐ *Document 10.1: Arthur Koestler in Ukraine, 1932–3*

The train puffed slowly across the Ukrainian steppe. It stopped frequently. At every station there was a crowd of peasants in rags, offering ikons and linen in exchange against a loaf of bread. The women were lifting up their infants to the compartment windows – infants pitiful and terrifying with limbs like sticks, puffed bellies, big cadaverous heads lolling on thin necks. I had arrived, unsuspecting, at the peak of the famine of 1932–33, which had depopulated entire districts and claimed several million victims ... My Russian travelling companions took pains to explain to me that these wretched crowds were *kulaks*, rich peasants who had resisted the collectivization of the land and whom it had therefore been necessary to evict from their farms.

In Kharkov, Koestler described the bazaar:

This was a permanent market held in a huge, empty square. Those who had something to sell squatted in the dust with their goods spread out before them on a handkerchief or scarf. The goods ranged from a handful of rusty nails to a tattered quilt, or a pot of sour milk sold by the spoon, flies included. You could see an old woman sitting for hours with one painted Easter egg or one small piece of dried up goat's cheese before her. Or an old man, his bare feet covered with sores, trying to barter his torn boots for a kilo of black bread and a packet of mahorka tobacco ...

Officially, these men and women were all *kulaks* who had been expropriated as a punitive measure. In reality, as I was gradually to find out, they were ordinary peasants who had been forced to abandon their villages in the famine-stricken regions. In last year's harvest-collecting campaign the local Party officials, anxious to deliver their quota, had confiscated not only the harvest but also the seed reserves, and the newly established collective farms had nothing to sow with. Their cattle and poultry they had killed rather than surrender it to the *kolkhoz*; so when the last grain of the secret hoard was eaten, they left the land which no longer was theirs. Entire villages had been abandoned, whole districts depopulated; in addition to the five million *kulaks* officially deported to Siberia, several million more were on the move. They choked the railway stations, crammed the freight trains, squatted in the markets and public squares, and died in the streets; I have never seen so many and such hurried funerals as during that winter in Kharkov. The exact number of these 'nomadised' people was never disclosed and probably never counted; in order of magnitude it must have exceeded the modest numbers involved in the Migrations after the fall of the Roman Empire.[15]

In spite of the devastation it caused, the party leaders had good reason to regard collectivization as a success. Table 10.2 gives the crucial figures. Figure 10.2 graphs columns A and B.

These figures and the graph show that though total agricultural production fell in the early 1930s, the proportion of agricultural produce at the disposal of the government increased. In 1928, procurements accounted for 15 per cent of the harvest. By 1933 they accounted for 33 per cent, and by 1938 for over 40 per cent. The government gained twice, for by 1933 it was reselling grain in the towns at four times the price it paid to collective farmers.[16]

The collective farms had failed as efficient producers of agricultural goods. However, they had succeeded as mobilizers of resources. The reason is simple. Instead of dealing with 25 million independent farms, the state now dealt with about 250 000 collective farms, each headed by a state-appointed manager. These it could control in a way it could never control millions of private farms. By law, collective farms had to sow what government planners told them to sow. Then they had to hand over their planned procurements to the state and to the MTS before paying or feeding their own members.

Once it had broken the peasantry, the government could afford some modest, but significant, concessions. These increased the fiscal efficiency of the *kolkhozy* by reconciling the peasantry to the new institutions. The crucial concession allowed collective farmers to keep a small plot of land

Table 10.2   *The meaning of collectivization*

| Year | Harvest (m. tonnes) | Procurements | | Cattle (m.) |
| | | m. tonnes | % of Harvest | |
	A	B	C	D
1921	42.0	3.8	9	43.7
1922	54.0	6.9	13	40.9
1923	56.6	6.5	11	41.8
1924	51.4	5.2	10	47.3
1925[a]	72.5			51.2
1926[a]	76.8			54.0
1927[a]	72.3			56.5
1928	73.3	10.8	15	66.8
1929	71.7	16.1	22	58.2
1930	78.0	22.1	28	50.6
1931	68.0	22.8	34	42.5
1932	67.0	18.5	28	38.3
1933	69.0	22.6	33	33.5
1934	72.0	26.1	36	33.5
1935[b]	77.0	27.5	36	38.9
1936[b]	59.0	27.5	47	46.0
1937	98.0	31.9	33	47.5
1938	75.0	30.0	40	50.9
1939	75.0	30.0	40	53.5
1940	86.2	36.4	42	47.8
1941[c]	56.3	24.4	43	54.8

Notes:
[a] Procurements figures for 1925–7 are missing from Clarke's table.
[b] Procurements figures for 1935–6 and 1938–9 are averages.
[c] Grain figure for 1941 are from Clarke, p. 112.

Sources: Column A: S. G. Wheatcroft, figures cited in R. T. Manning, 'The Soviet Economic Crisis of 1936–1940 and the Great Purges', in J. Arch Getty and R. T. Manning (eds), *Stalinist Terror: New Perspectives* (Cambridge University Press, 1993) p. 120; Columns B and D: R. Clarke, *Soviet Economic Facts 1917–1970* (London: Macmillan, 1972) pp. 113, 129. Clarke uses unprocessed figures from Soviet sources.

for their private use and to sell the produce at free market prices. This was a faint echo of the concessions made in 1921. The 1935 Collective Farm Charter described the private plots as follows:

> A small tract of land shall be allocated from the collectivized landholdings for the personal use of each household in the collective farm in the form of a house-and-garden (vegetable garden, orchard).

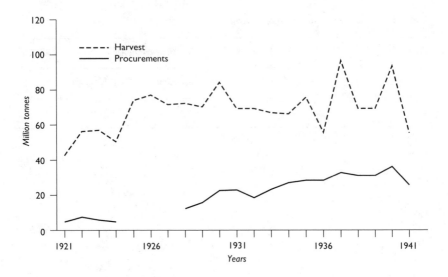

Figure 10.2 *The meaning of collectivization*
Note: Data missing 1925–7; based on information in Table 10.2

The size of plots assigned for individual use by households (exclusive of the site of the house) may vary from one-quarter of a hectare to one-half of a hectare and, in certain districts, to one hectare, depending on regional and district conditions.[17]

The private plots saved many peasants from starvation. They also represented one of the few areas of legal private entrepreneurship that survived in the Soviet Union. Collective farm markets, selling produce from the private plots at free market prices, existed in all Soviet towns. However the government always restricted their activities. It limited the amounts of land peasants could use, taxed their produce, and banned the employment of hired labour to make a profit.

By permitting private plots, the government had recreated in modern forms the nineteenth-century peasant *usad'ba*. Only those who worked on a *kolkhoz* could receive a private plot. To receive private plots, collective farmers had to work *kolkhoz* land and supply labour for which they received virtually nothing. As most collective farms coincided with pre-revolutionary communes, the parallels with serf villages were close. The ban on travel without the permission of the *kolkhoz* chairman or the local Soviet reinforced the impression that there had emerged a new form of serfdom.[18] Peasants joked, bitterly, that the initials of the All-Union Communist Party (VKP in Russian) spelt out 'second serfdom' (*Vtoroe Krepostnoe Pravo*). From the government's point of view, collectivization was a victory because it gave the government direct control of the countryside. The government could now mobilize the vast human and material resources of the Soviet countryside directly. In this way, direct mobilization through the massive use of coercion offered a solution to the problems of the 1920s. As Stalin's colleague Lazar Kaganovich (1893–) wrote, procurements were the 'touchstone on which our strength and weakness and the strength and weakness of our enemy were tested'.[19]

■ Industrialization

The party had committed itself to rapid industrialization even before it knew how it would pay for its ambitious projects. One idea was clear, though. Marxists had always believed in what they called 'planning' of the economy. Marx had argued that a socialist society would be free of the arbitrary control of market forces, or the self-interested control of the capitalist class. Instead, socialist society would control resources directly and plan production to meet the real needs of its people.

What this meant in practice was not so clear. The Civil War had provided some brutal experience of planning under conditions of crisis and economic breakdown. In *Vesenkha*, the Supreme Council of National Economy (see Chapter 8), there existed a body supposed, in principle, to plan the entire economy. However, in 1921 the government gave up this first attempt at planning. In the same year the government created *Gosplan*, the body that eventually took over the task of long-term planning. *Gosplan*'s mainly non-Bolshevik economic staff began to explore some of the theoretical and practical problems of long-term planning. They began to prepare the theoretical groundwork for an entirely new project, that of planning the inputs and outputs of an entire economy.

The political decision to implement a long-term plan was taken only in 1927. At the same time, the government embarked on a number of huge prestige projects, such as the Dnieper hydroelectric dam and the TurkSib railway, which was to link western Siberia and Central Asia. As party members became more concerned at the slow progress of industry under NEP, planners came under pressure to raise their targets. The government made planners prepare the first Five-Year Plan, which was to run from the end of 1928, in two drafts: an optimal version and a more modest version. In reality, no one had the statistical information or the theoretical understanding needed to predict the workings of a whole economy over five years. At best, the plans could set more or less realistic targets for growth. As Stalin became more impatient with slow rates of growth under NEP, careful planning gave way to the demands of politics. Instead of a 'planned' economy running according to carefully formulated plans, there appeared a 'command' economy, running according to the orders and priorities of the government. Where the plan conflicted with the government's priorities, the plan was adjusted. As collectivization showed, the political will and determination now existed to fulfil targets, whatever the economic and human cost. As a result, the first three Five-Year Plans (1928–40) succeeded much better than many planners expected, at least in some key areas.

The following analysis of the achievements and costs of the industrialization drive relies mainly on the statistics in Tables 10.2 to 10.5.

Statistics for this period are unreliable. Methods of collecting statistical information were primitive. Besides, figures for output look different depending on the prices used. Statistics that use 1928 prices yield high rates of growth, while those based on 1937 prices yield lower rates of growth. For example, Western calculations of the growth rate of the Soviet GNP (gross national product, a rough measure of total production) range from 4.8 per cent per annum (using 1937 prices) to 11.9 per cent per annum (using 1928 prices). These figures imply that after ten years of growth the Soviet GNP was between 1.6 and 3.1 times its size in 1928.

There is a further problem with Soviet statistics. From the late 1920s, the government began to manipulate statistics for propaganda effects. However, Soviet statistics are the only ones available, so we must make the best use we can of them. Helping us is the fact that Soviet planners needed accurate figures on the details of the country's economic performance. Roughly speaking, this means that detailed Soviet statistics are more trustworthy than very general statistics such as those on total national output, which were of greater use to propagandists than to planners. So western specialists have recalculated the general figures using detailed Soviet statistics. The figures used here come mostly from western recalculations of Soviet statistics.

Given the difficulties of using Soviet statistics, we must not expect precision. It is the broad picture that interests us. However, the most important changes are so spectacular that they show up despite these difficulties. The most general measure (though it is also one of the least reliable) tries to calculate the growth of Soviet National Income. Soviet estimates claimed that Soviet national income in 1940 was 5 times as large as in 1928.[20] These figures set an upper limit to available estimates. The most influential Western estimates, those of Abram Bergson, suggest that national income in 1940 was 2.75 times the 1928 level if one uses 1928 prices, and only 1.6 times that level using 1937 prices.[21] In other words, depending on the price index used, the economy had grown by between 175 per cent and 60 per cent of the 1928 level. At the lowest end of these estimates are the recent figures of the Soviet economist, G. I. Khanin, who argued that, on 1937 prices, Soviet National Income increased by only 50 per cent between 1928 and 1940.[22] What these figures suggest is a significant rate of economic growth in the 1930s, but a rate far slower than official Soviet claims have implied. Tables 10.4 and 10.5 show some more detailed results as calculated by Western scholars.

Table 10.3 covers the period from 1928 to 1980. Table 10.4 offers some general measures of growth during the first three Five-Year Plans. Table 10.5 shows how these changes, taken together, altered Russia's economic position in international terms. It compares the gross national product of different economies at three dates. Finally, the Soviet victory over Nazi Germany during the Second World War showed that economic and industrial growth could translate into military strength. These tables illustrate five important aspects of the industrialization drive. Roughly

Table 10.3   *Index numbers of Soviet economic development, 1928–80 (1928 = 1.00)*

Year	Popn	Nos in towns	Nos in em- ployment	Grain harvest	Nos of cattle	Meat prod.	Total consumption
	A	B	C	D	E	F	G
1928	1.00	1.00	1.00	1.00	1.00	1.00	1.00
1932	1.05	–	1.97	0.95	0.64	0.57	–
1937	1.06	–	2.33	1.15	0.79	0.61	0.97
1940	1.25	2.29	2.62	1.01	0.80	0.96	0.93
1945	1.12	–	–	0.62	0.91	0.53	0.64 (1944)
1950	1.16	2.51	–	1.06	0.97	1.00	1.11
1965	1.49	4.38	6.63	1.04	1.45	2.04	1.85 (1958)
1980	1.73	6.05	9.70	2.62	1.85	3.08	–

Year	Iron	Steel	Coal	Oil	Electric power	Motor vehicles
	H	I	J	K	L	M
1928	1.00	1.00	1.00	1.00	1.00	1.00
1932	1.88	1.37	1.81	1.84	2.70	29.88
1937	4.39	4.12	3.61	2.46	7.24	249.88
1940	4.552	4.26	4.67	2.68	9.66	181.25
1945	2.67	2.86	4.21	1.67	8.66	93.38
1950	5.82	6.35	7.35	3.27	18.24	453.63
1965	20.06	21.16	16.27	20.94	101.34	770.38
1980	32.42	34.42	20.17	51.98	258.80	2748.75

Source: Statistical Appendix for cols A–F and H–M; Col. G, is based on J. G. Chapman, 'Consumption in the Soviet Union', in M. Bornstein and D. Fusfeld (eds) *The Soviet Economy*, 2nd edn (Homewood, Ill.: R. D. Irvin, 1966) pp. 323–34.

speaking, the first three aspects reveal achievements, while the last two reveal costs.

First, Soviet production of industrial goods increased rapidly. Table 10.4, row A, suggests that total industrial output in 1940 was 2.6 times the level of 1928. Production of individual sectors of heavy industry, such as iron, oil and electricity (rows B to D), increased even more rapidly.

Second, as industrial output increased, so did the size of the urban population and the paid workforce (rows N and O). The size of the proletariat grew rapidly. Third, industrialization altered the international economic ranking of the Soviet Union. Table 10.5 shows that Soviet industrial output grew spectacularly when compared with the major capitalist economies, all of which suffered during the Depression. On these relatively optimistic figures, Soviet gross national product almost tripled in nine years. No other major economy even doubled output. These changes altered the economic ranking of the great powers. In 1928,

Table 10.4   *Increases in output between 1928 and 1940 (1928 = 1.00)*

		1937	(% p.a. increase)	1940ᵃ	(% p.a. increase)
Industry					
A	*Total industrial production*			2.63	(8.39)
B	Iron	4.39	(20.31)	4.52	(13.40)
C	Oil	2.46	(11.91)	2.68	(8.56)
D	Electric power	7.24	(28.08)	9.66	(20.80)
Agriculture					
E	*Total agricultural production*			1.05	(0.41)
F	Grain harvest	1.15	(1.76)	1.01	(0.08)
G	Nos of cattle	0.79	−2.90)	0.80	(−1.84)
Living standards					
H	*Total production of consumer goods*	1.81	(5.07)		
I	Consumption per caput	0.97	(−0.38)	0.93	(−0.60)
J	Meat production	0.61	(−5.99)	0.96	(−0.34)
K	Living space per caput			0.78	(−2.05)
L	Real wages			0.54	(−5.01)
Population and the workforce					
M	*Population*			1.25	(1.88)
N	No. in towns			2.29	(7.15)
O	No. in wage-earning employment	2.33	(11.15)	2.62	(8.36)

Note: ᵃ Some figures for 1940 are inflated by the absorption of the Baltic provinces, and parts of Poland and Romania during 1939 and 1940.

Table 10.5 *Comparative historical aggregate levels of GNP (in billions of 1964 $US)*

Year	1928	(% p.a. increase) 1928–37)	1937	(% p.a. increase) 1937–50)	1950	(% p.a. increase) 1928–50)
USSR	33	(11.93)	91	(2.41)	124	(6.20)
Britain	45	(2.46)	56	(4.50)	68	(1.89)
France	46	(−1.01)	42	(1.35)	50	(0.38)
Germany	34	(2.64)	43	(1.17)	50	(1.77)
Japan	28	(3.15)	37	(−1.11)	32	(0.61)
USA	203	(1.30)	228	(4.15)	387	(2.98)

Sources: Tables 10.4 and 10.5 are based on the Statistical Appendix and Table 10.3. In addition, A. Nove, *An Economic History of the USSR*, 3rd edn, (Harmondsworth: Penguin, 1992); S. Cohn, 'The Soviet economy: performance and growth', in W. L. Blackwell (ed.) *Russian Economic Development from Peter the Great of Stalin* (New York: New Viewpoints, Franklin Watts Inc, 1974) pp. 32–58; S. Cohn, *Economic Development in the Soviet Union* (Boston, Mass.: Heath & Co, 1967).

Soviet output was comparable to that of second rank capitalist countries, such as Germany, France and Britain. By 1937, it was second only to the United States. By then, the Soviet Union had twice the productive power of the major European powers.

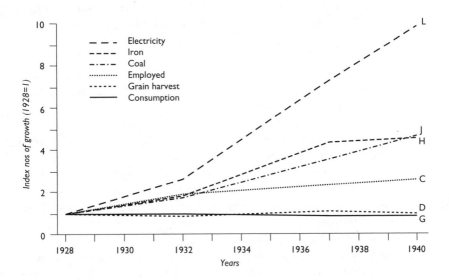

Figure 10.3 *Soviet economic growth, 1928–1940*
Note: Based on information in Table 10.3

These figures, together with the Soviet victory in the Second World War, show that in some sense the Soviet Union had solved the problem of industrialization and overcome its military weakness. By 1945 the Soviet Union was well on the way to being a superpower.

However, rapid industrial growth was not matched by improvements in the sectors of the economy that most affected the life of Soviet citizens – agriculture, consumer goods and housing.

Our fourth conclusion concerns agriculture. Agricultural production (Table 10.4, rows E to G) barely rose at all, and livestock numbers remained below the 1928 level until the 1950s. Even productivity did not rise significantly, despite more modern technology. In 1953 the farm labour force was only slightly smaller than in 1928.[23]

Fifth, statistics on Soviet living standards are even less impressive. While production of consumer goods rose, average consumption levels per caput (a crude measure of material living standards, but the only one available) declined. So did the quality of the diet and of housing, as well as the level of real wages (rows H to L).

Despite these limitations, the results of the first three Five-Year Plans suggested that the Soviet government had indeed found the alternative engine of growth they were looking for in the 1920s. Was this a new type of growth? If so, how did it work?

The government claimed that its successes were due to central planning. But as we have seen, in practice the government ignored its own plans where they conflicted with priority targets. Indeed, Stalin treated the entire planning system with some contempt, preferring to rely instead on the *praktiki* – those willing to obey orders and get things done. Economics as an independent discipline ceased to exist. For twenty years, there did not even exist an official textbook on political economy.[24] The most helpful model is not that of a plan, but of a war, for the new system owed more to the experiences of the First World War and the Civil War than to the economic theory of the 1920s.

How did the 'command economy' work? The best way of answering this question is to ask whether it relied on intensive or extensive growth. Did it achieve high growth rates by increasing inputs (of labour, money and resources), or by increasing the efficiency with which inputs were used?

The natural way to answer such a question is to examine changes in inputs and compare them with changes in total output. If inputs increase less rapidly than total production, then clearly the inputs are being used more efficiently. If the inputs increase as rapidly as total production, then economic growth is clearly dependent on the mobilisation of more resources and labour. Economists describe the relationship between inputs and outputs as a 'production function'. If outputs are divided by a measure of inputs in the form of labour, capital and land, the result is a quantity known as 'total factor productivity'. An increase in 'total factor productivity' suggests an increase in the efficiency with which resources are used.[25] Such calculations are extremely tricky, but most recent attempts to calculate changes in total factor productivity between 1928 and 1940 suggest that the real gains in output came not from increased efficiency, but from 'an increasing mobilisation of capital and labour'.[26] Improved efficiency counts, on the best estimates, for no more than 24 per cent of growth in this period, and probably much less, perhaps as little as 2 per cent.[27]

More detailed analyses of different types of input point to the same conclusion. Labour is the 'input' into production whose quantity and quality most directly affected the life of Soviet citizens. How did changes in the expenditure of labour compare with the changes in total output already summarized? Did Soviet men and women work more, or did they work more efficiently?

There clearly were gains in the productivity of labour. The government invested heavily in education during the 1930s, and the educational level of Soviet society rose sharply. Between 1928 and 1940, the number of high school students increased from 169 000 to 811 000. The numbers in classes eight to ten rose from 170 000 to 2.5 million.[28] The rate of literacy rose as well, from 51 per cent in 1929 to 81 per cent in 1940, as a result of mass literacy campaigns aimed mainly at the young. By 1939, of those aged between nine and forty-nine only 6 per cent were illiterate in the towns and 14 per cent in the villages.[29]

However, despite these changes, productive methods remained wasteful and inefficient. Table 10.6 uses calculations of rates of increase of inputs between 1928 and 1940, by the American economist, A. Bergson. Bergson's figures suggest that output per worker rose at between 0.5 per cent and 5.4 per cent per annum, as compared to rates of between 4.2 per cent and 9.3 per cent per annum for total output. These figures imply that improved labour productivity can account for at most one-half of the increased output in this period. That suggests that people not only worked more efficiently; they also worked harder. That this is so is particularly clear on the farms. Between 1926 and 1939, the numbers of people working on the farms declined from 61.6 to 48.2 millions, which suggests that productivity per worker increased by about 28 per cent. However, recent calculations have shown that those who stayed on the farms worked much harder. The total number of days worked rose from 9.8 million days in 1928 to 10.5 million days in 1937, despite the decline in the number of workers.[30]

Economists use a statistic known as the 'participation rate' to measure the proportion of the working-age population (aged from fifteen to sixty-four) engaged in wage-earning employment. Between 1928 and 1937 the

Table 10.6   *Output per unit of labour and capital, 1928–40*

Category of Output	Average annual rates of growth	
	1937 prices	*1928 and 1937 prices[a]*
Net national product (NNP)	4.2	9.3
NNP per worker	0.5	5.4
Fixed Capital	9.8	11.0
NNP per unit of fixed capital	–5.1	–1.6

Note: [a]This column used 1928 prices up to 1937 and 1940 prices from 1937–40.

Source: D. A. Dyker, *Restructuring the Soviet Economy* (London and New York: Routledge, 1992) p. 5.

Soviet participation rate increased at an astonishing rate, from about 57 per cent to about 70 per cent. There is no precedent for so rapid an increase in the participation rate in any other industrialising country.[31] Almost 20 million peasants flooded into the cities between 1926 and 1939, turning the Soviet Union's cities into what Ordzhonikidze described as a vast 'nomadic Gypsy camp'.[32] Most of the new arrivals found work, as did the remaining urban unemployed, because enterprise directors, desperate to meet rapidly rising plan targets, hired all the labour they could find. Plan targets for the size of the labour force were amongst the few targets to be overfulfilled during the first Five-Year Plan.

Cold statistics reflect harsh changes in the daily life of Soviet people. There were two main trends. The first was a vast influx of peasants into the towns to find wage-work. Their arrival transformed the industrial working class, lowering its levels of skill and experience, and weakening traditions of working-class solidarity. The second trend was a vast increase in the number of women in the wage-earning labour force. During the second Five-Year Plan and the Great Patriotic War, women provided most new recruits to the urban workforce. Declining real wages were the main lever that forced women into the paid workforce, for families found they could no longer live on a single income. Between 1928 and 1937 real wages probably declined by 20–40 per cent.[33] As a result of these changes, the percentage of women in wage-earning employment increased from 27 per cent in 1932 to 35 per cent in 1937, to 53 per cent during the war.[34] Women now entered industries that men had dominated before, though they usually took up the worst-paid jobs.

These changes meant that men and women, peasants and proletarians, all worked harder. Peasants had to adapt to the more regular work rhythms of urban factories. Women had to work both inside and outside the household. We can be sure that women worked harder because the government did little to ease their domestic burden. Nor did it do anything to persuade Soviet males to help around the household. The persistence, with government encouragement, of traditional ideas about male and female work ensured a particularly rapid increase in the burden carried by women. Clearly, the industrialization drive succeeded at least in part because Soviet citizens were working harder than before. They produced more because they worked harder.

How did the government mobilize labour on this scale? In the countryside, collective farms forced their members to spend more time and labour supplying the government with cheap grain. Collectivization also drove many peasants off the land into the towns, beginning with dekulakized *kulaks*. Between 1928 and 1932, 8.5 million of the 11 million who joined the urban workforce were peasants.[35] Once they had arrived in the towns, the government locked them in by reintroducing internal passports. These were a tsarist bureaucratic device that the Provisional Government had proudly abolished in 1917. The Soviet government furtively reintroduced them in 1932. The passports gave the government much greater control over where people lived and worked, for they enabled it to tie workers either to the town or the countryside. Instead of depending partly on factory wages, partly on a peasant farm, workers now had to choose to live either as peasants or as proletarians. The 'economic amphibians' of the late nineteenth century finally vanished. In their place, there emerged a class of urban workers, most of whom were disorientated by the sudden transformations in their lives, and still clung to peasant ways of thinking.

Once workers were in the paid workforce, managers had to discipline them to ensure they got full value from their labour. However, the immense demand for labour during the 1930s made this task difficult. After 1930, unemployment ceased to be a threat, for there was plenty of work. Unemployment had stood at 1.7 million in April 1929. By early 1931 it had dwindled almost to nothing. Rapid labour turnover now became the most serious problem. Without the 'economic whip' of unemployment, the government had to find other ways of disciplining the workforce. With government support, managers fined workers, threatened to deprive them of living quarters, or took away their ration cards after the reintroduction of rationing in 1929.[36] In 1930 the government abolished unemployment benefits on the grounds that unemployment no longer existed. The government borrowed many of its techniques directly from capitalism. Lenin had admired the work of F. W. Taylor, the pioneer of time-and-motion studies. His work inspired, among other devices, the introduction of piece-work, which tied wages closely to actual output. Under this system, managers paid workers not for hours worked but for the amounts they produced.

As war threatened from 1938, the government introduced more ferocious penalties for indiscipline. It made workers carry work books which included a complete record of an employee's career and behaviour. Workers could lose health and maternity rights for six months if they arrived late for work. The government raised average hours of work from seven to eight hours a day. It also introduced a six-day working week. Such legislation affected women more harshly than men as most women returned from work to a heavy domestic burden, made worse by overcrowded housing conditions and the need to stand in long queues to shop. Finally, as Hitler invaded France in June 1940, the government abolished the right to leave a job without permission. The same law made it a criminal offence to arrive at work more than twenty minutes late. Within six months, almost 30 000 people had been sentenced to labour camps for breaching these new laws.[37] This extraordinary law survived until 1956, although it had fallen into disuse well before then.

Not all the government's methods were punitive. It also found incentives to encourage hard work. Traditionally, socialists had believed in egalitarianism. They had always believed there should be as small a gap as possible between the richest and the poorest members of society. In June 1931 Stalin denounced this ideal as a sign of 'petit-bourgeois egalitarianism'. Incentives for increased productivity began to rise, as did wage differentials. Model workers received better wages, higher status, better housing and special allocations of consumer goods.

National campaigns encouraged workers to over-fulfil the norms set by the plans. The most famous of these 'shock workers' was a coal miner, Alexei Stakhanov. In 1935, Stakhanov produced fourteen times his planned output of coal through a combination of hard work, help from other workers, and some cheating. He and other so-called 'Stakhanovites' received star treatment and large material rewards for their achievements. Many of their fellow-workers detested them as 'norm-busters'. In 1936 work norms were, indeed, increased by 25 to 50 per cent in many industries. These and many other devices helped mobilize and discipline the hidden reserves of labour that existed in a poor, but populous country.

As with labour, so with resources. Increased output depended as much on increased inputs as it did on greater efficiency. Between 1928 and 1932, the percentage of national income devoted to capital investment rose from 19 per cent to 30 per cent.[38] One measure of the efficiency with which the government used these funds is the output achieved for every rouble of capital invested. The figures in Table 10.6 suggest that total capital increased faster than total output between 1928 and 1940. This means that the efficiency with which capital was used actually fell in this period. On Bergson's figures, output per unit of capital fell. Its 'growth' rate was between –5.1 per cent and –1.6 per cent per annum.

Such figures reflect in part the immense wastage of the early years of the industrialization drive. Plants were built before machinery was ready for them. Peasants wrecked machines they did not understand. Workers left machines idle for lack of spares or raw materials. The chaos and confusion of these years is indescribable. Looking back, it is astonishing that anything was built.

Where did the government find the vast sums of money needed for this wasteful strategy of growth? Much came from the countryside. In 1935, one-third of government revenues came from the resale of agricultural procurements purchased at artificially low prices.[39] This was why collectivization was so crucial to the industrialization drive. Indeed, some have argued that this was the main source of investment funds for industrialization. N. Valentinov, an economist who worked in the planning agencies in the 1920s, claimed that Stalin had solved the problem of industrialization using the methods of Tamerlaine. 'The financial basis of the first Five-Year Plan, until Stalin found it in levying tribute on the peasants, was extremely precarious ... [It seemed that] everything would go to the devil.'[40]

It is now clear, however, that resources did not just flow from countryside to town. On the contrary, there was a vast flow of money and resources in the opposite direction. Peasants earned extra income by selling the produce of their private plots in the towns at free market prices. In addition, in the early years of collectivization, the government had to invest heavily in agriculture, mainly in the production of tractors to replace the livestock killed during collectivization (see Table 10.3, row M). These factors directed resources back from the town to the countryside. Building the new fiscal apparatus of the collective farms was so costly that some economic historians have doubted whether the economy gained anything at all. However, these could be regarded as construction costs, just as the massacres of 1237–40 were the costs of setting up the Mongol fiscal machinery in the thirteenth century. By the late 1930s the collective farms worked extremely effectively as a way of pumping resources from the countryside to the government.[41]

In any case, the town population paid as well. The turnover tax on grain hit urban consumers as well as rural producers. The government also taxed vodka, matches and salt, as well as many other consumer goods. During the 1930s Soviet citizens came under intense pressure to buy 'voluntary' government bonds. Finally, like the tsarist government during the First World War, the Soviet government resorted to the printing press, so that Soviet consumers suffered from taxation by inflation. It is therefore not enough to say that the Soviet Union industrialized at the expense of the peasantry. It industrialized at the expense of both peasants and proletarians. Living standards declined in both the towns and the countryside. In both areas, declining consumption levels released resources for investment. The resources that fuelled industrialization came from the consumption fund of Soviet society as a whole. In 1928, about 82 per cent of national income was consumed by households. By 1937 the proportion had dropped to 55 per cent.[42] These figures measure a spectacular diversion of resources from consumption into investment.

One symptom of this was the decline in housing conditions. In the 1920s the government had invested heavily in new housing. In the 1930s and 1940s it invested very little in housing, diverting funds into heavy industry instead. As a result, the housing conditions of Soviet citizens declined drastically, as more and more people crowded into small, badly built, poorly equipped apartments. In Moscow, in 1935, 6 per cent of renting families occupied more than one room, 40 per cent had a single room, 24 per cent occupied part of a room, 5 per cent lived in kitchens and corridors, 25 per cent lived in dormitories.[43] Conditions in provincial towns were often far worse. What was true of housing was true in other areas as well. In the 1930s, there was a direct, though inverse, relationship between rising investment and declining living standards.

This was a revolution in the relationship between the new ruling group and the people it ruled. The industrialization drive depended on a huge increase in the government's power to mobilize labour, money and raw materials. It is hardly surprising that some contemporaries compared the early 1930s with the Mongol invasions of 700 years before.

We must not exaggerate. Productivity increased in many areas and there was plenty of innovation. Whole new industries appeared as the Soviet Union began to produce its own machine tools, synthetic rubber, high-grade cements and steels. These new industries depended at first on foreign models and foreign expertise, but it was mainly Soviet engineers and scientists who adapted foreign models to Soviet conditions. Sometimes they improved on them, particularly in weapons technology. In the T-34 tank or the Katyusha rocket launcher the Soviet Union produced some of the finest military equipment in the world. Indeed, Soviet engineers and scientists were themselves amongst the best in the world. The educational level of the workforce also rose rapidly. Between 1928 and 1941 the number of trained engineers rose from 47 000 to more than 900 000.[44]

However, the command economy encouraged heroic effort in priority areas rather than the widespread but small-scale cost-cutting innovations typical of capitalism. To produce and introduce new technologies, the planners had to make a special effort. By 1935 the Soviet Union spent 0.6 per cent of national income on organized research and development, while the USA spent only 0.35 per cent.[45] Planned innovation could achieve spectacular results, as it did later in the Soviet nuclear technology and space programmes. But the results were concentrated in specific areas, and spread with great difficulty to other areas of the economy. Diffusion was particularly slow from the military to the civilian sector, partly because of official secrecy, partly because civilian industries had little reason to change existing methods, particularly when innovation threatened existing plan targets.[46]

So, though there was plenty of innovation in the 1930s, the Soviet industrialization drive depended more on extensive than on intensive forms of growth.

■ The Stalinist 'Engine of Growth'

In the 1930s, under the brutal but purposeful leadership of Stalin, the Soviet government discovered the 'engine of growth' it had been looking for in the 1920s. What was new about the Stalinist 'engine of growth'? Very little. Most of its features would have seemed quite normal in the pre-modern world. In its main lines, Stalin's strategy was identical to that of Peter the Great. Both depended on the ability of a powerful state to mobilize resources. Stalin seems to have half-admitted this when, in November 1928, he praised Peter the Great's Industrialization drive as an 'attempt to leap out of the framework of backwardness'.[47]

Why did the Soviet government choose such an archaic strategy? It did so by a process of elimination. It had to find a strategy of growth of some kind if the Soviet Union was to defend itself and build a viable socialist society. Yet its own ideology ruled out many elements of the capitalist engine of growth. During NEP, the Soviet government experimented with an economy that used some elements of the capitalist structure, but in a subordinate capacity. Markets existed, but the government reserved the right to fiddle with prices when necessary. Entrepreneurs existed, but the government reserved the right to tax them out of existence when their activities conflicted with its own goals. Such policies limited the ability of market forces to generate growth. To the extent that market forces succeeded, they were a threat to the government, for they recreated new forms of capitalism. To the extent that they failed, they were also a threat for they generated only sluggish growth.

By 1928 Stalin and many other party members had concluded that the half-and-half policies of NEP could not work. In 1929, they dismantled the capitalist engine of growth altogether, eliminating the Soviet Union's last capitalist entrepreneurs and suppressing market forces. That left one alternative: the engine of growth of the pre-modern world. Far from leaping ahead of capitalism, the Stalinist system had fallen back on the pre-modern methods of extensive growth. If there did indeed exist a socialist 'engine of growth', combining equitable social policies and rapid growth, the Soviet government had failed to discover it.

The Stalinist strategy set up a global competition between two very different engines of growth, and that competition was to shape world history for much of the twentieth century. One strategy of growth depended on extensive growth, the other on intensive growth. In the short run, the Stalinist strategy achieved much. But in the long run it was bound to fail because it was too wasteful of resources. Why?

Under strategies of extensive growth, measuring costs is less important than achieving a particular level of output. This was as true for Soviet planners and industrialists as it had been for feudal landlords. Enterprises did not pay for their capital resources, but lobbied for them from the planners. This meant that the capacity to fulfil plans depended more on connections and political influence than on efficiency. Once enterprises got the resources they needed, they treated them as 'free goods'.[48] What mattered was fulfilling the planned targets for gross output or '*val*' (*valovaya produktsiya*). How economically they did this was a secondary consideration. Besides, efficiency itself was hard to measure within the command economy, for without markets there could be no objective prices. This meant that the prices placed on labour, raw materials, land, water, were all arbitrary. All these factors encouraged an extremely wasteful approach to resources.

Protected from economic competition, Soviet managers and planners hoarded resources and squandered them to achieve their goals. As the economist, Nikolai Shmelyov, wrote:

> The [administrative system of management] ... by its very nature cannot provide for growth in the quality of output or for raising the efficiency of production or for achieving the greatest result with the least expenditure. It aimed at the necessary gross quantity, not in accord with objective economic laws, but contrary to them. And 'contrary' simply means, at the cost of inconceivably high expenses of material and especially human resources.[49]

Eventually, such an economy was bound to run out of resources. Meanwhile, the sheer extravagance of the command economy explains why it threatened to waste the natural wealth, ruin the health, and devastate the landscape of one of the richest countries in the world. The command economy constructed under Stalin deployed medieval strategies of growth on a twentieth-century scale. Such strategies could succeed in the era of Peter the Great, when levels of productivity were low throughout the world. But the challenge was much greater in the twentieth-century, when levels of productivity were so much higher and rates of change so much faster.

The Stalinist strategy succeeded for several decades, but only because it enjoyed specific short-lived advantages. First, the techniques it borrowed from abroad gave a sharp boost to productivity. Like Peter's strategy of growth, Stalin's raised levels of productivity by borrowing foreign technologies and foreign approaches to education. The Soviet government also borrowed many capitalist tricks for enforcing labour discipline. However, as in the time of Peter the Great, gains in productivity based on foreign techniques were not self-sustaining. What was missing was the social structure that drove the capitalist engine of growth. Low levels of productivity and sluggish innovation were to prove the Achilles heel of the Soviet command economy. In addition to foreign technology, the Soviet government enjoyed two other advantages. It ruled the largest country in the world. This meant that vast human and material resources were available if it could mobilize them. Finally, Russia's autocratic traditions made it easier to build a state capable of mobilizing resources on the heroic scale necessary for rapid industrialization. The next chapter describes how this was done.

■ Summary

By the late 1920s, the Soviet government faced some terrible dilemmas. With no world revolution, it had to try to build socialism in the economically backward lands it controlled. And it began to devise ambitious plans of industrial development before it knew how it would fund them. In 1929, Stalin abandoned the experiment of NEP and launched a massive campaign of collectivization whose real aim was to give the government direct control of the rural sector, the one sector still controlled by private entrepreneurs. Unlike private farms, which responded to market pressures, collective farms were managed by government-appointed managers, and operated according to government plans. Collectivization meant the end of market relations in the Soviet countryside, and a return to the direct mobilization of rural resources. After collectivization, the government itself could determine what happened to rural produce. Above all, it could decide how much was consumed by the peasants, how much was invested in agriculture, and how much was made available in the form of 'procurements', to fund industrial growth. Not surprisingly, the forcible take-over of peasant farms generated a covert civil war whose main victims were millions of *kulaks* and the millions more who died in the 1933 famine. Despite this huge cost, by 1934 the government had successfully taken control of the immense human and material resources of the Soviet countryside.

Simultaneously it embarked on ambitious plans for rapid industrialization. Though Soviet statistics exaggerate the success of the first three five-year plans, there is no doubt that the Soviet government made great progress in building up a modern industrial economy and a powerful defence base. However, the achievement relied far more on direct than on indirect methods of mobilization. A careful comparison of inputs and outputs suggests that the economic achievements of the 1930s depended more on an increase in inputs than on genuine increases in productivity. More people worked, and they worked harder. At the same time, resources were diverted from consumption to investment. Not surprisingly, living standards fell for the majority of the population. Collectivization allowed the government to divert resources from the countryside to the towns, but urban workers also paid a high price in declining real wages and living conditions. In short, despite its use of modern technology and a massive expansion of education, the Stalinist industrialization drive marked no leap forward beyond capitalism, but a return to the methods of direct mobilization typical of the pre-industrial era.

☐ *Further Reading*

There are good general surveys of the period in Nove, *Stalinism and After*, Fitzpatrick, *The Russian Revolution*, and Ward, *Stalin's Russia*. On economic matters, Nove's *Economic History* is still extremely valuable. However, in some respects it is now superseded by Davies, Harrison, and Wheatcroft, *The Economic Transformation of the Soviet Union 1913–1945*, which offers the most serious and thorough recent attempt to calculate reliable statistical series on Stalinist economic history. The most detailed account of collectivization is Davies, *The Socialist Offensive* and *The Soviet Collective Farm*. I have also used S. Cohn, 'The Soviet Economy: Performance and Growth', in Blackwell (ed.), *Russian Economic Development from Peter the Great to Stalin*. On the changing political atmosphere during the collectivisation drive, see S Fitzpatrick (ed.), *Cultural Revolution in Russia*. Andrle, *A Social History of Twentieth Century Russia* is very good on labour relations and life in the towns and factories of the Soviet Union in the 1930s.

☐ *Notes*

1. M. Reiman, *The Birth of Stalinism* (Bloomington: Indiana University Press, 1987) p. 106.
2. Cited in A. Nove, *An Economic History of the USSR*, 3rd edn (Harmondsworth: Penguin, 1992) p. 147.

3. L. Viola, 'The Second Coming: Class Enemies in the Soviet Countryside, 1927–1935', in J. Arch Getty and R. T. Manning (eds), *Stalinist Terror: New Perspectives* (Cambridge University Press, 1993) pp. 65–98.

4. V. P. Danilov, *Rural Russia under the New Regime*, trans O. Figes (London: Hutchinson, 1988) p. 47.

5. Ibid., p. 43.

6. B. Dmytryshyn, *USSR: A Concise History*, 2nd edn (New York: Scribner's, 1971) p. 419.

7. Nove, *Economic History*, p. 173.

8. See R. and Z. Medvedev, *Khrushchev: The Years in Power* (New York and London: Norton, 1978) pp. 24–5.

9. M. Lewin, 'The Immediate Background to Soviet Collectivisation', in *The Making of the Soviet System* (London: Methuen, 1985) p. 99; and S. F. Cohen, *Bukharin and the Bolshevik Revolution* (Oxford University Press, 1980) p. 316.

10. Cited in L. Viola, 'Bab'i Bunty', in *Russian Review*, vol. 45 (1986) p. 37.

11. S. G. Wheatcroft, R. W. Davies and J. M. Cooper, 'Soviet Industrialization Reconsidered', in *Economic History Review*, 2nd ser., XXXIX, no. 2 (1986) p. 284.

12. Nove, *Economic History*, p. 210.

13. See S. G. Wheatcroft, 'More light on the scale of Repression and excess Mortality in the Soviet Union in the 1930s' in Getty and Manning (eds), *Stalinist Terror*, p. 280.

14. R. W. Davies, M. Harrison and S. G. Wheatcroft (eds), *The Economic Transformation of the Soviet Union 1913–1945* (Cambridge University Press, 1994) p. 68.

15. A. Koestler, *The Invisible Writing* (London: Hutchinson, 1969) pp. 63–4, 69–70.

16. Nove, *Economic History*, p. 213.

17. M. Matthews, *Soviet Government: A Selection of Official Documents on Internal Policies* (London: Cape, 1974) p. 338.

18. R. and Z. Medvedev, *Khrushchev*, p. 28.

19. M. Lewin, 'Society, State and Ideology during the First Five-Year Plan', in S. Fitzpatrick (ed.), *Cultural Revolution in Russia: 1928–1931* (Bloomington: Indiana University Press, 1978) p. 64.

20. Davies, Harrison and Wheatcroft (eds), *The Economic Transformation of the Soviet Union*, p. 41.

21. Davies *et al.*, p. 44; these figures are estimates for the territory within the 1939 boundaries.

22. Davies *et al.*, pp. 36–7, 44.

23. D. A. Dyker, *Restructuring the Soviet Economy* (New York: Routledge, 1992) p. 31.

24. M. Lewin, *Political Undercurrents in Soviet Economic Debates* (London: Pluto Press, 1975) p. 116.

25. Davies *et al.*, p. 193

26. Ibid., p. 194

27. Ibid., p. 310

28. B. Kerblay, *Modern Soviet Society* (London: Methuen, 1983) p. 149.

29. J. N. Westwood, *Endurance and Endeavour: Russian History 1812–1980*, 2nd edn (Oxford University Press, 1981) p. 364.

30. Davies *et al.*, p. 129.

31. S. H. Cohn, 'The Soviet Economy: performance and growth', in W. Blackwell (ed.), *Russian Economic Development from Peter the Great to Stalin* (New York: New Viewpoints, Franklin Watts, 1974) p. 333.
32. Cited from Ward, *Stalin's Russia*, pp. 94–5.
33. Davies *et al.*, p. 152.
34. D. Atkinson (ed.), *Women in Russia* (Brighton: Harvester Press, 1978) p. 194.
35. S. Schwarz, *Labour in the Soviet Union* (New York: Prentice-Hall, 1951) p. 9.
36. See D. Christian, 'Labour in a non-capitalist economy: the Soviet counter-example,' in Jill Roe (ed.), *Unemployment: Are there Lessons from History?* (Sydney: Hale and Iremonger, 1985) pp. 85–104.
37. E. Bacon, '*Glasnost*' and the Gulag', *Soviet Studies*, vol. 44, no. 6 (1992) p. 1078.
38. Nove, *Economic History*, p. 197.
39. Figures on revenues in 1935 from Nove, *Economic History*, p. 213.
40. Nove, *Economic History*, p. 158.
41. Dyker, *Restructuring the Soviet Economy*, p. 31.
42. Davies *et al.*, p. 272.
43. Nove, *Economic History*, p. 254.
44. Ibid., p. 235.
45. S. G. Wheatcroft, R. W. Davies and J. M. Cooper, 'Soviet Industrialization Reconsidered', p. 279.
46. There is a good discussion of how these problems affected the post-Stalin economy in R. W. Campbell, *The Failure of Soviet Economic Planning* (Bloomington: Indiana University Press, 1992) ch. 5, 'Problems of Technical Progress in the USSR'.
47. Ward, *Stalin's Russia*, p. 78.
48. Dyker, *Restructuring the Soviet Economy*, pp. 17–18.
49. N. Shmelyov, 'Loans and Debts', cited from R. Daniels (ed.), *The Stalin Revolution*, 3rd edn (Lexington, Mass, 1990) p. 238.

■ *Chapter 11* ■

The Stalinist Political Order

This chapter describes the construction of the political system that drove the Soviet 'engine of growth'. The foundations of the Stalinist system were laid during the 1920s, but the system itself was erected in the early 1930s to deal with the twin challenges of collectivization and industrialization. Though the details of the system were new, the logic behind its creation was not. Building a powerful fiscal system generated massive popular discontent. To overcome resistance, it was necessary to build a powerful coercive apparatus. This needed the support of a united and disciplined ruling group. The previous chapter described the construction of the Soviet fiscal system and the methods it used to mobilize resources. This chapter describes resistance to the new system, the building of a powerful coercive apparatus, and the formation of a highly disciplined ruling group with an exceptionally powerful leader. It also describes how Stalin's government mobilized popular and elite support through a combination of calculated concessions and systematic propaganda.

■ The Impact of Collectivization and the First Five-Year Plan: 1928 to 1934

Measuring resistance to the Soviet government is not easy. During the early 1930s the government took over control of all forms of communication. It used its monopoly over newspapers, radio and official records of all kinds to hide evidence of all conflicts except those it chose to publicize itself. It even managed to hide most of the evidence of peasant resistance to collectivization. Besides, the government's pre-emptive strike on the peasantry during dekulakization reduced the scale of resistance.

Nevertheless, resistance was widespread and dangerous. Part of the evidence comes from the sheer scale of the coercive effort the government made during collectivization. The government understood perfectly well that it was fighting a virtual civil war against the peasantry. After the famine of 1932–3, a party official who had taken part in the collectivization process put it bluntly:

A ruthless struggle is going on between the peasantry and our regime. It's a struggle to the death. This year was a test of our strength and their endurance. It took a famine to show them who is master here. It has cost millions of lives, but the collective farm system is here to stay. We've won the war.[1]

Stalin himself saw collectivization as the critical struggle of his career. In a wartime conversation with Churchill, he implied that collectivization had been even more terrible than the war with Nazi Germany.

☐ *Document 11.1: Stalin on collectivization, 1945*

'Tell me,' [Churchill asked], 'have the stresses of this war been as bad to you personally as carrying through the policy of the Collective Farms?'

This subject immediately aroused the Marshal [Stalin].

'Oh, no,' he said, 'the Collective Farm policy was a terrible struggle.'

'I thought you would have found it bad,' said [Churchill], 'because you were not dealing with a few score thousands of aristocrats or big landowners, but with millions of small men.'

'Ten millions,' he said, holding up his hands. 'It was fearful. Four years it lasted. It was absolutely necessary for Russia, if we were to avoid periodic famines, to plough the land with tractors. We must mechanise our agriculture. When we gave tractors to the peasants they were all spoiled in a few months. Only Collective Farms with workshops could handle tractors. We took the greatest trouble to explain it to the peasants. It was no use arguing with them. After you have said all you can to a peasant he says he must go home and consult his wife, and he must consult his herder.' This last was a new expression to me in this connection.

'After he has talked it over with them he always answers that he does not want the Collective Farm and he would rather do without the tractors.'

'These were what you call Kulaks?'

'Yes,' he said, but he did not repeat the word. After a pause, 'It was all very bad and difficult – but necessary.'[2]

After 1933, the government held the whip hand. There is no more evidence of large-scale resistance. However, there was plenty of hidden conflict. We can measure its extent partly by the huge apparatus of police, labour camps and terror that the government erected to contain conflict.

The government was also acutely aware of the hostility it faced from foreign capitalist powers. The rise of Nazi Germany heightened the government's sense of danger. Stalin never forgot that foreign armies had invaded the Soviet Union during the Civil War. He understood that if it was to survive, the Soviet Union would have to deal with the military challenge from foreign capitalism. As early as 1931 he told Soviet industrial managers that the main task of the industrialization drive was to build up a modern defence establishment.

☐ *Document 11.2: Stalin's 1931 speech to industrial managers*

It is sometimes asked whether it is not possible to slow down a bit in tempo, to retard the movement. No, comrades, this is impossible. It is impossible to reduce the tempo! On the contrary, it is necessary as far as possible to accelerate it. To slacken the tempo means to fall behind. And the backward are always beaten. But we do not want to be beaten. No, we do not want this! ... The history of old Russia is the history of defeats due to backwardness.

She was beaten by the Mongol Khans.

She was beaten by the Turkish beys.

She was beaten by the Swedish feudal barons.

She was beaten by the Polish–Lithuanian squires.

She was beaten by the Anglo-French capitalists.

She was beaten by the Japanese barons.

All beat her for her backwardness – for military backwardness, for cultural backwardness, for governmental backwardness, for industrial backwardness, for agricultural backwardness. She was beaten because to beat her was profitable and could be done with impunity.

... Do you want our Socialist fatherland to be beaten and to lose its independence? If you do not want this you must put an end to this backwardness as speedily as possible and develop genuine Bolshevik speed in building up the socialist system of economy. There are no other ways. That is what Lenin said during the October Revolution: 'Either death, or we must overtake and surpass the advanced capitalist countries.' We are fifty to a hundred years behind the advanced countries. We must cover this distance in ten years. Either we do this or they will crush us.[3]

The government's awareness of the hostility it faced within and outside the Soviet Union forced it, and helped it, to build the coercive machinery and the habits of discipline and unity it needed to survive.

The main elements of the expanding coercive machinery were the army (which is discussed in Chapter 12) and the secret police. There was a long tradition of secret police agencies in Russia. But never had the secret police flourished as they did under Stalin. Lenin set up the first Soviet secret police agency, the Cheka, in December 1917. The Cheka flourished during the Civil War, as did the secret police agencies of the anti-Bolshevik governments, and all made systematic use of terror. With the end of the Civil War, the use of mass terror ended. In February 1920, Lenin explained the shift in policy:

We were forced to use terror because of the terror practiced by the [Anglo-French] Entente, when strong world powers threw their hordes against us, not avoiding any type of conduct. We would not have lasted two days had we not answered these attempts of officers and White Guardists in a merciless fashion; this meant the use of terror, but this was forced upon us by the terrorist methods of the Entente.

But as soon as we attained a decisive victory, even before the end of the war, immediately after taking Rostov, we gave up the use of the death penalty and thus proved that we intend to execute our own program in the manner that we promised. We say that the application of violence flows out of the decision to smother the exploiters, the big landowners and the capitalists; as soon as this was accomplished we gave up the use of all extraordinary methods.[4]

Now called the GPU, under NEP the secret police retained a large network of informers and controlled several labour camps. However, it diminished in size and lost the right to try and sentence at will.

During the crisis years at the end of the 1920s, the role of the secret police expanded again. Late in 1927 Stalin demanded the creation of a network of GPU agents throughout the government apparatus and even in the army. These were to hunt out external and internal opponents of the government. Stalin made systematic use of the GPU during the final stages of his struggle with the Left Opposition at the end of 1927, and this set the ominous precedent of secret police involvement in party affairs. Uncertain of the reliability of the army, the government also encouraged an expansion of GPU troops. In 1928 the GPU received new powers to deal with the procurements crisis in the countryside.

During collectivization the GPU took an active part in the suppression of *kulaks*, bourgeois 'wreckers', and dissident members of the old intelligentsia. It played a particularly important role in dekulakization, supervising the deportation of 5 million *kulak* men, women and children. The prison-camp population controlled by the secret police increased from about 30 000 in 1928, to more than 500 000 by 1934.[5] Forced labour began to play an important role in industrialization, particularly in large prestige projects such as the White Sea canal between Leningrad and the Arctic.

In 1930 the government established a special institution within the police to supervize the labour-camp population. This was the Main Administration of Corrective Labour Camps (Gulag). The first boss of the new organization was Genrikh Yagoda (1891–1938). When it first established labour camps, the Soviet government intended to use them to rehabilitate class enemies through useful labour. However, as Gulag's empire grew, conditions within the camps deteriorated. The work load increased; food rations declined in quality and quantity; discipline became more brutal; and more and more camps appeared in areas of extreme cold. As a child, Stalin's biographer, Dmitri Volkogonov, lived in a Siberian village to which his mother had been exiled after the execution of his father. Here he watched as soldiers and prisoners set up a new labour camp.

☐ *Document 11.3: Setting up a labour camp*

I grew up in the village of Agul, Irbei district, in the south of Krasnoyarsk region. In the distance one could see the majestic snows of the Sayan mountains and their spurs jutting out towards the Yenisei, the Kana and the Agala. This was the genuine, drowsy *taiga*, the land of the Kerzhaks, indigenous Siberians who had migrated from the western territories of Russia a century or two earlier. In 1937 or 1938 some soldiers turned up in our little village, followed by columns of prisoners. They started cordoning off zones, and in some six months camps were established in Agul and a number of neighbouring settlements. Barbed wire appeared and high fences behind which one could just make out the huts, the armed sentries on watch-towers and the guard dogs.

The locals soon began seeing long columns of exhausted people constantly arriving on foot from the railhead sixty miles away. It seemed the camps must be infinitely expandable. Later they understood what was happening. Long ditches started appearing beyond the outskirts of the settlements, and the corpses of dead prisoners would be taken on carts or sleighs, covered with tarpaulins, and buried there at night. Many died from the sheer hardship. Many were shot out in the *taiga*. Boris Frantsevich Kreshchuk, who was living then in Agul and whose father, a blacksmith, and elder brother had been shot, told me of the time he and some other boys were out looking for pine nuts when they suddenly heard the crack of gunfire nearby, 'just like the sound of a large canvas being ripped apart'. They ran to the place and from behind some bushes watched as the firing squad threw some twenty executed prisoners into a ditch. 'I remember one of them was clinging to the grass, obviously he wasn't dead. We ran away.'[6]

By the mid-1930s, conditions in labour camps were so harsh that many prisoners did not expect to live out their full term. Alexander Solzhenitsyn described these conditions vividly in *Gulag Archipelago*, and in his short novel, *One Day in the Life of Ivan Denisovich.*

In 1934 the secret police became part of the People's Commissariat of Internal Affairs (NKVD). The NKVD now managed all prisons and labour camps, all police and frontier guards, and all aspects of state security. All the institutions of internal coercion now belonged together in a single organization.

How did the ruling group itself change in this period? By 1929, the Soviet political system was already very centralized. After the removal of Stalin's last serious rival, Bukharin, Stalin emerged as undisputed leader of the Communist Party and the Soviet government. His power rested, first, on bureaucratic patronage exercised through the party. Through the Secretariat of the Central Committee, he controlled the more important appointments to the party *apparat*. The *apparatchiki*, in turn, controlled the *nomenklatura*. This gave them control of appointments to all positions of importance throughout Soviet society. Stalin made skilful use of the huge powers of patronage he controlled in this way during the political struggles of the 1920s.

However, his power also rested on support within the party, the government, the police and the army. The brutal and energetic policies he advocated appealed particularly to younger, less educated party members, most of whom had joined the party since the revolution. By 1929, his power was immense, and during the celebrations for his fiftieth birthday there emerged the first signs of the Stalin cult.

Collectivization reinforced the party's traditions of unity and discipline by creating an atmosphere of intense crisis. Collectivization transformed the atmosphere within the party. It placed it once more in the position of an occupying army, and this justified a return to Civil War methods and attitudes. Bukharin argued that collectivization had brutalized those party members who took part. In 1933 he told a friend that during the Civil War, he had seen

> things that I would not want even my enemies to see. Yet 1919 cannot even be compared with what happened between 1930 and 1932. In 1919 we were fighting for our lives. We executed people, but we also risked our lives in the process. In the later period, however, we were conducting a mass annihilation of completely defenceless men, together with their wives and children ... [This experience, he added, had caused] ... deep changes in the psychological outlook of those Communists who participated in this campaign, and instead of going mad, became professional bureaucrats for whom terror was henceforth a normal method of administration and obedience to any order from above a high virtue. [The whole process had caused] a real dehumanization of the people working in the Soviet apparatus.[7]

Collectivization was one aspect of a larger 'cultural revolution'. Between 1928 and 1932 the whole tone of Soviet life changed. Military metaphors invaded the language. The papers began to talk of 'industrial fronts', of 'storming', of 'saboteurs' and 'traitors'. The government clamped down on all forms of dissent. Trade unions lost their independence. Non-Marxists lost positions of influence in universities, government offices and industrial enterprises. Rigid censorship ended the broad-ranging debates of the 1920s. Using the notion of 'socialist realism', government officials even tried to harness the arts to the tasks of the revolution from above.

In these ways, the party projected its embattled and militaristic mood on the whole of Soviet society between 1928 and 1932. Such processes increased the power of the leader, for the many dangers facing the party made dissidents reluctant to destabilize existing structures. The brutalization of party life also prepared the way for a bloody resolution of internal conflicts.

However, in the early 1930s there were still limits to the unity of the elite and the powers of its leader. After the completion of collectivization and the first Five-Year Plan, many party members felt it was time to call a halt. At the upper levels of the party, even among Stalin's closest followers, many were unhappy about the events of these years. Collectivization itself had been a dangerous gamble and its social and political costs appalled many party members. Stalin had alienated many provincial party secretaries with sweeping party purges in 1929–30. His 'Dizzy with Success' speech in 1930 disorientated local party officials who might otherwise have been sympathetic to Stalin's policies. Collectivization also unnerved many in the army. The destruction of livestock posed serious difficulties for an army that still relied on horse-drawn transport, while the alienation of most of the peasantry undermined the morale of recruits.

However, analysing the extent and significance of opposition to Stalin is difficult because dissent became invisible. Russian traditions of solidarity, reinforced by Bolshevik traditions of discipline, prohibited the public expression of dissent. The exclusion of non-communist parties from political life, and the 1921 anti-faction ruling gave formal expression to this powerful convention. As in the past, such conventions did not end conflict. They merely drove it underground. Party members colluded in public displays of unity at formal ceremonies and in unanimous votes in public party meetings. At the same time, they engaged in furtive conflict behind closed doors, in whispers, or in hints and innuendoes. Hidden conflict reinforced the atmosphere of insecurity and suspicion generated by the crises of the early 1930s. Where enemies hid themselves, it was tempting to see enemies everywhere.

There are indirect signs of several attempts to limit Stalin's powers in the early 1930s. The best-known is associated with the name of M. N. Riutin (1890–1937). An army officer from Siberia, who joined the Bolsheviks in 1914, Riutin became famous as a guerilla fighter for the Communists during the Civil War. In the late 1920s he supported the Rightists, and in 1930 he criticized Stalin's policies in a personal interview with the leader. For this Stalin had him expelled from the party and arrested. However, within months he was released and reinstated as a party member. In 1932, he circulated a document addressed to all party members, in which he criticized Stalin's policies.

☐   *Document 11.4: Extract from the 'Riutin Platform', Summer 1932*

The adventurist tempos of industrialisation have involved a colossal reduction of the real wages of manual and clerical workers, unbearable open and concealed taxes, inflation, price increases and the decline in the value of the ruble. Adventurist collectivisation has been assisted by dekulakisation, directed in practice against the mass of middle peasants and poor peasants in the countryside. The countryside has been exploited by all kinds of imposts and compulsory collections of agricultural products. This has led the country to a very profound economic crisis, the monstrous impoverishment of the mass of the people, and famine ... The rights of the Party have been usurped by a tiny gang of unprincipled political intriguers ... Stalin and his clique are destroying the Communist cause, and the leadership of Stalin must be finished with as quickly as possible.[8]

In August Riutin met with other critics of Stalin's policies, and this group began to circulate Riutin's essay. Its readers included Zinoviev and Kamenev. Some days after their meeting, police got a copy of the essay and arrested Riutin and several of those who shared his views. Stalin demanded Riutin's execution. However, several members of the Politburo opposed Stalin, and Riutin received a ten-year prison sentence instead. Stalin got his revenge in 1937, when he had Riutin shot together with friends and members of his family. Meanwhile, these events showed the limits to Stalin's power in the early 1930s.

By 1934 when the seventeenth Party Congress met, there were hints that others hoped to limit Stalin's powers or even to remove him from office. According to Anastas Mikoyan (1895–1978), who was to join the Politburo in 1935, almost one-quarter of the deputies voted against Stalin's election to the Central Committee. Stalin learnt about this and insisted on recording only three hostile votes. At the same congress, several delegates asked the rising star, Sergei Kirov (1886–1934), to stand as General Secretary instead of Stalin. Kirov refused and told Stalin of the plan.[9] Dissidents could also take heart from the knowledge of what was now an open secret: that Lenin himself had wanted to remove Stalin.

However, the crisis atmosphere of the early 1930s put those who opposed Stalin in a difficult situation. Like liberal politicians during the First World War, they faced the terrible dilemma that V. Maklakov had described in his parable of the 'mad chauffeur' (see Chapter 6). The turmoil of industrialization, the hatred of the peasantry, and the hostility of foreign capitalist powers made it extremely dangerous to indulge in a leadership struggle. In 1933 a correspondent of Trotsky's said of the old Bolsheviks, 'they all speak about Stalin's isolation and the general hatred of him ... But they often add: "If it were not for that (we omit their strong epithet for him) ... everything would have fallen to pieces by now. It is he who keeps everything together'".[10] On his last trip abroad in 1936 Bukharin, who already knew he was doomed, said much the same to the exiled Mensheviks, Lydia and Fedor Dan. Of Stalin, he said: 'This is a small, wicked man ... no, not a man, a devil'. However, he added, 'He is something like the symbol of the party. The rank-and-file workers, the people believe him. We are probably responsible for it ourselves ... and this is why we are all ... crawling into his jaws knowing for sure that he will devour us'.[11] This sort of thinking paralysed Stalin's opponents. Twenty years before, members of the *Duma* had failed to move against Nicholas II because they, too, believed that a bad leader was better than no leader at all at a time of extreme crisis.

 Terror and Stalin's Rise to Domination: 1934–9

Stalin reacted to dissent with manoeuvres as subterranean as those of his rivals. However, Stalin had a stronger hand, and played his cards more decisively. The Riutin affair showed Stalin the limits of his power. Formally, his power rested entirely on the party machine. It depended on his ability to secure majority votes in the main party organs, from the party congresses to the Politburo. If Stalin was to increase his own power and crush those who threatened him, he had to extend his personal power base beyond the party apparatus. He did so partly by extending his influence within the secret police apparatus and increasing the power and influence of the secret police.

Before 1934, the police had only limited powers of arrest and sentence, and the Procuracy, the body responsible for legal supervision of government institutions, still retained some control over the police. In law, at least, the secret police could not carry out death sentences. Further, party members were beyond its reach unless the party expelled them. The police had arrested members of the former right and left oppositions, but treated them leniently by the standards of the time.

With the murder of Kirov on 1 December 1934, the position of the secret police changed radically. Kirov had replaced Zinoviev as head of the Leningrad party apparatus in 1926. He became a candidate member of the Politburo in the same year, and a full member in 1934. His murderer, Nikolayev, was a disgruntled party member. He shot Kirov in Smolny, the headquarters of the Leningrad party apparatus and the building from which the October Revolution had been launched seventeen years before. Though there is no firm proof, indirect evidence suggests that Stalin may have organized the murder. Khrushchev hinted at

Stalin's complicity in his Secret Speech of 1956. Amongst other details, Khrushchev pointed to the 'unusually suspicious fact that when the Chekist assigned to protect Kirov was being brought for interrogation, on 2 December 1936, he was killed in a car accident in which no other occupants of the car were harmed'.[12]

On hearing of Kirov's murder, Stalin left for Leningrad by train the same evening. Yagoda, the head of the NKVD, accompanied him. When Stalin arrived, he personally interrogated Nikolayev. Even more important, before leaving Moscow, Stalin issued a decree on new judicial procedures for dealing with terrorism. *Pravda* published it even before the full Politburo saw it. Two days later, the members of the Politburo lamely accepted the decree Stalin had issued. The crisis atmosphere in which the party found itself deprived its leaders of the will to oppose Stalin's personal authority. They had allowed Stalin to take decisions of fundamental importance without getting the agreement of the Politburo. By 1937 they no longer had the power to rein him in.

The so-called Kirov Decrees, first introduced in this arbitrary manner, remained in force for twenty years.

□ *Document 11.5: The Kirov Decrees*

The Central Executive Committee of the USSR decrees that the following amendments on the investigation and consideration of cases relating to terrorist organizations and terrorist acts against agents of the Soviet Government shall be introduced into the existing codes of the union republics.

1. The investigation of such cases must be terminated during a period of not more than ten days.
2. The indictments should be presented to the accused twenty-four hours before the hearing of the case in court.
3. The cases must be heard without participation of a defence counsel.
4. Appeal against the sentences and also petitions for pardon are not to be admitted.
5. Sentence to the highest degree of punishment [that is, the death penalty] must be carried out immediately after passing of the sentence.

President of the Central Executive Committee of the USSR
M. KALININ

Secretary of the Central Executive Committee of the USSR
A. YENUKIDZE[13]

The Kirov Decrees allowed the police to arrest political dissidents, try them in secret, and execute them immediately. Within days, the NKVD arrested and shot a hundred Leningraders accused of complicity with Nikolayev. It also arrested thousands more suspected dissidents, including Kamenev and Zinoviev. Stalin launched a simultaneous purge of party members. Originally, such purges had meant little more than expulsion from the party, but in the atmosphere of the 1930s, they came to mean something more terrifying. Soon the police began to arrest party members as a matter of course. This marked a sharp rise in the influence of the police and a decline in the independence of the party. As Stalin now controlled the police, it also marked a sharp increase in the leader's power.

By 1934 there had emerged a small nucleus of officials directly responsible to Stalin. They included N. I. Yezhov, who was to lead the secret police during the great purge. Stalin had also established a private secretariat of his own, headed by A. N. Poskrebyshev. This allowed Stalin to communicate directly with the police and other government agencies without going through the party bureaucracy. In addition, he had formed a special State Security Committee that included Poskrebyshev and Yezhov. In the early 1930s Yezhov headed the records and assignment department of the Central Committee. This was the body that kept records on the careers of all party members, and assigned them to new jobs. Slowly Stalin had prepared for the time when he could give orders to the secret police on his own authority and thereby use the police against the party.

The aftermath of the Kirov assassination showed that Stalin could now order the secret police to arrest members of the party. These changes marked a revolution in the political structure of Soviet Russia, for Stalin could now bypass the party if he chose to do so. The party, once the dominant political institution, now became one of several more or less equal political structures. All were now subject to the personal authority of Stalin. Khrushchev described these changes in his Secret Speech to the twentieth Party Congress.

☐ *Document 11.6: Extract from Khrushchev's Secret Speech of 1956*

What is the reason that mass repressions against activists increased more and more after the 17th Party Congress? It was because at that time [1934] Stalin had so elevated himself above the Party and above the nation that he ceased to consider either the Central Committee or the Party. While he still reckoned with the opinion of the collective before the 17th Congress, after the complete political liquidation of the Trotskyites, Zinovievites and Bukharinites, when as a result of that fight and socialist victories the Party achieved unity, Stalin ceased to an ever greater degree to consider the members of the Party's Central Committee and even the members of the Political Bureau. Stalin thought that now he could decide all things alone and all he needed were statisticians; he treated all others in such a way that they could only listen to and praise him.[14]

The clearest sign of the reduced authority and independence of the party was the irregularity with which its main institutions now met. Party congresses had been annual or biennial events in the 1920s. Then the gap between congresses began to widen. The fourteenth Congress met in 1925; the fifteenth in 1927; the sixteenth in 1930. The seventeenth did not meet until 1934; the eighteenth met in 1939; and the nineteenth did not meet until thirteen years had passed, in 1952. The Central Committee also ceased to meet regularly. So did the Politburo. Stalin would call individual members of the Politburo together for specific tasks, leaving other members in the dark. However, Stalin avoided the mistake of elevating the police in place of the party. On the contrary, the great purge ended in 1938 with a purge of the secret police and the execution of its leader, Yezhov. Stalin no longer depended on any single institution. He could now manoeuvre freely between the various institutions of power that dominated Soviet society.

In 1936 Nikolai Yezhov (1895–1939) replaced Yagoda as head of the NKVD. Then, between 1936 and 1938, the government launched what has come to be known as the Great Terror, or the *Yezhovshchina*.

To foreigners, the visible sign of the purge was a series of carefully staged show trials at which the defendants were leading party and government figures. Most defendants confessed publicly to crimes against the Soviet state. Their confessions wove a melodramatic tale of intrigue and treachery, involving foreign governments, and co-ordinated by the arch-villain, Trotsky. At the time, most observers did not know that the police got their confessions using torture and threats to defendants' families. Police interrogators also exploited the curious sense of loyalty to the party that many defendants retained to the bitter end. (This is described superbly in Arthur Koestler's novel, *Darkness at Noon*.)

At the first trial, in August 1936, the prosecution accused Zinoviev, Kamenev and other prominent old Bolsheviks of plotting with Trotsky to murder party leaders, including Kirov. After confessing to most of the charges, the defendants were shot. Massive publicity campaigns in the papers and on the radio accompanied the trials. Papers published thousands of letters, purporting to come from ordinary Soviet citizens and demanding the death sentence for the accused.

In January 1937 several other prominent Bolsheviks were tried and executed with similar publicity. In June there was a purge and show trial of military leaders. These included the dominant figure in the Red Army, Marshal M. N. Tukhachevsky (1893–1937). In March 1938 came the turn of Bukharin, A. I. Rykov (1881–1938), Yagoda, and several other old Bolsheviks. In 1938 Yezhov was himself executed. His replacement as head of the NKVD was Lavrentii Beria (1899–1953). This final purge of the secret police marked the end of the worst period of the pre-war purges.

Stalin apparently decided that the disruption caused by the purges was beginning to outweigh any advantage he might gain from them. However, the legal and institutional machinery of the purges remained in place and Stalin used it sporadically to the end of his life.

Beneath the surface (and largely invisible to foreigners) a holocaust was taking place. Proportionately, the purges hit the party worst of all. They hit both the pre-revolutionary generation of old Bolsheviks and many who joined during the Civil War or the early 1920s. Stalin clearly saw the main threat to his own position coming from these older, established sections of the Soviet ruling group. The abolition of the once prestigious 'Society of Old Bolsheviks' in 1935 was an ominous sign of what was to come. In the early 1930s, G. I. Petrovskii told another old Bolshevik, S. V. Kosior (1889–1939): 'for some reason [Stalin] has taken a dislike to old Bolsheviks; he's out to get them'.[15] In his Secret Speech of 1956, Khrushchev described the impact of the purges on the party elite.

□ *Document 11.7: Extract from Khrushchev's Secret Speech of 1956*

It was determined [by a special Party commission set up after Stalin's death to investigate the purges] that of the 139 members and candidates of the Party's Central Committee who were elected at the 17th Congress [1934], ninety-eight persons, i.e. seventy per cent, were arrested and shot (mostly in 1937–1938). [Indignation in the Hall.] What was the composition of the delegates to the 17th Congress? It is known that eighty per cent of the voting participants of the 17th Congress joined the party during the years of conspiracy before the revolution and during the civil war; this means before 1921. By social origin the basic mass of the delegates to the Congress were workers ...

The same fate met not only the Central Committee members but also the majority of the delegates to the 17th Party Congress. Of 1966 delegates with either voting or advisory rights, 1108 persons were arrested on charges of antirevolutionary crimes, i.e. decidedly more than a majority.[16]

Below this level, at least 200 000 party members died between 1936 and 1939, though some estimates have put the figure much higher.[17] Other sections of the elite also suffered. The purge of the army, for example, removed 65 per cent of the upper command, including three out of five marshals, thirteen out of fifteen generals, and sixty-two out of eighty-five corps commanders.

These figures give little idea of the impact of the purges at lower levels of Soviet society. The press and radio helped create an atmosphere of general paranoia. Public statements encouraged people to look for and denounce enemies, wreckers, possible spies, or even people whose relatives had been class enemies. In a frenzy of denunciations, the purges spread to include relatives, friends, and casual acquaintances of those arrested at first. Eventually, under pressure to fulfil quotas, the police began to arrest completely arbitrary victims.

> By and large, the Organs [the police] had no profound reasons for their choice of whom to arrest and whom not to arrest. They merely had overall assignments, quotas for a specific number of arrests. These quotas might be filled on an orderly basis or wholly arbitrarily. In 1937 a woman came to the reception room of the Novocherkassk NKVD to ask what she should do about the unfed unweaned infant of a neighbour who had been arrested. They said: 'Sit down, we'll find out'. She sat there for two hours – whereupon they took her and tossed her into a cell. They had a total plan which had to be fulfilled in a hurry, and there was no one available to send out into the city – and here was this woman already in their hands![18]

How many suffered during the purges? This is an important, if gruesome, question. Material released by the Soviet government in the late 1980s allows us, at last, to give some figures based on archival evidence. By and large, these tend to lower the estimates accepted by most Western historians ever since the publication of Robert Conquest's influential book, *The Great Terror*. However, these adjustments do nothing to excuse the horror of the purges.

How many people were arrested and executed during the purges? In 1990 Soviet researchers who had used KGB archives claimed, with what seems excessive precision, that between 1931 and 1953 government tribunals sentenced 3 778 234 people, of whom 786 098 were executed. Almost 700 000 of those executed died in 1937 and 1938, at the height of the purges.[19] At present, these are the best estimates available. However, we can be certain that many more died unrecorded, so these count as low estimates.

How many ended up in labour camps and how many died there? Archival material released late in the 1980s suggests that the numbers in camps rose from about 500 000 in 1934 to about 1.2 million in 1937, and to almost 2 million on the eve of war. During the war, the numbers fell to about 1.2 million by 1944. They then rose again to a post-war peak of 2.6 millions in 1950, and remained at that level until Stalin's death.[20] However, these figures do not include those in ordinary prisons or in exile. It is likely that the numbers exiled to so-called 'labour settlements', whose regimes were less severe than those in camps, were as high as 75 per cent of the numbers in camps.[21] These figures suggest that in the late 1930s and the 1940s, between 2 million and 4 million lived in labour camps or as exiles in labour settlements. Death rates in the camps were high, but, except during the war, they were probably not as high as the 10 per cent per annum that Conquest regards as the normal rate.[22] Recent archival research suggests that death rates in the camps reached 10 per cent per annum only in 1939, and again during the war. At other times, they ranged from 3.5 to almost 7 per cent per annum.[23]

It is worth noting that far fewer died during the purges of the late 1930s than during collectivization and the collectivization famine of 1933. Though historians have usually seen the purges as the height of Stalinist repression, it was collectivization that inflicted the greatest human cost. The difference is that the purges were a far greater shock to the Soviet elite, and its view of Stalinism has had a disproportionate influence on historical accounts of the period.

What sort of political system can inflict such brutality on its own population and survive? The simplest explanation of the purges sees them as a product of Stalin's determination to remove all possible rivals. There is undoubtedly some truth in this explanation. Stalin bears direct responsibility for much of what went on during the purges, for his signature appears on death warrants for many thousands of purge victims.

From Stalin's point of view, there was also a more positive aspect to this process. The purges did not merely remove potential enemies. They also raised up a new ruling elite which Stalin had reason to think he would find more dependable. Particularly important is the career of the so-called *vydvizhentsy*, those 'brought forward'. By the late 1920s, the government was beginning to worry that most people with technical, scientific and industrial skills were not party members. Many were of bourgeois origin, which made them, technically, class enemies. The Shakhty trial of 1928 gave full rein to these suspicions and helped make them a national obsession.

Stalin's solution was to speed up the training of a new generation of experts from the working class. These 'Red experts' would eventually form a new 'proletarian intelligentsia'. Between 1928 and 1932, the party drafted more than 100 000 young Communist workers into colleges and universities for engineering and industrial training. This generation of *vydvizhentsy* turned out to be of immense significance, for they provided many of the managers and officials who replaced those removed during the purges. By 1939, many *vydvizhentsy* had risen to dizzy heights. Stalin was well aware of the turnover of elites accomplished during the purges. At the eighteenth Party Congress, he described the emergence of a new Soviet intelligentsia:

> Hundreds of thousands of young people, offspring of the working class, the peasantry, and the toiling intelligentsia, went to higher school and tekhnikums and, returning from the schools, filled the depleted ranks

of the intelligentsia. They poured new blood into the intelligentsia and revitalised it in a new Soviet way. They radically changed the contours of the intelligentsia, remaking it in their own image.[24]

The career of Aleksei Kosygin (1904–80) is typical of the politicians of this generation. Born in 1904, he fought in the Red Army during the Civil War. He went on to a technical college, and worked in co-operative organizations in Siberia during the 1920s. In 1927 he joined the Communist Party. In 1931 he entered the Leningrad Textile Institute as one of the *vydvizhentsy*, and on graduating in 1935, he became a department head in a Leningrad textile factory. His career took off during the purge era. In 1937 Kosygin was a factory director. A year later he was the head of the executive committee of the Leningrad city Soviet. Early in 1939, at the age of thirty-five, he became people's commissar (that is, minister) for light industry for the entire Soviet Union. In 1940 he became deputy chairman of the Council of People's Commissars, co-ordinating all light industries. Kosygin remained at the pinnacle of the Soviet political hierarchy until his death in 1980.

Other *vydvizhentsy* rose as fast. By 1952 they made up 36 per cent of the Central Committee. By the early 1980s, 50 per cent of Politburo members came from this group. As Sheila Fitzpatrick has shown, this generation dominated Soviet politics from the late 1930s to the mid-1980s. It included Aleksei Kosygin, Leonid Brezhnev (1906–82), Nikita Khrushchev (1894–1971), Dmitrii Ustinov (1908–84), and Andrei Kirilenko (1906–82). The 'Stalin generation' of politicians left the Soviet scene only in the mid-1980s. The purges had, indeed, created a new ruling elite.

Stalin could hardly have succeeded in such a ruthless destruction of the Soviet ruling elite, if there had not been other factors that made the purges possible. The paranoia of the purge era reflected the workings of the entire system, not just of Stalin himself. As we have seen, driving conflict underground created an atmosphere of pervasive suspicion, and made it difficult to distinguish friends from foes. The real dangers faced by the Soviet government in the 1930s intensified the atmosphere of suspicion. The government itself exacerbated the popular mood by manufacturing conflicts where none existed. Ever since the Shakhty trial, it had diverted discontent from its own failings and on to foreign powers or internal saboteurs and 'wreckers' by creating an atmosphere of permanent and acute crisis. By putting foreign experts on trial in the Shakhty trial, the government planted the idea that foreign and internal enemies of the Soviet state worked together. As early as 1927 Stalin announced: 'We are a country surrounded by capitalist states. The internal enemies of our revolution are the agents of the capitalists of all countries'.[25] In the atmosphere of the 1930s, the plots the government claimed to have discovered during the purges appeared all too plausible to ordinary Soviet citizens. In 1988, a former collective farm chairman wrote to *Izvestiya*:

> We believed everything. I refer to people like myself from the village ... I can honestly say that when they told us about the conspiracy of Bukharin and the others, I did not doubt for a second that everything was like that. My soul sought for revenge. We believed everything, everything in the newspapers. After all, we read their own confessions. Moreover, the iron will of the exposures, the mercilessness, had the effect that I believed Stalin still more, blindly ... Everything was so obvious![26]

The same atmosphere undoubtedly encouraged Stalin's own paranoias. He could rarely be certain who was an enemy. However, he knew that he had enemies and he knew that they plotted in secret. The same was true for the many petty Stalins planted in local party cells, industrial enterprises or military units throughout the country. The social upheavals of the early 1930s ensured a receptive atmosphere for the government's own paranoid propaganda even amongst the working-class population. Particularly for peasants forced off the land and into the bewildering and threatening atmosphere of Soviet towns, it was all too easy to believe there were enemies everywhere.

The atmosphere of the 1930s also helps explain how the purges spread in a chain reaction from relatives of victims, to friends, to casual acquaintances to completely innocent bystanders. In a period of great turmoil, they offered many chances for the settling of old scores.

Historians have often taken the purges as proof of the power of the Soviet government. This is partly true. Yet it is also misleading. To lash out with such violence may also have been a sign of weakness. Recent studies of the era have shown that the government launched the purges, in part, out of an acute sense of its own weakness. Earlier attempts to purge provincial party officials had shown how little control the centre had over the lower levels of Soviet political life. The central leadership could replace local party bosses, local enterprise managers, and local police and army commanders but it was almost impossible to supervise the day-to-day activities of provincial party bosses. The Soviet bureaucracy was just not efficient enough to do this. In a society where telephones were a novelty and local officials often travelled by horse, the centre lacked the means to exercise detailed supervision over its own agents. The central party apparatus even found it difficult to control such elementary matters as party membership. Party files were chaotic throughout this period, which made the task of weeding out undesirables extremely difficult. In the following passage the historian, J. Arch Getty, describes the career of one Podol'skii-Fel'dman.

> Actually named Fel'dman, he joined the Komsomol [Communist Youth League] in the Ukrainian town of Korosten in 1931. Ambition took him to Baku, where he presented himself as Podol'skii, claiming that he had lost his Komsomol membership card. He turned up later that year in Piatigorsk and was soon expelled for violations of discipline. He stole his personnel file and went to Bukhara, where he rapidly rose through the Komsomol to candidate Party membership. Expelled there for criminal activity, Podol'skii-Fel'dman kept his Party card, stole three blank personnel file records, stamped them with the Party seal, and moved to the city of Dnepropetrovsk. Promoted there to full Party membership in 1932, his 'references' won him a position on the regional newspaper. Expelled from the Party for 'personal corruption,' he used a set of his blank documents, stamped them with the Dnepropetrovsk seal and moved on to Kiev. Passing unscathed through the Party purge of 1934, he was holding a responsible position in a district prosecutor's office in 1935.[27]

The limited reach of the central authorities left plenty of power in the hands of local bosses. To protect themselves, local leaders worked together in so-called 'family groups' held together by ties of friendship and sometimes, literally, by kinship. The dominant figures were usually the provincial party secretaries. However, they usually worked closely with local police chiefs, army commanders and industrial managers to magnify local successes and hide local failures.

Amongst other things, the purges were an attempt by the centre to break the power of these local fiefdoms. In 1937 the centre encouraged ordinary party members to denounce corrupt provincial officials. In the middle of the year most provincial party secretaries and many lower level party officials vanished. However, though the purges removed many local cliques, the same phenomena soon reappeared. Indeed local cliques, partly insulated from central control, became an endemic feature of the Soviet political system, for the system could hardly work without them.[28] The purges had shown the limits as well as the extent of central power.

When the purges ended, the Soviet political system had been transformed. In 1934, Stalin's power derived from his position as head of the party apparatus. Decisions flowed from the Politburo, through the party apparatus and then to the economic ministries, the secret police, the army, and the various other organs of government. By 1939 the party apparatus could no longer control Stalin. Stalin had achieved a personal authority independent of any single institution. He had established his right to issue orders on his personal authority, using any bureaucratic channels he chose. In particular, he could act directly through the secret police against the party, the army or the economic ministries. Yet there was nothing to stop him from acting also through other institutions against the secret police.

> [Stalin] developed a system of competing and overlapping bureaucratic hierarchies in which both the Party and the police, penetrating and watching each other, simultaneously pervaded and controlled the armed forces, the administration, and all other organized sectors of life. He reserved his own ultimate authority to direct and coordinate the system by providing no point of final resolution for differences and conflicts short of himself ... He capitalized on the diffusion of power among his subordinates to prevent them from challenging his own.[29]

We must not exaggerate Stalin's power. There always remained the slim chance that his own main supporters would ally against him. There are signs that members of the Central Committee opposed a continuation of the party purge at its February–March meeting in 1937. In 1938 Stalin apparently hoped to replace Yezhov, the head of the NKVD, with G. M. Malenkov (1902–88). However, the rest of the Politburo outvoted him, choosing instead Laurentii Beria.[30] Clearly divisions continued even within the Politburo, and often Stalin's role was to adjudicate between different positions within it. Besides, the inefficiency of the Soviet bureaucracy blunted his power at the regional level. Nevertheless, after 1936 his personal power was so extensive that it became almost impossible to move against him.

The changes that occurred between the meeting of the seventeenth Party Congress in 1934 and the eighteenth Party Congress in 1939 had transformed a one-party state with a powerful leader into a personal dictatorship. By 1939 Stalin himself was the most important single institution in Soviet political life.

■ Mobilizing Support

The coercive elements of Stalinism are so striking that it is easy to forget that the system depended also on a surprising degree of genuine support. This explains the resilience the Stalinist system displayed during the war.

Within the Soviet ruling group, many had powerful reasons to support Stalin despite the insecurities of the purge era. Stalin enjoyed the support, in particular, of the generation of younger party members, industrial managers, and government and police officials who benefited from the changes of the 1930s. These we can think of as the new, Soviet *dvoriane*. Like the service nobles of Muscovite Russia, they owed their status, privileges and power, not to birth or to past services. They owed them to their willingness to obey the state and its current leadership, and serve it with all the skill and energy they could muster. Their elevation transformed the nature and atmosphere of the party and *nomenklatura*.

The rapid social changes of the 1930s created many opportunities for ambitious young party members. For every party member who vanished during the purges, someone else gained a promotion. The very scale of the purges created openings for a new generation of Soviet leaders. For them, the 1930s were a period of dangers, but also of spectacular successes, both personal and national. Most striking of all is the career of the *vydvizhentsy*, but below them there were many others of working-class origin for whom the 1930s offered similar, if less dazzling opportunities. In the early 1930s at least half a million people of working-class origin moved into white-collar and managerial jobs. Here was the raw material for a new ruling group recruited largely from the working classes, but also including many from the former intelligentsia.[31]

Despite their working-class origins, the Stalinist elite soon formed a distinct group within Soviet society, separate from the rest of the Russian working class. Stalin encouraged this tendency by magnifying the privileges, the power and the status of the new elite. After attacking egalitarianism in 1931, Stalin encouraged the introduction of higher wages and special privileges for elite groups and skilled workers. The power and status of industrial managers increased particularly during the early Five-Year Plans.

> The creation of a hierarchical scaffolding of dedicated bosses, held together by discipline, privilege and power, was a deliberate strategy of social engineering to help stabilise the flux. It was born, therefore, in conditions of stress, mass disorganization, and social warfare, and the bosses were actually asked to see themselves as commanders in a battle. The Party wanted the bosses to be efficient, powerful, harsh, impetuous, and capable of exerting pressure crudely and ruthlessly and getting results 'whatever the cost'. Rudeness ... became a virtue and, more significantly, the boss was endowed with quasi-police power in the workplace: among his prerogatives were fines and dismissals, which meant deprivation of lodging and food, and he had the further resource (even more corrupting) of the local security organs and the public prosecutor. The formation of the despotic manager was actually a process in which not leaders but rulers were made. The fact that their own jobs and freedom were quite insecure made the tyrannical traits of their rule more rather than less capricious and offensive.[32]

Typical of this style is the advice given by Stalin's industrial troubleshooter, L. M. Kaganovich (1893–), to enterprise managers to behave so that 'the earth should tremble when the director walks around the plant'.[33]

A whole generation of petty Stalins emerged, their style and behaviour that of traditional Russian officials. Material privileges bound them together as effectively as political power. From 1931, the privileges of party leaders, industrial managers, shock workers, army officers, police officials, and intellectuals rose sharply. Wages were the least important of these privileges. Favoured groups had access to better housing, to government cars, to luxury goods inaccessible to anyone else, and to special stores. For long periods they even received secret wage packets that could double or treble their official wages.

Within this elite there appeared rigid hierarchies of rank and privilege. These affected the tone of public life as the Table of Ranks had in the eighteenth and nineteenth centuries.

☐ *Document 11.8: Koestler on privilege, 1933*

Among citizens of the privileged categories who travelled armed with *bronis* [special permits], the speed with which they obtained a train reservation depended on the 'strength' of their *organizacia* – meaning the administrative department, trust, factory, state-farm or other body for which they worked. The GPU [secret police] had absolute priority; next to it came the Party, then the government administration, army, heavy industry, light metal industry, consumer industries, trade unions, research centres, etc., approximately in that order. The same system of hierarchic priorities was applied to the allocation of flats, rooms, or a share in a room, through the city Soviet's Housing Department, and to the allocation of a bed in a hotel room, for travellers arriving in a town, by the Central Hotel Management Trust. The same system of priorities determined to which food cooperative you belonged; the same system decided whether you gained access to an official parade or theatre performance. The first question one was asked when applying for any commodity or facility, from railway tickets to ration cards, was always 'What is your *organizacia*?' The rights and privileges of the individual were entirely dependent on the rank which his 'organisation' occupied in the social pyramid, and on the rank which he occupied inside that organisation. There has never perhaps been a society in which a rigid hierarchical order so completely determined every citizen's station in life and governed all his activities.[34]

It was this new elite group that Trotsky described as the Soviet 'bureaucracy'. The Yugoslav Communist Milovan Djilas called it the 'new class'. This group not only dominated Soviet society politically and economically. It also set the moral and even the aesthetic tone of official Soviet life – its standards of behaviour, of ethics, of political morality.

Though the party was in eclipse, the *nomenklatura* still bound the ruling elite together.

How large was the new ruling group? If we accept that it coincides with the *nomenklatura*, we can estimate it roughly. In 1970, the *nomenklatura* included about 700 000 positions. If we include families, this represents about 3 million people, or 1.2 per cent of the Soviet population.[35] Assuming the proportions were similar in 1940, there should have been about 600 000 officials on the *nomenklatura*. Including families, this should represent about 2.3 million people.

For members of this group, the Stalinist system appeared progressive. For them the 1930s were a period of heroic achievement. This explains their inability to see the less pleasant sides of Stalin's system. Lev Kopelev knew the system from the inside. Here, he describes the psychology of its members.

☐ *Document 11.9: Lev Kopelev on the psychology of the Party*

We were taught, when we were young, that it was our duty as citizens and members of the Komsomol to denounce friends and relatives, if need be, and to keep nothing from the Party. I never believed that Bukharin and Trotsky were Gestapo agents or that they had wanted to kill Lenin, and I was sure that Stalin never believed it either. But I regarded the purge trials of 1937 and 1938 as an expression of some far-sighted policy; I believed that, on balance, Stalin was right in deciding on these terrible measures in order to discredit all forms of political opposition, once and for all. We were a besieged fortress; we had to be united, knowing neither vacillation nor doubt ... Therefore, the opposition leaders had to be depicted as deviationists and villains, so that the people would come to hate them.

Finding myself among those marked out for such hatred [Kopelev was arrested in 1945 while serving with the army in Germany], I did not lose my convictions ... In prison I became even more consistent a Stalinist. What I was afraid of, more than anything else, was that my sense of personal injury would impair my view of what remained most important to the life of my country and of the world. That vision was essential to me as a source of spiritual strength, of my conception of myself as part of a great whole. Without that conviction my life would lose its meaning - my past life and whatever lay ahead ... I also believed that the generals, the men of the NKVD, the judge and the jailers were all blood of my blood, bone of my bone; that we were all soldiers in one army. Only some were more intelligent and conscientious than others, and some were stupider and worse than they should be. Even if a majority of the NKVD men, the prosecutors and the judges were no good, the overall objectives of the sum total of their work were just and historically necessary. And so I believed that no amount of mistakes or miscalculations or injustices could alter the aggregate or halt the coming triumph of Socialism.[36]

Privilege was not confined to members of the new Soviet elite. Below them were millions for whom the turbulence of the 1930s created opportunities as well as dangers. In spite of the appalling living conditions in the towns and the personal disorientation many peasants experienced when they left the villages, materially town life was better than village life. During the second Five-Year Plan (1932–7), average real wages began to rise again, particularly in the towns. By 1937, they were 35 per cent above the levels for 1935, though still well below the levels for 1928.[37] Meanwhile the government's investment in 'communal consumption' – education, welfare services, medicine, public canteens, kindergartens – increased rapidly in the 1930s.

Propaganda also played a role in mobilizing support. Peasants, barely literate and confused and embittered by the changes they had endured, seized readily on the simple messages of government propaganda. Some of those messages seemed very plausible. The Soviet Union did have many enemies. The capitalist world in the 1930s did appear on the verge of collapse. The government's claim that the difficulties of the 1930s were the birth pangs of a new and better world was therefore credible to many Soviet citizens, as to many outside the Soviet Union.

In these ways, the Stalinist system created supporters as well as opponents and victims. This explains its remarkable durability in spite of its excesses and its brutality. As the dissident Soviet historian Roy Medvedev has written: 'Stalin did not rely on terror alone, but also on the support of the majority of the people; effectively deceived by cunning propaganda, they gave Stalin credit for the successes of others and even for "achievements" that were in fact totally fictitious'.[38]

The Soviet government also built support by adapting its own attitudes and methods to those of a still traditional and conservative society. In the 1930s, it made many concessions to the patriarchal and nationalistic attitudes of what remained a very traditional society. This meant abandoning many of its more radical ideals.

Marxism itself changed. Like Christianity in the later Roman Empire, an ideology of the oppressed became the ideology of a brutal and authoritarian ruling elite. In the hands of Stalinist propagandists, the complex and subtle arguments of a German philosopher turned into the ritualistic and dogmatic formulae of Stalinism. For many, ideology offered a partial substitute for traditional religion. Peasants placed pictures of Stalin or Lenin in the 'Red' Corner of their house, where they had once placed icons or pictures of the tsar. The demonology of the purges made sense to peasants, many of whom still lived in a world of good and evil spirits.

The retreat from socialist and democratic ideals affected the whole of Soviet life. Under the New Economic Policy, Soviet educationists led by

316 Imperial and Soviet Russia

Lenin's wife, Krupskaya, had experimented with new, more liberal approaches to education. Soviet attitudes to the role of women and to aspects of family law such as divorce and abortion were extremely advanced by the standards of the time. In the 1930s the government turned its back on the cultural and social experimentation of the 1920s. In education there was a return to discipline. Teachers had to emphasize traditional basic skills. In history they concentrated on the national and military history of Russia. In family law, the government began to stress traditional family values. The government abolished abortion once again, and made divorce more difficult. It also began to stress traditional family values. In a novel written in the 1930s, the leader of a delegation of women who visited Stalin in 1937 made the following speech:

> Our feminine hearts are overflowing with emotions and of these love is paramount. Yet a wife should also be a happy mother and create a serene home atmosphere, without, however, abandoning work for the common welfare. She should know how to combine all these things while also matching her husband's performance on the job.[39]

Stalin's response to this speech is: 'Right!'.

This fictional meeting conveys well the style of family life that the government began to advocate. The government was unwilling or unable to fund enough crèches or public canteens or laundries to free women from domestic labour. Dominated as it was by traditional working-class men, the government was also unwilling to encourage Soviet men to share in domestic tasks. Instead, it encouraged women to keep their traditional roles as housekeepers and mothers. Most women now had little choice but to carry a crippling double burden of domestic and wage-earning employment. While Alexandra Kollontai survived the Stalinist period (much of it as Soviet ambassador to Norway, Mexico and Sweden), her hopes for a genuine liberation of Soviet women did not survive. Soviet life assumed an old-fashioned, slightly puritanical, and even 'bourgeois' tone. This remained the characteristic style of the Soviet elite until the 1980s.

What emerged in the 1930s was a society very different from the socialist ideals of the October Revolution. Instead of a classless society, there emerged a hierarchical society dominated by a privileged elite organized around the party and *nomenklatura*. The democratic structures of the Soviets, though enshrined in the 'Stalin Constitution' (largely prepared by Bukharin and issued in 1936), counted for little in practice. The urban and rural working classes, freed from the exploitation of capitalist employers, found themselves driven as ruthlessly by new Soviet bosses. Instead of 'withering away', as Engels had hoped it would, the state became more formidable, more extensive, and more brutal than ever.

■ Was Stalin Really Necessary?

Was it all necessary? Could the Soviet government have built the industrial base for Socialism without the violence and coercion of Stalinism? The decisions the Soviet leadership took in the late 1920s had such momentous results for Soviet society, and for the rest of the world, that we must take such questions seriously. They are particularly important for those who take seriously the socialist vision of a society combining democracy, equality and a basic level of material affluence for all.

At the height of the Cold War, it was fashionable to argue that Stalinism followed automatically from Marxism. Few scholars would now accept this view undiluted. Certainly, there are authoritarian tendencies in the writings of Marx and of Lenin. However, there are also democratic, even anarchistic tendencies in their writings. It was Lenin, for example, who said in 1918, in a quotation from Ovid: 'The golden age is coming; people will live without laws or punishment, doing of their own free will what is good and just'.[40]

Paradoxically, Marx himself had already hinted at a better explanation for Stalinist authoritarianism when he argued that the attempt to build socialism in an environment of scarcity would simply revive 'all the old crap' of class struggle. As the Mensheviks had insisted in 1917, a premature revolution was very likely to result in a brutal dictatorship. Alec Nove argued a similar case in a famous essay entitled, 'Was Stalin Really Necessary?' first published in 1962.[41] Nove argued that, given the party's ideology and the difficulties it faced in the 1920s, forced collectivization was the only strategy that provided enough resources to fund rapid industrialization. Without it, the Soviet Union would surely not have survived the Great Patriotic War. So, collectivization was necessary once the Communists decided to try to build socialism in backward Russia, as was the authoritarian apparatus that imposed collectivization. However, Nove argued that there was no need for the purges. Far from aiding industrial growth they stifled it.

In the 1970s several scholars challenged the claim that Stalinism was, in some sense, 'necessary'. In a polemic with Nove, first published in 1976, J. R. Millar argued that even collectivization was unnecessary.[42] Millar offered two distinct types of argument.

The first stressed the wastefulness of the Stalinist growth strategy. Millar pointed to the immense destructiveness of collectivization. He argued that, far from increasing the resources available for industrial growth, collectivization reduced them. For example, the government had to pump vast sums of money back into agriculture just to replace lost livestock. The expansion in tractor production, of which the government was so proud, merely replaced the draught horses killed during collectivization. In the urban sector, the absurd pace of industrialization led to breakages of complex machinery. Valuable plant lay unused for lack of raw materials or skilled operators, while highly trained experts vanished during the purges.

Millar's second argument takes us back to the late 1920s. It appeared then that both the slowdown in industrial production and the 1927 procurements crisis proved the failure of the New Economic Policy. Millar argued that this may not have been true. The statistical information available to the government was extremely unreliable, and the government may well have exaggerated the seriousness of both problems.

Inadequate statistics probably exaggerated the slowdown in industrial production. The issue of procurements is more complex. At the time, the government believed it had no choice but to back down (by raising the price it paid for grain deliveries), or launch an assault on the peasantry. Such arguments assumed that the peasants could afford not to sell their grain indefinitely. However, as Millar pointed out, this may not have been true. Certainly, many peasants chose not to market their surplus grain as grain prices declined. Yet they increased their marketing of other products, in particular of small livestock for meat. Faced with falling grain prices and stable prices for other produce, they fed surplus grain to their pigs and cattle, and then sold the meat. They had to sell something, for by now they depended more than the government realised on purchasing industrially produced items no longer made in the villages. The Russian peasantry had ceased to be as self-sufficient as the government believed.

The implications of these rustic economics are profound. They suggest that there may have been a third way out of the procurements crisis for the Soviet government. It simply had to lower the price it paid for livestock produce *as well as for grain*. Peasants would have had to sell their grain. They would also have had to sell it cheaply, leaving the government sector with the profits it needed to finance rapid industrial growth.

This conclusion is not as trivial as it may appear. It implies that the government could have used market forces to extract more resources than it realized from the countryside. Peasants might have grumbled, but they need not have resisted actively, for such measures would not have affected their interests as much as collectivization did. In other words, there may have been a strategy of growth which would have made use of market forces while retaining socialist control of the 'commanding heights'. This strategy would have combined elements of Bukharin's strategy of growth with those of the left wing. Like Witte's strategy, it would have combined market forces with a considerable, but not extreme, degree of fiscal pressure from the government. It was a strategy that still relied on indirect mobilization. The peasantry would have been taxed harder; the rate of industrial growth could have increased; the country would have avoided the brutal and wasteful excesses of Stalinism; and the basic framework of the New Economic Policy would have evolved gradually into socialism as the socialist industrial sector expanded. As in the 1920s, the government would have been authoritarian, but not 'totalitarian'. During the era of *perestroika* such arguments were of great interest, for they seemed to point to a 'third way', combining elements of socialism and capitalism.

Such strategies were certainly available. However, the failure of *perestroika* suggests, as did the failure of NEP, that they were likely to be unstable. Finding a stable balance between direct and indirect forms of mobilization was bound to be extremely difficult under conditions of great social and economic strain. Besides, could such a strategy have generated enough growth, particularly in heavy industry, to sustain a war against Nazi Germany by 1941? The strength of the Stalinist system was its ability to mobilize resources – people, money, and goods – on a scale huge enough to compensate for its inefficiency. Would a social structure closer to that of the NEP period have survived the strains of the war years? It would have wasted fewer human and material resources than the Stalinist system. However, it could never have generated the full power of the capitalist engine of growth, for it would have entailed many restrictions on the activities of entrepreneurs. Stalin himself clearly believed that such strategies would have failed. When, in 1944, the Yugoslav Communist Milovan Djilas remarked: 'Without industrialization the Soviet Union could not have preserved itself and waged such a war,' Stalin replied, 'It was precisely over this that we quarrelled with Trotsky and Bukharin.'[43]

The argument presented in this book is close to the position of the Mensheviks or of Alec Nove. Under conditions of backwardness, the attempt to build Socialism was bound to be dangerous. It required rapid growth, yet the hostility of socialist ideologies to capitalism ruled out use of the capitalist strategy of growth. This left two alternatives. Either a half-and-half strategy such as NEP, or a strategy of direct mobilization. The first strategy required a delicacy of touch that the Bolsheviks lacked. Besides, the difficulties they faced allowed no time to learn how to manage so unstable an economic structure. Many Bolsheviks opposed such a strategy anyway, as an improper compromise with capitalism. This left only the strategy of direct mobilization. There was a certain simplicity about it. Most party members could understand its logic. And its approach to economics and politics was familiar. Indeed, it had deep roots in Russian tradition. In the circumstances, the emergence of an extremely authoritarian state, relying on Russia's traditional political culture, was extremely likely. Whether it need have reached the extremes of High Stalinism is, however, doubtful.

■ Summary

Only a very powerful state could mobilize resources on the colossal scale needed for the Soviet industrialization drive. It is no accident, therefore, that the Soviet industrialization drive was managed by one of the most powerful, coercive, and centralized state systems of the twentieth century. Building on Russia's autocratic political culture, Stalin created a modernized autocracy of immense power. Collectivization helped remilitarize the party, and led to a rapid expansion of the police and the labour camp system. In the mid-1930s, Stalin's authority grew to the point where he no longer depended on the party, but established a uniquely personal system of rule. Now elevated above the party, Stalin fought savagely against real and imagined rivals, most of whom he eliminated during the purges. He also encouraged the rise of younger officials who posed a lesser threat to the leadership than the older party members of Lenin's time. At lower levels of government, officials began to exercise a local authority similar to that of Stalin at the centre. They, too, purged their rivals with great brutality. The atmosphere of crisis created by collectivization, the purges, and fears of foreign attack, generated a paranoid mood which strengthened the leadership by making any form of opposition look like treachery. But despite its harshness, the Stalinist government also enjoyed much popular support. Many people did well during the purge era, particularly those who rose rapidly through the party's ranks. At the same time, many ordinary citizens seem to have accepted the patriotic promises of Stalinist propaganda.

The huge mobilizational effort of the 1930s achieved much, though at great human cost. It turned the Soviet Union into a great military and industrial power, and generated a surprising amount of popular support. Yet it also created new forms of legal and economic inequality that undermined the idealistic claims of Soviet socialism. While its economic achievements were immense, the brutal methods of Stalinism did much to discredit the ideals of socialism.

☐ *Further Reading*

The political and social history of Stalinism raises acute moral, political and ideological problems, and has generated a huge polemical literature. Isaac Deutscher's series of lectures, *The Unfinished Revolution*, provide a superb introduction to many of these issues. There are good, balanced, introductory surveys in Ward, *Stalin's Russia*, and Nove, *Stalinism and After*, while Andrle, *A Social History of Twentieth Century Russia* deals very well with the social history of the 1930s. There is a valuable collection of essays in Daniels, *The Stalin Revolution*. The most interesting biographies of Stalin are Deutscher, *Stalin*, and Volkogonov's recent *Stalin: Triumph and Tragedy*, which incorporates new archival material. Solzhenitsyn, *Gulag Archipelago*, and Medvedev, *Let History Judge*, are important studies of Stalinism written, at great risk, from within the Soviet Union, while Trotsky's *Revolution Betrayed* was a critique of Stalinism written by a former colleague and eventual victim. Conquest, *The Great Terror*, was for a long time the standard work on the purges, but recently a number of historians have offered revisionist accounts of both the scale and the mechanisms of the purges. For an introduction to revisionist accounts, see Getty and Manning, *Stalinist Terror*. The best account of the Stalinist system written within the totalitarian model was Fainsod's *How Russia is Ruled*, which should be compared with the revised (and revisionist) version, by Hough and Fainsod, entitled *How the Soviet Union is Governed*. Gill, *Origin of the Stalinist Political System*, is a fine recent account of the complexities of the Stalinist system, which takes into account revisionist analyses. Some of the social aspects of the Stalinist system are dealt with in the fine collection of essays by Lewin, *The Making of the Soviet System*.

☐ *Notes*

1. Victor Kravchenko, *I Chose Freedom* (London: Robert Hale, 1947) p. 130.
2. W. Churchill, *The Hinge of Fate* (Boston: Cassell, 1950) p. 498.
3. Maurice Hindus, *Mother Russia* (London: William Collins, 1943) pp. 62–3, from a speech delivered on 4 February 1931 at a conference of managers of Soviet industry.
4. Cited by Khrushchev in his Secret Speech in 1956. B. Dmytryshyn, *USSR: A Concise History*, 2nd edn (New York: Scribner's, 1971) p. 497.
5. R. Conquest, *The Great Terror* (Harmondsworth: Penguin, 1971) p. 454; and figures for 1934 from E. Bacon, '*Glasnost*' and the Gulag', *Soviet Studies*, vol. 44, no. 6 (1992) p. 1071.
6. D. Volkogonov, *Stalin: Triumph and Tragedy*, trans H. Shukman (Rocklin, Calif.: Prima Publishing, 1992) p. 563.
7. Conquest, *The Great Terror*, p. 50.
8. Cited in R. W. Davies, *Soviet History in the Gorbachev Revolution* (Bloomington, Ind.: Indiana University Press, 1989) p. 84.
9. Volkogonov, *Stalin: Triumph and Tragedy*, p. 200.
10. I. Deutscher, *Stalin*, rev. edn (Harmondsworth: Penguin, 1966) p. 349.
11. Cited in M. Lewin, *Political Undercurrents in Soviet Economic Debates* (London: Pluto Press, 1975) p. 28.
12. Dmytryshyn, *USSR*, p 496. However, recent evidence has failed to prove Stalin's complicity. See J. Arch Getty, 'The Politics of Repression Revisited', in J. Arch Getty and R. T. Manning (eds), *Stalinist Terror: New Perspectives* (Cambridge University Press, 1993) pp. 42–9.
13. M. Matthews, *Soviet Government: A Selection of Official Documents on Internal Policies* (London: Cape, 1974) pp. 252–3.
14. Dmytryshyn, *USSR*, p. 495.
15. R. Medvedev, *Let History Judge* (New York: Alfred A. Knopf Inc, 1971) p. 154.

16. Dmytryshyn, *USSR*, p. 495.
17. Stephen Wheatcroft, 'On assessing the Size of Forced Concentration Camp Labour in the Soviet Union, 1931–1956', *Soviet Studies*, vol. 33, no. 2 (April 1981) p. 286, and 'Towards a Thorough Analysis of Soviet Forced Labor Statistics', *Soviet Studies*, vol. 35, no. 2 (April 1983) p. 227. Robert Conquest's *The Great Terror*, p. 713, estimates party victims at 1 million.
18. A. Solzhenitsyn, *The Gulag Archipelago* (London: Fontana/William Collins, 1974) vol. 1, p. 11.
19. A. Nove, 'Victims of Stalinism: How Many?' in Getty and Manning (eds), *Stalinist Terror*, p. 270.
20. Bacon, '*Glasnost*' and the Gulag', p. 1071.
21. Ibid., p. 1071.
22. Conquest, *The Great Terror*, p. 710; and see J. Barber and M. Harrison, *The Soviet Home Front 1941–1945* (London and New York: Longman, 1991) pp. 116–19 and 217.
23. Bacon, '*Glasnost*' and the Gulag', p. 1080.
24. S. Fitzpatrick, 'Stalin and the Making of a New Elite, 1928–1939', in *Slavic Review*, vol. 38, no. 3 (1979) p. 399.
25. M. Fainsod, *How Russia is Ruled*, rev. edn (Cambridge, Mass.: Harvard University Press, 1963) p. 423.
26. *Izvestiya*, 2 and 3 August 1988, cited in Davies, *Soviet History in the Gorbachev Revolution*, p. 82.
27. J. Arch Getty, 'Party and purge in Smolensk: 1933–1937', *Slavic Review*, vol. 42 (1983) no. 1, pp 63–4. Fel'dman's home town, Korosten, had been the medieval capital of the Derevlians. See Chapter 1, Documents 1.1 and 1.2.
28. See G. Gill, *The Origins of the Stalinist Political System* (Cambridge University Press, 1990).
29. See Fainsod, *How Russia is Ruled*, p. 578.
30. B. A. Starkov, 'Narkom Ezhov', in Getty and Manning (eds), *Stalinist Terror*, p. 38.
31. S. Fitzpatrick, 'Stalin and the Making of a New Elite, 1928–1939', in *Slavic Review*, vol. 38, no. 3 (1979) pp. 377–402. See also, S. Fitzpatrick, 'Cultural Revolution as Class War', and M. Lewin, 'Society, State and Ideology during the First Five-Year Plan', in S. Fitzpatrick (ed.), *Cultural Revolution in Russia 1928–1931* (Bloomington, Ind.: Indiana University Press, 1978). See also J. F. Hough and M. Fainsod, *How the Soviet Union is Governed* (Cambridge, Mass.: Harvard University Press, 1979).
32. M. Lewin, 'Society, State and Ideology during the First Five Year Plan', in Fitzpatrick (ed.), *Cultural Revolution in Russia 1928–1931*, p. 74.
33. Fitzpatrick (ed.), *Cultural Revolution in Russia 1928–1931*, p. 62.
34. A. Koestler, *The Invisible Writing* (London: Hutchinson, 1969) pp. 73–4.
35. M. McCauley, *The Soviet Union since 1917* (London: Longman, 1981) p. 262.
36. L. Kopelev, *No Jail for Thought* (Harmondsworth: Penguin, 1979) pp. 121–2.
37. A. Nove, *An Economic History of the USSR*, 3rd edn (Harmondsworth: Penguin, 1992) p. 253.
38. R Medvedev, *On Stalin and Stalinism* (Oxford University Press, 1979) p. 161.
39. G. Lapidus, in D. Atkinson *et al.* (eds), *Women in Russia* (Brighton: Harvester Press, 1978) p. 131.

40. Cited in M. Feshbach and A. Friendly, *Ecocide in the USSR: Health and Nature under Siege* (New York: Basic Books, 1993) p. 27.
41. See A. Nove, *Was Stalin Really Necessary?* (London: Praeger, 1964). For Marx's view, See Ch. 5, note 13.
42. J. R. Millar and A. Nove, 'A Debate on Collectivisation', in *Problems of Communism*, Jul.–Aug. 1976, pp 49–62. See also the preface to S. Cohen, *Bukharin and the Bolshevik Revolution* (Oxford University Press, 1980).
43. M. Djilas, *Conversations with Stalin* (Harmondsworth: Penguin, 1963) p. 62.

■ *Chapter 12* ■

The Great Patriotic War

The ultimate challenge for any ruling group is to defend its territory against external as well as internal enemies. We have seen that this task was peculiarly difficult in the cold flatlands of the Eurasian plain, where agriculture was hard and there were few natural defensive barriers. Indeed, the difficult task of defence did much to shape the autocratic political culture of Russian society. Judged by this test, imperial Russia was a great success before the mid-nineteenth century. However, the defeat in the Crimea (1853–5) marked the beginning of a period of decline. This culminated in the defeats of the First World War, revolution, and the humiliating Treaty of Brest-Litovsk. In international terms, the Brest-Litovsk Treaty was the worst humiliation a Russian government had faced since the foreign intervention of the early seventeenth century.

How successful was the new Communist ruling group in solving the difficult defensive problems that faced all Russian ruling groups?

■ Foreign Policy, 1917 to 1941

When the Bolsheviks led the October Revolution, they believed it would be the first in a series of anti-capitalist revolutions. Their conception of foreign policy was therefore simplistic. They hoped to turn the war between nations that began in 1914, into a war between classes. In a socialist world, nation states would be irrelevant. So would traditional foreign policy. When asked by Lenin to act as commissar for foreign affairs, Trotsky claimed the job would be easy. He would issue a few proclamations and then 'shut up shop'.

Within weeks of seizing power in 1917, the Bolsheviks realised that this was naive. If revolution did not break out abroad, they would have to reach an arrangement with foreign capitalist powers, because they were too weak to do anything else. This was particularly true of Germany, whose armies posed an immediate threat to the revolution. So, on 3 March 1918, after much heart-searching, the Soviet government signed a 'pact with the devil' at Brest-Litovsk. This was its first formal treaty with a capitalist government.

The dilemmas of Brest-Litovsk haunted Soviet foreign policy for many years. Should the Soviet government support a revolutionary overthrow of its capitalist enemies by helping foreign revolutionary movements? Or should it defend the socialist homeland through a policy of 'peaceful coexistence' with foreign capitalism, even if this meant betraying the international revolution?

During the Civil War, these two approaches – the revolutionary and the traditional – were represented by different foreign policy institutions. In March 1919, the Communist government held the first Congress of the 'Communist International' (*Comintern*). The Soviet government intended this to replace the 'Second International', which had collapsed in 1914. *Comintern* provided a single organization to unify the activities of revolutionary socialist parties throughout the world. Its members immediately accepted Soviet leadership.

There also existed a more conventional instrument of Soviet foreign policy. This was the Commissariat (Ministry) of Foreign Affairs. Trotsky headed it before the fiasco of Brest-Litovsk. His successor was G. V. Chicherin (1872–1936). After the Civil War, the Commissariat began to act like a traditional foreign ministry, negotiating and even signing alliances with foreign capitalist governments. *Comintern* and the Commissariat of Foreign Affairs symbolized the deep ambiguities of Soviet foreign relations.

In the 1920s, Soviet foreign policy tried to combine conventional diplomacy and revolutionary activism. Through the Commissariat, the Soviet government maintained normal diplomatic relations with major capitalist governments. As early as March 1921, it signed a trade treaty with Britain. In 1922 it negotiated an alliance with Germany. As a symbol of the traditional nature of official Soviet diplomacy, Soviet delegates appeared at their first international conference in 1922, wearing top hats and silk gloves.[1]

However, *Comintern* remained active. Under the New Economic Policy it tried to work through broad, left-wing coalitions, like those that had supported the Provisional Government in early 1917. This led to some contradictions. In China, it meant co-operating with the non-communist Chiang-Kai-Shek who, in 1927, turned on his communist allies and massacred them. Relations with Britain broke down for opposite reasons. Here, the propaganda activities of *Comintern* and Soviet encouragement for the general strike of May 1926 undermined the efforts of the Commissariat of Foreign Affairs to establish stable political and economic relations at the official level. In 1927, Britain broke off relations with the Soviet Union, causing a brief war scare.

The war crisis of 1927 helped the Stalin faction to remove left-wing critics such as Trotsky, who had argued for a more revolutionary foreign policy. Simultaneously, the new government borrowed the foreign policy ideas of the left opposition. The collapse of the alliance with Chiang-

Kai-Shek in China and worldwide economic depression persuaded the government that foreign communist movements should once again aim at revolution. *Comintern* demanded that foreign communist parties break all links with moderate socialist parties and prepare for revolution alone, as the Bolsheviks had done in the autumn of 1917.

However, the tactics that had worked in Russia in 1917 would not necessarily work for foreign communist parties in the early 1930s. On the contrary, the new tack proved disastrous for the world communist movement. Instead of working with other left-wing groups against the growing menace of fascism, communist parties concentrated their fire on moderate socialist parties. By doing so they weakened the entire left-wing of politics in Europe. In Germany, this tactic helped the Nazis gain power in 1933.

The mid-1930s saw another shift in Soviet foreign policy during Maxim Litvinov's (1876–1951) term as commissar for foreign affairs from 1930 to 1939. The growing threat from Nazi Germany and the Japanese conquest of Manchuria in 1931–2 persuaded the government to seek closer defensive alliances. The most important of these was with France in 1932. In 1933 the Soviet Union gained diplomatic recognition from the United States and joined the League of Nations. In line with this new policy, *Comintern* abandoned its 'revolutionary' direction. Instead, it encouraged foreign communists once more to seek broad alliances with other left-wing groups, in 'popular fronts'. This triumph of traditional over revolutionary foreign policy was characteristic of the 'great retreat' of the mid-1930s. By then, rhetoric was all that survived of the revolutionary foreign policy advocated during the Civil War and the 1920s. There remained only the forlorn hope that a socialist revolution might still occur in the advanced capitalist countries and break the isolation of the Soviet Union. *Comintern* itself held no more congresses after 1935, and Stalin formally abolished it in 1943.

In the 1930s traditional great power calculations shaped Soviet foreign policy. The immediate effect of collectivization and the first Five-Year Plans was to weaken the Soviet Union. It embroiled the army in a vicious conflict with the Soviet peasantry, its main source of recruits. Meanwhile, collectivization caused the slaughter of millions of horses at a time when the army still made great use of cavalry and of horse-drawn transport. During this period of weakness, the Soviet government had to avoid a major war. How could it best achieve this result? Through the anti-fascist alliance that emerged in the early 1930s? Or through alliance with Fascism? The democratic states revealed their weakness when they negotiated the Munich agreement in September 1938. After this, Stalin began to reconsider the second option. Hitler also wanted to avoid the war on two fronts which had been Germany's downfall in the First World

War. On 23 August 1939, after a year of tentative (and secret) soundings, the Soviet government signed a ten-year non-aggression pact with Nazi Germany. The two sides also concluded a trade pact. In a secret protocol to the pact, the two powers carved up Eastern Europe. The appointment of Stalin's close follower, V. M. Molotov (1890–1986), as minister of foreign affairs in May 1939 prepared the way for this abrupt switch in Soviet foreign policy.

On 1 September, with his eastern front secure, Hitler attacked Poland. He understood that this meant war with France and Britain. Two weeks later, Soviet armies occupied the eastern half of Poland. In June 1940, they occupied the Baltic States and the Bessarabian provinces of Romania. Lithuania, Estonia, Latvia and Moldova were to remain parts of the Soviet Union until 1991. The Soviet Union had regained with interest the territorial losses of Brest-Litovsk and the Civil War.

As it turned out, the Nazi–Soviet pact merely gave the Soviet Union a two year breathing space. The war the Soviet government had dreaded for so long began on 22 June 1941.

■ The Soviet Union in 1941

The industrialization drive of the 1930s had given the Soviet Union a substantial industrial base by 1941. In this general sense, the Stalinist system had done much to enhance the military potential of the Soviet Union.

Equally important, the methods used to industrialize increased the power of Soviet governments to mobilize labour and resources. The Soviet ruling elite was more powerful, more united, and better led than the tsarist ruling elite in 1914. As the danger of war came closer, the government redirected its mobilizational effort towards defence. In 1933, 3.4 per cent of the Soviet budget went towards defence. By 1937 this figure had risen to 16.5 per cent, and by 1940 to 32.6 per cent.[2] By 1940 the output of munitions industries was seventy times as great as in 1928.[3]

However, the economic achievements of the 1930s hid three serious weaknesses. First, the Soviet Union's industrial heartland remained dangerously close to its western borderlands. Most industry remained around Moscow and Leningrad, in Ukraine, and in the Caucasus and the Urals. During the 1930s the government continued to invest in these areas, rather than in Siberia. Planners began to build up industrial centres further east, particularly in the area linking the iron ore of the Urals and the coking coal of the Kuzbas area around Novosibirsk. However, the early months of the war showed that not enough had been done to relocate defence industries.

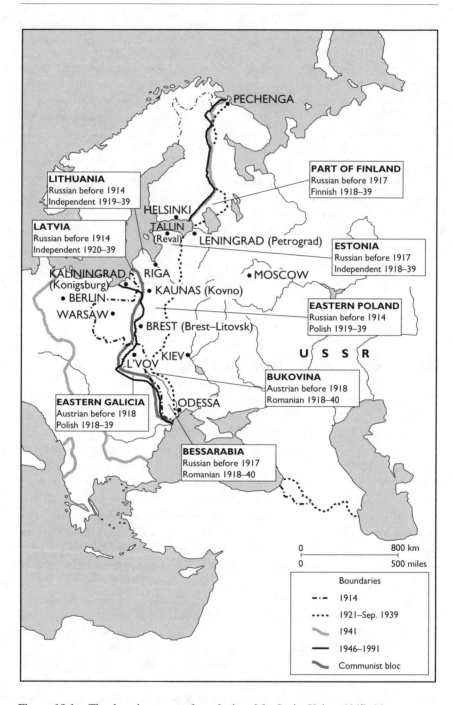

PECHENGA

LITHUANIA
Russian before 1914
Independent 1919–39

PART OF FINLAND
Russian before 1917
Finnish 1918–39

LATVIA
Russian before 1914
Independent 1920–39

HELSINKI

TALLIN
(Reval)

LENINGRAD (Petrograd)

ESTONIA
Russian before 1917
Independent 1918–39

KALININGRAD
(Konigsburg)

RIGA

• **MOSCOW**

• **BERLIN**

WARSAW •

• **KAUNAS (Kovno)**

EASTERN POLAND
Russian before 1914
Polish 1919–39

• **BREST (Brest–Litovsk)**

KIEV •

U   S   S   R

L'VOV •

BUKOVINA
Austrian before 1918
Romanian 1918–40

EASTERN GALICIA
Austrian before 1918
Polish 1918–39

ODESSA

BESSARABIA
Russian before 1917
Romanian 1918–40

0 — 800 km
0 — 500 miles

Boundaries

—·— 1914

···· 1921–Sep. 1939

〜 1941

— 1946–1991

〜 Communist bloc

Figure 12.1   *The changing western boundaries of the Soviet Union, 1917–46*

Second, during the purge era, the rate of economic growth slowed, even in crucial defence industries such as vehicles, oil, and iron and steel. (See the Statistical Appendix and Tables 10.3 and 10.4. Compare, in particular, rows B to D of Table 10.4, between 1937 and 1940.) The slowdown reflected the disruption caused by the purges. Experienced managers and specialists had vanished, and their replacements were often inexperienced and ill-educated. Further, the atmosphere of terror discouraged initiative and experimentation.

Third, and most disastrous of all, was the poor quality of much of the equipment supplied to the army. Most Soviet tanks and planes were inferior to those of the Germans. The problem was no longer one of technological inferiority. Plans existed for equipment such as the T-34 tank or the Katyusha rocket launcher that was superior to anything the Germans produced. However they were not yet in full production at the start of the war. Perhaps most catastrophic of all was the lack of motor transport (see the Statistical Appendix, column N). In 1941, the Red Army still used horses to haul much of its artillery and heavy equipment.[4] In these areas, Soviet planning for war was deplorable, and the Soviet government wasted the years gained by the Nazi–Soviet pact. Millions of Soviet citizens and soldiers paid with their lives for these blunders by Stalin's government.

Trotsky had largely created the Red Army. In the early 1930s, General M. N. Tukhachevsky presided over its modernization. Under his leadership, the army took to heart the strategic ideas of Liddel Hart, who foresaw the importance of tank armies. The Red Army also pioneered other forms of modern warfare, such as the use of parachute troops. By the mid-1930s, it had a reputation as one of the most advanced armies in the world.

The purges changed this. They removed much of the army's leadership and stifled initiative at all levels. Between 1937 and 1938 about 34 000 officers, or about 10 per cent of all officers, were discharged from the army and air force. At least 8000 of these were arrested by the NKVD. By 1940, about 30 per cent of those discharged had been reinstated.[5] The post-purge leadership abandoned Tukhachevsky's reforms and broke up his tank armies. Commanders such as Voroshilov and Budenny, whose military experience went back to the primitive cavalry battles of the Civil War, now took command of the Soviet defence establishment.

The shocking truth can be stated quite simply: never did the officer staff of any army suffer such great losses in any war as the Soviet army suffered in this time of peace. Years of training cadres came to nothing … At the beginning of 1940 more than seventy per cent of the division commanders, about seventy per cent of regimental commanders, and sixty per cent of military commissars, and heads of political divisions had occupied these positions for a year only. And all this happened just before the worst war in history.[6]

Internationally, too, the purges had disastrous results, for they convinced Hitler that defeating the Red Army would be easy. This is why, in 1941, he risked a war on two fronts. The disastrous performance of Soviet armies in the brief 'winter war' with Finland in 1939 and 1940 reinforced Hitler's belief. In December 1939, after analysing the pitiful performance of the Red Army in Finland, the German General Staff concluded that the Soviet Army was 'no match for an army with modern equipment and superior leadership'.[7] Hitler put it more bluntly: 'You have only to kick in the door and the whole rotten structure will come crashing down!'.[8]

Other weaknesses reflected the chaos of the purge years. Training, particularly of tank crews and pilots, was superficial. In June 1941 many Soviet tank crews went into battle with less than two hours experience in handling their tanks. Many pilots fought with less than fifteen hours flying experience.[9] Characteristically, they made up for this with desperate courage. Some just rammed enemy planes.

Stalin and the high command also made serious strategic blunders. Before 1939, army engineers had built a formidable defence line along much of the western border. After the Nazi–Soviet pact, the Soviet frontier moved west and the army abandoned the old defensive line. Yet it did little to fortify the new borders in Poland, the Baltic and western Ukraine.

Stalin contributed much to the initial catastrophes. He seems to have decided that the Soviet Union could not fight the Germans until 1942 at the earliest. As a result, he concentrated less on preparing for war, than on attempts to appease Hitler. He received repeated warnings about the imminence of a German attack from Soviet intelligence, from the British, and even from Nazi deserters. Yet he chose to ignore them, partly because he also received very different information, some of which represented deliberate Nazi disinformation. Until the war began Stalin would not let the army prepare any contingency plans for fear of antagonising Hitler. As a result, Soviet armies had no plans for a defensive war. Meanwhile, official propaganda persuaded the Soviet population and army that war was unlikely. A young Pole living in Rostov at the outbreak of war remembered:

> The people of the USSR were living as if anaesthetized ... put to sleep by their own leaders who repeated to them only ten days before the start of hostilities that the Germans would respect their treaty commitment to refrain from any aggression.[10]

Militarily, the lack of preparation was disastrous. In June 1941 Soviet army units had to wait several hours after the Germans attacked before receiving orders to return fire. Even worse, most Russian aircraft were on the ground and concentrated in a few airfields. Within hours, German planes destroyed 1200 Soviet combat aircraft. This deprived the Red Army of air cover for the first six months of the war.[11]

The Soviet Union had many weaknesses in 1941. Yet it also had many long-term strengths. It had immense reserves of labour, both military and civilian. Most remarkable of all, the war showed that it enjoyed the loyalty of most Soviet citizens. Further, the Stalinist system had an exceptional ability to hold together under strain and to mobilize resources in a crisis. By 1940 the Soviet government had more experience of centralized industrial production and rapid mobilization of resources than any other government in the world. These long-term strengths meant that if it could survive the first months of a German blitzkrieg, the Soviet Union's situation would slowly, but surely, improve.

■ The War

Germany and its allies attacked on 22 June 1941 with 5.5 million men, 2500 tanks and 5000 planes.[12] The Soviet armies had 2.9 million front-line troops equipped with 1800 mostly obsolete tanks.[13]

Soviet soldiers fought with desperate ferocity. A few days after the fighting began, a Soviet staff officer, Ivan Krylov, was told by a colleague:

> The men have been ordered not to die before taking at least one German with them. 'If you are wounded,' the order says, 'sham death, and when the Germans approach, kill one of them. Kill them with your rifle, with the bayonet, with your knife, tear their throats out with your teeth. Don't die without leaving a dead German behind you. ... Russians are terrible fighters. They like it and they have a contempt for death. If we can keep them armed the Germans will leave their own corpses scattered all over the steppes as so many have done before them'.[14]

Brutal military discipline played a role in this desperate heroism. Special troops from a section of the secret police called '*Smersh*' ('death to spies') stood behind advancing Soviet units with machine guns ready to shoot deserters. In August Stalin ordered that all soldiers captured alive by the Germans were to be treated as deserters, and their families would lose their military pensions.[15] The secret police took this order seriously, and treated captured Soviet soldiers as deserters even if they later escaped from the Germans. For less major infractions of military discipline, commanders placed soldiers in special penal battalions. They sent these units into battle without camouflage to draw enemy fire, or used them to clear minefields.[16] Civilians were not spared. In September 1941, as the German army approached Leningrad, they forced captured civilians to beg the defenders to sue for peace. Here is Stalin's response.

> It is said that the German scoundrels approaching Leningrad are sending ahead of their troops old men and old women, women and children, delegates from areas occupied by them to ask the Bolsheviks to surrender Leningrad and make peace. My advice is: don't be sentimental, but hit the enemy and his auxiliaries, willing or unwilling, in the teeth. War is merciless, and it will bring defeat in the first instance to him who shows weakness and vacillation ... No mercy to the Germans and their delegates, whoever they may be.[17]

Courage, desperation and savagery alone could not win the war. In the early days of the war even Stalin despaired. A tape-recording from these days records Stalin as saying, with characteristic brutality: 'Lenin left us a great inheritance and we, his heirs, have fucked it all up!'.[18] For a few days he was extremely depressed and could not take decisions. Even the basic idea of creating a State Defence Committee came from a nervous delegation of Politburo members. Mikoyan described this episode in his memoirs.

☐ *Document 12.1: Stalin during the first week of the war*

We decided to go and see him. He was at the nearby dacha.

Molotov said that Stalin was in such a state of prostration that he wasn't interested in anything, he'd lost all initiative and was in a bad way. Voznesensky, appalled to hear this, said, 'You go on ahead, Vyacheslav [Molotov], and we'll be behind you.' The idea was that, if Stalin was going to continue to behave in this way, then Molotov ought to lead us and we would follow him. We were sure we could organize the defence and put up a proper fight. None of us were downcast in mood.

We got to Stalin's dacha. We found him in an armchair in the small dining room. He looked up and said, 'What have you come for?' He had the strangest look on his face, and the question itself was pretty strange, too. After all, he should have called us in.

On our behalf, Molotov said power had to be concentrated in order to ensure rapid decision-making and somehow get the country back on its feet, and Stalin should head the new authority. Stalin looked surprised but made no objection and said 'Fine'.[19]

Not until 3 July did Stalin broadcast to the Soviet people. The speech he made that day had a profound effect, and helped transform Stalin into a popular leader of national resistance. Even the beginning of the speech implied a new relationship between government and people. He began: 'Comrades, citizens, brothers and sisters, fighters of our Army and Navy! I am speaking to you, my friends!'. Stalin explained the extent of the German attack and gave some idea of Soviet losses. He demanded total mobilization for the war effort. He called for partisan war behind German lines and demanded the destruction of all resources that could not be evacuated. He also ordered the formation of militia (*opolcheniye*) units. A Soviet novel written by Konstantin Simonov in the late 1950s gives a vivid description of the impact of Stalin's speech. The narrator is a wounded soldier lying in a field hospital.

> Stalin spoke in a toneless, slow voice, with a strong Georgian accent. Once or twice, during his speech, you could hear a glass click as he drank water. His voice was low and soft, and might have seemed perfectly calm, but for his heavy, tired breathing, and that water he kept drinking during the speech ...
>
> There was a discrepancy between that even voice and the tragic situation of which he spoke; and in this discrepancy there was strength. People were not surprised. It was what they were expecting from Stalin ...
>
> Stalin did not describe that situation as tragic; such a word would have been hard to imagine as coming from him; but the things of which he spoke – *opolcheniye*, partisans, occupied territories, meant the end of illusions ... The truth he told was a bitter truth, but at least it was uttered, and people felt that they stood more firmly on the ground.[20]

Diplomatically, the situation improved with the immediate British offer of a military alliance. The US government offered economic aid in September. After its first shock, the government moved quickly to repair some of the damage it had caused. In 1941, it released 420 000 men from the camps to join the army, and in the rest of the war it released another 555 000.[21] Many went straight to the front to take command of retreating units. The high command also began to reassemble the tank armies of the early 1930s.

However, in the short-term, disaster was unavoidable. By the beginning of December, German armies had reached a line running from Rostov in the south to Moscow and Leningrad in the north. In late November German units reached within 25 kilometres of Moscow. German generals later reported that they could see Moscow itself 'through a pair of good field glasses'.[22] German armies isolated Leningrad. The prolonged siege that followed was one of the most savage in modern history. During its twenty-eight months, 1 million of Leningrad's 3 million inhabitants died.[23]

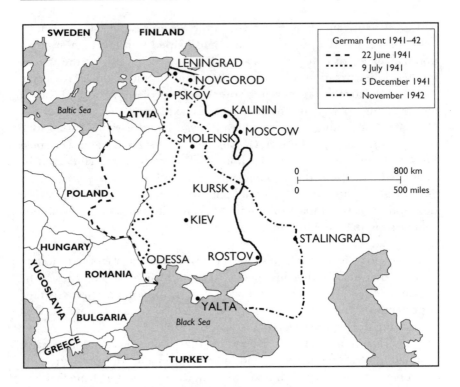

Figure 12.2 *The Great Patriotic War, 1941–5*

In the first six months of the war, the Red Army lost more than 5 million killed, wounded or captured. The Germans lost 1 million.[24] The territory lost to the Germans in the first five months had produced about 60 per cent of Soviet coal, iron, steel and aluminium, and included 40 per cent of the railway network. In November 1941 Soviet industrial production fell to 50 per cent of the level a year before.[25]

During this disastrous period, the Soviet Union began the vast mobilization effort that eventually won the war. The reorganization began at the top, with the setting up of the State Committee of Defence, headed by Stalin, on 30 June. In August Stalin became the supreme commander of the Soviet armed forces.

Particularly spectacular was the evacuation of industry to the east. On 24 June, in one of the few clear-headed decisions it took in these early days, the government set up a Committee on Evacuation to supervise the process. Despite incredible hardships, 1523 industrial enterprises had been moved east by November, and with them 10 million workers and evacuees, all carried in 1.5 million wagon loads. Whole factories were stripped down, dismantled, transported east and rebuilt. After a critical

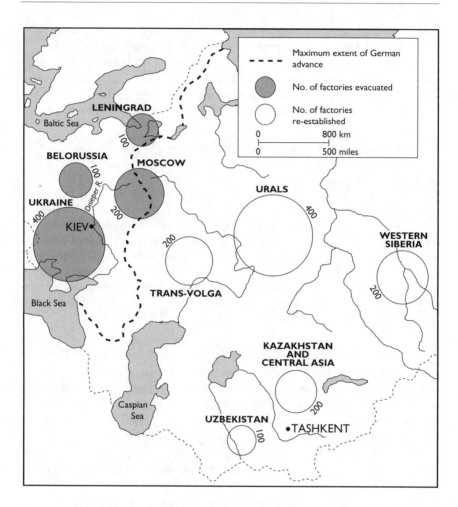

Figure 12.3 *Evacuation of Soviet industry to the east*

period of a few months during which evacuation reduced the output of industry, output of military equipment began to rise in 1942. In that year, Soviet factories produced 24 688 tanks – 270 per cent more than in 1941. In total during the war, 3500 new industrial enterprises were built, and 136 800 planes, 489 900 guns and 10 500 tanks were produced. By maintaining supplies through the critical winter of 1941, the evacuation process played a vital role in the war effort.

The United States also sent 9600 guns, 18 700 planes and 10 800 tanks under the lend-lease programme. This required no payment until after the war.[26] Allied supplies began arriving in large quantities in 1943, after the battle of Stalingrad. They did little to help during the initial German onslaught, but helped greatly during the march on Berlin.

Equally important was the conversion of civilian to military production. During the 1930s the government made all factories prepare advance plans for conversion. It had also encouraged defence planners to subcontract to civilian producers. These preparations help explain the remarkable, if bizarre, achievements of the conversion process.

☐ *Document 12.2: Conversion to military production*

This is what happened in Moscow: a children's bicycle factory began making flame-throwers. A die-stamping works where teaspoons and paper clips were made switched to entrenching tools and parts for anti-tank grenades. A woodworking shop producing abacuses and screens changed over to making pistol cartridges. A furniture factory started turning out anti-tank mines, cartridge boxes and stretchers. A typewriter works began making automatic rifles and ammunition. In Leningrad, by early July, civilian factories were starting to manufacture tanks, artillery, mortars and flame-throwers. A toy factory and a stove works (among others) were producing grenades; anti-tank mines were being made in place of musical instruments and perfumes.[27]

Soviet people worked astonishingly hard to increase output. This was particularly true of Soviet women, who replaced male workers drafted into the army. During the war women accounted for 53 per cent of the Soviet workforce. They were an even larger proportion of the rural workforce. It was largely their labour that kept Soviet armies supplied with foodstuffs.[28] To feed themselves, civilians had to fall back on their own devices. The government helped by increasing the size of private plots and encouraging town-dwellers to farm allotments. A Canadian diplomat described how, 'Each Sunday morning during the month of May the streets of Kuibyshev were full of men, women and children carrying spades and other tools and proceeding to the railway station, the Volga ferry or the streetcar stops to go out to their allotments'.[29]

Mobilization for war took a huge toll. The following description of work at the Kirov works in Leningrad (the pre-revolutionary Putilov works) suggests something of the human cost of supplying the armies. In September 1943, while Leningrad was still under siege, an English war correspondent interviewed a manager of the Kirov works.

☐ *Document 12.3: Industrial labour during the war*

Well [he said] you are certainly finding us working in unusual conditions. What we have here isn't what is normally meant by the Kirov Plant ... Before the war we had over 30 000 workers; now we have only a small fraction of these ... and sixty-nine per cent of our workers are female. Hardly any women worked there before the war. We then made turbines, tanks, guns; we made tractors, and supplied the greater part of the equipment for building the Moscow–Volga canal ... Before this war started, we began to make tanks in a very big way, as well as tank and aircraft engines. Practically all this production of equipment proper has been moved to the east. Now we repair diesels and tanks, but our main output is ammunition, and some small arms ...

The workers of the Kirov Plant ... were in reserved occupations, and hardly anybody was subject to mobilisation. Yet no sooner had the Germans invaded than everybody without exception volunteered for the front. If we had wanted to, we could have sent 25 000 people; we let only 9000 or 10 000 go. Already in June 1941 they formed themselves into what was to become the famous Kirov Division. Although they had done some training before the war, they couldn't be considered fully trained soldiers, but their drive, their guts were tremendous. They wore the uniform of the Red Army, but they were in fact part of the *opolcheniye*, except that they were rather better trained than other *opolcheniye* units ... many tens of thousands of them went out from here to meet the Germans, to stop them at any price ... It is no secret – a large proportion of the Workers' Divisions never came back ...

However, our most highly skilled workers, who were badly needed in Siberia and the Urals, were evacuated by air, together with their families. They were flown to Tikhvin, but after the Germans had taken Tikhvin, we had to fly them to other airfields, and from there the people had to walk to the nearest railway station, walk through the snow, in the middle of a bitter winter, often dozens and dozens of kilometres ... The people who left here in October were already working at full speed in their new place, 2000 kilometres away, by December! ...

[The winter months] were terrible ... On December 15 everything came to a standstill. There was no fuel, no electric current, no food, no tram-cars, no water, nothing. Production in Leningrad practically ceased. We were to remain in this terrible condition till the first of April. It is true that food began to come in February across the Ladoga Ice Road. But we needed another month before we could start any kind of regular output at the Kirov Works. But even during the worst hungry period we did what we could ... We repaired guns, and our foundry was kept going, though only in a small way. It felt as if the mighty Kirov Works had been turned into a village smithy. People were terribly cold and terribly hungry. Many of our people died during those days, and it was chiefly our best people who died – highly skilled workers who had reached a certain age when the body can no longer resist such hardships ...

We tried to keep people going by making a sort of yeast soup, with a little soya added. It wasn't much better, really, than drinking hot water, but it gave people the illusion of having 'eaten' something. A very large number of our people died. So many died, and transport was so difficult, that we decided to have our own graveyard right here.[30]

Even worse was the condition of those in labour camps mobilized for the war effort. The NKVD made almost one-quarter of a million camp inmates available for war industries by 1944.[31] This was only part of the NKVD's huge, but often unrecognized, role in the war effort. Throughout the war, it kept up a low-level purge aimed at incompetents, the disloyal, the lazy, and in particular anyone who had spent time behind enemy lines. It also took part in the evacuation of industry and the organization of partisan war. Characteristically, Stalin spent more time dealing with the NKVD than with the army, and his correspondence with NKVD officials dominates his wartime correspondence.[32]

The government also strengthened its monopoly over the machinery of persuasion. It immediately ordered Soviet citizens to hand in all private radios; it disconnected private telephones and it began to censor private letters. The government's Soviet Information Bureau, the only official source of news, deliberately misrepresented the situation at the front, downplaying defeats and exaggerating successes.

As the war progressed, the desperate improvisations of the first year gave way to more systematic planning. Improvisation achieved much during the emergencies of the early months. Eventually, however, it was necessary to balance different sectors of the economy more carefully, for by 1942 the army was absorbing such immense human and material resources that it threatened to undermine its own sources of supply. The increasing influence of N. A. Voznesensky (1903–50), the head of Gosplan from 1942, marked a return to the more systematic mobilizational techniques of the 1930s.

The first major victories came in December 1941, during the Soviet counter-attack around Moscow. This began on 5 December under the direction of Marshal G. Zhukov. The Germans were ill-prepared for a winter campaign. Soldiers lacked proper winter clothing and the engines of their tanks froze. Once it was clear that Japan would not attack the Soviet Union, the government began assembling fresh troops from Siberia. The Moscow counter-offensive forced German armies back, up to 300 kilometres at some points, along a front stretching for 1000 kilometres. This was the first major defeat for the German army. It showed that the *blitzkrieg* had failed. It was the beginning of the process by which the Russians, in Churchill's vivid phrase, 'tore the guts out of the German army'.[33]

After the failure of the *blitzkrieg*, the balance began to tip in favour of the Red Army. A longer, more savage war enabled the Soviet Union to exploit its reserves of raw materials and labour, and its unmatched ability to mobilize resources. In this sense, the battle of Moscow was a turning point.

At the time, this was less obvious. The Russian counter-offensive petered out by March 1942. In the summer, Hitler overrode the advice of his generals to renew the attacks on Leningrad and Moscow. Instead, he decided to attack in the south, to secure the agrarian and mineral wealth of Ukraine and the Caucasus. He was particularly interested in the oilfields of Baku. In the summer of 1942, German armies advanced rapidly in the south, entering the Caucasus and reaching Stalingrad on the Volga in September. This was the limit of the German advance. Increasing Russian resistance combined with shortages of supplies and the beginnings of winter, to check further progress. In Stalingrad vicious street fighting lasted for several months. In November the Red Army launched an offensive that took the Germans by surprise and surrounded the German 6th Army under General von Paulus. At the end of January von Paulus and the remains of his army surrendered. This was the most disastrous defeat the Germans had suffered, and it proved a turning point in the war.

With minor reverses, Soviet armies now drove the Germans steadily back. By the end of 1943 the Germans had retreated to the river Dnieper. Something of the savagery of the fighting is conveyed by Marshal Konev's account of the German defeats at Korsun-Shevchenkovsky, south of Kiev, in February 1944.

> He described, somewhat gleefully, Germany's latest catastrophe: some eighty, or even a hundred thousand Germans had refused to surrender and had been forced into a narrow space, then tanks smashed their heavy equipment and machine-gun posts while the Cossack cavalry finally finished them off. 'We let the Cossacks cut them up for as long as they wished. They even hacked the hands off those who raised them to surrender!' the Marshall said with a smile.[34]

Milovan Djilas, the Yugoslavian Communist who reported the conversation, adds: 'I must admit that at that moment I also rejoiced over the fate that had befallen the Germans'.

Late in 1944 Soviet armies advanced beyond the 1939 borders, and at many points beyond those of 1941. The final Soviet assault began in January 1945. Berlin fell on 2 May, and the Germans surrendered unconditionally on 9 May (Moscow time).

After the initial disasters, the Soviet system handled the crisis of war effectively, despite its economic and technological backwardness. It did so partly because of the energy, courage and ingenuity of its citizens, and the immense human and material resources available to it. Even more important, the government mobilized these resources successfully because it had more experience of direct mobilization than any other combatant nation. This was vital, for warfare is one form of competition in which direct mobilization can count for as much as indirect mobilization, even in the modern world. 'Effective in dealing with crises and in concentrating the country's resources on the task of achieving victory, the wartime system of government may have been; efficient in the use of human and material resources it was not.'[35]

However, in retrospect we can see that the Soviet victory fostered a dangerous, and eventually fatal illusion. The spectacular successes of the command economy in wartime persuaded many that it would succeed equally well in peace. Victory over Nazi Germany made an archaic political and economic system seem more successful than it really was. It encouraged Soviet leaders to persist with the Stalinist gamble on extensive growth for far too long. It hid the deeper flaws of the command economy and discouraged fundamental reform. In this paradoxical way, the victory of 1945 prepared the defeat of 1991.

■ The Impact of War

The Soviet system had survived the war, but at what cost? Soviet people paid a far heavier price than their western allies or even the Germans. At least 9 million died in battle or in prisoner of war camps, and 18 million were wounded. Another 19 million died among the civilian population. Deaths during the siege of Leningrad alone were greater than all the civilian and military deaths of the British Empire, the Dominions and the USA.[36]

The material damage was also huge. The fighting destroyed about half of all urban housing in the occupied areas. Seventy thousand villages and vast numbers of industrial enterprises lay in ruins. The war destroyed much of the achievement of the 1930s. Production figures for 1940 and 1945 give a partial measure of the decline in production (see the Statistical Appendix).

Politically, however, the war was a triumph for the Stalinist system. As Stalin said in a speech in February 1946: 'Our victory means, first of all, that our Soviet social system has triumphed, that the Soviet social system has successfully passed the ordeal in the fire of war and has proved its unquestionable vitality'.[37]

The war also made the Soviet government a popular national government. This change was the product of three distinct developments. One was the spontaneous reaction of millions of Soviet citizens to the German invasion. Even many who had little reason to love Stalin's government rallied round. Army officers who had languished in the camps after the purges, returned without hesitation to commanding positions after the German attack. Marshals K. K. Rokossovsky and L. A. Govorov are the best-known commanders of this group. During the war, a flood of anti-German novels reflected a genuine popular revulsion at the German invasion and its brutal methods.

Second, the government itself actively encouraged the Soviet people, and the Russians in particular, to see it as a national government. The process began during the cultural retreat of the 1930s. Official propaganda started to emphasize Russian patriotism in films such as Eisenstein's *Alexander Nevsky* and *Ivan the Terrible.* History textbooks adopted an increasingly nationalistic tone. They began to glorify Russia's military traditions and the exploits of generals such as Kutuzov and Suvorov, who had fought Napoleon. These changes may have reflected Stalin's own sense of Russian patriotism, which was strong despite his Georgian origins. The Yugoslav Communist Milovan Djilas noted in 1944 that, in conversation, 'Stalin used the term Russia, and not Soviet Union, which meant that he was not only inspiring Russian Nationalism, but was himself inspired by it and identified himself with it'.[38] In 1943, the government replaced the 'Internationale' as the Soviet national anthem. The new anthem ignored the internationalism of traditional Marxism and emphasized Soviet patriotism.

The government made great efforts to ensure the loyalty of the army. Patriotic slogans replaced party slogans. Instead of 'loyalty to the international proletariat', a revised military oath made soldiers promise to defend 'my homeland, the USSR'.[39] On 7 November 1941, Stalin reviewed the annual parade in memory of the revolution, with German troops only kilometres away, and their artillery already audible. He declared: 'Let the manly images of our great ancestors – Alexander Nevsky, Dmitri Donskoy, Kuzma Minin, Dmitrii Pozharsky, Alexander Suvorov, and Mikhail Kutuzov – inspire you in this war'.[40] Many of those who heard this speech were at the front within hours.

Other concessions to the military were more direct. The government revived many pre-revolutionary traditions. After reintroducing political commissars in the armed forces in July 1941, the government abolished them in October 1942. This enhanced the independent authority of officers. The army formed special clubs for officers, and increased their rates of pay and material privileges. The government introduced new patriotic medals. Stalin even re-established the elite guards regiments that Peter the Great had founded in the eighteenth century, and which had been disbanded only after the revolution. The government also tried to bring the party and the army closer together. It made it easy for soldiers and officers to join the party, so that by May 1945 25 per cent of all members of the armed forces were Party members, and 20 per cent more belonged to the party's youth movement, the *Komsomol.*[41]

The government even made tentative and mainly symbolic concessions to the peasantry. This was important militarily. Peasants made up almost as large a proportion of Soviet as they had of tsarist soldiers, since industrial workers found it easier to gain exemptions from military service. The party eased restrictions on the size and use of private plots on collective farms. However, this was its only material concession to the peasantry. The main concession was religious. Stalin himself is said to have remarked: 'We will never rouse the people to war with Marxism–Leninism alone'.[42] He downplayed anti-religious propaganda, and in 1943 he permitted the Church to summon a church council, or *Sobor*. The *Sobor* elected Metropolitan Sergius as the first Patriarch of the Russian Church (apart from a brief period after 1917) since the late seventeenth century. The new patriarch reciprocated by describing Stalin in a *Pravda* article as the 'God-chosen leader of our military and cultural forces'. Muslim and Jewish leaders soon followed suit.[43] These concessions were part of a large-scale political and ideological retreat similar to the fiscal retreat of 1921.

The final cause of the government's new-found popularity was the behaviour of the Germans in the territories they occupied. Hitler had reason to believe that non-Russian areas in the Baltic and the Polish provinces, and some of the collectivized peasantry, as well as nationalist intellectuals in Ukraine, might welcome the Germans as liberators. However, the Germans themselves soon alienated these groups by their brutal and exploitative treatment of occupied areas. The occupation authorities deported almost 3 million inhabitants of occupied territories to Germany as slave-labourers. Those left behind were not much better off. In October 1941, Marshal Reichenau announced that: 'To supply local inhabitants and prisoners of war with food is an act of unnecessary humanity'.[44] To maintain grain production, the Germans refused to dismantle the collective farms. They also refused to set up the national governments desired by nationalists in the occupied territories.

In international terms, the war was a triumph for the government and the Soviet system. Though devastated by war, the Soviet Union had proved itself a great military power. It had made good the territorial losses of 1918, and retained all the regions it occupied during the Nazi–Soviet pact. It also took additional territory from Finland, Czechoslovakia, Japan and Germany. Furthermore, the presence of Soviet armies in Bulgaria, Romania, Hungary, Czechoslovakia, Poland and East Germany assured the Soviet Union effective control over the borderlands of Eastern Europe, through which Russia had so often been invaded. The Soviet government used this control to set up sympathetic governments throughout Eastern Europe. To its internal empire (The Soviet Union), it now added an external empire in Eastern Europe. In a speech in Fulton, Missouri, in March 1946, Churchill christened the borders of the new Soviet Empire the 'Iron Curtain'.

In this unexpected way the Soviet government broke the ring of capitalist powers that had circled it since 1917. After the independent successes of the Communist armies of Mao Zedong in China in 1949, perhaps half of the world's population lived under Communist governments. For a time, at least, even China allied with the Soviet Union, and treated it as the leader of the socialist world. The successful testing of a Soviet atom bomb in 1949 further reduced the vulnerability of the world's first socialist state. By the early 1950s, the Soviet government controlled a larger area than any previous Russian government. Stalin's government had re-established the Soviet Union as a world power.

■ Reconstruction and Cold War

These achievements should have reduced the need for authoritarian government. In the eighteenth and early nineteenth centuries, military successes had led to a slow loosening of the political system of Peter the Great. Military success allowed the ruling group to relax its own internal discipline and the pressure it exerted on the population as a whole. Would the same happen after the successes of 1945?

Many in Soviet society at large and perhaps even within the elite expected liberalization after the war. The poet Alexis Surkov expressed this mood when he wrote: 'After the victory we shall call a halt, drink a cup, and rest to our heart's desire'.[45] Liberalization might have allowed the maintenance of friendly relations with the United States, the other major victor. It might have permitted liberal treatment of occupied Eastern Europe. Finally, it might have allowed the reconstruction of the Soviet economy using American loans. This would have greatly reduced the strain on the exhausted Soviet population. We know that during 1945 Stalin himself twice asked for huge reconstruction loans from the Americans.

However, it is unlikely that Stalin considered this option seriously. On the contrary, Stalin saw the victory, first of all, as a triumph for his strategy of direct, coercive mobilization. It justified his belief that Soviet Russia could solve its military and industrial problems without foreign help. He had little reason to change a system that had succeeded so spectacularly. Besides, he was too old to change the political methods he had used for so long. Finally, the Soviet Union still faced threats from abroad, particularly from an aggressive United States, which had emerged from the war wealthier and more powerful than ever.

For these reasons, the last years of Stalin's life saw a return to the methods of the 1930s. For Soviet citizens, the years between the end of the war and Stalin's death in 1953 were probably the bleakest of the whole Stalin period. Two problems dominated these years: security and reconstruction. Stalin tackled them in characteristic style.

By 1945 Soviet armies occupied much of Eastern Europe. Here was the opportunity, at last, to solve the security problems that have haunted all governments of Russia. Victory offered two new ways of defending the Soviet Union's precarious borders. First, it allowed the creation of a large buffer zone of weak or friendly states. Second, victory spread socialism, and thereby ended the isolation of the world's first socialist state. In these ways, Stalin determined to avoid any repetition of the catastrophe of 1941. In 1945, he remarked: 'This war is not as in the past; whoever occupies a territory also imposes on it his own social system. Everyone imposes his own system as far as his army has power to do so. It cannot be otherwise'.[46]

This approach meant emphasizing the basic conflicts between socialist and capitalist nations; conflicts that the wartime alliance had masked. However, this approach to defence also implied something else that Western governments missed. It set clear limits to Soviet expansionism. Stalin knew he could not control areas such as Iran or Greece, not directly occupied by Soviet armies. His government lacked the taste and the resources for further expansion while its own country lay in ruins. Beyond the lands occupied by Soviet troops Stalin conceded power to the western allies. Within them, he conceded nothing. Stalin's aim now was 'to seize opportunity but to dodge confrontation, to avoid war at all costs, and to retrench around the Motherland when all else failed'.[47]

Differences among the wartime allies, particularly over the treatment of occupied territories, emerged early. They appeared even at the wartime summit conferences at Teheran (November–December 1943), Yalta (February 1945), and Potsdam (July–August 1945). In May 1945, the new United States president, Harry Truman, abruptly ended Lend-lease. This increased Soviet determination to go it alone. So did the testing of an American atom bomb a month later, and the American refusal to grant the Soviet Union a large reconstruction loan. The Soviet government took no part in the Marshall Plan, which funded much of the reconstruction of capitalist Western Europe.

In Eastern Europe, Soviet armies were in occupation, and the left wing enjoyed temporary popularity because of its role in the resistance to Fascism. This allowed the establishment of pro-Soviet coalition governments. The Soviet Union set up a series of economic and defence alliances with eastern bloc countries. In the next few years, the government increased its influence over the economic and political life of Eastern Europe.

By early 1946 it was clear that the wartime alliance had broken down and a 'Cold War' had begun. Soon after Churchill's Iron Curtain speech, Harry Truman announced that the United States would aid any independent country threatened by Communism. In September 1947, the Soviet government revived, in the *Cominform*, a pale ghost of the *Comintern*. In June 1949, in response to the Marshall Plan, it created the CMEA (Council for Mutual Economic Assistance), a new Eastern European economic bloc.

Cold War antagonisms encouraged a new arms race. Immediately after the war, the Soviet government demobilized 9 million Soviet soldiers. But it soon changed its mind. In 1949, the Berlin blockade, the testing of a Soviet atom bomb, and the emergence of Communist China intensified the hostility between the two power blocks. In 1950, warfare broke out between US forces and Communist China in Korea. Both sides responded by beginning an arms build-up that continued until the 1980s. It exacted a heavy economic toll on both sides and forced an entire generation to live in the shadow of nuclear war.

For the Soviet government, the Cold War was extremely useful, for it helped revive the siege mentality of the 1930s. With the capitalist West cast as the Soviet Union's main enemy, the Soviet government could argue that it was still too early to relax. Instead, the government re-established the coercive mobilization structures of the 1930s during the reconstruction period.

The government re-established rigid control of collective farms and restricted the size of private plots. After announcing demobilization in June 1945, the government once more subordinated the army to the party and government. Recruitment of soldiers into the party slowed down. Political commissars reappeared. The government clipped the wings of popular and powerful Soviet generals, such as Zhukov.

There was also an end to the ideological retreat of the war years. Under Andrei Zhdanov, the Leningrad party boss, there was a savage purge of the Western influences on Soviet cultural life which had seeped in during the war years. Travel abroad became almost impossible for all but the most privileged of Soviet citizens. From 1947, the government prohibited marriage to foreigners. Finally, a new purge affected three main groups – the army, the party and the non-Russian nationalities.

Many soldiers who had been abroad, either with the army or as partisans or prisoners of war, returned home only to be sentenced to labour camps. This was the fate of Ivan Denisovich (the hero of Alexander Solzhenitsyn's novella, *One Day in the Life of Ivan Denisovich*) and of Solzhenitsyn himself.

The government purged the party to raise ideological standards, which had declined during the war. In 1947, it dismissed 27.5 per cent of all district party secretaries, mainly in areas occupied during the war. In 1948, after the death of Zhdanov, there was a purge of his followers in the so-called 'Leningrad affair'. Early in 1953 there were signs that a new purge might be under way. The government announced that several doctors who had treated prominent government officials were working for foreign intelligence. Nikita Khrushchev claimed later that Stalin saw the so-called 'doctors' plot' as the start of a new purge that would have removed most of his closest followers. Instead, Stalin's own death intervened on 5 March 1953.

The post-war purge struck whole national groups, particularly those suspected of collaboration with the Germans. The government deported some smaller national groups wholesale. These included the Volga Germans (the descendants of Germans who had settled in Russia during the reign of Catherine the Great) and the Crimean Tatars. Both groups were deported from their homelands to Siberia. In 1956, Khrushchev claimed that 'The Ukrainians avoided meeting this fate only because there were too many of them and there was no place to which to deport them'.[48] Nevertheless, the government deported millions from Ukraine and the Baltic States. After 1948 there was also a wave of anti-Semitism. As a result of these purges, the camp population grew even larger than in the late 1930s, to over two and a half million.[49]

Economic reconstruction began during the war itself. Formally, reconstruction began with the launching of the fourth Five-Year Plan, adopted in 1946. During the first year, demobilization, the need to gear industry once more to civilian needs, and a disastrous drought and famine in Ukraine slowed progress. After that, progress was rapid. (See the Statistical Appendix and Table 10.3.)

Why was growth so rapid? As in the early 1920s, part of the answer is that reconstruction is easier than construction. The Soviet Union also imposed savage reparations on its wartime enemies East Germany, Hungary, Romania and Finland, and it used the labour of 2 million prisoners of war. However, recovery depended mainly on the efforts and sacrifices of Soviet citizens. As in the 1930s, planners diverted resources from consumption to investment. A currency reform of 1947 reduced wage levels and devalued the savings of millions. In these ways, the government recreated the Stalinist 'engine of growth', which depended on direct mobilization of raw materials and human labour. During this period, 'A plan for an enterprise handed down from above had the force of law and non-fulfilment entailed political and criminal responsibility'.[50] Workers received savage punishment for lateness or minor breaches of discipline. Managers, too, worked long hours. Living standards remained extremely low. Worst of all were conditions on the collective farms, which planners exploited even more brutally than before the war. Many received less from the government than the cost of producing and delivering grain. The sociologist, Tatyana Zaslavskaya, studied life on collective farms in this period.

□ *Document 12.4: Tatyana Zaslavskaya on collective farms after the war*

In 1951, when I was looking through the aggregate annual accounts of collective farms in one of the regions of Kirghizia, I noticed that on average the collective farmers received one kopek for a day's labour, and for a year about two pre-reform roubles ... (the price of one kilogram of bread). In reply to my puzzled question as to what they lived on, it was explained to me that most of the families had a small flock of sheep and goats, which were pastured in the mountains, concealed from the tax authorities. So it was that I, a graduate of a university where I had been told about the advantages of the socialist distribution of income according to work done, first came up against the fact that a social class comprising about forty per cent of the population of the country was paid practically nothing for its work.[51]

Progress was fastest in heavy industry. However, there was also rapid growth in consumer goods industries. The difference was that industrial production had surpassed the 1940 level by 1950, while production in agriculture and consumer goods industries had merely returned to pre-war levels. By 1950, living standards in the towns had probably returned to the level of 1928, while industrial production had soared ahead of these levels. The Soviet consumer had yet to reap the material benefits of industrialization.

According to the statistics, recovery was complete by 1950. Was it not possible, at last, to ease the political and economic pressures that Soviet citizens had endured for two decades? By now, Stalin himself was the main barrier to change. His power and prestige were so immense that little could change while he remained in power. His death, on 5 March 1953, opened the way to rapid change.

■ Summary

From 1917, Soviet foreign policy was torn between the hope of generating a world revolution, and the desire to live in peace with capitalist neighbours while building the foundations of socialism. However, the Soviet government always knew that eventually it would have to face a military challenge from the west. With the rise of Hitler that threat came much closer. By the late 1930s the industrialization drive had turned into an armaments drive. Despite this, Stalin did not prepare the country well for the war that everyone knew was coming. The purges weakened the officer corps, while his own fear of provoking a conflict, particularly after the Nazi–Soviet pact in 1939, led him to avoid all overt preparations for war.

When the German attack came on June 22 1941, it was devastating. By December 1941, German armies had reached Leningrad and Moscow. In 1942, German armies advanced further South, reaching Stalingrad on the Volga river by September. However, the huge mobilizational system created by the Soviet government in the 1930s eventually began to show its value. The government transferred factories and their workers eastwards, and mobilized the equipment and men needed to replace the catastrophic losses of 1941. It sought popular support by negotiating concordats with the Soviet Union's various churches, by relaxing pressure on the peasantry, and by encouraging traditional forms of patriotism. After the victory at Stalingrad, in January 1943, Soviet armies pushed the Germany army back until the final German surrender in May 1945.

At the end of the war, many felt it was time to relax after fifteen years of socialist construction and war. However, Stalin returned to the methods that had seemed to work so well in the 1930s. The pace of reconstruction was intensified, and there were renewed purges, this time of captured soldiers and of whole nations that Stalin suspected of disloyalty. For Stalin, these were years of triumph. The Soviet Union was now a great world power, and when Stalin died, in 1953, the economy had largely recovered from the damage of war. Yet little had been done to ease the material and political conditions of the ordinary Soviet citizens who had borne the brunt of industrialisation and war.

☐   *Further Reading*

There is a good recent history of the Soviet Union at war in Barber and Harrison, *The Soviet Home Front*. Werth, *Russia at War,* is a fascinating account by a western journalist. Diplomatic issues are covered in Nation, *Black Earth, Red Star.* The best military history is Erickson, *Stalin's war with Germany,* though Clark, *Barbarossa,* is shorter and easier to read. See also the collection of essays in Linz (ed.), *The Impact of World War II on the Soviet Union.*

☐   *Notes*

1. R. C. Nation, *Black Earth, Red Star: A History of Soviet Security Policy* (Ithaca: Cornell University Press, 1991) p. 40.
2. A. Nove, *An Economic History of the USSR,* 3rd edn (Harmondsworth: Penguin, 1992) p. 230.
3. J. Barber and M. Harrison, *The Soviet Home Front 1941–1945* (London and New York: Longman, 1991) p. 5.
4. A. Werth, *Russia at War: 1941–1945* (New York: Avon Books, 1964) p. 147.
5. R. R. Reese, 'The Red Army and the Great Purges', in J. Arch Getty and R. T. Manning (eds), *Stalinist Terror: New Perspectives* (Cambridge University Press, 1993) pp 199–201.
6. R. Medvedev, *Let History Judge* (New York: Alfred A. Knopf, 1971) pp. 213–14.
7. Nation, *Black Earth, Red Star,* p. 106.
8. A. Clark, *Barbarossa* (Harmondsworth: Penguin, 1966) p. 70.

9. Werth, *Russia at War*, p. 149.

10. K. S. Karol, *Solik* (London: Pluto Press, 1986) p. 74.

11. M. McCauley, *The Soviet Union since 1917* (London, Longman, 1981) pp. 108, 110; Clark, *Barbarossa*, p. 76.

12. Barber and Harrison, *The Soviet Home Front*, p. 22.

13. McCauley, *The Soviet Union*, p. 108.

14. Ivan Krylov, *Soviet Staff Officer* (London: Falcon Press, 1951) pp. 115–16.

15. Barber and Harrison, *The Soviet Home Front*, p. 28.

16. J. N. Westwood, *Endurance and Endeavour: Russian History 1812–1980*, 2nd edn (Oxford University Press, 1981) pp. 344–5; and see Clark, *Barbarossa*, picture no 15.

17. Cited in Barber and Harrison, *The Soviet Home Front*, p. 67.

18. D. Volkogonov, *Stalin: Triumph and Tragedy* (Rocklin, Calif.: Prima Publishing, 1992) p. 410.

19. Cited in Volkogonov, *Triumph and Tragedy*, p. 411.

20. Cited in Werth, *Russia at War*, pp. 173–4.

21. E. Bacon, 'Glasnost and the Gulag', *Soviet Studies*, vol. 44, no. 6 (1992) p. 1079.

22. Werth, *Russia at War*, p. 250.

23. Ibid., p. 287.

24. R. Medvedev, *On Stalin and Stalinism* (Oxford University Press, 1979) p. 121.

25. Nove, *Economic History*, p. 276.

26. Ibid., pp. 275–81; Werth, *Russia at War*, ch. 9.

27. Barber and Harrison, *The Soviet Home Front*, p. 135.

28. D. Atkinson, *et al.* (eds), *Women in Russia* (Brighton: Harvester Press, 1978) p. 194.

29. W. Moskoff, *The Bread of Affliction: The Food Supply in the USSR during World War II* (Cambridge University Press, 1990) p. 109.

30. Werth, *Russia at War*, pp. 329–31.

31. Bacon, 'Glasnost' and the Gulag', p. 1081.

32. Barber and Harrison, *The Soviet Home Front*, pp. 52–3.

33. Cited in Werth, *Russia at War*, p. xvii.

34. M. Djilas, *Conversations with Stalin* (Harmondsworth: Penguin, 1963) pp. 46–7.

35. Barber and Harrison, *The Soviet Home Front*, p. 48.

36. Ibid., p. 40–2.

37. From the election speech of February 1946, cited in B. Dmytryshym, *USSR: A Concise History*, 2nd edn (New York: Scribner's, 1971) p. 452.

38. Djilas, *Conversations with Stalin*, p. 53.

39. M. Fainsod, *How Russia is Ruled*, rev. edn (Cambridge, Mass.: Harvard University Press, 1963) p. 477.

40. Dmytryshyn, *USSR*, p. 229.

41. McCauley, *The Soviet Union*, p. 121.

42. Medvedev, *Stalin and Stalinism*, p. 124.

43. Westwood, *Endurance and Endeavour*, p. 346.

44. Moskoff, *The Bread of Affliction*, p. 44.

45. A. Ulam, *Stalin: The Man and His Era* (New York: Viking Press, 1973) p. 615.

46. Djilas, *Conversations with Stalin*, p. 90.

47. Nation, *Black Earth, Red Star*, p. 194.

48. Dmytryshyn, *USSR*, p. 512.

49. Bacon, '*Glasnost*' and the Gulag', p. 1071. Volkogonov gives the higher figure of 3–4 million in *Triumph and Tragedy*, pp. 307–8.
50. T. Zaslavskaya, *The Second Socialist Revolution* (Bloomington, Ind.: Indiana University Press, 1990) p. 21.
51. Ibid., p. 23.

Chapter 13

Reforming the Stalinist System, 1953 to 1964

Stalin died early in the morning of 5 March 1953. A few days before, he had a stroke. Because of the 'doctor's plot', his own doctors were now in jail, so new doctors attended him. His daughter, Svetlana, remembered them 'making a tremendous fuss, applying leeches to his neck and the back of his head, making cardiograms and taking X-rays of his lungs. A nurse kept giving him injections …'.[1] Their treatment was a fitting symbol of Stalinism's strange and terrifying mixture of the archaic and the modern. So was the leave-taking of Stalin's servants.

☐ *Document 13.1: Saying farewell to Stalin*

My father's servants and bodyguards came to say goodbye. They felt genuine grief and emotion. Cooks, chauffeurs and watchmen, gardeners and the women who had waited at table all came quietly in. They went up to the bed silently and wept. They wiped their tears away as children do, with their hands and sleeves and kerchiefs. Many were sobbing. The nurse, who was also in tears, gave them drops of valerian … Valentina Istomina, or 'Valechka', as she was called, who had been my father's housekeeper for eighteen years, came in to say goodbye. She dropped heavily to her knees, put her head on my father's chest and wailed at the top of her voice as the women in villages do. She went on for a long time and nobody tried to stop her.[2]

The post-Stalin period of Soviet history falls into three main stages. The first was a period of instability and change. This lasted from 1953 until the mid-1960s. Khrushchev's fall from power in 1964 offers a symbolic end-point for this phase. During this period, reforming governments, led first by Malenkov, then by Khrushchev, dismantled much of the coercive and ideological scaffolding of Stalinism. They also began at last to redistribute some of the wealth generated by industrialization to the Soviet population at large. As a result, a new 'social contract' was negotiated between government and people. After the fall of Khrushchev, there followed a period of consolidation that lasted until the mid-1980s. Between 1964 and 1968, there was one last burst of reform, directed mainly at the economy.

351

After that, under the slogan 'stability of cadres', the government of Brezhnev tried to freeze change. Despite this, important economic, social and ideological changes took place beneath the surface of Soviet society. The third period begins with the rise to power of Mikhail Gorbachev in 1985. This was a period of even more radical reforms than those of the 1950s and 1960s. However, what began as an attempt to renovate the socialist system led, within seven years, to its collapse.

This chapter deals with the period of change that followed Stalin's death. Its dominant figure is Nikita Khrushchev.

Between 1905 and 1953, Russian and Soviet society had undergone massive, traumatic changes. Why should the post-Stalin leadership have launched new changes after his death? The short answer is that change was unavoidable, it was possible, and it was desirable.

Stalin's death made change unavoidable. Indeed his death itself represented a profound transformation of Soviet political life. Since the late 1930s, Stalin himself had become the central institution of the Soviet political system. All political threads led to his office. His death immediately raised the question: where does ultimate authority now reside? Political reform was unavoidable if only to clarify who ruled the country.

Stalin's death also weakened the political system. We have seen that strong leadership provides an index of the power of ruling groups. With Stalin gone, there was no longer a clear leader, or a final point for the resolution of conflict. As in the mid-1920s, a struggle for power at the top threatened to open deep fissures throughout the Soviet ruling group. Not only was the new leadership weak; it was also acutely aware of its weakness. Like the tsarist government in the 1850s, the new leaders projected these fears on to the population at large. Though there is little direct evidence of popular resistance to the system, the new leaders acted as if they had to ward off popular revolt. This explains the panic concessions they made after Stalin's death.

Paradoxically, it was Stalin's achievements that made possible a retreat from Stalinism. The Stalinist system had solved many of the problems Soviet governments had faced in the 1920s. It had created a large industrial base for the Soviet economy. It had almost abolished illiteracy and had raised the educational level of the entire population. Industrialization had also increased the size of the urban proletariat. Finally, the Soviet Union boasted a defence establishment capable not merely of defending the Soviet Union, but of making it a great world power. These changes gave the post-Stalin government options that had not been available in the 1920s. The industrial base of the Soviet economy was now large enough to permit considerable material concessions to the population without slowing economic growth.

Finally, change was desirable because the ruling group itself stood to gain from reform. As in the reign of Peter the Great, the creation of a powerful autocratic system had exacted a price even from the elites who benefited most from the process. It demanded high levels of discipline and created much tension and insecurity. It therefore devalued many of the benefits of belonging to a ruling group. Once it seemed that these sacrifices might no longer be necessary, elites had good reason to relax the tautness of the system. Soviet society was no longer a beleaguered fortress, and its elites no longer needed the barracks discipline of the 1930s. They could afford to ease the pressure both on themselves and the population at large.

Many pressures encouraged change. Yet the new leaders had good reason to limit its extent. The Soviet ruling group gained much from the existing system and had no reason to see it destroyed. So there were bound to be limits to the 'thaw' of the post-Stalin years. Above all, the *nomenklatura* elite had to preserve and defend its monopoly of state power and the state control over resources on which its material privileges depended. This meant preserving the one-party state and the command economy.

Negotiating these limits was complex and difficult. The government had to make concessions to the population. Yet how much could the ruling group concede without weakening its own grip on power? Could they allow a partial re-emergence of market forces? Could they make political concessions, or relax censorship, or reduce the power of the secret police? The tricky process of reforming the system while preserving the power and privileges of the elite explains the erratic progress of the reforms and the instability of the Khrushchev era.

■ Early Manoeuvres and Panic Concessions

In 1952 Stalin increased the size of the Politburo and renamed it the Presidium of the Central Committee of the Communist Party. This widened the circle from which his successor could be chosen. However, there was an inner group of politicians who held important positions and had been close to Stalin in his final years. The most influential of these were Georgyi Malenkov and Lavrentii Beria. Malenkov was a deputy chairman of the Council of Ministers and a leading member of the party Secretariat. This gave him influence within two of the most important bureaucracies – the party apparatus and the system of ministries. Beria headed the secret police. Other key members of the inner circle included Molotov, who headed the foreign policy bureaucracy, and Nikita

Khrushchev (1894–1971), who headed the Moscow party apparatus. Like Malenkov, Khrushchev also belonged to the party Secretariat.

Those present at Stalin's death looked for a testament or 'will' that might explain Stalin's wishes. They found nothing. Forced to take their own decisions, they summoned an *ad hoc* meeting of some twenty politicians from the Presidium, the Council of Ministers, and the Presidium of the Supreme Soviet. This technically unconstitutional group took some basic decisions about the distribution of authority. They reduced the size of the enlarged Presidium to the size of the former Politburo. They also presided over the first carve-up of leading positions.

The first division of political spoils looks like the result of a deal struck between Malenkov and Beria, the two obvious contenders for leadership. Malenkov retained his leading position in the Secretariat. On Beria's recommendation, he also became Chairman of the Council of Ministers. In this way, he gained the two positions Stalin had held since 1941. Of the two, it was the chairmanship of the Council of Ministers that appeared most important, for in his later years Stalin had preferred to rule through the ministerial apparatus. He had even abolished the post of General Secretary through which he had first risen to the leadership. In return for Beria's support, Malenkov proposed that Beria become head of a re-amalgamated ministry of internal affairs and state security, the MVD. This made Beria head, once more, of an immensely powerful secret police apparatus. If there was to be a *coup*, Beria was now in the ideal position to lead it. His troops controlled the Kremlin and made up the bodyguards of leading government officials. Stalin's funeral even allowed him to move MVD troops to the capital.

Like Trotsky in the early 1920s, Malenkov found that moving too fast was a mistake. A week later, after manoeuvres that remain obscure, Malenkov resigned his position in the Secretariat. Khrushchev was the main beneficiary of this change. Though he lost his position as head of the Moscow party apparatus, Khrushchev now became the leading figure in the Secretariat. This made him the leading figure in the party apparatus. However, as with Stalin in 1922, no one realized how much power this gave him. Malenkov, Beria and Molotov still seemed the main contenders for the leadership. Although Khrushchev chaired the committee that organized Stalin's funeral, Malenkov, Beria and Molotov made the main speeches.

These manoeuvres showed the uncertainty of the new leadership. The unity Stalin had provided for twenty-five years had gone. Stalin's heirs distrusted each other and lacked Stalin's prestige, his popularity, and his political skill and ruthlessness. The entire quality of leadership had changed. Announcing that there had been a return to the 'Leninist' principle of collective leadership did little to hide this reality.

Most people heard of Stalin's death with genuine grief. Tatyana Zaslavskaya remembers that: 'Many people honestly did not conceive how the country could continue to exist without its great teacher and friend. At memorial meetings the men were strained and grave and the women usually wept. I wept myself, although by that time my doubts about the correctness of Stalin's line were greater than my belief that he was right'.[3] There were few immediate signs that Stalin's death would encourage resistance to the oppressive system he had directed. Yet there were straws in the wind. In the summer there was a prolonged uprising of prisoners in labour camps in the Vorkuta region. In June there was an uprising in East Berlin.

However, as in the 1850s, the fear of popular resistance was more important than the reality. Stalin's successors understood that without Stalin they could no longer maintain the extreme pressure that had made the industrialization drive possible. The result was a series of hasty concessions. The element of panic explains the irrationality of some of these measures.

On 1 April 1953 the government announced price cuts averaging 10 per cent on basic items of consumption including food and clothing.[4] Some gestures were purely symbolic. It made no economic sense to reduce the price of already scarce goods such as meat. Doing so merely lengthened queues and raised black market prices. Other measures had an immediate impact on living standards. During 1953, a reduction in the size of compulsory purchases of government bonds, and an increase in nominal wages, raised real wages by 8 per cent. The government also raised planned output of consumer goods. In 1953 output of consumer goods increased faster than output of producer goods for the first time since the 1920s. Malenkov's pro-consumer policy soon became known as the 'new course'.

Improving food supplies and rural living conditions meant tackling the dreadful condition of Soviet agriculture. In some ways the situation was similar to that of March 1921. An exploitative policy towards the agricultural sector had deprived farmers of all incentives to increase output. The most important reform therefore reduced the tax on private plots and increased the prices paid for procurements from collective farms. Most striking of all was a sevenfold increase in the average prices the state paid for grains. Malenkov announced these concessions in August. Their impact was immediate. They transformed living conditions on collective farms, and output began to rise, particularly on the private plots that produced most of the country's potatoes, eggs and meat.

The government also made political concessions. Three weeks after Stalin's death, the new leadership announced an amnesty. This covered non-political prisoners sentenced to less than five years for minor crimes, as well as sick or aged prisoners. Almost 1.2 million people were released.[5] Some had highly placed relatives. They included Molotov's wife, Zhemchuzhina, and Mikoyan's son.[6] On 4 April, the Ministry of

Internal Affairs announced that there was no basis for the so-called 'Doctor's Plot'.

The early weeks set the pattern for the next few years. On the one hand, changes within the ruling group reorganized the political system. On the other hand, there occurred a profound change in the relationship between the ruling group and the rest of society. Both types of change reduced the tension and coerciveness of the Soviet system.

 # Political Changes and the Struggle for Succession

Further changes depended on the outcome of the precarious balance of power within the post-Stalin Politburo. Once Stalin had gone, did power lie with the party, the government apparatus headed by the Council of Ministers, or perhaps the police? After 14 March 1953, a member of the Presidium headed each of these bureaucracies, so the triangular power struggle that followed embroiled institutions as well as leaders.

With Malenkov's power reduced after 14 March, there was a real danger that Beria would complete the rise of the secret police that had begun in the early 1930s. This would have formally turned the Soviet Union into a police state. Beria's rivals found this prospect terrifying. So did most members of the Soviet elite, for they were more vulnerable than anyone else to police persecution. Most of Stalin's inner entourage had suffered from the purges. Molotov's wife had spent many years in camps, and was in exile in 1953. Lazar Kaganovich had lost a brother in the purges. Mikhail Kalinin had been the chairman of the Supreme Soviet, and formally head of state before his death in 1946, yet his wife spent seven years in labour camps. All those close to Stalin understood that they were vulnerable when the so-called 'Doctor's Plot' was announced early in 1953. In the circumstances, an anti-Beria alliance was a natural development. However, organizing such an alliance would not be easy.

In his memoirs, Khrushchev claimed to have started the delicate manoeuvres that led to Beria's arrest. Over several months he broached the subject, with extreme caution, to key colleagues. Once they had agreed on the idea, there remained some technical difficulties that Khrushchev described vividly in his memoirs.

☐ *Document 13.2: The decision to remove Beria*

Once we had formally resolved to strip Beria of his posts, who would actually detain him? The [Presidium] bodyguard was obedient to him. His Chekists would be sitting in the next room during the session [of the Presidium], and Beria could easily order them to arrest us all and hold us in isolation. We would have been quite helpless because there was a sizable armed guard in the Kremlin. Therefore we decided to enlist the help of the military. First, we entrusted the detention of Beria to Comrade Moskalenko, the air defense commander, and five generals ... Then, on the eve of the session, Malenkov widened our circle to include Marshal Zhukov and some others. That meant eleven marshals and generals in all. In those days all military personnel were required to check their weapons when coming into the Kremlin, so Comrade Bulganin [the Minister for the Armed Forces] was instructed to see that the marshals and generals were allowed to bring their guns with them. We arranged for Moskalenko's group to wait for a summons in a separate room while the session was taking place. [When Malenkov pressed a button to give the prearranged signal, the generals entered the room.] 'Hands up' Zhukov commanded Beria. Moskalenko and the others unbuckled their holsters in case Beria tried anything.[7]

On 28 June, the Presidium had Beria arrested on a trumped-up charge of working for British intelligence. His arrest led to the arrest of many other leading police officials. After an investigation and trial, Beria was executed in December 1953 under the Kirov Decrees.

Beria's removal placed the secret police once more under the authority of the party and government, as it had been before 1934. These critical changes made it possible to start dismantling the coercive machinery of the Stalin era. That process freed Soviet leaders and ordinary Soviet citizens from the extreme insecurity of the Stalin years.

There had already been an amnesty for some groups of prisoners. The stories they told of police methods and the regime in the camps helped ensure Beria's removal and execution. The investigations into police methods set up during Beria's trial produced evidence that even shocked tempered Stalinists like Khrushchev with their revelations of the extent and savagery of police repression under Stalin. Coupled with growing popular pressure, mostly from relatives of prisoners, this ensured that the assault on the police would not end with Beria's removal. Early in 1954 the government split the police apparatus once more. The Ministry of Internal Affairs retained control of the ordinary police. However, a separate committee of state security (KGB) now took control of the secret police. The new committee was subordinate to the Council of Ministers, but its first boss was a Khrushchev supporter, I. A. Serov. The Ministry of Internal Affairs also lost control of the economic empire represented by the labour camps. The Ministry of Justice now assumed control of the camps. The cancellation of the Kirov laws deprived the secret police of the extensive judicial powers they had exercized since 1934.

The new leadership also reduced the size of the secret police apparatus and its vast network of informers. The 'special sections', used by the police to spy on Soviet institutions and enterprises, were abolished. Most significant of all was the dismantling of the Gulag. The announcement of Beria's execution prompted thousands of people to demand the rehabilitation of relatives who had suffered imprisonment unjustly. The government responded by setting up several special commissions to investigate these cases, and the prosecutor-general's office began the vast job of investigating millions of appeals against unjust imprisonment. By the end of 1955 courts had released 10 000 to 12 000 people from the camps. They had rehabilitated many more posthumously. This was an important gesture, for it freed their relatives from the penalties of banishment, loss of party membership, and loss of residence rights they had suffered under Stalin.[8] The judicial review accelerated in 1956 and 1957, after the party had openly committed itself to destalinization at the twentieth Party Congress. New amnesty decrees freed most remaining political prisoners from the camps and cleared more posthumously.

These changes allowed a partial revival of the Soviet judicial system. Freed of police control, the Soviet judicial and legal system regained some independence. The idea of the 'rule of law' once more acquired real meaning, though the judiciary remained under party control.

The early reforms dismantled much of the Stalinist scaffolding of terror. Despite their limitations, they had a profound effect on Soviet life, quite apart from their direct impact on the lives of those released from the camps. Terror ceased to be a normal method of government, and the fear of arbitrary arrest and execution receded. The removal of the Stalinist terror apparatus made dissent possible once more.

Changes in the role of the secret police were part of a larger rearrangement of the balance of power within the Soviet political system. They led to a new balance of power similar to that of the 1920s, when the party apparatus had dominated the political system. At first, Stalin's successors proclaimed the principle of 'collective leadership'. The decree announcing Beria's arrest, declared that:

> The strength of our leadership is in its collective nature, its unity and monolithic character. Collective leadership is the supreme principle of leadership in our Party. This principle completely corresponds to Marx's well-known proposition on the harm and impermissibility of the cult of the individual figure ... Only the collective political experience and collective wisdom of the Central Committee, resting on the scientific basis of Marxist-Leninist theory, assures correct leadership of the Party and country, assures firm unity and closeness of ranks of the Party and success in building Communism in our country.[9]

In reality, the notion of 'collective leadership' merely papered over divisions within the Presidium. The removal of Beria left Malenkov and

Khrushchev as the main contenders for leadership. Their rivalry went back at least to the nineteenth Party Congress in 1952, when Malenkov openly criticized Khrushchev's proposals for agricultural reform. Personal differences added piquancy to what was also a struggle between institutions, between the party apparatus and the ministerial system.

The party gained most from Beria's fall. With the decline of the secret police, it became once more the only institution that could, through its powers of party discipline, influence and supervise the work of individuals throughout the political system. This enabled it to recover the dominant position it had held in the 1920s. Indeed, the party's control over individuals throughout the system made it the natural focus of power in the Soviet political system. As a result, power fell to the party as if by a basic law of Soviet political gravity. Though Stalin had suspended this law temporarily from the late 1930s, it reasserted itself naturally after his death.

In September 1953 Khrushchev strengthened his position as head of the party when he became its First Secretary. This made him the head of the party Secretariat. Using the influence this gave him, Khrushchev began to place his own followers in key positions within the party apparatus. By 1956, about one-third of Central Committee members had served under Khrushchev in Ukraine or the Moscow party apparatus. By late 1957, this group included most members of the Central Committee.[10] Nevertheless, the government apparatus appeared dominant for eighteen months after Stalin's death. Until late 1954, government decrees appeared first in the name of the government, and only then in the name of the party.[11]

Malenkov's dominance lasted until late 1954. Then things began to go very wrong. From August 1954, decrees began to appear in the name of the party and then the government. In December 1954, for the first time since the 1920s, the government paper, *Izvestiya*, disagreed with the party newspaper, *Pravda*, over economic policy. Finally, in February 1955, Malenkov resigned as chairman of the Council of Ministers. Malenkov's defeat left Khrushchev the dominant figure within the Presidium.

The defeat of Malenkov did not mean the final victory of Khrushchev or of the party apparatus. On the contrary, Khrushchev's increasing influence forced his opponents into new alliances, similar to those formed against Stalin in the late 1920s. In 1954 Khrushchev gained valuable support within the powerful ministries in charge of heavy industry when he complained that Malenkov's 'New Course' was starving them of funds. In the same year he launched a huge agrarian reform which he used to increase the influence of the party apparatus he now controlled.

By 1953, Khrushchev knew more about the real situation in the Soviet countryside than any other Presidium member. He also understood better than his colleagues the impoverishment and inefficiency of the collective farms. In 1954, he announced a plan to bring into cultivation large areas of 'virgin land' in the steppelands of western Siberia, northern Kazakhstan, and the northern Caucasus. He implemented this vast plan through the party and the *Komsomol*, rather than through the ministry of agriculture. Thousands of enthusiastic young party and *Komsomol* members set off for the virgin lands in 1954 to organize the new campaign. At first, the 'virgin lands' campaign was a huge success. By 1956 as many as 300 000 people had migrated to the state farms established in the new areas, and they had started farming 36 million hectares of steppe land, an area equal to the total cultivated area of Canada. The impact of these reforms on agricultural output appears clearly in the statistics. For the first time in Soviet history, agricultural production advanced well beyond the level reached in 1913. Gradually, the Soviet countryside ceased to be an exploited colony of the Soviet town. Instead, it became a massive recipient of investment resources and subsidies. The early success of the virgin lands programme boosted Khrushchev's prestige and increased the party's control over a crucial sector of the economy.

Khrushchev increased the power of the party even further through economic decentralization. In 1954–5, 11 000 enterprises that had been under central control were transferred to republican governments. Freed from the control of the Moscow ministries, party officials could exercise far more control over their activities. In 1957 Khrushchev decentralized the entire planning system by transferring most planning powers from Moscow to 105 regional economic councils, or '*sovnarkhozy*'. Most industrial ministries, except those producing defence equipment, now vanished. Within the *sovnarkhozy*, the crucial economic decisions came under the control of regional party officials. The most important of these officials were the regional party secretaries who came under the authority of the party Secretariat.

Colleagues on the Presidium watched these moves with apprehension. However, it was Khrushchev's famous 'Secret Speech' of 1956, and the events it triggered, that forced them to act against him.

In June 1955 the government announced that the party's twentieth Congress would meet on 14 February 1956. This would be the first congress since Stalin's death. It provided a chance for the new leadership to explain the policies it had adopted since the death of their old leader, and to clarify their attitude to the Stalinist period. This was clearly a sensitive issue. Though most members of the Presidium supported the dismantling of the Stalinist apparatus of terror, many had taken part in the purges themselves, and were reluctant to probe too deeply into the past. However Khrushchev argued that the leadership could no longer ignore the findings of the commissions set up to investigate police terror.

They had to clear the air at the congress. His colleagues, most of whom had been closer to Stalin than Khrushchev, were naturally uneasy about this. As a result, when the congress met, the Presidium had still not decided whether or not to debate Stalin's rule. Khrushchev secured his colleagues' reluctant consent to raise the issue only after threatening to speak out as a private delegate. They demanded only that he deliver his speech on Stalin at a secret session and that he take no questions from the floor.

In preparing his speech, Khrushchev used material assembled by a special commission of the Central Committee to investigate abuses committed under Stalin, which was headed by a historian and member of the Party secretariat, P. N. Pospelov. Khrushchev delivered his speech early in the morning of 25 February. To congress delegates, who had lived in Stalin's shadow for most of their careers, the speech was a bombshell. Its attack on Stalin destroyed the faith of many in the infallibility of the party and its leadership.[12]

Khrushchev attacked in particular the changes that had taken place after the seventeenth Party Congress in 1934. Above all, he criticized Stalin's elevation above the party and his ruthless purging of the party elite. Khrushchev used the catchphrase 'cult of the personality' to describe Stalin's arbitrary abuse of power and the exaggerated adulation paid to him. The speech hinted at Stalin's involvement in Kirov's murder, and described the brutal and arbitrary methods used to extract confessions. Khrushchev revealed Lenin's criticisms of Stalin in the last years of his life. He criticised Stalin's handling of the war and his disastrous decision to purge the military elite, claiming that these and other blunders had cost millions of unnecessary casualties during the first months of the war. He lampooned Stalin's ignorance of the country's real problems, particularly in agriculture. Finally, he attacked the mass deportations of whole nationalities from their homelands after the war.

What Khrushchev did not say reveals as much as what he said. He did not criticize Stalin's leadership before 1934. He did not mention the casualties of collectivization or the collectivization famines, or the early show trials between 1928 and 1931. On the contrary, he praised collectivization, the first Five-Year Plans, and the overthrow of the various oppositions as crucial stages in the building of socialism. Equally important, the speech gave no idea of the real extent of the purges, because it largely ignored the non-party victims who made up most of the casualties.

The speech defined the government's attitude to the Stalinist past in three distinctive ways. First, it defined those aspects of the Soviet past that Khrushchev regarded as legitimate elements of the system. These were: collectivization; rapid industrialization concentrating on heavy industry; a centralized command economy; strong leadership through a single party; and the elimination of factions. In short, Khrushchev declared the political, economic and social system that existed until 1934 to be sound, legitimate and normal. This remained the official verdict on the Stalinist period until the late 1980s.

Second, the speech criticized those aspects of the Stalinist system that most affected the Soviet ruling group, of which Khrushchev and most congress delegates were members. It attacked excessively autocratic leadership, the eclipse of the party, and the brutal suppression of party members. It also criticised Stalin's mishandling of the war. However, it largely ignored those aspects of the Stalinist years that most affected the ordinary population. He made less of Stalin's sacrifice of agriculture and the collective farmers, the decline and stagnation in living standards, or the purging of ordinary Soviet citizens. In spite of its radical implications, the speech represented a view from above. As Khrushchev put it (perhaps unwittingly) in 1962: 'We condemn Stalin because he drew his sword and wielded it against his own class, against his own Party'.[13]

Finally, the speech tried to distance the new leadership from the mistakes of the Stalin era. The phrase 'cult of personality' provided a convenient way of blaming Stalin for the horrors of the 1930s and 1940s while absolving most party members.

The impact of the speech was greater than Khrushchev had intended because it was leaked very rapidly and published abroad. For many outside the Soviet elite, his speech undermined the legitimacy of the last twenty years of Soviet rule. In Poland, and even more seriously in Hungary, it provoked rebellion against unpopular Stalinist governments. Outside the Communist bloc, many foreign Communists left the party in disgust at the revelations about the Stalinist era. In contrast, the Chinese leadership, which retained its admiration for Stalin, found Khrushchev's attack unforgivable. The Secret Speech marked the beginnings of divisions that led to a permanent rift between the two communist superpowers.

By the middle of 1957 Khrushchev's colleagues on the Presidium had had enough of his erratic style of leadership, and they voted him out of the Presidium. This time, however, the Presidium found it could not act alone. Khrushchev's supporters included the heads of both the army (Zhukov) and the KGB (Serov), so it was impossible to arrest him. Khrushchev appealed from the Presidium to the Central Committee, the body responsible in law for appointing and dismissing Presidium members. News of the confrontation leaked out. Central Committee members began arriving in Moscow, often with the help of the army, which flew many in from remote provinces. A delegation of Central Committee members, including Serov, demanded the right to take part in discussions about the leadership.

It has become known to us, members of the Central Committee, that the Presidium of the Central Committee is in continuous session. We have also learned that you are discussing the question of the leadership of the Central Committee and of its Secretariat. Matters of such great importance to the whole Party cannot be kept from members of the Central Committee plenum. We members of the Central Committee cannot remain indifferent to the question of the leadership of our Party.[14]

Serov, who controlled the Kremlin guard as head of the KGB, arranged for a delegation of Central Committee members to enter the Kremlin building in which the Presidium was meeting. When abused by Voroshilov, Serov grabbed him by the collar and threatened to call a meeting of the Central Committee with or without the permission of the Presidium.[15] Reluctantly, the Presidium agreed to a meeting and the Central Committee, now dominated by Khrushchev supporters, reversed the Presidium's original decision. It chose a new Presidium, dominated by Khrushchev allies such as L. I. Brezhnev.

Would there be a new purge? In a chilling reminder of what could have happened, one of Stalin's toughest 'enforcers', Lazar Kaganovich, phoned Khrushchev two days after the Central Committee meeting. 'Comrade Khrushchev, I have known you for many years. I beg you not to allow them to deal with me as they dealt with people under Stalin.'[16] Instead of executing them, the Central Committee demoted Khruschchev's opponents to minor government posts. Molotov became ambassador to Mongolia, and Malenkov the director of an electric power station. Members of the so-called 'anti-party' group suffered no further penalties until the twenty-second Party Congress in 1961, when they were expelled from the party.

By 1957 Khrushchev was first among equals. He was stronger than any of his colleagues and had more power to initiate policy. Now, like Stalin in the 1930s, he began to act as if he no longer needed the party that had brought him to power. In 1958, he became chairman of the Council of Ministers. This may have tempted him to rely less on the party apparatus, and to seek other bases for his power in the ministerial system or in the population at large. He sacked his ally Zhukov as minister of defence late in 1957 and began to dismiss his own supporters within the Presidium. By 1961, only six out of the thirteen supporters he had promoted to the Presidium were still there.[17] At lower levels, he began to remove regional party secretaries he had promoted in the early 1950s. After 1957, he began to take decisions without full consultation even in the Presidium. He also allowed the emergence of a minor cult of personality of his own.

The pace of destalinization particularly worried the Party's more conservative wing. At the twenty-second Party Congress, in 1961,

Khrushchev launched a new attack on Stalin without warning his colleagues. After Khrushchev's speech, the congress voted to remove Stalin's remains from the mausoleum on Red Square. Many towns and enterprises named after Stalin now changed their names. They included Stalingrad, which was known as Tsaritsyn before 1926, and now became Volgograd. There are signs that Khrushchev wanted to go further and rehabilitate some of the opposition leaders of the 1920s, such as Bukharin and Kamenev.[18] He also considered abolishing internal censorship.

Closer to home, his ill-thought-out administrative reforms threatened the power and privilege of party bosses. In 1962, against party resistance, he split the party at all levels into rural and urban sections. This halved the influence of regional and district party secretaries. In the same year, he introduced new party rules designed to limit the number of terms party officials could serve in public positions. If carried through, this reform would have destroyed the stranglehold on political power of the party apparatus.

It began to look as if Khrushchev wanted to increase popular participation in the formulation and execution of policy at the expense of the party elite. He encouraged a rapid increase in the size of the party from 7 million in 1956 to 11 million in 1964 (from 3.6 to 4.8 per cent of the population). This increased the proportion of working-class members and broadened the party's base in Soviet society, while diluting the power of the apparatus. Khrushchev encouraged popular participation in other areas too by increasing the role of local Soviets; by encouraging non-party members to take part in various forms of supervisory activity; and by inviting non-party members to party congresses.[19] Khrushchev also sought popularity outside the party through his economic policies and through his populist political style. His frequent visits to towns, enterprises and farms made him far more familiar than Stalin had ever been. All of this threatened the Soviet ruling elite.

However, unlike Stalin, Khrushchev failed to escape from the party's control. He was on holiday on the Black Sea when the Presidium decided to remove him. This time it had the full support of the Party Central Committee and the heads of the police and army. The Presidium summoned Khrushchev to an extraordinary session of the Presidium, which voted him out of office. At first he refused to retire, but the following day he agreed. When he returned home that evening, 'he threw his briefcase into a corner and said, "Well, that's it. I'm retired now. Perhaps the most important thing I did was just this – that they were able to get rid of me simply by voting, whereas Stalin would have had them all arrested"'.[20] His son, Sergei, later reported him as saying:

I'm already old and tired ... I've accomplished the most important things. The relations between us, the style of leadership has changed fundamentally. Could anyone have ever dreamed of telling Stalin that he no longer pleased us and should retire? He would have made mince-meat of us. Now everything is different. Fear has disappeared, and a dialogue is carried on among equals. That is my service. I won't fight any longer.[21]

The power struggles of the Khrushchev era reflected profound changes in the Soviet political system and the Soviet leadership. The terroristic, autocratic rule of Stalin had gone. In its place, there had emerged a system similar to that of the mid-1920s. As Khrushchev's removal had shown, the party was once again the dominant political institution. From the mid-1950s until the restoration of a multi-party system in 1990, the party dominated Soviet political life, and the party's first secretary (renamed the general secretary after 1966) became once again the most powerful Soviet politician. Party congresses began to meet regularly, and the party's leading institutions, the Presidium (renamed the Politburo in 1966) and the Central Committee, re-emerged as the central institutions of the political system. The dominance of the party limited the power of the secret police. The party also limited the power of its own leader.

These political changes were symptoms of deeper changes in the mood and structure of the Soviet ruling group. No longer did its members live as if in a beleaguered garrison. By 1964 they were confident enough of their own strength and that of the country they ruled to do without an absolute leader ruling through terror. This marked a significant decline in the discipline and unity of the ruling group. As we would expect, decline in the unity and discipline of the ruling group implied a decline in the fiscal pressure that the ruling group could exert on the rest of the population.

◼ Social, Economic and Ideological Reform

The less coercive government that emerged in the 1950s negotiated what many scholars have described as a new 'social contract' with Soviet society. Of course, there was no formal negotiation. However, as in the 1850s, the government was very sensitive to popular demands, and keen to prevent popular discontent. The unspoken contract negotiated during these years allowed the government to keep its monopoly on political power, to maintain tight controls on travel and the media, and to control economic planning. In return, the government began to raise material living standards, while guaranteeing full employment and an extensive, if low-grade, network of social services. Under this contract, Soviet consumers began to reap the benefits of their immense efforts during the industrialization drive.

After the panic concessions that followed Stalin's death, there came a series of more considered concessions as part of Malenkov's 'New Course'. However, Khrushchev soon stole Malenkov's policies. In September, Khrushchev announced large concessions to collective farmers. In 1954, he launched the virgin lands programme. This achieved great success in its early years and did much to improve Soviet diets. However, in its haste to mobilize resources the government made serious blunders. Agronomists had warned that the land to be farmed under the virgin lands scheme was fragile. Most lay on the edge of arid semi-desert. It needed irrigation and careful maintenance if it was to retain its fertility. However, under central government pressure, local officials competed to fulfil and overfulfil their plan targets to show quick results. Good harvests in the mid-1950s led to a sharp rise in the total grain harvest, from 82.5 million tons in 1953 to 125.0 million tons in 1956, to 134.7 million tons in 1958.[22] Then harvests began to stagnate. In the early 1960s wind storms destroyed 10 million acres in Kazakhstan and damaged 29 million more. Altogether these ruined half of the virgin lands.[23] The 1965 harvest was below that for 1956. In 1964, the Soviet Union purchased grain abroad. After that, the Soviet Union, a traditional exporter of grain, became a regular importer. Although agricultural output had risen and Soviet diets had undoubtedly improved, Khrushchev's methods of reform stored-up problems for the future.

Khrushchev also undertook other reforms that raised living standards above the level of 1928 for the first time. Statistics on the value of goods consumed by Soviet households tell a clear story. Living standards had declined sharply in the early 1930s. They returned roughly to the 1928 level by 1937, but fell sharply again during the war. By Stalin's death, they had recovered to the 1928 level, but this time the recovery continued, with the active encouragement of the new leadership. If the level of consumption in 1928 was 1.00, and the figure for 1950 was only 1.11, the equivalent figure for 1958 was 1.85. (See Table 10.3, column G.) So it was not until the 1950s that the Soviet consumer gained materially from the efforts made during the industrialization drive.

Other reforms included the abolition of tuition fees (introduced by Stalin) for secondary and higher education; improvements in pensions; and a shortening of the working day, combined with an increase in holiday entitlements. Housing was another crucial area in which there was radical change. Under Stalin, the government invested very little in housing, despite the massive increase in the urban population and the wartime destruction of housing. In 1957, Khrushchev launched a vast plan to build cheap, functional apartment buildings. The new buildings were not beautiful. Their construction explains the ugly suburban rings around most towns of the former Soviet Union. Yet Khrushchev's plan greatly improved Soviet family life, for it reduced the severe overcrowding that had been a feature of the Stalinist period. More and more families managed to settle in separate apartments, where they escaped the inconveniences and conflicts of 'communal' or shared apartments.

From 1956 Khrushchev began to reform the wage system, to reduce the extreme inequalities of the 1930s and 1940s. In 1946 the lowest salaries in the highest 10 per cent were 7.24 times as large as the highest salaries of the bottom 10 per cent. In 1963 the equivalent figure was only 3.35, and by 1968 it had declined to 2.83.[24] The changes affected collective farmers most of all, for they had been the most exploited section of the working population. Most of these changes reflected a raising of the lowest wages. However, they also reflected a slight decline in the embarrassingly generous wages and perks of the ruling group. For example, in 1957, the government abolished the secret supplementary pay packets that most state and party officials had received since the 1930s. However, the *nomenklatura* retained many privileges even in post-Stalinist Soviet society.

The 1950s saw a drastic reduction in the fiscal pressure on the population at large. This was a momentous turning point in Soviet history. If 1945 marked the arrival of the Soviet Union as a modern military power, the 1950s marked the arrival of the Soviet Union's civilian population as modern, urban consumers. An important symbolic measure of the change is the urbanization of Soviet society. From the early 1960s, for the first time, more than 50 per cent of the Soviet population lived in towns (see Figure 2.2).

Relaxation within the elite encouraged some to push the reforms further. There is, indeed, a striking parallel between the growth of liberalism and radicalism in nineteenth-century Russia, and the growth of dissidence in the Soviet Union since 1953. Both processes reflect the easing of discipline within an exceptionally cohesive ruling elite.

The Stalinist government's control of censorship provided a powerful device for hiding all public signs of conflict. It prevented public criticism of the government even through the traditional Russian vehicle of literature and literary criticism. With Stalin gone, there was immediate pressure to increase intellectual and artistic freedom. The Secret Speech set an example of criticism and gave impetus to this movement. In the early 1960s, Khrushchev gave the movement for liberalization further support in the second round of destalinization, begun at the twenty-second Party Congress. He personally gave permission for the publication of Solzhenitsyn's novel on the once taboo subject of life in a Stalinist labour camp, *One Day in the Life of Ivan Denisovich*. As we have seen, Khrushchev even contemplated abolishing censorship altogether.[25]

By the mid-1960s, the freedom available to artists, historians and social scientists, even in sensitive areas such as economics and sociology, had increased considerably. Nevertheless, limits remained. The government tolerated no public criticism of the bases of the socialist system. It set limits even to criticisms of Stalin. It also limited other artistic freedoms in defence of the stuffy moral and artistic ideas typical of the Stalin generation of politicians. The sculptor, Ernst Neizvestnyi, who was to carve Khrushchev's own tombstone at Khrushchev's request, describes a famous incident at an art exhibition held in 1962. It displays well Khrushchev's blunt but homely manner and the primitive cultural attitudes of politicians of his generation.

> *Document 13.3: Khrushchev and abstract art – the Manezh exhibition, 1962*

[Khrushchev] began his inspection in the room in which paintings by Bilyutin and some other friends of mine had been hung. He swore horribly and became extremely angry about them. It was there that he said that 'a donkey could do better with its tail' and remarked of Zheltovsky that he was a good-looking man but drew monsters. And it was there that I had my big clash with Khrushchev, the prelude to our subsequent conversation. It happened like this. Khrushchev asked, 'Who's the most important one here?' Ilyichev replied, 'This one,' pointing at me. I was motioned to come forward and stand in front of Khrushchev. He started shouting at me ... I said that I would only talk about my own work and turned away to go into the room where my work was on display, not imagining that Khrushchev would follow me. But follow me he did, and so did the whole of his entourage and the rest of the crowd.

That was when the fun and games began. Khrushchev said that I devoured the people's money and produced shit. I told him that he knew nothing about art. Our conversation was a lengthy one, but essentially it boiled down to this. I made it clear to him that he had been duped, as he was neither an artist nor a critic and was illiterate when it came to aesthetics. (I don't remember the actual words, but that was the gist of what I said.) He denied this. On what did he base his claim to expertise? I asked. He said: 'When I was a miner, I didn't understand. When I was a junior Party official, I didn't understand. At every level on my way up the ladder, I didn't understand. Today I am premier and leader of the Party: surely I'm able to understand things now, aren't I? Who do you work for?'

... My talk with Khrushchev ended like this. He said, 'You're an interesting man – I enjoy people like you – but inside you there are an angel and a devil. If the devil wins, we'll crush you. If the angel wins, we'll do all we can to help you.' And he gave me his hand.[26]

The party's decision to divert resources away from heavy industries and armaments producers after Stalin's death changed the workings of the command economy. Where there was a clear group of priority sectors, the crude command methods of the 1930s worked adequately. Choices about the allocation of resources solved themselves easily enough; if in doubt, spare resources went to heavy industry or defence. The changes of the 1950s complicated the planning problem by creating conflicts over resources between several different sectors. The government began to divert resources to consumer goods, to housing, and to agriculture. Khrushchev's reforms also weakened the power of the planning and ministerial system that had dominated the economy under Stalin. All this called for reforms of the command economy and its planning methods.

There were also deeper problems. Growth under Stalin depended on extravagant use of labour, cash and raw materials. However, everyone understood that though the Soviet Union enjoyed large reserves of these inputs such extravagant use could not continue forever. Eventually, levels of productivity would have to rise as well. In short, the Soviet economy had to make the change from extensive growth to intensive growth. By the 1950s labour was becoming a scarce commodity. In the 1930s, the government had tapped huge reserves of labour in the countryside and among women. By the 1950s it had used up these reserves. In addition, the rate of natural increase of the population was declining, and war casualties had further reduced the supply of labour. According to one calculation, the labour hours available between 1956 and 1960 grew at a mere 0.6 per cent per annum, while total GNP grew at 5.7 per cent.[27] In future, increases in available labour would have to come from increased productivity.

Shortages of other inputs were less acute in the 1950s. This meant that Khrushchev could persist with extensive methods. The virgin lands programme raised agricultural output by increasing the amount of land farmed. As oil production declined in the Caucasus, the government opened new oil fields in the Urals/Volga region. However, these were all short-term solutions. It was extremely worrying that the system was still using capital extravagantly. Western calculations suggest that output for every unit of capital invested declined in the 1950s at a rate of −2.7 to −3.6 per cent per annum.[28]

However Khrushchev, when faced with shortages, fell back naturally on the traditional Soviet ways of raising productivity: pressure and the technological fix. Both offered only short-term solutions. Sometimes they did not even offer that. In 1959, Ryazan *oblast* achieved such spectacular increases in livestock deliveries that Khrushchev held up their achievements as a model for other regions. Only later did it emerge that the local party secretary had forced local authorities to raise deliveries of livestock at any price. As a result, many collective farmers had slaughtered breeding stock and milk cows, which decimated livestock herds in the province. When the true story emerged, the regional party secretary committed suicide.

This showed the dangers of such campaigns. Yet they littered Khrushchev's career. In the mid-1950s, Khrushchev decided that maize was a miracle crop. Accordingly, he demanded that it be planted even in regions in which it could not possibly thrive. In the same period, he fell in love with systems of crop rotation that reduced fallow. He campaigned hard for the idea, without paying enough attention to local conditions and without ensuring that farmers who tried such rotations had adequate fertilizer and pesticides. The amount of land under fallow fell sharply, even in marginal regions such as the virgin lands. By the early 1960s, declining yields and increased erosion showed how mistaken this policy had been. Apart from their immediate effects, such campaigns disrupted the normal workings of enterprises and farms throughout the country.

The most spectacular example of such campaigns was the *sovnarkhoz* reform of 1957. Khrushchev saw, as did others, that decentralization might solve many problems. Much of the inefficiency of the economy reflected the sheer distance between the ministries in Moscow and the enterprises whose activities they planned in the provinces. By the mid-1950s, there were more than 200 000 industrial enterprises, and at least another 100 000 construction projects and it was impossible to plan everything they did from Moscow. Besides, each central ministry ran its own economic empire. 'A steamer belonging to one ministry would proceed up the river Lena full and return empty, while another steamer, transporting goods for a different ministry, went down-river full and up-river empty.'[29] Khrushchev argued that it made more sense to plan at a regional level.

However, the introduction of *sovnarkhozy* simply introduced new forms of inefficiency. Local planning authorities favoured their own enterprises at the expense of those in another region. Enterprises came under pressure not to deal with enterprises just over the border, but with enterprises in their own region. This cut well-established links. Even if Gosplan told it to produce a component for use in another region, what interest could a local *sovnarkhoz* have in fulfilling such a plan? Local plans were far more important.

As the weaknesses of the reform became clear, Khrushchev backed off. This made matters worse. The government transferred more and more power away from the *sovnarkhozy* and back to Moscow or to republican governments. Enterprises now found themselves serving several masters whose instructions often conflicted with each other. In 1963, the government merged many *sovnarkhozy* to form a total of forty-seven larger *sovnarkhozy*. Organizational chaos and a decline in agricultural output led to a general slowdown in growth. Khrushchev's successors abandoned the entire experiment with *sovnarkhozy* in 1965, a year after his fall.

Any genuine increase in productivity levels clearly demanded more than government pressure, and more than a few technological fixes. It required a reform in the workings of the entire command economy. But how? The theoretical aspects of the problem came onto the agenda for public debate in the 1950s. Under Khrushchev, economics revived as a serious discipline. Indeed, many of the reform ideas tried out over the next thirty years first emerged in discussions in the Khrushchev era.

In 1962, E. Liberman published a classic article on 'The plan, profits and bonuses'. This set the agenda for further reform. It argued that decentralization should extend to the individual enterprise. Planners should grant enterprises more autonomy in the way they used funds, but force them to live within their budgets. No longer could they treat capital as a 'free' good. Such ideas treated the Soviet enterprise almost like a traditional capitalist firm. Liberman argued that plans should set targets for profits rather than for output of specific goods. By doing so, they would solve two key problems. They would force enterprises to economise on resources. They would also encourage them to innovate, to introduce more efficient equipment and work methods.

Ideas such as these had little direct impact in the Khrushchev era. There was a first, crude approach to them with the introduction of cost reduction as a plan target for the first time in 1959. This required that enterprises achieve certain targets for cost-saving. However, as one of many plan indicators that often conflicted with each other, this could have little impact. In the context of the command economy, such measures simply encouraged enterprises to cut corners, which led to poorer quality. The problem of serious economic reform remained on the agenda for Khrushchev's successors.

▌ Foreign Affairs: The Soviet Union as a Superpower

The Great Patriotic War had shown that the Soviet Union could defend itself against a major European power. It had become a world power. Its main concern now was to defend its position, rather than to export revolution. The final year of the war was the main exception to this rule, the one period when expansion was possible, even unavoidable. With that exception, the Soviet Union usually had more to lose than to gain from a revolutionary or expansionist foreign policy. Stability abroad was the precondition for reform at home.

In the early 1950s, the concessions made internally had their counterpart in foreign policy. The new leadership abandoned an important part of the rhetoric of world revolution when Malenkov, and then Khrushchev, argued that nuclear weapons were so dangerous that future wars could benefit neither capitalism nor socialism. There was no alternative but for the two world systems to compete peacefully. The Soviet government envisaged peaceful co-existence as a policy of mutual tolerance in which different social systems would try to prove their superiority by improving the living conditions of their citizens. This implied that the future of socialism would depend more on the successes of the Soviet economy than those of its army.

A peaceful international climate was attractive to Soviet leaders for two main reasons. First, they had more direct experience of the real costs of war than their American counterparts. Second, the new social contract negotiated by the post-Stalin government meant devoting more resources to consumption and limiting the military budget. An aggressive foreign policy was hard to square with the need to satisfy growing consumer demand.

The twentieth Party Congress formally adopted the policy of peaceful co-existence. The government accompanied its change of heart with practical gestures. It signed an armistice in Korea. It tried to heal the breach with Yugoslavia. And it established closer ties with the West through the first visits of Soviet leaders to the West. In 1956, Khrushchev and Bulganin visited Britain, and in 1959, Khrushchev visited the United States.

The Soviet government even began to reduce the size of its defence establishment. As part of his 'New Course', Malenkov cut the defence budget, and reduced the size of the army. After Malenkov's resignation, Khrushchev briefly reversed these cuts, partly to maintain his alliance with the army and in particular with Marshal Zhukov. However, in the late 1950s he resumed a policy of reducing conventional armaments.

Yet the government still needed a cheap way of maintaining Russia's military strength as a world power. For a time, it seemed as if nuclear weapons might solve the problem. The Soviet Union tested its first atomic bomb in 1949 and its first hydrogen bomb in 1953. The launch of the world's first space satellite in 1957 showed that the Soviet Union now had the missile technology needed to deliver nuclear weapons. These developments raised the chimera of a cheap nuclear defence strategy. In the early 1960s, for the first time in Russian history, it seemed possible to solve the problem of defence without the extravagant expenditure of labour and resources that had always been demanded in the past. The absence of natural defensive boundaries became irrelevant in the age of nuclear missiles, and island powers such as Britain lost the natural defensive advantages they had enjoyed since the Middle Ages.

However, much of this strategy depended on bluff. Though it soon had enough missiles to attack Europe, the Soviet military found it harder to develop weapons that could threaten its major opponent, the USA. Besides, Khrushchev now began to pursue a more aggressive foreign policy. In 1962, the Soviet government suffered a humiliating rebuff when United States president J. F. Kennedy forced it to withdraw nuclear missiles it had tried to install in socialist Cuba. Khrushchev's failure to devise a cheap but flexible security policy may have been even more important than his domestic failures in bringing about his removal from office.[30]

After the foreign policy fiascos of the early 1960s, the Soviet government had to accept what many military leaders had been urging for some time. A build-up of conventional forces had to accompany the expansion of the Soviet Union's nuclear forces. This conclusion had far-reaching consequences. It meant abandoning any hope of maintaining great power status on the cheap. On the contrary, an adequate defence establishment would continue to cost vast amounts in human and material resources. Over the next two decades the burden of the Soviet Union's huge defence establishment worsened the country's economic problems and made it more difficult to maintain the 'social contract' negotiated in the 1950s.

■ A Balance Sheet: 1953 to 1964

What had changed since Stalin's death? A ruling group more confident of its power had deliberately dismantled the more extreme forms of autocratic rule. It had reduced the coercive powers of the secret police and weakened the power of its own leaders. The ruling group could afford these changes because it no longer needed to lean as hard on its population as it had in the Stalin era. It could now allow the Soviet population at large to enjoy many of the material benefits of industrial development. The reduction in tension benefited the entire population. It also reduced the pressure on members of the ruling group. Like the Tsarist ruling group in the eighteenth century, the post-Stalin leadership had begun to unravel a highly autocratic system. So far, they had managed to do this with reasonable success. They remained firmly in control of the government and the economy. And there seemed little doubt that, despite the reduction in central control, they had the political and economic means to sustain the Soviet Union's position as a great power.

However, a perceptive observer might have noticed some worrying signs. First, the economic reforms of the mid-1950s yielded only temporary gains. Improvements in agricultural output depended more on increased inputs of land and cash than on real improvements in agricultural productivity. Second, the Cuban missile crisis had dashed all hopes of reducing the defence budget. Finally, many in Soviet society had lost the profound faith in Socialism that had sustained them under Stalin. These three problems, still minor in the early 1960s, were the seeds of the crisis that was to bring the entire system down thirty years later.

■ Summary

At the end of his life, Stalin's authority was so immense and so personal, that his removal transformed the political situation. The system that emerged under his successors remained extremely centralized, but was less personal and less violent than that of Stalin. With Stalin removed, the party Secretariat reasserted its natural authority within the Soviet political system. Khrushchev, the dominant official within the Secretariat, used this power to win the struggle for succession. The mild treatment he handed out to his rivals after the 'anti-party' plot of 1957 suggested that, while the party would remain highly centralized, it now felt confident enough to dispense with the murderous methods of the purge era. Khrushchev's peaceful removal, in 1964, showed that a party oligarchy had now replaced the personal authority of Stalin.

Uncertain of its power, the immediate post-Stalin leadership began to negotiate a new relationship with the Soviet people. After the removal of Beria, they reduced the power of the secret police, and subordinated the police to the Party Central Committee. They made concessions to collective farmers and to consumers, devoting more resources to consumer goods, and investing more in areas such as housing and agriculture. Soviet living standards began to rise rapidly in the 1950s, and Soviet consumers began, at last, to benefit from the economic achievements of the Stalin era. Militarily, the Soviet Union's successes in rocketry and the manufacture of nuclear weapons sustained its position as a great power, though hopes of maintaining a cheap defence system based on nuclear weapons faded after the Cuban missile crisis of 1962.

The successes of the 1950s, after the harsh years of socialist construction under Stalin, generated a mood of optimism within the Soviet Union, and of corresponding pessimism in the West. For a time it seemed that the Soviet Union might really be building a society that was both more productive and more egalitarian than the capitalist societies of the west. However, in retrospect it is easier to see the long-term weaknesses of the Soviet system.

Committed as it was to raising living standards, and maintaining a huge defensive system, the post-Stalin leadership depended on sustained economic growth. Yet Soviet economists already understood that this would not be easy. They knew that the wasteful methods of the early five-year plans could not be sustained for ever, and began the search for new, and more productive ways of planning economic growth. Under Khrushchev, the government also began to search for new ways of raising productivity. Both economists and government officials understood that reform would require a degree of decentralization. Unfortunately, Khrushchev's initial attempts at reform undermined the workings of the planning system without significantly raising the productivity of Soviet factories, enterprises and farms. At his fall, in 1964, there were still no clear answers to these profound dilemmas.

☐ Further Reading

There is a general survey of the Khrushchev period in Nove, *Stalinism and After*. The economic history of the period is covered in Nove, *An Economic History of the USSR*, and foreign policy is dealt with in Nation, *Black Earth, Red Star*. There are good collections of essays in Cohen (ed.), *The Soviet Union since Stalin*, and McCauley (ed.), *Khrushchev and Khrushchevism*. The political history of the period is reviewed in Hough and Fainsod, *How the Soviet Union is Governed*. Aspects of social change are discussed in Kerblay, *Modern Russian Society*. Khrushchev's memoirs, published as *Khrushchev Remembers*, and the more recent *Khrushchev Remembers: The 'Glasnost' Tapes*, provide a very important primary source for this period. Khrushchev's 'secret speech' of 1956 is available in Matthews, *Soviet Government* and elsewhere. There are good biographies of Khrushchev by the Medvedev brothers, and a more recent biography by W. J. Tompson, *Khrushchev: A Political Life*.

☐ Notes

1. Svetlana Alliluyeva, *Letters to a Friend* (London: Hutchinson, 1967) p. 14.
2. Ibid., pp. 19–20.
3. T. Zaslavskaya, *The Second Socialist Revolution* (Bloomington, Ind.: Indiana University Press, 1990) p. 27.
4. A. Nove, *An Economic History of the USSR*, 3rd edn (Harmondsworth: Penguin, 1992) p. 333. This is the most useful source for the economic changes of this period, and much of the economic information in the rest of this chapter comes from it.
5. S. G. Wheatcroft, 'More light on the scale of Repression and excess Mortality in the Soviet Union in the 1930s', in J. Arch Getty and R. T. Manning (eds), *Stalinist Terror: New Perspectives* (Cambridge University Press, 1993) p. 300.
6. R. Medvedev, *Khrushchev* (Oxford: Basil Blackwell, 1982) p. 64; and R. and Z. Medvedev, *Khrushchev: The Years in Power* (New York and London: Norton, 1978) p. 19.

7. *Khrushchev Remembers*, trans S. Talbot (London: Sphere Books, 1971) pp. 301–3.
8. See Medvedev, *Khrushchev*, p. 83; and R. and Z. Medvedev, *Khrushchev: The Years in Power*, p. 19.
9. M. Matthews, *Soviet Government: A Selection of Official Documents on Internal Policies* (London: Cape, 1974) pp. 180–1.
10. M. McCauley, 'Khrushchev as Leader', in M. McCauley (ed.), *Khrushchev and Khrushchevism* (London: Macmillan, 1987) p. 13.
11. M. McCauley, *The Soviet Union since 1917* (London: Longman, 1981) p. 170.
12. The speech is available in *Khrushchev Remembers*; Dmytryshyn, *USSR*, and elsewhere.
13. Medvedev, *Khrushchev*, p. 212.
14. Cited in Medvedev, *Khrushchev*, p. 118.
15. This scene is described in Medvedev, *Khrushchev*, p. 118.
16. Cited from Khrushchev's memoirs, in Medvedev, *Khrushchev*, p. 119.
17. McCauley, 'Khrushchev as Leader', p. 21.
18. Medvedev, *Khrushchev*, p. 212. Both were rehabilitated at last in June 1988.
19. McCauley, *The Soviet Union*, p. 187.
20. Medvedev, *Khrushchev*, p. 245.
21. Cited by R. C. Nation, *Black Earth, Red Star: A History of Soviet Security Policy, 1917–1991* (Ithaca: Cornell University Press, 1992) p. 242, from a 1988 article in *Ogonek*, 20 (Oct. 1988), p. 27.
22. Nove, *Economic History*, p. 343.
23. M. Feshbach and A. Friendly, *Ecocide in the USSR: Health and Nature under Siege* (New York: Basic Books, 1992) p. 32.
24. D. Lane, *The End of Social Inequality? Class, Status and Power under State Socialism* (London: Allen and Unwin, 1982) p. 57.
25. Medvedev, *Khrushchev*, p. 245.
26. Cited from Medvedev, *Khrushchev*, pp. 217–18.
27. D. A. Dyker, *Restructuring the Soviet Economy* (New York: Routledge, 1992) p. 43.
28. Ibid., p. 43.
29. Nove, *Economic History*, p. 352.
30. Nation, *Black Earth, Red Star*, p. 242.

■ *Chapter 14* ■

Consolidation, Stagnation and Change, 1964 to 1982

Khrushchev's successors promised stability, particularly to the Soviet ruling group. This commitment helps explain the appearance of immobility that the Soviet Union presented to the rest of world in the 1970s and early 1980s. Yet appearances were deceptive. Beneath the surface, changes were taking place over which the leadership had little control. Educational levels rose, while popular susceptibility to propaganda fell. Increasingly, public conformity hid private cynicism. Abroad, technological revolutions in electronics and other fields widened the gulf between Soviet productivity levels and those of the leading capitalist countries. They also increased the burden of defence. Meanwhile, the rate of growth of the Soviet economy slowed.

The post-Khrushchev leadership offered few solutions to these problems. They may not even have understood how serious they were. Like the government of Nicholas I in the early nineteenth century, that of Brezhnev persisted with traditional, autocratic methods of rule, avoiding the many problems for which it had no solutions.

■ The Ruling Group

With Khrushchev gone, the positions of first secretary and chairman of the Council of Ministers were split. Leonid Brezhnev (1906–82) became first secretary of the Central Committee Secretariat. Aleksei Kosygin (1904–80) became chairman of the Council of Ministers. Brezhnev and Kosygin represented a distinctive generation of Soviet politicians and the features of that generation explain much about the politics of the Brezhnev era.

Talk of a distinct 'generation' of politicians is often merely metaphorical. Usually, a steady, gradual turnover blurs the lines between generations. However, in Soviet history the lines between generations of political leaders were drawn unusually sharply, for the catastrophes of revolution, civil war, and the purges destroyed entire cohorts of politicians. The impact of the purges was particularly striking. It removed from the upper levels of government most of the old Bolsheviks, the leaders of the pre-revolutionary party. Most of these had came from the intelligentsia. Those who replaced them were very different. Many came from a very specific group of politicians, the *vydvizhentsy*, whose origins are described in Chapter 11. These were young, working-class communists who had undergone crash training courses in the early 1930s as the government tried to create a new, 'Red' intelligentsia.

In retrospect, the most striking thing about this group of politicians is that they survived. There were smaller purges after the 1930s, but never again did an entire layer of politicians vanish. As a result, many who rose through the system in the purge era stayed there until the 1980s. The experiences of this generation of politicians were to have a profound impact on Soviet society. Its members dominated Soviet politics for almost fifty years. They also set the tone of Soviet official life, shaping official ideologies, official moral and cultural attitudes, and official attitudes to the outside world. Because their experiences were so distinctive, it is possible, with only slight exaggeration, to compile a collective biography of this group of politicians.

There was a clear difference in age between the 'Stalin' generation and the 'Leninist' generation that they replaced. Most members of the Stalin generation were born in the first decade of the twentieth century, while most members of Lenin's generation were born in the 1870s and 1880s. There was also a striking class difference. Most leading politicians of the Leninist generation came from the intelligentsia, but members of the Stalinist generation came from the proletariat or the peasantry. In part, this was a matter of policy. In the 1920s the party deliberately recruited from the proletariat and peasantry. It chose the *vydvizhentsy*, in particular, for their class background. Their working-class background explains their lack of formal education. Few had completed secondary education, and hardly any had tertiary education of any kind before the crash courses of the early 1930s. Some members of the Stalin generation had barely completed primary education.

We can take as an example a member of this generation who never quite rose to the very top: N. S. Patolichev (1908–89). Patolichev was born into a peasant family. His father served in the army and died fighting in the Civil War. Patolichev went to his village school, but did not complete primary education. At the age of sixteen he began to work in a chemical plant, where he undertook an apprenticeship. Here he joined the *Komsomol* and in 1928 he became a member of the party. He took part in the collectivisation drive in 1930. In 1931, as part of the *vydvizhentsvo*, he entered the Mendeleev Chemical-Technological Institute in Moscow.[1]

Tertiary training and the purges opened dazzling opportunities for working-class party members like Patolichev. To seize them, they had to be ready to work hard, to take some risks, to cut some corners, and, most important of all, to obey orders. By 1939 Patolichev, who was still only thirty-one, became the regional party secretary in the important industrial province of Yaroslav. As a regional party secretary, he now belonged to the group of 400 to 500 top politicians who controlled Soviet society. In the late 1940s he entered the Secretariat of the Central Committee. In the early 1950s, he became a candidate member of the Presidium/Politburo. In 1958, he became Soviet minister of foreign trade, and he retained this post until 1985, when Gorbachev assumed office.

The life experiences of this entire generation shaped their psychology and outlook. They entered adulthood and began political activity during the years of revolution and civil war. This was a savage introduction to politics, and it explains their readiness to accept the brutal political methods of Stalinism. It also explains why they naturally experienced politics as conflict rather than as negotiation. Unlike members of the Lenin generation, few from the Stalin generation had travelled abroad or learned foreign languages. Their first experience of international politics was during the Civil War, when foreign troops had invaded Soviet Russia at a time of extreme weakness. The crises of the Civil War also imbued them with a strong sense of national weakness. These early experiences made it natural for them to see themselves as members of a besieged garrison. Their limited education also shaped their approach to Marxism. For them Marxism was a set of instructions for building a better society. Few members of the Stalin generation had much patience for the ideological subtleties of Lenin's generation.

Their experiences in the 1930s also shaped them as politicians. Most took part in collectivization, and then tackled the task of building an industrial economy and a powerful defence establishment from scratch. They learnt the brutal methods of mobilization that characterized the Stalinist industrialization drive. They also learned that these methods worked. During the Great Patriotic War, they turned to the same methods. In the 1950s and 1960s, when faced with the very different problem of economic reform, they did so once again. The success of the industrialization drive, and victory over Nazi Germany, combined with the success of their personal careers ensured that they would think positively of the Stalinist era. Despite the dangers they had faced, for them the Stalin years were a time of national and personal triumph. Though they willingly removed the more extreme features of Stalinism under Khrushchev's leadership in the 1950s, none had any reason to dismantle the entire system. Nor did they have any interest in probing too deeply into the blunders and crimes of collectivization or the purges, for most were deeply implicated in these events.

Finally, despite their lack of education and their working-class origins, they found themselves in control of Soviet cultural life. The heritage of

Russian culture was something many approached with the reverence of those whose childhood experiences left little room for high culture. They treated cultural life with a stuffy combination of reverence and utilitarianism that set the tone of official culture for many decades.

When they rose to the top of the Soviet political system, members of the Stalin generation were still young. The average age of those who entered the Politburo in the late 1930s was forty-three. The average age of newly appointed ministers in this period was only thirty-six.[2] With little further turnover at the very top of Soviet political life, members of the Stalin generation grew old in office. By 1980, the average age of Politburo members was seventy; that of the Secretariat was sixty-seven; while that of the Council of Ministers was sixty-five.[3] When Khrushchev fell from office, most members of this generation were already old. They could no longer provide the dynamic, creative leadership needed by a society very different from that which had shaped them as politicians. This helps explain the most important aspect of policy-making in the Brezhnev years: its immobility. Now, at last, members of the Stalin generation could enjoy in peace the powers and privileges that many doubtless believed they had earned in a lifetime of dangerous and exhausting political service.

Leonid Brezhnev's style of leadership during his period as general secretary (1964–82) set the tone. Unlike Khrushchev, he was a consensus politician. Where Khrushchev had launched political initiatives without preparing his colleagues, Brezhnev took decisions only after careful consultation. For several years, he proved a competent, benign and dull manager of the affairs of the ageing Soviet ruling elite.

Stability at the top encouraged immobilism at lower levels of the ruling group. Despite the loss of some of their privileges under Khrushchev, the *nomenklatura* still enjoyed a distinctive lifestyle. In 1973, when the average monthly wage was 130 roubles, only 227 000 people received more than 500 roubles a month. A party first secretary received about 900 roubles, while directors of large enterprises earned anything from 450 to 600 roubles. A Marshal of the Soviet Union (the highest Soviet military rank), received as much as 2000 roubles.[4] However, in a society in which market forces played a subordinate role, cash incomes were only a partial guide to the distribution of wealth. Most upper-class privileges depended less on high incomes than on better access to scarce goods. These might include better quality housing and medical care, easier travel and holidays, and access to high-quality foreign goods, purchased in special shops. As a character in a Soviet novel, put it: 'Money is rubbish. Power gives the right to everything.'[5]

The elite also saw itself as separate from the rest of Soviet society. It had good reason to resist changes that might undermine its position. Arkady Shevchenko, a high-ranking Soviet diplomat who defected to the United

States in 1978, offers the following description of the *nomenklatura* class, to
which he had also belonged.

☐ *Document 14.1: The* nomenklatura *hierarchy*

Nomenklatura is a caste system that applies only to the elite class. Its many levels
enjoy varying degrees of privilege according to rank. For Politburo members there
is no limit or restriction on privileges. Below this level the grading structure
begins. The Central Committee defines the place of anyone eligible for inclusion
in the various categories: high party *apparatchiki*, Cabinet ministers, diplomats or
individuals with unusual abilities or exceptional talents such as artists, scientists,
Olympic champions and the like. Factory workers, farmers, engineers, lawyers,
doctors, store managers and other private citizens are excluded.

Members of the elite have extensive privileges: high salaries, good apartments,
dachas [privately owned holiday homes], cars with chauffeurs, special railway cars
and accommodation, VIP treatment at airports, resorts and hospitals off limits to
outsiders, special schools for their children, access to stores selling consumer
goods and food at reduced prices. They live far removed from the common man
and, indeed, have to go out of their way if they wish to rub elbows with the less
exalted. The highest group in the *nomenklatura* is separated from most citizens by a
barrier as psychologically imposing as the Great Wall of China. This class
constitutes virtually a state within a state.

Those designated under the system number many thousands. They form the
backbone of the status quo in the governmental and societal structure. They will
permit no one to transform that society or alter its foreign or domestic policy in
any way that may affect their perquisites. It is no small irony to know that this
fossilized elite controls the nation that calls on other countries to renounce
stability for revolution, to give up privilege for the blessings of proletarianism.[6]

Higher living standards shielded the *nomenklatura* elite from the problems
of ordinary Soviet citizens. Their privileges depended more on their
connections than on their productivity or efficiency. The failures of the
economy affected them much less than ordinary citizens and blinded
them to the difficulties faced by those they ruled.

The existence of this group justifies the claim that there existed a ruling
group in Soviet society. However, for all its privileges, this group was not
as privileged or as distinct from the rest of society as the ruling groups of
most capitalist societies. Although privileged parents could pass on some
of their privileges to their children, they had to do so informally,
exploiting connections and friendships. (Soviet colloquial usage referred
to these connections as *blat,* a term originally used by criminals. Under
Stalin, it was sometimes said that '*blat* is more powerful than Stalin'.)
Besides, even including the many non-monetary privileges of the elite,
their average incomes were only five to eight times the average wages in

the 1970s. The equivalent ratio for the United States was at least twelve times.[7] Part of the reason for this was that the egalitarian traditions of socialist ideology still carried weight in Soviet society. These traditions, reinforced by traditional peasant attitudes, inhibited the conspicuous display of wealth so apparent in capitalist societies.

Social Change, Dissidence and the Loss of Legitimacy

If the experiences of the Stalin generation, and the privileges of the *nomenklatura* explain the immobility of government policy in this era, the changes that occurred at lower levels of Soviet society explain why immobility was so inappropriate a governmental strategy. Soviet society changed greatly in the post-Stalin era, becoming more urbanized and better educated. By the 1970s, the Brezhnev generation was presiding over a society very different from the ill-educated society of peasants they had ruled in the 1930s.

When members of the Stalin generation first rose to power, they ruled a peasant country in a period of chaotic change. In the early 1920s, no more than 16 per cent of the Soviet population lived in cities.[8] The cities themselves, particularly the smaller ones or the outer suburbs of the larger ones, often looked like overgrown villages, and most of those who worked in them came from the countryside. Even in the 1960s, the childhood memories of most Soviet citizens were of the countryside, the village, and the peasant household.

In the 1930s, the urban population doubled from 26 million to 56 million.[9] Most of the newcomers were peasants. As a result, rapid urbanization led to a ruralization of Soviet cities. The disorientation so many experienced in the 1930s was, in part, the disorientation of peasants uprooted from the familiar world of the village. At Stalin's death, Soviet society was still, culturally speaking, a society of peasants, ruled by a thin layer of city-dwellers. In their attitudes and outlook, even most urban-dwellers still thought and behaved as peasants. Though they now worked in factories, most still engaged mainly in physical work. Even in 1959, 80 per cent of Soviet workers engaged in manual labour, either in the towns or on farms.

In the 1950s and 1960s new waves of migrants entered the towns. The urban population rose from 49 per cent of the Soviet population in 1959, to 65 per cent in 1972, and 70 per cent by 1985.[10] Between 1959 and 1980, the number of cities with over 100 000 inhabitants grew from 123 to 251.[11] By the 1970s, the Soviet Union was a country of cities and urban-dwellers.

It was also a country in which more and more people engaged in brain work. By the mid-1980s, brain workers and officials (described in Soviet literature as the 'intelligentsia') made up almost 40 per cent of the urban work force. Manual workers made up almost 60 per cent of the total work force, while collective farmers accounted for no more than 5 per cent.[12]

Education played a major role in changing the nature and outlook of the Soviet population. While levels of illiteracy fell sharply in the Stalin years, educational levels remained low. Even in 1959, 91 per cent of urban workers and 98 per cent of collective farm peasants had no secondary schooling. This meant they had completed no more than four years of primary schooling. By 1984 only 19 per cent of manual workers had no secondary education.[13] These figures reflect a quiet, but profound, cultural revolution in Soviet society. While the peasant manners and outlook of a Khrushchev or a Brezhnev continued to dominate at the top of the system, below them there emerged a sophisticated and highly educated modern society. By the 1970s and 1980s, the Stalin generation had less and less to offer a modern, highly urbanized and highly educated society.

The results of this mismatch between the Soviet government and its changing populations appeared most clearly in the realm of ideology. In the 1930s, the highly simplified Stalinist version of Marxism offered an intellectual handhold to peasants and workers caught up in the whirlwind of industrialization and then of war. Its very simplicity had the power to inspire. So did its incantational quality, and its growing nationalism, particularly during the war. But as educational levels rose, the appeal of so simplistic a set of ideas faded. For scientists, engineers, economists and journalists faced with the increasingly complex society of the 1970s, the old Stalinist formulae meant less and less. University students found compulsory courses in dialectical materialism tedious and insulting. Meanwhile, the partial relaxation of censorship under Khrushchev appeared to promise greater intellectual freedom to the growing numbers of the Soviet intelligentsia.

Under Khrushchev's successors, the ideological thaw came to an abrupt halt. Afraid of undermining their own legitimacy by criticism of the Stalin years, Khrushchev's successors adopted a more positive attitude to Stalin. In 1965 the government arrested and tried two writers, Yulii Daniel and Andrei Sinyavsky, for publishing abroad articles critical of the Soviet Union. Early in 1966, courts condemned them to terms of five to seven years in labour camps. In 1967 the government insisted on the dismissal of A. M. Nekrich, a military historian who published a book critical of Stalin's handling of the war. Censors withdrew his book, *22 June 1941*, from circulation. With the help of the KGB, the government began to clamp down on dissident members of the intelligentsia.

Dissidents responded with *samizdat* or 'self-publishing'. Readers of dissident works made extra copies before passing them on to others, so that copies multiplied like chain letters. The other option was *tamizdat* or publication abroad. A *samizdat* journal, the *Chronicle of Current Events*, began to appear in 1968 and survived despite KGB harassment until 1982. Also in 1968, the nuclear physicist Andrei Sakharov (1921–89) published his manifesto, *Reflections on Progress, Coexistence and Intellectual Freedom*. Though it gained much coverage in the Western press, the conflict that began between government and intellectuals had little resonance beyond the government and the more highly educated sectors of Soviet society. In the same year, the government prosecuted Alexander Ginzburg and Iurii Galanskov for illegally publishing material on the Daniel and Sinyavsky trial. Just over 700 people signed public protests against this trial. Of these, 50 per cent were academics or students. Another 22 per cent were engaged in the arts, 13 per cent were engineers and technicians, and 9 per cent were doctors, lawyers, teachers, journalists or employees of publishing houses. Only 6 per cent were workers.[14]

Despite the isolation of the intelligentsia, their prolonged battle with censorship marked a profound change in Soviet cultural life. In the 1930s and 1940s, official ideology had mobilized the support of much of the emerging Soviet intelligentsia. By the 1970s, it could not longer do so. Increasing numbers of educated Russians began to treat official propaganda with disdain. Even those who did not engage directly in dissident activity became cynical about the promises and achievements of the Soviet government. Increasingly, members of the intelligentsia lived double lives. Outwardly conformist, inwardly they despised rulers whose competence and education no longer matched that of the society they ruled. By the late 1970s, there had reappeared the sort of gulf between government and educated society that had so weakened tsarist governments in the early twentieth century.

After the appointment of Yu. V. Andropov (1911–84) as head of the KGB in 1967, the secret police conducted the struggle against dissident opinion with efficiency and skill. With little popular support, dissident attempts to organize, though heroic, could not succeed for long. By the early 1980s, it seemed that the KGB had won the battle. In retrospect, Andropov's was a hollow victory. He had merely driven dissident opinion underground. The powerful machinery of persuasion that the Soviet government had controlled for so long seemed to be losing its potency. As Andropov crushed the dissident movement, the liberal, critical and reformist views they had defended spread amongst the educated. One of the greatest shocks of the early Gorbachev years was the discovery that dissident opinion had become the orthodoxy even within the *nomenklatura*. Many of Gorbachev's early pronouncements said officially what dissidents had been saying, at the risk of imprisonment and exile, since the 1960s.

The disillusionment of the intelligentsia was one expression of a wider demoralization in Soviet society at large. There were practical reasons for popular disillusionment in the Brezhnev years. The post-Stalin government had struck a new social contract with the Soviet population. The expectation of rising standards combined with secure employment and a cheap and extensive welfare network was part of the deal. To keep some popularity the government had to hold to its side of the bargain.

There is no doubt that it tried hard to do so, sometimes at great cost. Low agricultural productivity meant that in the 1970s it could maintain supplies of meat only by importing grain for cattle feed. Combined with increasing subsidies to other areas of agriculture, this meant that agriculture, instead of being a source of investment funds, became a drain on the budget. Keeping prices of basic consumer goods low was also costly. Subsidies on the retail price of transportation, of books, on rents and domestic electricity, consumed a growing portion of the state budget.

However, Soviet consumers got poor value from this massive and growing expenditure. After the sharp improvements in living standards in the 1950s and 1960s, improvements in living standards began to slow down. Prices stayed low in the state sector, but free market prices for collective farm produce and black market goods rose steadily. Even some official prices rose as the government withdrew cheap, low-grade products and substituted more expensive goods supposed to be of higher quality. (In the early 1970s, there appeared a new, and more expensive brand of vodka called EKSTRA. Older, cheaper brands soon vanished from the shops. Consumers discovered that the new brand was in reality of inferior quality. Some claimed that 'EKSTRA' stood for '*Ekh! Kak Sud'ba Tyazhela Russkogo Alkogolika*, or 'Oh, how sad is the fate of the Russian alcoholic!') Official indices showed a 7 per cent rise in the cost of living between the 1950s and the late 1980s. Soviet scholars have since estimated that the real increase was at least 100 per cent.[15]

Levels of consumption continued to rise throughout this period. Consumer durables such as televisions and fridges became common. More and more people lived in separate, rather than communal apartments. However, the rate of growth of consumption fell after the heady rises of the 1950s. Between 1966 and 1970, per caput consumption of all goods and services rose at 5.1 per cent each year. In the early 1970s the rate fell to 2.9 per cent, and by 1981 it had fallen to 1.8 per cent.[16] As productivity fell in agriculture, supplies of food became more erratic from the mid-1970s. This led to periodic shortages of particular foods and the occasional resort to local rationing. So serious was the food situation that one of the last initiatives of Brezhnev's career was a major programme to improve food supplies, launched in 1982.

As important as the slowdown in the improvement of living standards, was the perception of decline. Increasing knowledge of conditions in the industrialized capitalist countries, and increasing contacts with western tourists and western consumer goods, persuaded many Soviet citizens that their living standards lagged well behind those in the west. The experiences of the sociologist, Tatyana Zaslavskaya, are typical, though she encountered the West earlier than most Soviet intellectuals.

My first trip abroad took place at this time – to Sweden in 1957. It made a very great impression indeed on me; before me was another, a different way of life, people with different values, needs, opinions, and different ways of organizing the economy and solving social problems. This experience not only broadened my mental outlook, it threw additional light on our own domestic problems. My own personal impressions shattered the idea I had been given that the life of working people in the West consisted mainly of suffering. We saw that, in fact, the countries of the West had in many instances overtaken us and we had lively discussions about ways of overcoming our own weaknesses.[17]

Attempts to compare Soviet consumption levels with those in other industrialized countries are extremely difficult. For what they are worth, they suggest that even in the late 1970s, average per caput consumption levels in the USSR were no more than one-third the levels for the USA. Comparisons over time suggest that: 'Although the gap between Soviet living standards and those of Western industrial societies narrowed during the 1960s, in the 1970s it began to widen'.[18] The trouble was, in part, that the successes of the 1950s had created rising expectations. As an American observer put it: 'Nothing fails like success: the regime's earlier success, its welcome promise to provide the good life, generated even greater expectations and contributed to the current perception of failure'.[19]

Harder to measure are the continued frustrations of daily life in Soviet society. Shopping remained a nightmare. Shoppers, mainly women, had to spend hours in queues every day to obtain the most basic foodstuffs. The absence or poor quality of labour-saving devices in the home ensured that housework remained exceptionally burdensome. Crowded transportation and poor quality crèches made day-care a torment. The following is from an interview with Liza, a twenty-eight-year-old single parent and editor in a publishing house. The interview was recorded in 1978. When asked how she had spent the previous day, she began:

☐ *Document 14.2: A mother's journey to work in Moscow*

I woke at six, pulled my child out of bed, packed a bag full of stuff for the whole week, and then he and I took off for the subway. The two of us were practically knocked down. A woman was sitting and reading and wouldn't give up her seat, even though my son was squashed against the doors. He almost fell on her, and I tightened my grip to keep him from falling and getting hurt. ... It took us fifty minutes to get to the day-care center.

I took him inside and undressed him and then I had to rush off to work. He cried, 'Mama, I don't want to stay here. I want to go home.' I said, 'Emil, sweetheart, please stay in the day-care center now. I'll come and get you soon. I'll pick you up on Friday.' And yesterday was Monday. It was terrible, but I had to hurry off to work.

I left him crying. The teachers took him by the arm and brought him over to the group because I couldn't stay to comfort him. I picked up my things and put my shawl over my head. Outside it was still rush hour. And I was going to the opposite end of Moscow. It was another hour's trip, and I was already late for work.[20]

Soviet society had promised women much. It gave them full legal equality and equal wages. By the end of the Great Patriotic War, as many women were in paid employment as men. This was liberating for some women, but not for all. Without any increase in the willingness of Soviet men to share domestic burdens, full employment simply meant that Soviet women took on a grinding double burden. This ensured that women could not climb as high as men in most professions. Women did most of the manual labour on farms, while men drove tractors and harvesters and sat in directors' offices. Women made up 85 per cent of those employed in medicine, but only 50 per cent of those in leading positions. So, despite formal equality in wages, average women's wages were only 65 per cent those of men in the early 1980s. Perhaps most important of all, women did not control the levers of power. Women accounted for only 27 per cent of party members in the late 1970s, and only 4 per cent of local and regional party secretaries and Central Committee members. Before 1985, only two women served at the very pinnacle of power. Ekaterina Furtseva (1910–74) was the only woman ever appointed to the Presidium. Aleksandra Kollontai was the only woman ever appointed as a Soviet ambassador.[21]

Tatyana Zaslavskaya was one of only five members of the Soviet Academy of Sciences. Yet, despite her success, she paints a bleak portrait of the life of Soviet women. Her account also suggests how little impact western feminism had on women's attitudes in the Soviet Union before the late 1980s.

☐   *Document 14.3: Women's work*

It would seem that the high level of employment of women in social production is socially unjustified. It has had a negative effect both on the birth rate and on the upbringing of children. In the towns, and now sometimes in the villages as well, the one-child family is becoming the prevalent model, which does not even ensure that the population reproduces itself and is damaging to the upbringing of children in a family. Social habits are being lost, together with the custom of sociable work done together and help given by older siblings to the younger ones, which are characteristic of families with several children.

What then is the cause of the very high level of employment of women which forces them to a certain extent to neglect their social and family functions? In the first instance, it is the low wages paid to men, most of whom cannot today maintain a family on their own, even for the few years that the children are growing up. It must be added that non-working women, even those with children, have a low status in the eyes of most people. A woman is regarded as a complete individual, not inferior in any way to a man, and therefore obliged to have a profession and to work. Of course, women themselves have developed the need to work and to have social contacts at work, and to belong to a particular group of workers. ... [Yet] Sociological research has shown that, given the choice, up to 40 per cent of women would give up full-time employment and would prefer to work part-time. To make this possible, however, men's wages must be raised.[22]

One of the most worrying signs of changing living standards was the deterioration in general levels of health. In the late 1970s, researchers in the West began to realise that many indicators of public health that had improved steadily throughout Soviet history, had begun to deteriorate. Between 1950 and 1971, deaths during the first year of life had fallen from 80.7 per thousand to 22.9 per thousand. Then they started to rise once again. By 1987 they had risen to 25.4 per thousand, though real rates may have been higher.[23] The Soviet Union appears to be the only industrialized country in which there has been such a sharp reversal in rates of infant mortality. At the same time life expectancy for Soviet males dropped from 66.1 years to 62.3 between 1960 and 1980, while the equivalent figures for the USA were, respectively, 66.8 and 70.4.[24] Among adults of working age, death rates rose by 20 per cent between 1970 and 1989, from 399 per thousand to 480.[25]

To some extent these changes reflect better reporting of mortality. However, there can be little doubt that, particularly in the late 1970s, there was a real decline in health standards. Many factors account for this shocking change. It reflected the poor training of doctors, inadequate medical equipment and drugs, pervasive alcoholism, poor diets, poor sanitation and high levels of pollution in many towns and regions of the Soviet Union. Alcoholism was a particularly serious problem. This was hardly surprising, for the Soviet government, like the tsarist government before it, continued to raise huge revenues from alcohol sales. In 1980, alcoholic drinks accounted for 22 per cent of the total value of all consumer goods produced.[26]

By the 1980s, Soviet citizens had good reason to feel that the government was not keeping its side of the social contract negotiated in the 1950s. This added to the cynicism and demoralisation caused by the government's oppressive handling of ideological matters. By the early 1980s, the Soviet system could no longer count on the support of most of its citizens. The patriotic, optimistic tone of life in the 1950s had given way to a pervasive sense of despair. The government's loss of legitimacy meant that, like the tsarist government in the early twentieth century, its power rested, increasingly, on the bureaucracy and the police. The social contract of the 1950s no longer sustained it.

 # Economic Stagnation and the Problem of Economic Reform

The clearest sign that the Soviet government was not coping with its many economic problems, was a slowdown in growth rates. Until the late 1950s Soviet growth rates had been impressive. On the basis of these rates, Khrushchev had predicted that the Soviet economy would overtake that of the USA during the next few decades. However, Soviet growth rates began to decline precisely in the late 1950s. Improvements in the efficiency and overall productivity of the economy also slowed. Sluggish improvements in labour productivity were in some ways the most worrying index of all. Had not Lenin himself written that: 'Labour productivity is, in the last analysis, the main, the most important factor for the victory of the new social system'?[27]

It is possible that the figures in Table 14.1 flatter Soviet economic performance. In 1987, two Soviet economists, V. Selyunin and G. Khanin, calculated that national income per head of population actually fell in the early 1980s.[28] In 1988, Gorbachev admitted that in recent years the appearance of economic growth had been sustained only because of 'trade in oil on the world market at the high prices that were established then, and the totally unjustified increase in the sale of strong drinks. If we look at the economic indicators of growth omitting these factors, we will see that practically over four Five-Year Plan periods [that is, for two decades] there was no increase in the absolute increment of the national income, and it even began declining in the early eighties'.[29]

Meanwhile, the government's room for manoeuvre had diminished. The social contract negotiated in the Khrushchev years required the

Table 14.1   *The slowdown – Soviet economic growth, 1951–85 (average annual rates of growth, official data, %)*

Year	Produced national income	Gross industrial prodn	Gross agricultural prodn	Labour productivity in industry	Real income per head
	A	B	C	D	E
1951–55	11.4	13.2	4.2	8.2	7.3
1956–60	9.2	10.4	6.0	6.5	5.7
1961–65	6.5	8.6	7.2	4.6	3.6
1966–70	7.8	8.05	3.9	6.8	5.9
1971–75	5.7	7.4	2.5	6.8	4.4
1976–80	4.3	4.4	1.7	4.4	3.4
1981–85	3.6	3.7	1.0	3.4	2.1

Source: Table 14.1 and Figure 14.1 based on S. White, *Gorbachev in Power* (Cambridge University Press, 1990) p. 85; figures from *Narodnoe knozyaistvo SSSR 1922–1972 gg.* (Moscow, 1972) 56; and *Narodnoe khozyaistvo SSSR za 70 let* (Moscow, 1987) pp. 58–9.

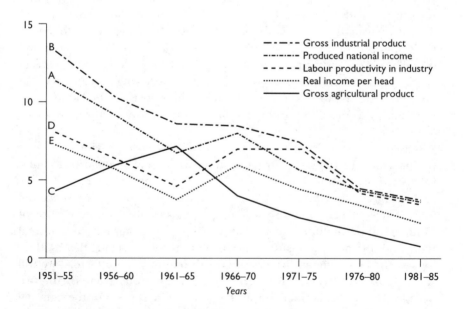

Figure 14.1   *Declining growth rates, 1951–85*
Note: Based on information in Table 14.1

government to spend money not just on heavy industry and defence, but also on consumer goods, housing and agriculture. No longer could the government solve economic problems by diverting resources from consumption into investment. Without a healthy rate of growth, the government would have difficulty maintaining the huge defence establishment that made it a superpower and the rising living standards that allowed it to rule without the extreme coercion of the Stalin years.

In capitalist economies, growth occurred in long waves. During recessions pressure increased on both entrepreneurs and workers to raise productivity. This, in turn, encouraged the innovations that fuelled a new wave of growth. Did equivalent mechanisms exist in the command economy of the Soviet Union? The answer of most economists who explored the problem was that they probably did not. The mechanisms that had generated the rapid growth rates of the 1930s could work only once. Further growth would require new engines of growth. As early as the 1950s, officials and economists realised that this meant moving from extensive growth to intensive growth. How could this be done? Could the structures of the Soviet command economy generate intensive growth as effectively as they had generated extensive growth?

The first step to reform was to allow economists to discuss the problem. In the late 1950s, economics had reappeared as a serious discipline in Soviet Universities and Institutes. The pioneers in these discussions were economists such as Ye. G. Liberman (1897–1983), V. S. Nemchinov (1894–1964), L. V. Kantorovich (1912–86) and V. V. Novozhilov (1892–1970). Kantorovich and Novozhilov had already done pioneering work in the 1930s. However, Stalin's government buried their results, and they were lucky to stay above ground themselves. The emerging signs of an economic slowdown set economists a fundamental theoretical and practical challenge.

They immediately focused on the problem of prices, for it was impossible to improve efficiency without knowing what resources really cost. Where markets did not set prices by balancing supply and demand, bureaucrats had to set them. Yet planning officials in Moscow had no objective way of measuring the real 'value' of anything. This raised the complex theoretical issue of 'value'. Marx had insisted that value reflected the labour used to produce a commodity. Estimating the value of the labour that went into production was hard enough. Yet Marx's theory had another drawback. It encouraged planners and managers to ignore the cost of the capital, raw materials and natural resources also used in production, and to neglect the problem of scarcity. It therefore encouraged the extravagant use of natural resources such as land, water and coal.

This wasteful approach to natural resources helps explain some of the ecological tragedies left behind by the Soviet system. In recent decades, more than 50 per cent of all water use went to irrigation, and cotton was the main user of irrigation.[30] Yet, astonishingly, farms did not pay for the water they used. Naturally, they used water wastefully. In Central Asia, excessive water use for cotton irrigation led to an ecological disaster. Since 1960, excessive drainage of water from the Amu Darya and Syr Darya rivers caused the Aral Sea to shrink by almost 50 per cent. In the same time, its level fell by 47 feet (approximately 14.3 metres), and the amount of water draining into it fell to one-ninth of the 1960 level.[31] Water draining off inefficiently irrigated fields carried into the Aral Sea high levels of salt, and high concentrations of pesticides and fertilizers. The poor quality of drinking water in the lands around the Aral Sea caused an increase in disease. Local doctors claimed that it was a major cause of the increase in local infant mortality rates to double those for the rest of Soviet Union.

Poor pricing policies also made it impossible to take rational decisions about energy use. With no Soviet market in energy, planners set prices that were insensitive to real costs. There were some very sophisticated attempts to calculate true costs, or 'opportunity costs' (that is, the costs of one source of energy in comparison to others). However, even these came up with prices well below world prices. These misleading calculations affected some basic decisions about energy use. Should planners continue to use coal, or should they prefer gas and oil? Should they continue using existing oil wells or should they invest more in exploration for gas and oil in Siberia? Without the guidance provided by objective market prices, planners took these decisions in ways that wasted the country's abundant resources of energy.

> With an industrial output no more than three-quarters the size of the United States in 1975, Soviet industry used almost as much energy as did US industry. In the same year, despite an agricultural output no more than eighty to eighty-five per cent of the US level, Soviet agriculture used appreciably more energy than US agriculture. Soviet automotive equipment has long had fuel efficiency considerably inferior to western equipment even before the rapid rise of energy costs in the 1970s.[32]

For Soviet economists, the task was to find a way of pricing that placed an objective value on labour, raw materials, capital and natural resources. Could they do this without a return to the market? In searching for objective ways of setting prices, Soviet economists had to rediscover, within the terminology of Marxist theory, much of the price theory taken for granted in the economics of the capitalist world.

Arbitrary prices were one symptom of a deeper problem. The command system encouraged waste in many ways. First, it encouraged inefficient use of existing capacity. Planners sent draft plans to enterprises for comment. Enterprises had every reason to negotiate plans downwards, to ease the task of fulfilling plan targets. So managers invariably underestimated what they could produce, and their workers colluded. As a result, managers and workers combined in a chronic 'go-slow'. The problem was that punishments for underfulfilment were severe (under Stalin, it could be treated as a criminal offence), while incentives for raising productivity were weak. In a capitalist economy, the eventual penalty for low productivity was bankruptcy. In the command economy, this threat did not exist, for the government gained nothing from closing down an enterprise in which it had invested effort and cash. So it continued to subsidize thousands of loss-making enterprises. Meanwhile, managers of loss-making enterprises or collective farms understood that if they raised productivity too much, they would lose these subsidies.

The same mechanisms discouraged innovation. The most important sign of success within the command economy was the ability to meet targets and occasionally overfulfil them. (Excessive overfulfilment was dangerous for it might encourage planners to raise plan targets next time.) Anything that disrupted the normal functioning of an enterprise made it difficult to meet planned targets. Yet innovation was certain to interrupt production. Installation of new plant or new production methods meant a temporary break in production. Further breaks to deal with temporary breakdowns were equally certain. For managers, innovation offered few advantages and many dangers. Naturally, they put up fierce resistance to pressure from planners to introduce new equipment or production methods.

Setting targets from above also encouraged the wasteful use of labour. Enterprises had an incentive to underestimate labour productivity, to ensure they always had enough labour on hand to meet planned targets. This encouraged them to hoard labour. So did the fact that the central authorities planned and paid basic wages. This gave managers little incentive to economise on wages. The result was that Soviet enterprises needed workers more than most workers needed employment. Under such conditions, it was impossible to create a disciplined and efficient work force. The system of planned targets also affected workers directly. Workers employed to unload bricks worked to plans that set time limits for each task. So they threw the bricks off the truck and many broke.[33] Like serfdom, the command economy could make people work hard but could not make them work efficiently.

The command system also undermined the entire notion of 'utility' or usefulness. Enterprises produced goods to meet plans, not to satisfy customers. In the North Caucasus in the 1960s construction enterprises laid drainage pipes too close to the surface because their plans were set in metres of pipe laid. As a result, 'backflows occurred, and sometimes too much water was supplied, so that land had subsequently to be drained'.[34] One can give many examples of this type. Trucking companies trying to fulfil plans measured in distances travelled, sent their trucks out empty during the final days of a plan period. Companies producing nails had to meet targets measured by weight. This encouraged them to use weaker alloys that increased the weight of nails, even if the nails broke at the touch of a hammer. In technologies such as electronics, it was even harder to devise plans that encouraged high quality products.

Problems arose not just in implementing plans. The plans themselves were also irrational. The sheer mathematics of the problems planners faced were daunting. They had to calculate all the inputs and outputs of thousands of enterprises producing for 200 million people. In the early 1960s some argued that computerization would solve the problem. It is now clear that the mathematics of such a problem are far beyond the capacity of even the most powerful computers. Yet planners had to make decisions with or without such help. In practice, they got many of their calculations wrong. Enterprises found that the plan had not provided for crucial inputs. Or suppliers produced to the wrong specifications. This, too, was a source of waste.

The failures of planning forced enterprises and consumers to circumvent the plans. Most enterprises used the services of *tolkachi*. These were agents who would get hold of goods enterprises needed to fulfil planned targets, in return for hefty bribes. Strictly, their activities were illegal, but the economy could not have functioned without them. Consumers resorted to black or 'grey' markets of various kinds, often at considerable cost in cash and in time. Here was one more source of waste. Both enterprises and consumers had to spent much of their effort in circumventing the regulations of the command economy. The pervasiveness of illegal economic activities also contributed to the demoralization of Soviet society by encouraging an almost universal disregard for official laws and norms.

In short, the traditional command economy encouraged wasteful use of resources, and the production of useless, or poor quality goods and services. No major economy, however rich in resources, could continue to waste resources at such a rate. The main aim of reform, therefore, was to find ways of making planners, enterprises and workers use resources more economically and more productively. Nemchinov warned, in 1965: 'An economic system so fettered from top to bottom will put a brake on social and technological progress, and will break down, sooner or later, under the pressure of the real processes of economic life'.[35]

Diagnosing the problem was hard enough. The step from diagnosis to remedy was harder. Certain general principles emerged from the economic debates of the 1950s and 1960s. The most important was that the command economy would have to borrow some of the techniques of market economies. The command economy lacked the concern for cost-cutting and efficiency that drove the capitalist engine of growth, for its entrepreneurs and its workers were free from competition. Enterprises did not compete with each other for markets because they all belonged to the same, monopolistic, state sector. Workers did not compete for work as enterprises hoarded surplus labour so that unemployment was not a serious threat. The absence of competition was perhaps the most fundamental difference between the command economies of the socialist world and the market economies of the capitalist world. The capitalist structure punished both workers and entrepreneurs for low productivity and rewarded them both for high productivity. In the command economy, productivity counted for little.

Most Soviet economists agreed that the command economy had to incorporate some elements of the market economy. This idea represented a return to the realities of the 1920s. Not surprisingly, many economists who took part in these discussions referred to the debates of the 1920s. Many found that Bukharin, in particular, had much of interest to say about the economics of Socialism. However, until his rehabilitation in 1988 they had to use his ideas with discretion.[36]

Any return to the use of market mechanisms meant decentralization. Khrushchev's reforms had been a step in the right direction, but they had not gone far enough. In 1962, Ye. G. Liberman had argued for decentralization to the level of enterprises. Enterprises had to enjoy the advantages and face the penalties of budgetary autonomy if they were to work more efficiently. Planners had to allow them more control over their own profits; they also had to let them go bankrupt if they failed.

However, implementing such ideas was immensely difficult, for they threatened the entire edifice of the command economy. How much independence could planners allow enterprises? Should they be able to choose their own suppliers or decide what they produced? Yet how could planners draw up plans if they did not know who was producing what, or how enterprises were to get their supplies? And how could enterprises take good commercial decisions while officials in Moscow continued to set prices? It made little sense to give enterprises more independence unless that independence was genuine, and they could trade with other independent enterprises. Yet this undermined the authority of the planners. Those in the planning system and the ministries in Moscow were bound to resist such ideas.

The dangers of reform went even deeper. Could the government grant autonomy to enterprises without granting it to ordinary citizens? Could it continue to repress information and ideas through censorship while encouraging enterprise managers to take informed economic decisions? The government understood all too well that in relaxing the centre's grip over the economy, it would also be relaxing its grip on Soviet culture and Soviet politics.

Under a government reluctant to embark once more on basic reform, the outcome of these conflicts was, predictably, a compromise. Instead of making enterprises fully autonomous, they would remain part of a larger command economy. However, planning targets would change. Planners would put less emphasis on gross output or *val*, and more on 'profits'. This meant using the principle of *khozraschet*, or 'self-financing'. (This was an acronym for *khozyaistvennyi raschet*, or 'economic calculation'.)

In 1963, the government began, experimentally, to place several enterprises on a 'self-financing' basis. This meant that their main plan target was to achieve a certain level of profit, rather than a specific level of gross output. In addition, managers received more control over the enterprise's budget, and more influence over contracts with suppliers.

In 1965, the government introduced the same principles throughout the economy. Aleksei Kosygin, the new chairman of the Council of Ministers, presided over the reform. It increased the number of economic decisions that enterprise managers could take, and increased the importance of profit as a plan indicator. Managers received more control over what they did with profits and how they controlled bonus payments. The reform even gave managers some room to negotiate with alternate suppliers. Simultaneously, the government began a reform of the pricing system. By introducing interest charges and other charges on resources, this attempted to force enterprises to use capital and resources more economically. The intention was that the new prices would give a better indication of scarcity. Finally, a reform in 1969 gave managers greater power to fire workers, though it also encouraged them to find these workers new employment.

Figures on output in these years show that the decline in growth rates slowed in the late 1960s and early 1970s. It is tempting to think that the Kosygin reforms may explain this improvement. However, few enterprises exploited the increased flexibility the reform allowed them. For example, few went outside the command economy in looking for supplies. Wholesale markets remained insignificant, accounting for only 0.3 per cent of national income in 1969.[37] The basic problem was that the reforms did so little. Enterprises remained subordinate to ministries, and ministries found it much easier to judge their efforts by traditional criteria. Managers also found it easier to work in familiar ways. The threat of bankruptcy was still remote. Most prices were still set by administrative decisions rather than market forces. Commands still dominated market forces throughout the economy. The slight improvements in the late 1960s may owe as much to good harvests and the increased use of new energy sources such as gas and Siberian oil, as to the economic reform.

If economic reform was to have an impact, it had to go further. Yet the post-Khrushchev leadership lacked the energy for radical reform. Events in the late 1960s confirmed them in their caution, and stifled any hope of genuine reform. Most important of all, the reform movement in Czechoslovakia showed how dangerous radical economic reforms could be for the existing political system. In Czechoslovakia economic reforms in the mid-1960s led to rapid decentralization of decision-making. This, in turn, stimulated demands for liberal reforms during the 'Prague Spring' of 1968. During his brief period in office from January to August 1968, Alexander Dubcek abolished censorship, established independent trade unions, and allowed the formation of non-Communist political parties. These reforms undermined the entire command economy. Even more important, the Czechoslovak government began to talk of leaving the Warsaw pact. This posed a threat to Soviet security. The Soviet leadership decided that the Czech experiment in 'Socialism with a human face' threatened the survival of Communism. On 21 August 1968, Soviet troops crushed the experiment when they led 250 000 Warsaw Pact troops into Prague.

After this experience, the government's approach to the problem of economic reform was more cautious. Discussion of reform continued in institutes and within the planning bureaucracy, as discussions of serfdom had continued within the bureaucracy of Nicholas I. However, radical solutions to the country's economic problems had to await the removal of the Stalin generation itself in the mid-1980s.

■ A Superpower in Decline

Warsaw Pact troops invaded Czechoslovakia in 1968. During the late 1960s, United States troops took part in the prolonged civil war in Vietnam which ended only in 1975. These events raised the level of tension between the superpowers. However, at no point did the two powers engage in direct conflict. In the 1970s, they began to co-operate more closely during the era of détente. Détente offered the Soviet government the prospect of solving some of its economic problems by importing foreign technology. However, superpower rivalry made western allies reluctant to export technology with any possible military value. Besides, the cordiality of détente vanished in the early 1980s. The new Cold War began in 1979 with the NATO decision to station Cruise and

Pershing missiles in Europe, and the Soviet decision to send troops to Afghanistan to prop-up a beleaguered Marxist government.

Diplomatic rivalry in the Third World accompanied the cooler relations of the late 1970s. In the contest for Third World allies the Soviet government suffered from serious strategic weaknesses. Its own economic weakness made it difficult to establish flourishing trading and commercial links with Third World powers. Usually, Soviet aid took the form of huge, government-to-government joint projects. This made it very easy to sever links with the Soviet Union after a change of government, as Egypt did in 1972 and Somalia in 1977. Severing links with capitalist powers was more difficult for these came with a whole array of public and private commercial and financial ties. The limited scale of the Soviet economic aid programme also weakened its ties with Third World clients. In the late 1970s, the Soviet Union provided only 3 per cent of foreign aid and its share of world trade with Third World countries was only 5 per cent.[38]

For the Soviet government, the most threatening development in international relations was the acceleration in the arms race. This continued despite the continuous negotiations towards arms limitation throughout this period. By 1969 the Soviet Union could claim equality in nuclear weaponry. Yet the initiative in most areas of research and development remained with the western allies. This meant that the burden of defence was greater for the Soviet Union than for the West. The share of GNP devoted to defence was probably at least twice as high in the USSR in the 1970s as in the USA.[39] This makes sense, for Soviet GNP was just over half that of the USA in the same period. Technological backwardness also raised the cost of defence. Despite the sophistication of some Soviet military equipment, on the whole Soviet weaponry was less advanced and more costly than that of the West. For example, Soviet missiles were far less accurate than Western equivalents, so the Soviet military needed more and bigger weapons to be equally confident of hitting a target. Defence was placing ever-increasing demands on an economy whose productivity was declining. The Soviet Union was suffering from what the diplomatic historian, Paul Kennedy, has called 'imperial overstretch'.[40] Its economic might was inadequate for a huge imperial power with vast international commitments.

■ Summary

After the revolutionary upheavals of the Stalin and Khrushchev eras, the Soviet Union seemed to enter a period of relative stability. Yet the apparent stability of the 'Brezhnev' era masked social, economic and military changes that were, in their way, as profound as those of the Stalin era. Society itself was changing. Education levels rose, creating a better educated public, less amenable to the crude propaganda methods of the 1930s, and less tolerant of authoritarian rule. Society also became more urbanized. Abroad, the microchip revolution threatened to make much Soviet military technology obsolete.

Meanwhile, the ruling group that had emerged in the 1930s remained in charge, and continued to use the methods of rule learned under Stalin and Khrushchev. As the leadership aged, its capacity to respond creatively to new problems declined. At the same time, rates of economic growth began to decline. The basic problem, as most Soviet economists understood, was simple. The Soviet economy could not go on using resources as extravagantly as it had in the past, for eventually, it would run out of materials, labour and cash. If it was to keep raising living standards, and maintaining its huge and costly defence establishment, the government had to find ways of raising productivity and encouraging productivity-raising innovation. Doing this would almost certainly involve a degree of decentralization. The difficulty was to find a way of doing this within the existing political and economic system. As the Czech reforms of 1968 demonstrated, decentralization in economic matters was liable to lead to political decentralization and the unravelling of the whole socialist system.

In the 1970s, living standards rose more and more sluggishly, disillusionment and cynicism began to set in, and Soviet military analysts began to warn of a growing technological gap between the USA and the USSR. However, the government had no new ideas to offer. By the 1980s, the Soviet Union's aged leadership had abandoned any serious attempt to solve these perplexing and dangerous problems.

We must not exaggerate the problems. The government remained powerful and stable. Few doubted its capacity to control Soviet society. It could still count on great reserves of patriotism, and many still believed in the socialist project. However, as with the tsarist government in the 1850s, the most perceptive observers understood that serious problems lurked beneath the surface of the monolith. In the 1850s, a change of leadership had brought reformist politicians to the top of the tsarist system, and they launched the 'Great Reforms' of the 1860s. In the 1980s a similar change of leadership launched even more radical reforms in the Soviet Union.

☐ *Further Reading*

Nove, *Stalinism and After* and Hosking, *The First Socialist Society* contain good general surveys. There are useful collections of essays in Cohen (ed.) *The Soviet*

Union since Stalin; Brown and Kaser (ed.), *The Soviet Union since the Fall of Khrushchev*, and *Soviet Policy for the 1980s*; Byrnes (ed.), *After Brezhnev*; and Cracraft (ed.), *The Soviet Union Today*. One of the best introductions to the problem of economic reform is Lewin, *Economic Undercurrents in Soviet Economic Debates*, though Nove's *Economic History of the USSR* is briefer. Lewin's *The Gorbachev Phenomenon* is very good on changes in social structure and attitudes, as is Kerblay, *Modern Russian Society*. Andrle, *A Social History of Twentieth-Century Russia* is good on social change. The fascinating series of interviews in Hansson and Liden, *Moscow Women*, give a vivid insight into the texture of Soviet life in the 'era of stagnation', as does Smith's *The Russians*. Once again, Nation, *Black Earth, Red Star* is good on foreign policy.

□   *Notes*

1. S. Fitzpatrick, 'Stalin and the Making of a New Elite, 1928–1939', *Slavic Review*, vol. 38, no. 3 (Sep. 1979), p. 386.
2. S. Bialer, *Stalin's Successors: Leadership, Stability, and Change in the Soviet Union* (Cambridge University Press, 1980) p. 89.
3. Ibid., pp. 83–4.
4. D. Lane, *The End of Social Inequality? Class, Status and Power under State Socialism* (London: Allen & Unwin, 1982) p. 57.
5. V. Maksimov, *The Seven Days of Creation*, cited in A. Nove, *Political Economy and Soviet Socialism* (London: Allen & Unwin, 1979) p. 203.
6. Arkady N. Shevchenko, *Breaking with Moscow* (New York: Alfred A. Knopf, 1985) quoted in *Time*, 11 Jan. 1985, p. 24.
7. Lane, *The End of Social Inequality?*, p. 58.
8. M. Lewin, *The Gorbachev Phenomenon* (Rocklin, Calif.: Hutchinson, 1988) p. 15.
9. Ibid., p. 31.
10. Ibid.
11. Ibid., p. 32.
12. Ibid., p. 51. Different sources will give slightly different figures depending on the definitions used. Here, it is the general trends that are more important than the details..
13. Ibid., p. 47.
14. Figures from Andrei Amalrik, *Will the Soviet Union Survive until 1984?* (New York: Harper and Row, 1971) p. 15.
15. A. Nove, *An Economic History of the USSR*, 3rd edn (Harmondsworth: Penguin, 1992) p. 388.
16. G. Lapidus, 'Social Trends', in R. F. Byrnes (ed.), *After Brezhnev* (Washington, DC: Centre for Strategic and International Studies, 1983) p. 193.
17. T. Zaslavskaya, *The Second Socialist Revolution* (Bloomington, Ind.: Indiana University Press, 1990) p. 29.
18. G. Lapidus, 'Social Trends', p. 194.
19. John Bushnell, in S. Cohen *et al.* (eds), *The Soviet Union since Stalin* (Indiana: Indiana University Press & Macmillan, 1980) p. 190.
20. C. Hansson and K. Liden, *Moscow Women* (London: Allison & Busby, 1983) pp. 4–5.

21. Figures in this paragraph from M. E. Fischer, 'Women', in J. Cracraft (ed.), *The Soviet Union Today*, 2nd edn (University of Chicago Press, 1988) pp. 334–53.
22. Zaslavskaya, *The Second Socialist Revolution*, p. 95.
23. M. Feshbach and A. Friendly, *Ecocide in the USSR: Health and Nature under Siege* (New York: Basic Books, 1992) pp. 4–5.
24. Ibid., p. 274.
25. Ibid., p. 189.
26. *SSSR v tsifrakh v 1989 godu* (Moscow: Finansy i statistika, 1990) p. 7.
27. Cited in M. Lewin, *Political Undercurrents in Soviet Economic Debates* (London: Pluto Press, 1975) p. 131.
28. Cited in S. White, *Gorbachev in Power* (Cambridge University Press, 1990) p. 86.
29. 'The Ideology of Renewal for Revolutionary Perestroika', from *Pravda*, 19 Feb. 1988, cited from J. L. Black (ed.), *USSR Documents Annual 1988: Perestroika the Second Stage* (Gulf Breeze, Fla, 1989) p. 27.
30. See R. Campbell, *The Failure of Soviet Economic Planning* (Bloomington, Ind.: Indiana University Press, 1992) ch. 7.
31. Feshbach and Friendly, *Ecocide in the USSR*, p. 74.
32. Campbell, *Failure of Soviet Economic Planning*, p. 51.
33. Lewin, *Political Undercurrents*, p. 148.
34. D. A. Dyker, *Restructuring the Soviet Economy* (New York: Routledge, 1992) p. 34.
35. Cited in Lewin, *Political Undercurrents*, p. 157.
36. The use they made of these writings is explored in Lewin's superb book, *Political Undercurrents in Soviet Economic Debates*.
37. Dyker, *Restructuring*, p. 51.
38. R. C. Nation, *Black Earth, Red Star: A History of Soviet Security Policy, 1917–1991* (Ithaca: Cornell University Press, 1992) pp. 272–3.
39. Estimates of the size of the defence budget in the late 1980s range from 15–30 per cent. See Ben Eklof, *Soviet Briefing: Gorbachev and the Reform Period* (Boulder, Colo.: Westview, 1989) p. 100.
40. Paul Kennedy, *The Rise and Fall of the Great Powers* (London: Unwin Hyman, 1988) pp. 488–514.

■ *Chapter 15* ■

Perestroika and the End of the Soviet Experiment, 1982 to 1991

By the 1980s Soviet politicians and economists understood the need for basic reforms that would raise the level of productivity. However, they also understood that reform would threaten the existing command economy and the political and social structures that sustained it. When it finally came, reform led to the collapse of the entire system created after the October Revolution. This chapter tries to explain the complex, but mainly peaceful, revolution that ended the Soviet experiment.

■ The Interregnum

As in the 1850s, reform could only begin once the older generation of politicians had gone. The change of generations occurred between 1982 and 1985. Brezhnev died on 10 November 1982. For the last year or two of his life, he was senile. He was also surrounded by scandal, as rumours circulated of his daughter Galina's corrupt connections. On 12 November a plenum of the Gentral Committee elected Yuri Andropov as general secretary.

Yu. V. Andropov (1914–84) is a paradoxical figure. In the West he was known as the Soviet ambassador in Hungary during the 1956 uprising, and the head of the KGB during its prolonged battles with dissidence. In the Soviet Union, he was known as the most reform-minded member of the leadership since the late 1950s. His period as head of the KGB may have increased his sense of the need for reform for, like Nicholas I's police chief, Benkendorff, he gained a unique insight into the popular mood. Even many of his opponents respected his efficiency and honesty. Those who knew him were not surprised when, as general secretary, he embarked on a programme of reform.

This programme had two elements. The first was an attack on the corruption and indiscipline that had flourished during the Brezhnev years. Andropov began to apply to corruption the methods he had used earlier to suppress political dissidence. He attacked corruption even amongst members of Brezhnev's family, a gesture that the old guard saw as an attack on the entire Stalin generation. He also attacked indiscipline at lower levels of Soviet society. In 1983 the government launched a campaign against absenteeism and alcoholism at work. Police began picking up pedestrians during working hours and asking them to explain why they were not at work. These measures broke with long-standing customs which allowed Soviet workers to shop during work hours while colleagues covered for them. Indeed queuing was so time-consuming that most people had to shop in work hours. Andropov's attack on corruption and indiscipline was part of a larger programme to improve economic efficiency. In the middle of 1983 he announced reforms that tightened success indicators and increased the pressure on enterprises and workers to fulfil plans to the letter.

There was a second element to the Andropov reforms. Like the Kosygin reforms of the 1960s, they tried to increase the autonomy of enterprise managers. The government gave managers of selected enterprises greater control over their budgets, in particular over the use of bonus funds for workers, and the disposal of profits. Andropov began to talk of 'socialist self-management'.

In retrospect, the Andropov reforms were far too restricted. For example, enterprise managers found that when they tried to spend extra funds on new buildings, they could find no one to do the construction work, as the extra work did not appear in anyone's plans. Andropov's was a cautious and conservative approach to reform. Nevertheless, it showed the government's awareness of the need for prompt action.

Andropov was already ill when he assumed office, and he died on 9 February 1984 before the reforms could have much effect. They are important in part because they were managed by Mikhail Gorbachev (1931–). Gorbachev had been the Central Committee secretary in charge of agriculture since 1978. From 1982 his responsibilities were broadened to include the economy as a whole. Gorbachev learned much from Andropov's attempts at reform. He also benefited from Andropov's support. Andropov had been a patron of Mikhail Gorbachev since the 1970s, and it may have been through his influence that Gorbachev first entered the Central Committee Secretariat in 1978. While Andropov led the party, he was clearly grooming Gorbachev for the succession.

However, after Andropov's death, the remnants of the old guard, worried by Andropov's assault on their easy-going privilege, and keen to avoid instability, handed power to one of their own. The new leader was Konstantin Chernenko (1911–85), an old friend and client of Brezhnev's. (A biographer of Gorbachev refers to him as 'Brezhnev's political valet'.)[1] It is likely that the various factions struck a deal. This left Gorbachev considerable power and guaranteed him the succession once Chernenko died.

By late 1984 Chernenko was already too ill to run the country and Gorbachev became the most influential member of the Politburo. He became the formal leader of the party after Chernenko's death on 10 March 1985. The next day, a plenum of the Central Committee elected him secretary general of the Communist Party.

There followed a rapid changing of the guard. Within one year, the new leadership had replaced 70 per cent of ministers. Of the fourteen Politburo members in March 1981, only four survived to the twenty-seventh Party Congress in March 1986. Of the twelve-member Politburo elected at the twenty-seventh Congress, five had entered the Politburo in the year after Gorbachev came to office and another two in 1983. The new appointments included Eduard Shevardnadze (1928–), who replaced Andrei Gromyko (1909–89) as foreign minister; Nikolai Ryzhkov (1929–), who replaced the aged Tikhonov (1905–) as prime minister; Boris Yeltsin (1931–), who replaced Viktor Grishin (1914–) as head of the Moscow party organisation; and Yegor Ligachev (1920–). In this way, Gorbachev cleared out the Stalin generation and those who thought like them. He replaced them with a new generation of leaders that we can think of as the 'Gorbachev' generation.

Under Gorbachev, the new leadership launched a series of basic reforms, which came to be known as *perestroika*. The word means 'rebuilding' or 'restructuring'. The image, drawn from building, suggested an entire renovation of the Soviet economy and of Soviet society. As the reforms progressed the issue became whether or not it was possible to renovate the building at all.

To understand why the new generation of leaders launched such radical reforms, it will help to compare their collective biography with that of the Stalin generation. Gorbachev's career is typical. He was born in 1931, of peasant parents, in Stavropol province in the northen Caucasus. He was an adolescent during the Great Patriotic War, so his young experiences were of a threatened, but powerful Soviet Union. Despite the disruption of war, he completed secondary education, then went on to tertiary education in Moscow University. He joined the Communist Party in 1952. In Moscow, he met his future wife, Raisa Titarenko (1932–), who was completing a degree in philosophy. She later completed a doctorate and published a book on the life of collective farm peasants in Stavropol province.

The major political experience of Gorbachev's youth was destalinization. After university, he returned to Stavropol province. Here he climbed through the ranks of the *Komsomol* and the party apparatus until in 1970 he became the regional party secretary. Being regional secretary of a province with many resort towns, he came to know prominent politicians such as Andropov when they holidayed in the south. In 1978 Gorbachev was summoned to Moscow to become the Central Committee secretary in charge of agriculture. He became a full member of the Politburo in 1980.

Several aspects of this biography were typical of leading politicians of his generation. First, most leading politicians of Gorbachev's generation benefited from a complete education extending to university. They were better educated and more sophisticated than members of the Stalin generation. They lacked the rough peasant style of a Khrushchev or a Brezhnev. This explains the surprise many westerners felt when they encountered Soviet leaders who were sophisticated, well-educated technocrats. Second, politicians of Gorbachev's generation entered politics when the Soviet Union was already a superpower. They did not experience the extreme sense of vulnerability of those who fought in the Civil War or the early months of the Great Patriotic War. They lacked the paranoias of the Stalin generation, and their extreme caution in dealing with the capitalist world. Third, the formative experience for politicians of this generation was destalinization. Their first political experiences were of dismantling Stalinism rather than constructing it. As a result, they felt less inhibition about criticizing Stalin himself and the political and economic structures he had established. The central problem of their careers was to reform an existing system, while the central problem of the Stalin generation had been to build something from scratch. Fourth, this meant that they spent their careers not in the brutal tasks of construction, but in the more delicate task of improving the workings of an existing system. Their education, their personal histories and their professional experiences ensured that they would see efficiency as the central problem of their careers. The life experiences of members of Gorbachev's generation made them advocates of intensive rather than extensive growth. Unlike their predecessors, they understood that mobilization could not compensate indefinitely for low productivity.

Finally, the Gorbachev generation rose slowly through the ranks because the Stalin generation blocked their path. They had many years to ponder the reforms the system needed. Their formative experiences ensured they understood the need for reform. Their relative youth gave them the energy needed to tackle reform seriously. Youth also meant that they would have to tackle the task of economic reform in their own lifetimes. The frustrations of not being at the top made it likely that they would move fast when they finally arrived.

These collective experiences explain why reform came so swiftly onto the political agenda once the Gorbachev generation took power. The launching of *perestroika* was not a personal whim of Gorbachev. It was a natural result of the emergence of a new generation of leaders.

■ The Beginnings of Reform: 1985 to 1987

Gorbachev understood even before taking power that the root of the malaise that had taken hold of Soviet society was the slowdown in economic growth. This is how he described the problem in 1987.

☐ *Document 15.1: Gorbachev on the economic roots of* perestroika

At some stage – this became particularly clear in the latter half of the seventies – something happened that was at first sight inexplicable. The country began to lose momentum. ... A kind of 'braking mechanism' affecting social and economic development formed. And all this happened at a time when scientific and technological revolution opened up new prospects for economic and social progress.

Something strange was taking place: the huge fly-wheel of a powerful machine was revolving, while either transmission from it to work places was skidding or drive belts were too loose.

Analyzing the situation, we first discovered a slowing economic growth. In the last fifteen years the national income growth rates had declined by more than a half and by the beginning of the eighties had fallen to a level close to economic stagnation. A country that was once quickly closing on the world's advanced nations began to lose one position after another. Moreover, the gap in the efficiency of production, quality of products, scientific and technological development, the production of advanced technology and the use of advanced techniques began to widen, and not to our advantage. ...

It became typical of many of our economic executives to think not of how to build up the national asset, but of how to put more material, labor and working time into an item to sell it at a higher price. Consequently, for all 'gross output' there was a shortage of goods. We spent, in fact we are still spending, far more on raw materials, energy and other resources per unit of output than other developed nations. Our country's wealth in terms of natural and manpower resources has spoilt, one may even say corrupted, us. That, in fact, is chiefly the reason why it was possible for our economy to develop extensively for decades.

Accustomed to giving priority to quantitative growth in production, we tried to check the falling rates of growth, but did so mainly by continually increasing expenditures: we built up the fuel and energy industries and increased the use of natural resources in production.

As time went on, material resources became harder to get and more expensive. On the other hand, the extensive methods of fixed capital expansion resulted in an artificial shortage of manpower ... The inertia of extensive economic development was leading to an economic deadlock and stagnation.[2]

Like Andropov, Gorbachev began with attempts to improve discipline and efficiency. These early reforms took shape under the slogan of 'acceleration' (*uskorenie*), which he first mentioned at the Central Committee plenum of April 1985.

Typical of this phase was the government's attack on alcohol abuse. Consumption of distilled liquor had steadily risen in recent decades, partly because the government itself benefited from the revenues alcohol generated. In the early 1980s, alcohol sales accounted for some 12 per cent of total budgetary revenue. Yet economists estimated that alcoholism cost Soviet society the equivalent of 10 per cent of national income.[3] Alcoholism also reduced work efficiency and caused many industrial and traffic accidents. It lay behind the growing problem of domestic violence and family breakdown.

On 17 May 1985, the government issued a decree reducing alcohol production and restricting sales. Soviet embassies abroad began to offer their guests mineral water and soft drinks, and officials privately started calling the new 'general secretary' the 'mineral secretary'. In the wine-growing regions of the south, over-enthusiastic officials began to cut down ancient vineyards. Like Nicholas II's ill-fated experiment with prohibition, the short-term effects of the reform were promising. Sales of alcohol halved between 1984 and 1988.[4] Alcohol-related crimes and accidents fell sharply, and hospitals found themselves treating fewer alcoholics. However, even in the medium-term the reform failed. Declining revenues forced the government to print extra money, which gave a boost to inflation. Meanwhile, drinkers turned to illegal distillers (*samogonshchiki*) or to surrogates. Official figures reported 11 000 deaths from consumption of illicit liquor or surrogates such as perfume in 1987 alone.[5] Soldiers in Afghanistan drank the anti-freeze used in tank engines. Others drank insecticides, varnish and cleaning fluids. Perfume disappeared from the shops, and so did sugar, the main raw material used by *samogonshchiki*. In 1987 the government relaxed the campaign, and finally abandoned it in 1989. Vodka reappeared in state shops and foreign embassies.

Other early reforms included the creation of a super-ministry to deal with the many problems of the agricultural sector. (Its name, *Gosagroprom*, displayed the planners' traditional flair for elegant acronyms.) Another important centralizing reform was the creation, in 1986, of *Gospriemka*. This was a government organization with the power to check on the quality of goods produced by enterprises. It replaced the ineffective quality control sections which existed within all enterprises. These had depended so much on plan fulfilment that, far from rejecting poor quality goods, their main role was 'to convince the customer that the output was acceptable despite departures from standards and specifications'.[6] *Gospriemka* set about its work enthusiastically. Early in 1987 it rejected up to 20 per cent of output from 1500 enterprises. This temporarily reduced industrial output. It also caused an outcry from workers and managers who lost bonuses. The high economic and political costs of real quality control soon forced the government to cut back on the activities of the new organization.

These failures showed that the centre could not handle reform on its own. Somehow, it had to stimulate enterprises and individuals to take responsibility for improved efficiency. In a phrase first put into circulation by Tatyana Zaslavskaya, it had to 'mobilize the human factor'.

The burden of defence made economic reform extremely difficult. Yet the announcement of the US Strategic Defence Initiative (SDI) in 1983 suggested that in future the defence burden would increase. The 'star wars' programme proposed to use the technology of the electronics revolution to neutralize the Soviet nuclear threat. To counter the 'star wars' programme, the Soviet government would have to spend vast sums on computerization and laser technology, in which it lagged behind the West. As a western scholar put it: 'A nation which can outproduce the world in steel, cement and coal is, in effect, panting along, one industrial revolution behind its major rivals, its preponderance in conventional arms liable to be nullified by the deployment of new weapons it cannot hope to match'.[7]

The alternative to a new round in the arms race was disarmament. As early as 1984, the Soviet foreign minister, Andrei Gromyko, argued that the time had come to rethink Soviet foreign policy. He suggested the need for 'New Thinking' on defence, in a phrase first used by Bertrand Russell and Albert Einstein in 1954.[8] Under Gorbachev, 'New Thinking' came to symbolize a genuine reorientation of Soviet foreign policy. It meant recognizing that in the nuclear age, and with modern communications, nations were more interdependent than ever before. An attitude of confrontation was no longer appropriate. In future, Soviet foreign policy would assume the need for co-operation between the major powers to preserve the future of a common human civilization, and a common planetary home.

This reorientation of official attitudes made possible a reduction in the burden of defence. From the very beginning, Gorbachev saw disarmament as an important counterpart to internal reforms. In an interview in *Time* magazine in September 1985, he said:

> You ask what changes in the world economy could be of benefit to the Soviet Union. First of all, although this belongs more to politics than economics, an end to the arms race. We would prefer to use every ruble that today goes for defence to meet civilian, peaceful needs. As I understand, you in the US could also make better use of the money consumed nowadays by arms production.[9]

Though the West reacted cautiously, Gorbachev made some serious moves towards radical disarmament. On 7 April 1985 he announced that the Soviet Union would no longer try to counter the NATO rearmament programme in Western Europe. In August, the Soviet Union unilaterally ended nuclear testing. Gorbachev had a first summit with US president Reagan in November 1985, and in January 1986 he announced plans for the abolition of all nuclear weapons by the year 2000. However suspicious western governments were of his real intent, Gorbachev had transformed the issue of disarmament, and Soviet negotiators had seized the high ground in the nuclear arms debate.

Reforming the Command Economy: 1987 to 1989

The reform process gathered momentum between 1986 and 1989. At the twenty-seventh Party Congress, early in 1986, the party committed itself to a thorough modernisation of the economy. Gorbachev announced that economic reform was 'the key to all our problems, immediate and long-term, economic and social, political and ideological, domestic and foreign'.[10]

The government announced its intention to decentralize economic structures. Gosplan would concentrate more on long-term forecasting, while enterprises and farms would be encouraged to respond to market pressures. To do this they needed more control over their own budgets, over pricing, and over employment. The government announced plans to relax central control of prices and to permit small cooperative enterprises. The central idea of reform was still that of the Kosygin reforms: the creation of autonomous enterprises, functioning on the basis of 'full cost accounting' within a planned socialist economy. But the approach was much more decisive. In 1987 Gorbachev wrote: 'The essence of what we plan to do throughout the country is to replace predominantly administrative methods by predominantly economic methods. That we must have full cost accounting is quite clear to the Soviet leadership'.[11]

In the early years of *perestroika*, there was much interest in NEP, for Soviet society in the 1920s offered a model of how central planning could be combined with market mechanisms. The comparison was appealing, for it suggested that economic growth would occur naturally as the government relaxed its grip on the economy. This made the task of reform appear reasonably simple. As the government relaxed its grip on sector after sector, private initiative would take over in a smooth changeover to a socialist market. It is no coincidence that the government rehabilitated Bukharin in 1988 and began to publish his writings.

In foreign trade the government retreated even further than Lenin had in 1921. Ever since the revolution, the Soviet government had controlled foreign trade through the ministry of foreign trade. From 1 January 1987 the ministry lost its monopoly. The government permitted several other ministries and several large associations of enterprises to trade directly with foreign countries. New regulations allowed them to negotiate directly with foreign enterprises and to keep some of the foreign currency they earned. Within two years the government extended these rights to all Soviet enterprises. By early 1988, Soviet enterprises handled 18 per cent of exports and 30 per cent of imports directly. A decree of January 1987 allowed the creation of 'joint enterprises' with foreign companies. By the middle of 1990, there were already more than 1800 joint ventures.[12] These changes forced Soviet enterprises to face the reality of market competition, if only, as yet, in international markets.

More cautiously, the government tried to introduce internal competition as well. In June 1987, the government passed a new law on enterprises, replacing the laws passed in 1965. The new law took effect from January 1988. Though the law required enterprises to fulfil 'state orders', it gave them much greater freedom in deciding how to do so. It also gave them more freedom to negotiate with other enterprises. Finally, the law allowed for unsuccessful firms to go bankrupt. Though state orders continued to dominate the business of most enterprises, in principle they were now more autonomous and more vulnerable. To mobilize the interests of workers within enterprises, the law provided mechanisms by which workers could elect their directors.

New laws also permitted the creation of entirely new types of enterprises. A law that came into effect in May 1988 allowed the formation of co-operative enterprises. These operated largely outside the command economy, though they could supply government enterprises, and remained subject to certain government controls. Though most operated semi-legally, cooperatives proved much better at filling small commercial niches than existing state enterprises. By early 1989 there were almost 80 000, mainly in service sectors such as restaurants or hairdressing.[13] By early 1990 co-operatives employed more than 3 million workers or 2.4 per cent of the entire workforce. They accounted for about 3 per cent of total GNP.[14]

Agriculture remained the most backward sector of the Soviet economy. However it was a sector in which Gorbachev had long taken an interest. Indeed, he had presided over the cautious agricultural reforms of the early 1980s. The most original element in these reforms was the revival of the 'link' method. The idea was an old one. A 'link' was a small group, often a family group, which assumed responsibility for a particular piece of land or a specific agricultural task. When properly handled, the link system gave families a real stake in more efficient farming, and some saw it as a tentative step towards private peasant farming. Gorbachev himself had encouraged similar systems in Stavropol province.

The 1982 reform revived the link system under the notion of 'collective contracts'. These allowed collective farms to grant some autonomy to small groups of farmers. The collective farm would grant land and supplies, in return for an agreement to supply certain goods at contract prices. Like peasant farms under NEP, the links had freedom to dispose of surpluses. When he became party leader, Gorbachev tried to extend the system of collective contracts. The government instructed the new agricultural ministry, *Gosagroprom*, to encourage the system. It also tried to stimulate the activities of private plots, which were still by far the most productive sector of agriculture. Early reforms also gave collective farms greater freedom to dispose of produce on free markets.

However, the new agricultural ministry turned into one more bureaucratic monster. Its bureaucratic regulation of agriculture and the authority of local collective farm chairmen were enough to stifle most forms of small-scale enterprise. The government finally abolished the super ministry in 1989.

A more important break with past practice came in October 1988, when the government introduced the principle of leasing. New regulations allowed families to take out long leases on plots of land. They could even pass these on to their children. In theory, at least, this was a step towards the decollectivization of Soviet agriculture. In practice, collective farmers did not rush to take out leases. As under the Stolypin reforms, many peasants feared the difficulties of independent farming. They also knew that local collective farms and Party officials would harass them mercilessly, as their successes would threaten the future of traditional Soviet farming methods. By early 1990, less than 10 per cent of Soviet farms had allowed leases to be taken up. Part of the problem was that in 1988 Gorbachev had put his conservative rival, Yegor Ligachev, in charge of agriculture. Politically, this was a clever move, for it removed Ligachev from the centre of political debate. However, it did little for the reform process in agriculture. In early 1990, Ligachev said in an interview on British television, that he would allow the decollectivization of Soviet agriculture 'over his dead body'.[15]

With these measures, the government had exposed the command economy to a modest degree of external and internal competition. Yet most of the old structures remained in place. Increasingly, the government came up against resistance from members of the *nomenklatura* whose interests were bound up with the existing system. Conservative officials and managers at all levels of government tried to strangle the new institutions at birth. Pressure grew to restrict the activities of co-operatives. New regulations in December 1988 excluded them from certain types of activities such as trading in video films and forbade them to use foreign currency. Local authorities used safety regulations to close co-operatives which competed with state businesses and retail outlets. Enterprises trying to trade directly with foreign companies also faced many obstacles. They found it difficult to get supplies of goods within the existing system. Most important of all, in a financial system not geared to commerce, they found it difficult to raise money.

There was also growing opposition to reform from the Soviet population. Any reform that threatened to raise prices of basic consumer goods was bound to be unpopular. This accounts, in part, for the unpopularity of co-operatives, many of which offered improved services, but at free market prices and using corrupt methods.

Though normally seen as an aspect of foreign policy, it makes sense to regard disarmament as an aspect of economic reform. Disarmament negotiations stalled after the Reykjavik summit in 1986. However, there was more progress in 1987. The Soviet government agreed to negotiate separately on the reduction of Intermediate Nuclear Forces, and an INF treaty was signed in December 1987. This was the first disarmament treaty of the nuclear age which did not simply limit the growth of nuclear weapons, but actually reduced their numbers. The agreement planned to eliminate all nuclear weapons in the European theatre.

In the middle of 1987, after a young German pilot, Matthew Rust, flew undetected through Soviet air defences and landed in Red Square, Gorbachev sacked several top Soviet commanders and replaced them with his own nominees. This reduced resistance within the defence establishment to radical disarmament proposals. Late in 1988, at the United Nations, Gorbachev announced unilateral cuts in Soviet conventional forces and the withdrawal of Soviet troops from Afghanistan. The last troops left Afghanistan a year later, in February 1989. The negotiations conducted in this period prepared the way for the more radical cuts in nuclear and conventional arms of the 'START I' treaty, concluded in September 1991.

By 1987 Gorbachev understood how important it was to mobilize support from below. This was necessary, first to overcome resistance, and second because the success of reform would depend on the energy and creativity of the entire population.

☐ *Document 15.2: The need for democracy*

The weaknesses and inconsistencies of all the known 'revolutions from above' are explained precisely by the lack of such support from below, the absence of concord and concerted action with the masses. And, since all these things were lacking, a greater or lesser degree of coercive pressure from above was needed. This led to deformities in the course of changes, and hence their high socio-political and moral 'cost'.

It is a distinctive feature and strength of *perestroika* that it is simultaneously a revolution 'from above' and 'from below'. This is one of the most reliable guarantees of its success and irreversibility. We will persistently seek to ensure that the masses, the 'people below,' attain all their democratic rights and learn to use them in a habitual, competent and responsible manner. Life convincingly confirms that at sharp turns of history, in revolutionary situations, the people demonstrate remarkable ability to listen, understand and respond if they are told the truth. This is exactly how Lenin acted at even the most trying moments after the October Revolution and during the Civil War, when he went to the people and talked to them frankly. This is why it is so important that *perestroika* maintains a high level of political and labor energy amongst the masses.[16]

In a famous article published in 1987, the economist, G. Popov, had argued that the 'Great Reforms' of the mid-nineteenth century had failed because the government of Alexander II had imposed them from above, without mobilizing popular support. Popov's article was called, 'The Façade and the Reality [literally, the 'Kitchen'] of the Great Reform'. In this spirit, Gorbachev began to link the success of economic reform to the progress of political and ideological democratization.

Abandoning the efforts of their predecessors to repress dissident thought and ideas, the new leadership encouraged a ferment of discussion. As in the 1850s, it was suddenly possible to discuss topics that had long been taboo. The policy of '*glasnost*', or 'openness', reflects once more the distinctive experiences of the Gorbachev generation, with their higher educational levels and their respect for expertise. As early as 1984, Gorbachev insisted that: 'Broad, up-to-date and honest information is a sign of trust in people, respect for their intelligence and feelings, and their ability to make sense of developments.'[17] At the twenty-seventh Party Congress, early in 1986, the government openly criticized the stagnation of the Brezhnev years.

One of the events that forced the government to become more honest with its own population was the explosion at a nuclear plant in Chernobyl in Ukraine, on 26 April 1986. During the two critical days after the explosion, no one would admit anything. This hindered the process of evacuation, and hid the dangers from those at home and abroad affected by the huge cloud of radiation that issued from the crippled reactor. The decision to publish honest information about the disaster, after the initial delays, was itself a breakthrough in a country whose government had long suppressed news of major disasters.

In 1987, more and more sensitive topics entered public debate. They included the crimes of Stalin, a subject downplayed in the official press since the late 1960s. In their attitude to Stalin, the formative influence of the Khrushchev thaw on members of the Gorbachev generation was clear. The new leadership now had the chance to finish the work begun in Khrushchev's Secret Speech. Gorbachev announced that there must be no more 'blank spots' in people's understanding of Soviet history. While encouraging historians and journalists to probe more deeply into the Soviet past, the government set up a commission to investigate Stalin's 'crimes'. In 1988, the government rehabilitated most of those sentenced during the purge trials of the 1930s.

Meanwhile, the government ended its persecution of dissidents. In December 1986, Gorbachev personally phoned the great nuclear physicist and peace activist, Andrei Sakharov, who had been in exile in the town of Gorky since 1980. Gorbachev told Sakharov that he was free and encouraged him to support the reform process. Novels long denied publication began to appear in print, including Anatolii Rybakov's *Children of the Arbat* and Mikhail Bulgakov's *Heart of a Dog*. In 1987, Tengiz Abuladze's film, *Repentance*, with its thinly disguised satire on Stalin, played to packed cinemas throughout the country. In 1988, Boris Pasternak's novel, *Dr Zhivago*, appeared officially. So did other once banned works, including Vasilii Grossman's *Life and Fate*, the memoirs of Nadezhda Mandelshtam, and the novels of Vladimir Nabokov. In 1989, the journal, *Novyi Mir* began publication of Solzhenitsyn's account of camp life under Stalin, *Gulag Archipelago*.

The official press and media began to publish honest discussion on a whole range of sensitive topics, from crime, to alcoholism, to prostitution, to drugs. Official statistics that the government had suppressed in recent years, such as census figures or figures on agricultural output, reappeared. Papers which had carried nothing but good news about the successes of the Soviet system began to condemn its failings as violently as any western cold warrior. This made heady reading and viewing for the Soviet public. Soon they got used to media which had little good to say for the Soviet system, but idealized the capitalist West. By 1990, the fear that prevented Soviet citizens from honest debate with foreigners had vanished entirely. Intellectually, Soviet citizens had joined the community of educated citizens throughout the world.

Democratization allowed Soviet citizens greater freedom of political action, as *glasnost'* allowed them greater freedom of thought. As with the policy of *glasnost'*, the government was at last conceding what many within the intelligentsia had been demanding for years. Indeed, despite the difficulties, Soviet citizens had never been entirely passive even earlier. Most successful of all had been the public battle, waged over twenty years, to save Lake Baikal from industrial pollution. The government finally banned cellulose production and restricted timber felling around the lake in 1987 as a result of the activities of a movement which received little publicity in the West.

However, the crucial changes came from above. There was some talk of the need for democratization at the twenty-seventh Party Congress in 1986, but the issue of political reform came firmly on to the agenda at the Central Committee plenum held in January 1987. Gorbachev announced that economic reform could not progress further without democratization. 'A house can be put in order only by a person who feels that he owns this house'.[18] At the January 1987 plenum, Gorbachev announced plans to introduce multi-candidate elections for local Soviets. In Soviet elections in June, a small number of constituencies witnessed contested elections. This was no more than a testing of the water. Nevertheless, in a society in which single-candidate elections had been the rule for seventy years it marked a radical change.

A Central Committee plenum in June 1987 agreed to the summoning of a party 'conference' in 1988. Though party congresses had met regularly, this would be the first party 'conference' in half a century. Its task was to discuss ways of democratizing the Soviet political system. Gorbachev's book, *Perestroika*, appeared in the autumn of 1987. It offered a cautious description of the aims of political reform. 'One of the prime political tasks of the restructuring effort, if not the main one, is to revive and consolidate in the Soviet people a sense of responsibility for the country's destiny.'[19] The book proposed reviving the independence of Soviets, increasing the independence of trade unions and enterprises, and reviving democratic elections within all three types of institution.

The decisions of the nineteenth Party Conference, which met in June 1988, mark a critical turning point in the history of *perestroika*. Gorbachev proposed the creation of a genuine parliamentary body, the Congress of People's Deputies, with 2250 deputies. One-third would be elected by the population at large, one-third by the different nationalities, and one-third by social and political organisations such as trade unions and the Communist party. The Congress, in turn, would elect a smaller Supreme Soviet, made up of 542 of its members. Like the former Supreme Soviet, this was to consist of two chambers, a Soviet of the Union and a Soviet of Nationalities. Heading the new government would be a president, chosen by the Supreme Soviet, but with functions similar to those of a US president. The effect of these rules would be to remove power from the party *apparat*, and return it to the elected institutions which, in theory, had held power under all Soviet constitutions since 1918. Remarkably, the existing Supreme Soviet accepted these proposals in December 1988. The heated debates at the nineteenth Party Conference were themselves a sign of growing democratization within the party.

These discussions raised in an acute form the issue of the party's role. Where there were multi-candidate elections, could the party keep its monopoly of power? Or could other parties contest elections formally? Many party members approved of a broadening of democracy within the party, but were nervous about weakening the party itself. Contested elections were held within the party as early as 1987. Their effect was to undermine the system of co-option that had bound the party apparatus together since the Civil War. Party officials lost the security they had once taken for granted. The *nomenklatura* system, which had bound the Soviet ruling group together, began to break down.

Meanwhile, new 'informal' social organizations began to appear. By 1988 some of these organizations already looked like embryonic political parties. They included '*Memorial*', an organization dedicated to full disclosure of Stalin's crimes; the Russian patriotic and anti-semitic organization, '*Pamyat*'' ('Memory'); liberal, anti-socialist organizations such as the 'Democratic Union'; and nationalist organizations, such as the popular fronts that emerged first in the Baltic provinces. Under the 1988 constitutional reforms, some 'informals' received the right to put up candidates at Soviet elections. However, the principle that the Communist Party was the ruling party of the Soviet Union survived in the constitution until February 1990.

Elections to the Congress of People's Deputies were held in the spring of 1989. The conflicts these created provided a fascinating education in democratic methods. Though popular participation varied from region to region, many elections were fiercely contested. Despite pressure from above, electors refused to elect powerful party bosses in region after region. The congress met on May 1989 and duly elected Mikhail Gorbachev president, though not after some tough questioning and the elimination of two rival candidates. The congress immediately began to grill government members and to criticise many aspects of government policies. The prime minister, Nikolai Ryzhkov, presented a new team of ministers, and the congress accepted the new ministry only after close questioning of all the nominees. Within the congress, some delegates moved towards the formation of political parties. In July, there emerged the so-called 'inter-regional' group. This included Boris Yeltsin – who had been dropped from the Politburo at the end of 1987 for his criticisms of the pace of reform – and Andrei Sakharov.

Millions watched these lively debates on television. For Soviet citizens, they were a revelation. Here was the first proof that genuine change was taking place. By now, there could be little doubt that the reforms had galvanized ordinary citizens into action. Whether they would act as the government wanted was another matter.

■ Crisis: 1989 to 1990

In 1990 the reform process began to fall apart. The government let slip the empire it had inherited from the tsarist government, and the even larger empire it had acquired after the Great Patriotic War. At the same time, the economic reforms ground to a halt and the Soviet economy began to disintegrate. Finally, the government lost its grip on political power. These changes guaranteed that the reforms of the 1980s would go further than those of the 1860s or the 1950s. In 1990 the initiative passed from the government to forces over which the government had less and less control.

Since the sixteenth century, the Russian Empire had absorbed many non-Russian peoples, from Slavic Ukrainians, to Christian but non-Slavic Georgians and Armenians, to Turkic and Islamic Azerbaijanis or Kazakhs. By 1900, the Russian Empire was a bewildering patchwork of nationalities, languages, cultures and histories. Committed, formally, to national independence, the Bolsheviks created what they thought of not as an empire, but as a union of socialist nations. The Soviet Union, formally created in 1924, included many different types of national status. In the late 1980s there were fifteen Union Republics. Within them there were twenty Autonomous Republics, eight Autonomous Regions and ten Autonomous Areas. The Union included at least 150 distinct peoples, and many more smaller ethnic groups. Though Russians made up over 50 per cent of the population of the Soviet Union, it was the Communist Party that dominated politically, rather than the Russian nation. Indeed, by the 1980s, many Russians believed that the empire had become a burden on the Russian Republic.

Formally, the Republics of the Union had always enjoyed the right to secede. In reality, this had been impossible since the 1920s. Yet paradoxically, the administrative structures of the Union had kept alive, and in some areas had created, a sense of nationalism among the different peoples of the Union. Democratization in the late 1980s allowed these nationalisms to take public form.

After 1945, the Soviet Union had also gained an external empire in Eastern Europe. In the late 1980s the Soviet government lost control of its external empire and then of its internal empire. *Perestroika* within the Soviet Union revived democratic movements long forced underground in Eastern Europe. Indeed, the Soviet government actively encouraged reform in Eastern Europe. In Poland, a near-revolution had been averted in 1981 by the imposition of martial law. The Polish government at the time saw this as the only alternative to Soviet intervention. By the late 1980s, the Soviet government no longer had the will to intervene. It made no protests when, in 1989, elections in Poland led to the appointment of a non-communist prime minister, Tadeusz Mazowiecki.

Meanwhile, in Hungary the parliament legalized opposition groups, and began to prepare for general elections. In the autumn of 1989 events in Eastern Europe moved with incredible speed. Once it became clear that the conservative communist governments of Eastern Europe lacked the support of the reformist government of the Soviet Union, they became more vulnerable than ever before. In October, anti-government demonstrations broke out in East Berlin and other cities in Eastern Germany, and the East German leader, Erich Honecker, resigned. His successor, Egon Krenz, agreed to allow East Germans to travel abroad, and the Berlin Wall fell on the night of 9 to 10 November. Demonstrations in neighbouring Czechoslovakia led to the fall of the communist leadership in November. In Bulgaria, Todor Zhivkov fell after ruling the country since the early 1950s. In Romania, a popular uprising in December led to the arrest and execution of the dictator, Nicolae Ceausescu. By January 1990 every pro-Soviet government in Eastern Europe had fallen.

Nationalism also began to threaten the integrity of the Soviet Union's internal empire. In December 1986, when the Politburo appointed a Russian as head of the Communist party of Kazakhstan, there was an outbreak of rioting in the Kazakh capital, Alma-Ata. In June 1987, Crimean Tatars, deported from their homeland by Stalin, demonstrated in Red Square to demand the recreation of a homeland in the Crimea. In August there were demonstrations in the Baltic republics, protesting against their illegal incorporation within the Soviet Union in 1940. In October, demonstrations in Armenia demanded the return of the mainly Armenian region of Nagorno-Karabakh, which lay inside the neighbouring Republic of Azerbaijan.

In 1988, savage conflicts broke out between Armenians and Azerbaijanis over the status of Nagorno-Karabakh. In the Baltic provinces, nationalist 'popular fronts' emerged. Local government officials, and even some local communist parties, began to support local independence movements, and to insist on the autonomy of republican governments. In November 1988, the Supreme Soviet of Estonia declared that its laws took priority over those of the USSR. In 1989 the other Baltic republics declared their sovereign status. The fiftieth anniversary of the Nazi–Soviet pact provoked massive demonstrations throughout the Baltic. Other ethnic conflicts emerged in Central Asia. There also emerged nationalist movements in Moldova and Ukraine. By the middle of 1990, even the Russian and Ukrainian Republics had proclaimed their sovereignty.

While Gorbachev did not resist the idea of independence entirely, he insisted on negotiating the terms on which the republics could gain independence. This demand led to direct confrontation with the Baltic republics and required complex negotiations with the other republics of the Union.

A successful economic reform would have strengthened the hand of the Soviet government. Instead, economic reform led to a decline in production and a breakdown in supplies. What had gone wrong? The trouble was that in some ways the reforms did not go far enough, while in others, they went too far.

On the one hand, the reforms dismantled much of the old planning system, without putting anything in its place. In the late 1980s, it became clear that NEP did not provide the appropriate model for reform. Markets had flourished as soon as the government legatised them in 1921, because they had flourished before the Civil War. In 1990, the preconditions for a viable market no longer existed. There no longer existed the attitudes, the commercial habits, or the legal and financial structures necessary for markets to flourish. This meant that it was not enough to dismantle the existing economic structures. Unless the government began creating the legal and financial preconditions for a viable market, the dismantling of the existing structures could lead only to collapse.

The difficulty became clear as the planning mechanism came apart. Managers lost confidence in the plans and began to ignore them. Attempts to decentralize weakened the capacity of the centre to guarantee enterprises the supplies and funding they needed to keep producing. More and more, enterprises had to look for suppliers on their own. Yet there did not exist the flourishing wholesale markets that capitalist enterprises rely on. Instead, enterprises had to rely on traditional ways of getting around the inefficiencies of the planning system. Most used the services of the increasing numbers of *tolkachi* or 'fixers', to get hold of supplies. With or without such help, enterprises engaged in barter deals, for few had the spare cash to pay for supplies not supplied under the plan. Even sub-sections within enterprises began to rely on barter rather than cash. In Minsk, the repairs section of an enterprise producing industrial lighting equipment hired its services to other enterprises in return for supplies of consumer goods such as vodka or sausages. These it distributed to its own members, or used to barter for other goods, like nineteenth-century workers' artels.[20] If such deals competed with the demands of the plan, so much the worse for the plan. By the middle of 1990, the Soviet Union presented the astonishing spectacle of a modern industrial superpower, much of whose business was conducted without cash.

Yet barter was an extremely inefficient way of running the economy. Without flourishing markets managers lacked the information needed to estimate costs. Without legally binding contracts, they could never be certain that barter deals would be honoured. The emergence of barter showed that enterprises now had greater autonomy, but it also revealed the absence of the legal and financial preconditions for genuine markets.

Table 15.1   *Annual rates of growth of the Soviet economy, 1986–91*

Year	Growth in NMP (Soviet estimates) (%)	GDP (Western estimates) (%)
1986	4.1	2.4
1987	2.3	1.5
1988	4.4	1.5
1989	2.4	–
1990	4.0	–4.0
1986–90	1.8	0.3
1991 (estimates)	5.0	–5.0

Note: NMP (Net Material Product) and GDP (Gross Domestic Product) are different ways of summing up the total output of the Soviet economy in a given year.
Source: cited from D. A. Dyker, *Restructuring the Soviet Economy* (London and New York: Routledge, 1992) p. 172; western estimates from *The Economist* intelligence unit.

    Under such chaotic conditions, total production began to decline (Table 15.1). A Soviet economist, Grigory Khanin, argued that real output was declining even in 1988.[21]

    As production declined, the supply system began to break down. The planning system could no longer handle the complex business of distributing supplies from one region to another. Yet markets were not developed enough to take up the slack. By 1990, local officials simply ignored inconvenient orders from the centre, and regional authorities began to hoard scarce goods rather than send them to other regions. There emerged a regionalization of the economy reminiscent of Khrushchev's experiment with *sovnarkhozy*. Moscow and Leningrad in particular suffered from shortages as a result of the localism of party officials in the agricultural regions which normally supplied them. Yet the large cities contributed to the breakdown of exchange by requiring purchasers of foodstuffs and other scarce goods to show local residence permits.

    While the economic breakdown reflected, in part, the disintegration of the planning system, it also reflected the government's failure to take reform far enough. If the government hoped to generate the dynamism of a market system, it had to do more than grant enterprises some autonomy. It had to allow the emergence of real markets and of genuine competition between entrepreneurs and workers. Yet real markets could not exist without real prices, and these could only emerge once the government stopped setting prices. Creating genuine competition between enterprises meant allowing unsuccessful enterprises to go bankrupt. Finally, creating competition between workers meant allowing companies to dismiss surplus workers, thereby creating what Marx called a 'reserve army of the unemployed'. Each of these steps was bound to create opposition both from the Soviet ruling elite and from the population at large.

Members of the *nomenklatura* resented the break up of the planned economy from which they derived their powers and privileges. Gorbachev had to move against the *nomenklatura* with great caution, for his own power derived from the political structures they represented. Like Khrushchev before him, he tried to sidestep them by creating new forms of support through the dangerous gamble of democratization. In this way, Gorbachev kept the political initiative. However, he found it almost impossible to deal with the quiet sabotage of reform conducted by local party officials, by the managers of large enterprises and collective farms, or by banking officials. Few enterprise or collective farm managers took up the freedoms offered by the reforms. Most preferred to continue dealing with the central planning authorities or with regional authorities as long as they could. This offered familiar methods, familiar contacts, and a familiar system of supplies. It also protected them from bankruptcy.

Ordinary citizens feared unemployment and a decline in living standards. Under the social contract that emerged in the 1950s, the government promised Soviet citizens rising living standards, job security, subsidized prices and cheap welfare services. In return, Soviet citizens surrendered political and intellectual freedom. This was a deal that offered most to the traditional working classes and least to the intelligentsia. Though the old social contract was already breaking down under Brezhnev, *perestroika* threatened to end it entirely. In its place the reforms offered a new social contract that promised greater economic, intellectual and political freedom in return for reduced material and employment security. A deal of this kind had considerable appeal to the Soviet intelligentsia, but even they would suffer from the dismantling of the older contract. On balance, support for a new social contract was weaker than fears about the ending of the old social contract.[22]

Resistance from above and below explains why the government's reforms began to grind to a halt in the late 1980s.

Formally, *perestroika* increased pressure on enterprises to shed surplus labour. On paper, some 3 million industrial workers had lost their jobs by the end of 1986.[23] In reality, most had either retired or been re-employed, for unemployment not only offended accepted social norms; it was also counter-balanced by the traditional managerial habit of hoarding spare labour. Despite this, there were some losers, mainly among women, the sick, and those seen as less efficient or less productive.

The reforms also threatened loss-making enterprises with bankruptcy. In 1987, the government's own figures suggested that one-quarter of all Soviet enterprises operated at a loss, or made insufficient profits to survive without government support.[24] Yet despite the introduction of greater enterprise autonomy from the beginning of 1988, the government allowed very few enterprises to go bankrupt. There were often good reasons for propping up loss-making enterprises. Some lost money because the government kept the price of their products artificially low. Sometimes the costs of allowing enterprises to go into liquidation would have been too high. This was particularly true where enterprises were the sole employees for whole towns or regions, or where their products, like the electricity produced by power stations, were needed by other enterprises. Under such pressures, the government backed down late in 1988, and decided to continue subsidizing loss-making enterprises. Though it cost money the government could no longer spare, this decision postponed the unpleasant and dangerous prospect of mass layoffs. It thereby preserved much of the traditional social contract, and protected the traditional managerial elite.

Workers resisted reforms of the wage system which abolished traditional bonuses and threatened a higher level of wage discipline. By the middle of 1988, strikes against poor working conditions were common. Many were organized by newly established independent unions. The new unions were particularly strong in mining. Many strikes took aim at the quality control organization, *Gospriemka*, which, in its early days, rejected much poor quality produce, thereby threatening the bonuses of both managers and workers. Breakdowns in the supply system triggered other strikes.

Even more dangerous for the government was the issue of price reform. If prices were to reflect real costs, and the government was to reduce its deficit, it had to reduce subsidies on the price of basic goods and services. Price reform was, indeed, a basic requirement of economic reform. In principle, it was also one of the simpler reforms. The government simply had to let prices float up towards more realistic levels. Yet the government approached the issue with great caution, promising to compensate consumers for rises in the price of foodstuffs, housing and transport, by raising wages and pensions. Its caution was understandable, for however it was done, price reform was bound to depress living standards. The issue threatened to turn the entire population against reform.

When it came to the crunch, the government lost its nerve. In 1989 it postponed basic price reforms. As a result, even in 1990, a quarter of government expenditure still went on subsidizing basic consumer goods and services.[25] In 1989, subsidies on agricultural products, mainly meat and dairy produce, reached 90.2 billion roubles. This was similar to the government's total budget deficit, and represented 12 to 14 per cent of national income.[26]

The reforms halted just as they threatened to breach the old social contract. By 1990, the reform process had hit a wall. While the government talked of the need for a 'market economy', it preserved the main features of the command economy. In 1990 government orders still accounted for 85 per cent of all industrial production. As the economist, Gavriil Popov, put it, the government was still trying to 'tell hens how many eggs to lay'.[27]

The government's loss of nerve suggests a striking analogy with the behaviour of the tsarist government in its final years. That government had also lost legitimacy, for a modernizing society was no longer willing to accept its autocratic methods of rule. The power of the government rested less and less on a widespread sense of its legitimacy and more on more on naked power. This made the government unwilling to test the limits of its power. Consequently, it lost its fiscal nerve. When it needed to raise revenue, it did not dare impose the costs directly on the population at large. For the tsarist government, the challenge came with the First World War. For the government of Gorbachev it came in the late 1980s.

The rising costs of preserving the traditional social contract through subsidies to industry and subsidies on consumer goods and services showed up clearly in the rising budget deficit (Table 15.2). Like the tsarist government during the First World War, Gorbachev's government found it could no longer balance income against expenditure. A serious budget deficit appeared soon after Gorbachev took office. The anti-alcohol campaign may have lost the government up to 10 billion roubles a year (as prohibition had lost the tsarist government revenue in 1914). The sharp fall in world oil prices in 1985 and 1986 lost it some 20 billion in export

Table 15.2 *Growth of Soviet budget deficits (billion roubles)*

Year	Official Soviet figures	CIA estimates
1984	–	11.0
1985	18.0	17.0
1986	47.9	49.8
1987	57.1	64.4
1988	90.1	68.8
1989	92.0	
1990	60.0	

Source: D. A. Dyker, *Restructuring the Soviet Economy* (London and New York: Routledge, 1992) p. 177.

revenues.[28] By 1990, republican governments were refusing to pay to the central budget their shares of revenue.

The Soviet government began to look for painless ways of raising revenue. It considered borrowing money, but Soviet governments had always been reluctant to borrow abroad, and they could not borrow at home because there was no domestic money market. This left one alternative. Like the tsarist government during the First World War, it began to print money.

The result, in both cases, was inflation. While official prices remained low, supplies in state stores became unpredictable and this forced consumers to buy in collective farm markets, co-operatives, or the black market, where prices rose rapidly. Meanwhile, even the government could not resist some price rises. Some state enterprises used their increasing control over prices to raise their prices. Others passed on the costs of wage rises introduced in response to growing union pressure and strikes.

■ Collapse: 1990 to 1991

In 1990, the Communist party lost its grip on the levers of power. The party gave up its constitutional monopoly on power early in February 1990. This allowed the formal emergence of other political parties. In July, the party gave up its monopoly over the media. In April, a leading reformer, Gavriil Popov, was elected mayor of Moscow, and in May, another reformer, Anatolii Sobchak was elected mayor of Leningrad. In Russia, the newly elected parliament of the Russian republic chose Boris Yeltsin as its chairman. Immediately, the new Russian parliament began to challenge the Soviet government for control over the finances and the property of the largest republic within the Union. At the May Day celebrations that year, the crowd booed Gorbachev. He now came under attack from the right, which accused him of destroying the Soviet system, and from the left, which accused him of propping it up. In July, Boris Yeltsin, now *de facto* leader of the Russian republic, announced his resignation from the Communist Party. So did Popov in Moscow and Sobchak in Leningrad. The communist government headed by Gorbachev was losing control of the reform process and of the government.

This was a fundamental turning point. Increasingly, reformers who had lost all hope of preserving the Soviet system were taking control of the reform agenda. For radicals, it was now clear that reform meant installing a 'market economy' and abandoning the ideal of socialism. Meanwhile, conservatives now understood that the reforms challenged the very survival of socialism. The 'third way' no longer seemed a real option. As in the early days of Soviet history, there appeared a stark choice between capitalism and socialism.

During 1990 and 1991 the government's own behaviour became increasingly erratic as it manoeuvred between powerful opponents to the right and left. As it lost its grip on power, as the economy fell apart, and as it saw its external and internal empires slip from its grasp, the government dithered. The crucial issues were price reform and relations between the Soviet government and the various Union republics.

In May 1990, the embattled prime minister, Nikolai Ryzhkov, presented a plan for price reform that provoked an outcry amongst conservatives and a wave of strikes among workers. Meanwhile, radical reformers criticized Ryzhkov for caution and indecision. In August, the Russian parliament began to consider a much more radical plan of reform, produced by a team headed by the economist, Stanislav Shatalin (1934–). This called for 'shock therapy', a rapid reform of the economy over a period of 500 days. It demanded the freeing of prices, which would allow them to rise quickly to realistic levels. It also called for the rapid privatization of state owned enterprises. Simultaneously, it demanded social security measures to protect those such as pensioners who would suffer most during the transition to a market economy.

In the autumn of 1990, the Soviet and Russian governments tried without success to negotiate a compromise programme. At the end of the year, Gorbachev found his own room for manoeuvre narrowing. In December, his foreign minister, Eduard Shevardnadze resigned in response to growing attacks from conservatives. As he resigned, he warned of the danger of a conservative *coup*. To allay that danger, Gorbachev began to ally more closely with conservative forces. In December, he replaced Nikolai Ryzhkov as Prime Minister with a more traditional figure, Valentin Pavlov (1937–). In the first half of 1991, Pavlov took several crude and ineffective steps towards price reform, without ever making the decisive break with past practices that was now necessary. On 2 April (on 1 April everyone would have taken it for a joke), he introduced a price reform which allowed prices to rise by an average of 300 per cent. However, the government was still trying to control prices.

The other nightmare Gorbachev faced in 1990 and 1991 was the issue of relations between the republics of the Soviet Union. With the support of his foreign minister, Shevardnadze, Gorbachev had willingly surrendered the external empire in Eastern Europe. He was less willing to surrender the internal empire. He also knew that conservatives would regard this as a final act of treachery. So he resisted the claims of the various republics for autonomy. Sometimes this required the use of force. Soviet troops fired on crowds in Georgia (1989), in Baku (January 1990), and in Latvia (January 1991). Gorbachev insisted throughout this period on the need for a negotiated process of change. His aim was the negotiation of a new 'Union Treaty' to replace the treaty of 1924 that had created the Soviet Union. Gorbachev hoped that such a treaty would preserve central control over defence, foreign policy, banking, transportation and energy supplies, while ceding most other powers to republican governments. Attempts at negotiation continued throughout the first half of 1991. Slowly, it became clear that the republics held the upper hand.

In June 1991 electors in the Russian republic chose Boris Yeltsin as their President. This made him the first popularly elected leader ever to rule Russia. With Moscow itself now under the control of a non-communist mayor and a Russian parliament headed by a non-communist president, the Soviet government became increasingly irrelevant. In July, the power of the Communist Party was further reduced when it lost the right to operate party cells within the police and the army. Meanwhile, increasing numbers of party members were following the example of prominent party figures such as Yeltsin and Shevardnadze, and resigning from the party.

The final blow to the old order came in August 1991. Difficult negotiations during the summer led to agreement on a draft union treaty, and republican governments agreed to sign the new treaty on 20 August. Fearing this would mark the end of the Soviet Union, several leading conservative politicians decided to act before the treaty could be signed. On 18 August, while Gorbachev was on holiday at Cape Foros in the Crimea, they tried to persuade him to introduce a state of emergency and cancel the signing of the treaty. He refused, and they placed him under house arrest. In the morning of 19 August, they announced that Gorbachev had been taken ill and that government was now in the hands of a 'committee for the state of emergency' led by the vice-president, Gennadi Yanayev (1937–). The committee's members included the prime minister, Valentin Pavlov; the head of the KGB, Vladimir Kryuchkov (1924–); the minister of internal affairs, Boris Pugo (1937–91); and the minister of defence, Marshal Dmitri Yazov (1923–).

The organizers of the *putsch* seem to have acted at short notice and without careful preparation. Though troops took up positions at many points in Moscow, they did not control the 'White House' in which the Russian parliament met. They also failed to arrest its leader, Boris Yeltsin. Several military units, including crack KGB troops ordered to arrest Yeltsin, refused to obey the committee's orders. Some of the tank units ordered to surround the Russian parliament promptly announced that they would defend the building. Yeltsin inspired popular opposition to the emergency committee in a dramatic speech of defiance on top of a tank whose crew were now defending the Russian parliament. Journalists set up a transmitter inside the parliament building. From here they transmitted reports which western news services broadcast back to the Soviet Union. After some initial confusion, foreign governments refused to acknowledge the new committee. Meanwhile, its members had made a very poor showing at a press conference. All looked ill-at-ease, and Yanayev's hands trembled visibly as he spoke. Within three days the *putsch* was over. The leaders flew to the Crimea where they begged the forgiveness of Gorbachev. Gorbachev flew back to Moscow, chastened, and with his prestige and power severely shaken. The leaders of the *putsch* were arrested.

The *coup* finally discredited the Communist party and the old regime. On his return, Gorbachev ordered the suspension of Communist Party activities and the confiscation of party property and records. One by one, the republican governments began to assert their independence, ignoring Gorbachev's continuing efforts to negotiate a new union treaty. In December, the leaders of the three Slavic republics, Russia, Ukraine and Belarus (former White Russia), ended these efforts by negotiating a new agreement to form a commonwealth with no central authority. A week later, at a meeting in Alma-Ata in Kazakhstan, eight other republics joined them in the new Commonwealth of Independent States. (The only absentees were the Baltic republics and Georgia.)

The signatories to the new commonwealth announced that the Soviet Union no longer existed. Gorbachev had no choice but to resign as President. The hammer and sickle came down over the Kremlin for the last time on 25 December 1991. In its place was raised the red, white and blue flag of the Russian republic.

The new commonwealth was extremely fragile. It inherited many of the economic problems and the ethnic tensions of the old Soviet Union. However, its new leaders were free of much of the ideological baggage of the old order. Most also enjoyed, for a time at least, the prestige of having been elected by the population, and having led their various nations to independence. However, the history of the new, post-Soviet governments of what had been the Soviet Union takes us beyond the agenda of this book.

■ Summary

As in the 1850s, it took the emergence of a new leadership group to tackle problems that had accumulated for decades. Brezhnev died in 1982. In March 1985, after a three-year interregnum, Gorbachev became the first leader of a new generation of politicians. Like many politicians of his generation, he was well-educated, familiar with the economic problems of the Soviet economy, undogmatic, and young enough to support an energetic programme of reform. During his first two years in office, Gorbachev evolved a programme of radical economic, ideological and political decentralization designed to stimulate the creativity of Soviet managers, scientists and citizens. Drawing his inspiration from the early successes of the NEP period, he seems to have believed that, as the government relaxed its grip on the economy and society, citizens would take up the slack. As planners did less planning, entrepreneurs would emerge to fill the economic niches no longer filled by government planners. Enterprises and collective farms were given more economic autonomy, and independent co-operative enterprises were permitted. In this way, he hoped to create a market socialism which would enjoy the economic dynamism of the market, together with the social responsibility of socialism.

The reforms soon generated a momentum of their own. By 1989 it was becoming clear that the NEP analogy was deceptive. Political reforms and ideological relaxation allowed the appearance of new opposition groups whose aims were very different from those of the government. Particularly threatening was the appearance of nationalist movements committed to the break-up of the Warsaw Pact and even the USSR. The economic reforms also failed in their aims. Though the planners relaxed their grip on the economy, few entrepreneurs appeared to take their place. Instead, the economy began to break down. Economic reform also proved painful for most sections of the population. The relaxation of subsidies on consumer goods, housing, transportation and other goods hit consumers hard, as did the slow decline in production, while the declining authority of the government threatened the privileges of government officials. In these ways, the reform programme generated new forms of opposition amongst most sectors of Soviet society.

When the government began to understand the scale of the crisis its reforms had created, it no longer had the power to act decisively. Gorbachev tried to manoeuvre between radicals and conservatives. In 1990, with the consent of the Soviet leadership, Eastern Europe broke away from the Warsaw pact. In 1991, the Soviet Union itself broke up. In December, the Soviet flag was lowered over the Kremlin for the last time. Within the various Soviet Republics there appeared anti-communist governments mostly led by ex-party leaders, but committed now to the building of a viable capitalism in Russia. The Soviet experiment had ended.

☐   *Further Reading*

The dust has barely settled on the era of '*perestroika*', and many of the books written the 1980s have dated rapidly. The best introductions to the era of *perestroika* are Hosking, *The Awakening of the Soviet Union*, and Lewin, *The Gorbachev Phenomenon*. On economic reform, see Dyker, *Restructuring the Soviet Economy* and Nove, *An Economic History of the USSR*. On foreign policy, see Nation, *Black Earth, Red Star*. Kennedy, *Rise and Fall*, puts the decline of the Soviet Union as a great power in a global perspective. Political issues are covered well in White, *Gorbachev in Power*, but the most recent account is Archie Brown, *The Gorbachev Factor*. Buckley (ed.) *Perestroika and Soviet Women* discusses the complex changes experienced by Soviet women in the reform era. Davies, *Soviet History in the Gorbachev Revolution* gives some insight into changing Soviet views of Soviet history. The crucial primary source is Gorbachev's book, *Perestroika: New Thinking*.

□ *Notes*

1. C. Schmidt-Hauer, *Gorbachev: The Path to Power* (London: Pan, 1986) p. 98.
2. M. S. Gorbachev, *Perestroika: New Thinking for Our Country and the World* (London: Collins, 1987) pp. 18–20.
3. S. White, *Russia Goes Dry: Alcohol, State and Society* (Cambridge: Cambridge University Press, 1996) pp. 37, 52.
4. Ibid., p. 102.
5. Ibid., p. 128.
6. R. Campbell, *The Failure of Soviet Economic Planning* (Bloomington, Ind.: Indiana University Press, 1992) p. 94.
7. G. Hosking, *The Awakening of the Soviet Union* (Harmondsworth: Penguin, 1991) p. 2.
8. R. C. Nation, *Black Earth, Red Star: A History of Soviet Security Policy, 1917–1991* (Ithaca: Cornell University Press, 1992) p. 288.
9. *Time*, 9 Sep. 1985.
10. Cited in S. White, *Gorbachev in Power* (Cambridge: Cambridge University Press, 1990) p. 23.
11. M. S. Gorbachev, *Perestroika*, p. 88.
12. D. A. Dyker, *Restructuring the Soviet Economy* (London and New York: Routledge, 1992) p. 91.
13. White, *Gorbachev in Power*, p. 98.
14. Dyker, *Restructuring*, p. 95.
15. Ibid., p. 125.
16. M. S. Gorbachev, *Perestroika*, pp. 56–7.
17. Cited in White, *Gorbachev in Power*, p. 58.
18. Ibid., p. 24.
19. Gorbachev, *Perestroika*, pp. 102–3.
20. Based on conversations with the author in 1990.
21. White, *Gorbachev in Power*, p. 102.
22. L. Cook, 'Brezhnev's "Social Contract" and Gorbachev's Reforms', *Soviet Studies* (1992) vol. 44, no. 1, pp. 37–56.
23. Cook, 'Brezhnev's "Social Contract"', p. 40.
24. Ibid., p. 42.

25. *A Study of the Soviet Economy*, 3 vols (Paris: IMF, World Bank, OECD and European Bank for Reconstruction and Development, 1991) vol. 1, p. 265.
26. Dyker, *Restructuring*, p. 178.
27. Ibid., p. 175.
28. White, *Russia goes Dry*, p. 150; Dyker, *Restructuring*, p. 178.

Conclusion

■ The Failure of the Soviet Experiment

The socialist experiment ran into trouble in Russia for reasons that Marx himself had predicted. Marx had insisted that socialism could be built only under conditions of abundance and high productivity. Without a high level of abundance, he argued, the attempt to create a more egalitarian society would impoverish as many as it would enrich. This would ensure the persistence of social and political conflict. In launching a socialist revolution in backward Russia, the Bolsheviks knew they were flouting this basic principle. They did so in the conviction that the revolution would be world-wide, and that the high levels of productivity necessary for building socialism did exist in the advanced capitalist countries. However, the failure of the world-wide revolution left them high and dry. They now had to build socialism in an environment in which even Marx had insisted the project was impossible. This is the 'Menshevik' explanation for the failure of the Soviet experiment. As early as 1917, Mensheviks argued that the October Revolution was premature. It was doomed as soon as the world-wide revolution failed. In this view, Stalinism fulfilled Marx' gloomy prediction that the attempt to build socialism under conditions of backwardness would generate violent social conflict.

However, once embarked on the experiment, the Bolsheviks persisted despite the failure of the world revolution. If the Bolsheviks were to prove the Mensheviks wrong and justify the October Revolution, they had to use their own resources to build up the productive resources of Soviet society. They had to do this both to defend the Soviet Union and to lay a foundation for socialism. Could they do it? Was there a strategy of growth as successful as the capitalist strategy, but compatible with the egalitarian goals of socialism? This was the challenge Stalin took on.

By the end of his life, he almost certainly believed that he had found this alternative strategy of growth. The Soviet command economy had generated spectacular rates of growth. Though Stalin's strategy exacted a high cost from Soviet citizens, it offered in return the promise of national strength and a better life in the future. These successes convinced many within the Soviet Union and elsewhere that the Bolsheviks had indeed found a non-capitalist route to modernity. For a time in the mid-twentieth century, this route was particularly attractive to the governments of many Third World countries.

The trouble is that the successes proved to be more temporary than the failures. Like a piece of pre-industrial machinery, the Stalinist engine of growth could maintain modern rates of production only at great cost or in selected areas, such as defence. The failures of Stalinist socialism posed moral as well as economic problems. If the Stalinist strategy could not compete with capitalism, it could hardly justify the immense costs it had imposed on the Soviet people. As early as the 1950s, Soviet economists and politicians began to suspect that the Stalinist strategy could generate extensive growth much better than intensive growth. Yet sustained growth clearly demanded intensive growth. From the 1950s until the late 1980s, successive Soviet governments sought a strategy that would generate intensive as well as extensive growth within the Soviet planned economy. They never found such a strategy.

Did Soviet governments miss something? Was there a 'third' way to modernity which avoided the inequalities of capitalism but generated equally rapid growth? Or was the socialist project itself unrealistic?

Those who have argued that the Soviet government missed the right strategy have focused on two turning points: NEP and *perestroika*. In each case, it appeared that there might be chances to exploit the dynamism of the market within the structures of a socialist society. In each case, governments made mistakes. However, the failure of the experiment with market socialism on both occasions also shows how difficult the project was. Markets and planning always threatened to destabilize each other. Market forces undermined planning mechanisms, while plans imposed from above stifled business activity. A restricted market could only generate slow growth, while an unrestricted market economy was bound to create new forms of inequality. There was a clear trade-off between equity and growth.

Does this mean that it is impossible to combine markets and planning? Not at all. Most modern economies do precisely that. Most communist economies incorporated elements of the market. And most capitalist societies planned, for most accepted some of the social justice goals of socialism and used planning mechanisms to redistribute wealth to the unemployed or the poor. However, in all modern economies one element is dominant. Either the planners dominate the market (as in the socialist economies of Eastern Europe and China), or market forces dominate, and all too often undermine, attempts to plan. Markets and plans can co-exist. Yet a society in which they are equal forces is likely to be unstable, like Soviet society in the late 1920s or the late 1980s. In such a society, it is also likely that neither planning nor markets will operate with maximum potency. Markets cannot generate intensive growth if planners harass entrepreneurs and distort pricing mechanisms. Within a planning system, the capitalist engine of growth could only work at half throttle. On the other hand, the experience of modern capitalist societies shows that attempts to redistribute wealth more equally tend to be undermined by market forces unless they are so determined that they begin to throttle growth.

This suggests that there is, indeed, no 'third way' in the modern world. There is no stable balance of planning and markets. Instead, there is a wide range of systems in which one of these two elements dominates the other. And, looking back from the end of the twentieth century, it appears that systems in which the market dominates are best at generating sustained growth.

These conclusions suggest that in the modern world the goals of growth and social equity may be incompatible. Marx had hinted at this possibility already. This is why he concluded that the creation of a society free of oppression required the overthrow of capitalism. Further, of the two goals, it is growth that generates the most power in the modern world. The rapid economic growth of capitalist societies threatened traditional societies because it generated both wealth and military power. To choose equality over growth was, therefore, to choose weakness. In this sense, the socialist project of building a more equitable society was probably doomed, at least under twentieth-century conditions.

■ The Future of the Socialist Project

Does this mean that growth will always win out over equality? If so the attempt to build a more egalitarian society is doomed and the ideals of socialism are Utopian. This is certainly the conclusion many have drawn from the collapse of the Soviet experiment. Socialism has been tried and has failed.

In reality, things are not so simple. In the capitalist world, growth rules. Paul Kennedy has shown how economic growth sustained the power of all the great imperial powers of the modern world.[1] Will this always be true? There is good reason to think it will not. We have seen that the Soviet planned economy was immensely wasteful of resources, and that its wastefulness had severe ecological results. Because of its in-built principle of 'economy of inputs', capitalism is more restrained in its use of resources. However, the social structures of modern capitalism require constant growth. So do the social contracts in place in most of the advanced capitalist societies. So do the demands of military power. In the long run, the capitalist system may prove even more extravagant in resource use than the socialist command economies, for it requires constant expansion of output. It may already be pushing at the limits of

sustainable growth in many areas.[2] Growing signs of a world-wide
ecological crisis suggest that capitalism is in danger of repeating the
mistakes of the Soviet command economy. It, too, is exploiting resources
at a rate that is not sustainable.

Will the world-wide capitalist system run into a brick wall as the Soviet
system did in the 1980s? It is hard to see a way around this outcome. What
will happen then? There are many possible scenarios, most of them
unpleasant. However, there are some less unpleasant scenarios. In these,
human societies will deliberately tame growth. They will abandon the
assumption that each generation must be larger and consume more than
its predecessor. The rates at which societies use resources, and the rates at
which populations grow will slow to a steady state. As this happens, further
growth will appear dangerous and improper. Where growth no longer
rules international relations, issues of equity will assume greater
importance than they do today. No longer will the demands of growth
undermine the demands of equity. Social justice will no longer weaken
states. On the contrary, it may become a condition of survival. In such a
world, the ideals of socialism will appear once more on the agenda for
serious political debate. And the successes and the failures of the socialist
experiments of the twentieth century will be examined with renewed
interest.

☐ *Notes*

1.   Paul Kennedy, *The Rise and Fall of the Great Powers* (London: Unwin Hyman,
     1988).
2.   See, for example, D. and D. Meadows, and J. Randers, *Beyond the Limits: Global
     Collapse or a Sustainable Future* (London: Earthscan Publications, 1992).

Statistical Appendix

☐ *General notes*

1. *Territorial changes* The territory controlled by the Russian and Soviet governments was significantly smaller between 1921 (after the Brest-Litovsk Treaty) and 1940 (after the Nazi–Soviet pact, which allowed the Soviet government to reoccupy the territory lost in 1918). Most figures between 1917 and 1940 reflect the contraction in territory.
2. *Reliability* It is hard to be accurate about statistics of this kind. Directly or indirectly all statistics for the Soviet period derive from Soviet sources, which may be inflated. For earlier periods, the collection of statistical information was extremely haphazard. And in any case, statistics are always very rough and ready, based much more on guesswork than statisticians would generally like us to believe. So, for all these reasons, other sources may give slightly different figures. It is, however, the long-term trends that are important, and these are not so much affected by the inaccuracies of detail, which are certainly present in these figures.
3. *Dates* I have not been able to choose regularly spaced dates. Instead, I have picked those dates that highlight the important changes in Russian and Soviet economic and social history.
4. *Gaps* Where there are gaps this means either that the given commodity was not in production (for example, there were no televisions in 1917), or that figures are not available for that year. The context should make the distinction obvious.

Table A.1 Russia in the nineteenth and twentieth centuries: population and agriculture

Year	Population — Population m. (A)	Population — In towns (%) (B)	Population — Literate (%) (C)	No employed (industry, mines, railways) (m.) (D)	Grain harvest 3-year averages (m. tonnes) (E)	Agriculture — Cattle (m.) (Eur Russia) (F)	Agriculture — Meat production (m. tonnes) (G)
1861	73.6	6 (1860)		0.871	28.2		
1871	85.4	11 (1870)			32.9	21.4 (1870)	
1881	100.0				33.9	23.8 (1882)	
1891	119.0			1.432	34.4	25.3	
1896	125.1	15 (1897)	21		42.5	29.5	
1901	134.8				48.9	31.9	
1906	146.4				45.9	30.5	
1913	170.9	18 (1914)	28	3.915	61.7	32.0	5.0
1916	181.5				50.6		4.3 (1917)
				(workers & clerical)		(USSR incl. Siberia)	
1921	130.9	16 (1920)		6.2	47.9	43.7	3.3
1928	154.3	18 (1929)	51	11.6	72.6	60.1	4.9
1932	162.4	21 (1931)		22.9	69.2	38.3	2.8
1937	164.0	24 (1933)		27.0	83.2	47.5	3.0
1940	193.0	33	81	30.4	73.6	47.8	4.7
1945	170–75		45.2	54.8	2.6	4.9	
1950	178.5	39	almost 100	76.7	58.1		
1965	229.3	53		76.9	148.1	87.2	10.0
1980	266.6	63		112.5	190.0	111.0	15.1
1989	286.6	66		115.9	c. 200.0	119.6	20.0

Notes to Table A.1

A: P. A. Khromov, *Ekonomicheskoe razvitie Rossii v XIX–XX vv.* (Moscow: Nauka, 1951) up to 1916; R. Clarke, *Soviet Economic Facts* (London: Macmillan, 1972) up to 1940; *SSSR v tsifrakh v 1981* (a Soviet statistical publication), after 1940; figures for 1932 and 1937 from R.W. Davies M. Harrison and S.G. wheatcraft *The Economic Transformation of the Soviet Union 1913–1945.* Cambridge: Cambridge University Press, 1994, p. 269.

B: Clarke; B. Kerblay, *Modern Soviet Society* (London: Methuen,1983) p. 55; *SSSR v tsifrakh*

C: Kerblay, pp. 147–8

D: O. Crisp, 'Labour and Industrialisation in Russia', in *Cambridge Economic History of Europe*, vol. 7, pt. 2, Cambridge University Press, 1978, p. 332 up to 1913; *SSSR v tsifrakh*; and F. Lorimer, *The Population of the Soviet Union* (Geneva: League of Nations, 1946) pp. 219 ff. The figures before and after 1917 are not, strictly, comparable, as the definitions used changed. But they give a very rough impression of the stages in growth of an urban working class.

E: A. S. Nifontov, *Zernovoe proizvodstvo vo vtoroi polovine XIX veka* (Moscow, 1974) pp. 117, 183, 267, up. to 1900; Khromov, pp. 453–4 up to 1916; Clarke for 1913 and 1921–65; A. Nove, in A. Brown and M. Kaser (eds), *Soviet Policy for the 1980s* (London: Macmillan, 1982) p. 170 for 1980 harvest. Apart from the last, these figures give three-year averages (that is, the average of the year listed and those before and after), in order to highlight the long-term trends rather than the annual fluctuations.

F, G: B. R. Mitchell, *European Historical Statistics* (London: Macmillan,1975) to 1913; Clarke to 1965.

Table A.2 Russia in the nineteenth and twentieth centuries: producer goods and consumer goods

| | Producer goods | | | | | | Consumer goods | | |
| | Railways (000 km.) | Iron (m. tonnes) | Steel (m. tonnes) | Coal (m. tonnes) | Oil (m. tonnes) | Electric power (milliard kW h.) | Motor vehicles (000s) | Refrigerators (000s) | TVs (000s) |
Year	H	I	J	K	L	M	N	O	P
1861	2.2	0.3	0.002	0.3	0.004				
1871	13.6	0.4	0.007	0.8	0.3				
1881	23.1	0.5	0.3	3.5	0.7				
1891	30.7	1.0	0.4	0.2	4.6				
1896	39.5	1.6	1.0	9.4	7.1				
1901	56.4	2.9	2.2	16.5	12.0				
1906	63.6	2.7	2.5	21.7	8.9				
1913	70.2	4.2	4.2	29.2	10.3	2.0			
1916	80.1	3.8	4.3	31.3 (1917)	10.0	2.6			
1921	71.8	0.1	0.2	9.5	3.8	0.5			
1928	76.9	3.3	4.3	35.5	11.6	5.0	0.8		
1932	81.8	6.2	5.9	64.4	21.4	13.5	23.9		
1937	84.9	14.5	17.7	128.0	28.5	36.2	199.9		
1940	106.1	14.9	18.3	165.9	31.1	48.3	145.0	3.5	0.3
1945	112.9	8.8	12.3	149.3	19.4	43.3	74.7		
1950	116.9	19.2	27.3	261.1	37.9	91.2	362.9	1.2	11.9
1965	131.4	66.2	91.0	577.7	242.9	506.7	616.3	1675.0	3660.0
1980	142.0	107.0	148.0	716.0	603.0	1294.0	1327.0	5932.0	7528.0
1989	147.4	114.0	160.0	740.0	607.0	1722.0	1217.0	6465.0	9938.0

Notes to Table B

H: Khromov and Mitchell.
I: Khromov and Clarke and *SSSR v tsifrakh.*
J, K, L: B. R. Mitchell, *European Historical Statistics*, to 1913; Clarke to 1965.
M, N, O, P: Clarke to 1965; *SSSR v tsifrakh* for 1980.
Figures for 1989 from *SSSR v tsifrakh* for 1989.

Annotated Bibliograpy

This is not an exhaustive bibliography, but a list of books that I have found useful myself, or have referred to in the lists of readings at the end of chapters. It includes few of the many fine detailed monographs on this period.

For those new to the history of Russia and the Soviet Union, the best short introduction is Kochan and Abraham, *The Making of Modern Russia*. The standard textbook is Riasanovsky, *A History of Russia*. Pipes, *Russia under the Old Regime* goes up to the end of the nineteenth century, while Westwood, *Endurance and Endeavour*, covers the nineteenth and twentieth centuries. For the Soviet period, the standard short history is Hosking, *The First Socialist Society*. Nove's *Stalinism and After* is a more interpretative study. There is a very fine economic history by Nove, *An Economic History of the USSR*; and a good recent social history by Andrle, *A Social History of Twentieth Century Russia*. The best short study of the revolutionary epoch is Fitzpatrick, *The Russian Revolution*, though Kochan, *Russia in Revolution* is also very good for the pre-revolutionary decades. The best encyclopedia of Russian and Soviet history is the multi-volume *Modern Encyclopedia of Russian and Soviet History*.

☐ *History*

Acton, E., *Rethinking the Russian Revolution* (London, 1990); good recent survey of the historiography
—— *Russia: The Tsarist and Soviet Legacy*, 2nd edn (New York/London: Longman, 1995); a recent general history
Adams, A. (ed) *Imperial Russia after 1861: Peaceful Modernization or Revolution?* (Lexington, Mass.: D. C. Heath & Co., 1965); documents and articles
Anderson, M. S., *Peter the Great* (London: Thames & Hudson, 1978)
Andrle, V., *A Social History of Twentieth-Century Russia* (London/New York: Edward Arnold, 1994); the only general survey of its subject
Ascher, A., *The Revolution of 1905*, 2 vols (Stanford, Calif.: Stanford University Press, 1988, 1992); standard
Atkinson, D. *et al.* (eds) *Women in Russia* (Brighton: Harvester Press, 1978); a pioneering collection of essays
Auty, R. and D. Obolensky, *An Introduction to Russian History* (Cambridge University Press, 1976); textbook account, contains detailed bibliography and a good description of Russian geography
Barber, J. and M. Harrison, *The Soviet Home Front 1941–1945* (London and New York: Longman 1991); very fine survey of the USSR at war
Black, C. *et al.* (eds) *The Modernization of Japan and Russia* (New York: Free Press, 1975); compares Russian and Japanese history
Blackwell, W. L. (ed.) *Russian Economic Development from Peter the Great to Stalin* (New York: New Viewpoints, Franklin Watts, 1974); good collection of essays

Blum, J., *Lord and Peasant in Russia from the Ninth to the Nineteenth Century* (Princeton, NJ: Atheneum, 1961); still the best history of Russian serfdom

Bottomore, T (ed.) *A Dictionary of Marxist Thought*, 2nd edn (Oxford: Blackwell, 1991); superb short essays on Marxist ideology

Brown, A. (ed.) *The Cambridge Encyclopedia of Russia and the Soviet Union*, 2nd (rev.) edn (Cambridge and New York: Cambridge University Press, 1992)

—— *The Gorbachev Factor* (Oxford University Press, 1996); a comprehensive account of the *perestroika* years

—— and M. Kaser (eds) *The Soviet Union Since the Fall of Khrushchev*, 2nd edn (London: Macmillan, 1978); collection of essays

—— and —— (eds) *Soviet Policy for the 1980s* (London: Macmillan, 1982); collection of essays

Buckley, M. (ed.) *Perestroika and Soviet Women* (Cambridge University Press, 1992)

Bushnell, J., *Mutiny amid Repression: Russian Soldiers in the Revolution of 1905–1906* (Bloomington, Ind.: Indiana University Press, 1985); crucial on the role of the army

Byrnes, R. (ed.) *After Brezhnev* (Washington, DC: Center for Strategic and International Studies, 1983); collection of essays

Carr, E. H., *The Russian Revolution from Lenin to Stalin 1917–1929* (London: Macmillan, 1979); a summary of Carr's encyclopaedic *History of Soviet Russia*, 14 vols (Harmondsworth: Penguin, 1966–76)

Chamberlin, W. H., *The Russian Revolution: 1917–1921*, 2 vols (New York and London: Macmillan, 1935); a classic still worth reading

Channon, J. (ed.) *The Penguin Historical Atlas of Russia* (Harmondsworth: Penguin, 1995); attractive maps, very up-to-date

Clark, A., *Barbarossa* (Harmondsworth: Penguin, 1966); good short history

Clements, B. E. *et al.* (eds) *Russia's Women: Accommodation, Resistance, Transformation* (Berkeley, Calif.: University of California Press, 1991); a recent collection of essays

Cohen, S., *Bukharin and the Bolshevik Revolution* (Oxford University Press, 1980); a classic, crucial on the 1920s

—— *et al.* (eds) *The Soviet Union since Stalin* (Bloomington, Ind: Indiana University Press, 1980); collection of essays

Conquest, R., *The Great Terror: A Reassessment* (London: Pimlico Press, 1990); revised version of a classic study, whose conclusions and approach have recently been subject to some criticism

Cracraft, J. (ed.), *The Soviet Union Today*, 2nd edn (University of Chicago Press, 1988); collection of essays

—— (ed.), *Peter the Great Transforms Russia* (Lexington, Mass.: D. C. Heath & Co., 1991); collection of essays

Crisp, O., 'Labour and Industrialization in Russia,' in *Cambridge Economic History of Europe*, vol. VII, pt 2 (Cambridge University Press, 1978); a pioneering study of working-class life in the pre-revolutionary era

Crummey, R., *The Formation of Muscovy 1304–1613* (London and New York: Longman, 1987); the best short history of this period

Daniels, R., *The Stalin Revolution: Fulfilment or Betrayal of Communism?*, 3rd edn (Lexington, Mass.: D. C. Heath & Co., 1990); documents and articles

Danilov, V. P., *Rural Russia under the New Regime*, trans O. Figes (London: Hutchinson, 1988); by the best Soviet historian of the Soviet peasantry

Davies, R. W., *The Socialist Offensive. The Collectivization of Soviet Agriculture, 1929–1930* (London, 1980); and *The Soviet Collective Farm, 1929–1930* (London, 1980); standard, very detailed accounts

—— *Soviet History in the Gorbachev Revolution* (London, 1989); on the impact of *glasnost* on Soviet views of Soviet History

—— (ed.) *From Tsarism to the New Economic Policy* (Ithaca: Cornell University Press, 1990); collection of essays

—— M. Harrison, and S. G. Wheatcroft, *The Economic Transformation of the Soviet Union 1913–1945* (Cambridge University Press, 1994); now the basic reference work on the economics of Stalinist industrialization

Deutscher, I., *Stalin*, rev. edn, (Harmondsworth: Penguin, 1966); a classic biography of Stalin, still very readable

——, *The Unfinished Revolution* (Oxford University Press, 1967); a series of lectures that pose the fundamental questions raised by Stalinist history

Dolukhanov, P. M., *The Early Slavs: Eastern Europe from the Initial Settlement to the Kievan Rus* (Longman, 1996); the most recent account of the prehistory of the eastern Slavs

Dukes, P., *A History of Russia*, 2nd edn (London: Macmillan, 1990); recent survey history

Dyker, D. A., *Restructuring the Soviet Economy* (London and New York: Routledge 1992); good on the economic problems of the Soviet Union

Eklof, B. and J. Bushnell (eds) *The 'Great Reforms'* (Bloomington, Ind.: Indiana University Press, 1994); collection of essays

—— and S. P. Frank (eds) *The World of the Russian Peasant: Post-emancipation Culture and Society* (Boston: Unwin Hyman, 1990); an up-to-date collection of the best recent articles on peasant society

Emmons, T. (ed.) *Emancipation of the Russian Serfs* (Hinsdale, Ill.: Dryden Press, 1970); collection of essays

Erickson, J., *Stalin's War with Germany* (London: Weidenfeld & Nicolson) vol. 1, *The Road to Stalingrad* (1975); vol. 2, *The Road to Berlin* (1982); standard work, very detailed

Erlich, A., *The Soviet Industrialization Debate 1924–1928*, (Harvard, Mass., 1960); despite its age, the best survey of Soviet discussions of industrialization in the 1920s

Fainsod, M., *How Russia is Ruled*, rev. edn (Cambridge, Mass.: Harvard University Press, 1963); a textbook account of the Soviet political system written from the 'totalitarian' perspective

Falkus., M., *The Industrialisation of Russia: 1700–1914* (London: Macmillan, 1972); very valuable survey, though getting dated

Field, D., *The End of Serfdom. Nobility and Bureaucracy in Russia, 1855–1861* (Cambridge, Mass.: 1976); standard detailed account of the politics of reform

Figes, O., *Peasant Russia, Civil War: The Volga Countryside in Revolution (1917–1921)* (Oxford University Press, 1989); the best study on the peasantry during the revolution and civil war

Fitzpatrick, S. (ed.) *Cultural Revolution in Russia, 1928–31* (Bloomington, Ind.: Indiana University Press, 1978); collection of essays

——, *The Russian Revolution: 1917–1932*, 2nd edn (Oxford University Press); a modern classic

—— (ed.) *Russia in the Era of NEP: Explorations in Soviet Society and Culture* (Bloomington, Ind.: Indiana University Press, 1991); collection of essays

Florinsky, M. T., *The End of the Russian Empire* (New York: Collier Books, 1961); superb, written by a historian who fought in the tsarist army

Frankel, E. R. (ed.) *Revolution in Russia: Reassessments of 1917* (Cambridge University Press, 1992); collection of essays

Franklin S. and J. Shepard, *The Emergence of Rus 750–1200* (London and New York: Longman, 1996); the most recent survey of Medieval Rus'

Gatrell, P., *The Tsarist Economy 1850–1917* (London: Batsford, 1986); covers recent research on the economic history of tsarism

Gerschenkron, A., 'Agrarian Policies and Industrialization, Russia 1861–1917', in *Cambridge Economic History of Europe* vol. VI, pt 2 (Cambridge University Press, 1966); detailed study of the impact of reform in the Russian countryside

——, 'Problems and Patterns of Russian Economic Development', in M. Cherniavsky (ed.), *The Structure of Russian History* (New York: Random House, 1970) pp. 282–308; classic essay on the distinctive features of industrial development in Russia

Getty, J. Arch and R. T. Manning (eds) *Stalinist Terror: New Perspectives* (Cambridge University Press, 1993); a collection of revisionist essays

Gilbert, M., *Russian History Atlas*, rev. edn (London: J. M. Dent, 1993)

Gill, G., *Origin of the Stalinist Political System* (Cambridge University Press, 1990); very detailed recent study which shows the limits of central power in Stalinist Russia

—— *Stalinism* (Basingstoke: Macmillan, 1990); textbook account by a specialist

Gooding, John, *Rulers and Subjects: Government and People in Russia 1801–1991* (London: Hodder/Arnold, 1996)

Gorbachev, M. S., *Perestroika: New Thinking for our Country and the World* (London: Collins 1987)

Haimson, L. 'The Problem of Social Stability in Urban Russia, 1905–1917', in M. Cherniavsky (ed.) *The Structure of Russian History* (New York: Random House, 1970); a key essay in debates over the causes of revolution

Hansson, C. and K. Liden, *Moscow Women: Thirteen Interviews* (London: Alison & Busby, 1983); vivid insight into the life of Soviet women

Harding, N., *Lenin's Political Thought*, 2 vols (London and Basingstoke: Macmillan, 1977 and 1981); the best modern study

Hasegawa, T., *The February Revolution: Petrograd 1917* (Seattle and London, 1981); detailed account

History of the USSR (Moscow: Progress Publishers, 1977); for a Soviet account that has little more than curiosity value nowadays

Hoch, S. L., *Serfdom and Social Control in Russia: Petrovskoe, a Village in Tambov* (Chicago, 1986); vivid insight into peasant life in the early nineteen century

Hosking, G., *The Russian Constitutional Experiment: Government and Duma, 1907–1914* (Cambridge University Press, 1973); still the best study of its subject

—— *The Awakening of the Soviet Union*, 2nd edn (London: Mandarin, 1991); one of the best accounts of *perestroika*

—— *The First Socialist Society: A History of the Soviet Union from Within* (London: Mandarin, 1993); a standard history

Hough, J., and M. Fainsod, *How the Soviet Union is Governed* (Cambridge, Mass.: Harvard University Press, 1979); detailed post-totalitarian account of Soviet politics

Kaiser, D. H. (ed.) *The Workers' Revolution in Russia: 1917 The View from Below* (Cambridge University Press, 1987); collection of essays

Katkov, G. and E. Oberlander (eds) *Russia Enters the Twentieth Century* (London: Methuen, 1971); collection of essays

Kennedy, P., *The Rise and Fall of the Great Powers: Economic Change and Military Conflict from 1500 to 2000* (London: Unwin and Hyman, 1988); sets the Soviet period in its international context.

Kerblay, B., *Modern Soviet Society* (London: Methuen, 1983); by far the best sociological account of contemporary Soviet society

Khrushchev Remembers, trans S. Talbot (London: Sphere Books, 1971); *Khrushchev Remembers: The Last Testament*, trans S. Talbot (Boston, 1974); and *Khrushchev Remembers: The Glasnost' Tapes*, trans J. L. Schechter and V. Luchkov (Boston, 1990); Khrushchev's memoirs

Kingston-Mann, E. and T. Mixter (eds), *Peasant Economy, Culture, and Politics of European Russia, 1800–1921* (Princeton, 1991); a collection of recent essays on the Russian peasantry

Kochan, L., *Russia in Revolution: 1890–1918* (London: Granada, 1966); still one of the best short books on the period it covers

—— and R. Abrahams, *The Making of Modern Russia* (Harmondsworth: Penguin, 1983); the best short history of Russia

Koenker, D. (ed.) *Party, State and Society in the Russian Civil War* (Bloomington, Ind.: Indiana University Press, 1989); collection of essays

Kolchin, P., *Unfree Labor: American Slavery and Russian Serfdom* (Cambridge, Mass.: Harvard University Press, 1987); superb, compares Russian serfdom and American slavery

Lapidus, G., *Women in Soviet Society* (Berkeley, Calif.: University of California Press, 1978); a fine, detailed study

Lewin, M., *Lenin's Last Struggle* (London: Pluto Press, 1975); much more important than its title suggests

—— *Political Undercurrents in Soviet Economic Debates* (London: Pluto Press, 1975); very fine on the problem of reforming the command economy

—— *The Making of the Soviet System* (London: Methuen, 1985); a fine collection of essays on Soviet social and political history

—— *The Gorbachev Phenomenon* (Rocklin, Calif.: Hutchinson, 1988); despite its title, a superb short social history of the Soviet Union

Lichtheim, G., *A Short History of European Socialism* (London: Fontana, 1975); good general introduction to socialist thought

Lincoln, W. B., *The 'Great Reforms': Autocracy, Bureaucracy, and the Politics of Change in Imperial Russia* (De Kalb, Ill.: Sphere Books, 1990); a good survey by a specialist

——, *Red Victory* (London: Sphere Books, 1991); good recent history

Linz, S. J. (ed.) *The Impact of World War II on the Soviet Union* (Totowar, NJ, 1985); collection of essays

McCauley, M., *The Soviet Union since 1917* (London and New York: Longman, 1981); textbook survey

——. (ed.) *The Russian Revolution and the Soviet State 1917–21* (London: Macmillan, 1975); documents on 1917 and the Civil War

—— (ed) *Octobrists to Bolsheviks: Imperial Russia 1905–1917* (London: Edward Arnold, 1984); documents on the late imperial period

—— (ed.) *Khrushchev and Khrushchevism* (London: Macmillan, 1987); collection of essays

McNeal, R. (ed.) *Russia in Transition: 1905–1914* (New York: Holt, Rinehart & Winston, 1970); collection of essays

Mandelstam, N., *Hope against Hope* (Harmondsworth: Penguin, 1971); a brilliant memoir of life during the 1930s

Martin, J., *Medieval Russia 980–1584* (Cambridge University Press, 1995); a recent history by a specialist

Matthews, M., *Class and Society in Soviet Russia* (London: Allen Lane, 1972); good on class structure

—— *Privilege in the Soviet Union* (London: George Allen & Unwin, 1978); good on the Soviet elite

—— (ed.) *Soviet Government. A Selection of Official Documents* (London: Cape 1974); collection of documents

Mawdsley, E., *The Russian Civil War* (Boston and London: Allen & Unwin, 1987); a standard recent history

Medvedev, R., *Khrushchev* (Oxford: Blackwell, 1982)

——, *Let History Judge*, rev. edn (Oxford University Press, 1989); a remarkable account of Stalinism by a dissident Soviet Marxist historian

—— and Z. *Khrushchev: The Years in Power* (New York and London: Norton, 1978)

Nation, R. C., *Black Earth, Red Star: A History of Soviet Security Policy, 1917–1991* (Ithaca: Cornell University Press, 1992); the best up-to-date history of Soviet defence and foreign policy

Nettl, J., *The Soviet Achievement* (London: Thames & Hudson, 1967); good illustrations and text

Nove, A., *Stalinism and After*, 3rd edn (London: George Allen & Unwin 1989); a very fine introduction to a complex period

——, *An Economic History of the USSR*, 3rd edn (Harmondsworth: Penguin, 1992); indispensable

Owen, T. C., *Russian Corporate Capitalism from Peter the Great to Perestroika* (Oxford University Press, 1996)

Parker, W. H., *An Historical Geography of Russia* (University of London Press, 1968); superb introduction to Russian geography for historians

Pipes, R., *Russia under the Old Regime* (London: Weidenfeld & Nicolson, 1974); an influential and readable interpretation of tsarist history, which includes a good account of the nineteenth-century class structure

Rabinowitch, A., *The Bolsheviks come to Power* (New York: Norton, 1976); one of the best studies of the October Revolution

Ransel, D. L. (ed.) *Village Life in Late Tsarist Russia: Olga Semyonova Tian-Shanskaia* (Bloomington, Ind.: Indiana University Press, 1993); very vivid insight into the life of a tsarist village

Reed, J., *Ten Days that Shook the World* (Harmondsworth: Penguin, 1966); vivid, partisan account of the October Revolution

Reiman, M., *The Birth of Stalinism* (Bloomington, Ind.: Indiana University Press, 1987); very important on the late 1920s

Riasanovsky, N. V., *A History of Russia*, 5th edn (Oxford University Press, 1993); standard textbook history

Rigby, T. H., *Lenin's Government. Sovnarkom: 1917–1921* (Cambridge University Press, 1979); the best study of the workings of government during the Civil War

Rogger, H., *Russia in the Age of Modernisation and Revolution 1881–1917* (London and New York: Longman, 1983); fine textbook account

Saunders, D., *Russia in the Age of Reaction and Reform 1801–1881* (London and New York: Longman, 1991); fine textbook account

Schapiro, L., *The Communist Party of the Soviet Union*, 2nd edn (London: Methuen, 1970); still the standard general history of the party

Service, R., *The Bolshevik Party in Revolution. A Study in Organizational Change. 1917–1923* (London: Macmillan, 1979); very good on the impact of civil war on the Communist Party

——, *Lenin: A Life*, 3 vols (London: Macmillan, 1985–)

—— *The Russian Revolution 1900–1927*, 2nd edn (Macmillan, 1991); textbook account

—— (ed.) *Society and Politics in the Russian Revolution* (New York: St. Martin's Press, 1992); collection of essays

Seton-Watson, H., *The Russian Empire: 1801–1917* (Oxford University Press, 1967); a standard textbook account, best on political and diplomatic issues

Siegelbaum, L., *Soviet State and Soviet between Revolutions, 1918–1929* (Cambridge University Press, 1992); a good survey of the critical era of the New Economic Policy

Smith, H., *The Russians* (London: Sphere Books, 1983) and *The New Russians* (New York: Random House, 1990); vivid and informed accounts by an American journalist of Soviet life in the 1970s and the 1980s

Smith, R. E. F., and D. Christian, *Bread and Salt: A Social and Economic History of Food and Drink in Russia* (Cambridge University Press, 1982); on the tsarist period

Solzhenitsyn, A., *The Gulag Archipelago*, vol. 1 (London: Fontana/William Collins, 1974); classic dissident study of the camps

Steinberg, M. D. and V. M. Khrustalëv, *The Fall of the Romanovs: Political Dreams and Personal Struggles in a Time of Revolution* (New Haven and London: Yale University Press, 1995); documents and commentary

Stone, N., *The Eastern Front: 1914–17* (London: Hodder & Stoughton, 1976); a provocative study of tsarist Russia at war

Subtelny, O., *Ukraine: A History* (Toronto University Press, 1988); now the standard history of Ukraine

Suny, R. G. (ed.) *The Russian Revolution and Bolshevik Victory* (Lexington, Mass.: D. C. Heath & Co., 1990); documents and articles

Tompson, W. J., *Khrushchev: A Political Life* (Macmillan, 1995); good recent biography

Trotsky, L., *The History of the Russian Revolution*, 3 vols (New York: Sphere Books, 1967); very vivid partisan account

—— *The Revolution Betrayed* (New York: Pathfinder, 1977); the classic Marxist critique of Stalinism

Tucker, R. C. (ed.) *The Marx–Engels Reader*, 2nd edn (New York: W. W. Norton, 1978); the best short collection of writings by the founders of Marxism

Venturi, F., *Roots of Revolution: A History of the Populist and Socialst Movements in Nineteenth Century Russia* (New York: University Library, 1966); still the best detailed history of its subject

Vernadsky, G. *et al.* (eds) *A Source Book for Russian History from Early Times to 1917*, 3 vols (New Haven, Conn.: Yale University Press, 1972); by far the best collection of documents on pre-revolutionary Russia

Volkogonov, D., *Stalin: Triumph and Tragedy* (Rocklin, Calif.: Prima Publishing, 1992); translation of a Soviet biography of Stalin published during the era of *glasnost'*

——, *Lenin, A new Biography* (1994)

Von Laue, T., *Why Lenin? Why Stalin?* (New York: J. B. Lippincott, 1964); a classic now appearing in a 3rd edition as *Why Lenin? Why Stalin? Why Gorbachev?* (New York: Harper Collins, 1993); an interpretation that concentrates on the issue of modernization

Walicki, A., *A History of Russian Thought from the Enlightenment to Marxism* (Stanford, Calif., 1979); the best modern survey of its subject

Ward, C., *Stalin's Russia* (London: Edward Arnold, 1993); very good recent survey

Werth, A., *Russia at War: 1941–45* (New York: Avon Books, 1964); vivid account of the Soviet Union at war

Westwood, J. N., *Endurance and Endeavour. Russian History 1812–1992*, 4th edn (Oxford University Press, 1993); a good general history, detailed, and with good bibliographies

White, J. D., *The Russian Revolution 1917–21* (London/New York: Edward Arnold, 1994); probably the best post-*perestroika* study

White, S., *Gorbachev and After*, 2nd edn (Cambridge University Press, 1991); a good study of *perestroika*

Wildman, A., *The End of the Russian Imperial Army* (Princeton University Press, 1980); the crucial study on the collapse of the tsarist army

Worobec, C., *Peasant Russia: Family and Community in the Post-Emancipation Period* (Princeton, NJ, 1991); superb account of peasant life

Zaionchkovsky, P. A., *The Abolition of Serfdom in Russia* (Gulf Breeze, Fla, 1978); the standard Soviet account

Zuckerman, F. S., *The Tsarist Secret Police in Russian Society, 1880–1917* (London: Macmillan, 1995)

☐ *Literature and history*

Auty, R. and D. Obolensky, *An Introduction to Russian Language and Literature* (Cambridge University Press, 1977)

Hingley, R., *Russian Writers and Society 1825–1904* (London: Weidenfeld & Nicolson, 1967); very good on the role of literature in tsarist Russia

——, *Russian Writers and Soviet Society* (London: Hutchinson, 1979); very good on the role of literature in Soviet life

Here is a list of literary works (in roughly chronological order) that illuminate aspects of Russian and Soviet history. I have not included poetry, for, though one of the glories of Russian literature, it translates poorly.

Pushkin, A., *The Captain's Daughter* (a short novel set during the Pugachev uprising of 1773–4)

Gogol, N., *The Inspector General* (a satire on the bureaucracy during the reign of Nicholas I); *Dead Souls* (a satire on the provincial nobility in the 1930s)

Herzen, A., *My Life and Thoughts*, vol. 1 (on the intellectual debates of the 1840s)

Turgenev, I., *A Huntsman's Sketches* (on the peasantry under serfdom); *Fathers and Sons* (on the radical intelligentsia)

Tolstoy, L., *War and Peace* (a historical novel set in the Napoleonic era); *Anna Karenina* (set in the 1870s)

Chekhov, A., any of the plays or short stories; for an account of peasant life in the late nineteenth century, read *Peasants*

Gorky, M., *My Childhood*; *Amongst the People*; *My Universities* (autobiographical accounts of working-class life in the late nineteenth century)

Sholokhov, M., *And Quiet Flows the Don* (on life amongst the Don Cossack communities between 1900 and the New Economic Policy era)

Babel, I., *Red Cavalry* (set during the Polish campaign of 1920)

Pasternak, B., *Dr Zhivago* (on the fate of an intellectual during the years of revolution and civil war)

Ilf, I. and E. Petrov, *The Twelve Chairs* (a satire on life during the New Economic Policy)

Bulgakov, M., *Heart of a Dog*; *Master and Margarita*; *The White Guard*

Simonov, K., *Days and Nights*; *The Living and the Dead* (both set during the Great Patriotic War)

Ehrenburg, I., *The Thaw* (on the period after Stalin's death)

Solzhenitsyn, A., *August 1914* (historical novel set at the beginning of the First World War); *One Day in the Life of Ivan Denisovich* (set in a Stalinist labour camp)

Rybakov, A., *Children of the Arbat* (set in the 1930s)

Grossman, V., *Life and Fate* (set in the Great Patriotic War)

Voinovich, V., *The Life and Unexpected Adventures Of the Soldier Ivan Chonkin* (a satire on Soviet life at the beginning of the Great Patriotic War); *The Ivankiad* (an autobiographical account of life on the fringes of the *nomenklatura* elite)

Richards, D. (ed.) *The Penguin Book of Russian Short Stories* (Harmondsworth: Penguin, 1981)

Milner-Gulland, R. and M. Dewhirst (eds), *Russian Writing Today* (Harmondsworth: Penguin, 1977)

Chronology

*c.*862	According to *Russian Primary Chronicle*, invitation to Riurik to rule Novgorod
*c.*882	Kiev becomes capital of first Russian state
*c.*945	Death of Prince Igor and Olga's Revenge (*Docs 1.1 and 1.2*)
*c.*957	Conversion of Olga to Christianity
*c.*988	Prince Vladimir accepts Christianity
1019–54	Prince Yaroslav the Wise
1037–41	Building of St Sophia cathedral in Kiev
1065	Foundation of Caves Monastery in Kiev by St Theodosius
*c.*1037–1118	Composition of *Russian Primary Chronicle*, mainly by monks of the Caves Monastery in Kiev
1113–25	Vladimir Monomakh Grand Prince of Kiev (*Doc. 1.3*)
11th and 12th centuries	Decline of Kievan Russia
1147	First mention of Moscow
1206	Temuchin elected 'Genghis Khan' (universal khan) of Mongol tribes
1237	Mongols capture Riazan (*Doc. 1.4*)
1240	Kiev sacked by Mongol armies
1241	Khan Batu establishes Tatar capital at Sarai, on Volga
1246	Khan Guyuk elected sovereign of Mongol tribes
1257	First census, conducted by Chinese experts
1325–40	Reign of Ivan I ('Moneybags') of Moscow
1326	Russian Orthodox Church makes Moscow its metropolitan centre
1327	Ivan I leads Tatar army against Tver (*Doc. 1.6*)
1380	Tatar Khan Mamai defeated by Muscovite army under Grand Prince Dmitrii Donskoi, at Kulikovo Polye
1386	Polish and Lithuanian dynasties unite
1462–1505	Reign of Ivan III
1478	Conquest of Novgorod by Moscow
1480	Formal rejection of Tatar rule
1505–33	Reign of Vasilii III
1533–84	Reign of Ivan IV, 'The Terrible'
1547	Ivan IV crowned 'tsar'
1564–72	*Oprichnina*; power of *boyare* weakened
1581–1639	Initial conquest of Siberia
1598	Death of Tsar Fedor I; end of Riurikid dynasty
1598–1613	'Time of Troubles': Polish and Swedish armies invade, civil war, peasant uprisings including Bolotnikov uprising (1606–7)
1613	*Zemskii Sobor* elects Mikhail Romanov tsar (*Doc. 1.10*)
1613–45	Reign of Mikhail Romanov

1645–76	Reign of Alexei Mikhailovich
1649	New *Ulozhenie* (Law Code); consolidation of serfdom
1654	Treaty of Pereiaslavl; beginnings of incorporation of Ukraine in Muscovy
1666	Beginnings of church schism (*Raskol*)
1670	Peasant war led by Stenka Razin
1682–1725	Reign of Peter the Great (co-ruler until 1696)
1697–8	Peter travels to Europe
1700	Charles XII of Sweden defeats Russian army at Narva on the Baltic
1703	St Petersburg founded on the Baltic; becomes capital in 1712
1709	Russian victory over Charles XII at Poltava
1721	Treaty of Nystadt; Russia now dominant in Eastern Europe; Peter assumes title of emperor
1722	Table of Ranks introduced (*Doc. 1.12*)
1724	Poll tax established
1741–61	Reign of Elizabeth I
1761–2	Reign of Peter III
1762	Manifesto freeing nobility from compulsory service. Peter overthrown and murdered in palace *coup* led by his wife, Catherine
1762–96	Reign of Catherine the Great
1772	First partition of Poland
1773–4	Peasant war led by Emelyan Pugachev
1775	Establishment of provincial government institutions
1785	Charter to the nobility
1793–5	Second and third partitions of Poland
1796–1801	Reign of Paul I
1801	Paul I murdered
1801–25	Reign of Alexander I
1801–12	Discussions of constitutional reforms; influence of Speransky
1812	Napoleon invades Russia; burning of Moscow
1814	Russian armies reach Paris
1825	14 December: Decembrist uprising
1825–55	Reign of Nicholas I
1840s	Westerniser/Slavophile debates (*Docs 2.8 and 2.9*)
1842	Potato riots (*Doc. 3.3*)
1843–4	Baron Haxthausen visits Russian Empire (*Doc. 2.6*)
1848	Revolutions in Europe
1849	Russian armies help Austria suppress Hungarian uprising
1853–5	Crimean War
1856	Treaty of Paris ends Crimean War
1855–81	Reign of Alexander II
1856	*Glasnost'* and public discussion of reforms (*Doc. 3.4*)
1861	Emancipation of serfs; peasant insurrections (*Docs 3.5 and 3.6*); revolutionary manifestos (*Docs 3.7 and 3.8*); foundation of *Zemlya i Volya* revolutionary organization

1862	Budgetary reform; nobles of Tver province demand national assembly
1863	Polish uprising; university reform; introduction of liquor excise
1864	Judicial reform; establishment of *zemstva*
1865	Censorship reform
1866	D. Karakozov attempts to assassinate Alexander II
1873–4	'To the People' (*Doc. 3.9*)
1874	Military reform: compulsory military service for all
1877–8	Russo-Turkish War
1878	Congress of Berlin
1878–81	Wave of assassinations
1879	Foundation of '*Narodnaya Volya*' ('The People's Will')
1881	1 March: Alexander II assassinated in St Petersburg
	Withdrawal of Loris-Melikov's limited projects of constitutional reform
1891–4	Reign of Alexander III
1887	Poll tax abolished
1889	Land Captains established
1891	Vyshnegradskii tariff; famine
1892–1903	Sergei Witte minister of finance (*Docs 4.1 and 4.2*)
1894–1917	Reign of Nicholas II
1897	Russian currency put on gold standard; strikes in St Petersburg
1898	Renewed peasant uprisings (*Doc. 5.3*)
1900	Slump; Marxist paper *Iskra* ('The Spark') published abroad by Lenin and Plekhanov; Socialist Revolutionary Party formed
1901–3	Zubatov unions (*Doc. 5.2*)
1902	Peasant revolts in Poltava and Kharkov provinces; liberal newspaper *Liberation* published in Stuttgart
1903	Russian Social Democratic Party founded; splits into Menshevik and Bolshevik factions
1904	(January) to August 1905: Russo-Japanese War
	January: Union of Liberation formed (*Doc. 5.5*)
1905	9 January: Bloody Sunday (*Docs 5.6 and 5.7*)
	May: first Soviet formed, Ivanovo;
	October: general strike led by St Petersburg Soviet (*Doc. 5.8*)
	17 October: October Manifesto, grants civil rights and elected legislative assembly
	October: Kadet Party formed
	November: mutinies in army and navy
	3 December: St Petersburg Soviet closed
	December: Octobrist Party formed, Moscow workers' uprising suppressed
1906–11	P. A. Stolypin chairman of Council of Ministers
1906	3 April: international loan negotiated
	23 April: publication of 'Fundamental Laws' (*Docs 6.1 and 6.2*)
	26 April to 8 July: first *Duma* (*Doc. 5.9*)
	10 July: 'Vyborg Manifesto'; renewed mutinies in army and navy
	November: Stolypin introduces agrarian reform by decree

1907	Redemption payments cancelled
	February to June: second *Duma* meets; 3 June: Stolypin changes electoral law by decree
	November: third *Duma* meets, dominated by Octobrists, lasts to 1912
1911	Stolypin assassinated
1912	Lena goldfields massacre
1914	July: general strike
	5 August: Russian offensive in Galicia
	20 July: declaration of war (*Docs 6.3 and 6.4*)
	13–17 August: Battle of Tannenberg, Russian retreats
1915	May: WIC set up
	June: *ZemGor* set up
	August: Progressive Bloc formed; Nicholas leaves to lead army at front
	September: Maklakov's article on 'the Mad Chauffeur' (*Doc. 6.6*)
	After Russian retreats from Poland, Ukraine, Lithuania, front line stabilizes
1916	22 May to 31 July: Brusilov offensive in Galicia
	1 November: Milyukov's speech to *Duma* (*Doc. 6.7*);
	16–17 December: assassination of Rasputin
1917	February: demonstrations and troop mutiny in Petrograd
	27 February: Provisional Committee of *Duma* formed
	1 March: Petrograd Soviet meets (*Doc. 7.1*), Soviet's 'Order No 1'
	2 March: Nicholas II abdicates in favour of his brother, Grand Duke Mikhail; Provisional Government formed after agreement with Soviet
	3 March: Grand Duke Mikhail abdicates in favour of Provisional Government
	April: land seizures (*Doc. 7.2*)
	3 April: Lenin returns, April Theses (*Doc. 7.6*)
	Milyukov (foreign minister) resigns from government
	June: first All-Russian Congress of Soviets
	18 June: demonstrations in Petrograd (*Doc. 7.7*)
	18 June–mid July: 2nd Brusilov offensive
	3–7 July: 'July Days', unsuccessful Bolshevik uprising
	8 July: Prince L'vov resigns as prime minister, Kerensky becomes prime minister
	25 August–1 September: Kornilov *coup* (*Doc. 7.4*)
	9 September: Bolshevik majority on Petrograd Soviet
	13 September: Lenin demands preparation for an uprising (*Doc. 7.8*)
	10 October: decision of Bolshevik Central Committee to attempt uprising
	25–6 October: Provisional Government overthrown while second All-Russian Congress of Soviets meets (*Doc. 7.9*)

26 October: second Congress assumes power (*Doc. 8.1*); new Soviet government formed, headed by Lenin; issues decrees on land and peace

December: armistice negotiated with Germany, Cheka formed, creation of *Vesenkha*

1918   5 January: Constituent Assembly meets and is dispersed

21 January: repudiation of tsarist debts

1 (14) February: Gregorian calendar introduced

3 March: Treaty of Brest-Litovsk

6–8 March: seventh Party Congress, Bolshevik Party renamed Communist Party

12 March: capital moved to Moscow

25 May: Czech army seizes trans-Siberian railway

Spring: anti-Bolshevik governments formed in Samara, in western Siberia, in Arkhangel'sk

10 July: first Soviet constitution

16–17 July: murder of royal family, at Ekaterinburg in Urals

1 August: British troops land at Arkhangel'sk

6 August: fall of Kazan to Czech and White forces; battle of Sviyazhsk (*Doc. 8.2*)

1919   March: eighth Party Congress, Party Secretariat and Politburo established (*Doc. 8.3*), foundation of *Comintern*, creation of *Zhenotdel*

April–October: Admiral Kolchak directs three-pronged attack from Siberia, Ukraine, Baltic October: Red counter-attacks; by November, all White attacks defeated

1920   April: Polish armies attack towards Kiev, General Wrangel attacks from Crimea; Soviet counter-attack reaches Warsaw

October: Polish counter-attack November: armistice and evacuation of Wrangel's army from Crimea

1921   February: demonstrations in towns, rural insurrections (*Doc. 9.2*)

March: Kronstadt uprising (*Doc. 9.3*); tenth Party Congress (*Doc. 9.5*), introduction of New Economic Policy

1922   Treaty of Rapallo with Germany

May: Lenin's first stroke, Stalin becomes general secretary of Central Committee

December: USSR formed

1924   Death of Lenin

1925   Trotsky dismissed as commissar of war

1927   Procurements crisis and Urals–Siberian method

1928–32   First Five-Year Plan (*Doc. 11.2*)

1929   November: decision to begin mass collectivization

1930   March: 'Dizzy with Success'; collectivization continues (*Doc. 11.1*)

Foundation of 'Gulag'

1931   Stalin attacks 'petit-bourgeois egalitarianism' (*Doc. 11.8*)

1932–3   Famine in Ukraine (*Doc. 10.1*); Soviet Union joins League of Nations, United States recognition; Riutin plan (*Doc. 11.4*)

1933–7   Second Five-Year Plan

1934	Seventeenth Party Congress, 'Congress of Victors', signs of opposition to Stalin; December, murder of Sergei Kirov, issue of Kirov Decrees (*Doc. 11.5*)
1935	Beginnings of Stakhanovite movement
1936	N. Yezhov becomes head of secret police; beginning of Great Terror (*Docs 11.3, 11.7 and 11.9*); Stalin constitution; August, trial of Zinoviev, Kamenev
1937	June: trial of Marshal Tukhachevsky and military purge
1937–41	Third Five-Year Plan
1938	March: trial of Bukharin
1939	Eighteenth Party Congress
	23 August: Nazi–Soviet pact
	1 September: Hitler invades Poland
	September: Soviet armies occupy eastern Poland
1940	June: Soviet armies occupy Baltic states and Bessarabia
1941	22 June: Germany attacks Soviet Union (*Doc. 12.1*)
	3 July: Stalin's broadcast to the nation
	November: German armies reach line from Rostov to Moscow to Leningrad (*Doc. 12.3*)
	5 December: first major Soviet counter-attack outside Moscow
1942	March: Soviet offensive ends, renewed German offensive in south
	September: German armies reach Stalingrad on Volga, street fighting
	November: Soviet counter-attack at Stalingrad
1943	January: German 6th Army surrenders
	May: *Comintern* disbanded
	July: Kursk tank battle
1944	Soviet advances
1945	February: Yalta conference
	2 May: Berlin falls
	9 May: Germany surrenders
	July–August: Potsdam conference
	6 August: United States drops nuclear bomb on Hiroshima
1946	March: Churchill's 'Iron Curtain speech, Fulton, Missouri; fourth Five-Year Plan
1948	February: Communists take power in Czechoslovakia
1949	25 January: Comecon formed
	March: 'Leningrad affair'
	April: CMEA formed
	June to May: Berlin blockade
	July: break with Yugoslavia
	September: first Soviet atom bomb tested; Communist government in China
1950–3	Korean War
1952	Nineteenth Party Congress
1953	5 March: Stalin dies (*Doc. 13.1*); Malenkov becomes chairman of Council of Ministers

1 April: price cuts
17 June: Berlin uprising
28 June: Beria arrested (*Doc.13.2*), and executed December
July: end of Korean War
August: first Soviet H-bomb
September: Khrushchev becomes first secretary of Central
Committee

1954 — Virgin lands programme; Ilya Ehrenburg's 'The Thaw' and
beginnings of thaw; KGB formed; Kirov Decrees repealed

1955 — February: Malenkov resigns
May: Warsaw Pact formed

1953–7 — Amnesties release millions of camp inmates

1956 — 25 February: Khrushchev's Secret Speech to twentieth Party
Congress; peaceful co-existence
Khrushchev visits Britain
October: revolt in Hungary, Soviet intervention

1957 — February: decentralization of economic planning, *Sovnarkhozy*
June: anti-Party plot
October: launch of Sputnik

1959 — Khrushchev visits United States

1961 — Twenty-second Party Congress

1962 — October: Cuban missile crisis
November: publication of Solzhenitsyn's *One Day in the Life of
Ivan Denisovich*, Manezh exhibition (*Doc. 13.3*)
Party split into rural and urban sections

1964 — Soviet Union imports grain
October: Khrushchev voted out of office by Politburo; Brezhnev
becomes general secretary, Kosygin becomes chairman of
Council of Ministers

1965 — Kosygin economic reforms; arrest of writers Daniel and Sinyavsky

1968 — 25 August: Soviet troops invade Czechoslovakia; retreat from
economic reforms

1977 — October: adoption of new Soviet Constitution

1979 — December: Soviet troops invade Afghanistan

1982 — 10 November: death of Leonid Brezhnev; succeeded as general
secretary by Yurii Andropov

1984 — 10 February: death of Yurii Andropov; succeeded as general
secretary by Konstantin Chernenko

1985 — 11 March: death of Konstantin Chernenko, succeeded as general
secretary by Mikhail Gorbachev, first Soviet leader from the post-
Stalin generation
23 April: 1st plenum of CC under new leadership, commitment
to '*uskorenie*'
17 May: decrees against alcoholism
July: plenum of CC, changes in leadership, Shevardnadze
becomes minister of foreign affairs
September: Ryzhkov becomes prime minister
23 November: creation of '*Gosagroprom*'

1986	February–March: twenty-seventh Party Congress criticises 'era of stagnation', adopts twelfth Five-Year Plan
	26 April: explosion at Chernobyl
	12 May: creation of '*Gospriemka*'
	11–12 October: Reykjavik summit
	December: release of A. A. Sakharov from internal exile, nationalist riots in Alma-Ata
1987	1 January: decrees abandoning government monopoly on foreign trade, and permitting 'joint enterprises'
	5 February: decrees on cooperative enterprises
	27–28 February: plenum of CC, Gorbachev proposes multi-candidate elections to Soviet
	28 May: Matthew Rust lands plane in Red Square, shake-up of military leadership
	June: plenum of CC announces 'radical restructuring' of economy and elections to local Soviets
	30 June: new law on enterprises to apply from January 1988
	August: nationalist demonstrations in Baltic republics
	September: publication of Gorbachev's book, '*Perestroika* and New Thinking'
	October: demonstrations in Armenia demanding return of Nagorno-Karabakh from Azerbaijan
	11 November: Boris Yeltsin dismissed as head of Moscow party apparatus
	December: signing of INF treaty, Washington; Abuladze's anti-Stalinist film, 'Repentance'
1988	February: plenum of CC, Yeltsin dismissed from Politburo
	March: reforms of agriculture
	13 March: article of Nina Andreeva in *Sovietskaya Rossiya*
	6–7 June: celebration of millennium of conversion to Christianity
	June: rehabilitation of Zinoviev, Kamenev, Bukharin and others purged in 1930s
	28 June–1 July: nineteenth Party Conference
	September: plenum of CC approves political reforms, including elected parliament
	1 December: Supreme Soviet approves creation of Congress of People's Deputies
	Publication of Pasternak's *Dr Zhivago*, and Grossman's *Life and Fate*; appearance of 'informal' organisations including '*Memorial*' and '*Pamyat*', and popular 'fronts' in Baltic republics; fighting between Armenia and Azerbaijan over Nagorno-Karabakh; in November, Estonia declares its sovereignty
1989	15 February: last Soviet troops leave Afghanistan
	March–April: elections to Congress of People's Deputies
	25 May: opening of Congress, Gorbachev elected President
	30 July: formation of 'Inter-Regional Group', including Sakharov, Yeltsin, G. Popov, Yu. Afanasev

August: publication of first part of Solzhenitsyn's *Gulag Archipelago*

12–24 December: Congress passes thirteenth Five-Year Plan after stormy debates

Autumn: collapse of communism in Eastern Europe

1990   February: abolition of Communist Party monopoly on power

April–May: reformers (G. Popov, A. Sobchak) elected as mayors of Moscow and Leningrad

May: Ryzhkov announces price reforms

29 May: Yeltsin elected president of parliament of Russian federation

12 June: Russian parliament announces sovereignty of Russian republic

July: Twenty-eighth Party Congress

12 July: Yeltsin announces resignation from Communist Party

15 July: Communist control of radio and television ended

16 July: Ukrainian parliament decrees Ukrainian sovereignty

August: Russian parliament begins debating Shatalin plan

December: Shevarnadze resigns, warning of danger of *coup*, Ryzhkov replaced as prime minister by Pavlov

1991   2 April: Pavlov announces price reform; negotiations on new 'Union Treaty'

June: Yeltsin elected president of Russian republic, first elected leader of Russia

July: Party surrenders right to maintain party cells within state apparatus and army

18–21 August: failed putsch in Moscow

September: START 1 treaty signed;

December: announcement of new Commonwealth of Independent States (CIS)

25 December: Soviet flag lowered over Kremlin, end of USSR

Glossary

apparat – Communist Party 'machine'; professional party members, mainly party secretaries

autocracy – government by a single individual whose power is not limited in law

barshchina – feudal dues paid in the form of labour services

Bolsheviks – faction of Russian Social Democratic Party formed after 1903 split; led by Lenin; in 1918 renamed Communist Party

bourgeoisie – classes who live off profits from ownership of capital, or industrial, commercial, or landed property; by 1917, often applied to all members of upper classes

boyar (pl. *boyare*) – hereditary nobles, usually descended from princely families of Kievan Russia; archaic by nineteenth century

CC – Central Committee of Communist Party; standing committee elected at party congresses

Cheka – The first name for the Soviet secret police (1917–22); still used unofficially (see also secret police)

chernozem – fertile black steppeland soils of Ukraine and Central Russia; began to be farmed in the eighteenth century

CIS – Commonwealth of Independent States; established in December 1991 to link eleven former republics of the Soviet Union

CMEA – Council of Mutual Economic Aid; established in 1949 to co-ordinate economic planning of Eastern European countries

Comintern – Third, or 'Communist International'; leading body of world Communism, 1919–43

commissar – term used for government minister, 1917–46

commissariat – term used for government ministry, 1917–46

commune – *obshchina, mir*, the tsarist village community; collectively responsible for the land allocated to its members, and for the payment of taxes

Congress of People's Deputies – elected Parliament, first met in 1989, disbanded 1991

Cossacks – Free warrior-peasants settled on the southern borders of Muscovy and Russia; formed special cavalry units in army and used for internal policing in the nineteenth century

CPSU – Communist Party of the Soviet Union; official title of Soviet Communist Party since 1952

demesne – under serfdom, the area of land set aside to support the landlord

dessyatin – measure of area, 1.09 hectares

druzhina – military retinue of princes of Kievan Russia

Duma – elected parliamentary assembly, 1905–17

dvorianin (pl. *dvoriane*) – service nobility; by the nineteenth century, the general term for 'noble'

factory committees – committees of workers from a single factory; first appeared in the late nineteenth century; flourished during 1917; declined after 1918 *glasnost'* – open debate, lack of censorship, used of government policies in the 1850s and again in 1980s

GNP – Gross National Product; an estimate of the total production of a nation's economy in a year

Gosplan – Soviet planning agency, established in 1921

gubernator – governor of a *guberniya*, or province, linchpin of local government in imperial Russia; term reintroduced in 1991

guberniya – Province; an administrative division of imperial Russia; survived in Soviet Union until 1930

Gulag – main directorate of labour camps, established in 1930

iarlyk – charter granted by Tatars in the thirteenth to fifteenth centuries, confirming the authority of Russian princes

intelligentsia – In tsarist period, a social category referring to those who were educated but belonged neither to the bureaucracy nor the nobility; in the Soviet period it refers to all white-collar workers

izba – wooden house; main form of peasant housing

Kadets – Constitutional Democratic Party; main left-wing liberal party, founded 1905

KGB – Committee of State Security; official name of Soviet secret police since 1954 (see also secret police)

khozraschet – the self-financing or financial independence of enterprises

khutor – individual (non-communal) peasant farm

kolkhoz – collective farm

kolkhozniki – members of *kolkhoz*

kolkhozny rynok – collective farm market; market in Soviet towns where *kolkhozniki* sell produce from private plots

kormlenie – 'feeding', the right of Muscovite officials to live off the territory they administered

kormlenshchik – Official granted a *kormlenie*

krepostnoe pravo – serfdom

kulak – rich, semi-capitalist peasant; literally 'fist', in sense of 'money-grabber'

kustar – domestic industry, crafts

Mafia – used of criminal organizations that emerged during *perestroika*

Mensheviks – faction of Russian Social Democratic Party founded after 1903 split

meshchanin (pl. *meshchane*) – Legal term in tsarist Russia for poorer categories of town-dwellers; included shop-keepers, labourers

MGB – ministry of state security, official name for Soviet secret police, 1946–53 (see also secret police)

mir – see commune

Mongols – leading tribes of the Turkic peoples of medieval Siberia

MTS – Machine Tractor Stations, established in 1930 to supply equipment and technical expertise to collective farms

Narodnaya Volya – revolutionary populist party, founded 1879; assassinated Alexander II in 1881

NEP – New Economic Policy; mixture of capitalist rural sector and socialist urban sector, 1921–*c*.1929

NEP men – private entrepreneurs, small capitalists, during NEP

NKVD – ministry of internal affairs (after 1946, MVD); included secret police between 1934 and 1946 (see also secret police)

nomenklatura – List of key government positions to which officials are appointed by the Communist Party; or those appointed to these elite positions; first emerged in 1920s

oblast – from 1930, Soviet equivalent of *guberniya*, or province

obrok – feudal dues paid in cash

obshchina – see commune

Octobrists – union of 17 October, main right-wing liberal party, founded 1905

OGPU – Unified State Political Administration, official name for Soviet secret police 1922–34 (see also secret police)

Okhrana – main institution of tsarist secret police 1881–1917 (see also secret police)

opolcheniye – national militia or partisans

oprichnik (pl. *oprichniki*) – servants of tsar, within *oprichnina*

oprichnina – territory owned absolutely by Tsar Ivan IV, from which *boyare* were expelled, 1564–72

otkhod – 'going away', the term for temporary migration in search of wage-work

pech – brick stove in most peasant houses in the nineteenth century

perestroika – rebuilding or restructuring; used of the reforms of the 1980s

podzol – the poor soils of central and northern Russia

pogrom – anti-Semitic riot

Politburo – 'political bureau', established 1919; a sub-committee of the Central Committee of the Communist Party; since then, the main executive institution of Soviet government

poll tax – tax on all males (or 'souls'), established by Peter the Great in 1724

pomeshchik (pl. *pomeshchiki*) – Owner of a *pomest' ye*; later the general term for noble landowners, 'gentry'

pomest' ye – land grant in return for service (usually military)

pood – measure of weight – 16.38 kilograms

Populism – form of agrarian socialism that dominated Russian revolutionary movement in the nineteenth century and remained influential in the early twentieth century

procurements – rural supplies (mainly of grain) demanded by government; see *zagotovki*

prodrazverstka – method of grain requisitioning during Civil War

proletariat – urban wage-earning working classes

rada – Ukrainian national assembly

raion – from 1930, Soviet equivalent of *uezd*, or district

Raskol – the religious schism of the seventeenth century

raskolniki – 'Old Believers', religious dissenters who emerged after the *Raskol*

Raznochintsy – people of mixed ranks, a social category in Tsarist Russia including those who were literate but could not be fitted easily into the Table of Ranks

samizdat – 'self-published', illegal literature, copied by readers and circulated by hand

Secretariat – Secretariat of Central Committee of Communist Party, established 1919; in charge of Party personnel and appointments; the head of the Secretariat (general secretary or first secretary) has led the party since 1920s

secret police – see Cheka, KGB, MGB, NKVD, OGPU, Okhrana, Third Section

serfdom – legal and social system under which landlords have a right to tax their peasants in labour, kind, or cash (see *krepostnoe pravo*)

Slavophiles – intellectuals who disapproved of Western European culture and admired the religious traditions of Russia's past; mainly 1840s

smychka – alliance of workers and peasants; in Lenin's thinking, the social basis for the October Revolution

Socialist Revolutionaries (SRs) – populist political party formed in 1900

souls – legal term in imperial Russia for males of tax-paying classes, those subject to poll tax

Soviet – a working-class-elected council; first appeared as a strike committee in Ivanovo in May 1905; modelled on commune

sovkhoz – state farm

sovnarkhoz – regional economic councils; regional planning bodies introduced in 1957; abolished in 1965

Sovnarkom – Soviet of People's Commissars; the cabinet of the Soviet government under Lenin

SRs – see Socialist Revolutionaries

Stakhanovites – shock workers, who produced more than their 'norm' or quota; after Aleksei Stakhanov, a coal miner who achieved record norms in 1935

State Council – 1810–1905, advisory council appointed by tsar; 1905–17, upper house of parliament, included some elected members

table of ranks – list of ranks for all nobility, established in 1722

taiga – forested zone of northern Russia

Tatars – collective name for the Turkic tribes led by Mongols

terem – women's quarters; the segregated areas in which women lived in upper-class Muscovite houses

Third Section – Third Section of His Majesty's Chancellery, founded in 1826, official name for secret police to 1880 (see also secret police)

tolkachi – 'pushers', or 'fixers'; suppliers who operated outside the command economy, helping enterprises to acquire scarce goods

tsar – monarch, or emperor; from 'Tsezar', or 'Caesar'; used of Russian monarchs from sixteenth century

uezd – until 1930, a district, subdivision of a *guberniya*

Ulozhenie – code of laws

usad' ba – in tsarist Russia, the plot of land on which a peasant's house was sited; included outhouses and vegetable gardens

USSR – Union of Soviet Socialist Republics, formed 1922

val (*valovaya produktsiya*) – gross output; the most important single target indicator for most enterprises under the command economy

Varangians – vikings

veche – town meeting in city-states of medieval Russia

verst – Measure of length – 1.07 kilometres

Vesenkha – Supreme Council of National Economy; planning organization established in 1917

voevoda – provincial military/administrative official in Muscovy; forerunner of *gubernator volost* – administrative district in Muscovite and imperial Russia; a subdivision of an *uezd*

vydvizhentsy – 'those brought forward', working-class party members trained as technical specialists in early 1930s

WIC – War Industries Committee; semi-official organization set up by *Duma* in 1915 to co-ordinate war supplies; included representatives of factory managements and labour

zagotovki – procurements

ZemGor – all-Russian union of *zemstva* and town councils; semi-official body set up in 1915 to co-ordinate war effort

Zemlyachestva – associations of workers from the same province or region

Zemskii Sobor – 'Assembly of the Land'; a national assembly that met in the sixteenth and seventeenth centuries; similar to the various parliamentary bodies of western and central Europe.

zemstvo (pl. *zemstva*) – elected local government institutions established in 1864; became a focus for liberalism

Zhenotdel – women's department of Communist Party, established 1919

Index

abortion, 211, 316
Abuladze, T. Ye., 414, 454
Academy of Sciences, 387
aeroplanes, 329–31, 335, 337
Afghanistan, 108, 398, 407, 412, 453–4
agriculture, 7–8, 10, 13, 15, 16, 43–56,
    68, 73, 86, 110–12, 114–19, 122,
    124–5, 157–8, 161, 165, 213, 236,
    241, 244–8, 262, 278–80, 324, 347,
    355, 359, 361–2, 369–70, 373–4,
    385–6, 390–2, 403, 405, 407,
    410–11, 414, 420, 422, 436, 454
    commercial, 73, 114, 118, 121, 165,
      244
    see also collectivization, grain,
      harvests
alcohol, 15, 30, 31, 49, 59, 68, 82, 86,
    123, 165–6, 385, 388–9, 403, 407,
    414, 423, 449, 453
    see also vodka
Alekseev, general, M. V., 175, 189, 213
Alexander I, 34, 61, 65, 66, 76, 79, 448
Alexander II, 71, 76, 77, 80, 82, 87, 93,
    95–7, 117, 139, 413, 448–9, 457
Alexander III, 95, 96, 449
Alexandra, Empress, 161, 169, 171
Alexei, tsarevich, 154, 169
Alexei Mikhailovich, tsar, 102, 448
Allilueva, Svetlana, 351
Alma-Ata, 258, 418, 427, 454
anarchists, 224, 226, 238
Andropov, Yu. V., 162, 384, 402–3, 405,
    407, 453
anti-communists, *see*, whites
anti-faction rule, 253–5, 259, 299, 362
anti-party plot, 362–3, 374, 453
anti-semitism, 96, 156, 346, 458
apparat, 255–8, 261, 298, 301, 309–10,
    353–4, 356, 358–9, 363–4, 381,
    404, 415–16, 456
April Theses, 196–8, 450
Aral Sea, 47, 108, 392
Arkhangel'sk, 22, 214, 225, 227, 230,
    451
aristocrats, *see* nobles, landowners
Armenia, 418, 454
armaments, *see* industry, military
arms race, 101, 345, 397–8, 408–9, 412

army, 15, 17
    Kievan, 10, 13–15
    Mongol, 17–21
    Muscovite, 21, 24, 25, 26–9, 31, 37,
      101
    Imperial, 31–4, 36–7, 39–40, 58–9,
      60–1, 65–6, 68, 71, 73–8, 80,
      85–8, 95, 96, 100, 102, 124,
      128–31, 133, 141, 143–9,
      158–65, 168–71, 173–6, 180–1,
      183–5, 187–91, 196–201,
      208–12, 378, 448–50
    Soviet, *see* Red Army
Arsenev, K. I., 39, 40, 42, 64, 265
art, 133, 217, 298, 368, 384
artels, 121–2, 419
artisans, 39, 41, 68, 102, 137
assassination, 78, 95, 139–41, 154, 156,
    209, 258, 301, 303, 314, 449–50,
    457
Astrakhan, 22, 29, 32, 227
August putsch, 426–7, 455
Australia, 46
autocracy, 18, 20–1, 23–31, 34–7, 61–4,
    66–8, 71, 80, 85, 87, 91, 93, 97,
    101–2, 107, 110, 115, 126, 128,
    130, 133–5, 143, 145–6, 150–1,
    153–6, 168, 172, 175–7, 180,
    183–4, 193, 196, 231, 254–5, 260,
    289, 320, 324, 353, 365, 373, 377,
    423, 456
Azerbaijan, 417–18, 454

Babel, I. E., 116, 217, 235
backwardness, 73–4, 92, 96, 100–1, 103,
    116, 126, 164, 181–2, 194–6, 204,
    207, 235, 242–4, 246, 262, 287,
    289, 295, 317, 319, 339, 398–9, 431
Baikal, lake, 22, 47, 108, 415
Baku, 105–6, 108, 227, 310, 339, 425
Balkans, 7, 140
Baltic provinces/republics, 32, 82, 96,
    140, 213, 226, 230, 327, 330,
    342, 346, 416, 418, 427, 451–2,
    454
    see also Estonia, Latvia, Lithuania
Baltic sea, 10, 22, 47, 105, 108, 141,
    239, 334–5, 448

461

bankruptcy, 77, 82, 393, 395–6, 410,
    421–2
banks, 71, 73, 82, 104, 117, 133, 145,
    150, 168, 172, 189, 209, 220, 241,
    424, 426
  barshchina, 56, 57, 58, 73, 456, 459
Batu, khan, 16–20, 447
Belarus, 8, 335, 427
Belgium, 109
Belinsky, V. G., 66
Belorussia, *see* Belarus
Benkendorff, count, 74, 75, 78, 162,
    402
Beria, L. P., 304, 311, 353–4, 356–9,
    374, 453
Berlin, 140, 234, 328, 335, 339, 345,
    355, 418, 452–3
Bessarabia, 327–8, 452
Bezborodko, prince, 34–5
black earth, 47, 48, 50, 89, 114, 118,
    143, 456
Black Hundreds, 156
black market, 224, 355, 385, 394, 424
Black Sea, 11, 22, 34, 47, 104–6, 108,
    143, 165, 214, 225, 227, 334–5, 364
Bloody Sunday, 141–3, 159–61, 449
Boer war, 128
Bolotnikov uprising, 31, 447
Bolsheviks, 4, 123, 139, 144, 147, 160,
    169, 172, 183, 187, 192, 194–201,
    203–5, 207–15, 217, 219–20, 231,
    235, 237, 242–3, 247, 251, 257–60,
    262, 299–300, 304–5, 324, 326,
    332, 377–8, 417, 431, 449–51, 456
  see also Communists
borderline groups, 40, 62–3, 119
bourgeois revolution, 181–2, 188,
    193–4, 197
bourgeoisie, 62, 118, 129–30, 132–3,
    137, 181–3, 189–90, 193–8, 204,
    211, 243, 254, 265, 307, 456
boyare, 20, 21, 24, 25, 26, 27, 29, 33, 35,
    36, 62, 260, 447, 456, 458
Breshkovskaya, C., 94
Brest–Litovsk, treaty of, 213–14, 217,
    221, 324–5, 327–8, 342, 435, 451
Brezhnev, L. I., 78, 308, 352, 363, 377,
    380, 382–3, 385–6, 398, 402–3,
    405, 413, 421, 427, 453
Britain, 62, 77, 80, 109, 119, 136, 164,
    193, 214, 220, 227, 229, 250, 279,
    295, 325, 327, 330, 333, 340, 357,
    372, 451, 453
Brusilov, general A. A., 185, 229

Budenny, S. M., 329
budget, 59, 86, 107, 154, 166–7, 327,
    372, 385, 395–6, 403, 407, 409,
    423–4, 449
Bukharin, N. I., 192, 244–7, 249–52,
    257–8, 270, 297–8, 301, 303–4,
    309, 314, 316, 318–19, 364, 395,
    410, 452, 454
Bulavin, 32
Bulgakov, M. A., 414
Bulganin, N. A., 357, 372
Bulgaria, 334, 342, 418
bureaucracy, 21, 33, 36, 60–2, 85, 86,
    87, 133–4, 142, 144, 158, 161, 183,
    193, 197, 209–11, 218, 230, 256–7,
    311, 313, 389, 391, 397, 411, 457
  see also officials
Byzantium, 10, 11, 13, 15
  see also Constantinople

calendar, 6
Canada, 10, 336, 360
capital, 104, 107, 109, 128, 193, 211,
    280–2, 284–5, 288, 369, 371,
    391–2, 396, 456
Capital, 136
Capitalism, 1, 4, 5, 6, 42, 90, 91, 100–4,
    113, 116–19, 121, 124, 126, 136–8,
    150, 153, 181, 192–5, 199–200,
    231, 234, 240–4, 246–8, 252, 262,
    265, 283, 286–90, 294–5, 315, 319,
    324–5, 372, 374, 377, 381–2, 386,
    391, 393, 395, 405, 414, 425, 428,
    431–4
capitalists, 104, 124, 133, 137, 142,
    153–4, 156, 160, 188–90, 197, 219,
    243, 247, 265, 275, 287, 296
  see also bourgeoisie, entrepreneurs,
    merchants
cash, 42, 54, 56, 57, 74, 103, 110, 114,
    120, 220, 243, 280, 285–6, 369,
    399, 419, 458–9
Caspian Sea, 11, 22, 29, 47, 105–6, 108,
    227, 335
Catherine II, 34–6, 57, 60–1, 72, 74, 78,
    174, 346, 448
cattle, 16, 44, 50, 88, 115, 120, 130–1,
    186, 268, 270–3, 277–8, 318, 369,
    385, 436
Caucasus, 7–9, 11, 22, 96, 105, 130,
    140, 213–14, 227, 230, 271, 327,
    339, 360, 369, 394, 404
cavalry, 20, 28, 173, 223, 226, 228, 326,
    329, 339, 456

Caves monastery, Kiev, 13, 447
censorship, 63, 66, 71, 86, 96, 101, 184,
    210, 217, 253, 265, 298, 338, 353,
    364, 367–8, 383–4, 396–7, 424,
    449, 455, 457
census, 18, 30, 32, 39, 128, 414, 447
Central Asia, 8–9, 16, 258, 271, 275,
    335, 392, 418
Central Committee, 139, 200–1, 209,
    254–5, 257, 261, 300, 303–5, 308,
    311, 353, 358–9, 361–5, 374, 377,
    381, 387, 402–5, 407, 415, 450–1,
    453–4, 456, 458
Central Producer Region, 110, 114–15,
    158, 165, 177
ceremonial life of peasants, 30, 54, 123
Chayanov, A. V., 120
Cheka, 210, 214, 221, 235, 295, 302, 456
Chekhov, A., 87
Chernenko, K. U., 403–4, 453
Chernobyl, 413, 454
Chernov, V. M., 139, 187, 189, 213–14,
    225
Chernyshevskii, N. I., 92
Chicherin, G. V., 325
child care, *see* crèches
China, 7, 16, 100, 106, 108, 128, 140,
    325–6, 342–3, 345, 362, 432, 447,
    452
Christianity, 13, 14, 15, 19–21, 23, 34,
    53, 67, 315, 447, 454
    Nestorian, 19
chronicles, 10, 12, 13, 16, 17, 19, 447
church, 13, 14, 15, 17, 20, 25, 30, 31,
    33, 44, 60, 134, 186, 188, 269, 342,
    348, 447–8
Churchill, W., 294, 338, 342, 344, 452
CIS, *see* Commonwealth of
    Independent States
civil war, 27, 191, 210, 214–31, 234,
    237, 239–40, 242, 251, 253–7,
    259–62, 265, 267, 275, 280, 294–5,
    298–9, 305, 308, 325–7, 329,
    377–9, 405, 413, 416, 419, 447, 458
classes, 3, 39, 40, 41, 42, 56, 60, 67,
    85–6, 93, 116–24, 129–32, 134,
    136–7, 142, 150, 163, 182–3, 196,
    211, 265–6, 313, 316
    see also intelligentsia, nobles,
        peasants, privilege, ruling
        group, working classes
clergy, 14, 17, 39, 40, 59, 60, 63, 75, 92,
    141–3, 147, 265–6, 268–9
climate, 7, 15, 16, 28, 36, 49

CMEA, 344, 452, 456
coal, 105, 107, 125, 236, 277, 284, 334,
    391–2, 408, 437
coercion, machinery of, 2, 3, 180–1,
    183–5, 191, 196, 198, 201, 207,
    209–13, 215, 266, 293–5, 357, 373,
    413, 423
    see also army, police
Cold War, 195, 317, 344–5, 397
collective farms, 265–70, 272–4, 281,
    283, 285, 289, 294, 309, 342,
    345–7, 355, 360, 366–7, 369–70,
    374, 383, 385, 387, 393, 404, 409,
    411, 421, 424, 428, 457
collective leadership, 354, 358
collectivization, 122, 248, 251, 265–76,
    283, 285, 289–90, 293–4, 296,
    298–300, 307, 317–18, 320, 326,
    361, 378–9, 451
colonies, 100, 106
Cominform, 344
Comintern, 325–6, 344, 451–2, 456
command economy, 220, 265, 275,
    280, 286, 288, 340, 353, 362,
    368–9, 371, 391–7, 402, 409–11,
    423, 431–4, 459
commanding heights, 241, 318
commissars, political and military, 203,
    209, 215–16, 219, 222–3, 230, 239,
    257–8, 308, 324–6, 341, 345, 456,
    459
Committee for the State of Emergency,
    426–7
Commonwealth of Independent States,
    427, 455–6
commune, 51–3, 81, 84, 89, 90, 92, 93,
    107, 110–11, 114, 117–18, 131,
    143, 145–6, 148, 157–8, 184, 186,
    274, 456–7, 459
Communism, 1, 2, 5–6, 138, 180, 219,
    241–2, 262, 342–5, 358, 397
    see also Marxism, socialism
Communist International, *see* Comintern
Communist Party, Communists,
    215–21, 224, 226, 228–31, 234–5,
    237–43, 249, 252–62, 265–70, 274,
    297–300, 303–4, 307–14, 320, 326,
    341–2, 345, 353, 358–65, 378, 387,
    404, 409, 415–18, 424, 426–7, 451,
    455–6, 458, 460
    see also Bolsheviks
competition, 4, 121, 288, 395, 410–11,
    420–1
    see also innovation, markets, prices

computers, 394, 408
Conference of Communist Party, 198, 415–16, 454
Congress of Soviets, 181, 198, 201, 208–11, 217, 450–1
Congress of People's Deputies, 415–16, 454–6
Congresses of Social Democratic/Communist Party, 139, 192, 199, 218–19, 238–40, 253–5, 258–9, 261–3, 300–1, 303–5, 307, 311, 358–65, 367, 372, 404, 409, 413, 415, 451–4, 456
Conquest, R., 306–7
Constantine Porphyrogenitus, 13
Constantinople, 13, 105, 164
　see also Byzantium
Constituent Assembly, 145–6 175, 180, 182, 186, 189, 204, 209, 212–14, 229, 451
constitution, 134–5, 145–7, 154–8, 169, 176–7, 217, 265, 316, 415–16, 448–9, 451–3
consumer goods, consumption, 109, 113–15, 125, 137, 165, 167, 245–6, 248, 250, 267, 277–80, 284–6, 313, 318, 346–7, 355, 366–7, 369, 372, 374, 381, 385–6, 389–91, 394, 412, 422–3, 428
co-operatives, 409–10, 412, 424, 428, 454
cordon detachments, 235–8, 240
corruption, 60, 218–19, 310, 394, 402–3, 412
Cossacks, 29, 30, 32, 40, 41, 76, 131, 143, 173, 212–13, 226, 339, 456
cotton, 113, 118, 236, 392
courts, 51, 57, 60, 76, 83, 84, 85, 86, 96, 133
crafts, 44, 49, 54, 55, 68, 74
　see also domestic industry
crèches, 315–16, 386
Crimea, 79, 80, 96, 225–6, 234, 418, 426–7, 451
Crimean war, 5, 73, 75–7, 79, 80, 82, 104, 162, 324, 448
Cuba, 373–4, 453
cult of personality, 298, 358, 361–3
cultural revolution, 298–9, 382–3
culture, political, 64, 65, 66, 255, 266, 319–20, 324
　see also autocracy, ruling group
Czech Army of Liberation, 214–16, 225, 227, 451

Czechoslovakia, 342, 397, 399, 418, 452–3

de Custine, Marquis, 61
Decembrists, 65, 66, 78, 448
defence, 5, 15, 23, 31, 36, 116, 242, 246, 248, 250, 262, 266, 280, 287, 290, 295, 317–19, 324, 327, 329, 343–4, 352, 360, 368, 371–4, 377, 391, 398–9, 408, 412, 426, 431–2
dekulakization, 265, 268–72, 283, 293–4, 296, 298, 300
democracy, democratization, 35, 134–5, 183–4, 186–7, 191, 193–4, 196, 207, 217–18, 237, 253, 256, 259–60, 262, 316–17, 412–17, 421
democratic centralism, 139, 217–18, 255–7, 259
demography, *see* population
Denikin, general A. I., 213, 224–9
desert, 7, 46, 47, 366
destalinization, 358, 360–1, 363, 367–8, 404–5
Dictatorship of the Proletariat, 196, 254
diets, 28, 44, 49, 280, 366, 388
disarmament, 408–9, 412, 454–5
discipline
　in factories, 122–3, 185, 187, 190, 211, 220, 237, 240, 252, 283–4, 289, 346, 393, 403, 407, 421–2
　in army, 16, 31, 32, 75, 76, 144–9, 158, 160–1, 163–4, 168, 173–5, 181, 184–5, 187–9, 211, 215–17, 228, 231, 251, 257, 331–2
　of political parties, 95, 138–40, 192, 194, 209, 217–18, 228–31, 253–62, 298–9, 312–14, 359, 403
　of ruling groups, 16, 18, 21, 23–8, 31–36, 62–4, 66, 128, 132–3, 153, 156, 158–9, 168, 175–6, 183, 211, 215, 217–18, 228–31, 253–62, 266, 293, 295, 305, 312–14, 327, 343, 352–3, 365, 367, 416
dissent, dissidents, 62, 63, 255, 296, 299–303, 315, 358, 367, 383–5, 402–3, 413–14, 453
distilling, 86, 118, 407
　illegal, *see* samogon
district, 36, 62, 458–60
divorce, 211, 316
Djilas, M., 313, 319, 339, 341
Dmitrii Donskoi, prince, 23, 341, 447

Dnieper River, 11, 13, 19, 22, 105, 275, 339
doctors' plot, 345, 351, 356
domestic industry, 54–5, 68, 97, 103, 113, 118, 120–2, 125, 457
Don river, 11, 105
Donets River, 11, 105, 252
druzhina, 10, 12, 13, 14, 18, 24, 222, 456
dual power, 183–4
Dubcek, A., 397
Duma, 118, 134, 145, 147–50, 154–8, 160–2, 166, 168–71, 173–7, 180, 182, 204, 301, 449–50, 456, 460
Durnovo, P. N., 162
dvoriane, 24–9, 33, 35, 36, 62, 312, 456
Dzerzhinskii, F. E., 214

economic amphibians, 119–20, 122, 283
economists, 4, 6, 72–4, 280, 371, 375, 391–2, 399, 402, 407, 423, 432
educated classes, 65–7, 72, 93, 97, 104, 119, 133, 147, 149–50, 155, 158, 160, 164, 169–71, 175–7, 180, 182–3, 185–93, 204, 384
see bourgeoisie, intelligentsia
education, 45, 46, 53, 60–5, 86, 87, 93, 94, 102, 119, 131, 133, 140, 217, 259–60, 281, 286, 289–90, 315–16, 352, 366, 377–9, 382–3, 399, 404–5, 413, 423, 427
see also, schools
egalitarianism, 284, 312, 382, 431–4, 451
Eisenstein, S. M., 341
Ekaterinburg, 105, 214, 227, 451
elections, 85–6, 93, 134–5, 142, 144–6, 150, 154–6, 189, 211–12, 217, 229, 237–8, 256, 415–18, 426–7, 450, 454–5
see also suffrage
electricity, 236, 241, 248, 275, 277–9, 385, 422, 437
electronics, 377, 394, 399, 408
emancipation of serfs, 5, 71, 74, 75, 77–85, 88–91, 92, 94, 95, 96, 97, 104, 115, 117–19, 129, 132, 448
Emperor, 32, 154–5
see also tsar
Engels, F., 79, 136, 207, 316
engines of growth, 3, 5, 42, 90, 91, 103, 243, 280, 287–9, 293, 317–19, 346, 391, 395, 431–4
England, *see* Britain

Enlightenment, 34–5
entrepreneurs, 3, 4, 5, 42, 57, 72, 74, 88, 91, 97, 100, 102–4, 106–7, 117–18, 124–5, 133, 150, 153–4, 156, 187, 193, 240, 243–4, 262, 274, 287, 289, 319, 391, 395, 420, 428, 432, 457
estates, *see* classes
Estonia, 79, 82, 225, 230, 327–8, 418, 454
Eurasia, 7–9
  Outer, 7–8
  Inner, 7–9, 29, 101, 324
Europe, 5–6, 7, 15–16, 28–9, 34, 36, 42, 49–50, 57, 61, 65–7, 73, 77–9, 92, 96, 100, 102–4, 106, 113, 116, 118, 122, 126, 137, 181, 191, 194–5, 200, 204, 210, 225, 235, 242, 262, 344, 372, 398, 409, 412, 448
  Eastern Europe, 327, 342–4, 417–18, 425, 428, 432, 448, 455–6
European culture, 33, 34, 35, 52, 61, 62, 64, 66, 67, 101, 459
Executive Committee of the Congress of Soviets, 208, 217

factories, 56, 94, 95, 102, 113, 117–18, 120–4, 144, 172, 174, 177, 182–3, 190, 195, 198, 201, 204, 211–12, 219–21, 235, 247, 334–6, 340, 348, 370–1, 375
factory committees, 183, 187, 189–90, 198, 211, 219–20, 237, 456
factory workers, *see* working classes, *proletarians*
family groups, 310
famine, 48, 49, 50, 81, 88, 109–11, 114, 128, 235, 241, 262, 271–2, 274, 289, 293–4, 300, 307, 337, 346, 361, 449, 451
Fascism, 156, 326, 344
see also Nazis
February Revolution, 5, 116, 172–7, 180–1, 185, 204, 221, 239, 248
Fedor I, 27, 447
feminism, 211, 387–8
fertilizer, 50, 53, 114, 120, 161, 370, 392
feudal dues, 42, 49, 56–9, 68, 79, 83, 84, 87, 90, 91
  see also barshchina, obrok
films, 217, 341, 414
financiers, 62, 117, 177, 188

Finland, 96, 105, 140, 149, 199, 213,
    226–7, 328, 330, 334, 342, 346
Finnic speakers, 8, 10
First World War, 5, 115, 116, 118, 154,
    158–72, 175, 177, 184–9, 195–8,
    204, 208–9, 213, 244, 248, 280,
    285, 300, 324, 326, 423–4, 450
fiscal retreat, 145, 239–41, 245, 342
fiscal system, *see* taxation
fishing, 10, 44, 49, 52, 53
Five-Year-Plans, 267, 275–7, 280, 282,
    285, 290, 299, 312, 315, 326, 346,
    361, 375, 389, 451–2, 454–5
Florinsky, M. T., 185–6
foreign policy, 105, 140–1, 185, 209,
    213, 248–50, 324–7, 347, 371–3,
    408, 412, 426
foreigners, 101–2
forests, 8, 10, 44, 46, 47, 48, 50
    see also taiga
France, 62, 65, 77, 80, 109, 158, 164,
    193, 211, 214, 229, 279, 284, 295,
    326–7
French Revolution, 64, 91, 158, 193,
    211
fridges, 385, 437
Frunze, M. V., 225
Fundamental Laws, *see* constitution
furs, 10, 13, 103
Furtseva, E. A., 387

Gapon, priest, 130, 141–3
garrison troops, 146–7, 164, 168,
    172–4, 181, 184, 198–201, 203–4,
    210, 212, 231
gas, 392, 397
gender division of labour, 50–1, 282–3,
    387
General Secretary, 257, 259–60, 262,
    265, 300, 354, 359, 365, 377, 380,
    402, 404, 407, 451, 453, 458
Genghis Khan, 16, 18, 24, 222, 252, 447
gentry, 61, 85, 132, 134, 146, 148, 157,
    229, 270, 458
    see also landowners, nobles
geography, natural, 15
Georgia, 213, 333, 341, 417, 425, 427
Germany, 134, 161–2, 164–5, 185, 188,
    191, 195–6, 199, 213–15, 220, 231,
    234, 252, 277, 279, 294, 314, 319,
    324–6, 329–42, 346–7, 379, 418,
    450–2
Gerschenkron, A., 115–16, 125
glasnost', 80, 413–14, 448, 457

Glavlit, 253
GNP, 116, 276–9, 286, 369, 389–90,
    398, 406, 407, 410, 420, 423, 457
Gogol, N., 42, 61
gold, 109
Golden Horde, 17–21, 23, 447
Golovachev, A. A., 85
Gorbachev generation, 404–6, 413–14,
    427–8, 453
Gorbachev, M. S., 80, 82, 87, 352, 379,
    384, 389, 403–16, 418, 421, 423–8,
    453–4
Gorbacheva, R. M., 404
Gosagroprom, 407, 411, 453
Gosplan, 243, 275, 338, 370, 408, 457
Gospriemka, 407–8, 422, 454
governors, 62, 75, 76, 86, 184, 255, 457,
    459
GPU, 252, 260–1, 296, 313, 458
grain, 43, 44, 48–51, 73, 104, 110–12,
    114, 120, 125, 186, 355
    yields, 16, 50, 110–12, 114–15, 236,
        245, 270, 370, 374, 436
    exports, 73, 104–5, 107, 109, 112,
        114, 165, 243, 245, 248
    imports, 366, 385, 453
    supplies, 164–8, 172–3, 177, 189–90,
        198, 209, 221, 235, 237, 239–41,
        243–5, 248, 250–2, 267–8, 283,
        285, 318, 386, 419–20
    see also diets, *prodrazverstka*,
        procurements, rye, wheat
grain requisitioning, *see* procurements,
    prodrazverstka
great debate, 241–9
great retreat, 315–16, 326, 341–2, 345
Great Patriotic War, 6, 277, 280, 282,
    294, 306–7, 311, 317, 319, 331–43,
    347–8, 361–2, 371, 379, 383, 386,
    404–5, 417
Great Reforms, 71–91, 96, 97, 100, 113,
    115, 125, 131, 399, 402, 413, 427,
    448–9
Greece, 13, 334, 344
Grishin, V. V., 404
Gromyko, A. A., 404, 408
gross output, *see* val
Grossman, V. S., 414, 454
growth, economic, 3, 4, 5, 6, 73, 96, 97,
    100–7, 109–17, 124–6, 128, 150,
    161, 187, 193, 245–50, 262, 265,
    276–90, 317–20, 329, 375, 377,
    389–91, 396–7, 399, 406, 409,
    418–20, 431–4, 436–7

extensive, 3, 4, 6, 101–3, 112, 280, 287–8, 340, 369, 391, 399, 405, 432–3

intensive, 3, 4, 6, 100–3, 112, 114, 116, 242, 245, 280, 287–8, 369, 375, 391, 405, 432–3

guberniya, see provinces

Guchkov, A., 117–18, 146, 169–71, 180–1, 185, 187–8

Gulag, 296–7, 358, 451, 455, 457

Guyuk, khan, 18, 447

Haimson, L., 175

harvest, 29, 30, 50, 51, 54, 56, 105, 109–11, 114, 121–2, 128, 130, 161, 165, 235–6, 241, 251, 262, 267, 270–4, 277–80, 360, 366, 390, 397, 436

Haxthausen, baron, 46, 48, 52–3, 448

health, *see* diets, medicine, welfare

heavy industry, 107, 111–13, 115–16, 124–5, 161, 244, 246, 248, 250, 277–9, 286, 290, 313, 327, 346–7, 355, 359, 361, 368–9, 391, 437

see also industry

Herberstein, 25

Herzen, A., 92

historians, Soviet, 71, 72, 75, 341, 383, 414

western, 71, 72, 306

Hitler, A., 284, 326–7, 330, 338, 342, 347, 452

Hobbes, T.

honey, 10, 13

horses, 12, 15, 17, 23, 28, 29, 50, 53, 88, 115, 120, 222, 270–1, 299, 309, 317, 326, 329

household, 43, 44, 45, 46, 50–5, 60, 68, 84, 97, 103, 110, 113–15, 117–18, 120–2, 143, 157–8, 269, 271, 273–4, 283, 286, 316, 366, 382, 387

housing, 168, 252, 278, 280, 284, 286, 313, 340, 366–7, 369, 374, 380, 385, 391, 422, 428

see also izba

Hsiung-nu, *see* Huns

Hughes, J., 105

Hungary, 105, 215, 234, 334, 346, 362, 402, 418, 448, 453

Huns, 7–8

hunters and gatherers, 7

hunting, 10, 14, 15, 52, 53

iarlyk, 17

ideologies, 1, 6, 134

see also Populism, Socialism, Liberalism, Marxism, Leninism, Nationalism

Igor, prince, 10, 12, 14, 447

imperialism, 100, 140, 181, 195, 197, 210, 249

India, 7

industrial managers, 220, 252, 283, 288–9, 295, 307, 310–13, 329, 346, 380, 393, 395–6, 403, 408, 411, 419, 422, 428

industrialists, 117, 122–4, 129, 169, 180, 187–9, 193, 195, 219, 229

industrialization, 74, 90, 97, 104–17, 125, 126, 128, 138, 243–50, 261, 265, 267, 275–90, 293, 295–6, 300, 317–20, 327, 347–8, 351–2, 355, 361, 365–6, 373, 379, 383

see also modern revolution

industry, 63, 67, 94, 102–7, 109, 111–16, 118, 122, 124, 133, 161, 164, 187, 208, 220, 228, 230, 236, 241, 245–6, 248, 259, 327, 334–8, 340, 390, 437

military, 101–3, 111, 115–16, 161, 164–5, 167, 169, 172, 176, 185, 221, 230, 242, 246, 248, 250, 261, 277, 280, 286–7, 327, 329, 334–7, 347, 360, 368–9, 372, 398, 408

textiles, 102–5, 113–14, 117–18, 129, 143, 172, 236, 245, 308

see also coal, heavy industry, iron, oil, steel

inequality, 2–6, 91, 92, 137, 195, 320, 367, 380–2, 432–4

inflation, 81, 165, 167–8, 189–90, 220, 285, 300, 407, 424

informal organisations, 416, 454

informers, 266, 296, 314, 357

innovation, 4, 6, 53, 96, 286–7, 289, 371, 391, 393, 399, 406

intellectuals, *see* intelligentsia

intelligentsia, 41, 52, 60, 62–3, 94, 119, 126, 132–3, 135, 138–40, 150, 154, 156, 160, 162–3, 180, 182, 192, 207, 218, 229, 259, 261, 265–6, 296, 307–8, 312–13, 378, 383–6, 414, 421, 457

international revolution, *see* world revolution

International Women's Day, 172

investment, 128
  see also loans
Irkutsk, 22, 47, 108, 215, 225
iron, 102–3, 105–7, 111–12, 125, 128,
    236, 246, 248, 277–9, 329, 334, 437
iron curtain, 342, 452
Iskra, 139
Islam, 19, 21, 23, 342, 417
Italy, 116, 214, 227
Ivan I, '*kalita*', 20, 447
Ivan III, 21, 23, 24, 25, 447
Ivan IV, 'The Terrible', 25, 26, 27, 28,
    29, 101, 260, 341, 447, 458
Ivanovo, 105, 143, 459
izba, 43, 44, 45, 48, 53, 83, 88, 457
Izvestiya, 309, 359

Japan, 108, 125, 140–1, 153, 214, 226,
    279, 295, 326, 338, 342
Jews, 96, 144, 159, 342
joint enterprises, 410, 454
journalists, 414, 426–7
judicial reform, 85, 86, 96, 449
July days uprising, 187, 199, 201, 450

Kadets, 146–7, 155, 157, 169, 187–8,
    449, 457
Kaganovich, L. M., 275, 313, 356, 363
Kalinin, M. I., 302, 356
Kamenev, L. B., 192, 196, 201, 203,
    208–9, 257–8, 270, 300, 303–4,
    364, 452, 454
Kankrin, count E. F., 73
Kantorovich, L. V., 391
Kazakhstan, 8–9, 247, 270, 335, 360,
    366, 417–18, 427
Kazan, 21, 22, 29, 101, 216, 225, 227, 451
Kerensky, A. F., 170, 180, 182, 187–8,
    199–201, 203, 208, 212, 450
KGB, 306, 357, 362–3, 383–4, 402, 426,
    453, 457
Khabalov, general S. S., 172–4
Kharkov, 105, 131, 144, 227, 271–2, 449
Khazars, 10, 11
khozraschet, 396, 409, 457
Khrushchev, N. S., 160, 301–3, 305,
    308, 345–6, 351–4, 356–75, 377,
    379–80, 383, 389, 395, 398–9, 405,
    414, 420–1, 453
khutor, 157–8, 186, 457
Kiev, 10–13, 15, 17, 19, 22, 47, 105,
    310, 328, 334–5, 339, 447, 451
Kievan Rus', 10–21, 29, 36–7, 46, 447,
    456

kinship, 24, 310
Kireevskii, I. F., 66
Kirilenko, A. P., 308
Kirov Decrees, 302, 357, 452–3
Kirov, S. M., 300–4, 361, 452
Kirov works, *see* Putilov works
Klyuchevskii, V. O., 48
Koestler, A., 271–2, 304, 313
Kokovtsov, count V., 147, 174
Kolchak, admiral A. V., 225, 229, 451
kolkhozy, *see* collective farms
Kollontai, A. M., 211–12, 253, 316, 387
Komsomol, 310, 314, 341, 360, 378, 404
Konev, marshall I. S., 339
Konovalov, A. I., 160, 180, 187
Kopelev, L. Z., 314
Korea, 140–1, 345, 372, 452–3
kormlenie, 23, 457
Kornilov, general L. G., 188–9, 191,
    199–200, 213, 450
Kosygin, A. N., 308, 377, 396, 403, 409,
    453
Kremlin, 354, 357, 363, 427–8, 455
Kronstadt, 146, 149, 198, 237–40,
    253–4, 451
Krupskaya, N. K., 316
Krymov, general A. I., 171
Kryuchkov, V. A., 426
kulaks, 118, 120, 148, 154, 157–8, 177,
    214, 221, 224, 241, 247, 250–1, 265,
    268–72, 283, 289, 294, 296, 457
Kulikovo, 21, 23, 447
Kursk, 143, 334, 452
kustar, *see* domestic industry
Kutuzov, general, 341

labour, 3–4, 6, 56, 72–3, 81, 165, 243,
    280–6, 288, 290, 346, 369, 389–93,
    399, 406, 420–1, 436
  see also wage labour, wage-earning,
    work-rhythms
labour camps, 5, 271, 294, 296–7,
    306–7, 320, 333, 337, 345–6,
    355–8, 367, 383, 414, 451, 453, 457
  see also Gulag
labour, forced, 72, 74, 77, 78, 87, 102,
    104
  see also serfdom, slavery, labour
    camps
land redistribution, 50–53, 93, 148,
    155, 157–8, 162, 182, 184–6, 189,
    195, 197–8, 204, 208–9, 211–12,
    219, 221–2, 229, 235, 450–1
  see also repartition of land

land shortage, 54, 88–9, 110, 119–20, 126, 130–1, 137, 148–50, 155, 157–8, 160, 177, 247
Land Captains, 96, 110, 184, 449
landowners, 3, 28, 29, 30, 31, 32, 35, 41–2, 44, 46, 50, 55–62, 73, 74, 81–4, 86–91, 93, 94, 97, 109, 114, 116–17, 130–3, 146, 150, 154, 156–7, 159, 177, 180, 186–7, 193, 195, 197, 211, 219, 224, 229, 247, 265–6, 268, 270, 294, 296, 456, 458
  see also boyare, dvoriane, gentry, *kulaks*, nobles, *pomest'ye*
Latvia, 79, 227, 327–8, 334, 425
law, 35, 41, 71, 91, 119, 145, 211, 358
  martial, 86, 133, 149, 216, 417
Law Codes, 29, 30, 448, 459
League of Nations, 326, 451
left opposition, 258, 296
legitimacy, *see* persuasion
Lena River, 22, 47, 108, 159, 370
Lenin, V. I., 74, 118–19, 128–9, 138–9, 157–8, 191–201, 203–4, 208–11, 213–15, 220, 222–6, 229, 231, 239–41, 243, 246, 249, 253, 255, 257–8, 260, 262, 267, 283, 295, 300, 314–17, 320, 324, 332, 361, 389, 410, 413, 449–51, 456, 459
Leningrad, 6, 257, 296, 301–3, 308, 327–8, 332–6, 338, 340, 345, 347, 420, 424, 452
Leninism, 192–8, 260, 342, 354, 358, 379
Liberalism, liberals, 4, 34, 41, 64, 78, 80, 85, 86, 90, 91, 92, 93, 118, 133–5, 140–1, 143, 145–7, 160, 169–70, 184, 367, 416, 449, 457–8, 460
Liberation movement, 134–5, 141, 182, 193, 449
Liberman, E. G., 371, 391, 395
Liddel Hart, general, 329
Ligachev, Ye. K., 404, 411
List, F., 109
literacy, 56, 64, 131, 217, 249, 281, 352, 383, 436
literature, 64, 235, 253, 367, 414, 445–6
Lithuania, 19, 20, 28, 79, 81, 227, 295, 327–8, 447, 450
Litvinov, M., 326
livestock, 7, 44, 45, 49, 50, 53, 55, 115, 120, 165, 186, 248, 268, 270–3, 277–8, 280, 285, 299, 317–18, 347, 369, 436

living standards, 110, 114–15, 119, 125, 167–8, 177, 189–90, 246, 248, 271, 280, 285–6, 290, 315, 346–8, 355, 362, 365–6, 372, 374, 385–6, 388–91, 399, 421–2
loans, 73, 83, 87, 88, 109, 128, 147, 167, 214, 244, 246–8, 343–4, 424, 449
local government, 36, 62, 71, 85, 86, 132, 169, 184–5, 209, 256, 309, 421
Lunacharsky, A. V., 203
L'vov, prince G. E., 180, 187, 450

machine tractor stations, 269–70, 272, 457
magic, 53, 54
Makhno, N., 224–6, 228
Maklakov, V. A., 170–1, 176, 300, 450
Malenkov, G. M., 311, 351, 353–9, 363, 366, 372, 452–3
Mamontov, S. I., 133
managers, *see* industrial managers
Manchuria, 22, 108, 140–1, 145, 147, 162, 326
Mandelstam, N. Ya., 414
Mao Zedong, 342
markets, 3, 4, 5, 42, 54, 56, 68, 72, 73, 74, 88, 89, 91, 92, 94, 97, 100, 103, 104, 106, 110, 114, 117, 120–1, 124–6, 165, 195, 220, 240, 243–6, 248–51, 260, 262, 271–4, 275, 285, 287–9, 318, 353, 380, 391–2, 395–6, 409–12, 419–20, 423–5, 428, 432–3, 457
  see also black markets
marriage, 21, 25, 45, 46, 51, 52, 57, 59, 83, 103, 122–3, 211, 316, 345
Marshall plan, 344
Martov, Yu. O., 129, 138–9
Marx, K., 4, 79, 119, 129, 136–9, 181, 193–4, 196, 220, 242–3, 317, 358, 391, 421, 431, 433
Marxism, Marxists, 1, 71, 72, 129, 134–9, 144, 192, 193–4, 201, 243, 275, 315, 317, 341–2, 358, 379, 383, 392, 449
  see also communism, socialism
Mayakovsky, V. V., 217
meat, 30, 49, 240, 271, 277–8, 318, 355, 385, 422, 436
medicine, 45, 53–4, 63, 86, 119, 387–8
Medvedev, R. A., 315
Memorial, 416, 454

Mensheviks, 139, 144, 155, 181–2, 187, 190, 192, 194, 198, 203, 208, 217, 253, 301, 317, 319, 431, 449, 457
merchants, 10, 20, 27, 28, 39, 40, 41, 59, 60, 62, 63, 93, 102–4, 110, 114, 117, 125–6, 132–3, 150, 268
meshchane, 39–41, 128, 457
MGB, 457
migratory work, 43, 44, 46, 54–7, 73, 121–6, 128–9, 131, 165
  see also otkhod
Mikhail Aleksandrovich, grand duke, 175, 180, 450
Mikhail Romanov, 27, 101, 447
Mikoyan, A. I., 300, 332, 355
military specialists, 215–16, 256
Military-Revolutionary Committee of Petrograd Soviet, 203, 207
militia, 13–14, 184, 186, 211, 215, 333, 337, 458
Miliutin, D., 76, 77, 86
Miliutin, N., 82
Milyukov, P. N., 132–4, 143, 146–7, 170–1, 180, 185, 187–8, 450
mining, 56, 113, 122, 160, 247–8, 284, 422, 436
ministries, ministers, 59, 60, 62, 81, 106–7, 109, 118, 144, 154–6, 162, 166, 169–70, 174, 180–1, 187, 189–90, 208–9, 243, 308, 310–11, 325–7, 353–4, 356–7, 359–60, 363, 369–70, 377, 379–81, 396, 404, 410, 416, 452–3
Minsk, 227, 419
mir, see commune
mobilization, direct and indirect, 2–6, 10, 12, 13, 18, 24, 29, 32, 36, 37, 56–60, 63, 68, 71, 72, 77, 96, 101–3, 107, 115–16, 164–71, 177, 215, 220–1, 230–1, 239–40, 243–6, 250, 261–3, 267, 272, 275, 280–9, 318–20, 327, 331, 333–4, 338–9, 343, 346–8, 379, 405
mobilizing the 'human factor', 408
modern revolution, 1, 2, 4, 42, 60, 62, 64, 67, 71, 72, 74, 87, 90, 92, 96, 97, 100–2, 107, 110, 119, 124–6, 133, 136–7, 141, 150, 153, 241–9, 261, 267, 431
modernization, *see* modern revolution
Moldova, 26, 80, 327, 418
Molotov, V. M., 327, 332, 353–6, 363
monasteries, 17, 67
Mongolia, 8–9, 16, 108, 363

Mongols, 11, 15, 16–21, 23, 32, 37, 58, 285–6, 295, 447, 457
Moscow, 17, 20, 21, 22, 24, 47, 48, 61, 66, 80, 89, 102–5, 108, 110, 115, 117–18, 130, 133, 143, 146–7, 160, 165, 175, 188, 199–200, 210, 213–15, 218, 225, 227, 230, 237–8, 252, 257, 286, 302, 327–8, 333–6, 338, 347, 354, 359, 362, 370, 391, 395, 404–5, 420, 424, 426–7, 447–8, 451–2
motor vehicles, 277, 313, 329, 381, 392, 437
MTS, *see* machine tractor stations
Murmansk, 214, 227, 259
Muscovy, 20–31, 46, 48, 50, 66, 101
  expansion, 22, 23, 29, 32, 34, 101
mutiny, 76, 143–9, 162–3, 173–4, 177, 237–9, 253–4, 449–50
MVD, 354–7, 458

Nabokov, V. V., 414
Napoleon, 34, 39, 64, 65, 71, 341, 448
Narodnaya volya, 95, 139–40, 449, 457
Narva, battle, 31, 448
national income, *see* GNP
nationalism, 93, 95, 134, 140, 341–2, 348, 383, 399, 416–18, 428, 454
nationalities, non-Russian, 96, 134–5, 140, 147, 182, 209, 213, 257, 342, 345–6, 361, 417
nationalization, 182, 197, 211, 214, 220
NATO, 397, 409
navy, 39, 102, 141, 145, 449
Nazi-Soviet pact, 327, 329–30, 342, 347, 418, 435, 452
Nazis, 277, 294, 319, 326–7, 330, 340
Neizvestnyi, E. I., 368
Nekrich, A. M., 383
Nemchinov, V. S., 391, 394
neolithic, 8
NEP, *see* New Economic Policy
NEP men, 240–1, 244, 247, 250, 254, 265, 268, 457
New Economic Policy, 5, 236, 239–53, 262–3, 267, 275, 287, 289, 296, 315, 318–19, 325, 395, 409–11, 419, 428, 432, 451, 457
New Thinking, 408, 454
newspapers, 94, 132–3, 139, 144, 148–9, 168, 172, 176, 201–3, 210, 216–17, 243, 252, 257, 293, 304, 309–10, 338, 414, 449
  see also press

Nicholas I, 61, 66, 73, 74, 76, 78, 80, 89, 377, 397, 402, 448
Nicholas II, 110, 128, 134, 140, 142–5, 149–50, 153–6, 159, 161–2, 165–6, 168–77, 189, 301, 407, 449–51
Nizhny-Novgorod, 227, 414
NKVD, 297, 302, 304, 306, 311, 314, 329, 337–8, 458
nobles, 5, 20, 23, 24, 25–30, 33–6, 39–42, 59, 60–3, 68, 73–4, 78–88, 90–4, 96–7, 102, 114, 117–19, 124–6, 132–5, 150, 153–4, 156, 159, 211, 260–1, 265–6, 456–9
see landowners, gentry, *boyare, dvoriane*
nomadism, 7, 8, 10, 15, 16
nomenklatura, 256–7, 261, 266, 298, 312, 314, 316, 353, 367, 380–2, 384, 411, 416, 421, 458
Nove, A., 271, 317, 319
Novgorod, 11, 15, 20, 22, 23, 25, 334, 447
Novikov, N., 78
Novosibirsk, 47, 327
Novozhilov, V. V., 391
nuclear industry and weapons, 286, 343–5, 372, 374, 397–9, 408–9, 412–13, 452–3
Nystadt, treaty, 32, 448

oblast', 458
obrok, 56, 57, 59, 68, 73, 117, 458–9
October Manifesto, 145–6, 155, 158, 449
October Revolution, 4, 6, 180, 192, 200–5, 207–11, 216, 240, 257, 265, 295, 301, 316, 324, 341, 377, 379, 402, 413, 431, 450, 459
Octobrist party, 118, 146, 156–7, 161, 169, 187, 449–50, 458
Odessa, 104–5, 118, 143, 227, 328, 334
officials, 33, 36,39, 40, 57, 58, 60, 61, 62, 63, 74, 80, 81, 84–6, 90, 93, 96, 97, 119, 132–4, 140, 142, 156, 181, 184, 209, 218, 235, 265–6, 313, 383
see also bureaucracy, Soviet
OGPU, *see* GPU
oil, 104–6, 246, 277–9, 329, 339, 369, 389, 392, 397, 423, 437
okhrana, 458
Old Believers, 31, 32, 33, 458
Olga, princess, 12–13, 447
oprichnina, 26, 27, 28, 260, 447, 458
Order No. 1, 174, 181, 184, 187, 450
Ordzhonikidze, G. K., 282

Orgburo, 255, 257
otkhod, 44, 458
see also migratory work
Ottoman Empire
see Turkey

Paleologue, M., 163
Pamyat', 416, 454
parliamentary institutions, 90, 93, 142, 144–5, 150, 154, 169, 197, 213, 418, 424, 426–7, 449, 454–6, 460
see also Congress of People's Deputies, *Duma, rada, Zemskii sobor*
parties, political, 134, 162, 397, 424
see also Kadets, Octobrists, Bolsheviks, Mensheviks, Trudoviks, Progressive party, Communists
participation rate, 281–2
partisans, 225, 256, 333, 338, 345, 458
Party, *see* Communist Party
Party secretaries, 255–7, 260–1, 299, 309–10, 345, 360, 363–4, 369, 379–80, 387, 404–5, 456
passports, 283
Pasternak, B. L., 235, 414, 454
pastoralism, 7, 8
pastoral nomads, 7, 8, 10, 15, 16, 32, 36, 48, 101
Patolichev, N. S., 378–9
Patriarch, 33, 342
patronage, 255–6, 259–60, 262, 298, 416
Paul I, 61, 76, 78, 448
Pavlov, V. S., 425–6, 455
peace arbitrators, 84
peaceful coexistence, 246, 325, 347, 372, 408, 453
peasant uprisings, 31, 32, 34, 58, 74–7, 79–83, 86, 88–90, 92, 95, 115, 129–31, 143, 146, 148–9, 156–8, 186, 227–9, 235, 240–1, 249–51, 262, 270, 293–4, 447–9
peasants, 5, 29–32, 39, 40–60, 65, 67, 68, 72–6, 79, 81–5, 87–9, 91, 92, 94, 95, 97, 103, 109–10, 113–22, 124–6, 128–9, 131, 133, 135, 137, 139, 142–3, 145–6, 148, 150, 154, 156–60, 162–3, 165, 167, 177, 180, 183–4, 189–98, 204, 207–12, 219–24, 229, 235, 238–41, 244–54, 260–2, 265–71, 282–5, 289, 293–4, 299–300, 307, 309, 315, 318–19, 326, 341–2, 348, 378, 381–2, 404, 411, 457, 459

poor, 14, 15, 49
  see also serfs
Penza, 131, 215, 227
People's Will, *see Narodnaya volya*
perestroika, 6, 71, 319, 352, 404–27, 432,
  454, 457–8
Peresvetov, 26
Perm, 105, 227
permanent revolution, 193, 249
persuasion, machinery of, 2, 3, 13, 19,
  23, 31, 33, 133–4, 164, 176, 184,
  216–17, 253, 265, 315, 338, 384,
  389, 423
  see also propaganda
Peter I, 31–6, 59, 60–1, 64–7, 102, 104,
  107, 115–16, 125, 211, 243, 256,
  260–1, 266, 287–9, 341, 343, 353,
  448, 458
Peter III, 35, 78, 448
Petrograd, 6, 161, 165, 167, 172–5, 181,
  185, 196, 198–203, 205, 210,
  212–13, 225, 227, 230, 235–9, 257,
  450
Petrograd Soviet, 174, 181–5, 187,
  190–2, 198–200, 202–4, 207–8,
  258, 450
Petrunkevich, I. I., 134–5, 146
planning, 220, 241, 243, 267, 275–6,
  280, 287–8, 338, 346, 365, 366,
  369–71, 375, 391–7, 403, 409–10,
  419–21, 423, 428, 432–3, 453, 457,
  459
Plehve, V. K., 141
Plekhanov, G. V., 138–9, 449
Pobedonostsev, C. P., 95, 96
podzols, 15, 48, 458
Poland, 19, 27, 29, 32, 34, 60, 89, 93,
  95, 96, 105, 140, 213, 225–6, 234,
  295, 327–8, 330, 334, 342, 362,
  417, 447–52
police, 36, 51, 62, 65, 74, 75, 81, 87, 88,
  94, 130, 139, 142–4, 146, 148, 156,
  159–60, 162, 167, 173, 181, 184,
  186, 193, 197, 209–11, 215, 217,
  252, 260–1, 265, 270, 294–5, 298,
  300–4, 306, 310–13, 320, 331,
  353–60, 364–5, 373–4, 384, 389,
  403, 426, 452, 456–9
  see also Cheka, GPU, KGB, MGB,
    MVD, NKVD, *Okhrana*, Smersh
Politburo, 255, 257–8, 300–4, 308,
  310–11, 332, 353–4, 356–65,
  379–81, 387, 404–5, 416, 418, 451,
  453–4, 458

  see also Presidium
poll tax, 32, 51, 59, 68, 73, 103, 448–9,
  458–9
Poltava, 32, 131, 448–9
pomest'ye, 24, 25, 29, 458
Popov, G. K., 413, 423, 424, 454–5
popular fronts, 326, 418, 454
population, 3, 7, 8, 9, 16, 27, 29, 32, 39,
  45–6, 50, 61, 89, 103, 110–12, 114,
  120, 128, 140, 235, 277–8, 369,
  388, 392, 434, 436
Populism, populists, 52, 53, 92, 94, 95,
  113, 117–18, 129, 135–6, 138–9,
  214, 448, 457–9
Port Arthur, 22, 108, 140–1
Poskrebyshev, A. N., 303
Pospelov, P. N., 361
potatoes, 49, 75–6, 240, 355
potato riots, 75–6, 448
Potemkin, battleship, 143, 449
Potsdam, 344, 452
praktiki, 260, 280
Pravda, 257, 302, 342, 359
Preobrazhensky, E. A., 246–8, 250
President, 415–16, 426–7, 454
Presidium, *see* Politburo
press, 85, 106, 132–3, 176, 184, 201–3,
  210, 216–17, 238, 253, 256–8,
  304–5, 309, 414
  see newspapers
prices, 109–10, 121, 161, 165, 167–8,
  172, 189, 221, 239, 248–50, 262,
  267, 272–3, 276, 285, 287–8,
  318, 355, 385, 391–3, 395–6,
  409, 412, 420–4, 425, 432, 453,
  455
priests, *see* clergy
primitive accumulation, 119, 247
private plots, 272–4, 285, 336, 341–2,
  345, 348, 355, 411, 457
privatisation, 157–8, 240, 425
privilege, 2, 3, 4, 6, 14, 18, 20, 24, 26,
  34, 35, 40, 60–3, 87, 93, 126,
  175–6, 186, 196, 207, 218–19, 237,
  259, 261, 312–16, 320, 345, 353,
  380–2, 421, 428
procuracy, 301
Procurator of the Holy Synod, 33
procurements, 165, 221, 250–2, 258,
  262, 265, 267–75, 285, 289, 296,
  318, 355, 451, 458, 460
prodrazverstka, 221–4, 231, 235, 239–41,
  458
production function, 280–1

productivity, 3–6, 7, 16, 68, 73, 74, 76, 81, 90, 100–1, 104, 111–12, 114–17, 124, 126, 136–8, 157–8, 161, 187, 193, 242, 245, 247–8, 268, 280–90, 369, 371, 374–5, 377, 381, 385, 389–95, 398–9, 402–3, 405–6, 411, 431

profits, 3–4, 100, 102, 118, 195, 240–1, 245, 371, 395–6, 403, 456

Progressive Bloc, 169–71, 176, 182, 450

Progressive Party, 160

prohibition, 165–6, 407, 423

proletarian revolution, *see* socialist revolution

proletariat, 52, 79, 83, 90, 91, 92, 104, 117, 119, 122–4, 126, 128–30, 137–8, 150, 155–6, 160, 180, 193–8, 212, 235, 242, 246–7, 249, 254, 262, 265–6, 278, 282–3, 352, 378, 383, 395, 458
see also workers, wage-earners

propaganda, 95, 106, 131, 164, 184, 216–18, 230, 238, 253, 276, 293, 315, 320, 325, 330, 341, 377, 384, 399

proto-industrialisation, 103, 113

provinces, 36, 62, 81, 86, 184, 255–6, 261, 309–10, 448, 457–9
see also local government

Provisional Government, 118, 174–5, 180–92, 196–200, 203–4, 208, 210–12, 220–1, 283, 325, 450

Pskov, 11, 23, 25, 175, 334

Pugachev, E., 34, 74, 78, 82, 448

Pugo, B. K., 426

purges, 219, 259, 299–300, 303–11, 314–15, 317–18, 320, 329–30, 338, 340, 345–8, 356, 360–3, 374, 377–9, 414, 452, 454

Pushkin, A. S., 42

Putilov works, 141, 172, 202, 336–7
see also Kirov works

queues, 168, 190, 252, 284, 355, 386, 403

rada, 20, 213, 458

Radek, K. B., 254–5

Radishchev, A., 35–6, 78

railways, 5, 73, 77, 82, 104, 105–7, 109, 111–13, 115, 123–5, 128, 133, 140, 144–5, 165, 175, 181, 200, 210, 212, 217, 219–20, 230, 236–7,

239–41, 243, 247, 271–2, 275, 302, 313, 334, 336–7, 436–7
see also trans-Siberian railway

rainfall, 7, 46, 48

ranks, *see* Table of Ranks

Raskol, 31, 33, 448, 458

Rasputin, G., 169, 171, 450

raw materials, 6, 106, 164, 243, 280, 286, 288, 346, 369, 391–2, 399, 406

Razin, Stenka, 31, 448

raznochintsy, 39–41, 63, 92, 133, 458

Reagan, R., 409

recruitment, 3, 32, 57, 58, 59, 86, 87, 162–6, 215–16, 231, 249, 251, 299, 326, 341, 345, 449

Red Army, 211, 215–19, 221–31, 234–5, 237–9, 242, 249, 251, 257–9, 261, 267, 270, 295–6, 298–9, 304–5, 308, 310–11, 313, 326–7, 329–41, 344–5, 347–8, 357, 361–2, 364, 372–4, 380, 397–9, 407, 412, 425–6, 451–5

Red Guards, 201–3, 210, 212

Red Square, 364, 412, 418, 454

redemption payments, 83–4, 88, 90, 107, 109, 110, 145, 148, 156, 450
see also emancipation

Reed, J., 188–90, 202–4

religion, 2, 53, 64, 67, 123, 184, 269, 315, 342, 348
see also Christianity, church, Islam, Old Believers

repartition of land, 50–53, 93, 117–18

Republics, 417–18, 424–8

resistance, 16, 19, 20, 32, 128–9
see also peasant uprisings, revolutionary movement

retinue, *see druzhina*

Reutern, M. Kh., 82

revolution
of 1848, 79, 104, 135, 137, 193, 448
of 1905, 88–90, 114, 124, 126, 128–51, 154, 160–4, 167, 174, 176–7, 183–4, 192–4, 239, 249, 459
see also socialist revolution, bourgeois revolution, February Revolution, October Revolution

revolutionaries, revolutionary movement, 41, 63, 64, 65, 75–6, 86, 89, 91–7, 129–31, 133, 137–9, 147, 149, 159–60, 162, 164, 172, 192–3, 259, 325

Riabushinskii, P. P., 188

Riazan', 15, 17, 370, 447
Riga, 105, 163, 328
Riurik, 447
Riurikid dynasty, 447
Riutin, M. N., 299–301, 451
Rodzianko, M. V., 161, 169, 173, 180, 188
Romania, 105, 327, 334, 342, 346, 418
Romanov dynasty, 27, 28, 175, 447
Rostov, 227, 296, 330, 333–4, 452
Rostovtsev, general, 82
Rostow, W., 115
ruling group, 2, 3, 15–16, 21, 324
    Kievan, 10, 14–16, 20
    Mongol, 17–19, 21, 23
    Muscovite, 20, 21, 23, 24, 25, 26, 27
    Imperial, 31–5, 40, 41, 56, 58, 60–8, 87, 103, 117–18, 128, 131–4, 153–6, 158–9, 168, 170–2, 175–6, 180, 183, 203, 207, 211–12, 229–30, 235, 238, 260–1, 265–6, 324, 327, 343, 373
    Soviet, 6, 180, 207, 215, 218, 229–31, 253–61, 265–6, 270, 286, 293, 297, 305, 308, 311–15, 324, 327, 343, 352–3, 356, 362, 364–5, 367, 373, 377–82, 399, 416
Rurik, 15, 27
Rus', *see* Kievan Rus'
Russian Empire, 1–2, 5, 7–9, 29, 31–6, 71, 87, 89, 101–2, 107, 111–12, 115–16, 119, 134, 140, 144, 153, 188, 191, 207–9, 213, 224, 226, 262, 324, 417, 448
Russian Republic, 8, 417–18, 424–7, 455
Russification, 140
Russo–Japanese war, 108, 125, 128, 140–2, 145, 150, 161, 165, 449
Ruzsky, general N. V., 175
Rybakov, A. N., 414
rye, 44, 49, 51, 110, 186
    see also grain
Rykov, A. I., 304
Ryzhkov, N. I., 404, 416, 425, 453, 455

Sakharov, A. D., 384, 414, 416, 454
salt, 30, 31, 54, 59, 103, 285
Samara, 108, 186, 214, 225, 227, 451
samizdat, 384, 458
samogon, 166, 407
Sarai, 11, 17, 447
Saratov, 186
Schism, *see Raskol*

schools, 46, 53, 140, 144, 281, 381
    see also education
science, 66–7, 259
scissors crisis, 248–9
Scythians, 7
SDI, Strategic Defense Initiative, 408
Sebastopol, 80
Second International, 325
Second World War, *see* Great Patriotic War
secret speech, 301, 303, 305, 360–2, 367, 414, 453
Secretariat of CC, 255–9, 261, 298, 353–4, 359–61, 363, 374, 377, 379–80, 403, 451, 458
serfdom, 5, 29–32, 35–7, 41–2, 46, 56–8, 66, 68, 72–80, 83–5, 87, 94, 96–7, 102, 274, 393, 397, 448, 457, 459
    abolition of, *see* emancipation
serfs, 3, 25, 29, 30, 32, 40–2, 45, 46, 56, 57, 58, 60, 61, 62, 63, 68, 72, 73, 79, 83–6, 88, 91, 117–18
    household, 57, 83, 94
    industrial, 102
Serov, I. A., 357, 362–3
Shatalin, S. S., 425, 455
Shevardnadze, E. A., 404, 425–6, 453, 455
Shevchenko, A. N., 380–1
Shingarev, A. I., 166
Shipov, D. N., 134
Shlyapnikov, A. G., 253
Sholokhov, M. A., 235
show trials, 252–3, 304, 307–9, 314, 361, 452
Siberia, 8, 9, 16, 22, 29, 41, 47, 57, 95, 101, 104, 108, 114, 138, 147, 158–9, 192, 196, 214–15, 225–6, 230, 251, 270, 272, 275, 297, 299, 308, 327, 335, 337–8, 346, 360, 397, 447, 451
Sino–Japanese war, 140
slavery, 3, 10, 12, 13, 18, 30, 32, 57, 73, 78, 342
Slavophiles, 66, 67, 78, 92, 448, 459
Smersh, 331
Smith, Adam, 4, 72, 74
Smolensk, 11, 48, 49, 334
Smolny, 202–3, 208–9, 301
smychka, 196, 246–7, 249, 252, 459
Sobchak, A. A., 424, 455
social contract, 351, 365, 372–3, 385, 389, 391, 421–3, 433

social support, 184–5, 191, 196, 201, 207, 209–10, 212, 215, 228, 230, 315–16, 320, 331, 340–2, 348, 389, 399, 412–13, 423

Social Democratic Party, 138–9, 156, 449, 456–7
  German, 195
  see also Bolsheviks, Mensheviks, Communists

socialism, 4, 5, 52, 53, 91, 92, 118, 129, 134–40, 155, 157, 160, 162, 169, 172, 174, 181–2, 187, 191–2, 194–9, 204, 207, 212, 214, 219–20, 224, 235, 241–4, 246–50, 253, 262, 275, 287, 289, 314, 317, 319–20, 343–4, 347, 361, 372–3, 395, 414, 424–5, 428, 431–4
  see also Populism, Marxism

Socialism in One Country, 249, 260, 263

socialist realism, 298

socialist revolution, 5, 91–6, 129, 136–9, 162, 181, 193–201, 204, 207–8, 248, 431

Socialist Revolutionary Party, 94, 135, 139–40, 181–2, 187, 189, 198–9, 203, 208, 210, 212–14, 217, 225, 229, 253, 459

socialists, *see* socialism

soils, 15, 16, 36, 46, 47, 48, 49, 52, 56, 73

soldiers, *see* army

soldiers' committees or soviets, 181, 184, 187, 211, 216

Solzhenitsyn, A. I., 297, 345, 367, 414, 453, 455

Soviet Empire, 1–2, 7–8, 29, 342–4, 417, 425

Soviet Union, 1, 5–6, 7, 192, 246–7, 250, 252, 257–60, 263, 265, 274, 278–9, 315, 317, 320, 324–8, 330–1, 334, 338, 341–4, 348, 352, 371–4, 377, 383, 388, 391, 398–9, 404–5, 408–9, 417–19, 424–8, 431, 451–3, 455–6, 459

Soviets, 143–4, 147, 181–5, 188, 190, 196–200, 204, 208–11, 217, 219–22, 231, 237–8, 253, 274, 308, 316, 364, 415–16, 449, 451, 454, 459
  see St. Petersburg Soviet, Petrograd Soviet

Sovkhozy, see state farms

Sovnarkhozy, 360, 370, 420, 453, 459

Sovnarkom, 209, 217, 229, 459

space programme, 287, 372, 453

SRs, *see* Socialist Revolutionary Party

St. Petersburg, 6, 32, 47, 61, 66, 81, 93, 102–3, 105, 108, 124, 129–30, 134, 141–3, 144, 146, 149, 160–1, 448
  see also Leningrad, Petrograd

St. Petersburg Soviet, 143–4, 146–7, 449

stagnation, 71, 74, 78, 80, 352, 380, 389–99, 406, 413, 454

Stakhanov, A. G., 284, 452, 459

Stalin generation, 308, 368, 377–80, 382–3, 397, 399, 403–5

Stalin, J. V., 5, 6, 102, 115–16, 125, 196, 217, 231, 244, 249–52, 257–63, 265–70, 275, 280, 284–5, 287–9, 293–321, 325–7, 329–34, 338–45, 347–8, 351–69, 373–4, 379, 381–3, 391, 393, 398–9, 405, 414, 416, 418, 431–2, 451–2

Stalingrad, 17, 334–5, 339, 347–8, 364, 452

Stalinism, *see* Stalin

state capitalism, 220, 240

State Council, *see Duma*

State Defence Committee, 332, 334

state farms, 265–6, 269–70, 313, 360, 459

state peasants, 39, 40, 56, 57, 59, 68, 79, 83, 84

statistics, 39, 43, 63, 111–12, 119, 129, 235–6, 275–9, 290, 318, 329, 340, 347, 390, 435–7

steam engines, 104

steel, 106, 125, 236, 246, 248, 277, 329, 334, 408, 437

steppes, 7–8, 15, 29, 36, 43, 46–8, 50, 101, 360

Stolypin, P. A., 149, 154, 156–9, 177, 449–50
  reforms, 154–61, 177, 411, 449

streltsy, 28, 31, 101

strikes, 110, 128–31, 141–7, 149–50, 159–61, 168, 172–7, 182, 189–90, 325, 422, 424–5, 449–50, 459

Stroganov, 103

Struve, P. B., 74, 134

students, 92–4, 143, 159, 174, 384
  see also education

subsidies, 106, 385, 393, 421–3, 428

suffrage, 134–5, 142, 145, 154, 156, 211

Sukhanov, N. N., 181, 198–9, 209–10, 212, 258

Supreme Soviet, 354, 356, 415, 418, 454
Suzdal, 11, 20
Sverdlov, Y. M., 255
Sviyazhsk, 216, 225, 227, 451
Sweden, 27–9, 31–2, 196, 295, 316, 334, 386, 447–8
Switzerland, 138, 192

Table of Ranks, 33, 39–41, 61, 62, 64, 211, 256, 313, 448, 458–9
Taganrog, 121
taiga, 20, 47, 297, 459
Tambov, 45–6, 50, 56, 227, 235
tanks, 329–31, 333, 335–9, 407, 426
tariffs, 107, 109, 449
    see also taxation, customs
Tashkent, 47, 335
Tatars, 346, 418, 457, 459
    see Mongols
Tauride Palace, 174, 182
taverns, 31
taxation, 3, 4, 13, 16, 17, 18, 20, 21, 23, 30, 42, 49, 51, 54, 56–60, 71, 73, 93, 96, 102, 107, 109–12, 115, 119, 125–6, 128, 130–1, 142, 145, 149, 164, 166–7, 215, 221, 239–41, 243, 245–8, 250, 266, 285, 293, 300, 318–19, 365, 423
    customs, 59, 60, 107, 109, 165
    direct, 32, 56, 58, 59, 84, 103, 109–10, 145
    government revenue, 31–32, 58, 59, 60, 68, 73, 77, 96, 102–3, 107, 110–12, 115, 128, 145, 165–7, 285, 407, 423–4
    income, 167
    indirect, 30, 31, 56, 58, 59, 60, 86, 103, 109, 167, 272, 285, 389, 407
    local, 86
    see also feudal dues, *prodrazverstka*, poll tax, redemption payments, tribute, turnover tax
Taylor, F. W., 283
technological innovation, *see* innovation
technology, foreign, 28, 30, 32, 33, 101–3, 245–6, 286, 289, 377, 397
telephones, 201–3, 309, 338
televisions, 385, 435, 437
terem, 25, 34, 459
terror, 18, 86, 95, 139–40, 149, 294–6, 298, 302, 315, 329, 358, 360, 365, 374, 452
    see also purges

third element, 119
Third World, 113, 398, 431
tiaglo, 30, 51, 56
Tikhonov, N. A., 404
Time of Troubles, 27, 29, 37, 145, 153, 175, 324, 447
tolkachi, 394, 419, 459
Tolstoy, L. N., 61
totalitarianism, 319
    see also, Stalin, Stalinism
tractors, 269–70, 285, 294, 317, 337, 387
trade, 3, 8, 10, 11, 13, 15, 103, 107, 117, 164–5, 220–1, 224, 235, 239–41, 245–6, 248–52, 262, 267, 325, 379, 395, 398, 410
Trade Unions, 129–31, 141–3, 189, 212, 220, 222, 238, 253, 298, 313, 415, 422, 424, 449
trans-Siberian railway, 107–8, 113, 128, 140–1, 146–7, 161, 214–15, 225, 227, 451
transportation, 104, 107, 115–16, 172–3, 385–7, 422, 426, 428
Trepov, D. F., 157
Tretyakov, P., 133
tributes, 3–4, 8, 10, 12–14, 16–18, 20–21, 23, 221–2, 247, 251–2, 285
Trotsky, L. D., 144, 159, 188, 193–4, 199, 201, 203, 208–11, 213, 215–16, 219, 225, 228, 239–40, 246, 248–9, 252, 256–8, 300, 303–4, 313–14, 319, 324–5, 329, 354, 451
Trudovik party, 148, 170
Truman, president, 344
tsar, 25, 26, 27, 28, 33, 35, 57, 58, 60–2, 65, 66, 75, 80, 85, 93, 95, 102, 133, 140, 142–6, 148, 153–6, 159, 161–2, 168–77, 185, 196, 214, 230, 315, 447, 451, 459
Tukhachevsky, general M. N., 225, 239, 304, 329, 452
Tula, 101–3, 105, 230
tundra, 46, 47
Turks, 8, 10, 15, 31, 417
Turkey, 32, 77, 80, 164, 258, 295, 334, 449
turnover tax, 272, 285
Tver, 19, 20, 23, 85, 93, 105, 134, 447, 449

uezd, *see* district
Ukraine, 8, 19, 22, 29, 30, 35, 41, 43, 48, 50, 94, 96, 105, 114, 121,

130–1, 140, 144, 213–14, 221,
224–7, 235, 247, 270–1, 309, 327,
330, 335, 339, 342, 346, 359, 413,
417–18, 427, 448, 450–1, 455–6,
458
Ulozhenie, see Law Codes, 448, 459
Ulyanov, V. I., *see* Lenin
unemployment, 128, 282–3, 365,
395–6, 421, 432
Union of Liberation, *see Liberation
movement*
Union treaty, 417, 425–7, 455
United Nations, 412
universities, 63, 86, 92, 132, 143–4, 174,
298, 307, 347, 378, 383, 391,
404–5, 449
upper classes, *see* nobles, educated
classes
Urals, 8–9, 11, 16, 22, 30, 32, 36–7,
102–3, 105, 214–15, 225, 227, 251,
327, 335, 369
Urals-Siberian method, 251–2, 267, 451
urbanization, 43, 67, 111–12, 116,
122–3, 126, 266, 277–8, 282, 367,
382, 399, 436
USA, 57, 73, 78, 104, 109, 123, 141,
143–4, 203, 214, 227, 241, 279,
286, 326, 333, 335, 340, 343–5,
372–3, 380, 382, 386, 389, 392,
397–9, 408–9, 415, 451, 453
usad'ba, 44, 83, 274, 459
Uskorenie, 407, 453
USSR, *see* Soviet Union
Ustinov, D. F., 308
Uzbeq, khan, 20

val, 288, 396, 406, 459
value, 391–2
Varangians, 459
Vasilii III, 25, 447
veche, 19, 20, 459
vegetables, 30, 44, 49, 51, 273
Vesenkha, 220, 275, 451, 459
Vikings, 8, 10, 447, 459
villages, 8, 13, 17, 43, 44, 45, 46, 48, 52,
53, 54, 56, 59, 68, 120–4, 131, 157,
160, 183–6, 217, 221–2, 226, 235,
239, 249, 251–2, 269, 272, 281,
309, 315, 318, 340, 382, 388, 456
virgin lands, 360, 366, 369–70, 453
Vladimir, city, 11, 14, 105, 113
Vladimir I, prince, 13, 447
Vladimir Monomakh, Grand Prince,
14, 447

Vladivostok, 22, 47, 108, 146, 214
vodka, 30, 31, 53, 54, 59, 60, 68, 73, 76,
82, 86, 103, 109, 123, 165–6, 239,
245, 285, 385, 388–9, 419
see alcohol
voevody, 15, 19, 26, 459
Volga river, 10, 11, 17, 19, 22, 29, 47,
56, 105, 108, 115, 143, 214, 216,
224–5, 271, 335–6, 339, 346–7,
369, 447
Volgograd, *see* Stalingrad
Volkogonov, D. A., 297
Voroshilov, K. Y., 329, 363
Voznesensky, A. A., 332, 338
vydvizhentsy, 307–8, 311–12, 320, 378,
460
Vyshnegradskii, I. A., 107, 449

wage-earners, wage-earning, wage
labour, 4, 42, 54–7, 68, 72, 74, 79,
81, 83, 91, 94, 95, 100, 102–4, 110,
112–14, 117–25, 128–33, 137–8,
142, 147, 154, 157, 167–8, 172–3,
177, 180, 265, 277–9, 281–4, 300,
316, 386–8, 391, 395–6, 420–1, 436
see also proletariat, labour
wages, 4, 54–7, 68, 72, 81, 91, 97,
119–23, 128, 131–3, 147, 167–8,
177, 189, 237, 265, 270, 278, 280,
282–3, 290, 300, 312–13, 315,
346–7, 355, 367, 380–1, 386, 388,
393, 403, 422, 424
war, 14–16
see also Crimean war, Napoleon, First
World War, Great Patriotic War,
Korea, Russo–Japanese war,
Russo–Finnish war,
Sino–Japanese war,
Russo–Polish war, civil war
War Communism, 215–24, 231, 237,
239–40, 242, 251, 256, 261–2, 267
Warsaw, 105, 225, 227, 451
Warsaw pact, 397, 428, 453
weaving, 113, 117, 120
welfare services, 5, 45, 212, 283, 315,
365, 380, 385–8, 392, 421, 425
Wells, H. G., 234–5
westernization, 33, 34, 78
Westernizers, 66, 67, 92, 448
wheat, 44, 51, 118
see also grain
White Russia, *see* Belarus
Whites, 213–15, 217, 224–31, 234–5,
239, 254, 268, 295–6, 451

WIC, War Industries Committee,
169–71, 174, 176–7, 450, 460
Witte, S. Yu., 106–7, 109, 110, 115–16,
118, 125, 133, 141, 144–5, 147,
150, 157, 161, 243–4, 246, 318, 449
women, 25, 34, 44, 45, 46, 50, 51, 52–5,
59, 66, 94–5, 120–2, 134, 172, 190,
211–12, 270, 282–4, 316, 336–7,
386–8
wood, 43, 44, 48, 52, 88, 120, 222
work rhythms, 54–55
workers' control, 195, 209, 211–12, 219
working classes, workers, 43, 112,
122–4, 128–32, 134–9, 142–4,
146–9, 153, 156–60, 167, 172–3,
175–6, 181–3, 185–6, 189–98, 201,
204–5, 207–12, 215, 220–2, 228,
230, 235, 237–9, 253, 260–2, 265,
305, 307, 309, 312, 316, 364,
378–9, 381–4, 410, 413, 420–1, 458
see also peasants, wage-earners,
proletariat
Workers' Opposition, 253
world revolution, 194–5, 199–200, 204,
210, 225–6, 231, 234, 242, 248,
262–3, 289, 324–5, 347, 372, 431
World War II, *see* Great Patriotic War
Wrangel, general P. W., 225–6, 234,
451

Yagoda, G. G., 296, 302, 304
Yalta, 334, 344, 452
Yalu river, 140–1
Yanayev, G. I., 426–7
Yanushkevich, general, 163
Yaroslav, prince, 13, 447
Yazov, marshall D. T., 426
Yeltsin, B. N., 404, 416, 424, 426, 454–5
Yenukidze, A., 302
Yezhov, N. I., 303–4, 311, 452
Yudenich, general, N. N., 225
Yugoslavia, 334, 372, 452
Yurii Dolgorukii, prince, 20
Yuzovka, 105, 160

Zablotskii, A. P., 41–2, 58, 72, 73
zagotovki, see procurements
Zaslavskaya, T. I., 346, 355, 386–7, 408
ZemGor, 169–71, 177, 450, 460
Zemskii sobor, 27, 28, 447, 460
zemstva, 85, 86, 88, 95, 119, 132–5, 143,
169–71, 184, 449, 460
Zhdanov, A. A., 345
Zhenotdel, 211, 451, 460
Zhukov, marshal G. K., 338, 345, 357,
362–3, 372
Zinoviev, G. Y., 192, 199, 201, 209,
257–8, 300–1, 303–4, 452, 454
Zubatov, S. V., 130, 146, 449